GENDER IN MODERN EAST ASIA

GENDER IN MODERN EAST ASIA

An Integrated History

BARBARA MOLONY
Santa Clara University

JANET THEISS
University of Utah

HYAEWEOL CHOI
Australian National University

A Member of the Perseus Books Group

Published by Westview Press,
A Member of the Perseus Books Group
2465 Central Avenue
Boulder, CO 80301
www.westviewpress.com

Cover Image: *Songbook for "Song of the Milky Way"* (altered detail) from the Shochiku film Milky Way, 1931, artist unknown, color lithograph, inks on paper. Published by Shochiku kinema gakufu shuppansha, Printed by Noguchi Tsurukichi, 26.5 x 19 cm. From The Levenson Collection, and drawn from the exhibition "DECO JAPAN: Shaping Art and Culture, 1920–1945" organized and circulated by Art Services International, Alexandria, Virginia.

Image page 16: Photograph © 2016 Museum of Fine Arts, Boston. Attributed to: Emperor Huizong, Chinese, 1082–1135, ruled 1100–1125. Court ladies preparing newly woven silk, (detail). Chinese, Northern Song dynasty, early 12th century. Ink, color, and gold on silk 37.1 x 145 cm (14 5/8 x 57 1/16 in.) Museum of Fine Arts, Boston, Special Chinese and Japanese Fund, 12.886.

Image page 238: Tipsy, Kobayakawa Kiyoshi, Japanese, 1889–1948. Shōwa period, 1930. Woodblock print; ink and color on paper, 17 1/4 x 10 5/8 in. (43.8 x 27 cm). Honolulu Museum of Art, Gift of Philip H. Roach, Jr., 2001 (26926).

Design and composition by Eclipse Publishing Services

Library of Congress Cataloging-in-Publication Data

Names: Molony, Barbara, author. | Theiss, Janet M., 1964- author. | Choi, Hyaeweol, author.
Title: Gender in modern East Asia / Barbara Molony, Santa Clara University, Janet Theiss, University of Utah, Hyaeweol Choi, Australian National University.
Description: First Edition. | Boulder, CO : Westview Press, 2016. | Includes bibliographical references and index.
Identifiers: LCCN 2016004201| ISBN 9780813348759 (paperback) | ISBN 9780813348766 (ebook)
Subjects: LCSH: Women—East Asia—History. | Gender identity—East Asia. | Sex role and globalization—East Asia. | Feminism—East Asia. | BISAC: HISTORY / General. | HISTORY / Asia / General. | HISTORY / Asia / China. | HISTORY / Asia / Japan. | HISTORY / Asia / Korea. | HISTORY / Modern / General.
Classification: LCC HQ1760.5 .M65 2016 | DDC 305.4095—dc23 LC record available at http://lccn.loc.gov/2016004201

PB ISBN: 978-0-8133-4875-9
EBOOK ISBN: 978-0-8133-4876-6

10 9 8 7 6 5 4 3 2 1

We dedicate this book with love and gratitude to our mothers.

Dorrit Molony
Judith E. Theiss (1939–2011)
Hong Haeng (1930–2012)

Contents

Preface

This book covers the history of gender—both femininities and masculinities, but with a greater emphasis on women—in the Chinese, Korean, and Japanese cultural and political realms. Beginning with an overview of the ancient and medieval eras, the book treats the history of gender in both national and transnational contexts in the early modern and modern eras by examining the dynamic histories of sexuality; gender ideology, discourse, and legal construction; marriage and the family; and the gendering of work, society, culture, and power.

The dual approach of locating gender history within a society's national history as well as describing its role in an integrated regional history of East Asia is novel in the field of women's and gender history. In addition, this book examines the global context of historical changes in the three countries and, where appropriate, highlights cross-cultural themes that transcend national boundaries within and outside the region. We discuss themes and concepts such as writing and language, the body, feminism, immigration and diasporas, and Confucianism as part of an integrated history. The proximity of these three countries (now five, including Taiwan and North Korea) has long permitted the flow of ideas, people, materials, and texts throughout the region. (This flow has extended significantly beyond East Asia in the past 150 years.) At the same time, the authors are conscious of the potential problem of seeming to lump East Asian gender issues into a monolithic (and therefore incorrect) whole, and thus stress the historical contexts of both differences and similarities wherever they occur in the three countries.

An integrated history borrows much from the growing field of transnational history, which also focuses on the movements of people and material and ideas, as well as on issues of war, peace, imperialism, and economics. In this book, key issues highlight this integrative transnational approach. They include such topics as Confucian texts for men and women, gender performance, the role of the state in gender construction, nationalism, sexuality and prostitution, New Women and Modern Girls, feminisms, "comfort" women, imperialism and empire, and Japanese (and later East Asian) neologisms based on Western concepts but using the shared Chinese-based writing system to express them. Other transnational approaches are comparative, such as an examination of differing notions of the "family" and a study of the impact of Christianity on feminist movements and gender history in each of the three countries.

Structure of the book

Gender in Modern East Asia contains eleven chapters that treat each country's gender history in a separate section thematically linked to the sections dedicated to the other two countries. Years of teaching courses on women's and gender history have persuaded the authors that chronology must undergird a thematic approach, both to enhance students' comprehension of the material and to emphasize the contemporaneous and integrated experiences of the countries studied. In addition, each chapter opens with a brief examination of global context. We ask what is happening elsewhere in the world that drives the region's history and discuss how the cultural, economic, and social developments discussed in each chapter are approached in studies of Europe, the Americas, and Africa during the same years. East Asia does not exist in a vacuum, and we hope students will be able to see appropriate regional and global similarities and dissimilarities.

During the early modern and modern eras, the three countries alternated in exerting greater regional influence. This alternation is reflected in the organization of each chapter. Until the nineteenth century the flow of culture and ideas, although always multidirectional, originated most often in China, and thus discussion of China leads off in those chapters. From the late nineteenth century through World War II, that flow shifted and Japan became most influential. The direction of the flow of culture shifted again in the postwar era, and thus Korea joins Japan as leading off in the latter chapters of the book. Regardless of which country is discussed first in each chapter, coverage of all three is balanced throughout the book.

This volume is the first book-length work that focuses on gender in modern East Asia from both a transnational perspective at the macro level and an intersectional perspective at the level of the individual. There are numerous historical monographs and articles as well as translations of literary and other forms of artistic culture for each of these East Asian societies. Other works link East Asian gender practice and discourse with global movements of ideas, images, artifacts, and capital. But no single text has brought all these topics together in a comprehensive way accessible to undergraduates. This volume is intended as a response to changing approaches to teaching and research in the histories of gender and of East Asia by offering an integrated analysis of the region through the lens of gender.

Hyaeweol Choi would like to thank Dan Devitt, Sun Joo Kim, Ksenia Chizhova, Suzy Kim, and Robert Eskildsen for their helpful feedback on early drafts of her contributions to the volume. She would also like to acknowledge a generous grant from the Academy of Korean Studies (AKS-2011-BAA-2106), which afforded her teaching release that was of great help in securing time for writing. She is also grateful to Routledge for granting permission to reprint "Declaration of the Establishment of Kŭnuhoe," which originally appeared in Hyaeweol Choi, *New Women in Colonial Korea: A Sourcebook* (London: Routledge, 2013), pp. 199–200.

When one undertakes a project of this scope, unforeseen events almost inevitably interfere with plans. We would like to thank the editorial staff at Westview for their indulgence and understanding in accommodating delays that occurred in our original schedule.

Barbara Molony
Janet Theiss
Hyaeweol Choi
January 2016

KAZAKHSTAN
RUSSIA
Ertis
Yenisey
Angara
Lake Balkhash
MONGOLIA
CHINA
KYRGYZSTAN
Lake Issyk-Kul
Ürümqi
Turpan
Kashgar
XINJIANG
TAJ.
PAK.
Taklamakan Desert
GANSU
Gobi Dese
GREAT WALL
Xining
Lanzhou
QINGHAI
Himalayan Mountains
Indus
Yangtze
XIZANG (TIBET)
SICHUAN
Nu
Mekong
Chengdu
Maquan
Lhasa
Mt Everest 29,028ft
Ganges
NEPAL
BHUTAN
INDIA
Brahmaputra
Guiyang
BANGLADESH
Kunming
Ayeyarwady
YUNNAN
0 200 mi
0 200 km
MYANMAR
LAOS
Bay of Bengal
THAILAND
© AVALON TRAVEL

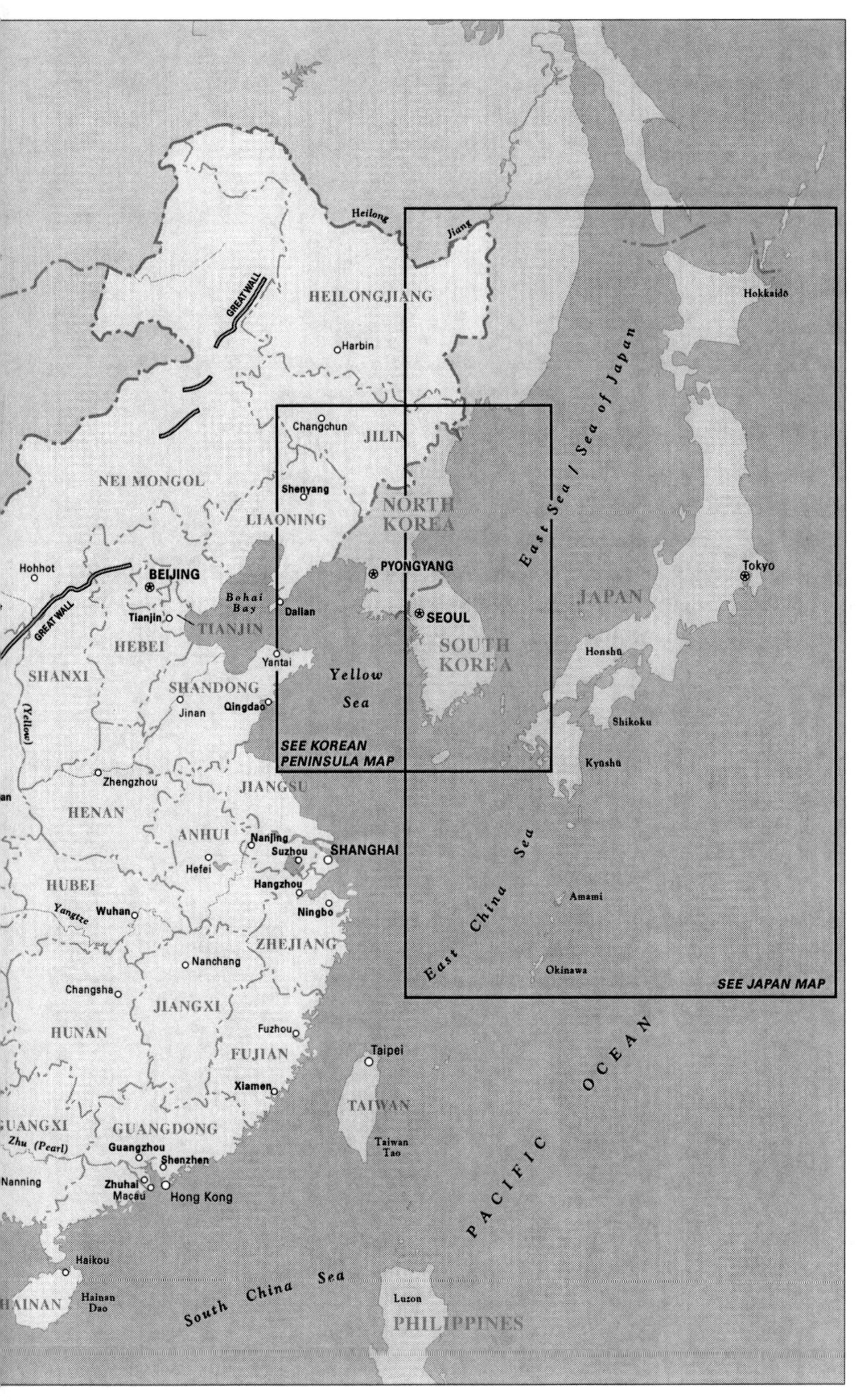

Heilong
Jiang
HEILONGJIANG
GREAT WALL
Harbin
Hokkaidō
Changchun
JILIN
NEI MONGOL
Shenyang
NORTH KOREA
LIAONING
East Sea / Sea of Japan
Hohhot
BEIJING
PYONGYANG
Tokyo
Bohai Bay
Dalian
SEOUL
JAPAN
Tianjin
TIANJIN
GREAT WALL
HEBEI
SOUTH KOREA
Honshū
Yantai
SHANXI
Yellow Sea
SHANDONG
Jinan
Qingdao
Shikoku
(Yellow)
SEE KOREAN PENINSULA MAP
Kyūshū
Zhengzhou
JIANGSU
HENAN
ANHUI
Nanjing
Suzhou
SHANGHAI
Hefei
East China Sea
HUBEI
Hangzhou
Amami
Yangtze
Wuhan
Ningbo
ZHEJIANG
Nanchang
Okinawa
SEE JAPAN MAP
Changsha
JIANGXI
HUNAN
Fuzhou
FUJIAN
Taipei
PACIFIC OCEAN
Xiamen
TAIWAN
GUANGXI
GUANGDONG
Taiwan Tao
Zhu (Pearl)
Guangzhou
Shenzhen
Nanning
Zhuhai
Macau
Hong Kong
Haikou
South China Sea
HAINAN
Hainan Dao
Luzon
PHILIPPINES

KOREAN PENINSULA
CHINA
Fushun
Sonbong
Musan
Hamgyong Mountains
Chongjin
Hyeson
Manpo
Kanggye
Chosan
Taedong
Kangnam Range
Kimhyonggwon
Kilchu
Kimchaek
Sinuiju
Hamhung
Hungnam
NORTH KOREA
Chongju
Taedong
Sin-Ni
Sunchon
Munchon
Wonsan
PYONGYANG
Anbyon
EAST SEA/ SEA OF JAPAN
Korea Bay
Nampo
Imjin
Sariwon
Diamond Mountains
Changyon
Pyongsan
DEMILITARIZED ZONE
Sokcho
Haeju
Ongjin
Kaesong
Chuncheon
Gangneung
Goyang
SEOUL
Ulleungdo Island
Incheon
Namhan
Wonju
Ansan
Suwon
Eumseong
Cheongju
Soback Mountains
Andong
SOUTH KOREA
YELLOW SEA
Geum
Daejeon
Nakdong
Pohang
Gunsan
Iksan
Daegu
Jeonju
Gyeongju
Ulsan
Nam
Gwangju
Seomjin
Changwon
Busan
Mokpo
Yeosu
Tsushima Island
JAPAN
0 50 mi
0 50 km
Jeju Strait
Kitakyushu
Korea Strait
Jeju
Jeju Island
© AVALON TRAVEL

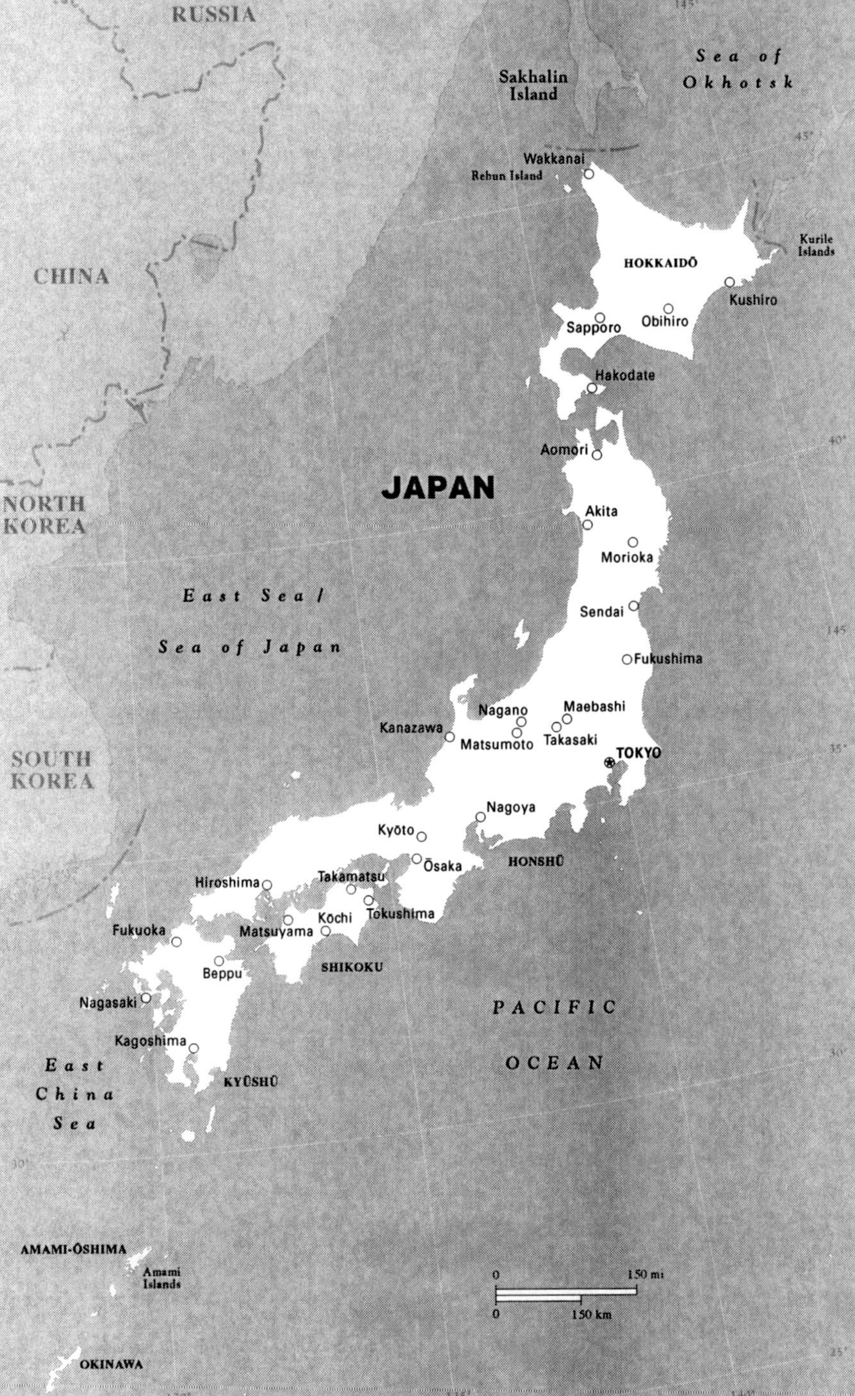

RUSSIA
Sakhalin Island
Sea of Okhotsk
Wakkanai
Rebun Island
Kurile Islands
HOKKAIDŌ
Kushiro
Sapporo
Obihiro
Hakodate
CHINA
Aomori
JAPAN
NORTH KOREA
Akita
Morioka
East Sea / Sea of Japan
Sendai
Fukushima
Nagano
Maebashi
Kanazawa
Matsumoto
Takasaki
TOKYO
SOUTH KOREA
Nagoya
Kyōto
Ōsaka
HONSHŪ
Hiroshima
Takamatsu
Kōchi
Tokushima
Fukuoka
Matsuyama
Beppu
SHIKOKU
Nagasaki
PACIFIC OCEAN
Kagoshima
East China Sea
KYŪSHŪ
AMAMI-ŌSHIMA
Amami Islands
0
150 mi
0
150 km
OKINAWA

1

Gender in Ancient and Medieval East Asia Before 1600

GLOBAL CONTEXT

Gender and sexuality in East Asian societies, as elsewhere throughout the world, have varied over time and among societies. They have been framed in the varying historical contexts of secular and religious ideas, the evolution of economic activities, bureaucratization and governance, the increasing complexities of social life, and war and peace. The mobility of people and cultures has meant that no society has been so isolated from others that it developed unique and unchanging ways of defining gender and sexuality.

The movement of ideas and people before 1600 was much livelier and more deliberate between neighboring societies than between distant societies. So it is no surprise that what are now the modern nations of China, Korea, and Japan, all located in Northeast Asia, can be seen as an integrated region because of the flow of cultures and people over time. Until the nineteenth century, the movement of ideas, cultures, and religions tended to be from west to east—from China to Korea to Japan—while trade and human migration were more multidirectional. One of the key mediators that facilitated such movement was the Chinese writing system. From late antiquity on, the Chinese writing system came to be used by the elites and ruling classes in all three areas. As a result, it was seen until the late nineteenth century as a "truth language," much as Latin was in Western Europe before the rise of vernacular writing in the Renaissance. This allowed Chinese ideas, including gender norms, to be influential throughout the region for hundreds of years. But it would be a mistake to assume that intraregional mobility of ideas and people erased all local differences in the construction of gender and the performance of sexuality. Each society had its own history and thus its own historically inflected notions of gender.

People in modern societies generally think of sex (male/female) and gender (masculine/feminine) as binary, that is, as being divided into two categories. Recently this binary divide has been challenged by the increasingly accepted view that both sex and gender exist on a continuum, without a rigid division into just two categories. To be sure, the concept of gender as a way of categorizing people is itself fairly recent. Less than thirty years ago, it was typical to divide society into two immutable sexes, rather than into genders that were historically and socially constructed and, therefore, open to reconstruction. Although societies' laws and customs were created in the past as if sex was an unchanging characteristic with which people were born, the notion that gender was constructed has been much more consistent with historians' view that things change over time. It was a tremendous scholarly breakthrough to add women and gender to the study of history, so viewing gender as a "useful category of historical analysis" was revolutionary (Scott 1986). Scholars will not go back to the days of ignoring sex and gender. For that reason, we need to find the origins and development of these categories.

Sex and gender have not always been more important social and legal categories than other ways of classifying people. Marital status, family or clan membership, social class (especially the relationship to the ruling class), occupation, caste, and other categories were at times more important. Unlike gender, sexual practice has long been acknowledged as taking many different forms, although the concept of sexual identity (lesbian, gay, bisexual, transgender, queer) and its linkage with one's choice of sexual partners has a much more recent history. Sexuality includes not just sexual practice but also intimate relations, family formation, commodification (sale) of sex, marriage rituals, and reproduction, all of which must be considered in their historical contexts.

When and why did gender become so central to social organization?

One way to look at the development of gender in societies is economic. Prehistoric people needed food, shelter, and protection from predators, and formed small communities to deliver those necessities. Some members hunted animals, some gathered plants to eat. These roles were not initially gendered, but over time, in many places, it became more likely for men to hunt and women to gather. So gender could be defined by labor choices, a pattern that became increasingly important as societies and economies developed. Gender hierarchy was not evident in most hunter-gatherer societies. With the advent of agricultural development, however, gender dynamics began to shift toward more male-dominant structures and practices.

Later, gender was also defined by religion, including belief in the supernatural. As societies came to see themselves as entities distinct from neighboring groups, many created myths to explain where they came from. In most of these creation stories, nonhumans or gods interacted with humans, and those humans or their descendants went on to found one's country or civilization. In all of these cases, some sort of familial relationship played a part: Adam and Eve in the Judeo-Christian Bible, the Greek and Roman gods' sexual bonding with humans, the foundation of Old Chosŏn (Korea) by a descendant of the son of the Heavenly King and a woman transformed from a bear, the founding of Japan by descendants of the sun goddess Amaterasu, the large variety of Native American creation stories, and so on. The family and family relationships were thus at the center of the ways most human societies explained their origins as organized communities or states. In many cases, both men and women played significant roles in these myths. Later, more structured religions created rituals, doctrines, and belief systems, and many of these came to define men and women as different and often unequal.

Religion-based inequality often paralleled social inequality, but which came first is not clear. In any case, a civilization's level of complexity seems to have played a part in creating gender differences. The more complex a society was—with planned cities, bureaucracies, organized government, and culture—the more likely it was that people's status was classified by their sex (that is, male and female). In some cases, constructed notions of gender placed individuals in the classes of empowered and disempowered. But similar stages of social complexity did not always lead to similar levels of equality. Four thousand years ago, in ancient West Asia (Mesopotamia, Israel, and other civilizations), men and women did not have equal legal status. Around the same time, in ancient Egypt, sex did not define legal status; rather, whether one was free or a slave was more important.

In increasingly sophisticated civilizations, religion and philosophy came to create more specifically defined binary sex/gender divisions. These divisions were, in turn, used to create governments that were based on sex/gender differences. Athens's "democracy" was crafted by Solon, known as "the lawgiver," in the sixth century BCE as a way to arrange the disorganized Greek matrimonial system of his day in a patriarchal (male-dominated) manner. This created a government by free men only, so stipulating who was male and who was female was necessary. The esteemed Athenian philosopher Aristotle (384–322 BCE) claimed that men were intellectually and physically superior to women; perfecting masculinity was the basis of democracy. In fact, as the historian Thucydides (c. 460–c. 395 BCE) noted, the good woman was the one who was "least talked about among the men, whether for good or for bad" (quoted in Halsall 2004, 290). In Rome a few hundred years later, patriarchal dominance was embedded in the rule that fathers had complete control over their families. Medieval European Christianity also gendered society and placed men over women. But all of these societies were characterized by slavery and serfdom as well, so there were multiple forms of inequality. Religion and philosophy played a significant role in constructing gender and other inequalities in East Asia in antiquity and the medieval era too, as we shall see in this chapter.

Sexuality has varied over time and place. Ancient and medieval governments tended to care little about one's sex partners (and often valued same-sex relations, as in ancient Greece), but they did care about marriage. Marriage was linked to power and to inheritance, and messing with marriage could disrupt society. Formal marriage rituals and divorce procedures were developed. Some focused on matrilocal residence and inheritance (as in Korea and Japan in antiquity and the early medieval era), but many stressed the dominance of the husband's family in residence and inheritance (as in China). Some marriages involved more than two people. In some areas of Tibet, one bride could have several husbands, while under Islam, a man could marry up to four wives if he could care for them all equally. The Catholic Church claimed the right to regulate marriages of the elite and of clergy in the fourth century CE (Catholic clergy could marry until the eleventh century) and began to regulate commoners' marriages in the thirteenth century. In Southern and Eastern Europe from 1000 to 1500 CE, grooms tended to be much older than their brides, and the couple often lived with one set of parents until she matured. Northern European couples at that time usually married when both partners were much older, setting up their own households right away. In some societies religious rites were required; in others all that was required was an exchange of wine cups or a contract written by a hired scribe. In some West African areas, marriages were gendered, but female "husbands" could marry female "wives." Marriages took many different forms throughout the ancient and medieval world. As this chapter will show, these forms, which were linked to notions of gender, varied throughout East Asia as well.

CHINA

Dynasties in China

Zhou (c. 1000–256 BCE)
Qin–Han (221 BCE–220 CE)
Sui–Tang (581–907)
Song (960–1279)
Yuan (1260–1368)
Ming (1368–1644)
Qing (1644–1911)

The earliest evidence of gender systems in East Asia comes from the territory of what is today China. Increasingly rich archaeological evidence from Neolithic cultures (c. 5000–1766 BCE) depicts the fragmented emergence of complex societies in different regions demonstrating striking variety in material culture. Yet despite this regional diversity, Neolithic cultures appear to have shared key elements of later Chinese gender order: the linkage of status to kinship roles, the great significance of mortuary rituals in expressing kinship relations, the lower status of women compared to men of the same rank, and the large difference in gender roles of elites and non-elites. In excavated burials there are many fewer women than men, women are commonly buried with fewer grave goods, and there are gender distinctions in body positioning and grave goods assemblages, with women getting spindle whorls and domestic items and men getting weapons and ritual items. There is some mortuary evidence of women being buried with their natal families, which suggests that while gender hierarchies and divisions of labor were well established, patrilineal patterns of family organization may not have been universal (Linduff and Sun 2004).

The clear dominance of patrilineal principles accompanied the development of state structures in the Yellow River valley of the north in the Shang period (c. 1766–1045 BCE). The Shang royal ancestral cult focused on the male line of succession and made the king's family matters essential affairs of state. Ideas about gender difference and patrilineal descent were integral to expressions of state power and legitimacy. The earliest extant Chinese texts were oracle bones used by the Shang rulers for divination rituals querying royal ancestors about important matters. They depict the royal consorts of the polygynous Shang kings engaging in ritual sacrifices and military affairs, show the importance placed on their health, childbirths, and dreams, and indicate that sacrifices were made to honor them as ancestors in dedicated temples.

The royal consort Fu Hao (c. 1250 BCE) led armies of more than ten thousand troops in battle and was honored in death with one of the most sumptuous Shang tombs yet discovered, including hundreds of elaborate bronze vessels, weapons, and ritual objects, hundreds of objects in jade, bone, stone, and shell, and sixteen human sacrifice victims including men, women, and children. Yet Fu Hao's exceptional power and wealth, like those of the other documented consorts, derived from her marriage to the king, and she was clearly subordinate to him. The oracle bone texts show that the Shang ancestor cult focused more on men than on women: fewer women were venerated (and then only if they had borne sons for the king), women received fewer rituals than men, and women had smaller tombs (Linduff and Sun 2004).

The Emergence of a Confucian Gender Orthodoxy

The Shang were conquered and succeeded by a rival polity, the Zhou (1045–221 BCE), whose rulers extended their power by bestowing titles on loyal nobles who then acknowledged their ongoing fealty through elaborate rituals. Strategic marriages between the Zhou royal family and noble lineages and among nobles were a key mechanism for securing political alliances. In a context where political relations were highly ritualized and intertwined with kinship bonds, the first codification of norms of gender and family hierarchy took the form of ritual rules (*li*) governing behavior. To understand gender roles, the most salient of these codifications is the *Li Ji* (*Book of Rites*), compiled in its current version in the Han period (206 BCE–220 CE), based on content developed in the Zhou period. Reflecting the fact that the Zhou political system was based on kinship relations, this text articulated the paradigm of the family as an analogy for the state and presented prescriptions for the conduct of family and state affairs that were the foundation for the ethical system promoted by Confucius (c. 551–479 BCE) and his followers. By the third century BCE, the lineage system of the Zhou was being replaced by state bureaucracies staffed by officials who were not related to the ruler by blood or marriage. As the Qin (221–206 BCE) and Han (206 BCE–220 CE) dynasties unified China under a centralized bureaucratic state, they promoted homogenization of customs that expressed an emerging state orthodoxy based on what came to be called Confucian norms. The Han state promoted Confucian education among literate male elites across the empire to create a pool of potential officials that shared its values and political vision. The Han law code enforced Confucian family principles of gender and generational hierarchy and filial piety, that is, the reverence and obedience that children, especially sons, owed to their parents. But although such core patrilineal principles and beliefs about death and the afterlife that inspired Confucian ancestral rituals were part of a common Chinese culture shared across social classes, marriage, funerary, and other rituals varied widely, as did practice of gender norms such as sex segregation. Despite its pretension to social regulation, the state did not have much influence in everyday family life. The household was the key economic and social unit in a largely agrarian society, and the lives of most men and women were regulated through kin groups (Hinsch 2010).

The *Book of Rites* explicates the core elements of the family system that informed Han law and set an ideal standard for the population. The family was defined by patrilineal principles of descent from a common male ancestor and structured by age and gender hierarchies. Under the rubric of filial piety, men and women were all supposed to be subservient first to their living parents and grandparents, in addition to performing ongoing respect for previous generations of elders through ancestral rituals. Marriage was patrilocal. The husband's parents chose a bride to bring into the family as a strategy to ensure the success and perpetuation of the patriline. Women were additionally subordinate to men according to the rubric of the Three Obediences, which prescribed subservience to their fathers before marriage, to their husbands in marriage, and to their sons in widowhood. In a state system where loyalty to the ruler was cemented through marriage ties with powerful elite families, which were then able to exercise power through daughters married into the court, political bonds and sexual bonds were conflated: a wife's loyalty to her husband was equivalent to a court minister's loyalty to his ruler. The resulting tension between an inner court dominated by the ruler's consorts and their natal families and an outer court controlled by male officials became a central feature of the political system as China entered its imperial period.

To deal with this tension, the *Book of Rites* provided an elaborate template for orderly gender relations based on two binary pairs: the cosmological concepts of yin and yang and the notion of inner (*nei*) and outer (*wai*) realms. The polarity of yin and yang was a rubric for describing the dynamism of the natural and human worlds in terms of the shifting relationship between complementary opposites. When the concepts first appeared in texts of the Zhou period, they were not necessarily hierarchical, nor did they correlate with female and male. But in the middle of the Han dynasty in the first century BCE, when scholars solidified a Confucian orthodoxy that saw the human body, the family, the state, and the cosmos as analogous and mutually reinforcing, yin and yang came to be hierarchically correlated with earth and heaven and with female and male. The hierarchical interpretation would

BOX 1.1

Confucianism

There is no single Chinese term for the philosophical system that we, in English, call Confucianism. The term refers to the ethical ideals and practices expressed in a canon of Chinese classical texts. Five ancient texts that Confucius was said to have compiled, based on earlier precedents, made up the core of this canon: the *Book of Rites* (a manual of rituals guiding everyday life), the *Book of Poetry* (a collection of the earliest extant poems and songs), the *Book of Changes* (a divination manual), the *Book of History*, and the *Spring and Autumn Annals* (the latter two chronicle the history of China's earliest kingdoms). Interpretations of these texts varied over the many centuries that Confucian thought represented the dominant ideological framework in China.

The ultimate goal of Confucian ethics is to establish a harmonious and hierarchical social and political order by cultivating a spirit of filial piety originating in the family and emanating outward to the realm. According to the *Book of Filial Piety*, a primer for children, "Filial piety is the root of virtue and the source of civilization. . . . [It] begins with serving our parents, continues with serving the ruler, and is completed by establishing one's character." The *Book of Filial Piety for Women*, authored by a Miss Zheng, probably in the mid-Tang dynasty, explained the application of this core virtue for women and girls, emphasizing their critical role as moral exemplars for all members of their families. Structured as a conversation between Ban Zhao (discussed later) and a group of women and enlivened with sample stories from the Han period, *Admonitions for Women* became one of the most popular didactic texts for girls in the later Ming and Qing dynasties. Highlighting reciprocity in marital relations, the text demonstrates the nuances of Confucian notions of gender hierarchy. Here is a sampling of its teachings:

prevail in later gender discourse with the important exception of medical theories that typically described men and women's bodies as fundamentally identical, made up of the same yin-yang polarities.

The binary of inner and outer realms expressed the hierarchical formulation of yin and yang in social practice. The activities of women and men were to be distinct but complementary, and rigorously separated spatially and socially to avoid casual contact even among family members. Women were to be confined in the inner quarters of the household, occupied with the

With regard to a woman's service to her parents-in-law, she is as reverent as to her own father, as loving as to her own mother. . . . In the winter she checks that [her parents-in-law] are warm enough, in the summer cool enough. In the evening she checks that they are settled, in the morning that they are getting up.

The husband is heaven. . . . In antiquity, when a woman went to be married, she was said to be going home. She transfers her heaven to serve her husband. . . . When women follow the nature of heaven and earth . . . then they can bring success to their families. On this basis, a wife acts first to extend love broadly, then her husband will not forget to be filial to his parents. She sets an example of rectitude and virtue and her husband enthusiastically copies it. She takes the initiative in being reverent and yielding, and her husband is not competitive. . . . If she indicates the difference between good and evil, her husband will know restraint.

The women said, "May we ask if a wife who obeys her husband's orders can be called worthy?" Lady Ban replied, "What kind of talk is this? . . . If [the ruler] had ministers to point out his errors to him, he would not lose his empire, even if he were imperfect. . . . If a gentleman had a friend to point out his errors to him, he would not lose his good name. If a father had a son to point out his errors to him, he would not fall into doing wrong. And if a husband had a wife to point out his errors to him, then he would not slip into incorrect ways. . . . Thus, when a husband might do something wrong, a wife warns against it. How can following a husband's orders be considered wise?" (Translated in Mann and Cheng 2001, pp. 47–69)

domestic matters of providing food and clothing and attending to children and elders. Men were to focus on the affairs of the outside world. In sum, "outside affairs should not be talked of inside the threshold [of the women's apartments], nor inside affairs outside it" (cited in Raphals 1998, 224).

Instructional texts for women interpreted the gender paradigm established in the *Book of Rites* for succeeding generations. The first of these was *Admonitions for Women*, written by Ban Zhao (c. 45–115 CE), a highly erudite woman from a prominent family of court scholars. Using the hierarchical language of yin and yang, she argued that gender differences are essential: "Yin and yang have different natures; men and women have different conduct. Yang is deemed powerful by virtue of hardness; yin is deemed useful by virtue of flexibility. Men are deemed honorable by virtue of their strength; women are deemed beautiful by virtue of their frailty" (cited in Raphals 1998, 242). Invoking Han cosmology correlating human actions with the workings of heaven, she advocated that women be subordinate to their husbands, because a husband is a woman's heaven. Herself a widow, she cited ancient precepts in advocating that widows not remarry since "it is said of husbands as of Heaven that as certainly as people cannot run away from Heaven, so surely a wife cannot leave [a husband's home]" (Swann 2001, 78). She prescribed ideals of female conduct in four categories, womanly virtue, womanly words, womanly bearing, and womanly work, emphasizing that women need not have "brilliant talents" but should be humble, yielding, modest, chaste, and industrious at domestic work.

Although the text appears at many points to be a codification of a rigid gender hierarchy, Ban Zhao embodied the contradictions built into the Confucian gender order from its inception. Ironically, despite her rhetoric on containing women within the inner quarters and limiting their speech, she was herself a court scholar and tutor who had received the highest level of education available to anyone, male or female, and she staunchly advocated education for women equivalent to that of men. There are many theories about the meaning of the mixed messages sent by this foundational text. Perhaps she was promoting Confucian orthodoxy for a broader audience for whom literacy was not essential but wanted to emphasize that it was permissible. Perhaps she was couching a strong argument for women's education in the guise of conservative norms to make it more palatable to the Confucian elite. Perhaps she was offering advice primarily to aristocratic women like her and her relatives in the inner court, for whom humility, yielding, wifely loyalty, obedience to parents-in-law, and literacy were all essential survival skills. Later writers would use Ban Zhao as a model for different norms of womanhood: as a chaste widow, as the model for Confucian gender orthodoxy, and as an exemplar of female scholarly talent.

Gender in Social Practice

Evidence of the lives of women at various social levels in this early period shows that the prescriptive norms of elite texts like these did not describe the daily practices of most people. Although women's core activities in this predominantly agricultural society centered on production of food and textiles to support the household economy and family rituals, there are many accounts from the Zhou and Han periods of women participating in political and intellectual life, advising rulers and husbands, and deploying expertise in agriculture, archery, astronomy, navigation, ritual, law, medicine, crafts, music, and dancing outside the home, at court, and in aristocratic and commoner society. Although married women joined their husbands' families and took their name and rank from their husbands, there is plenty of evidence that women of all ranks, from commoners to imperial consorts whose families accessed political power through their daughters' royal marriages, maintained close ties with their natal families.

As mothers (especially of sons), mothers-in-law, and widows, women exercised considerable power within the family. Indeed, contrary to the dictates of the Three Obediences, the requirement that sons show respect to their parents led sons to be obedient to their mothers. Despite Ban Zhao's eloquent arguments for widow chastity, remarriage was the widely accepted norm for widows and for divorced women, both of whom typically returned to their natal families to make the new match. While husband and wife were both supposed to prioritize obedience to his parents over their marital bond, accounts of conflict between daughters- and mothers-in-law and of tension between marital devotion and filial duty were common in historical and fictional sources. Yet another challenge to the marital bond was the practice of concubinage, a form of polygyny that was very common among wealthy elites. According to law and ritual regulation, men were allowed to have only one legal wife, but the filial mandate to produce sons justified "marriage" to additional women. Concubines were legally and ritually inferior to wives and were not allowed to succeed to the wife's position even if she died. But concubines' children were full heirs who were to recognize the legal wife as their mother and were entitled to the same property rights and ritual status as the legal wife's own children. Tension between wives and concubines would become a commonplace of Chinese family life, posing continual challenges to marital hierarchy and loyalty (Hinsch 2010).

Buddhism and Daoism in China's Middle Period

The Han imperial order collapsed in the third century CE, and for the next three centuries China was politically divided into varying configurations of rival kingdoms. Many of those based in the north were multiethnic polities governed by non-Chinese rulers with strong cultural and economic ties to the Inner Asian polities along the Silk Road trade routes. Political fragmentation, weak governments, warfare, and increasing social inequality that resulted from the unchecked growth of aristocratic power at the local level caused widespread disillusion with the Confucian worldview, the ultimate goal of which was stable secular governance and which revered rulers and officials as models of virtue. Amid this ideological crisis, Buddhism was filtering into China from the Indian subcontinent, spread by missionary monks and Silk Road merchants. Buddhism introduced the new notion of reincarnation through cycles of rebirth governed by individual karma, the accumulated effects of good and bad deeds during one's life. The ultimate spiritual goal was release from the recurring cycles of rebirth into a world characterized by suffering through attainment of enlightenment or salvation (also called nirvana). The path to enlightenment required living an ethical life focused on spiritual cultivation to overcome the attachments and desires that cause despair and human strife. As Buddhism was adopted across China, Chinese believers adapted the traditional Confucian-based family values of filiality and loyalty to the patriline to fit with new Buddhist values and institutions. This required some adjustment; we shall see below that new ideas such as Buddhism required adaptations in Korea and Japan as well. Buddhism valorized celibacy for men and women, in direct conflict with the Confucian mandate to produce sons to carry on ancestral rituals. It created alternative social roles and paths to literacy and authority outside the family and the state for women as nuns, for men as monks, and for both as Buddhist laypeople who gained religious merit and social recognition for patronage of monasteries and nunneries.

In response to the moral challenges of the era and the model of Buddhist institutions and cosmology, Daoism, China's third important school of thought in addition to Confucianism and Buddhism, also became an organized religion in its own right, with elaborate notions of sin; heaven and hell; a scriptural canon; male and female clergy; and ritual practices inspired by localized folk religion. Descended from the ancient philosophy of the Zhou period, it focused on attainment of longevity and perfection through various techniques including breath and diet control, meditation, and sexual practices designed to unify yin and yang forces to achieve harmony with the Dao. Within Daoist cosmology women embody the cosmic force of yin, the essential complement to the male yang, and the Dao itself is often described as a universal mother. Goddesses and female immortals, like the Queen Mother of the West, are prominent in the Daoist pantheon (Cahill 1995). Like Buddhism, Daoism provided new opportunities for women to seek literacy and spiritual authority, but because its practitioners married, it did not pose a challenge to patrilineal family norms (Despeux and Kohn 2005).

To address the social and ideological tensions created by the integration of Buddhism into Chinese society, sutras (scriptures) and morality tales created exemplary sons and daughters who demonstrated a Buddhist form of filial piety by helping their parents attain salvation. The story of Mulian tells of a bodhisattva (an enlightened being who refrains from full attainment of nirvana so as to be able to help other beings on their spiritual journey) who rescues his sinful mother from the tortures of hell and, through the power of his faith in the Buddha and his filial devotion, manages to get her reborn into heaven. This tale is framed as an explanation of the origins of the ghost festival, an annual celebration during which families made food offerings to feed the hungry ghosts of ancestors languishing in the underworld. The twelfth-century tale of the Princess Miaoshan identified a real woman as an incarnation of the bodhisattva Guanyin (Sanskrit: Avalokitesvara; Japanese: Kannon; Korean: Kwanŭm) and dramatized the conflict between filial obedience and Buddhist piety for women. Miaoshan defied her father's wishes and refused to marry so that she could devote herself to Buddhist spiritual cultivation. Her angry father expelled her from the family, killed her and her entire community of nuns, and for his sins was stricken with a horrible sickness. Restored to life by the gods, Miaoshan offered her eyes and arms to cure him and, through her great compassion, converted him to Buddhism. In the end, she was apotheosized at the Great Compassionate Guanyin of the Thousand Arms and Eyes (Mann and Cheng 2001, pp. 31–44).

Buddhism and Daoism reached the peak of their political influence and cultural prestige during the Sui (581–617) and Tang dynasties (618–907), which reunited China into the medieval world's most powerful and prosperous empire. It was in the Tang period that Chinese political institutions, law, arts and letters, and cultural values would become a model for Korea and Japan. With large parts of the Silk Road under Tang control, foreigners and their ideas and products streamed into China. Chang'an, the Tang dynasty's cosmopolitan capital, had large communities of merchants, envoys, and Buddhist pilgrims from Central Asia, India, Japan, Korea, and Tibet. Foreign fashions in clothing, hairstyles, music, dance, decorative arts, and furnishings pervaded the city's lively entertainment quarters and daily life. To extend the power of the state to local areas controlled by strong local elites, the Sui and Tang developed a system of examinations to test would-be officials' literary abilities and knowledge of the classical Confucian scholarly canon. While aristocratic families still dominated the upper ranks of government, talented men from less prominent families could now aspire to official positions. Literary accomplishment and cultural refinement became essential components of idealized masculinity alongside the martial skills of horsemanship and archery that had long been hallmarks of aristocratic manhood. In a new genre of short stories, male authors romanticized effete young male scholars and explored the dangers of love through tales of their affairs with courtesans, prostitutes, and occasionally young women of respectable families, who distracted them from their studies. In fiction and in biographical literature, Tang courtesans and upper-class women embodied idealized notions of femininity, literary refinement, and beauty.

The anomalous figure of the empress Wu Zetian (624–705) is often used to symbolize the potential for power and danger that women represented in the Tang. She entered the palace as a concubine of the emperor Gaozong, who shunted aside his first empress in favor of his concubine in flagrant violation of protocol. Wu systematically eliminated rivals to her power, including her sons, and after the emperor's death in 663 took over as ruler, declaring herself emperor of a new dynasty in 690, the only woman in Chinese history to take this male title. Though ruthless, she was highly educated and very effective as a ruler, extending the boundaries of the empire in the northwest, expanding the scope of the examination system, suppressing rebellions, and effectively promoting Buddhism to legitimate her rule. However capable and, indeed, manly in the ruthless exercise of power, no woman could be a truly legitimate ruler according to Chinese patrilineal principles of succession, and Empress Wu was viewed by later commentators as a usurper who exemplified the evils of women's influence in politics and thus the need for strict separation between the inner realms of the court, where women resided, and the outer rooms, where men conducted government business (Rothschild 2015).

Below the level of the court, legal texts and other documents from oasis trading cities in the far northwest such as Dunhuang and Turfan confirm the ongoing divergence between Confucian gender ideals and women's actual lives. These documents show the importance of filial respect toward parents-in-law, female subordination, and seclusion as ideals, especially for elite women. Conversely, they also depict women engaging actively outside the home in a wide variety of economic activities, including trading, weaving, and pawning, and religious activities, such as organizing worship and charity. These activities allowed women to control considerable amounts of money and to enter into legal contracts of all sorts, often as household managers or heads of household with taxpaying responsibilities in their own right (Deng 1999).

Neo-Confucian Revival in the Song, Yuan, and Ming Dynasties

The transition from the Tang to the Song dynasty in the tenth century was marked by major political and economic transformations—chiefly commercialization of the economy and institutionalization of the examination system—that had huge effects on family life and gender order. By expanding the examination system based on Confucian texts as the dominant mechanism for recruiting government officials, the Song dynasty (960–1279) curtailed hereditary access to office, rank, and their privileges, bringing the old aristocracy to an end and creating an expanding class of upwardly mobile families. The new elite comprised officials and scholars who dedicated years of their lives to passing the rigorous series of state-run examinations upon which family status and success were now based. They promoted a revitalized Neo-Confucianism that was highly critical of the pervasive influence of Buddhism on Chinese society. With a metaphysical theory of the workings of morality in the cosmos, Song Neo-Confucians advocated social reform centered in the family and local communities to reestablish core Confucian principles of family ethics: gender differentiation, generational hierarchy, and diligence in the service of family interests. In this competitive new sociopolitical order, standards of masculinity and femininity shifted away from the martial and artistic markers of prestige in the Tang and toward the education, diligence, and frugality that were required for family success. Song-era men needed literate, capable wives who could manage their households and finances while they studied or pursued government careers, and who could provide early education for sons as a foundation for later examination success. Inspired by a new dedication to Neo-Confucian ethics and political philosophy that emphasized the family as the foundation of harmonious and ethical social order, this new scholar-official elite valorized a model of womanhood very different from the Tang beauty. The ideal Song woman of the elite was a wife who was industrious and serious-minded, literate enough to provide primary education for her sons and manage family accounts, and devoted to her husband's family. Song men recognized that their success depended on wives being dependable partners. But their respect for women's accomplishments in this regard came along with a heightened focus on women's loyalty to a husband's patriline (Ebrey 1993).

Commercialization of the economy and expansion of cities created new roles for women and changed the significance of their labor. Women's weaving, sericulture, and food production were no longer just for household use and tax payments, but for the market as well. Picking tea and selling cloth, thread, fish, vegetables, and fruit brought in cash income for their families.

This painting attributed to Song Emperor Huizong (1082–1135) depicts the annual palace sericulture ritual in which the empress led palace ladies through all stages of silk production from silkworm processing to sewing dresses to show the importance of textile work for women of all statuses. COURT LADIES PREPARING NEWLY WOVEN SILK (DETAIL) PHOTO © 2016 MUSEUM OF FINE ARTS, BOSTON

Women assisted in family businesses such as inns, restaurants, and shops, and some widows served as proprietors. The ranks of female entertainers in urban centers expanded to serve a widened audience of officials and merchants, who purchased female servants to work in their large extended family compounds as well as household courtesans trained in music, singing, and dancing to assist with the entertainment of male friends and colleagues, an activity deemed essential for the maintenance of social and professional networks. Prior to the Song, women entertainers were usually from families with hereditary debased status, but with the increasing fluidity of economic and political order, household courtesans were likely to be contractual labor and might even come from formerly elite families that had fallen on hard times. Such women often became concubines, and if they bore sons, they could elevate their status and secure their position within elite families. As a consequence of the incorporation of courtesan entertainers into elite households, the practice of footbinding, which apparently started among Tang-era dancers to enhance the beauty of their feet, spread to elite women, who, perhaps feeling a sense of competition with alluring young entertainers in their households, adopted the dancers' fashions. After its establishment as a sign of respectability and upper-class style, footbinding became a nearly universal practice among Chinese commoner women in subsequent dynasties. Ironically, Neo-Confucian moralists associated the practice with eroticism, and although it restricted women's mobility in ways that supported the moralists' renewed emphasis on distinctions of inner and outer realms, they did not promote it. Indeed, in the competitive and fractious political environment of the Song, the presence of courtesans in elite households provided fodder for accusations of decadence and excess among politically divided male elites (Bossler 2013).

The Song were in a constant state of military crisis: the northern half of the empire was conquered by the Jurchen Jin dynasty in 1126, and the rest of the empire was taken in 1279 by the Mongols. As a result, political loyalty became the preeminent political virtue in an increasingly toxic political discourse infused with Neo-Confucian moral fervor. In the late Song a wife's loyalty to her husband became a potent metaphor for male political virtue. A growing number of men began to advocate that widows remain chaste, refraining from remarrying in order to continue service to a husband's patriline. Prior to this, widow chastity had occasionally been praised as exemplary, most notably by Ban Zhao during the Han dynasty, but it was rarely practiced. Amid the violence of the Mongol conquest, female chastity acquired new salience, as many women committed suicide to avoid being raped by soldiers. Their heroism was heralded as a model for men enjoined to fight to the death against the invaders.

As the Mongols completed their conquest of the Song empire and established their own Chinese-style dynasty, which they named the Yuan (1260–1368), female chastity and widow loyalty became the preeminent markers of ideal femininity for Han Chinese families and critical expressions of the survival of Han Chinese values under alien Mongol rule. Although the Mongols marginalized Han elites and abrogated many elements of Confucian political culture, such as the examination system, they were eager to consolidate their authority among the majority Han population. Thus, under advice from Neo-Confucian scholars, the Mongols established a state system for canonizing chaste widows as exemplars of Confucian morality, offering them awards and tax remission. The Yuan also discouraged widow remarriage through law, forbidding widows from taking their dowry property into a new marriage and dictating that if they did remarry, their first husband's parents were legally entitled to negotiate the match. This was a major change to law and practice, even among Song Neo-Confucian elites. Until the Yuan, if a woman was widowed or divorced, she typically returned to her natal family with her dowry and often with her children as well, so that her own parents could arrange a new marriage. According to the Mongol custom of the levirate, in contrast, a widow was supposed to remarry one of her husband's relatives so that she and her dowry remained with his family. Although the Chinese considered such marriages incestuous, the legal promotion of widow chastity reflected, in part, a convenient convergence between Neo-Confucian patrilineal principles and Mongol custom, amounting to a compromise that kept women and their property in the husband's family but prevented incestuous remarriage. This was the origin of a so-called cult of female chastity that made chaste widows exemplars of the highest and purest form of femininity and female virtue. It emerged out of the complex cultural politics of an alien dynasty and represented not simply a fulfillment of Neo-Confucian gender ideals but the encounter between those ideals and the gender norms of Mongolian steppe culture (Birge 2010).

As China began its late imperial period in 1368 with the founding of the Ming dynasty (1368–1644), the state placed unprecedented emphasis on promotion of orthodox family values and gender norms as a tool for social and political stability and a mechanism for reinvigorating a Chinese civilization that the Ming founder considered tainted by Mongol influences. The examination system vetting scholars for bureaucratic office was fully restored, with the curriculum focused on Song Neo-Confucian philosophy and political thought. An upwardly mobile class of scholar elites aspiring to get their sons into government office again saw the importance of harnessing women's labor and dowries for the success of the patriline. The Ming kept the Yuan statutes on widow property and expanded the system for canonizing chaste widows and chastity martyrs. Among the literati, female chastity continued to be a potent metaphor for self-sacrifice and political loyalty and also became a hallmark of family respectability. Male literati enhanced their own reputation and that of their families by commemorating chaste widows in hagiographies that circulated through the vibrant publishing market (Carlitz 1997). Promoted and rewarded by the state and extolled by male writers, the practice of widow chastity spread across the empire and to all social classes during the Ming dynasty. Poor women who resisted remarriage even though it would have improved their economic circumstances were upheld by elite men as particularly poignant exemplars of female virtue. The numbers of women formally honored by the state and local elites for their chastity skyrocketed, with local histories documenting them in their thousands. As the numbers grew, so too did the extremes of their chaste behavior. Increasing numbers of widows demonstrated their loyalty to their husbands by committing suicide to "follow their husband in death." Tales of their heroic deaths often depicted staunch and gruesome resistance to the attempts of family elders to keep them alive.

KOREA

Dynastic Lineages

Old Chosŏn (2333–194 BCE)
Wiman Chosŏn (194–108 BCE)
Three Kingdoms
Koguryŏ (37 BCE–668 CE)
Paekche (18 BCE–660 CE)
Silla (57 BCE–935 CE) (Silla unified Koguryŏ and Paekche in 668)
Koryŏ (918–1392)
Chosŏn (1392–1910)

Foundation Myths and the Emergence of Gender Hierarchy

Archaeological evidence from the Neolithic period suggests that the inhabitants of the Korean peninsula were organized in consanguineous groups that maintained communal economic activities, held shamanistic and ancestor worship rituals, practiced exogamy, followed matrilineal practices, and worshiped female deities. While there is evidence of a certain division of labor between men as hunters and women as gatherers, that division was not marked by a hierarchy at this point in history. Women's labor in weaving, making pottery, and gathering food must have been indispensable in the livelihoods of individual families as well as in the economies of the broader communities.

However, during the Bronze Age (from approximately the ninth to the fourth century BCE), with the emergence of enhanced economic productivity through agriculture and a rise in warring conflicts between communities, gender dynamics began to shift toward more male-dominant structures and practices. One of the signs that the society had stratified and a ruling class had emerged was the appearance of gigantic dolmen tombs for the interment of rulers. Some of these monuments had capstones as long as thirty feet and weighed as much as seventy tons; thus, it is quite clear that the construction of these tombs required the power and authority to deploy a large number of laborers and command economic resources. It is likely that tribal chieftains and their successors were buried in the dolmen tombs, along with bronze ornaments and tools that symbolized their power and wealth. The stratified societies of the Bronze Age eventually developed into the early form of state structure.

Old Chosŏn (2333 BCE–194 BCE) was one of the most advanced political structures to come out of the Bronze Age. The seat of the original state was located in the Taedong River basin at P'yŏngyang, the capital of present-day North Korea. It eventually developed into a large confederation by uniting other walled-town states scattered throughout the region between the Taedong and Liao Rivers. According to the foundation myth of Old Chosŏn, the Korean nation came into existence when Hwan'ung, son of the Heavenly King, descended from heaven to Mount T'aebaek. He brought with him three thousand loyal subjects as well as the ministers of the wind, the rain, and the clouds, delivering knowledge of agriculture, medicine, punishment, morality, and virtue. A bear and a tiger conveyed to Hwan'ung their desire to become human. Hwan'ung gave them garlic and bitter mugwort, and he told them that if they lived on these foods in an unlighted cave for one hundred days, they would be transformed. After twenty-one days the tiger succumbed to the conditions and left the cave, but the bear endured the test for the full length of the challenge and was transformed into a woman. The bear-woman then prayed for a husband, and Hwan'ung took the form of a man, lay with her, and begat a son, Tan'gun Wanggŏm, the mythical founder of Old Chosŏn.

There is no clear historical or archaeological evidence that will allow us to pinpoint the year that the Korean state was founded; however, some archaeological evidence and ancient histories of China and Central Asia help us infer that those who established Old Chosŏn came from a region that stretched from the Shandong peninsula and southern Manchuria. They are imagined to have brought with them a superior bronze culture that enabled them to gain power and authority over the native people on the Korean peninsula, who still adhered to a Neolithic material culture and totemic beliefs related to the bear and the tiger. The foundation myth is also indicative of the growing gender hierarchies and clear division of labor, with men taking up the public role and women in the private role. Tan'gun Wanggŏm, the mythical founder of Old Chosŏn, brings together the sacred, heavenly bloodline of his father, Hwan'ung, and the secular, earthly bloodline of his mother, the bear-woman. The creation myth implies that it is the role of men to rule a nation by virtue of their knowledge and morality, while it is women's role to endure hardships by virtue of their patience, as demonstrated in the mythic achievement of the she-bear. This type of gender-specific talent and the hierarchical order of men and women in society and the family came to be increasingly visible in the construction of more complex state structures shaped by the ongoing influence of Chinese political and cultural doctrines.

Continuity and Rupture in Confederated Kingdoms

The first major influence from China came in 108 BCE when Han China established the Four Commanderies on the Korean peninsula in the area north of the Han River. The Chinese colonial administration deployed labor services and commanded some level of control over the Korean population, but it also tended to allow the local population to exercise a degree of political freedom. Under Chinese colonial rule, Chinese culture made significant inroads on the Korean peninsula. In particular, Lo-lang, the commandery located near P'yŏngyang, served as a principal gateway for Chinese thought, culture, and material into the region through Chinese officials, merchants, and others. Through this dynamic flow, the earlier Bronze Age culture was gradually replaced by Iron Age culture. The metal cultures that had developed in the Taedong River basin spread in all directions and eventually contributed to the rise of the Yayoi culture in Japan.

The period of the Four Commanderies coincided with the establishment of several confederated kingdoms—most representatively Koguryŏ (37 BCE–668 CE), Paekche (18 BCE–660 CE), and Silla (57 BCE–935 CE). This era in Korean history is commonly referred to as the Three Kingdoms period. It was during this period that political and religious thought from China gained increasing prominence in Korea and had a far-reaching impact on Korea's subsequent history. By the fourth century, the establishment of institutions of Confucian teaching, such as T'aehak in Koguryŏ, had begun. Within a few decades, scholars affiliated with these institutions were transmitting Chinese ideas to Japan, thereby continuing the eastward spread of continental culture. According to Japanese historical accounts from the early eighth century, Wang In, a Confucian scholar of Paekche, was said to have brought Chinese writing and Confucian texts to Japan by the early fifth century. Confucianism enjoyed a burgeoning popularity among scholars and the ruling elite in Korea, who advocated it as a set of philosophical principles that provided good guidance for governing the country. When the Three Kingdoms were unified under Silla in 668, Confucian philosophy took on even greater significance as it came to be more fully adopted in order to strengthen the power of state rulers and reform government structures.

The adoption and growing influence of Confucianism had enormous implications for women. Over time the philosophy accelerated movement toward a male-centered political and social structure that promoted an idealized notion of labor divided along gender lines, with men taking on tasks in the public sphere and women assigned to the domestic sphere. Confucian philosophy prescribed certain gender norms, such as the Three Obediences (*samjong*) of a woman (to her father, husband, and son), which led to the emergence of new social attitudes about the proper behavior of men and women. Women's interference in public matters came to be frowned

Clay Figurine of a Woman in Childbirth. Silla Kingdom.
NATIONAL MUSEUM OF KOREA

upon. Preference for sons became increasingly visible, and it began to shape new family dynamics. During the Silla kingdom a pattern of household succession in which sons succeeded their fathers as the heads of families took root.

Despite the steadily growing influence of Confucian norms and regulations, indigenous traditions continued to be important in the areas of marriage and family, religion, and even politics. One prominent area in which powerful indigenous traditions were still evident was marriage customs. (As we shall see in the case of Japan later in this chapter, indigenous traditions in marriage and intimate relations continued for hundreds of years after Confucian ideas arrived there as well.) While the royal family and the ruling class in Korea began to adopt Confucian ways of marriage, diverse marital customs from the earlier period continued to be practiced during the Three Kingdoms period. In the Koguryŏ kingdom people followed the precept of the "son-in-law chamber" (*sŏok*), a practice in which the groom would move into the home of the bride's family upon marriage and stay until the couple's children were grown. This marriage custom continued through the Silla kingdom, through the Koryŏ dynasty (918–1392), and even into the early Chosŏn dynasty (1392–1910). The tradition of a married couple taking up residence in the home of the bride's family is suggestive of a matrilineal tradition. Matriliny is also implied by the fact that sons and daughters were relatively equal with regard to the inheritance of property and slaves from their natal family.

In the upper classes marriage was not seen simply as the union of a couple. Rather, marriage was strategically used to create political alliances. To cope with the southward aggression of the Koguryŏ kingdom, ruling families in the Paekche and Silla kingdoms allied themselves through marriage. Marital partners were also chosen for purposes of maintaining or enhancing family status. In general, people selected partners from similar social strata. This was especially true among royal and aristocratic families. Silla kings and queens recorded both paternal and maternal lineages, which suggests that marriage was seen as a partnership and that social status was of central importance.

Although strategic marriages were notable in this early period, love and marriage during the Three Kingdoms period were rather free in form, often taking place without a formal ceremony or ritual. In *Records of the Three Kingdoms*, a Chinese historical text from the third century, Chen Shou describes some aspects of Korean folk life at that time, including marital practices, and the description there suggests that marriage was based on romance rather than parental arrangement. Men and women freely associated in public, engaging with each other in such activities as singing and dancing. However, one can also detect the growing influence of Confucian propriety in shaping the practice of romance and marriage.

From that time there is the legendary love story of Ch'unch'u, who became King Muyŏl of Silla (r. 654–661), and Munhŭi, a woman from an aristocratic family. In the story, while participating in a sporting event with Ch'unch'u, Munhŭi's brother Yusin inadvertently steps on a ribbon trailing from Ch'unch'u's jacket. Feeling guilty for damaging his friend's garment, Yusin brings Ch'unch'u to his home, where he asks his sister, Munhŭi, to mend it. Ch'unch'u is immediately smitten with the girl, and he begins to frequent her house. When it is discovered that she has become pregnant through her relationship with Ch'unch'u, her brother, furious at her "immoral" behavior, decides that she must be immolated to restore the honor of the family. However, Queen Sŏndŏk, the aunt of Ch'unch'u, intervenes to rescue the young woman. A few days later, Munhŭi and Ch'unch'u are formally married. This episode reflects the reality that there was open romance in Silla. However, it also illustrates the growing power of Confucian ethics, which instructed women to be "proper" and "chaste" before marriage. It is apparent that marital practices such as love marriage saw significant retrenchment once Confucianism had become thoroughly instituted in later periods.

While Confucianism from China helped to shape political structures during the Three Kingdoms period, both indigenous religions and Buddhism, newly introduced on the peninsula, dominated spiritual and cultural life. The term "indigenous religions" refers to a spectrum of belief systems that prevailed on the Korean peninsula, including the worship of mountain spirits, dragon kings, heavenly gods, and ghosts. What is broadly referred to as "shamanism" is the most protracted, most influential religious tradition in Korea. The role of the shaman was to mediate between heaven and earth, drive away bad spirits, and bring good fortune. There are very few historical records that present a clear picture of the role women played in religious practices; however, the historical records that do exist suggest that local deities and mountain spirits were frequently embodied in female form. In addition, participants at seasonal festivals would worship goddesses or the mother of the founder of the state. Indeed, some religious rituals appear to have required women to preside over them. One of the best-known woman priests of the Silla kingdom was Aro, the daughter of the founder of Silla and the sister of King Namhae (r. 4–24). According to *Samguk sagi* (*History of the Three Kingdoms*), the oldest extant Korean history book, authored by Kim Pusik (1075–1151), Aro presided over ancestor worship rituals, especially in memory of her father. The fact that she took on the role of the highest religious leader, separate and distinct from her brother's political leadership, may indicate the existence of a division of labor beginning in the first millennium, with men in control of the state in the political arena and women in charge of the religious domain.

Buddhism was introduced into Korea via China in the fourth century and had become firmly established by the sixth century. Koguryŏ and Paekche accepted the religion without any major disturbance, but there was considerable resistance in the case of Silla, where Buddhism was not formally accepted until 527. The first woman to become a Buddhist in Silla was known only by her last name, Sa. She and her brother assisted a monk who had come from Koguryŏ on a mission to spread Buddhism in Silla nearly a century before the religion was officially accepted during the reign of Pŏphŭng (r. 514–540). After that, women of the upper class and royal families became major patrons of the religion, and some of them, especially widows, chose to become nuns.

Women were key in the spread of Buddhism, not only across Korea but also in Japan. Korean Buddhist nuns of the Paekche kingdom are particularly noteworthy. Paekche was responsible for transmitting the Chinese writing system, the technology for making iron weapons, and other significant advances to Japan. Buddhism was another prominent influence on Japanese culture that came through Paekche. According to the eighth-century classic history of Japan, *Nihon shoki* (*The Chronicles of Japan*), King Widŏk of Paekche dispatched several missions to the Japanese ruling family in the second half of the sixth century. These missions included Buddhist monks, nuns, and artisans. Widŏk also sent a variety of gifts, the most significant of which were Buddhist texts and statuary. Some members of Japan's ruling family were deeply impressed with this new religion, while others held firmly to the indigenous religious beliefs of Japan. This engendered conflict, which was resolved in favor of the supporters of Buddhism in 587. In the following year, Widŏk sent "an embassy bringing both gifts of Buddhist relics and a second, and even larger, contingent of Buddhist clerics and artisans for presentation to the Japanese throne" (Best 2006, 155–156). In addition, there are also records that indicate three Japanese nuns came to Paekche in 588 to receive novice precepts; they were ordained in 590. These three nuns became "the first members of the Japanese *sangha* [Buddhist monastic community] to receive training abroad" (Best 2006, 156–157; see also Cho 2011, 17–18). Women of status and wealth were also prominent patrons in establishing temples. Thus in a variety of ways, we see that women were vital in the introduction and spread of Buddhism on the peninsula and beyond it.

Women's contribution to the economy during the Three Kingdoms period is also evident. They were indispensable participants in agriculture, weaving, pottery making, and a number of other crafts. It was typically men who were primarily responsible for working the land to cultivate food, but women provided various forms of labor in the gathering and processing of grains. When wars were waged during the Three Kingdoms period and men were drafted into the military, it would fall to the women to take care of agricultural work. As in both China and Japan, one of the most significant areas of work for women was weaving and making clothes. States promoted the production of textiles as women's work. Even queens and women of the aristocratic class devoted some time to weaving. In Silla, the government employed skilled women workers to gather the raw materials for textiles, weave and dye the textiles produced, and then turn them into clothing. Women were a dominant force in the marketplace as well, selling and buying products. There are also examples of upper-class women from Silla who engaged in the import of raw materials such as wool from Tang China and the export of products to Japan.

BOX 1.2

Women Rulers in the Silla Kingdom

In the political arena, the most remarkable feature of the Three Kingdoms period is that there were three female rulers, all of whom reigned during the Silla kingdom (57 BCE–935 CE). After that no other woman ruled on the Korean peninsula until 2012, when Park Geun-hye was elected president of South Korea. One important sociopolitical feature that enabled women to ascend to the throne during Silla was the strict application of the so-called bone-rank system (*kolp'umje*), which governed aristocratic society. The top rank in the bone-rank system was "hallowed-bone" status (*sŏnggol*), followed by "true-bone" status (*chin'gol*), then "six-head," "five-head," and "four-head" statuses. Those who came from hallowed-bone and true-bone ranks constituted the ruling class in Silla. Hallowed-bone rank was held by a relatively small number of people. This was the class from which the rulers came. The first two queens, Sŏndŏk (r. 632–647) and Chindŏk (r. 647–654), came from the hallowed-bone rank. That rank, in effect, ceased to exist around the time Silla unified the Three Kingdoms in 668. At that time those who came from the true-bone rank were elevated and became eligible to take the throne. The last queen, Chinsŏng (r. 887–897), was from the true-bone rank.

The accomplishments and the failures of the three queens are recorded in *Samguk sagi* (*The History of the Three Kingdoms*), compiled in 1145, and *Samguk yusa* (*Memorabilia of the Three Kingdoms*), compiled in 1281. When Queen Sŏndŏk and Queen Chindŏk came to power, intense conflicts among the Three Kingdoms shaped the political dynamics, leading to shifting alliances. Both Queen Sŏndŏk and Queen Chindŏk had to bring in mediators from the Tang dynasty in order to quell Paekche. Queen Sŏndŏk, the most renowned of the three, is well regarded for her exceptional intelligence, wisdom, and compassion for the poor, which she displayed in her policies, her promotion of Buddhism, and her diplomatic skills in dealing with the Tang dynasty. In her last year as queen, Sŏndŏk found her authority as the head of state challenged by Lord Pidam, who led a revolt, claiming she did not have the leadership skills needed to govern the country.

Upon Sŏndŏk's death, her cousin Chindŏk ascended to the throne. At the time Silla was still engaged in a long and difficult conflict with Paekche. Taking the advice of her closest advisors, she sought military assistance from the Tang dynasty, and while her proactive collaboration with Tang laid the foundation for the unification of the Three Kingdoms, her reliance on foreign power has been criticized by historians. The court of the third queen, Chinsŏng (r. 887–897), has been described as corrupt and immoral, and it is said that this court "brought the kingdom to the brink of ruin" (Ilyon 1972, 128). However, it is not clear that Chinsŏng should bear total responsibility for the waning of the kingdom. By the time she came to the throne, Silla had already fallen into a rapid decline for a number of reasons: an extreme power struggle among aristocratic families, incessant peasant rebellions, and the growing power of local gentries who had built not only monetary wealth through private trading activities but also private military forces.

It comes as no surprise that the growing influence of Confucian philosophical and political thought toward the end of the Three Kingdoms period resulted in disapproval of the female rulers of Silla. Kim Pusik, author of *The History of the Three Kingdoms* and a Confucian scholar and statesman during the Koryŏ dynasty, expressed his discontent with the Silla practices that sanctioned women ascending the throne. He quite explicitly stated that "according to the cosmological principles, yang is strong and yin is gentle and thus men should be revered, and women should be despised. How can an old woman confined to the inner chamber [i.e., the queen] possibly govern the country? Silla granted women the capacity to rule the country, and the result was chaos. It was only pure luck that kept the country from ruin under female rulers" (*Samguk sagi*, Silla pon'gi 5: Queen Sŏndŏk). We can assume that his dismissive assessment of female governance came out of a Confucian worldview that presumed a clear division of labor in which the conduct of political and public affairs was exclusively in the realm of men.

Consolidation of Gender Hierarchy in Medieval Korea

When Wang Gŏn established the Koryŏ dynasty (918–1392), he was very deliberate in placating the former royal families of Silla and influential families of the gentry. He conferred land grants on those who contributed to the founding of the dynasty. He also strategically used marriage to establish alliances with powerful local landlords that would strengthen the dynasty by integrating various groups of regional elites. (Wang Gŏn himself had twenty-nine wives.)

Koryŏ was an aristocratic society with a government built on the foundation of Confucianism. By the eleventh century the state had succeeded in creating a centralized bureaucratic system for law, administration, and education, following the model of Tang and Song China. In particular, it instituted civil service examinations in the tenth century as a device for selecting government officials on the basis of their intelligence rather than family background. Although the civil service examinations did help to bring well-educated, thoughtful individuals into government service, they did not eliminate legacy appointments. The policy of protected appointments (*ŭmsŏ*) for the sons, cousins, and sons-in-law of aristocrats continued. Family background and a close-knit kinship network—both maternal and paternal—was still a more reliable asset in securing political power and material wealth than individual talent. And at the heart of this family network was marriage.

Arguably, the strategic use of marriage and kinship for consolidation and enhancement of political, economic, and cultural power reached its peak during the Koryŏ dynasty. (As we shall see below, what historians have called "marriage politics" similarly dominated the political and economic system in Japan in the ninth through eleventh centuries.) As indicated earlier in this section, maternal as well as paternal family lines were important in Koryŏ families. For instance, great accomplishments in a wife's family accrued to her husband and benefited his status. By the same logic, any misfortune or bad behavior in the wife's family negatively affected her husband. Rules for the inheritance of property also were more inclusive, recognizing family linkages created through marriage. A son-in-law could inherit the property of his wife's parents, and the son of a daughter was deemed a legitimate heir of property from his maternal grandparents. In this way, both paternal and maternal family networks were at the heart of political and economic power. Marriage could also be a vehicle for social mobility. This stands in stark contrast with the situation that had evolved in Silla, where the rigid "bone-rank" system made social mobility through marriage practically impossible, or in Chosŏn, where strict patrilineality was privileged over maternal family lines.

Koryŏ society was organized by distinct social classes. The ruling class was composed of civil service and military elites, collectively called *yangban*. Below them were commoners (*sangmin*), who were largely farmers. In the bottom stratum were the lowborn (*ch'ŏnmin*), which included slaves, artisans, peddlers, entertainers, shamans, butchers, and others. This social organization was based on a kinship unit that incorporated five generations, all of whom usually lived in the same village. The order of family succession was typically the eldest legitimate son, followed by the eldest legitimate grandson, the second legitimate son, any illegitimate son, the second legitimate grandson, any illegitimate grandson, and finally any female child. While daughters were not considered to be equal candidates for family succession, family registries from that time include both sons and daughters in the order of their birth rather than other alternatives, such as listing sons before daughters, irrespective of their birth order, or sons exclusively. Historical evidence also shows that women were sometimes allowed to head families. For instance, under certain circumstances when the head of the family died, his wife became head of the family even when there was an adult son.

Furthermore, with regard to the inheritance of property, women had rights that were fairly equal to those of men. Women could inherit land, houses, slaves, and other valuable commodities such as rice or jewelry. This relatively equal distribution of family wealth to sons and daughters is a result of the fact that daughters and sons shared responsibilities for ancestor worship equally. In Koryŏ, sons and daughters alternated the financing of ancestor worship rituals held at Buddhist temples. This Koryŏ tradition contrasts with the practice that was adopted during the Chosŏn dynasty (1392–1910), in which the eldest son was exclusively responsible for ancestor worship and thus inherited most of the family wealth. It is also notable that the status of sons-in-law was equal to that of sons in terms of property inheritance and family-related responsibilities. The deep integration of the son-in-law into his wife's family might have stemmed from an earlier marriage custom in which the future son-in-law moved into the home of his bride's family and continued to live there after marriage. Under these circumstances, the daughter was able to maintain a close relationship with her family and was equal to a son in matters of family inheritance.

These practices of equal inheritance and residential arrangement for married couples did not always benefit women. If a woman's family was poor and did not have the means to provide material resources for her marriage, she could not marry. Having no marital prospects, those women sometimes chose to become Buddhist nuns. Furthermore, since marriage was a crucial opportunity for men to gain wealth and status, there were a number of cases in which a husband abandoned his wife to enter into marriage with another woman whose family held more wealth and prestige. The state rarely punished men for such behavior. However, unlike later during the Chosŏn dynasty, there was no stigma in or prohibition against remarriage, so women who were abandoned or divorced weren't condemned to a solitary life. The fact that remarriage was an option did not necessarily mean that a woman had the power or freedom to choose her own life. Since marriage was often calculated as a political or social strategy, her parents were more than likely the ones making the calculations in seeking out a potential husband.

Confucian ethics and Buddhist ideas of salvation created conditions and attitudes that had a significant impact on the lives of women. The late Koryŏ dynasty saw more rigorous regulations placed on women's bodies and life choices. At this time Buddhism was under increasing scrutiny and Neo-Confucianism, introduced from China via the Yuan dynasty (1260–1368), was promoted by the emerging literati class of Confucian scholars and politicians who came to hold the central power in the new Chosŏn dynasty (1392–1910). The women of aristocratic families would have had direct exposure to Confucian ideals, having been educated using Confucian texts in Chinese that instructed them on appropriate behavior for women. Other segments of society were much more influenced by Buddhist ethics and practices. Significantly, Buddhist teachings during the Koryŏ dynasty did not contradict the state-sanctioned Confucian precepts; rather, in both Buddhist and Confucian teachings, the role of women was largely confined to domestic matters. They were socialized and instructed to comply with the expectations to cook, sew, manage the household, raise the children, and serve their husbands and parents-in-law. In particular, womanly virtues such as filial piety and chastity were promoted and celebrated through public recognition of exemplary women. Women were expected to keep their bodies pure and remain chaste while married. The implications of these expectations were most obvious in the reactions to adultery. In cases in which men were unfaithful to their wives, there were no serious sanctions against such behavior. In contrast, if a woman was discovered to have had an adulterous liaison, she would receive severe punishment.

In spite of these points of consensus, one can also see some major differences between Confucian and Buddhist teachings for women in the matters of marriage, remarriage, chastity, and filial piety. In Buddhism, marriage was a private matter and thus was the choice of individuals. It was completely acceptable for an unmarried woman to devote herself to serving her aging parents. Chastity was important, but after her spouse had passed away, a woman was free to remarry. Daughters, whether single or married, contributed to ancestor worship for the salvation of their parents. In contrast, in

Confucianism, marriage was an essential process in life in order to produce sons and carry out one's duty to serve one's parents and perform ancestor worship.

That women's primary duties were in the domestic arena did not mean that they were excluded from economic activities. Women of all classes actively participated in the family economy in various ways. In the case of the upper classes, the woman, as the manager of the family, oversaw a wide range of household matters, including supervising the slaves who worked in the home and on family farmlands. Some women showed exceptional talent in commercial and trading activities, earning profits for their families. The Yuan empire built an extensive trading route that connected Asia with Europe, and some Koreans took advantage of new commercial opportunities by trading Korean ginseng, ramie, and other native agricultural products for products from around the world.

Koryŏ was repeatedly invaded by the Mongols between 1231 and 1270, and a subsequent peace treaty between Koryŏ and the Mongols had a substantial impact on Korean politics as well as Korean culture and family structure. One significant change was intermarriage between Koryŏ kings and Yuan princesses, which turned Koryŏ into the "son-in-law nation" of Yuan. The first such case was King Ch'ungyŏl (r. 1274–1308), who married Princess Chegukdaejang, the daughter of Kublai Khan. In addition to the marital union of two royal families, Koryŏ was obliged to send women and artisans to Yuan to serve as ladies-in-waiting, eunuchs, or slaves.

One prominent example of a Koryŏ woman sent to Yuan was Lady Ki. As a young girl she attracted the attention of Emperor Shun while she was serving tea at his palace, and she became his favored consort. In 1365, despite extreme jealousy and strong opposition from Yuan's ruling elites, she ascended to the role of empress, the highest status possible. The ascendance of a foreign woman to such a position of prominence and authority is a remarkable story. However, Lady Ki is also a controversial figure in Korean history. Her family in Koryŏ abused their power and mistreated people in amassing their wealth. In addition, as Koryŏ began to adopt anti-Yuan policies under King Kongmin (r. 1351–1374), Empress Ki continued to be firmly pro-Yuan, placing her own interests above those of a nation full of Koreans. In other words, despite her renown, Lady Ki was an exception. For the vast majority of Korean women forced to leave their families and lead lives of subordination in a foreign country, the experience was a terrible ordeal. To avoid subjecting their daughters to such a fate, many parents arranged early marriages (*chohon*).

JAPAN

Historic Time Periods in Japan

Yayoi c. 300 BCE–c. 250 CE
Kofun c. 250–538
Asuka 538–710
Nara 710–784
Heian 794–1185
Kamakura 1185–1333
Muromachi 1336–1573
Warring States 1467–1600
Edo (Tokugawa) 1600–1868

Until the end of the last ice age, around twelve thousand years ago, what are now the islands of Japan were the easternmost edge of continental Eurasia. Rising sea levels after that time made migration of people and culture more difficult, although not impossible. Modern archaeologists' studies of gravesites in the western reaches of Japan show that a large number of people arrived from the Korean peninsula around 300 BCE, bringing with them crop agriculture and animal domestication. Gradually, the skills and techniques brought by these new settlers diffused to the fertile Kansai plain, the area around modern Kyoto and Osaka. Agriculture produced sufficient wealth to give rise to rulers and the communities that supported them.

The rise of these communities and rulers was not initially accompanied by a diffusion of continental religions, ideologies, or ideas about gender relations and sexualities. This began to change in the sixth century CE, when the Korean kingdom of Paekche sent Buddhist clerics, texts, and relics to Japan, and it accelerated in the seventh and eighth centuries, when Japanese rulers adopted Confucian-based legal codes from Tang China to centralize their monarchical authority. Even then, however, Chinese and Korean legal practices were adapted to existing Japanese culture in many ways.

The earliest historical records mentioning Japan were late third-century CE Chinese chronicles. The chronicles describe two female rulers, Himiko and Iyo, whose successful reigns were separated by the chaotic reign of a male ruler. Ancient rulers, both female and male, were expected to carry out spiritual functions such as communicating with deities that were associated with their clan—the Yamato family of Himiko and Iyo worshiped the sun goddess, Amaterasu, as their family's ancestor—as well as administrative functions such as ruling their community and carrying out diplomatic relations. Himiko's and

Iyo's communications with China's Wei and Western Jin dynasties indicate that Chinese rulers recognized female rule in Wa ("Wa" was an ancient name for Japan). A Wei dynasty emperor gave Himiko a medallion and referred to her as "king of Wa, friendly to Wei" (Tonomura 2009, 353). Women continued to carry out spiritual and administrative rule for several more centuries, accounting for eight of the sixteen imperial reigns from 592 to 770. Rulership was not identified primarily with male gender until the end of the eighth century.

As in the case of Korea, sexuality and marriage practices in ancient Japanese society differed from Chinese practices. Unlike the information about women rulers' role in diplomacy and administration gathered by Chinese observers in the third century, information about sexual practices comes to us from much later Japanese writers. These eighth-century writers were often provincial officials charged with collecting detailed information about culture and agricultural productivity in their regions for the imperial court. From their records, we learn that boys and girls engaged in songfests where they exchanged poems and songs as a way to select sexual partners. Sexual relations did not require a contractual agreement of marriage, and premarital relations were not morally censured. Families generally consisted of mothers and their children, with husbands more loosely connected to the family through sexual relations with the mother that could end at any time. Marriages were centered in women's homes; husbands visited their wives' homes for varying lengths of time. Some of these marriage practices paralleled marriage customs in Korea during the same period. As we shall see later in this section, Japanese marriages continued to be located primarily in wives' homes until the fourteenth century, long after the introduction of Confucian-based legal codes.

Early Medieval Laws and Practices in Japan

Continuing waves of Korean immigrants in the fifth and sixth centuries brought arts, culture, techniques of organizing the state, and the Buddhist religion to the Yamato rulers. Over time, these institutions helped the Yamato family consolidate its power as the leading royal family (this family came to be called the imperial family). At the beginning of the seventh century, the head of the immigrant Soga family, Prince Shōtoku, together with his aunt, Empress Suiko (r. 592–628), established diplomatic relations with China's Sui dynasty. Suiko and Shōtoku's actions ushered in a flood of deliberate borrowing from the Sui and Tang dynasties. This showed few signs of abating for more than two hundred years, even after the Soga were pushed aside in 645 by another family, the Fujiwara, as the leading advisors to the imperial family.

Chinese influences were evident in new official legal codes called the *ritsuryō* system (*ritsu* is criminal law; *ryō* is administrative law), new patterns of land ownership and taxation, and new ways of organizing government.

Sexuality, marriage, and construction of gender changed more slowly than the official codes, however, as continental ideas and practices were modified to blend with indigenous culture. In the imperial family, unlike most others, continental influences did make some inroads. Although before the thirteenth century most heterosexual marriages and other intimate relationships outside the imperial family were located in the woman's home and not the man's, by the end of the eighth century it had become the norm that male emperors' wives and lovers lived with the emperor in his residential palace. Emperors' wives, especially if their sons became heirs to the throne, eventually gained more influence than daughters of emperors. One aristocratic family in particular, the Fujiwara family, maintained power within the imperial system over a two-hundred-year period through its daughters becoming mothers of imperial heirs from the ninth to the eleventh centuries. These heirs, following Japanese custom, were born in their mothers' homes and were raised for several years by their (Fujiwara) maternal grandparents, even after their mothers returned to the imperial palace. By the time the children joined their mother and father in the palace, they had developed loyalty to their maternal lineage. Historians call this custom "marriage politics," a practice whereby some of the daughters of major aristocratic families came to be more valued than their brothers because of their ability to link their family to the throne through sexuality and marriage.

Chinese models were also at the heart of new ways of organizing society and economy in the seventh and eighth centuries, although these models were modified due to persisting gender norms. The official *ritsuryō* legal codes established a landholding system that placed all arable land under the emperor's ownership. The emperor's officials would then redistribute the land to the farmers, with allocations based on each family's composition as listed in the family registry. But the registry system—also newly created at this time—used a Confucian-style definition of the family, which assumed a male head of household, patrilineal inheritance and marital location, formal rites to designate marriage, and laws against premarital sex and wives' adultery. This Confucian-style model was alien to Japanese practices at the time and had little effect on how families were formed or lived their lives, except when it came to land allocation.

Because the family registry was used to redistribute land, families made adjustments to best serve their needs. Under *ritsuryō* law around the year 700, each able-bodied adult male listed in the family's registry received two *tan* (a unit of land measurement) of land, and each woman received two-thirds of the man's allotment. But women were exempt from three onerous taxes that men had to pay: the labor service tax, the military service tax, and the head tax (the head tax was often paid with cloth made by the family's women, although it was levied on the men). Because men's taxes were higher, many men registered as women, giving up some land to avoid paying those taxes. Over time, the throne's ownership of land eroded, and the allotment system itself faded away within a century. Private ownership of land began to take its place, and title deeds show both male and female ownership of land, with husbands and wives often having separate holdings. The military service tax was also soon abandoned by the government. The fact that masculinity had been identified with military service in the eighth century would, however, contribute in later centuries to a gender structure in which women were disadvantaged when a class of economically and politically empowered warriors called samurai arose.

Much of our information about gender and sexuality in the early medieval period derives from the extensive literary output by women of the Heian court and aristocracy. The Heian period (794–1185) is named for the location of the imperial capital at Heian-kyō (meaning "Capital of Peace and Tranquility"), the modern city of Kyoto. Because literacy in Japan, as elsewhere in the medieval era, was limited to the upper classes, we know much more about courtly and aristocratic society (about twenty thousand people at that time) than about commoners (six to seven million people). Occupations, residency (urban or rural), and status were as significant in the defining of social rank as gender.

Servants and officials of the court came from the aristocratic classes, and unlike the case in some other courts around the world at that time, a large proportion of these were women. Although many of the more prestigious bureaucratic positions at court were occupied by men in the early eighth century, women officials also carried out important functions in the inner palace, such as sending out imperial announcements and assisting with ceremonies. By the end of the ninth century, male officials, noting the importance of these jobs carried out by women, began to take over many of them, and by the end of the tenth century, a large number of the court's women were limited to household duties such as lamplighting and cleaning. A few had coveted jobs as ladies-in-waiting to empresses, and two of these ladies, Sei Shōnagon and Murasaki Shikibu, were among the greatest writers of the early eleventh century. We shall return to them later in this section.

In addition to losing their ability to rule as emperors and perform as important officials at court, women lost status within religious practice as well. Women continued to occupy leading roles in Shinto, the ancient religion of the early rulers and their clans, serving as heads of convents and as shamans, but they lost much of their earlier status in Buddhism by the ninth century. Buddhism arrived in Japan from the Korean kingdom of Paekche in the sixth century, and, according to the *Nihon Shoki* (*Chronicles of Japan*, completed in 720), the first Japanese to be ordained as Buddhist clergy were the nun Zenshin'ni and two other nuns. Many monasteries and convents were established in the seventh and eighth centuries, and numerous men and women were ordained as monks, priests, and nuns. Nuns performed Buddhist ceremonies at the imperial court until 772, when new regulations stipulated that ten male clerics would carry out those functions. In 806, rules for ordination inaugurated by the acclaimed monk Saichō (767–822) on his return from studies in China further limited women's roles in Buddhism. Nunneries were abandoned as nuns died off, and some convents were taken over by monks. The number of women lay practitioners of Buddhism continued to grow during the Heian period, however. Women produced Buddhist paintings and writings, and increasing numbers of women became "lay nuns," who cut their hair and retreated into a life of prayer and contemplation without being formally ordained.

Aristocratic men and women were prolific writers. It was customary for men to use both classical Chinese and vernacular Japanese writing for their works, while women wrote mostly in Japanese. Japanese vernacular script (*kana*) had been invented in the early ninth century, supplementing the more awkward ways of expressing the Japanese language with Chinese characters that had been the style for three hundred years before that time. While men continued to write administrative and legal documents using Chinese characters—the official language of government until the late nineteenth century—both sexes wrote poetry and prose in Japanese. Ki no Tsurayuki, an esteemed literary critic, government official, and poet, when tasked by the court to edit a collection of Japanese poetry in 905, collected more than a thousand works by both male and female poets. His high regard for women writers was apparent when he wrote the travelogue *Tosa Nikki* (*The Tosa Diary*) in 940, claiming he was a woman author. In the preface, he wrote: "It is generally a man who writes what is called a Diary, now a woman will see what she can do" (Ki no Tsurayuki 1981, 13). Ki no Tsurayuki was being ironic, as women were already among the greatest writers of the day. Although the distribution of their works was limited to courtly and aristocratic readers, many have now been translated into modern Japanese and dozens of world languages.

None of these writers has left a greater legacy than the contemporaries Sei Shōnagon (c. 966–1017/1025) and Murasaki Shikibu (978–1014/1025). Each of these women served in one of the courts of the two rival wives of the emperor around the year 1000, and they wrote scathingly of each other as snobbish or unskilled. Sei Shōnagon's most famous work, a witty collection of essays called *The Pillow Book*, included instructions for proper and tasteful lovemaking, showed her attitudes toward beauty and refinement, expressed snobbishness toward country folk and commoners, and offered dozens of intimate portraits of the Heian-period elite.

Young men and women from puberty on were expected to enjoy romantic liaisons, and society looked askance at those who avoided sex altogether. They were trained to choose their partners carefully and to conduct their trysts under cover of night until the young lady and her family accepted as a husband the young man who visited her. (First marriages were often among

BOX 1.3

Sei Shōnagon: A Lover Should Know How to Make His Departure

In this witty passage, Sei Shōnagon suggests that sexuality was freely practiced and that lovers abided by strict rules of taste.

> *A lover should know how to make his departure. . . . One likes him to behave in such a way that one is sure he is unhappy at going. . . . He should not pull on his trousers the moment he is up, but should first of all come close to one's ear and in a whisper finish off whatever was left half-said in the course of the night. . . . Then he should raise the shutters, and both lovers should go out together at the double doors. . . . [A]fter he has slipped away, she can stand gazing after him, with charming recollections of those last moments. . . . If he springs to his feet with a jerk and at once begins fussing round, tightening in the waistband of his breeches, or adjusting the sleeves of his court coat, hunting jacket, or what not, collecting a thousand odds and ends, and thrusting them into the folds of his dress . . . one begins to hate him. (Sei Shōnagon 1955, 138–139)*

young teens.) When the couple was considered "married," the young man could come and go freely during the day. He lived at his wife's house, was outfitted for court by her family, and often adopted the name of her house as his own; a head of the powerful Fujiwara family of the early eleventh century noted that "a man's career depends on his wife's family" (Nickerson 1993, 452). Although children inherited membership in their father's clan, their residency, as well as their father's, was with their mother. Daughters usually inherited the houses they lived in.

The aristocratic marriage pattern of the Heian period was quite different from the Confucian-style pattern stipulated in the *ritsuryō* codes. In the Heian period, virginity was not a virtue, and boys and girls were permitted multiple sex partners until they made a primary marriage. While married, men continued to have latitude in sexual relations, including making secondary marriages and other liaisons, although women did not. Marriages could end easily and both partners could remarry without stigma. Husbands usually lived with and were supported by their wives' families, but a husband did not lose his patrilineal descent group identity upon marriage, although he was often known to society by his wife's house name. And finally, daughters, rather than sons, usually inherited the family residence. Thus, marriage and inheritance practices in Heian Japan, while not gender-neutral, did not overwhelmingly favor sons and husbands, as they would in later centuries.

Murasaki Shikibu's *Tale of Genji*, one of the world's greatest early novels, deals with the life, loves, and sorrows of the sensitive and talented Prince Genji, depicted as a paragon of male virtue, as well as those of Genji's male friends and his wife, Murasaki. From *The Tale of Genji*, we learn of the importance of male friendship—for example, Genji's brother-in-law and best friend, Tō no Chūjo, visits Genji, at great political risk to himself, when Genji is in exile due to a misdeed—as well as the power of romantic love, both male-female and male-male. While most of the sexual liaisons in *The Tale of Genji* and other Heian literature involved men and women, tales of men's same-sex love were neither infrequent nor seen as secondary to heterosexual love. In *Genji* we learn that weeping was the most heartfelt expression of both manly and womanly compassion and sentimentality. Murasaki Shikibu also shows the power of beauty and refinement. Lack of skill at poetry, calligraphy, and playing musical instruments would doom a potential love match for both men and women, and Murasaki's prose novel is replete with the beautiful poems she had her characters write to prove their love for each other.

Women were courted by men who observed them wearing perfectly matched garments—up to twelve layers of robes in winter—because culti-

The Tale of Genji described tasteful courtship among refined ladies wearing multiple layers of gowns and men with hats called eboshi. The lady waits behind her screen for her lover. ANDO HIROSHIGE, GENJI MONOGATARI 54, 1852. LIBRARY OF CONGRESS, LC-USZC4-10706

vated beauty, which showed refinement and training, was as highly valued as physical beauty. But it was not only aristocratic women who were judged by the beauty of their clothes. Both sexes wore loose clothing that could be worn by either gender; lovers often exchanged under and outer garments as a token of intimacy. Gender was highlighted in fewer ways than we are accustomed to, with women's floor-length hair and men's very tall hats being two of the few ways of unmistakably distinguishing men's and women's dress. As far as professional clothing was concerned, male courtiers wore loose pants called *hakama* starting in the sixth century (they adopted from China's Sui and Tang dynasties the practice of wearing trousers for court duty), and women courtiers began wearing the same *hakama* for professional duties from the eighth century on. Men and women used drawstrings of different colors to tie their trousers, but men and women generally wore similar clothes, their appearance differing mainly in women's long hairstyles and men's headgear.

The fact that men and women could wear one another's clothes made tales of gender-bending believable to Heian-period aristocrats. *Torikaebaya* (*The Changelings*) was one of a number of stories written in the late Heian period that show the flexibility of gender. The protagonists were a brother and sister who served at the highest ranks in the court, dressing and behaving as their sibling's sex. The (biological) sister's pregnancy eventually led the two to quietly swap their assumed identities and resume their birth sexes, but the exchangeability of clothing had permitted the two to pretend they were their sibling's sex for years.

Changes in Gender Practices in Late Medieval Japan

By the end of the twelfth century, private owners, rather than the imperial throne, controlled over half the arable land of Japan. The form of ownership was complex, with multiple layers of local officials and aristocrats in the capital having claims, called *shiki*, to income from the land. These property rights were held by men and women alike, and late twelfth- and thirteenth-century records of legal cases over disputes about ownership rights show that both sexes were allowed to subdivide their property among their heirs. Some women's inherited property rights were limited to their own lifetimes, however, and they had to give their inheritance back to their birth family (possibly to a brother's family) on their death. This reflected the fact that children at that time usually—although not always—inherited their father's family membership even if they inherited property from their mother's side of the family. Many parents of daughters were reluctant to allow their family property to pass to another family through a son-in-law's children. A legal dispute might arise if a woman with limited inheritance rights wished to name her own heirs and resisted the demand that she return her land to her family, or one might arise if her husband's family tried to claim her land. Legal disputes also arose in cases where the wife held unconditional rights and her husband tried to distribute the land without her required permission. These kinds of cases show that women still held rights to *shiki,* although male ownership was increasingly common by the thirteenth century.

Private landowners—who emerged after the land distribution system stipulated in the *ritsuryō* codes began to fall apart—needed to protect their holdings. As we have seen, the government ceased to require military service by the ninth century, leaving the countryside undefended, so private armed guards, called samurai, began to appear. The number of samurai grew enormously over the next three centuries. When disputes over imperial succession at the capital broke out in the 1180s, massive bands of these samurai warriors were called on to join contending military supporters of the feuding royal factions. The winning side in these battles, led by Minamoto Yoritomo, set up a new system of military-dominated rule. Minamoto Yoritomo and his successors continued to recognize the prestige of the imperial court in Heian, which was increasingly called Kyoto (meaning "capital city"). He needed the court to legitimize his actual assumption of power, so he got the court to designate him "shogun," a term of military authority that would be applied to the military rulers of Japan for the next seven hundred years. Emperors continued to sit on the throne, and on several occasions during those seven centuries an emperor would attempt to assert his right to rule against a military overlord. But these attempts did not succeed. In addition, the aristocrats of Heian society no longer set the standards or reflected the patterns of male-female relationships. As the samurai- and shogun-led political order became dominant, the relationships in samurai families set new gender standards in Japan.

The Minamoto shogun offered land rights, called *jitō-shiki*, to men and sometimes widows of men who performed meritorious service in the wars that led to the shogun's assumption of power. These rights came with responsibilities of guard duty or other military service, regardless of gender, and they could be subdivided and bequeathed to one's heirs. Throughout the thirteenth century, however, the process of divided inheritance and the need for heirs to perform military service ran up against a new imperative to consolidate family resources. This was made evident at the time of the Mongol invasions in 1274 and 1281, when the shogun called on samurai families to send their (male) warriors to the battlefield, well equipped with expensive armor and weapons that could be bought only if the soldier's family had sufficient resources. These costs militated against subdividing inheritances. A small number of women were praised in thirteenth-century war chronicles, but they were described as exceptions to the common practice that warriors were men. From the time of the Mongol invasions, women's ability to inherit—as well as that of sons other than a single primary heir—rapidly declined. Thus, as in China and Korea, the coming of the Mongols had a significant impact on gender relations in Japan.

Parallel to the decline in property rights, women also lost status within marriage in the late thirteenth century. Court cases show that many women were simultaneously owners of property and treated as property themselves. For example, sexual violence against a married woman was ruled a violation of her husband's rights. Rape of a married woman led to punishment of the rapist; fortunately, the victim was not punished herself. But, sad to say, this would change by the fifteenth century, when harsh punishments, including a possible death penalty, could be meted out against a rape victim. Another example of the declining status of women in marriage was the *ritsuryō* assumption, increasingly common after the Mongol invasions, that a woman would marry into her husband's family rather than the converse, which had been the norm in earlier centuries. Interestingly, the beginnings and endings of marriages were not yet marked by formal ceremonies, nor was remarriage after divorce or a husband's death uncommon or disdained.

The shogunal government established by Minamoto in the late twelfth century and maintained by the family and allies of his powerful and politically active widow, Hōjō Masako, lasted until the 1330s, when another civil war brought in a new shogunal government under different leaders. The tales of this fourteenth-century war give us a glimpse into that era's view of masculinity: men's war injuries were recorded as a mark of their loyalty and were duly rewarded. When the even longer-lasting Warring States period began in 1467, decentralized bands of warriors struggled against their neighbors to claim control of territories, villages, and military manpower. In that period of endemic warfare, which lasted until 1600, women of the samurai class had little power.

Whatever power samurai women had was in their service to their husband's family. There they educated the children, handled ceremonial matters, and carefully maintained proper etiquette to avoid offending allied or rival families and thereby possibly triggering a war. But in other ways, their status could be abysmally low. The greatest of the warlords of the Warring States period used their female family members as pawns in political linkages with other families. Both a woman's natal family and her married family expected utmost loyalty, and when political alliances changed precipitously, as they often did in this era, the wife was left in an unsustainable position between the two families, trusted by neither. Some of the great warlords forced their female family members to marry and divorce frequently as their alliances shifted.

Gender relations outside the top ranks of the samurai class also underwent changes, although the decline in non-samurai women's status was less steep. Written records documenting peasants' lives and economic conditions from the Warring States era show that men, women, and children all participated in communal village activities such as dancing and singing at religious festivals. Young men and young women engaged in intimate activities, which sometimes led to marriage. As in the case of the samurai, marriage, divorce, and remarriage were acceptable in Japanese farming communities. Some villages had women's community halls, where women could relax with other women or prepare food for festivals or survival. In addition, women were often responsible for spring rice planting and fall threshing. Many sold farm products at local markets. In short, the medieval household required the gendered work of both men and women, and families valued the economic contributions of both sexes. This does not mean that the genders were equally empowered in the village, however. As the village became increasingly important as a unit of autonomous governance in the Warring States era, men were far more likely than women to participate in the religious and governing associations that determined prestige and authority in the village. In most cases, women could participate in these organizations on behalf of their family only in the absence of a male family member.

The arts and culture began to spread among farming folk as well as the elite from the fourteenth through the sixteenth centuries, and both men and women took part in the production and consumption of this culture. Itinerant storytellers, many originally Buddhist monks and nuns, traveled the byways of Japan to bring their presentations, which included songs, instrumental performance, puppets, and illustrations, to wealthy mansions and poor villages alike. Traveling throughout the country, these men and women helped to create and disseminate a national culture to a politically fragmented society. In time, some of these individual itinerant artists formed larger performing groups, and some towns and villages built theaters for their performances. Although women were forbidden from performing on the stage beginning in the seventeenth century, throughout the sixteenth they continued to present plays and dances, often claiming to be nuns to avoid being taken for prostitutes—which, despite their protestations, many of them in fact were.

CONNECTIONS

To understand gender in modern East Asia, we begin this book by describing and analyzing the similarities and dissimilarities in gender and sexuality in China, Korea, and Japan from antiquity until the beginning of the early modern period. The movements of people and ideas, particularly the philosophy of Confucianism, the religion of Buddhism, and arts and culture, could be said to be an early form of transnationalism—that is, a form that existed before the nation-state came into being in East Asia in the late nineteenth century. These "transnational" movements from west to east affected constructions of gender and intimate relations, although, as we have seen in this chapter, marriage and sexuality retained their indigenous character many centuries after government institutions in Korea and Japan were first influenced by Chinese notions of the state and social relations. Most important were the philosophies developed by Confucius (sixth century BCE) and his followers and the significant modifications called Neo-Confucianism in the eleventh century CE of these philosophies. Confucianism and Neo-Confucianism were complex, broad in scope, and highly esteemed over the centuries by the ruling classes in all three countries, but as far as gender was concerned, they insisted on binary sex divisions in society, and stipulated that the female was subordinate to the male.

Other areas of similarity in the history of gender in all three countries were the impact of the Buddhist religion and the role of women in its transmission; different types of "marriage politics" in the three countries; and the significant impact on gender relations of the Mongols, who set up a government in China in the thirteenth and fourteenth centuries and invaded Korea and Japan in the thirteenth century. But differences in the construction of gender and the gendered body for both men and women in these societies continued in the medieval and early modern periods despite the dominance of ideas of Chinese origin.

REFERENCES AND SUGGESTIONS FOR FURTHER READING

GLOBAL CONTEXT

Halsall, Paul. 2004. "Early Western Civilization Under the Sign of Gender: Europe and the Mediterranean." In *A Companion to Gender History*, edited by Teresa A. Meade and Merry E. Wiesner-Hanks. Oxford: Blackwell.

Kent, Susan. 2004. "Gender Rules: Law and Politics." In *A Companion to Gender History*, edited by Teresa A. Meade and Merry E. Wiesner-Hanks. Oxford: Blackwell.

Ko, Dorothy, JaHyun Kim, and Joan R. Piggott. 2003. *Women and Confucian Cultures in Premodern China, Korea, and Japan.* Berkeley: University of California Press.

Scott, Joan W. 1986. "Gender: A Useful Category of Historical Analysis." *American Historical Review* 91, no. 5: 1053–1075.

Wiesner-Hanks, Merry. 2004. "Structures and Meanings in a Gendered Family History." In *A Companion to Gender History*, edited by Teresa A. Meade and Merry Wiesner-Hanks. Oxford: Blackwell.

CHINA

Birge, Bettine. 2010. *Women, Property and Confucian Reaction in Sung and Yüan China (960–1368).* Cambridge: Cambridge University Press.

Bossler, Beverly. 2013. *Courtesans, Concubines and the Cult of Female Fidelity.* Cambridge, MA: Harvard University Press.

Cahill, Suzanne E. 1995. *Transcendence and Divine Passion: The Queen Mother of the West in Medieval China.* Stanford, CA: Stanford University Press.

Carlitz, Katherine. 1997. "Shrines, Governing-Class Identity, and the Cult of Widow Fidelity in Mid-Ming Jiangnan." *The Journal of Asian Studies* 56, no. 3: 612–640.

Deng, Xiaonan. 1999. "Women in Turfan during the Sixth to Eighth Centuries: A Look at their Activities Outside the Home." *The Journal of Asian Studies* 58, no. 1: 85–103.

Despeux, Catherine, and Livia Kohn. 2005. *Women in Daoism*. Cambridge: Three Pines Press.

Ebrey, Patricia Buckley. 1993. *The Inner Quarters: Marriage and the Lives of Chinese Women in the Sung Period*. Berkeley: University of California Press.

Hinsch, Bret. 2010. *Women in Early Imperial China*. Lanham, MD: Rowman and Littlefield.

Holmgren, Jennifer. 1995. *Marriage, Kinship and Power in Northern China*. Aldershot, UK: Variorum.

Linduff, Katheryn M. and Yan Sun, editors. 2004. *Gender and Chinese Archaeology*. Walnut Creek, CA: Altamira Press.

Mann, Susan, and Yu-Yin Cheng, eds. 2001. *Under Confucian Eyes: Writings on Gender in Chinese History*. Berkeley: University of California Press.

Raphals, Lisa. 1998. *Sharing the Light: Representations of Women and Virtue in Early China*. Binghamton, NY: State University of New York Press.

Rothschild, N. Harry. 2015. *Emperor Wu Zhao and Her Pantheon of Devis, Divinities, and Dynastic Mothers*. New York: Columbia University Press.

Swann, Nancy Lee. 2001. *Pan Chao: Foremost Woman Scholar of China*. Ann Arbor: University of Michigan Press.

Wang, Robin, ed. 2003. *Images of Women in Chinese Thought and Culture: Writings from the Pre-Qin Period through the Song Dynasty*. Indianapolis, IN: Hackett.

KOREA

Best, Jonathan W. 2006. *A History of the Early Korean Kingdom of Paekche: Together with an Annotated Translation of* The Paekche Annals of the Samguk sagi. Cambridge, MA: Harvard University Press.

Cho, Eun-su, ed. 2011. *Korean Buddhist Nuns and Laywomen: Hidden Histories, Enduring Vitality*. Albany, NY: SUNY Press.

Committee for the Compilation of the History of Korean Women. 1979. *Women of Korea: A History from Ancient Times to 1945*, edited and translated by Yung-Chung Kim. Seoul: Ewha Womans University Press.

Duncan, John B. 2000. *The Origins of the Chosŏn Dynasty*. Seattle: University of Washington Press.

Eckert, Carter J., Ki-baek Lee, Young Ick Lew, Michael Robinson, and Edward W. Wagner. 1990. *Korea Old and New: A History*. Cambridge, MA: Harvard University Press.

Kim, Pusik. 2012. *The Silla Annals of the Samguk Sagi*, translated by Edward J. Shultz and Hugh H. W. Kang. Seoul: Academy of Korean Studies Press.

———. 2011. *The Koguryo Annals of the Samguk Sagi*, translated by Edward J. Shultz and Hugh H. W. Kang. Seoul: Academy of Korean Studies Press.

Ilyon. 1972. *Samguk Yusa: Legends and History of the Three Kingdoms of Ancient Korea*, translated by Ha Tae-Hung and Grafton K. Mintz. Seoul: Yonsei University Press.

Lee, Ki-baek. 1984. *A New History of Korea*, translated by Edward W. Wagner with Edward J. Shultz. Cambridge, MA: Harvard University Press.

Lee, Peter, ed. 1993. *Sourcebook of Korean Civilization, vol. 1: From Early Times to the Sixteenth Century*. New York: Columbia University Press.

Pai, Hyung Il. 2000. *Constructing "Korean" Origins: A Critical Review of Archaeology, Historiography, and Racial Myth in Korean State-Formation Theories*. Cambridge, MA: Harvard University Press.

JAPAN

Farris, William Wayne. 2009. *Japan to 1600: A Social and Economic History*. Honolulu: University of Hawai'i Press.

Ki no Tsurayuki. 1981. *The Tosa Diary*. Translated by William N. Porter. Boston: Charles E. Tuttle.

Nickerson, Peter. 1993. "The Meaning of Matrilocality: Kinship, Property, and Politics in Mid-Heian." *Monumenta Nipponica* 48, no. 4: 429–467.

Sei Shōnagon. 1955. "Pillow Book." In *Anthology of Japanese Literature*, edited by Donald Keene. New York: Grove Press.

Ruch, Barbara. 1997. "Medieval Jongleurs and the Making of a National Literature." In *Japan in the Muromachi Age*, edited by John Whitney Hall and Toyoda Takeshi. Berkeley: University of California Press.

Takeda, Sachiko. 1999. "Menswear, Womenswear: Distinctive Features of the Japanese Sartorial System." In *Gender and Japanese History*, vol. 1, edited by Wakita Haruko, Anne Bouchy, and Ueno Chizuko. Osaka: Osaka University Press.

Tonomura, Hitomi. 1990. "Women and Inheritance in Japan's Early Warrior Society." *Comparative Studies in Society and History* 32, no. 3: 592–623.

———. 1994. "Black Hair and Red Trousers: Gendering the Flesh in Medieval Japan." *American Historical Review* 99, no. 1: 129–154.

———. 1999. "Sexual Violence Against Women: Legal and Extra-Legal Treatment in Premodern Japan." In *Women and Class in Japanese History*, edited by Hitomi Tonomura, Ann Walthall, and Wakita Haruko. Ann Arbor: University of Michigan Press.

———. 2009. "Women and Sexuality in Premodern Japan." In *A Companion to Japanese History*, edited by William M. Tsutsui. Malden, MA: Wiley-Blackwell.

Yoshida, Kazuhiko. 2005. "Religion in the Classical Period." In *Nanzan Guide to Japanese Religions*, edited by Paul L. Swanson and Clark Chilson. Honolulu: University of Hawai'i Press.

2

Gender and Sexuality in Early Modern East Asia

GLOBAL CONTEXT

Multicultural empires were the dominant form of government in much of the world before the seventeenth century. In West Africa, a series of empires rose and fell, including the empires of Ghana (eighth to eleventh century) and Mali (thirteenth and fourteenth centuries). The empires of the Aztecs and Incas dominated the Americas until they were defeated by Europeans and their diseases in the sixteenth century. Eurasia was under the rule of five powerful empires at the dawn of the early modern era: in the north, Russia; in the south (India), the Mughals; in Persia, the Safavids; in West Asia and Eastern Europe, the Ottomans; and in the east, the Ming dynasty. Following wars and revolutions, none of these empires would exist by the first decades of the twentieth century. But they were already being supplanted in some areas by new state formations in the seventeenth century.

On the Eurasian periphery, in Western Europe and in Korea, monarchies were steadily consolidating their control of smaller regions into "nations"—that is, linguistic and ethnically cohesive realms. Japan would join that group as a separate and relatively unified realm in the seventeenth century. The creation of this new type of state, which initially took the form of an absolute monarchy, had profound effects on gender and sexuality. Although it was one of the great multiethnic empires, China's Ming (and later Qing) dynasty shared certain characteristics with European monarchical nation-states, particularly the use of ideology about gender, the family, and sexuality in framing the state. As we will see in this chapter, Neo-Confucianism was employed as the basis for creating the Qing, Chosŏn, and Tokugawa states, and it linked those states' polities with gendered laws, regulations, and customs.

Sexuality was increasingly controlled by the state in the late medieval and early modern periods. Marriage was defined in the law and came to be viewed by states as a way of restraining social disorder (adultery and extramarital sex were often punishable by death). Throughout Europe and North America until the eighteenth century, marriage was most often seen as a way of promoting family continuity, through both production and reproduction. To be sure, family members loved one another, but marriages were generally not contracted for love. Love-based marriages emerged after improved medicine and public health began to allow more spouses and children to survive and when the notion of the individual and individual happiness became accepted in European and North American thought in the eighteenth century.

In European, Ottoman, and Chinese law, the family included a patriarch who had legal control of the family's women and children; early modern states codified in law religious and customary patriarchal practices. In addition, codification of inheritance laws in Europe and North America often stripped away women's abilities to control their own property and to inherit. In essence, by codifying some customary practices as law in order to regulate society, the early modern state was based on a gender structure that eroded the position of women. Women's loss of inheritance and other rights in the family occurred somewhat earlier in East Asia, as the codification of Neo-Confucian marriage rules in Korea and the Japanese shogun's response to the Mongol invasions (as we saw in Chapter 1) led to a more rigid and male-centered definition of marriage.

The early modern European state was constructed on a basis of political theory in which gender played a significant role. The British case is an informative example. Confronting notions that women rulers "defiled, polluted and profaned the throne of God," as John Knox stated in 1558 (Hardwick 2004, 354), Queen Elizabeth I downplayed her femininity, dressing androgynously when she was a young woman and never marrying. A century later, as pro-monarchy and pro-Parliament forces struggled for political domination in the English Civil War, political theorist Robert Filmer articulated the view, taken as natural by the royalists, that the king's rule over his subjects paralleled the husband's unquestioned rule over his wife. Just as the wife could not terminate her marriage, the people could not break their contract with the king. But his was not the only view at the time. John Locke theorized that the state was based on a voluntary social contract among individuals, and marriages were, too. Thus both could be dissolved if necessary. It would take several centuries before these ideas of the state and individual rights would be expanded upon and used for both political and gender rights around the world, including East

Asia. Mary Astell wrote presciently in 1706, "If all men are born free, how is it that all women are born slaves?" (Hardwick 2004, 356).

Early modern economic developments also strengthened the gendering of society. As Europe became more urban, craft guilds, many of which excluded women by the mid-fifteenth century, played a larger role in the economy. Guilds of skilled craftsmen became quite powerful, and merchants sought cheaper production methods with less skilled labor. They developed ties to small rural producers, many of them women, in a "putting-out system." That is, merchants might bring wool to a farm woman, who would spin it into yarn; then the merchants would take that yarn to a weaver (often a man), then market the cloth. Each producer would be paid for his or her work, although the women's work was often seen as an extension of her household duties. The existence of urban skilled workers and rural unskilled workers increased the gendering of the work force. Fifteenth- and sixteenth-century Europeans were so accustomed to this gender division that they were surprised to see that women and not men wove cloth in Central America, a practice paralleled throughout East Asia.

CHINA

Early Modern Commerce, Urban Culture, and Gender in the Ming Period, 1368–1644

Establishing a new dynasty after the decades of disorder that accompanied the collapse of the Mongol empire, early Ming rulers set about reinstating the components of Chinese political order, most importantly the system of regular civil service examinations. However, the dynastic founder Ming Taizu, also known as the Hongwu emperor, an uneducated peasant who rose to power as a ruthless rebel commander, was deeply distrustful of literati and merchants. He envisioned the empire as a society of self-sufficient villages living harmoniously and virtuously according to Confucian ideals of social and gender order that the emperor proclaimed routinely through hortatory edicts. Enacting policies to centralize political control and enhance the authority of the emperor, Taizu eliminated the post of prime minister, used his palace guard as a secret police force to spy on officials, and carried out political purges that took tens of thousands of lives. The political marginalization of the literati resulted in the rise of a shadow palace bureaucracy of eunuchs, much to the chagrin of scholar-officials, who saw eunuchs as illegitimate political players that violated Confucian norms by choosing castration—thereby rejecting the filial act of continuing the family line—to pursue wealth and power. The late Ming was consumed with factional conflict among literati as well as between literati and the emperor and eunuchs at court.

These political fights became entangled in philosophical debates, framed as conflicts between those who stood for the revival of orthodox ethics propagated through instruction by Confucian teachers and others who advocated a more liberal, egalitarian understanding of Confucianism that assumed moral knowledge to be innate to everyone and focused on individualized paths to self-cultivation. For embattled male literati, the tragically self-sacrificing figure of the female chastity martyr, who committed suicide upon the death of her husband, became an exemplar of moral purity and the noblest form of loyalty to rightful authority. Literati men expressed their frustrations with what they considered the moral turpitude of their day through promotion of the chastity cult. They enhanced their own reputations by publishing biographies of chaste women of their own families and communities, building shrines to honor them, and promoting their canonization by the state. Responding to the dramatic surge in numbers of chaste widows and chastity martyrs, the Ming state expanded the categories recognized for canonization, tightened eligibility criteria, and systematized award procedures, but the real impetus for the explosion of widow suicides and the widespread exaltation of chastity as the core element of virtuous femininity was the work of local literati.

Despite the despotism of imperial rule, the Ming state did not, in fact, exercise the systematic control over society that its founder, Taizu, envisioned. As the dynasty progressed, developments in the economy began to undermine the orthodox hierarchies he promoted, challenging in particular the status and identity of male literati and norms of gender propriety. The stability created by the new regime fostered developments in the agricultural sector and expansion of domestic and foreign trade that together radically transformed Chinese society. Since the Ming did not control the Inner Asian trade routes that linked China to markets farther west, the dynastic shift from Yuan to Ming in the fourteenth century entailed a major shift in the geographic focus of China's foreign trade from the overland routes to the sea routes off the southeast coast. Ship transport enabled much greater volume of trade, and with the opening up of new trade routes across the Pacific via Manila in the sixteenth century, China's exports of silk, porcelain, tea, and other products greatly increased. The most obvious indicator of this expansion of trade was the influx of Japanese and Mexican silver used to purchase Chinese products. As the economy became increasingly monetized, the Ming state was forced to monetize its own operations in a series of reforms that commuted taxes and payments from grain and silk to silver.

At the same time, there was a dramatic expansion in domestic markets fueled by the commercialization of agriculture in core regions linked to domestic and foreign trade routes: North China along the Grand Canal, the Lower Yangzi delta (Jiangnan), and the southeast coast of Fujian and Guangdong. In these regions farmers turned in large numbers to production of cash crops such as sugar, cotton, silk, tea, and handicrafts. They came to rely on networks of rural markets to sell their produce for money to pay land rents and taxes and to purchase staple items that they no longer grew for themselves. As peasant families engaged more deeply with the market, women's production of cotton and silk thread and woven cloth for sale became a vital part of household income that fueled China's economic development.

With the commercialization of the economy came greater prosperity, population growth, and greater access to education. This meant that the ranks of elite families and thus the number of men competing in the civil service examinations increased. As the number of successful candidates remained constant, an individual's odds of passing declined steadily. In a late Ming population that numbered approximately two hundred million people, there were approximately a hundred thousand students who had passed the lowest level of examinations. At most, 10 percent of these would pass the next level, becoming eligible for a government post. At any given time there were only between two thousand and four thousand men who had passed the next, highest level of the exams.

At the same time merchants grew in number, wealth, and status. The traditional distinction between merchants and literati whose wealth was based in land blurred and in some cases disappeared as the two groups intermarried. Expanding markets created opportunities for literati families to make money in the land market. Growing numbers of literati families in rich regions such as Jiangnan became absentee landlords and moved to cities. In some regions, such as Huizhou in Anhui Province, rural literati families took up long-distance trade as a core occupation, sending male family members to sojourn for months and years at a time in cities across the empire.

Like cities in seventeenth-century Japan, China's cities also grew in number, size, and complexity during this period, functioning not only as administrative seats for the state but also as centers of commerce and culture, full of merchants, literati, artisans, and entertainers. The last included courtesans (elite sex workers, many of whom were versed in literary and performing arts) and cross-dressing male opera performers, who provided companionship, sex, and cultural capital for literati and merchant patrons sojourning far from home. The commercial publishing industry expanded tremendously, churning out mass quantities of books of all sorts and prices: Confucian classics, exam preparation materials, Buddhist and Daoist religious tracts, practical manuals, and vernacular fiction and plays that catered to the tastes and sensibilities of a growing urban reading public. The short stories written and edited by Feng Menglong (1574–c. 1645) captured the social fluidity and moral ambiguity of the late Ming "floating world," which paralleled that of Tokugawa Japan, discussed later in this chapter. Exploring the emotional lives and moral conundrums of ordinary women and men, these stories valorized the notion of *qing* ("sentiment" or "love") over orthodox ritual propriety and complicated normative assumptions about the relationship between social status and morality, for example, by depicting courtesans who killed themselves when a patron died or abandoned them as chastity martyrs who exemplified the highest form of female virtue. The playwright Tang Xianzu's 1598 masterpiece, *The Peony Pavilion*, a love story featuring the cloistered daughter of an official and an aspiring young scholar whose eroticized passion was powerful enough to overcome the constraints of orthodox morality and even death, generated an enthusiastic following among elite women, growing numbers of whom were literate.

These popular literary works fueled a cult of *qing* that posed a profound challenge to the precepts of the cult of chastity and inflected it with new emotional intensity. Biographies of widows who followed their husbands in death praised the depth of women's emotional attachment to their husbands and the intensity of their suicidal intent with graphic, melodramatic narration of the violence of their deaths and their resistance to attempts by family members to dissuade them. Late Ming anthologies of chastity martyr biographies were often published in fine editions richly adorned with the same woodcut illustrations used to depict the less edifying suicides of fictional heroines (Carlitz 2001). The infusion of the chastity ethos with *qing* was most dramatically evident in the phenomenon of so-called faithful maidens who were so passionately committed to the ideal of marital fidelity that they committed suicide to follow fiancés who died before the wedding, young men they usually had never met face-to-face, according to dominant rules of premarital propriety (Lu 2008). Some literati extolled faithful maidens as paragons of wifely fidelity who should be eligible for state canonization, but others criticized their suicides as selfish acts of *qing* that prioritized marital devotion over filial service to parents-in-law.

The competition, mobility, and moral ambiguity engendered by the commercialization of the economy and its social effects created anxieties about downward mobility and transgression of gender and status boundaries.

Across the most developed regions of the country, elite families responded to the challenges and opportunities of the age by constructing lineage organizations modeled on those advocated by Neo-Confucian scholars in the Song period to pool resources and provide a cushion in times of adversity. As in the Song, Neo-Confucian ideology linked family economic success and their sons' performance in the examination system to the family's moral propriety. Lineage leaders sought to cultivate habits of filial obedience to patrilineal authority, maintenance of proper distinctions between women and men, diligence, frugality, and, for women, chastity. They admonished their sons to devote themselves to study or, as a second choice, to commerce, and to resist the temptations of urban pleasure quarters and leisure activities. Concerned about the potential for sexual transgression among women left behind by husbands sojourning for official appointments, the examinations, or trade, they taught their daughters to seclude themselves within the women's quarters of the family compound, working diligently to care for children and aging parents, managing the household, and engaging in spinning, weaving, or embroidery.

The vibrant commercial publishing industry that fostered the emergence of popular fiction and drama also facilitated education for literate elites by churning out primers, didactic books for boys and girls, books for examination preparation, and compilations of biographies of exemplary women. In elite families, boys started their education as early as three years of age by memorizing the *San zi jing* (*Trimetrical Classic*) and other primers that taught core Confucian precepts along with recognition of characters necessary for formal study of Confucian classical texts in preparation for the exams. By the middle of the Ming a growing number of elite families, especially in the wealthy and urbanized Jiangnan region, were also educating their daughters to read the canonical Confucian texts supplemented with classic texts on women's virtue, including foundational works such as Liu Xiang's *Biographies of Exemplary Women*, Ban Zhao's *Admonitions for Women* from the Han dynasty (see Chapter 1), and numerous later moral handbooks and collected biographies of chaste women based on them. Communal gender norms were commonly conveyed to literate and nonliterate family members through ancestral rituals (often accompanied by didactic operas), recitation of lineage rules codified in the family genealogy, and established punishments for misbehavior.

Gender and Empire-Building in the Qing Dynasty

In the middle of the seventeenth century, Ming rule disintegrated as the politically dysfunctional regime failed to deal with fiscal crisis, corruption, and spreading rebellion. In 1644, the forces of a newly formed dynasty, the

Qing, poured across the Great Wall and conquered the Ming capital, Beijing. The Qing ruling elites were Manchus, an ethnic group from the northeast distinct from the majority Han ethnic group. The Manchus, like many non-Han conquerors of China before them, recognized the political utility of Chinese political and social systems and adopted much of the Ming state structure. However, they saw themselves not as Chinese emperors but rather as universal rulers of a multiethnic empire in the tradition of the Mongols, who had unified the peoples of Inner Asia.

The Manchus also believed that maintenance of political cohesion among the minority elite as it built a multiethnic empire required cultivation of their distinct ethnic identity. In the early stages of the conquest they established the banner system, which incorporated Chinese and Mongols who allied with them into "banners," military units that became the foundation for a hereditary ruling caste acculturated to Manchu ways whose members were forbidden to intermarry with the Chinese commoner population. Maintenance of distinctive Manchu gender norms was an essential part of this identity, along with Manchu language and family customs. In contrast to Han male literati culture, which the Manchus perceived to be decadent and effeminate, banner men were required to learn the skills of archery and horseback riding and to practice frugality. All male subjects of the Qing imperium, whatever their ethnicity, were required to display their loyalty to the regime by wearing the queue hairstyle—shaving the front part of their heads and braiding the hair into a single long braid. Early in the dynasty the Qing authorities attempted to ban footbinding, which was not a Manchu practice, but, unable to enforce this among their Han subjects, they settled for forbidding it among banner women (Elliot 1999).

The Qing conquest gave new political salience to the chastity cult, as women committed suicide to avoid rape in the midst of warfare and men and women loyal to the Ming martyred themselves rather than surrender to the new rulers. Since the chastity martyr became one of the most potent symbols of Ming loyalist opposition to Qing rule, the Manchus could not simply adopt the Ming system of canonization for the chaste and filial. As outsiders to the Confucian cultural order, they were willing to challenge established norms and cherished ideals. They saw the chastity awards system as a tool for the civilizing mission of their universal empire. That mission included the reform of barbaric customs and the promotion of a unified standard of virtue, defined by the state, and applicable to all social classes. For Manchu emperors, the Chinese practice of widows following their husbands in death was tainted both by conflation with Ming loyalism and by its similarity to a Manchu tradition that the Qing wished to abandon because it appeared uncivilized. The Qing criticized suicide in the name of any sort of virtue as barbaric, inhumane, and unnecessary, describing it as "taking life lightly," and forbade state honors both for widow suicides and for death resulting from extreme acts of filial piety such as *gegu* (cutting flesh from one's body to feed a dying parent). They extended eligibility for honors in approved categories (chaste widows, women who died resisting rape, and filial daughters) to Manchus, Mongols, and other ethnic groups on the frontiers as well as groups previously considered unworthy of such honors, including Daoist nuns, wives of criminals, freed bondservants, and women from hereditary debased families. Over the course of the dynasty the precise rules of eligibility shifted and exceptions, even to the ban on honors for widow suicide, were not infrequent, but such variations were always vetted by the emperor and confirmed the prerogative of the state to define orthodox behavior (Theiss 2001). While the numbers of canonized women exploded, the proportion of widow martyrs recorded in *difangzhi* (local gazetteers that compiled information on local history, geography, economy, and customs and included biographies of local worthies and local literature) dropped significantly.

Over the latter half of the seventeenth century, Qing rulers pacified opposition to their rule and turned their attention to expansion of the empire into non-Han frontier regions and perfecting state control over its resources, personnel, and society at large. As imperial conquests proceeded in the eighteenth century, policy makers developed a paradigm of the imperial civilizing mission aimed at transforming the customs of newly incorporated non-Han peoples (like the Miao and Dai in the remote southwest regions), including casual social and sexual interactions between men and women in public, courting and marriage choice, matrilocal residence, female attire that did not cover the body, and women's labor in the fields. The imperial state also aimed to curb heterodoxy among Han subjects in the heartland through law, ritual regulation of marriage, Confucian state honors, reform of local customs, suppression of heterodox religious sects, education, and promotion of the gender division of labor encapsulated in the slogan "Men plow, women weave." While they deployed traditional statecraft mechanisms, these policies were unprecedented in scope and complexity, reflecting a new early modern vision of a morally activist state that positioned itself as the central arbiter of normative order by inserting itself into family and community life through interventionist social reform policies.

The chastity cult, reformed to reflect the values of the new regime, was a critical mechanism for this civilizing project. Under the Yongzheng (1723–1736) and Qianlong (1736–1796) emperors, the state became for the first time the chief patron of the cult of chastity, which was thoroughly bureaucratized with newly detailed regulations on eligibility and procedures for applications to receive imperial monies to construct commemorative arches. Yongzheng ordered that shrines to the chaste and filial be constructed next to the official Confucian temple at every provincial, prefectural, and county seat in the empire in accordance with imperial regulations on design and funding and that presiding officials conduct twice-yearly sacrifices in them.

BOX 2.1

The Yongzheng Emperor's Edict Against Widow Suicide

In an edict reiterating the dynasty's opposition to widow suicide, Yongzheng casts the chaste woman as a model of imperial subjecthood: civilized to adhere to state-defined norms of propriety by a benevolent ruler and expressing absolute loyalty to the imperial social and political order through obedience and dutiful service to family and state.

> *Widow martyrs die to martyr themselves for their husbands, nobly following them down under the earth. This is certainly difficult for people to do. Yet . . . chaste widowhood is even more difficult. For those who follow in death show resolve only for a moment, while those who maintain chastity [for a lifetime] must have perpetual regard for their husbands. Those who follow in death sacrifice their lives and that is the end of it. Those who maintain chastity must be prepared to undergo hardships. Moreover, the circumstances under which widow martyrs martyr themselves for chastity . . . vary. Some suicides are pressured by poverty and lack of means of support. Some occur out of indignation and failure to think about the future. [These women] do not realize that after the husband has died, the duties that a wife must fulfill are even greater [than before]. Above her are her parents-in-law whom she must serve and nurture as a substitute in the way of the son. Below her are her descendants whom she must educate as a substitute in the way of the father. If she prepares sacrifices and manages household affairs, her duties are countless. This is why the honoring of chaste widows is stipulated in the laws and regulations [of the dynasty]. But widow martyrs are not mentioned in the statutes . . . . If many people imitated them, then there would be great loss of life, a prospect that we cannot tolerate. (Theiss 2001, 33–34)*

The dynasty used routine awards, which numbered up to fifteen hundred a year, to demonstrate the paternalistic presence of the state as the most visible and consistent patron of female chastity in local society. The strategic designation of chastity martyrs followed by shrine construction in the wake of pacification of rebellions or conquest of non-Han peoples highlighted the political role of the chastity cult in the expansion of the empire.

The canonization system itself was only one of an array of state technologies deployed to transform customs in line with state orthodoxy. Eighteenth-century Qing officials, most of them Chinese, shared the dynasty's vision of a paternalistic and reformist state and energetically advanced new regulations, policy initiatives, and laws to intervene in diverse realms of social life and promote proper gender order and social hierarchy. They identified myriad social problems as targets for moral transformation (*jiaohua*), including declining filiality and respect for family hierarchy, female infanticide, heterodox religious sects that encouraged wanton mixing of the sexes, lack of interest in the primary occupations of farming for men and weaving for women, improper marriage and funerary rituals, kidnapping of women for marriage, prostitution, sexual slander resulting in female suicide, forced widow remarriage, women going on pilgrimages and visiting temples, and even lack of sex segregation in prisons. They advocated improved moral education by local magistrates and lineage leaders, but the most commonly recommended strategy for *jiaohua* was expansion and refinement of the law. During the latter half of the eighteenth century the Qing legal code expanded dramatically, with dozens of new substatutes in the sections of the code dealing with illicit sex, illegal marriage, homicide related to sexual assault, adultery, prostitution, and causing a woman to commit suicide through improper behavior. These new substatutes clarified with unprecedented precision state norms of proper family behavior and gender relations and signaled a new understanding of the law not just as a source of punishment but as a tool for molding behavior (Theiss 2004).

This legal discourse clarified the parameters of a new state vision of sexual order within which the basic social unit was the commoner peasant family, whose stability required protection of the chastity of its women and the masculine integrity of its men (Sommer 2000). Already in the late Ming, literati commentators surveying the social effects of rapid commercialization noted with concern the phenomenon of itinerant single men unattached to structures of family authority, who might seduce or assault women left home alone by sojourning husbands. By the middle of the eighteenth century, sex ratios skewed by female infanticide, polygyny among the elites, and widow chastity meant that a very large proportion of the poor male population could not find wives (Sommer 2015). Marriage was not merely a Confucian ideal but a hallmark of respectability, and it was out of reach for the poorest men. Much of the new legislation on illicit sex was implicitly or explicitly directed at controlling such men, labeled as "rootless rascals" or *guanggun* (literally, "bare stick"), and protecting respectable commoner families from their predations, despite the fact that, as in most times and places, most sexual assaults involved familiars, not strangers.

The Qing inherited from the Ming the basic judicial category of illicit sex defined as sex outside of marriage. Men who committed rape, or "coerced illicit sex," were punished by strangulation; attempted rape was punishable by one hundred blows of the heavy bamboo and life exile. The punishment for adultery, or "consensual illicit sex," was eighty blows of the heavy bamboo for both partners, ninety if the woman was married. The law allowed a husband to expel his wife for failure to give birth to a son, adultery, unfiliality toward his parents, loquaciousness, theft, jealousy, or contagious disease, though he was forbidden to do so if she had performed three years' mourning for his parents, had no family to take her back, or if he became wealthy during the marriage. However, buying or selling a divorce (that is, selling a wife to another man as the latter's wife) was illegal and punishable with flogging for all parties involved. As in the Ming, widow remarriage was legal for all except wives of senior officials as long as the widow observed the proper three-year mourning period for her husband, but remarriage resulted in the widow losing her dowry, control of her husband's property, and, often, access to her children. Forcing a widow to remarry was a crime; punishment depended on the relationship of the perpetrators to the widow and whether the widow's family gained financially from the bride price paid by the new husband's family. In conflicts between widows and their in-laws over control of a dead husband's property, which occurred frequently, Qing jurists firmly defended the property rights of the widows and in 1774 codified explicitly a widow's right to name an heir (Bernhardt 1999).

Qing law produced two significant innovations in the policing of sexual behavior. The first was to make prostitution illegal for all subjects of the realm, effectively holding everyone to a single standard of sexual virtue. Ming law prohibited men from allowing or forcing their wives, concubines, or daughters to engage in illicit sex, and for "respectable" commoners sale of sex was punished in the same way as adultery. But prostitution was legal for women from hereditary debased groups, registered by the state as entertainer or musician families. In 1723, Yongzheng abolished this centuries-old juridical status, thus making debased people commoners who would now be held to universal standards of sexual propriety. In theory, this new policy criminalized all sex work, regardless of one's status. In practice the law was directed mostly at poor, rural women, who lost access to a source of income, while courtesan establishments patronized by elite men were left alone.

A second major set of changes was made to the statute on causing a woman to commit suicide. Amid the rising tide of moral concerns about sexual transgressions, Ming jurists created a new substatute mandating punishment for causing a person to commit suicide in connection with illicit sex. Women who killed themselves to avoid begin raped or died resisting rape were also eligible for canonization as chastity martyrs. In 1733, Yongzheng took the unprecedented step of allowing women who killed themselves in response to a sexual proposition to be canonized and subsequently authorized a new substatute mandating strangulation for causing a woman's suicide due to attempted rape or unwanted flirtation (Theiss 2004). Over the rest of the century, some fifteen additional substatutes were created to elaborate the range of circumstances under which a man would be deemed responsible for the suicide of a woman, including unintended sexual insult or "improper familiarity"; "indecent remarks," "dirty jokes," or "obscene gestures" made in her presence or about her; adultery; prostitution; incest; or gossip arising out of any such incidents. These substatutes not only criminalized sexual harassment and unintended sexual insult but also made a woman's reaction to them (that is, whether she committed suicide or not) the critical determinant of his guilt. Similarly, if a widow chose suicide to avoid remarriage, those responsible for trying to force her to remarry would be sentenced to strangulation, decapitation, or military exile, depending on the closeness of their relationship to the widow. These were much heavier penalties than they would receive if she did not kill herself.

The Qing paradigm of sexual order extended to men through new laws on sodomy. The late Ming code for the first time criminalized sex between men, but the term for sodomy was not introduced into the code until the early Qing, when it was categorized as a crime of illicit sex that, like other forms of sexual assault, was an attack on vulnerable junior members of respectable families. The substatute reads, "If evil rascals gather in a gang and abduct the son or younger brother of a commoner family and use coercion to sodomize him, then the ringleader shall be immediately beheaded, and the followers shall all be sentenced to strangulation" (Sommer 2000). In 1734, amid the explosion of new substatutes designed to define female virtue and assaults against it with ever greater precision, the substatute on sodomy was similarly expanded to elaborate in parallel manner all the possible variations of age, number of perpetrators, nature of coercion, and exchange of money that jurists imagined could shape the crime of sodomy. While consensual sex between men, like heterosexual adultery, was illegal, it was usually prosecuted only in the context of more serious cases of homicide or assault. The dalliances of elite men with servants, opera performers, or other male paramours were never prosecuted. The codes never mentioned sex between women.

Classic Confucian norms of gender and family propriety constructed marriage as the fulfillment of filial duty to serve one's parents and continue the family line. They emphasized the primacy of the patrilineal authority of fathers and family elders over that of husbands. In a conflict between obedience to a husband and obedience to parents-in-law, a wife was supposed to choose the latter. The late imperial chastity cult, infused with the ethos of *qing*, elevated the status of the conjugal bond and intensified its allure. Though the goal of the Qing policy makers was to reinforce patriarchal family order as they institutionalized the chastity cult as a technology of state building and used law to promote chastity as a universal virtue in the eighteenth century, they unwittingly exacerbated tensions between conjugal and patrilineal notions of family patriarchy that existed widely in social practice. Conflicts over female virtue often pitted women against family authorities pushing for widow remarriage, trying to prevent chastity suicides, or ignoring sexual affronts in order to avoid disgracing the family. The Qing state allied itself with widows fighting remarriage and victims of sexual assault and harassment and made their own interpretations of chastity and insults to it central to adjudication.

KOREA

Neo-Confucianism as Political and Moral Doctrine in Korea in the Chosŏn Dynasty

Historian Martina Deuchler refers to the transition from the Koryŏ dynasty (918–1392) to the Chosŏn dynasty (1392–1910) as the "Confucian transformation of Korea" (Deuchler 1992). During Koryŏ, Buddhism provided the essential guiding principles not only for religion but for politics, economy, and culture as well. In contrast, the Chosŏn dynasty saw the adoption of Neo-Confucianism broadly as the governing philosophy, ethics, and legal code, in an attempt to rationalize and systematize state affairs based on stricter moral and ethical principles. First introduced in Korea in the late Koryŏ dynasty, Neo-Confucianism became prominent during the Song and Ming dynasties in China. It appealed to a new class of scholar bureaucrats in Koryŏ who were critical of the hereditary aristocratic families and of their abuse of power and unrestrained, indulgent lifestyles. Led by Yi Sŏnggye (1335–1408), a military commander who became the founder of the Chosŏn dynasty, this reform-minded literati class emerged as the ruling force in shaping a new dynasty centering on Neo-Confucianism as its moral, ethical, and philosophical foundation.

Throughout the Koryŏ dynasty and even in the early part of the Chosŏn dynasty, women had rights of inheritance, access to divorce and remarriage without stigma, and considerable freedom to move around in public without restraint. Daughters were listed in the family genealogies, and both sons and daughters were listed by order of birth. Furthermore, second marriages of women of the upper class were also recorded (Wagner 1983). However, the active implementation of Confucian precepts that came with the establishment of the Chosŏn dynasty fundamentally weakened the rights and privileges of women.

This dramatic shift was justified on the basis of Neo-Confucian interpretations of the universe and human nature. Neo-Confucianism is based on a cosmological belief that the universe and society are governed by the forces of yin and yang and that achieving harmony between the two in both realms is the key to peace and prosperity. (For a discussion of yin and yang in China, see Chapter 1.) The logic of the philosophy may not in and of itself induce gender inequality, but the social value attached to yin and yang brought about such practices. According to Neo-Confucian precepts and the ways they were interpreted and adopted in Chosŏn, women (identified with yin) should be subordinated to men (identified with yang). The roles that women and men play in society should also be differentiated, with women assigned to the domestic arena and men to the public domain. Any transgression of that gendered boundary was considered a serious violation of proper behavior. Even the architectural design of residences (especially for upper-class families) reflected this gendered distinction of physical space, with floor plans split between inner chambers for women and outer chambers for men. It should be noted that despite the new dynasty's attempts to implement Confucian doctrine and practices, people continued to adhere to old customs and resisted prescriptions from the government. Thus it took several centuries for the "Confucian transformation" to prevail in Korean society, and it was only in the seventeenth and eighteenth centuries that Confucian precepts, legal codes, and cultural norms became firmly rooted as the dominant force. Throughout this long period of transition the rights of women were continually eroded, not only in the ideology of the time, but in actual legal, economic, and cultural practices.

Patrilineal Family System

The most significant factor for this dramatic shift in the status and rights of women was the adoption and implementation of a patrilineal social paradigm. This new paradigm began to transform the family into a singularly male-centered system that subordinated women to their husbands and their husbands' families. At the very beginning of the dynasty, newer practices that were intended to establish and enforce a patrilineal family system were ignored and people continued to practice the old customs. One of the first places where tensions between the old and new customs came to a head was in wedding rituals. Customary practice during the Koryŏ dynasty dictated that the groom come to the home of the bride for the wedding and take up residence with the bride's family. This custom allowed a woman to adjust to married life in familiar surroundings with support from her family. (Note the similarity with Japanese customs around the same time.) However, Confucian scholars and high-ranking officials began to criticize the custom as inappropriate because, from the Confucian cosmological standpoint, yin (woman) was supposed to follow yang (man). In their view, the practice in which the husband moved into the home of the wife had yang following yin, a distortion of the natural order of things. With the aim of setting an example of proper marital behavior, the royal family adopted the new wedding custom, in which the bride would go to the groom's home for the wedding ceremony and then live there; however, despite the model provided by the royal family and the strong condemnation of the traditional practice by leading Confucian scholars, this new wedding custom was not readily accepted, even by families of the upper class. It was only in the seventeenth century that this patrilocal marital custom became the norm.

The new marriage practice brought about significant changes in the lives of women. Unlike in our contemporary world, where "love marriage" is taken for granted, in Chosŏn Korea arranged marriages were the standard practice. Parents and relatives selected partners whom they deemed appropriate for their children. Prospective brides and grooms were not afforded any time to get to know each other, often meeting for the first time at their wedding ceremony. Imagine this scenario: a young woman who had until that point lived her entire life within the inner chambers of her family's home, having had contact with virtually no one from outside of her family, is one day removed from those safe and familiar environs and delivered to the home of a complete stranger, where by the end of the day she would be married to a man she had never met before and living with a family she did not know. Quite clearly, the separation from her natal family immediately after her wedding would have placed an emotional burden on the new bride. In addition, having to adopt a completely new role, one that put her at the beck and call of her new in-laws, while at the same time coping with the totally new culture of her husband's family, was inevitably an adjustment.

Another significant change came in the financial aspects of life. Throughout the Koryŏ dynasty and in the early and even middle parts of the Chosŏn dynasty (late sixteenth century to the beginning of the eighteenth), sons and daughters had equal inheritance rights (Peterson 1996, 6). Nor was birth order an important consideration for the distribution of an estate. Even after marriage, a woman was able to keep property or other assets in her own name rather than having her husband take control of them. If a woman had no children, her property would be returned to her natal family upon her death.

One justification for the relative equality between sons and daughters in terms of inheritance was the assumption under traditional practices that all children would share equally the responsibilities for ancestor worship. Family wealth was distributed to all children so that each of them would be able to underwrite ancestor worship rituals on a rotating basis. However, the idea that ancestor worship was a shared responsibility of all the children was gradually undermined with the spread of the Confucian doctrine that gave the eldest son primary responsibility for conducting the family's rites of ancestor worship. Over time, the rationale for daughters receiving an equal share of inheritance was lost. Gendered inheritance practices were clearly in evidence from the seventeenth century on, and by the end of that century, ancestor worship was firmly established as the sole responsibility of male heirs.

The radical shift toward a kinship system centered on male heirs was justified by Neo-Confucian doctrine. Male descendants were considered the only legitimate heirs of the family lineage. Family genealogical records (*chokpo*) clearly show that patrilineage was firmly in place by the end of the seventeenth century. Historian Mark Peterson describes patrilineage as "men related to men through men" (Peterson 1996, 3). Daughters and daughters-in-law became minor players in genealogy. Daughters were listed as "having married out and into another lineage," and daughters-in-law were described as "having come from" their natal lineage (Peterson 1996, 3–4). A married daughter was often referred to as "one who left the household and became a stranger" (*ch'ulga oein*).

The patrilineal system also created a clear distinction between primary and secondary wives. The primary wife had all the legal and familial rights and prestige, but no such rights or privileges were granted to secondary wives. This inequality led to complicated domestic dynamics not only because of the resulting emotional tensions between wives but also because of the competition between their children, whose status was completely dependent on the status of their mothers (Deuchler 2003, 143). For instance, sons of secondary wives were barred from taking the state examinations that were the key to getting into offices in the government. This kind of rigid discrimination against secondary wives and their offspring was unique to Korea. There was no parallel behavior found in China, nor were the children of secondary wives severely discriminated against in Tokugawa Japan (Deuchler 1992, 268).

Womanly Virtues in Everyday Life

Education was a very important part of the Confucian transformation in Chosŏn. From its beginning, the new dynasty emphasized the crucial role that educational institutions would play in cultivating Confucian ideals and virtues for the future of the state. However, formal education was reserved for boys and men. Women were excluded from any institutionalized education. Informal, family-based, individual education at home was the main source of instruction for women of the upper class, with mothers or grandmothers often acting as teachers. The central focus of the education given to girls at home was often on womanly virtue, proper behavior, and industriousness in the performance of their household duties. While they were not expected to be highly knowledgeable about Chinese classics, they still devoted time to reading and writing, and some of them read a variety of Chinese classics, including *The Classic of Poetry*. Im Yunjidang (1721–1793) is among the upper-class women who became exceptionally proficient in Confucian classics, so much so that they were able to engage in philosophical debate.

Confucian classics provided some justifications for gender-specific education. In the works of Mencius, one of the five cardinal human relationships outlined is the relationship between husband and wife, which was governed by virtue of their innate differences (*pubu yubyŏl*). This essential distinction between man and woman was the basic tenet in the socialization of the genders and dictated the nature of education. Men learned to guide women, while women learned to obey men. As noted in Chapter 1, a woman was subject to the Three Obediences: obedience to her father before marriage, to her husband during marriage, and to her son in widowhood. Along with instilling an obedient attitude toward the male figures in their lives, women's education also stressed weaving, making clothes, cooking, managing the household, preparing food for ancestor worship rituals, serving visitors, and labor that women could do at home, such as sericulture.

Confucian values and the principles of "womanly virtue" were broadly propagated through books, both printed and handwritten. The most influential textbook was *Elementary Learning* (*Sohak* in Korean, *Xiaoxue* in Chinese), compiled by the Chinese Neo-Confucian scholar Zhu Xi in 1189. As the title of the book indicates, it offered basic rules of personal conduct and interpersonal relationships, serving as a primer for the next level of learning. In 1518, the Chosŏn court printed thirteen hundred copies of *Elementary Learning* and distributed them to court officials and some members of the royal family. The justification for its distribution is found in 1517 in the *Annals of the Chosŏn Dynasty*:

> *The* Elementary Learning *is of critical importance in everyday use. Yet, the simple people in the alleys and the women who are unfamiliar with writing [Chinese] find it difficult to read and practice it. We beg that those books most instrumental for everyday use like the* Elementary Learning *be translated into the vernacular, printed, and distributed inside and outside the capital so that no one from the palace and the capital officialdom down to the little people in the alleys is ignorant of it and does not read it. If all the families in the land are corrected, the evil atmosphere will cease and heavenly harmony will prevail. (Deuchler 2003, 145)*

BOX 2.2

Women Reading and Writing in Vernacular Korean, *Han'gŭl*

The diffusion of Confucian precepts via Chinese classics such as *Elementary Learning* was hampered by the fact that the vast majority of the population could not read Chinese. In this regard, it cannot be emphasized strongly enough that the invention of the Korean writing system (*han'gŭl*) in 1443 served as a catalyst in the dissemination of Confucian norms and ethics to the wider population. Prior to the invention of *han'gŭl*, Koreans of the upper class used Chinese script exclusively for official and personal writings. Men studied Chinese classics, which were the main texts that needed to be mastered in order to pass the state examinations for holding office in the government. Chinese language had prestige. King Sejong (r. 1418–1450) found it deplorable that the vast majority of his people were illiterate and thus unable to express their views and concerns. To remedy that situation, King Sejong gathered

(continued)

together a group of scholars to help him create an easy-to-learn writing system that would conform to the phonetic aspects of the Korean language.

Men of the upper class did not readily adopt the Korean writing system or appreciate its value, as it had the effect of making literacy more widely accessible, which would undercut their status as elites. In contrast, women enthusiastically embraced the new Korean writing system because it was easy to master, enabling more women to learn to read and write than ever before. To be sure, there were women of the upper class who had been trained to read and write in Chinese. However, they were discouraged from communicating in written Chinese and often hid their Chinese literacy. Thus, the Korean writing system became the main medium for reading and writing among women, and translations of Chinese texts into vernacular Korean came to be the primary vehicle for the spread of Confucian-prescribed gender ethics. Some of the key texts that were translated were *Sohak* (Elementary learning), *Samgang haengsilto* (Illustrated guide for the conduct of the three bonds), and *Yŏsasŏ* (Four books for women). In addition to those Chinese texts, there were also Korean works. For example, *Naehun* (Instructions for women) was compiled by Queen Sohye (1437–1504), who had lamented the lack of written resources that would help women cultivate their minds and bodies. She selected some important passages from well-known Chinese books, including *Elementary Learning*, *Notable Women* (*Lienü*), *Lessons for Women* (*Nüjiao*), and *Mirrors of Sagacity* (*Mingjian*). Prominent Korean scholars of Confucianism also wrote instructional books for women, including *Kyujung yoram* (Brochure for the inner chambers) by Yi Hwang (1501–1570) and *Kyenyŏsŏ* (Instructions for women) by Song Siyŏl (1607–1689).

By the end of the seventeenth century the growth in literacy among women and the production and distribution of textbooks for women had had a significant impact on women's culture. Confucian precepts and "womanly virtues" came to be internalized as the ultimate guidelines for life not only among women of the upper class, who had historically had ready access to written textbooks, but also those from the commoner and even lower classes. Beyond that, their new literacy skills gave women the ability to express the agony and suffering they experienced under the oppressive patriarchal family culture. To be sure, the majority of women adopted and even advocated Confucian precepts, taking for granted women's devotion to and sacrifice for their husband's family. However, it is also important to recognize that women were able to make use of patriarchal gender ideology to empower themselves, especially through their morality, a point that is further discussed in Chapter 3.

Regulating Women's Bodies and Sexuality

The patrilineal social structure in Chosŏn began to be manifested in strict regulation of women's bodies and sexuality. One of the legal provisions implemented to control women's sexuality was banning remarriage for women. As discussed in Chapter 1, prior to the Chosŏn dynasty, remarriage had been freely practiced, so widows could remarry without stigma. However, under Neo-Confucian influence, a woman was expected to remain chaste for her husband, even after his death. A proposal at the beginning of the Chosŏn dynasty to outlaw women's remarriage was not immediately embraced. Officials sympathetic to the plight of women argued that enforcement of such a law would be viewed as overly harsh, especially in those cases where a woman had become a widow at an early age or had no place to go after her husband's death. However, discrimination against and stigmatization of remarried women began to take legal shape as time went on. During the reign of King Sŏngjong (1469–1494), sons of remarried women were legally prevented from holding positions in government. It is notable that a majority of the Confucian officials had opposed this legal provision, yet King Sŏngjong came down on the side of the minority view and authorized the statutory change in policy in order to consolidate Neo-Confucian doctrines as state ideology. This legal provision certainly had the effect of regulating women's sexuality. For the sake of their sons' futures, women submitted to solitary widowhood and remained faithful to their deceased husbands.

Another powerful measure taken to control women's sexuality was to confine them to the private space of the domestic sphere and limit their interactions to family members and close relatives. When upper-class women did go out into public areas, they had to cover their faces and wear long-sleeved clothing to avoid any improper male gaze.

However, such practices were not universally adopted. The different social classes varied in the degree to which they embraced the "inside-outside rule." While women of the upper class followed the strict rules of behavior, commoner and lower-class women were not expected to follow the same rigorous conventions. This class distinction is particularly evident in the legal codes that stipulated women's sexual conduct. For instance, if women of the upper class committed adultery, they were executed, while the law did not subject women of the lower classes to any such punishment (Kim 2015).

The increasing confinement of women of the upper class to the domestic arena also affected their religious lives. Unlike previous dynasties, Chosŏn systematically oppressed Buddhism as a matter of state policy. Despite this antagonism toward the religion, women continued to go to Buddhist temples

A woman with a cover. Painting of Sin Yunbok (1758–1817). NATIONAL MUSEUM OF KOREA

during the Chosŏn dynasty. Even women in the royal family continued to be devoted followers of Buddhism. Some married women sought sanctuary in temples rather than endure the abuse meted out by their husbands and in-laws. In the face of this broad and continuing adoption of the religion, Confucian-based anti-Buddhist state policy raised debate about the danger and moral depravity that women invited by visiting temples, and there was expression of alarm at the considerable number of young women who had become Buddhist nuns rather than marrying. This behavior of avoidance and escape was thought to disturb the harmonious energy of the universe. From the Confucian cosmological viewpoint, women should be in marital relationships no matter how harsh the circumstances. In addition, a common assumption by Confucian scholars was that the presence of laywomen among the male monks would inevitably lead to sexual encounters. These imagined encounters became accepted as the basis for forbidding women from visiting temples in the name of moral purity and chastity (Jung 2011).

Various textbooks meant to offer instruction for women on exemplary behavior emphasized the ideology of chastity. As in China, women were expected to remain chaste, no matter what circumstances they might be facing. The expectation of chastity was so great that some women committed suicide rather than face the social stigma of rape, especially during the invasions of Korea (1592–1598) by the Japanese general Toyotomi Hideyoshi and the two Manchu invasions that took place between 1627 and 1636. Those women who chose death over a bad reputation were held up as exemplary. Monuments were erected to them in villages, providing a reminder of the meaning of womanly virtue. These women brought glory upon themselves through their heroic efforts to preserve their virtue, but ultimately that glory was reflected in an elevation of the reputation of their husbands' families.

Women's Empowerment Within Limits

Confucian precepts did not invariably oppress women. Women also utilized these precepts to secure power and authority within the family. For example, by following the rigid injunctions for "womanly virtue," they were not merely complying with the dominant ideology of the time but also proactively attempting to achieve higher status through exemplary behavior and judicious life choices. One example that clearly demonstrates these twin aspects of the Confucian gender ideology and practice in Chosŏn can be found in the petition system. The Chosŏn dynasty instituted a petition system in 1401. It allowed people, regardless of their gender or class, to express grievances in either oral or written form. Initially, women were not frequent petitioners; in its early years, the system allowed petitioners to submit grievances only when they themselves were the subject of the complaint. However, by the early eighteenth century, when the categories of petitionable grievances and eligible petitioners were expanded, women took full advantage of the petition system and participated actively. Under the revised system, women were allowed to petition on behalf of husbands, unmarried daughters for their natal parents, and daughters-in-law for their parents-in-law. In this vein, "women emerged as legal agents who could seek justice for their family members," which brought about changes that were "nothing less than epochal" (Kim Haboush 2002, 246). The vast majority of the petitions submitted by women centered on family lineage issues, adoption, and restoration of a husband's reputation. It is clear that women petitioners exploited the public system to preserve or enhance the status of their families and thereby raise their own status as custodians of the family. Thus, rather ironically, women's proper role in the domestic arena brought them into the public domain. Indeed, women could fully justify their public engagement as a means of fulfilling their duties and responsibilities in the private, domestic arena. With the separation in which women were relegated to the "inner" sphere and men to the "outer" sphere, a woman could gain legitimate entry to the public arena as long as it concerned the well-being and prosperity of the family.

Women also found distinctive space within the domestic sphere to empower themselves. As mentioned previously, it was the custom during Koryŏ for young married couples to live with the bride's family for some time after their marriage. Under those circumstances, married women could maintain close ties with their natal families. However, during the Chosŏn era, this custom was gradually replaced. Upon marriage brides would move into the homes of their husbands' families, and they would have little or no contact with their own families. Under this new marital arrangement, which became prevalent beginning in the seventeenth century, women's lives and destinies depended on the connections, achievements, and prospects of their husbands, and that led to a new set of dynamics in the family. Once married, a woman had to adjust to a new and unfamiliar role in the culture of a new family, and in the face of all of that novelty she was expected to maintain a unique and pure family tradition.

The only historical records describing the status and roles of women in the family are those of the upper class. They show that women of the upper class proactively enforced the requirement of womanly virtue on themselves to ensure the prosperity of their families. They were deeply engaged in managing household affairs, educating children and grandchildren, and contributing to the building and maintenance of the family economy. There is an adage in Korea: "When a country is in crisis, a loyal minister is needed; when a family is in poverty, a good wife is needed." This proverb is indicative of the crucial role that women played in family finances. Men of the upper class remained at a remove from the actual, everyday affairs of the domestic sphere in order to cultivate their minds and study Chinese classics. As a result, women had to step in to take care of the family economy. In this context, women's resourcefulness and industriousness were highly valued and celebrated, especially in times of natural disaster or a decline in family fortunes.

The ideology of chastity and the wealth of records regarding "chaste women" are another example of how women appropriated a seemingly oppressive gender ideology to vindicate themselves. As described previously, women's sexuality was systematically regulated with a central focus on purity and chastity. A wide array of texts, most representatively the section on the "chaste woman" in *Samgang haengsilto* (Illustrated guide for the conduct of the three bonds), contributed to the reification of the ideal of chastity. Whereas the ideology of chastity certainly suppressed women from acting on their sexual desires and barred widows from remarrying, many women accepted chastity as a means by which they could assert their value and contribute to the maintenance or enhancement of their family's standing. When a woman committed suicide rather than face the social stigma that she would be subjected to after a rape or ungrounded rumors and slander, we need to ask what motivated that extreme choice. What did she want to achieve when she made the decision to end her own life? Was it a passive act to comply with the Confucian precepts? Or could it be better understood as an effort to take control of her own body? Using legal cases involving suicide by widows to preserve their chastity, historian Jungwon Kim argues that "the act of suicide was one response available to widows to counter sexual assaults, rumors, slanders and conflicts inside and outside of the family. It was the most powerful expression of the conjunction of violence and independence in relation to a widow's agency to control her own dignity, death and fate" (Kim 2014, 143–144).

JAPAN

The victory in 1600 by forces loyal to Tokugawa Ieyasu, the most powerful military overlord in Japan, brought an end to the Warring States period. To gain peacetime political legitimacy, Tokugawa had Japan's emperor—an official with no political power and only traces of prestige lingering from the ancient past—name him as the new shogun. Tokugawa and his successors as shoguns created a political structure that ruled over Japan until the middle of the nineteenth century. Historians of Japan refer to the two and a half centuries of Tokugawa rule as Japan's early modern era. Neo-Confucian doctrine was one of several tools used by the Tokugawa shoguns to consolidate their rule over Japan, and by the end of the seventeenth century, Neo-Confucianism had gained a foothold in early modern Japan, just as it had in Chosŏn Korea and, centuries earlier, in China.

To control Japan, Tokugawa Ieyasu set up a system of self-regulating status groups, with the shogun as the supreme ruler over these groups. The groups were, nominally, the four classes of the ancient Confucian texts, recast for Japanese use as samurai, farmers, artisans, and merchants. Self-regulating status groups contained more diversity than homogeneity; there were rich farmers and poor farmers, rich merchants and poor merchants, samurai who were powerful provincial rulers (called daimyo) and lowly foot soldiers, and men and women. Not all groups within society were equally Confucianized, and the impact of Confucian principles on gender relations, marriage, and sexuality varied among the status groups. These differences will be discussed in detail in this section. As status groups, their boundaries were less flexible than those of the social classes in China, where a young man's diligent study of Confucian classics could potentially earn him a spot in the ruling class.

In Tokugawa-period Japan, mobility among the bottom three status groups was not uncommon, since sons and daughters of farm families migrated as teenagers to find work either on nearby farms or in cities, towns, and castles, but it was nearly impossible, until the end of the Tokugawa period, for non-samurai to enter the samurai ruling class.

At the top of the ruling order, right under the shogun, were the daimyo. These were powerful and wealthy male military overlords who, like the shogun, controlled from several hundred to many thousands of samurai warriors as well as many farming villages whose revenues they taxed. Although the daimyo were part of the samurai status group, they were treated as a special category of warriors. The Tokugawa shoguns were most concerned with the daimyo because they were provincial leaders from whose ranks the shoguns themselves had emerged. In their consolidation of power in the early seventeenth century, the Tokugawa shoguns punished those daimyo who had fought against them in 1600 by either taking away some or all of their land or moving them to less desirable areas. More trusted daimyo were moved to territories closer to the Tokugawa capital at Edo, and less trusted daimyo were moved to the periphery of the islands. After these changes, the remaining daimyo were permitted to rule fairly autonomously within their own domains, collecting taxes and adjudicating legal disputes, as long as their laws and procedures were generally consistent with Tokugawa practice and they did not challenge the Tokugawa shoguns' authority.

The Tokugawa shoguns also kept an eye on the daimyo by controlling their marriages and family lives. After 1615, to prevent alliances of potential rivals to the shogun, members of daimyo families were required to secure the shogun's permission to marry. In addition, after the 1630s, the shogun implemented an "alternate attendance system" that required daimyo to travel back and forth annually between the shogun's capital at Edo (today's Tokyo) and the daimyo's own castles in their domain, taking with them a huge retinue of their samurai. Maintaining a castle at home and a mansion in Edo and feeding and lodging hundreds of samurai as they moved about the country cost the daimyo a large part of the taxes they raised from the farmers, guaranteeing that the daimyo would never have enough resources to successfully challenge the Tokugawa. While alternate attendance drained daimyo resources, however, it also brought many daimyo into the shogun's government as officials while they were in Edo.

In addition to depleting the daimyo's financial resources, the alternate attendance system also controlled the daimyo by making use of their bonds with their wives and children. Daimyo wives and children were required to remain in Edo, where they were, for the most part, hostages in the gilded cages of their mansions. Post stations were set up at frequent intervals along the roads leading to Edo—roads carried a constant stream of commercial traffic in addition to massive processions of daimyo performing their alternate attendance—to check for the movement of weapons into and women out of Edo. Nuns, entertainers, housewives on pilgrimages or personal travel, and other commoner women could move freely, but daimyo wives' movements were suspect and therefore strictly controlled.

The wives and daughters of daimyo and other high-ranking samurai families were not totally without employment possibilities while in Edo, however. Some were able to gain appointments to the women's quarters of the shogun's court, where they could act as palace functionaries, adding to their families' prestige by carrying messages, making alliances with women of other daimyo families, and serving the shogun and his wife in a variety of capacities, including entertainment, advice giving, and sexual service. Sexual service carried the possibility of becoming the mother of a shogunal heir, a powerful position at the shogun's court (Totman 1967, 89–110). The sons of daimyo families were also influenced by the control mechanisms of the alternate attendance system. Raised in Edo, the center of national culture by 1700, these sons helped to link the Japanese islands together culturally when they moved back to their families' domains as adult daimyo. The rough, rustic young daimyo sons of the Warring States period were soon tamed by Edo's urban culture, creating a new type of elite masculinity for the daimyo class.

The end of a century of warfare throughout the Japanese islands and a decade of incursions into Chosŏn also changed the meaning of life for countless samurai warriors of less than daimyo status after 1600. Over the course of a few decades, the daily practice of being samurai required them to become government bureaucrats, serving their daimyo or shogunal superiors in offices rather than as dashing warriors. At the same time, all samurai men were required to wear two swords, and nonchalant bad-boy behavior continued to be viewed as charming in samurai circles throughout the Tokugawa period. One seventeenth-century scholar even created a term for this type of cult of masculinity in his popular book on the "way of the warrior" (*bushidō*). The rowdier samurai initially resisted government authorities' attempts to remold them as scholars, gentlemen, and bureaucrats. This was especially true of masterless samurai, whose daimyo had been killed or dispossessed of all their land; many of these rootless young men roamed the streets making trouble, often as armed youth gangs. It took till 1650 for masterless samurai to be either defeated or co-opted into a life of responsible manly work, similar to the life of samurai who were under the control of successful daimyo. This created a new definition of masculinity in which literacy, education, and culture were as important as martial skills.

The Tokugawa State and the Regulating of Everyday Life

Before the rise of the Tokugawa shoguns, the liveliest intellectual tradition in Japan had been found in Buddhist theology. But the new period seemed to call for a new focus, one more practical than the introspective, faith-based learning of Buddhism. Chinese Neo-Confucian thought entranced a new generation of scholars. The Tokugawa shoguns saw one of the schools of Neo-Confucianism as particularly supportive of their claim to political power in Japan. In this Japanese approach to Neo-Confucianism, the Japanese shogun was equated with the emperor of China's Confucian ideology, while the Japanese emperor, who was in reality a figurehead with no political power, was equated with the Confucian concept of "heaven." The militarily powerful shogun's respect for the impotent Japanese emperor was used to justify the shogun's right to rule. This school of Neo-Confucianism also rationalized the four-status structure that placed the samurai on top and contended that the Confucian relationships, one of which was the husband's superiority to his wife, were natural and proper for all people and times. Small wonder that the shogun's government encouraged the samurai to study the same Confucian texts their counterparts in the Chinese bureaucracy studied in order to qualify for jobs as officials in Japan's early modern state. Only the samurai, who were expected to be part of the ruling class, were eligible to be educated at the government's expense. All women and commoners of both genders, and many samurai who sought specialized education, paid for their own education. Confucian ideas were often part of their education, but learning took a variety of forms for commoners and many samurai as well.

The basic educational texts for samurai were written in a form of Chinese that educated young men in Japan were expected to learn in the early modern era, even while a bourgeoning publishing industry cranked out popular literature for the masses in Japanese *kana* script. New and diverse types of schools, works of prose and poetry, theatrical works and the arts, and essays on philosophy and government created new ideals of masculinity and femininity. Many of these institutions and works of art were aimed at the samurai, but most found eager cross-status consumers.

The Tokugawa self-regulation system was extended to all status groups. Each village regulated itself, and cities and towns had a variety of means of governance. As long as the towns and villages paid their taxes, maintained the peace, and behaved in ways that roughly paralleled Tokugawa laws, farmers, artisans, and merchants generally governed themselves. The shogun's government involved itself as little as possible in the day-to-day oversight of most commoners.

But the shogunal government stepped into everyday life when it came to relations with foreigners. By the late 1630s, fear of Christianity and Christian missionaries led the Tokugawa to allow foreign trade only with Chinese, Koreans, Ryūkyū Islanders, and the Dutch (who promised not to send missionaries) and to restrict trade to limited places. To strengthen the ban on Christianity, all Japanese were required to register their families as members of a local Buddhist temple. As a result, there are extensive temple records of births, marriages, and deaths. Together with records kept by families themselves, these temple records give us a good overview of family formation and gender relations in the early modern period (Walthall 1991).

The government also involved itself in the construction of gender through social and economic policies as well as ideologies that affected people of different statuses in different ways. Even before the beginning of the Tokugawa period, Toyotomi Hideyoshi, a powerful daimyo who controlled most of Japan, decreed that armed farmer-warriors had to choose between giving up their arms to become full-time farmers and giving up their farmland to become full-time warriors. A man who chose to be a samurai had to live in or near his daimyo's castle. For his service to his daimyo (the service became increasingly bureaucratic in a time of peace) and to compensate for the loss of his land, he and his successors were paid a stipend. This policy was continued under the Tokugawa. Soon the forced movement of samurai led to the development of towns and cities called "castle towns." Merchants and artisans migrated to the castle towns to serve the now landless samurai, building homes and furnishings for themselves and the samurai, making clothing and armor, marketing food, running lodges and restaurants, carrying out banking, publishing books, creating arts and entertainment, and running a lively business in the sex trades. Men of the samurai status were not supposed to be involved in merchant or artisan activities, although some occupations, such as medicine and scholarship, were open to all statuses (only a small handful of practitioners in these fields were women; some women were midwives, teachers, poets, and painters).

By 1700, in most daimyo domains, about 6 to 7 percent of the population were urbanized samurai, an equal percentage were merchants and artisans, and about 85 percent were farmers. Japan's cities had grown enormously by 1700. Edo, the Tokugawa's own castle town, was the world's largest city, having grown from a tiny fishing village in 1590 to over a million residents. The population of Japan as a whole grew from twelve million in 1600 to thirty million in 1720, and then it stagnated for the next 140 years.

Samurai men were at the heart of the governmental service system. They received stipends for the service, and at times supplementary income if they were particularly talented. If a samurai died without an heir, his stipend was terminated. His wife and daughters were not allowed to inherit his stipend, and they were often left penniless. As a result, many samurai wives had to tolerate their husbands' concubines (secondary wives) to make sure there would be an heir to support them. Children born to concubines were acknowledged as legitimate, and a concubine's son inherited his father's stipends and property if he was the only son. The primary wife was the legal mother of a concubine's children, which placed the concubine in the lowest position in the household—below her own birth children. (Note that the legal status of secondary wives and of the children born to them differed significantly in Qing, Chosŏn, and Tokugawa Japan at this time.)

Adoption of children and adults as heirs was quite common as well. In the samurai class, marriages were arranged and their primary official purpose was producing an heir, but most families nevertheless had loving relationships. That is not to say that samurai men did not have emotional extramarital relationships in addition to those with their wives and concubines. They did, without a sense of impropriety or shame. Samurai women's extramarital affairs were strictly illegal, however, and popular novels and plays of the mid-Tokugawa period depict such affairs as ending in execution or suicide for the star-crossed lovers.

The everyday lives of the other two status groups in the cities—merchants and artisans—were intertwined with the samurai who patronized their shops, passed them daily on the streets, celebrated the same religious festivals, and sat next to them in the theaters. In some other ways, their lives did not mingle. Intermarriage of samurai and commoners was highly unusual before the nineteenth century, and commoner boys' and girls' training for adulthood was different from that of the samurai. Commoner children of both sexes expected to play a role in commercial or artisanal houses as adults, and both needed to be literate. Marriage partners were chosen for their compatibility, and the young people themselves often played a role in choosing their mates, unlike the common practice of arranged marriages among the samurai.

Education for non-samurai urban children was varied and focused on practicality. Many children were educated at schools run by priests at local Buddhist temples or at small private schools run by both married and unmarried women. Many teenage boys served apprenticeships with merchant houses outside their own family, and in some cases the most talented apprentice married the boss's daughter, usually with the daughter's approval. That young man would become a part of his boss's family—a practice that echoed the earlier matrilocal marriage patterns of the elite, described in Chapter 1—and the young couple would later inherit and run the business together. Other urban boys might attend one of many private academies run by famous intellectuals for any student who could pay the tuition, regardless of their status as samurai or commoner. Some academies focused on science and mathematics; others stressed Confucian virtue. The most famous of these was the Kaitokudō Academy, founded in 1726, which expanded the principles of orthodox Confucianism to teach that the governing responsibilities of samurai and the economic activities of merchants were equally important in the community and larger society. Many boys took the Kaitokudō's courses in reading, accounting and abacus use, and simple Confucianism (loyalty and filial piety). Those who advanced to further study analyzed Confucian texts (Smith 1988; Najita 1977).

Boys and girls over the age of seven or eight rarely studied together, as the skills they needed for adulthood were different. Urban daughters usually received less formal education than their brothers, although an unlettered young woman could not make a good marriage. Many girls were taught to read and write and especially to use the abacus and do the simple math needed to keep the family and business accounts. Urban women were expected to work in the family business; even in the richest families, brides, who did not have to perform difficult house maintenance chores, were called upon to serve their parents-in-law. Girls' earliest education, like that of their brothers, was often in temple schools or small schools run by women teachers. Girls studied texts called *jokun* (precepts for women) that stressed filial piety and obedience to one's husband and in-laws. Some well-to-do merchant families paid upper-class samurai families to take their daughters in as servants to train them in etiquette and manners (a chaperone was often sent to make sure the daughter would be well cared for). A daughter's education could cost up to 5 percent of her family's total income. By the end of the Tokugawa period, approximately 50 percent of men and 15 percent of women throughout Japan were literate; the majority of literate women lived in the cities. While these literacy rates seem very low to us today, they were among the world's highest in the nineteenth century.

The texts men and women studied included references to the Confucian idea of women's inferiority. Many of the *jokun* used in temple schools, the most famous of which was *Onna daigaku* (*Greater Learning for Women*), described the ideal woman as loyal to her husband and parents-in-law, passive, submissive, cheerful, and hardworking in her role as a wife. *Onna daigaku*—long believed to have been written by Confucian scholar Kaibara Ekiken (1630–1714)—was read by millions of girls from the early eighteenth century until the early twentieth century. It was considered by Japanese feminists in the late nineteenth century to be one of the reasons for women's subordination. Yet when first published in 1716, it was just one part of a larger work, *A Treasure Chest of Greater Learning for Women* (*Onna daigaku takara bako*), that discussed numerous occupations for women, training of children, practical skills, ways to deal with medical emergencies, and literature and poetry, in addition to its notorious list of women's shortcomings. Many scholars now stress that the message of subordination in *jokun* such as *Onna daigaku* paled by comparison with the empowering role of literacy promoted by their use as textbooks (Tocco 2005).

It cannot be ignored, however, that these works were part of girls' education, that fewer girls than boys received education, and that women's legal status was far below men's. Yet that does not mean that women were not prized for what they did do. While women of samurai status were viewed as servants of their parents-in-law and childbearers for their husbands, merchant women's status relative to their husbands was often higher. They had business roles to play in their families, and many merchant-status parents allowed their daughters to express their opinions in the selection of their husbands because family harmony was essential to the success of their firms.

Sexuality and the Arts

Early modern urban life, in which samurai, merchants, and artisans participated, cannot be understood outside the context of sexuality. The Tokugawa government sought to control the boundaries of sexuality; *uncontrolled* sexuality was of great concern to them. Their reaction to the rise of kabuki theater is a good example of the government's anxiety over uncontrolled sexuality. In 1603, a woman dancer named Okuni introduced to Kyoto residents a new form of sensual dance performance—this was an early form of kabuki. At first all the performers were women, and female kabuki troupes became very popular in Kyoto, Edo, and Osaka. But onlookers often became excited by the dancers, which could lead to fights, so the authorities forced the performances to the outskirts of cities in 1608. Soon a lively sex trade involving actors and would-be performers followed the kabuki troupes, leading the government to outlaw all female stage performers in 1629. Boy actors then took over the women's roles, but the government found that this did not solve the problem of audiences' overly enthusiastic reactions to the actors. Many of the boys were as attractive to the male theater-goers as the women had been. Believing the audience members' adulation of this new type of actor was as problematic as the previous type, the government went one step farther and in 1653 restricted the performance of female roles to adult males rather than boys. Theaters were moved to officially designated sexuality districts that had been set up in 1617 in Edo (the Yoshiwara district), in 1629 in Osaka (Shinmachi), and in 1641 in Kyoto (Shimabara). In these districts the sex industry was cordoned off from the rest of the city.

Brothels, mostly staffed by women and girls (though some also offered boys as sex workers), were required to move to those districts. The sexuality zones attracted all sorts of arts and culture: in addition to brothels, there were teahouses, artists' and writers' studios, theaters, and restaurants. Street performances—including exotic animals, jugglers, musicians, and entertainers of all sorts—enlivened the zones. These zones, called "pleasure districts" (*yūkaku*), had been created to marginalize and control sexuality so the samurai could focus on carrying out their duties to their daimyo or the shogun. In practice, these zones attracted samurai and commoner alike. They aimed primarily at male pleasure, but many of the zones' residents were women—sex workers, servants, teahouse attendants, and the like. Wives and daughters of families not in the entertainment business, who did not live in the zones, also entered to attend plays and other attractions.

Adult male actors had to shave their heads in the style of adult male samurai. At first they wore small scarves to cover their bald patches and later were allowed to wear wigs to perform female roles. But they continued to be objects of audience members' desire. Indeed, many theater-goers, performers, and critics at the time believed that male actors performed femininity better than women could. The government did not mind same-sex attraction or male-male sexual relations as long as they followed proper rules of sexual etiquette. The performance of sex was part of the accepted process of adult male mentoring of samurai boys in the seventeenth century, practiced by the Tokugawa family itself, the daimyo, and all ranks of warriors. Merchant and artisan townsmen took part in sexual relations with young protégés as well. Many urban adult men had marital relationships with their wives and more casual sexual relationships with both male and female prostitutes. In the Tokugawa era, sexual practice did not define sexual identity—that is, as heterosexual or homosexual—as it would in the late nineteenth century (Pflugfelder 1999).

BOX 2.3

Ihara Saikaku, "The Umbrella Oracle"

In 1685, comedic writer Ihara Saikaku (for more on his life and work, see Chapter 3) mocked the provincial ignorance of gullible villagers far from his cosmopolitan birthplace, Osaka. In this sketch, we see the view of sophisticated urban people toward rural sexual attitudes.

> *To the famous "Hanging Temple of Kwannon" . . . someone had once presented twenty oil-paper umbrellas which . . . were hung beside the temple for the use of any and all who might be caught in the rain or snow. . . . One day in the spring of 1649, however, a certain villager borrowed one of the umbrellas and, while he was returning home . . . the umbrella was blown completely out of sight, and though the villager bemoaned its loss, there was not a thing he could do.*
>
> *Borne aloft by the wind, the umbrella landed finally in the little hamlet of Anazato, far in the mountains of the island of Kyushu. The people of this village had from ancient times been completely cut off from the world and—uncultured folk that they were—had never even seen an umbrella! All the learned men and elders of the village gathered around to discuss the curious object. . . . Finally one local wise man stepped forward and proclaimed . . . , "Though I hesitate to utter that August Name, this is without a doubt the God of the Sun!"*
>
> *All present were filled with awe. . . . The whole population of the village went up into the mountains and . . . built a shrine that the*

Sex with a serving maid within the home or a boy who was a protégé could be practiced privately anywhere, but the shogun's government confined sex for purchase to the segregated pleasure districts. Young women far outnumbered young men in legally licensed brothels. To be sure, life for sex workers was not pleasant. Pleasure districts were surrounded by moats and gates, preventing the sex workers from leaving. Girls sold to brothels as very young children led difficult lives, their often elegant clothing and genteel manner merely a part of the performance of sexuality. Sex workers were ranked by their artistic skills and training. The highest-ranked entertainers, called geisha, were, like their Korean counterparts (*kisaeng*), literate, musically skilled, and witty courtesans. They consorted with men of means, often high-ranking officials and merchants. But like their low-ranking, less skilled *deity's spirit might be transferred hence from Ise. When they had paid reverence to it, the divine spirit did indeed enter the umbrella.*

At the time of the summer rains the site upon which the shrine was situated became greatly agitated. . . . When the umbrella was consulted, the following oracle was delivered: "All this summer the sacred hearth has been simply filthy, with cockroaches boiled in the holy vessels. . . . Let there not be a single cockroach left alive! I also have one other request. I desire you to select a beautiful young maiden as a consolation offering for me. If this is not done within seven days . . . I will rain you all to death, so that the seed of man remains no more upon the earth!"

Thus spake the oracle.

The villagers were frightened out of their wits. . . . The young maidens, weeping and wailing, strongly protested the umbrella-god's cruel demand. . . . They cried, "How could we survive even one night with such a god?" for they had come to attach a peculiar significance to the odd shape that the deity had assumed.

At this juncture a young and beautiful widow [said], "Since it is for the god, I will offer myself in place of the young maidens." All night long the beautiful widow waited in the shrine, but she did not get a bit of affection. Enraged, she charged into the inner sanctum, grasped the divine umbrella firmly in her hands and, screaming, "Worthless deceiver!" she tore it apart, and threw the pieces as far as she could! (Keene 1955, 354–356)

sisters in the sex trades, even geisha were indentured to their houses and required to pay off their contracts if they wished to change their profession.

Sex workers outside the government-licensed brothels had a much tougher time. The government did not permit unregulated sex work, whether by males or females, so people who engaged in unlicensed sex for hire were arrested if caught. Sadder yet, burial records indicate that the leading cause of death for prostitutes was syphilis. The average age of death for serving girls at roadside post stations, who often engaged in unregulated sex, was twenty-one; those in the licensed sex market suffered similar fates.

And yet, in these crowded areas of sexuality, gender oppression, and artistic license, urban culture flourished. Because so many people found themselves at the mercy of the uncertainties of life and fortune, the world of the arts and sexuality in the late seventeenth century came to be called the "floating world" (*ukiyo*), a concept of life's impermanence familiar to all Japanese from the teachings of Buddhism. Life expectancy, especially for entertainers, was short, and for many people in urban areas, gender, far from being "real" or "natural," was constituted through performance onstage and in the brothels.

Gender and Farm Families

Gender relations among the overwhelming majority of Japanese who were farmers differed from those of the urbanized samurai and commoners and were far less influenced by Confucian propriety. Farm women's roles depended on their families' wealth and on local customs that varied throughout Japan. As in China and Korea, Japanese farm wives, husbands, children, and other members of the family contributed to the family's well-being (productive work) and continuity (reproductive work). Mothers bore children (reproductive work) but also had the primary responsibility for planting and threshing rice, spinning thread, and sewing clothing (productive work). Japanese fathers took charge of early childhood education and even infant care (reproductive work), and also went out to their fields daily to maintain their farms and, at harvest season, to gather in the grain and other crops (productive work). Children of six or seven years carried their siblings on their backs while playing or attending school, while their parents and their grandparents (if they were still vigorous) worked in the fields. No member of the average farm family could avoid either reproductive or productive work. Some tasks were more likely to be performed by one sex or the other, but if a woman was not available for planting or a man for harvesting, no one sacrificed family welfare and continuity on the altar of sex differences (Uno 1991).

Representation in village communal associations—the heart of local governance for the self-regulating farming status—was a different story. Farm women usually took part as representatives of their families only when a suitable male relative was not available, although from time to time a senior member of a family favored a daughter over any of the sons and sent her to village association meetings. Village endogamy (marriage within the village) was the most common practice in early modern Japan, but when young people did migrate to a neighboring village for marriage, it was usually women who did that. Villages generally did not allow "outsiders" to attend meetings of the village's shrine association, an important sign of inclusion. Women were more likely to be excluded from village leadership because they were "outsiders," and also because of the villagers' preferences for male leadership.

In the medieval and early modern periods, farm women planted rice seedlings in straight rows while men prepared the rice paddy.
"The Farmer Planting the Rice Sprouts." The Miriam and Ira D. Wallach Division of Art, The New York Public Library /NYPL catalog ID: b11818701

Rural boys and girls were less likely to attend school than their urban counterparts, but a significant number did gain rudimentary reading skills. Some learned to read at home, while others attended the same kinds of temple schools or small schools run by women that were found in the cities and towns. Many more village boys than girls attended these schools. Most girls also learned household skills from their mothers or the families into which some of them were apprenticed. Starting in early adolescence, girls spent time in village "girls' rooms," where more senior girls and young women guided younger girls in practical skills such as sewing and good manners. Girls enjoyed learning skills alongside their female friends and having a chance to socialize at festival time, away from their parents' eyes, with the "boys' rooms" in the village. In some areas of Japan, this socializing among teenagers led to romance and marriage. Young people in villages were much freer to choose their own marriage partners. Families esteemed harmony, so a couple's compatibility and the wife's ability to get along with her marital family and contribute to its productivity were critical components of a marriage. Divorce was common among farm families when these conditions were not met, and remarriage was not stigmatized. Temple and family documents offer good records of family formation, dissolution, and reformation.

Despite the legal dominance of males as family heads and representatives in village governance, farmers were pragmatic. Samurai families could be dissolved in the absence of a male heir, but farm families could collapse without good men, women, boys, and girls to carry out their functions. Both sexes and all age groups were viewed as necessary. Unlike in samurai families, female infants were welcomed with birth celebrations and feted on particular birthdays, as were their brothers. While infanticide was practiced (illegally) by farm families, girl babies were no more likely than boys to be targeted, as families sought gender balance as well as optimal family size. Widows were not seen as superfluous. Many older women, both widows and those still married, were relieved, after a few decades of backbreaking farm work, to turn over the administration of their households to their daughters-in-law and begin to travel on pilgrimages with other similarly situated women. They could now relax with a cup of tea; the government periodically issued bans on tea drinking by women under forty to make sure they did not sit around unproductively. Because this prohibition was issued so frequently, it is clear that it could not be strictly enforced, but it is an example of the social requirement that young women work hard, leaving relaxation as a reward for senior members of the family (Walthall 1991).

CONNECTIONS

Gender, family, and sexuality were used in the construction and framing of early modern states in China, Korea, and Japan. In each of these cases, Neo-Confucian ideas were used by governing officials to help define the relationship of individuals and families to the state. To varying degrees, the people of those states adapted to their states' principles and practices; in some cases, they either passively or actively resisted them.

Marriage, which had earlier been more informal in some cases, was a critical relationship that was increasingly defined by law and customary practices. In China, the cult of chastity limited—though it did not completely eliminate—widow remarriage. In Chosŏn Korea, the matrilocal marriages and female inheritance of earlier centuries gave way to a banning of widow remarriage. In Japan, remarriage was acceptable after divorce and widowhood. Women's abilities to choose their own marriage partners and their rights within marriage varied greatly by class status in Japan. In all three countries, a wife's status relative to her husband was lower among the more elite classes than among farmers. For example, only among upper-class women was adultery punishable by death in Korea. While each of these countries permitted men to have only one primary wife, they all tacitly accepted the practice of men having concubines, or secondary wives. The status of concubines and their children differed significantly among the three countries. In China, itinerant unmarried men were viewed as dangerous "rootless rascals." In Tokugawa Japan, the shogun controlled the highest feudal lords, the daimyo, by controlling whom they married. Thus, marriage in a variety of forms was seen as critical to the state.

The early modern period was a time of great urban growth in all three countries. This was accompanied by increasing levels of literacy and access to the arts and entertainment by a wider segment of society. Many boys and girls either attended school or were trained at home to read, and their textbooks focused on instilling moral and ethical gender roles as defined by Neo-Confucianism. The urban-based arts were practiced in what was considered a "floating world" in each of these countries. This world included theaters and the commodification of sex. In all three countries, the government sought to contain the sale of sex, which they did by permitting high-status performers—geisha in Japan, *kisaeng* in Korea, and courtesans in China—while outlawing the unregulated sale of sex (prostitution). Prostitution was, however, practiced everywhere.

Masculinity also varied over time and among social classes. Confucian scholars were concerned about the role of eunuchs in China; samurai gave up being warriors and became bureaucrats during the Tokugawa peace in Japan. Masculine same-sex love was practiced and featured in literature in China and Japan, though much less is known about female same-sex love in the early modern period.

REFERENCES AND SUGGESTIONS FOR FURTHER READING

GLOBAL CONTEXT

Frader, Laura Levine. 2004. "Gender and Labor in World History." In *A Companion to Gender History*, edited by Teresa A. Meade and Merry E. Wiesner-Hanks. Oxford: Blackwell.

Hardwick, Julie. 2004. "Did Gender Have a Renaissance? Exclusions and Traditions in Early Modern Western Europe." In *A Companion to Gender History*, edited by Teresa A. Meade and Merry E. Wiesner-Hanks. Oxford: Blackwell.

Nye, Robert. 2004. "Sexuality." In *A Companion to Gender History*, edited by Teresa A. Meade and Merry E. Wiesner-Hanks. Oxford: Blackwell.

CHINA

Bernhardt, Kathryn. 1999. *Women and Property in China, 960–1949*. Stanford, CA: Stanford University Press.

Carlitz, Katherine. 1997. "Shrines, Governing Class Identity, and the Cult of Widow Fidelity in Mid-Ming Jiangnan." *Journal of Asian Studies* 56, no. 3: 612–640.

———. 2001. "The Daughter, the Singing Girl, and the Seduction of Suicide." In *Passionate Women: Female Suicide in Late Imperial China*, edited by Paul. S. Ropp, Paola Zamperini, and Harriet T. Zurndorfer. Leiden: E. J. Brill.

Elliot, Mark C. 1999. "Manchu Widows and Ethnicity in Qing China." *Comparative Studies in Society and History* 41, no. 1: 33–71.

Elvin, Mark. 1984. "Female Virtue and the State in China." *Past and Present* 104: 111–152.

Lu, Weijing. 2008. *True to Her Word: The Faithful Maiden Cult in Late Imperial China.* Stanford, CA: Stanford University Press.

Sommer, Matthew. 2000. *Sex, Law and Society in Late Imperial China.* Stanford, CA: Stanford University Press.

———. 2015. *Polyandry and Wife-Selling in Qing Dynasty China: Survival Strategies and Judicial Interventions.* Berkeley: University of California Press.

Tang, Xianzu. 2002. *The Peony Pavilion.* Translated by Cyril Birch. Bloomington: Indiana University Press.

Theiss, Janet. 2001. "Managing Martyrdom: Female Suicide and Statecraft in Mid-Qing China." In *Passionate Women: Female Suicide in Late Imperial China*, edited by Paul. S. Ropp, Paola Zamperini, and Harriet T. Zurndorfer. Leiden: E. J. Brill.

Theiss, Janet M. 2004. *Disgraceful Matters: The Politics of Chastity in Eighteenth-Century China.* Berkeley: University of California Press.

KOREA

Cho, Eun-su, editor. 2011. *Korean Buddhist Nuns and Laywomen: Hidden Histories, Enduring Vitality.* Albany, NY: SUNY Press.

Deuchler, Martina. 1992. *The Confucian Transformation of Korea: A Study of Society and Ideology.* Cambridge, MA: Harvard University Press.

———. 2003. "Propagating Female Virtues in Chosŏn Korea." In *Women and Confucian Cultures in Premodern China, Korea, and Japan*, edited by Dorothy Ko, JaHyun Kim Haboush, and Joan Piggott. Berkeley: University of California Press.

Jung, Ji-Young. 2011. "Buddhist Nuns and Alternate Space in Confucian Chosŏn Society." In *Korean Buddhist Nuns and Laywomen: Hidden Histories, Enduring Vitality*, edited by Eun-su Cho. Albany, NY: SUNY Press.

Kim, Jisoo. 2015. *The Emotions of Justice: Gender, Status, and Legal Performance in Chosŏn Korea (1392–1910).* Seattle: University of Washington Press.

———. 2009. "Individual Petitions: Petitions by Women in the Chosŏn." In *Epistolary Korea: Letters in the Communicative Space of the Chosŏn, 1392–1910*, edited by JaHyun Kim Haboush. New York: Columbia University Press.

Kim, Jungwon. 2014. "'You Must Avenge on My Behalf': Widow Chastity and Honour in Nineteenth-Century Korea." *Gender and History* 26, no. 1: 128–146.

———. 2007. "Negotiating Virtue and the Lives of Women in Late Chosŏn Korea." PhD dissertation, Harvard University.

Kim Haboush, JaHyun. 2002. "Gender and the Politics of Language in Chosŏn Korea." In *Rethinking Confucianism: Past and Present in China, Japan, and Vietnam*, edited by Benjamin A. Elman, John B. Duncan, and Herman Ooms. Los Angeles: UCLA Asia Pacific Monograph Series.

———. 1995. "Filial Emotions and Filial Values: Changing Patterns in the Discourse of Filiality in Late Chosŏn Korea." *Harvard Journal of Asiatic Studies* 55, no. 1: 129–177.

Kim, Sun Joo, and Jungwon Kim. 2014. *Wrongful Deaths: Selected Inquest Records from Nineteenth-Century Korea.* Seattle: University of Washington Press.

Kim, Youngmin, and Michael Pettid, eds. 2011. *Women and Confucianism in Chosŏn Korea: New Perspectives.* Albany, NY: SUNY Press.

Oh, Young Kyun. 2013. *Engraving Virtue: The Printing History of a Premodern Korean Moral Primer.* Leiden: E. J. Brill.

Peterson, Mark. 1996. *Korean Adoption and Inheritance.* Ithaca, NY: East Asia Program, Cornell University.

Research Center for Asian Women. 1986. *Women of the Yi Dynasty.* Seoul: Sookmyung Women's University.

Wagner, Edward W. 1983. "Two Early Genealogies and Women's Status in Early Yi Dynasty Korea." In *Korean Women: View from the Inner Room*, edited by Laurel Kendall and Mark Peterson. New Haven, CT: East Rock Press.

Walraven, Boudewijn. 2002. "Popular Religion in a Confucianized Society." *In Culture and the State in Late Chosŏn Korea*, edited by JaHyun Kim Haboush and Martina Deuchler. Cambridge, MA: Harvard University Press.

JAPAN

Keene, Donald. 1955. *Anthology of Japanese Literature: From the Earliest Era to the Mid-Nineteenth Century.* New York: Grove Press.

Najita, Tetsuo. 1977. *Visions of Virtue: The Kaitokudō Merchant Academy of Osaka.* Chicago: University of Chicago Press.

Pflugfelder, Gregory M. 1999. *Cartographies of Desire: Male-Male Sexuality in Japanese Discourse, 1600–1950.* Berkeley: University of California Press.

Smith, Thomas C. 1988. "'Merit' as Ideology in the Tokugawa Period." In *Native Sources of Japanese Industrialization, 1750–1920*, edited by Thomas C. Smith. Berkeley: University of California Press.

Tocco, Martha. 2005. "Made in Japan: Meiji Women's Education." In *Gendering Modern Japanese History*, edited by Barbara Molony and Kathleen Uno. Cambridge, MA: Harvard University Asia Center.

Totman, Conrad. 1967. *Politics in the Tokugawa Bakufu, 1600–1843.* Cambridge, MA: Harvard University Press.

———. 1993. *Early Modern Japan.* Berkeley: University of California Press.

Uno, Kathleen S. 1991. "Women and Changes in the Household Division of Labor." In *Recreating Japanese Women, 1600–1950*, edited by Gail Lee Bernstein. Berkeley: University of California Press.

Walthall, Anne. 1991. "The Life Cycle of Farm Women in Tokugawa Japan." In *Recreating Japanese Women, 1600–1945*, edited by Gail Lee Bernstein. Berkeley: University of California Press.

3

Urban and Rural Lives in the Early Modern Era

GLOBAL CONTEXT

By the middle of the nineteenth century, Europe and America were emerging as the center of a new imperial order. Just one century earlier, China and India together produced about three-quarters of the world's goods. Technological superiority in textiles and porcelain made Indian and Chinese products attractive in global markets. Specialized products such as spices and indigo were desired by consumers outside the Asian region. More efficient agriculture in Asia also produced cheaper food, which allowed workers on farms and in workshops to maintain the same standard of living as their European counterparts but at a lower, more competitive cost. Standards of living varied by region both in Europe and in East Asia, but overall the greater efficiency of agriculture and the resulting lower cost of food consumed by producers of export goods in East Asia enhanced East Asian dominance in global markets before the Industrial Revolution in the nineteenth century. Europeans used precious metals and other natural products of the New World, which was under European colonial control from the sixteenth century on, to buy Indian cotton textiles in the seventeenth century and Chinese tea, porcelain, and silk in the seventeenth, eighteenth, and nineteenth centuries.

Worried about the effect of Indian textiles on British producers, however, England outlawed imports of Indian cloth in the early eighteenth century. These limits severely damaged the Indian textile industry. Also in the eighteenth century, Briton James Watt's patented steam engine and the discovery in England of easily accessible coal vastly increased the amount of energy available to Britain's economy. These developments, together with plentiful cotton produced cheaply by enslaved Africans in the American South, made

England a major producer of cotton textiles by the mid-eighteenth century. This was the beginning of England's Industrial Revolution. By the 1830s, the United States was the second country to undergo the Industrial Revolution, followed several decades later by other European countries and Japan.

Despite their success at surpassing India as a textile producer, England continued to suffer a drain of silver, its main currency, as Britons consumed large quantities of Chinese tea. Britain's silver problem was solved in the early nineteenth century by a complicated arrangement that involved the sale of Indian opium to China (parts of India were by then under British colonial control), resulting in a net outflow of China's silver to Britain despite the continuing export of tea to England. The reversed direction of the currency flow, the debilitating effect of widespread opium addiction in China, and China's defeat at the hands of Britain in the Opium War (1839–1842) led to a sharp decline in China's fortunes, just as Western nations were growing steadily as industrial and imperial powers.

In addition, from the dawn of the early modern period, new and powerful military weapons and naval vessels accompanied changes in the political landscape of Europe. These new military technologies were critical to the rise of nation-states. In time, they also threatened many parts of the world outside Europe and were a necessary part of imperialism by conquest between the seventeenth and nineteenth centuries.

The confluence of the massive increase in productivity of Western industry as a result of the Industrial Revolution, the stagnation of China's economy, and the improvement of military technology in Europe and the United States produced a tremendous shift of power from East Asia to Europe and the United States. This, in turn, led to the influence of Western ideologies and social and political practices in East Asia in the late nineteenth century (this influence will be discussed in Chapter 4), with important implications for gender and sexuality.

The Industrial Revolution drew large numbers of women and children into factory labor, with long hours, unhealthy workplace conditions, and miserable pay. Despite the development of a discourse of "domesticity" throughout Europe, the Americas, and Australia that claimed that women's place was in the home, in fact women and children dominated in some types of industrial production, primarily in spinning. But the notion that women's proper role was in the household was pernicious, leading to lower wages for female workers. Types of machinery were also gendered in people's minds, with no particular reason for that gendering—for example, weaving looms were men's machines, while spinning machines were women's. (Weaving paid much more than spinning.) Types of occupations were gendered as well. Coal mining, a dirty and dangerous job, was gendered as male in Western nations by protective legislation that removed women from the mines in Europe and the United States in the mid-nineteenth century. Very young children were removed from the factories by varying forms of mandatory education. By the middle of the nineteenth century in Europe and North America, a large number of states required several years of schooling, although the content differed by the child's gender (in some areas, girls were taught household skills rather than literacy).

The late eighteenth and early nineteenth centuries were also the era of the birth of women's rights movements in the West. The stirring language of individual rights in revolutionary movements in France and the United States in the late eighteenth century (although initially intended to apply only to white males), the notion that the family was bound by emotional ties and was more than an economic and reproductive unit, and even the discourse on domesticity, which seems on its face to limit women's options in the world of work, opened up space for women who used the language of women's special qualities to justify women's rights as a way to serve the nation. At the same time, throughout Europe, Australia, and the Americas, sexuality was becoming increasingly regulated. The regulation of prostitution and the rise of public health went hand in hand. Regulation was linked to the growth of empires and the resulting contact between people of European origin and people who were racially and culturally distinct from them.

Were there similar developments in East Asia at the end of the early modern period? As in the case of industrial employment, the development of military technology, the gendering of education, the ideology of women's rights, the regulation of sexuality, and the development of public health also took root in East Asia by the end of the nineteenth century. As we shall see in this chapter, fertile ground for those changes had been sown in China, Korea, and Japan in the two centuries before that time.

CHINA

The expansion of the monetary economy and the social fluidity it produced were hallmarks of China's early modern era and shaped daily life in complex ways. In the eighteenth century, economic prosperity and political stability created the conditions for tremendous population growth. The most developed areas of the country had some of the highest consumption levels and life expectancies in the early modern world. At the same time, much of the country suffered impoverishment as a result of the diminution of land and water quality and loss of forests that provided fuel and other resources. Population pressure in many regions increased competition for land and work, and skewed sex ratios that were a result of female infanticide made marriage impossible for many men.

Society was mobile geographically and economically, and mobility was distinctly gendered. Elite and commoner families strategized to advance and maintain their status in an era when movement up the socioeconomic ladder was possible but downward mobility was a constant threat. Men were highly mobile geographically, leaving home for work as officials, merchants, hired laborers, and peddlers. Most women, with the exception of those trafficked, moved once, into the household of their husbands, where their lives were centered. The texture of everyday life was shaped by marriage and work, both of which varied across the country's diverse geographic regions and underwent significant change in the early modern period.

Marriage and Family Life

Commercialization increased social stratification, and while its effects varied by class and region, across the social spectrum family life at the most intimate level was shaped by market forces. The preferred mode of marriage, practiced by families with sufficient means to maintain or aspire to respectability, involved an exchange of bride price, paid by the family of the groom, for dowry, provided by the parents of the bride. For many poorer families, perhaps the majority, however, this equal exchange of property was not possible. Marriages among the poor were often contracted without dowries, but the acceptance of bride price in exchange for a bride was described as "selling a daughter in marriage," indicating its lack of respectability. Many poor families gave a daughter to a prospective husband's family as a "little daughter-in-law" (*tongyangxi*) to be reared in her fiancé's household until she reached an age appropriate for consummation of the marriage, usually about fifteen. Blurring the boundaries of respectable marriage still further was the practice of concubinage, in which families sold a daughter to become a secondary wife subordinate to the main wife even though her children were legal and ritual equals of the first wife's. (By contrast, as we saw in Chapter 2, in Chosŏn Korea, the children of secondary wives had different statuses.) At the bottom end of the market, poverty-stricken families sold their daughters as maids or prostitutes.

Marriage was thus a key marker of social status, and families that had sufficient funds invested heavily in dowries for their daughters that would match or, better yet, exceed the bride price, so as to avoid the appearance of selling them. For many families marriage offered at least the possibility of improving a daughter's social status: a large dowry might attract a groom of higher social standing, and families lacking dowry might sell a girl as a concubine to a family of much higher status. Dowry inflation along with the fact that daughters married out of the family meant that raising daughters was considered more expensive than raising sons. As a result, the practice of female infanticide spread widely across Chinese society. It was used by the poorest as a desperate measure to stave off starvation and debt and by families of modest means to control the spacing and sex ratio of their offspring so as to maximize family assets and ensure ongoing prosperity. The resultant skewing of sex ratios combined with the stigma attached to widow remarriage and the monopolization of marriage-aged girls by elite men purchasing concubines and maids meant that although marriage of some sort was all but universal for women, it was impossible for a large proportion of the poorest men. Heterodox and even illegal forms of marriage became increasingly common among the poor. These included widow remarriage and its illegal variant of the levirate (a form of marriage in which a widow was required to marry her deceased husband's brother), the selling of a wife to another husband (known as "selling a divorce"), marrying a husband into a woman's household, and polyandry (in which women had two husbands, providing domestic service and heirs to both) (Sommer 2015).

The nature of marriage determined much about the quality of daily life for women and men. At the age of fifteen girls underwent the hair-pinning ritual, a coming-of-age rite parallel to the capping ceremony for boys that marked the onset of adulthood and readiness for marriage. For a bride of any class, marriage was a bittersweet occasion at best, as it sent a young woman away from her own family into a household of strangers. The literary culture of the day extolled sentiments of love and fostered the emergence of a new ideal of companionate marriage, manifested in the efforts of many families to betroth highly educated daughters to young men of equivalent accomplishment and sensibilities. While marital affection was not uncommon, for the typical young bride the potential for happiness in her new home depended greatly on her relationship with her mother-in-law, who in most cases was in charge of the domestic sphere where she would spend the rest of her life.

At the top of the social hierarchy were literati and merchant families, the wealthiest of which were concentrated in the highly urbanized Lower Yangzi River delta region of Jiangnan. These elite families typically lived in multigenerational households that included parents; sons and their wives, concubines, and children; and unmarried daughters. The families occupied walled compounds that were large enough to provide space for secluded inner quarters for women and small children, usually at the back. Such households also included large numbers of purchased or hired male and female servants, some of whom were contractual laborers with fixed terms of service and others of whom were hereditary or indentured bondservants or slaves. (This type of extended family had parallels among wealthy farm families in seventeenth- and eighteenth-century Japan as well.)

As in Chosŏn Korea, in China during this period the paradigm of distinction between "inner" and "outer" framed discussion of the spatial, social, economic, and behavioral dimensions of female propriety and gender roles in prescriptive literature, social commentary, and official discourse. The idealized woman of virtue spent her days secluded in the inner quarters, diligently engaged in "womanly work" (textile work and other domestic chores) and sheltered from casual contacts with people outside her family, including not just men but also potentially corrupting women such as Buddhist and Daoist nuns, fortune-tellers, and midwives. At the upper levels of society, family authorities indeed enforced norms of spatial separation, gender differentiation of work, and segregated social life. By the age of six or seven, after a briefly shared early childhood, boys began formal schooling and girls had their feet bound, setting them on their separate paths of examination study and domestic work. By the age of ten, elite girls in the Qing era were confined to the inner quarters to learn the skills of domestic textile production and the techniques of food preparation for family rituals.

Small feet, known as "lotus feet," were a critical bodily marker of respectability for Chinese women, essential for marrying well. Footbinding also constrained women's mobility, facilitating seclusion and the habituation of young girls to the rigors of textile work in the home (Gates 2015). Elite women had the most tightly bound feet. Although the practice also became widespread among peasant women during the Qing, in regions where women participated in agricultural work and other tasks requiring mobility, feet were not bound as tightly. Many non-Han ethnic groups, including the Manchus from the northwestern frontier and the Hakka in South China, did not practice footbinding at all.

Very few women outside of the literati and merchant elites had the means to aspire to the strict gender separation that was universal among elites. Urban and rural families of more modest means typically had smaller households, perhaps with elderly parents and children occupying a single house and courtyard. While many peasant dwellings were surrounded by a wall separating the household from the outside world and had interior walls or curtains to demarcate inner, female space, they were not large enough to allow women to live in seclusion. Yet the inner/outer distinction was a critical part of ideas about femininity and women's virtue for most women and their families, even when work and other activities of daily life took them outside their gates and into contact with outside men. In a society where status and respectability were mutable, where women could be sold into and out of marriages, concubines could become wives, and courtesans mimicked the talents and virtues of elite women (discussed later in this chapter), chastity-centered virtue exhibited by adherence to some semblance of an inner/outer divide was a crucial marker of female propriety, demonstrating that a family had means and morals.

Work

Expansion of domestic and foreign trade spurred commercial production of agricultural products such as cotton, silk, and tea as well as manufactured goods such as porcelain and finished silk and cotton textiles. By the 1500s women's production for the market was a key factor in household income and economic growth more broadly, though historians debate the effects of their textile work on the quality of their lives and their families' living standards. In a country of continental size and geographic diversity such as China, there were major regional differences in the nature of agricultural and handicraft production and culture that affected gender divisions of labor. Market expansion fostered regional specialization, and economic development was uneven as some regions commercialized and urbanized faster than others. Under the classic rubric "men plow, women weave," the Qing state actively promoted the dual development of grain production and silk and cotton textile production across the empire. Officials assumed that this idealized paradigm of gender distinction was also optimal for maximizing households' potential to pay their taxes. In reality, the model was better suited to some regions than others. Even in grain-producing regions, women and men worked together as members of households, doing what needed to be done to sustain the family and improve its prospects without worrying about adhering strictly to state orthodoxy.

In many regions the inner/outer divide was irrelevant, and in others it was fulfilled with labor involving products other than textiles. Working women's lives were generally more home-centered than those of men. They worked spinning and reeling silk or cotton thread; weaving; sewing; raising silkworms; making shoes, baskets, reed mats and hats, straw or bamboo splint hats, or paper umbrellas; brewing soy sauce; processing tea, tobacco, sugar, or other foods; cooking; and caring for small children and elderly parents-in-law. But in many regions of China, women also worked in the fields picking cotton and transplanting rice or sugarcane; collected and processed bast fibers such as ramie, hemp, and kudzu for cloth production; picked tea; gathered firewood; herded animals in nearby forests and pastures; tended vegetable gardens; fetched water from village wells and streams; sold textile products and purchased household goods; and carried noonday meals to male kin working in the fields. These activities took them not only outside their gates but into the company of men outside their families.

Textile production was most conducive to female seclusion, though it was often a family enterprise in which women, men, and children worked side by side. Women's home production of yarn and woven fabric for market sale or subsistence was essential for household economies across China, although the finest luxury fabrics were produced primarily by men. In Jiangnan, the earliest and largest center for production of cotton and silk textiles, women's weaving (not spinning or reeling) often brought in more income than men's agricultural work growing rice or cotton. China's inheritance system mandated equal division of property among sons, so as the population grew, the size of individual farms shrank, resulting in lower income from agriculture. In many households young girls and elderly women spun and reeled yarn that their mothers or daughters-in-law wove into cloth to maintain family income. Here the orthodox formulation had real economic utility, although there are many references to men weaving as well. In North China, where farming was increasingly difficult and not as lucrative due to environmental degradation, women largely worked in seclusion, but in quite a number of households men also wove and sometimes spun cotton thread with their wives. Many families produced cotton cloth only for their own use. Scattered evidence from other regions—the fertile lowland regions of interior provinces or the rugged mountain regions of the far south that the Qing empire conquered and pacified in the eighteenth century—suggests that gender divisions of labor in agriculture and textile production varied depending upon income potential (Pomeranz 2005).

In other kinds of household-based handicraft production, inner/outer distinctions were still salient but families interpreted them flexibly to maximize everyone's labor participation. In papermaking villages, for example, men typically harvested bamboo, which required mobility outside the village, and did the tasks requiring more physical strength and continuous labor—working the steamers that cooked the fibers, processing the fiber into pulp, and

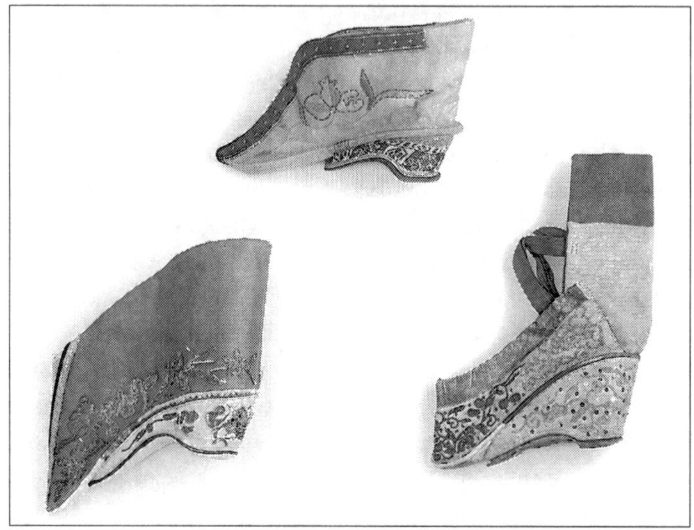

Women's production and embroidered decoration of shoes for themselves and their relatives was a ubiquitous form of self-expression, artistry, and productivity.
Shoes for Women's Bound Feet, 19th century. Brooklyn Museum, Frank L. Babbott Fund, 37.371.104.1-.2

molding the pulp into sheets pressed into piles. Women and old men separated the sheets, brushed them onto walls on the outside of houses or in drying sheds, and, once they were dry, smoothed, cut, folded, and packed them for sale. These tasks were physically demanding and took up long hours but could be interrupted for domestic duties such as cooking and child care and did not require as much mobility, though brushing often had to be done on exterior walls or in shared drying sheds, where women encountered men unrelated to them. Local cultural conventions forbade idle conversation between men and women or their sitting together in such situations (Eyferth 2009).

Gendered divisions of labor in the book publishing industry, which had centers in diverse regions such as rural Fujian, Jiangxi, Guangdong, and Sichuan and the cities of the Yangzi delta, were determined by economic factors as well as notions of gender propriety. From the industry's beginnings in the Song dynasty, women had been employed to do the work of carving characters and pictures into woodblocks for printing, a task that was considered low-skilled and did not require literacy, since the characters were written onto paper pasted on the blocks. In centers of book production in the Ming-Qing period, women in publishing lineages or households cut woodblocks and often did most of the printing and binding of books, while male family members managed the business and handled sales, tasks that required more literacy and travel away from home (Brokaw 2007). Publishing houses contracted out the carving, printing, and binding work to families in specialized villages, who used it to supplement their agricultural income. Since women's labor was significantly cheaper than men's, many of these hired laborers were women. Occasionally women in publishing, mercantile, or scholar-official families took on managerial roles, overseeing accounts, landed property, and labor as widows or while their husbands were sojourning far from home for months or years at a time. In cities and towns women worked in family enterprises—restaurants, inns, and shops.

The tea industry developed yet another mode of allocating the labor of men and women. By the beginning of the eighteenth century, tea was China's top export commodity, purchased in growing quantities for European markets, especially Britain. In the tea-producing households and tea firms across the hilly regions of Fujian, Hunan, and Sichuan, women and men picked, sorted, and cured tea leaves, but in many areas much of the tea production was done primarily by women as household or wage labor while men focused on other agricultural work. Harvesting was tedious and physically demanding work involving long hours of picking during three or four harvest periods throughout the year and carrying baskets of tea leaves up and down rugged hillsides. In peak seasons, whole families worked late into the night to sort and cure the leaves before they rotted. Despite the complete absence of even a semblance of female seclusion in tea regions, Qing poets romanticized the lively culture of hardworking female tea pickers fanning out across the hills as the harvest season began:

Above the poplar trees white clouds lie thickly;
In the guyu season [beginning of tea picking time] the sprouting tea shoots are as thin as pine needles.
Singing songs, village women with lotus feet walk steadily;
Carrying baskets on their backs, they climb the highest peak.
(Lu 2001, 235)

Women's Culture

Because of their leisure, elite women were expected to demonstrate skill and diligence in textile work, usually embroidery, which was in huge demand to embellish clothing in wealthy households and was emblematic of refined seclusion. Yet even in elite circles, the inner/outer distinction was blurred by the boom in women's publishing and artistic production. Beginning in the seventeenth century, significant numbers of elite families, especially in the Jiangnan region, gave girls the same education in classical literacy as their brothers. Many girls, tutored in the inner quarters by mothers, sisters, and other female and male relatives, took up writing, especially of poetry. Female poets, who, between the seventeenth and nineteenth centuries, numbered in the thousands, played a prominent role in the cultural life of early modern China. Elite women also made names for themselves with painting, calligraphy, and "embroidered painting." Like writing, these were genteel activities that connected women to networks outside their boudoirs and could also provide income for families that encountered hard times. (These women had a parallel in Japan's *bunjin,* discussed later in this chapter.)

Male commentators often remarked on the particular talent of women for writing poetry and noted how life in the women's quarters, secluded from the political world of men, was especially conducive to the poetic contemplation of emotions and inner life. For many, women's poetry was the quintessential expression of the cult of *qing* ("emotion" or "love"; see Chapter 2) and a clear refutation of the commonly stated view that for women talent was incompatible with virtue.

Women's poetry documents the paradoxes and complexity of their lives, describing the events and emotions of family life and revealing the richness of women's culture within the inner quarters. One young woman from Jiangsu, Liu Wanhuai, taught together with her brother by her poet mother, invokes the iconically virtuous activity of sericulture as a metaphor for her literary pursuits in a poem titled "Sitting at Night Discussing Poetry with My Brother":

Writing a poem is like making a friend.
You want to see inside to the true liver and gall.
Why enlist ornament or decoration
When art and feeling will pour out spontaneously together?
A spiritual energy charges my brush;
An enlightened mind shuts out worldly cares.
Compare it to a silkworm spinning thread;
Liken it to a stone holding gems in a matrix.
(Mann 1997, 108–109)

Through publishing and exchanging poetry, women indeed made many friends inside and outside the inner quarters. In the seventeenth century, women's literary circles included courtesans and singing girls as well as male literati. The late Ming gentry poetess Xu Yuan praised the beauty of a talented courtesan friend:

Lotus blossoms as she moves her pair of arches,
Her tiny waist, just a hand's breadth, is light enough to dance on
a palm.
Leaning coyly against the east wind,
Her pure color and misty daintiness fill the moon.
(Ko 1995, 170)

In this poem a respectable woman for whom bound feet were a marker of propriety celebrates the bound feet of a courtesan as an emblem of beauty and sensuality, demonstrating both intimacy across social boundaries and conflicting interpretations of the practice of footbinding, which incarnated the inner/outer dichotomy.

BOX 3.1

Women's Poetry

Highly educated elite women in the Ming and Qing dynasties used poetry to express their thoughts and feelings about daily life, family matters, and life course rituals such as marriage, the birth of children, and deaths of those close to them. Poetry was also an important vehicle for communication among women writers and between women and distant family members. Upon marriage a woman moved permanently into the house of her husband, and if his home was far from her own she rarely, if ever, had the chance to see her natal family again. Marriage was thus a bittersweet moment for women, and their poetry reveals the sadness that often accompanied their passage to adulthood.

In one poem, titled "To My Sisters, In Memory of Times Past," published in Wanyan Yun Zhu's anthology, *Correct Beginnings*, a woman named Fang Jing ponders the pain of separation from her sisters and of growing old. She references a poem about marriage, 'Tao yao,' from the ancient *Book of Odes* (see Chapter 1) to highlight the complexities of women's emotional lives.

As little girls, we matched shoulders to line up according to height,
How hard to forget those splendid days of our childhood!

(continued)

By a window draped in blue gauze were crammed a thousand books,
Incense of aloeswood encaged a whole bed's quilt.
When spring reached the loft of our house, we embroidered there together.
We made linked verse beneath the flowers, our lines spreading fragrance of their own.
Laughing and chattering freely at our parents' side,
How could we know that the poem 'Tao yao' threatened eternal sorrow?
The glow of companionship had not lasted long, when suddenly autumn grew dark.
Frosts and snows came out of the season and took our father's life.
Like ranks of snowgeese disturbed by the wind, we grieved to lose our orderly formation.
Like swallows with mud in our beaks after the rain [that is, trying vainly to build a nest], we lamented the dying spring.
Once we enjoyed a happy meeting, but each of us had grown old.
Even if we could return to the old days, the path back is all worn away.
The white head cannot bear to dwell on what happened long ago,
My poem takes shape, each word a taste of bitter sorrow.
(Translated in Mann 1997, 110)

Amid the mounting crises of the nineteenth century, women used their poetry to comment on events and express political sentiments. In 1842, at the height of the Opium War (discussed later in this chapter), Zhang Qieying (1792–ca. 1863), whose natal and marital families were full of prominent officials, reveals a budding proto-nationalist consciousness in the poem "Moved by Events," written to venerate the heroism of the official Lin Zexu (1785–1850), who first confronted the British opium traders. The piece is full of allusions to virtuous heroes from history.

A glowing autumn just at its peak,
When drifting clouds suddenly cover the sun!
No sooner clear than rain returns,
Transforming the face of autumn into chaos;
Song Yu's grief at autumn was so rightly bitter!
My ears roar with autumn squalls,

My breast fills with distress and indignation,
But how can my soundless words make any difference!
The flowing current, how I long to turn it back!
How can I bear the pain of these passing years?
My eyes search abroad, the wilted grass laden with frost,
Amid desolate smoke, a lone tree,
Shaking, spent, utterly without direction.
The shrieking partridge cries "You can't go on!"
But my slip of a heart is hard to pour out....
What can I do? Swallow my anger forever?
(translated in Mann 1997, 104)

As increasing numbers of women acquired a "public" presence through their published works, debates emerged over the propriety of women's writing and its potential to foster transgression of norms of female seclusion, neglect of domestic responsibilities, and indulgence in illicit passions. The prominence of highly educated courtesans among these women writers in the seventeenth century enhanced the taint of the improper attached to women's writing. Thus, in the eighteenth century, status-conscious families increasingly emphasized the importance of classical education for their daughters to ground their literacy in Confucian ethics and set them apart from courtesans and other women of questionable status, such as nuns. Wanyan Yun Zhu (1771–1833), wife of a Manchu aristocrat, who compiled the most important anthology of women's poetry, *Correct Beginnings*, encapsulated the moralistic turn in attitudes about women's learning in the volume's "Editorial Principles":

> *In compiling this anthology, I have attached the greatest importance to purity of emotional expression. . . . As for female adepts and Buddhist nuns, among whom are many able poets, they are not fit to appear in the ranks of respectable ladies and accordingly I have not included them. . . . Poems about sexual love and romance by courtesans, those fallen women of the green chambers [i.e., brothels], whom earlier compilers anthologized profusely and rhapsodized over, are not included here. (Mann 1997, 98)*

Yun Zhu's comment on female adepts and nuns points to the significance of Buddhism and Daoism in women's daily lives, despite the challenges they posed for the gender orthodoxy of the day and Confucian moralist disparagement of the bad influences of the "three aunties and six grannies" (Buddhist nuns, Daoist nuns, fortune-tellers, medicine sellers, midwives, matchmakers, shamanesses, procuresses, and brothel "mothers"). Because of their gender, these skilled women of the lower classes (with the exception of the last two, associated with prostitution) could and did visit respectable households and were usually tolerated because they offered services that were much in demand. Criticism of their bad influences on women stemmed from the fraught status of female medical practitioners and of Buddhist, Daoist, and folk religious practices in a society dominated by Confucian norms.

Medical treatment of women and children was largely handled by female healers, including "grannies" such as shamanesses, midwives, and medicine sellers, and also female physicians from medical lineages and other elite families educated in the classical medical tradition dominated by male doctors. But male doctors routinely disparaged the knowledge and skill of such women and claimed superior authority as experts not only on women's illnesses but also on pregnancy and childbirth, despite the fact that most families preferred to rely on midwives for the latter two (Wu 2010).

Similarly, while many literati men steeped in the Confucian canon were highly critical of Buddhist, Daoist, and folk religious traditions, most people, commoners and elites alike, engaged in devotional practices associated with all of them. Within the inner quarters, women chanted and copied sutras, practiced meditation, fasted, burned incense and prayed to Daoist deities like the Queen Mother of the West, and embroidered Buddhist images, such as the figure of the bodhisattva Guanyin, who was a particularly popular focus for women's devotional practices. Once their child-rearing years had passed, many older women in elite families took up concentrated pursuit of Buddhist enlightenment or Daoist inner alchemy, including celibacy, vegetarianism, and textual study, sometimes under the mentorship of a male teacher. Women's ritual lives also included family ancestral rites and folk celebrations such as the Double Seven Festival, held on the seventh day of the seventh lunar month, which marked the annual romantic reunion of the Weaving Maid, patron deity of women's textile work, and the Cowherd. The story, emblematic of affectionate marriage between a diligent wife and husband despite long periods of separation, had particular resonance for women whose husbands sojourned far from home (Mann 1997).

Women of all classes also regularly participated in festivals at local temples on special days such as the birthdays of Guanyin, the Buddha, and local deities. They also made pilgrimages farther afield to temples and monastery complexes such as the religiously eclectic Mount Tai, whose female deities were appealed to for fertility and safe childbirth. These religious activities drew constant criticism from Confucian moralists because they placed women in mixed company with men, sometimes involved overnight stays, and were perceived by some as excuses for leisure outside the home or, worse yet, illicit relations with monks, rather than genuine acts of devotion. The central state, provincial, and local officials issued numerous and repeated bans on various forms of temple-going for women, but these had little effect. The state was equally ineffective in its efforts to root out flourishing Catholic communities founded in coastal Fujian province by Spanish missionaries who arrived with trade ships from Manila in the early seventeenth century. With the support of these communities, lay religious women called *beatas* took vows of chastity and shunned marriage to devote themselves to religious pursuits that offered opportunities for spiritual independence and authority, including teaching, charitable work, and family mediation. Although this religious pathway to female empowerment was not unlike those available within Buddhist and Daoist traditions in the medieval period, such rejection of marriage and motherhood was rare in the early modern era (Menegon 2009).

Sex Work and Entertainment

In 1673 the Qing state abolished the system of government-sponsored prostitutes that provided entertainment for official functions, and in 1723 the Yongzheng emperor (r. 1722–1735) abolished the hereditary debased legal category of entertainer households, whose women were legally allowed to work as prostitutes. This in effect made prostitution illegal. However, sex work continued to flourish under other guises. Sojourning and wealth created a vast market for sexual services and entertainment in the pleasure quarters in commercial cities, where women worked as singing girls, prostitutes, actors, and storytellers in teahouses, wine shops, pleasure boats, and brothels. At the high end, talented courtesans (much like Japanese geishas), accomplished in music, poetry, dance, acting, and refined conversation, provided companionship, including sex, and entertainment for wealthy scholar-officials and merchants who came to relax, develop business relationships, cultivate their artistic tastes and reputations as refined gentlemen, and find women they might purchase as concubines. The city of Yangzhou, centrally located in the Yangzi delta region, was famous as a market for beautiful and talented girls who were educated by their parents or sold to merchant "foster families" who educated them and then sold them again to wealthy men as maids or concubines or to brothels as courtesans and singing girls (Finnane 2004).

The world of opera, the most pervasive and popular performance genre across urban and rural China, presented another set of challenges to orthodox gender norms. Most actors in troupes that performed in public venues—village festivals or urban theaters, teahouses, and merchant halls where men gathered—were men. Poverty-stricken parents sold young boys into indentured status in opera troupes to be trained as actors. Eroticized connoisseurship of beautiful cross-dressed boys who played popular female roles was one of the main pleasures of participation in the opera demimonde, and it was common for wealthy merchants and literati to form relationships of sexual patronage with them. Unlike Japan in the Tokugawa period, where same-sex relationships were common among men, this was the only context in which same-sex relationships were publicly accepted in the Qing period.

Unlike the case in Japan, described later in this chapter, respectable women did not go anywhere near public entertainment venues, and women were explicitly forbidden to enter the playhouses in Beijing that dominated opera culture in the eighteenth and nineteenth century. Women did attend the operas that always accompanied temple fairs and village festivals, and within their homes elite women enjoyed salon performances by troupes that were privately commissioned or actually owned by their families. Even in such domestic settings, though, they usually sat separated from their menfolk by a screen or curtain that maintained an illusion of proper gender segregation. Much to the consternation of moral purists, however, this screen could not prevent male actors from glimpsing the women or shield women from the influence of tales of illicit love that were common operatic fare (Goldman 2013). Elite women also commissioned women storytellers and ballad singers to entertain them in the inner quarters with tales of romance between gifted scholars and talented beauties. Women themselves authored the poetic narratives called *tanci*, long and intricate stories that featured talented and sometimes unconventional female characters, including cross-dressing heroines who fell in love with other women, and presented critiques of traditional patriarchal norms (Guo 2015).

Mid-Qing fiction explored the contradictions and complexities of the gender order and even raised questions about them. The greatest novel of the eighteenth century, *Dream of the Red Chamber*, depicted life within the inner chambers of a wealthy official family at the top of the social hierarchy, highlighting the tensions between gender propriety and family obligation, on one hand, and human emotions, on the other. The early nineteenth-century novel *Flowers in the Mirror* deployed the story of a man marooned on an island of women to poke fun at footbinding and other restrictions on women's activities.

Rebellion and Social Instability

The gender system was flexible and resilient enough to make room for such critiques, but by the end of the eighteenth century China's long period of political stability had been ruptured by a rebellion of the White Lotus sect that swept across north and northwestern China between 1796 and 1804, followed by the Eight Trigrams rebellion in 1813. These rebellions were fueled by growing poverty resulting from competition for land and employment due to population pressure and environmental degradation (including exhaustion of land fertility, erosion, and flooding). Such economic problems were compounded by widespread official corruption.

Yet mid-Qing social and political instability was also distinctly gendered. The White Lotus religion, which emerged in the sixteenth century, borrowed elements from Buddhism and Daoism but was banned as heterodox by the state in large part because of its transgression of dominant gender norms. It was centered on millenarian belief in a female deity, the Eternal Mother, and fostered social and devotional practices that violated principles of sex segregation. Periodically White Lotus followers launched rebellions against state authorities triggered by emissaries of the Eternal Mother who announced the end of the cosmic age, bringing the arrival of the Maitreya Buddha and salvation for believers. Believers gathered in small mixed-sex congregations around a teacher to chant White Lotus scriptures together or meditate and practice martial arts. Some formed celibate same-sex residential communities for men sojourning away from home or for widows. Many women were attracted to the religion because it offered opportunities for religious leadership, literacy, and independence from family. White Lotus sects were also attractive to men detached from normative family life, such as itinerant laborers, migrants, and the unmarried. The Qing state successfully suppressed these rebellions, but in doing so it depleted central state reserves and was distracted from the looming threats posed by piracy and British encroachments on the southeast coast.

Over the course of the eighteenth century British imports of Chinese goods expanded rapidly, and Chinese tea, in particular, became a national beverage, with imports topping twenty-eight million pounds annually by the early nineteenth century. To balance this trade the British began to smuggle opium cultivated on plantations in its Indian colony into China. The Qing state banned sale and use of the drug in 1729, but the illegal trade continued, with increasing quantities of silver flowing out of China to pay for it, a rapid increase in the numbers of opium addicts, and the growth of a vast criminal underworld that thrived on smuggling the drug across China. Opium consumption spread widely across the society, affecting both women and men. Tobacco smoking had long been respectable for women of all social levels and it was not uncommon for women to take up opium smoking in their boudoirs. The drug became an integral part of the culture of courtesans and their clients. Women often bore the brunt of the destructive effects of male opium addiction on family life when they were forced to make up for a husband's lost income, sometimes through prostitution. Addiction was also a commonly noted reason for men to sell their daughters.

In 1839 the Qing decided to crack down on opium smuggling, confiscating the stocks of foreign merchants in the port city of Guangzhou. The British, already chafing at restrictions on their access to Chinese markets, retaliated by launching the First Opium War, in which they readily defeated Qing forces that were ill prepared for naval warfare. The war concluded in 1842 with the Treaty of Nanjing, the first in a long series of unequal treaties that exacted huge indemnities, trade concessions, and legal privileges for Western powers from a Qing state increasingly weakened by war and fiscal crisis. The treaty opened up five so-called treaty ports, cities where Westerners could reside and engage in unrestricted trade; foreigners' extraterritorial legal status meant that they were not subject to Chinese law. Both the war and the treaty caused enormous disruption of the economy of southeast China. The shift of trade centers to cities up the coast from Guangzhou caused widespread unemployment as the illegal opium trade grew and a weakened Qing government proved unable to deal with rising banditry and social unrest. These were the conditions for the largest civil war in human history, which was going to radically transform Chinese society, including, not least, gender order.

KOREA

During the Chosŏn dynasty, Korea was a predominantly agrarian society. The government made a concerted effort to promote agricultural production by introducing advanced methods of land cultivation, developing irrigation technologies, and distributing farming manuals to the peasants. In contrast to the support the government provided for agriculture, commerce was strictly controlled by the state. In fact, the authorities generally discouraged commercial activities. Confucian scholars and officials regarded commerce "as an unproductive branch that existed at the expense of farming" (Lee 1993, 575). In contrast to the highly regulated commerce that went on in the capital, a different kind of marketplace emerged in the rural areas at the end of the fifteenth century as local people regularly came together to exchange goods in informal markets. For instance, farmers and peddlers in a region might set up a one-day market that would be open for transactions every five days. Especially in times of famine and economic distress, such markets were crucial for survival. By the late Chosŏn dynasty, there were around a thousand periodic markets around the country.

The agriculture-centered economy underwent major transformations after Korea was invaded first by the Japanese (1592–1598) and later the Manchus (in 1627 and 1636). After those conflicts, famine and disease were widespread. Land records and census registers had been destroyed, making it difficult for the government to collect taxes and enforce corvée levies. There were numerous local uprisings, adding to the chaos. These escalating problems were compounded by factional strife between competing political cliques and the concentration of governmental power in a few prominent families.

Government officials and scholars responded to these conditions by putting forward ideas for reform. To tackle the financial disarray and widespread poverty, the government enacted the Uniform Land Tax Law (*taedongpŏp*). This law allowed people to pay taxes in rice, coin, or cotton. Peasants found some additional relief with the abolition of the tribute tax system, which had been collected on local specialty crafts and agricultural products from small farmers and artisans. The elimination of the tribute tax ultimately helped to stimulate the economy (Lee 1996, 71).

The steady growth of the population and the limited amount of arable land also prompted people to think about new ways to cultivate crops. In the early seventeenth century, advanced techniques in agriculture—in particular, the technique of transplanting rice seedlings—became available. Irrigation systems that supplied water more effectively were also developed. In the end, these new farming techniques and improved irrigation helped farmers to increase crop yields with far less labor. Some successful farmers were able to trade their agricultural output in the marketplace, creating a class of "agricultural entrepreneurs" (Lee 1984, 227). Consumption was no longer limited to staple necessities; luxury items were actively bought and sold, especially in the capital. Furthermore, certain agricultural products, such as ginseng, tobacco, and cotton, were not only raised for domestic consumption but also exported to China and Japan. This vital development of agriculture went hand in hand with the development of markets and trade routes that established active commercial networks throughout the country. Trade routes, in turn, stimulated various additional activities such as banking, storage, innkeeping, and transportation that added to the growth of the economy. This integration of advanced agricultural techniques with the use of urban consumer markets paralleled similar developments in early modern Japan and China.

Women as Producers, Managers, Entrepreneurs, and Consumers

Women contributed significantly to the economy as producers of both agricultural products and commercial goods, as household managers, as consumers, and even as entrepreneurs. The vast majority of women from the commoner classes, largely peasants, were active in agricultural production. To help support their families they worked the land, generally doing seeding and weeding rather than the more physically demanding tasks of cultivating the rice fields and harvesting. As in China and Japan, textile production was another economic sector in which women played an essential role. Women of the commoner class had always spun thread and woven textiles to make clothing for their families, but those textiles also came to have exchange value, so they could be used to add directly to the family finances. As noted earlier, textiles were also an alternative form of payment for the uniform land tax. Thus, women's labor in textile production was a central part of the family economy.

Historical records indicate that some women amassed considerable wealth through their business acumen. One route for the accumulation of wealth was silkworm cultivation. Many women produced silk thread and cloth and traded these products through commercial networks. While the case of Kim Mandŏk (see Box 3.2) illustrates philanthropy and working for the good of others, other women utilized their accumulated wealth to restore or strengthen the status of their extended families. The contribution that women made to their families' finances was commonly acknowledged. One bit of evidence for this is that there were legal statutes prohibiting a man from divorcing his wife if her contribution to the family's wealth was significant.

The main task for women of the upper class was to manage the household. With their husbands occupied by other demands—either preparing for the public service examination or residing in official postings away from home—wives managed the household, including overseeing agricultural production and supervising servants who resided either within the house or on outer properties. The management of servants in particular required a great deal of skill and wisdom to keep them maximally productive without feeling abused.

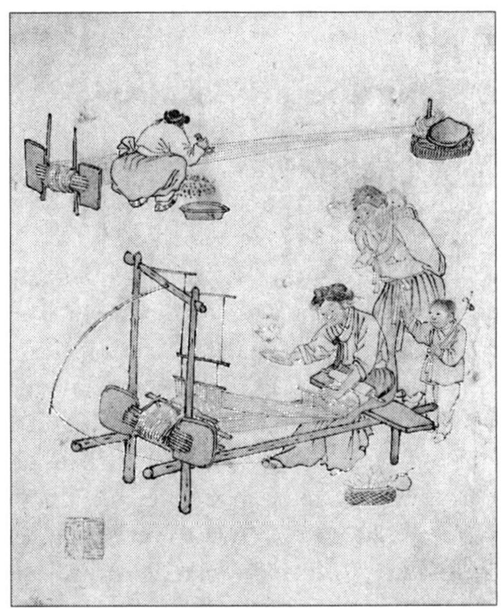

Pinp'ung ch'ilwŏldo. Yi Pang'un. The painting shows women working at weaving and dyeing textiles. NATIONAL MUSEUM OF KOREA

Aside from the task of supervising servants' performance, the most significant responsibility that upper-class women had was to keep the ritual calendar and do all of the necessary preparations for ancestor worship rituals. There were several manuals offering specific instruction to women on the techniques and attitudes needed to carry out the ancestor worship rites. With the increasing emphasis on and institutionalization of the patrilineal social system in Chosŏn society, ancestor worship became the central part of family affairs, as it was an essential mechanism in the recognition and acknowledgment of family lineage. The supervision and preparation of memorial rituals was viewed as an essential task that required extensive planning, ingenuity, and the utmost care. By the mid-Chosŏn period, the majority of upper-class families memorialized four generations of ancestors in elaborate rituals. This meant that the woman of the household had to prepare eight rituals every year. In addition to these memorials, there were other seasonal rituals, such as those for New Year's Day and Autumn Harvest Day, not to mention birthdays for elderly family members. These numerous occasions throughout the year required women to keep track of dates, to prepare elaborate feasts for the ritual celebrations, and, most important, to budget family resources to ensure that there would be appropriate resources available for each rite.

Beyond maintaining the calendar of ancestor rites, women were expected to host guests. A family's reputation and status were dependent on the manner

BOX 3.2

A Woman CEO of Chosŏn? The Story of Mandŏk

There are a few prominent examples of commoner women that show how wildly successful they could be in commercial activities. If they had been born into the contemporary world, they most likely would have been lauded for their entrepreneurial skills. One of the best-known examples is Kim Mandŏk (1739–1812). Kim was born on Cheju Island into the commoner class. She was orphaned at age ten when an epidemic swept through the entire country. She was adopted by an entertainer (*kisaeng*), and she herself was soon registered as a *kisaeng*, which made her a member of the lowest social stratum in Chosŏn. However, she never considered herself an entertainer, and in the end she succeeded in getting the local government to remove her name from the roster of entertainers, no easy task in a society that strictly observed a hierarchy of social strata. She was twenty-three years old when she regained her status as a commoner.

Instead of getting married, as was typically expected of women her age, she created a new life as an innkeeper for merchants. Through her business she developed exceptional skills in trading Cheju specialties, such as oysters, abalone, seaweed, and horsehair, for products from the mainland. She had a knack for identifying products that people would want to buy and that would help her keep a central position in the marketplace. Over time, she accumulated significant wealth. When the island was hit by a long period of drought beginning in 1792 and food relief from the central government was lost at sea, she became a major benefactor of the people of Cheju, donating a significant portion of her wealth to purchase rice from the mainland to be distributed to the famished population.

King Chŏngjo (r. 1776–1800) heard of her benevolence, which went far beyond anyone's imagination, and he wanted to reward her. He urged the governor of Cheju Island to ask her what her fondest wish might be and grant her wish no matter what. She replied that her greatest desire was to tour the palace and visit Diamond Mountain—something unthinkable at that time, as women on Cheju were strictly banned from leaving the island, in order to maintain the island's population. Yet Mandŏk's bold wish was immediately granted by the king. When she arrived in the capital in the autumn of 1796, she met high-level ministers and paid a visit to the queen, who praised Mandŏk for her unmatched benevolence. Her deed was recorded in the annals of the Chosŏn dynasty as well as in the writings of Confucian scholars. Mandŏk is affectionately referred to as the "Grandma of Cheju Island" by contemporary Koreans.

in which guests were treated and the amount and assortment of foods and wines they were served. Unlike in our contemporary world, where there are abundant public spaces for both formal and informal meetings, such as cafés, bars, and restaurants, in the Chosŏn dynasty such gatherings typically took place in the outer chambers of private homes, and it was the responsibility of women to offer the men of their families and their male visitors food, wine, or tea. In those spaces, over wine and food, men established and enhanced their sociopolitical networks, which in turn could help them secure positions in the government.

Women of the upper class and those with disposable income were also vitally important as consumers. In the seventeenth century, the capital city, Seoul, became a bustling center of commerce. Luxury items such as silk, jewelry, artwork, and other decorative items for the home became increasingly available. Expensive and rare items were imported from China. In a society where frugality had always been idealized, Confucian scholars became gravely concerned about the growing tendency to indulge in luxury. The annals of the Chosŏn dynasty are filled with reports of both men and women of the upper class wearing silk clothing, building luxurious houses, and spending exorbitant amounts of money on weddings and funeral rituals. Books for women warned of the evils of a luxurious lifestyle and commended the industrious and frugal life. In an attempt to curtail what many saw as inappropriate spending on frivolous indulgences, King Yŏngjo (r. 1724–1776) went so far as to ban the wearing of the *tari,* a popular hair accessory for women that gave the hair a fuller appearance.

Women in the Public Domain

According to the dominant Confucian gender ideology prevalent during the Chosŏn dynasty, women's proper place was in the domestic sphere. However, there were specialized professions for women in the public domain. Women could receive training to work as palace women, doctors, and entertainers (*kisaeng*).

The term "palace woman" refers to those who served the royal family in the palace. Palace women were ranked according to seniority and the specific function they served (e.g., attending to the private chambers of the members of the royal family, cooking, washing, or sewing). In early Chosŏn, daughters of the commoner class were considered eligible to work as palace women, but by the eighteenth century they were barred by law from filling these positions. Instead, with only a few exceptions, the majority of palace women were recruited from the class of servants. Some of them were brought into the palace at a young age to receive training in Korean literacy and palace etiquette. The general rule was that palace women should remain single. In some cases, these young women became targets for the king's sexual advances. If they became pregnant from one of these assignations, they might be promoted to the status of consort. One of the best-known examples is Lady Chang (Chang Hŭibin), who became the queen of King Sukchong (r. 1674–1720), although for only a very short time. Her turbulent life story has become well known, inspiring a number of creative works in popular culture in South Korea.

Some of these palace women left important literary works in vernacular Korean. Examples include *The Tale of Queen Inhyŏn* and *The Diary of the Year Kyech'uk* (1613). Both works are anonymous, but from the level of detail they report about everyday life in the palace as well as the intrigues and intricate palace politics, it is inferred that they were authored by ladies-in-waiting (Kim Haboush 2003). *The Tale of Unyŏng*, a popular novel of the time, offers a vivid portrait of the inner emotional life of palace women. The author of the work is not known; however, it is inferred that this tale was authored by a man of the upper class. Written in literary Chinese in the early seventeenth century, the novel depicts a romance between a palace woman and a man of the upper class, even though such a relationship would have been prohibited in actuality because only the king would have had liaisons with palace women. One of the novel's distinctive elements is that it is written from the perspective of a female protagonist reporting her emotional experiences of love, passion, and despair within the context of the restricted freedoms palace women had to face in their day-to-day lives (Pettid 2009).

Female doctors were a necessity because of the prescribed segregation of the genders (known as the "inside-outside rule"). Under this rule, from an early age women and men were supposed to be separated in virtually every situation. This type of gender separation made it inappropriate for male doctors to have any contact with female patients, even for diagnostic purposes, so female doctors were needed to treat female patients. Beginning in 1406, the government established a curriculum for medical training, set criteria for evaluating doctors after training, and stipulated a ranking system for female doctors depending on their performance. Perhaps the most interesting thing about female doctors, who were recruited from the lower classes between the ages of ten and fifteen, is that in order to receive medical training, they had to learn Chinese so they could read the standard medical texts. Literacy in Chinese was a privilege that was not commonly available to women of the lower classes. The annals of the Chosŏn dynasty include accounts of several excellent female doctors, including Changgŭm, who gained the complete trust of King Chungjong (r. 1506–1544) because of the medical skills she displayed in treating members of the royal family. Some historical documents also suggest that female doctors sometimes served as investigators in crimes when the suspects were women of the upper class or the royal family.

Another profession open to women was that of entertainer (*kinyŏ* or *kisaeng*). The terms originally referred to a woman with special talent, primarily in music and dance, but they also encompassed such skills as medicine and needlework. Entertainers belonged to the lowest status, but they had frequent contact with men of the upper class and foreign visitors. In early Chosŏn, some Confucian scholars submitted multiple petitions to abolish the *kisaeng* system, arguing that it was improper from the perspective of Confucian moral teaching. However, the government resisted closing down the system because of the concern that without it, women of the commoner class could become prey to male sexual desires. Women entertainers were classified into several groups based on the training they received, the class of clients they entertained, and the nature of the work they engaged in. In an era when most women were secluded in the inner chambers, women entertainers were free to move around in public spaces and enjoy outings with their clients. Some of them, especially the highest-status entertainers, were literate in Chinese or Korean in order to be fitting companions for the Confucian scholars who were their clients. Although, as public slaves, they occupied the lowest, most despised social rank, the *kisaeng* had opportunities that were unavailable to the vast majority of women during the Chosŏn dynasty. Some of them became famous for the intelligent, artful, and poignant poetry they wrote, inspired by their loving relationships with men of high status. Hwang Chini (1506–1560) is the best known among these literary *kisaeng*. She is a near mythic figure, celebrated in multiple imaginings in numerous works of popular culture.

Reading and Writing Women

It is impossible to know what the literacy rate was, but it is clear that literacy in classical Chinese and vernacular Korean was largely the privilege of women of the upper class (with some exceptions among the *kisaeng*), and thus when we talk about reading and writing culture, we almost exclusively refer to women of the upper class who produced and circulated didactic manuals, poems, and songs among their own lineage groups.

In literature, there was a distinction between a higher genre and a lower one. The higher genre was called "records" (*rok* or *ki*) and the lower genre was labeled "tales" (*chŏn*). Women of the upper class read books and manuals related to "womanly virtue" and Confucian-prescribed ethics, considered to be examples in the genre of *rok* or *ki*. They were also active in reading and writing lineage novels (*kajŏn sosŏl*) in vernacular Korean calligraphy, which was unique to premodern Korea (Chizhova 2015). The best known in the category of records is the *Memoirs of Lady Hyegyŏng*, which is a collection of autobiographical writings (1795–1805) by the crown princess, whose husband, Crown Prince Sado, was executed by his own father, King Yŏngjo (r. 1724–1776). The *Memoirs* are an indispensable historical and literary record that conveys both the political turbulence in the court and the complex emotional life of the royal families (Hyegyŏnggung Hong Ssi 1996).

Another important literary genre was *kyubang kasa* (songs of the inner chambers), which were written in vernacular Korean and became popular in the eighteenth and nineteenth centuries. Largely anonymous, *kyubang kasa* were very likely written by the wives of the literati class and passed down to succeeding generations. Tens of thousands of *kyubang kasa* are extant. These pieces cover a wide range of topics—not only didactic lessons based on Confucian norms but also laments about domestic life and exaltations of the pleasure derived from outings (Häussler 2004).

Popular vernacular Korean literature in the eighteenth and nineteenth centuries was an important medium for both the propagation of Confucian values and, whether intended or not, their undermining. If the orthodox Confucian texts served as hegemonic discourses, the popular vernacular literature conveyed alternative or even counterhegemonic discourses that challenged the conventional Confucian patriarchal order. For instance, the best-known love story in traditional Korea, *The Story of Ch'unhyang*, is about a forbidden love between a man of the upper class and the daughter of a *kisaeng*. The rigid system of social strata in Chosŏn would not have allowed a formal union between members of two different classes, let alone the son of a respectable upper-class family and the daughter of an entertainer. However, in *The Story of Ch'unhyang* the protagonist keeps her chastity even when the local governor threatens her with death for not submitting to him, thereby demonstrating her true love for her partner, Mongryong. Because of her exemplary display of morality, the couple is exempted from the usual social constraints of the highly class-bound society and is allowed to live happily ever after as a legally married couple. A casual reading of the story underscores the value that was placed on a woman preserving her chastity. Indeed, the figure of Ch'unhyang has become the epitome of the chaste wife. However, the story can also be interpreted as offering a social critique of the class-based hierarchy in its portrayal of people in power who abuse their authority. While chastity was highly valued for women in Confucian Korea, men of the elite class, represented by the local governor, scorned the idea of lower-class women preserving their chastity, revealing contradictions between the ideology held by the elite and their actual practice. The tale, in which the idealized love between Ch'unhyang and Mongryong is almost thwarted, can also be taken to imply that the socially constructed status system hinders true human love.

The Story of Simch'ŏng, which became popular in the late eighteenth century, is another example that mixes conventional Confucian virtues with an implicit subversion of the patriarchal system. The main theme is filial piety. Simch'ŏng, the daughter of a poor blind man, is the quintessential example of a filial daughter, a young woman who is willing to sacrifice her own life to help her father regain his sight. While that element of the story is in keeping with Confucian principles, other aspects of Confucian ideology are challenged. The father is portrayed as meek and powerless, contesting the invariant image of the authoritative father figure in the patriarchal family system of Chosŏn. In contrast, Simch'ŏng is a strong, courageous, and powerful female figure, which is "least expected in a complex, patrilineal, and patriarchal society such as Chosŏn Korea" and shows "the tensions between male normative power and female real power" (Kim Haboush 1995, 174). Given this, it is not surprising that from the perspective of Confucian scholars and the ruling authorities, the circulation of popular novels and women's obsession with them was cause for a great deal of concern.

New Challenges to the Old Dynastic Order in Nineteenth-Century Chosŏn Korea

Throughout the nineteenth century, as a result of a variety of circumstances both internal and external, Chosŏn Korea experienced one of its most volatile periods in terms of political, economic, and cultural changes, the foremost among these being the weakening of the Neo-Confucian doctrine that was the foundation of social order during this period. Following the death of King Chŏngjo (r. 1776–1800), there was a succession of weak kings, many of whom had ascended to the throne as boys. Under these circumstances, power came to be concentrated in the hands of the young kings' in-laws, a situation that led to political corruption and ineffective governance. Major sources of government revenue—namely, the land tax, the military service tax, and the grain loan system—were ravaged by corruption, usury, and abuse of power. Ultimately the people were the ones who suffered most from the disarray in national politics and had to bear the burden of corruption in the tax system. There was growing anger among the peasants at the corruption and injustice they were being subjected to, and it frequently boiled over into rioting during this period (Kim 2007).

Internally the political corruption and resulting social disruption helped to destabilize the Neo-Confucian foundations of the Chosŏn dynasty. Further destabilization came through the encounters with the West that began in the late eighteenth century. In particular, the introduction of Catholicism in Korea paved the way for a worldview that was vastly different from the Neo-Confucian orthodoxy. Korean envoys first encountered Catholic writings during their visits to China and brought back tracts and pamphlets in Chinese, the most important of which was *The True Teaching of the Lord of Heaven* (*Ch'ŏnju sirŭi* in Korean, *Tianzhu shiyi* in Chinese). The religion did not spread widely, but it did have a particularly strong impact in the capital and surrounding areas. The first Korean adherents to Catholicism were members of the upper class (*yangban*) and middle class (*chung'in*), who were drawn by intellectual curiosity, but the religion soon spread to the lower classes as well. Catholicism's rejection of the rituals of ancestor worship as false idolatry caused great concern among the power elite in Chosŏn. Some early converts were even executed for failing to perform ancestor worship rituals or burning their ancestral tablets. Despite these cases of severe government repression, however, Catholicism continued to spread. By the turn of the nineteenth century there were about ten thousand Korean converts to Catholicism. In an attempt to curtail the spread of the religion, the government launched a series of infamous persecutions of Catholic adherents beginning in 1801, when Catholicism was "officially declared to be treason" (Ledyard 2006, 39). These persecutions drove Catholic believers underground until 1871, when the persecutions finally ceased.

Women played a significant role in spreading Catholicism. Given that public proselytization was impossible, believers met in people's homes at night to study, pray, and discuss the religion. Wives and mothers actively utilized their domestic networks with lineage groups in distributing the new religion (Ledyard 2006). One of the best-known early Catholic women was Kang Wansuk, one of the twenty-nine women martyrs killed in the 1801 persecution. Kang became a very devout Catholic and took leadership in the organization of meetings and the conversion of new adherents to the religion. A prime target for her efforts at conversion was her husband, but those efforts were ultimately unsuccessful and the couple eventually divorced. On the other hand, she was successful in converting her mother-in-law, and after the divorce the mother-in-law decided to live with Kang in Seoul rather than stay with her own son. However, Kang is perhaps most renowned for her fortitude and resilience. Her capacity to endure physical pain during interrogation inspired one of her torturers to say of her, "This one is a god, not a human being!" (Ledyard 2006, 57).

There are no materials that offer direct insight into how Kang perceived the Catholic creed or what it meant to be a Catholic woman; however, her biography makes it clear that she led a life in which she did things from which women were generally excluded. Despite the paucity of reliable data, the lives of Kang and other Catholic women show us that the newly introduced Western religion shook some of the deep foundational precepts that had determined gender practices in Chosŏn society. Specifically, given the central role of ancestral rites in Neo-Confucian families and the key role women played in planning and performing those rituals, a woman's conversion to Catholicism implied a rejection of those rituals, which were the backbone of the Confucian doctrine. In addition, in a society where men and women of the upper classes were segregated from each other after the age of seven and hierarchical class distinctions were an unavoidable feature of social interaction, the practices of Catholicism offered release from those strictures. In Catholic communities, men and women of all classes met together for study and prayer. Furthermore, as shown in the case of Kang, some women took up leadership roles in propagating their new religion, although in secret. In this we might say that the introduction of Catholicism contributed to the undermining of the boundaries that defined the roles of men and women as well as the social code that distinguished between the various social classes in the nineteenth century.

Catholicism was a foreign religion whose spread and popularity were largely restricted to the area around the capital. In other regions of the country an indigenous religion called Tonghak (Eastern Learning) gained popularity among the peasants in the second half of the nineteenth century (Kallander 2013). Founded by Ch'oe Cheu (1824–1864), Tonghak drew its precepts from a variety of religious and moral traditions: Buddhism, Confucianism, Taoism, shamanism, and even Catholicism. The emergence of this religion was deeply rooted in that era's particular historical context, in which the rampant political corruption and economic exploitation perpetrated by the ruling class had devastated the lives of peasants. It was also driven, in part, by a growing awareness of the powerful military forces of the Western countries that were demanding trade and diplomatic relations. In particular, China's Opium Wars with Britain (1839–1842, 1856–1860) and its ultimate defeat resulted in daunting new realities in Korea, as they had in Japan. The founder of Tonghak wrote, "Our country is full of bad diseases, and the people have no peace. Suffering is the lot of the people. It is said that the West wins and takes whatever it fights for, and there is nothing in which it cannot succeed. . . . How can the plan of protecting the nation and securing peace for the people be made?" (Lee 1996, 317).

In a significant way, Tonghak was an indigenous response to the challenges that Korea faced at that time from both inside and outside the country. It propagated an ideal of equality for all human beings, regardless of class, gender, or age, in order to address long-standing social injustices, and at the same time it aimed to protect the nation from growing threats from foreign countries. The emphasis on social equality was an especially revolutionary ideal in a society that strictly conformed to a social hierarchy. However, Tonghak had limitations, especially when it came to gender relations. One of the phrases from the tracts of Tonghak, *puhwa pusun* (the husband treats the wife gently, the wife obeys the husband), expresses the traditional idea of the subordination of women to men. Concrete guidelines for how to practice "truth" at home taught women to obey their husbands. Nonetheless, the religion's advocacy of social equality for all human beings contributed to the questioning of hierarchical human relationships, a trend that would increase and have a strong impact in later decades.

JAPAN

Economic Transformations in Early Modern Japan

Economic, social, and demographic changes transformed Japan between the seventeenth and early nineteenth centuries. The coming of peace in the early seventeenth century permitted farmers to look forward to more reliable harvests; overseas trade with Korea and China, especially in the seventeenth century, put more goods in upscale consumers' hands; and the movement of people and goods throughout Japan that was a result of the alternate attendance system (see Chapter 2) and the government's need for currency to support that system grew the economy throughout the seventeenth century. Many people in addition to government officials moved around Japan. Traveling merchants introduced goods to rural areas, maritime shipping companies hauled rice and other heavy goods from the coastal regions to Edo and the Osaka/Kyoto region, pack-horse hauling companies sent thousands of horses onto the roads every day, and foot travelers carefully picked their way along the roads behind the horses (Gordon 2009, 26–27). Dozens of express messenger services made deliveries between Osaka and Edo, a distance of more than three hundred miles, in four days. Pilgrims and sightseers, many of them women over forty years of age, added to the lively travel between cities. Villagers along the highways scooped up marketable waste such as horse manure and solicited customers for food, lodging, sex, and souvenirs.

The expanding economy not only allowed the population of the cities, towns, and villages to grow—at least until the early eighteenth century, when the cities' population began to stagnate—but also increasingly linked the towns and countryside together. A blossoming urban consumer base encouraged farmers to plant a wide variety of specialty food crops and to produce cotton, silk, and other fabrics for urban and rural consumers' use. The villages closest to the cities and to the roadways used by the alternate attendance processions of the daimyo were more greatly influenced by urban ideas, culture, and products than villages in more remote areas. Their inhabitants were more likely to come into contact with city folk, either by migrating to cities for work or by going to market in nearby towns and cities. Itinerant merchants brought a variety of consumer products—pots and pans, books, personal products such as hair ornaments and cosmetics, and many more items—to towns and villages large and small. Gender and class relations in villages touched by urban culture changed significantly by the beginning of the nineteenth century, while remote villages in the hinterland changed barely at all. So, just as societal expectations for men's and women's lives, roles, and sexuality differed by status group (see Chapter 2), where one lived (geography and place) also played an important role in gender relations.

Changing Rural Men's and Women's Lives

As alternate attendance processions moved across Japan, towns and villages along the way lodged, fed, and entertained them. Money made its way from roadside inns and restaurants to the villages that supplied raw materials, food, and labor. That cash was used to buy what many farmers viewed as labor-saving farm products and technologies. As we shall see, rather than eliminating labor, these new tools and technologies allowed farmers, especially women and children, to redirect their labor to new types of work, thereby increasing their productivity. This shift in labor led to changes in class and gender relations within both the family and the village as a whole in the second half of the Tokugawa era (Smith 1959).

One of the new labor-saving products was commercial fertilizer (human and animal waste), which replaced the twigs and compost that farmers, especially women and children, had traditionally spent many hours collecting from communal woodlands owned by the village as a whole. Unlike commercial fertilizer, traditional fertilizers were acquired through investment in physical labor rather than expenditure of money. Once villagers were able to cut the time spent collecting fertilizer, they could refocus their time on more productive tasks. In addition, purchasing fertilizers allowed many of the old communal woodlands to be converted to new arable fields, which in turn increased the village's crop production and therefore its income.

Commercial fertilizer not only changed village life; it also forged an important nexus between cities and villages. That is, urban people bought and ate the food farmers produced, and farmers bought and applied the human waste, euphemistically called "night soil," produced by city people's consumption of that food, to grow more crops. Class and gender were taken into consideration when calculating the price of night soil. Waste collected from a male samurai fetched a higher market price than that produced by a commoner woman (Ebrey, Walthall, and Palais 2009, 285). While this seems to be a ridiculous example of class and gender bias, in most families men were fed higher-quality and more-varied food while women and children ate inferior or leftover food. And samurai diets were often richer and more varied than commoners' diets. Thus, samurai men's excrement *may* have indeed produced a better fertilizer, although the price differences were grounded in stereotypes about sex and class and not in any kind of scientific reasoning. As with new fertilizers, innovative irrigation devices were costly but useful new technologies. Irrigation opened previously less fertile fields to rice farming, which led both to higher crop yields and to more demand for farm labor. As we saw in Chapter 2, women did much of the planting of seeds and seedlings, while men and strong boys did most of the harvesting. So as new fields were brought into rice cultivation, the demand for the labor of both men and women to cultivate those new fields expanded.

Another new technology that appeared to be a labor-saving device was a rice thresher that resembled a comb several feet long. For many centuries, rice had been threshed by pulling harvested stalks, held in one hand, through huge chopsticks held in the other hand, and allowing the grains of rice squeezed out between the chopsticks to fall onto a woven mat. These outsized chopsticks required strong hands, and adult women had long been tasked with threshing the rice. But the new comb-like thresher could be handled by weaker members of the family, including children. This freed up the labor of stronger adult women (and men, many of whom also threshed grain) to work more strenuously in their newly opened fields or to undertake craft work and textile production, both of which increased the flow of urban cash into the village. Thus, what appeared to be labor-saving devices—tools that, like the thresher, permitted much greater output with the same input of labor—usually led to greater investment of family labor, as less skilled children could replace more skilled adults, especially women (Smith 1959). These women, in turn, could take on new and more difficult tasks, such as silk reeling and weaving, which were often more lucrative. Men also could use their labor more productively. As literacy spread in the seventeenth and eighteenth centuries, more farmers, especially men, read agricultural treatises about new agricultural technologies and seed information and applied those technologies to their farms.

The expanding economy connected villagers to the urban markets in additional ways. Demands for construction workers and artisans of all types in the rapidly growing towns and cities, for example, drew labor away from the villages. This forced peasants who remained on the land to work more efficiently after many of their sons migrated away. Nuclear families (parents and their unmarried children) that could mobilize the labor of all their members were found to be more productive than the large extended families that had been most common during most of the seventeenth century. Siblings and cousins of the family head, along with their families, as well as hereditary servants, all of whom had supplied labor to the large extended families that predominated in early seventeenth-century villages, were less willing to do heavy labor for the family head once the existence of an urban labor market increased the value of their labor. Some peripheral family members (cousins, hereditary servants, and the like) were priced out of farm families' economic ability to retain them. Spouses and children in nuclear families, on the other hand, could be more effectively mobilized to work hard for their immediate families, as the continuity of the family (*ie*) from generation to generation was highly prized. As we saw in Chapter 2, the welfare and continuity of the family were more important than any strict division of labor by gender—men could do what were traditionally women's tasks and vice versa, if necessary, in Japanese farm families. Family records stored in Buddhist temples show that married relatives and hereditary servants who had earlier been listed as part of large extended families were increasingly listed as separate nuclear families.

Thus, by the end of the seventeenth century, villages nearest to the highways experienced changes to the old village structure. Despite those changes, the new smaller families that had been the nucleus of the prestigious extended families of the past usually continued to be the village leaders, even if the number of people in their families had dropped from several dozen to just a half dozen. These leading old families dominated the village headship and the village council. Men from the leading families ran the council, with women taking a seat only when a family did not have a man available. Even if these prestigious families now had fewer family members, they often continued to own more land than they wished to farm with their own nuclear family's labor alone. As a result, many employed hired hands, who were usually the sons and daughters of their poorer neighbors, or rented out surplus fields to those neighbors. The old extended families had included both privileged and poor members, but all had been part of the same family. The new village structure included a variety of nuclear families, from desperately poor tenant farmers to rich landlords, with each family listed separately in the temple records. Vast differences in wealth produced greater class divisions in the village. The poorest families tended to have the smallest number of members, as they could afford to feed fewer mouths. Farm families regulated family size in several ways, including the timing of marriage and childbirth as well as infanticide, a practice that was illegal but not uncommon.

Some farm families with a lot of cash—often rental income from farmers who previously had been peripheral members of the landlords' extended families—set up small production facilities, such as cotton and silk spinning mills, which hired many teenage girls as wage laborers. When Japan began modern factory development in the late nineteenth century, the experience of daughters working away from home in the textile industry and sons working as wage laborers in other workshops and farms had a long precedent in the early modern era. This development of gendered work in the Tokugawa period was one of many factors that contributed, as we shall see, to the gendering of the industrial workforce in modern Japan. Thus, the course of political and economic development in the early modern centuries made long-lasting changes in the nature of the Japanese family and in the roles of rural men and women in society.

Gender and Culture in Japan's Cities

In the medieval centuries preceding the rise of the Tokugawa, Kyoto had been Japan's only large city. The removal of full-time samurai from the countryside in the late sixteenth century and the alternate attendance system in the seventeenth century changed that. Castle towns sprang up in every daimyo's domain; the Tokugawa shogun's capital at Edo became a political and cultural nexus; and Osaka emerged as a merchant-run consumption and marketing center. The populations of Edo and the castle towns were mostly half samurai, half commoner. Osaka's population consisted overwhelmingly of merchants and artisans. Kyoto harbored the old aristocracy and royal family as well as the realm's greatest artists, novelists, and playwrights in the seventeenth century until cultural centers emerged in the larger cities of Edo and Osaka in the eighteenth century.

At the dawn of the seventeenth century, urban culture had been samurai culture. By the end of that century, the arts were affordable for an expanding number of city folk, and the number of poets, playwrights, novelists, and wood-block artists increased rapidly to meet new consumer demand. There was an explosion of printing and literacy. More than seven hundred publishing companies were founded in Kyoto alone during the seventeenth century. Most men and women in the cities could read, attend the theater, and enjoy prints and other forms of pictorial art. Patronage of the arts by commoners made them the dominant arbiters of urban taste and culture, and representations of women and men, sexuality, and gender in printed and staged works of art not only reflected the values of merchants and artisans but also helped to frame them. In addition, those values influenced gender discourse throughout Japan, as books and other forms of culture were brought into the countryside by itinerant merchants and artists.

The last decades of the seventeenth century and the first decades of the eighteenth were a golden age of urban culture and arts in Japan. Of course, art continued to be produced in the last century and a half of the Tokugawa period as well, but the groundwork for the styles and themes of early modern art was laid in the years around 1700. Contemporaries greatly admired the poet Matsuo Bashō (1644–1694), novelist and storyteller Ihara Saikaku (1642–1693), wood-block artist Hishikawa Moronobu (c. 1620–1694), and playwright Chikamatsu Monzaemon (1653–1724). These four were men, but their subjects tell us much about the representation of both men and women around the turn of the eighteenth century.

Son of a minor samurai, Matsuo Bashō was the companion of his daimyo's son, who introduced him to *haikai*, a poetic form developed in the early seventeenth century. His friend's untimely death led Bashō to study *haikai* more formally, and by 1677 he was the major practitioner of the form. In the 1680s, he pioneered what later (in the nineteenth century) came to be called haiku—a poem of a single seventeen-syllable stanza—and published numerous volumes of his own and his students' work. His studies of Zen, Chinese literature, and medieval Japanese poetry informed his writing. His seventeen-syllable haiku used imagery to evoke mood and suggested the linkages between seemingly dissimilar objects.

On a withered branch
a crow has settled–
autumn nightfall. (Henderson 1958, 18)

On a journey, ill—
my dreams, on withered fields
are wandering still. (Keene 1955, 385)

In a society that enjoyed pilgrimages to holy spots and travel to scenic wonders, Bashō's poetic accounts gained a wide following, especially *Oku no hosomichi* (Narrow road to the north), a volume recounting his long journey in 1689 from Edo northward throughout Honshū, the largest island of Japan.

Although gender topics appeared less frequently in Bashō's poetry than in the works of the other artists to be discussed here, several of his haiku addressed the issue of women as prostitutes in roadside inns. He also observed farm children working late into the night.

Under the same roof
prostitutes, too, were sleeping—
the moon and clover. (Keene 1955, 373)

Peasant boy—
husking rice, he pauses
to gaze at the moon. (Bashō 2004, 60)

Bashō found the condition of an elderly, lonely woman to be pitiful:

Her face,
an old woman weeping alone:
moon as a companion. (Bashō 2004, 82)

In a poem that referred to sexuality, Bashō did not express a preference for same-sex love or heterosexual love, noting only their difference:

Plum and willow,
Young man or woman? (Pflugfelder 1999, 35–36)

Bashō's contemporary Ihara Saikaku, one of the most prolific prose writers of the late seventeenth century, addressed gender and sexuality in his novels and short stories far more often than did Bashō in his poetry. During his career as a prose writer, Saikaku grew increasingly concerned with the difficulties of life for city folk and always noted the darker aspects of human relationships, but even these concerns were filtered through his wit and eye for the risqué. His novels and short stories moved from one intimate encounter to another, comparing men and women as lovers.

Born in 1642 to a prosperous merchant family, Saikaku attended the theater and visited teahouses and brothels in his early years. His family manufactured swords for samurai, so Saikaku at first worked in his family's sword business. At the same time, he loved poetry and was a prolific *haikai* writer, balancing his avocation of writing with his work in the family business until his wife died in 1675, leaving him alone to care for his blind daughter. He focused on sword-making until his daughter died a few years later, after which he threw himself into writing. At first he primarily wrote poetry, but eventually he found that boring. So he turned to writing plays and commentaries on the sexual and theatrical skills of handsome young actors. His plays never enjoyed success, but his prose sketches and reviews of actors opened the door to a successful career as a prose writer focusing on the sexual lives of samurai, townsmen, and actors.

Traveling throughout Japan, as familiar with samurai—who had purchased his company's swords—as with merchants, Saikaku had a keen eye for human relations that made his stories enormously popular among his contemporaries. (See an excerpt from one of his short stories in Chapter 2.) His first collection of stories, *Kōshoku ichidai otoko* (*Life of an Amorous Man*, 1682), was so well received that readers clamored for more. Until his death a decade later, Saikaku wrote at an incredible pace. His first works, which also included *Nanshoku ōkagami* (*The Great Mirror of Male Love*, 1678), *Kōshoku gonin onna* (*Five Women Who Loved Love*, 1686), and *Kōshoku ichidai onna* (*Life of an Amorous Woman*, 1686), dealt primarily with love between men and women and between men—although not with female same-sex love. Gender relations, sexualities, and the daily lives of average people were addressed in these works.

The clash between love—referred to as "human emotion" (*ninjō*)—and social obligation (*giri*) was a central theme in Saikaku's tales. One of the tales in *Five Women Who Loved Love* recounts the humorous foibles of a young married woman who ran off with her husband's business assistant after the two mistakenly had sex (Keene 1955, 336–353). The fact that their first sexual encounter was a mistake is hard to believe, but we must keep in mind that Saikaku meant his stories to be humorous. The pair's escapades were undertaken out of love or human emotion—and, in Saikaku's telling, they were quite risqué and somewhat coarse—but the assistant had an overriding social obligation to his boss and the wife to her husband. In the end, the lovers were caught and brought to justice. *Life of an Amorous Man* granted the protagonist, a man whose sexual life began at age seven, a bit more license. The book follows him through numerous sexual adventures with women and men (he had more than two thousand partners) and ends with him sailing off happily in search of the "Island of Women" at age sixty. *The Great Mirror of Male Love* focused on male same-sex love, and its narrator wished that Japan could be an all-male "Island of Men."

Saikaku's collections on sex and love were witty and spicy, even if their hedonistic protagonists had to atone for often inappropriate sexual escapades between women and men that upset social obligations (male-male sex usually avoided upsetting marital social obligations and was therefore less dangerous). Saikaku's tone turned more pessimistic in his last years. A year before his death, Saikaku wrote a dark tale of poverty, *Seken munezan'yō* (*Worldly Mental Calculations*, 1692).

Pictorial art was closely connected to literature. Illustrated books combined the various genres, bringing art inexpensively to a wide readership. Wood-block prints were the new artistic form of the late seventeenth century. Hishikawa Moronobu elevated the humble wood-block print to a major art form. Like Saikaku, Moronobu created works that depicted average people—in fact, he illustrated Saikaku's *Life of an Amorous Man*. Like the hundreds of wood-block artists he inspired in the next two centuries, his works portrayed scenic locations, handsome actors, beautiful courtesans, gardens, urban street life, and very explicit erotic scenes. These works of art were quite cheap and accessible to the masses, unlike the paintings of an earlier era, which were created for the elite. Wood-block prints spread ideas of beauty, images of people at work and play, and notions of sexuality to city folk and villagers.

As in the case of poetry, prose, and art, theatrical works were written with commoner audiences in mind. Some plays were enacted by puppets (*jōruri* or *bunraku* theater), and others were staged by all-male casts playing both male and female roles (kabuki theater). Tokugawa-era audiences were comfortable with the idea that gender was constructed through performance rather than stamped on individuals by birth as boys or girls (see Chapter 2).

Chikamatsu Monzaemon was Japan's most esteemed playwright, writing about 130 plays during a long career. Some of his works dealt with political events, often masked as historical tales, such as *Goban Taiheiki* (Chronicle of Great Peace), the first theatrical treatment of the vengeance tale of the

Kitagawa Utamaro, known for his images of beautiful women, created this wood-block portrait of a famed geisha around 1800.
Kitagawa Utamaro, Ōgiya takihashi, 1800. Library of Congress, LC-DIG-jpd-02321

loyalty of forty-seven samurai to their disgraced feudal lord. This tale stressed a kind of masculinity based on devotion to one's "band of brothers" and one's feudal lord.

Chikamatsu's most popular works were dramas of suicide and other highly emotional topics. In these, his protagonists were ordinary people—prostitutes, shopkeepers, long-suffering wives—who faced painful moral dilemmas. Chikamatsu's characters, like Ihara Saikaku's, struggled with the conflict between human emotion and social obligation—in Chikamatsu's plays, the obligation was usually a Confucian principle such as filial piety or loyalty to one's superior. Although love suicides were against Tokugawa law, audiences were keenly aware that there was sometimes no other way to resolve the dilemmas of restrictive social principles, economic problems, and human feelings. In Chikamatsu's plays, the lovers confessed guilt for the sorrow their suicide would inflict on their parents and other loved ones, and professed their faith in Buddhist salvation before committing suicide. The need to satisfy one's emotional longing and the idea that those who attempted to do so could achieve salvation indicate Chikamatsu's (and his audience's) belief in the agency of ordinary men and women.

In addition to the commercial forms of art—published and marketed poetry and prose works, staged plays, and artworks printed in thousands of copies—amateur arts also proliferated in the Tokugawa period. The practitioners of amateur arts were called *bunjin* (literati). Though they were "amateur" in the sense that they were neither employed as artists in an official capacity by government officials nor recipients of commissions from wealthy temples, their level of accomplishment in painting, calligraphy, poetry, prose, tea ceremony, and other refined arts was extremely high.

Bunjin could be of urban or rural origin or residence; of samurai, farmer, or merchant background; and either male or female. Many supported themselves with another occupation, but some made a living as artistic advisors, designers, or illustrators. For example, a young Kyoto couple, Ike Taiga and Gyokuran, sold their amateur paintings for several years after their marriage in 1752 before the husband (Taiga) placed the family on more stable footing by taking in paying students. Though far outnumbered by men, women were not uncommon in the ranks of the *bunjin*. Inspired by the mid-Qing practice of encouragement of female learning in China, Japanese *bunjin* masters encouraged their daughters' and wives' cultural growth.

By the late eighteenth century, even girls without family ties to male *bunjin* could aspire to cultural development. One such young woman was Ema Saikō (1787–1861), who developed a national reputation as a *bunjin* artist (Fister 1991; see Box 3.3).

BOX 3.3

Ema Saikō

Ema Saikō grew up in a scholarly household—her father served as official physician to his daimyo. Saikō was a child prodigy whose skills in painting, calligraphy, and poetry convinced Dr. Ema to arrange for her to receive instruction from a painter in Kyoto. Saikō focused on developing her talents. When her father tried to arrange her marriage at age eighteen to a young doctor he planned to adopt as his heir, she refused the proposal in order to pursue her studies. The young doctor married Saikō's sister instead.

A few years later, Saikō met the renowned poet Rai San'yo. The two fell in love. Invited to help Saikō with her poetry, he wrote to a friend after his first meeting with her, "I've been asked to touch up her poems, but I'd love to touch up her whole body" (Lipman, Molony, and Robinson 2012, 131). Some scholars contend that Rai San'yo may have asked Dr. Ema for permission to marry his daughter, but this is unclear. They did not marry, but Saikō continued to visit Rai and the woman he later married. As artists, women and men *bunjin* could meet in poetry groups and were accorded generally equal treatment in their artistic lives. But in their social lives women did not have equal opportunities. Although many of Saikō's poems express her joy as an artist, others express sadness that women had to choose between a life as an artist and marital love. Commenting on a collection of verse by Chinese women poets, Saikō lamented her own loneliness:

> *The hushed night deepening, I can't take to my pillow:*
> *The lamp stirred, I quietly read the women's words.*
> *Why is it that the talented are so unfortunate?*
> *Most are poems about empty beds, husbands missed. (Ema 1998, 50)*

CONNECTIONS

The eighteenth and nineteenth centuries were a time of great economic development in the three East Asian countries, and this development brought about changes in gender relations in urban and rural areas. In all three countries, women and men produced goods for emerging rural and urban markets, managed small enterprises, engaged in new forms of labor, and were major consumers of the new products being produced. This new economic activity led to changes in family structures. At the same time, new opportunities for talented women, especially for poets, opened up. And in China and Korea in the first half of the nineteenth century, religious movements offered opportunities for women to breach the inner/outer paradigm that had kept women inside and pushed men outside.

"Men plow, women weave," a venerable expression of China's division of labor, was increasingly too narrow a description of what women actually did. Women's tasks varied regionally, and many, such as picking tea or cotton and work in restaurants and inns, took place outside the home. Of course, textile and food production inside the home, which could be accomplished with bound feet, continued to employ many Chinese women in varying ways. These types of jobs helped pay the family's taxes (an outside role). In urban areas, women worked in book publishing and other jobs. Maintaining the principle of the inner/outer distinction continued to be valued, but it was often difficult to practice.

This distinction was important in Chosŏn, too, but there were several categories of women who worked in the outer realm. The desire to maintain the inner/outer rule required female physicians for female patients, so some women studied medicine—in Chinese. Others worked as performers (*kisaeng*) or as palace employees, bringing them into contact with men. Others worked on farms, where new agricultural techniques led to higher productivity and, in turn, economic growth and opportunities for work as managers and producers. In Japan, economic growth tied the cities to the countryside. This led to an increased value for labor as people migrated to the cities to work. The rise in the cost of labor made the large extended families that were common in the seventeenth century in Japan too expensive to maintain in the eighteenth and nineteenth centuries. As cousins and servants moved away, the remaining members of the nuclear family used technical innovations to increase output by parents and children.

The role of women in religion was also significant in these centuries. In China, women played a central role in the White Lotus religious movement. The gender challenge of the White Lotus movement—as well as the White Lotus uprising—was a serious threat to the Neo-Confucian order. In Chosŏn, the coming of Christianity was perhaps even more of a challenge, as the Christian meetings where women and men sat together—some of the meetings were even led by women—undermined inner/outer propriety. In addition, women had been primarily responsible for carrying out the family's Confucian and religious rituals, and women's conversion to Christianity prevented them from carrying out this responsibility. Their involvement in the Tonghak religious movement was a further challenge to Confucianism.

In all three countries, educated, refined women found a niche they could exploit for personal development as artists in the eighteenth and nineteenth centuries. Although some men thought writing by elite women was unseemly, women's writing was highly regarded by many more.

In a variety of ways—economic development, new work opportunities, and respect for literate women—the eighteenth and early nineteenth centuries sowed the seeds for modernity and rapidly changing roles for men and women in the late nineteenth century.

REFERENCES AND SUGGESTIONS FOR FURTHER READING

GLOBAL CONTEXT

Frader, Laura Levine. 2004. "Gender and Labor in World History." In *A Companion to Gender History*, edited by Teresa A. Meade and Merry E. Wiesner-Hanks. Oxford: Blackwell.

Kent, Susan Kingsley. 2004. "Gender Rules: Law and Politics." In *A Companion to Gender History*, edited by Teresa A. Meade and Merry E. Wiesner-Hanks. Oxford: Blackwell.

Marks, Robert B. 2007. *The Origins of the Modern World: A Global and Ecological Narrative from the Fifteenth to the Twenty-First Century*. Lanham, MD: Rowman and Littlefield.

Miller, Pavla. 2004. "Gender and Education Before and After Mass Schooling." In *A Companion to Gender History*, edited by Teresa A. Meade and Merry E. Wiesner-Hanks. Oxford: Blackwell.

Nye, Robert. 2004. "Sexuality." In *A Companion to Gender History*, edited by Teresa A. Meade and Merry E. Wiesner-Hanks. Oxford: Blackwell.

Pomeranz, Kenneth. 2000. *The Great Divergence: China, Europe, and the Making of the Modern World Economy*. Princeton, NJ: Princeton University Press.

Tucker, Judith. 2004. "Rescued from Obscurity: Contributions and Challenges in Writing the History of Gender in the Middle East and North Africa." In *A Companion to Gender History*, edited by Teresa A. Meade and Merry E. Wiesner-Hanks. Oxford: Blackwell.

Valenze, Deborah. 2004. "Gender in the Formation of European Power, 1750–1914." In *A Companion to Gender History*, edited by Teresa A. Meade and Merry E. Wiesner-Hanks. Oxford: Blackwell.

Wong, R. Bin. 1997. *China Transformed: Historical Change and the Limits of European Experience*. Ithaca, NY: Cornell University Press.

CHINA

Bray, Francesca. 1997. *Technology and Gender: Fabrics of Power in Late Imperial China*. Berkeley: University of California Press.

Brokaw, Cynthia. 2007. *Commerce in Culture: The Sibao Book Trade in the Qing and Republican Eras*. Cambridge, MA: Harvard East Asia Center.

Cao, Xueqin. 1974. *The Story of the Stone*. Translated by David Hawkes. London: Penguin Classics.

Eyferth, Jacob. 2009. *Eating Rice from Bamboo Roots: The Social History of a Community Handicraft in Rural Sichuan, 1920–2000*. Cambridge, MA: Harvard East Asia Center.

Finnane, Antonia. 2004. *Speaking of Yangzhou: A Chinese City, 1550–1850*. Cambridge, MA: Harvard East Asia Center.

Furth, Charlotte. *A Flourishing Yin: Gender in China's Medical History, 960–1665*. Berkeley: University of California Press.

Gates, Hill. 2015. *Footbinding and Women's Labor in Sichuan*. New York: Routledge.

Goldman, Andrea S. 2013. *Opera and the City: The Politics of Culture in Beijing, 1770–1900*. Stanford, CA: Stanford University Press.

Guo, Li. 2015. *Women's Tanci Fiction in Late Imperial and Twentieth Century China*. West Lafayette, IN: Purdue University Press.

Ko, Dorothy. 1995. *Teachers of the Inner Chambers: Women and Culture in Seventeenth-Century China*. Stanford, CA: Stanford University Press.

Mann, Susan. 1987. "Widows in the Kinship, Class, and Community Structures of Qing Dynasty China." *Journal of Asian Studies* 46, no. 1: 37–56.

———. 1997. *Precious Records: Women in China's Long Eighteenth Century.* Stanford, CA: Stanford University Press.

Mann, Susan. 2007. *The Talented Women of the Zhang Family.* Berkeley, CA: University of California Press.

Mann, Susan, and Yu-Yin Cheng, eds. 2001. *Under Confucian Eyes: Writings on Gender in Chinese History*. Berkeley: University of California Press.

Menegon, Eugenio. 2009. *Ancestors, Virgins, and Friars: Christianity as a Local Religion in Late Imperial China*. Cambridge: Harvard University Asia Center.

Naquin, Susan. 1985. "The Transmission of White Lotus Sectarianism in Late Imperial China." In *Popular Culture in Late Imperial China*, edited by David George Johnson et al. Berkeley: University of California Press.

Pomeranz, Kenneth. 2005. "Women's Work and the Economics of Respectability." In *Gender in Motion: Divisions of Labor and Cultural Change in Late Imperial and Modern China, edited by Bryna Goodman and Wendy Larson.* Lanham, MD: Rowman and Littlefield.

Sommer, Matthew. 2015. *Polyandry and Wife-Selling in Qing Dynasty China: Survival Strategies and Judicial Interventions.* Berkeley: University of California Press.

Wu, Yi-Li. 2010. *Reproducing Women: Medicine, Metaphor, and Childbirth in Late Imperial China.* Berkeley: University of California Press.

KOREA

Chizhova, Ksenia. 2015. "The Subject of Feelings: Kinship, Emotion, Fiction, and Women's Culture in Korea, Late 17th–Early 20th Centuries." Ph.D. dissertation, Columbia University.

Committee for the Compilation of the History of Korean Women. 1979. *Women of Korea: A History from Ancient Times to 1945*. Edited and translated by Yung-Chung Kim. Seoul: Ewha Womans University Press.

Häussler, Sonja. 2004. "Kyubang Kasa: Women's Writings from the Late Chosŏn." In *Creative Women of Korea: The Fifteenth Through the Twentieth Centuries*, edited by Young-Key Kim-Renaud. Armonk, NY: M. E. Sharpe.

Hyegyŏnggung Hong Ssi. 1996. *The Memoirs of Lady Hyegyŏng: The Autobiographical Writings of a Crown Princess of Eighteenth-Century Korea*. Edited and translated by JaHyun Kim Haboush. Berkeley: University of California Press.

Kallander, George L. 2013. *Salvation Through Dissent: Tonghak Heterodoxy and Early Modern Korea*. Honolulu: University of Hawai'i Press.

Kim Haboush, JaHyun. 1995. "Filial Emotions and Filial Values: Changing Patterns in the Discourse of Filiality in Late Chosŏn Korea." *Harvard Journal of Asiatic Studies* 55, no. 1: 129–177.

———. 2003. "Versions and Subversions: Patriarchy and Polygamy in Korean Narratives." In *Women and Confucian Cultures in Premodern China, Korea, and Japan*, edited by Dorothy Ko, JaHyun Kim Haboush, and Joan Piggott. Berkeley: University of California Press.

Kim, Kichung. 1996. *An Introduction to Classical Korean Literature: From Hyangga to P'ansori*. Armonk, NY: M. E. Sharpe.

Kim, Sun Joo. 2007. *Marginality and Subversion in Korea: The Hong Kyŏngnae Rebellion of 1812*. Seattle: University of Washington Press.

Kim-Renaud, Young-Key, ed. 2004. *Creative Women of Korea: The Fifteenth Through the Twentieth Centuries*. Armonk: M.E. Sharpe.

Kwon, Soon-Hyung. 2014. "Did People Divorce in the Joseon Period?" In *Everyday Life in Joseon-Era Korea: Economy and Society*, edited by Michael Shin. Leiden: E. J. Brill.

Ledyard, Gari. 2006. "Kollumba Kang Wansuk, an Early Catholic Activist and Martyr." In *Christianity in Korea*, edited by Robert E. Buswell Jr. and Timothy S. Lee. Honolulu: University of Hawai'i Press.

Lee, Ki-baek. 1984. *A New History of Korea*. Translated by Edward W. Wagner with Edward J. Shultz. Cambridge, MA: Harvard University Press.

Lee, Peter, ed. 1993. *Sourcebook of Korean Civilization, Volume 1: From Early Times to the Sixteenth Century*. New York: Columbia University Press.

———, ed. 1996. *Sourcebook of Korean Civilization, Volume 2: from the Sixteenth to the Twentieth Centuries*. New York: Columbia University Press.

Pettid, Michael J. 2009. *Unyŏng-jŏn: A Love Affair at the Royal Palace of Chosŏn Korea*. Translated by Kil Cha and Michael J. Pettid. Berkeley: Institute of East Asian Studies, University of California.

Shin, Michael, ed. 2014. *Everyday Life in Joseon-Era Korea: Economy and Society*. Leiden: E. J. Brill.

JAPAN

Matsuo, Bashō. 2004. *Bashō's Haiku: Selected Poems of Matsuo Bashō*. Translated by David Landis Barnhill. Albany, NY: SUNY Press.

Ebrey, Patricia, Anne Walthall, and James Palais. 2009. *East Asia: A Cultural, Social, and Political History*. Belmont, CA: Wadsworth.

Ema Saikō. 1998. *Breeze Through Bamboo*. Translated by Hiroaki Sato. New York: Columbia University Press.

Fister, Patricia. 1991. "Female *Bunjin*: The Life of Poet-Painter Ema Saikō." In *Recreating Japanese Women, 1600–1950*, edited by Gail Lee Bernstein. Berkeley: University of California Press.

Gordon, Andrew. 2009. *A Modern History of Japan*. New York: Oxford University Press.

Henderson, Harold G. 1958. *An Introduction to Haiku*. New York: Doubleday.

Keene, Donald. 1955. *Anthology of Japanese Literature: From the Earliest Era to the Mid-Nineteenth Century*. New York: Grove Press.

Lipman, Jonathan, Barbara Molony, and Michael Robinson. 2012. *Modern East Asia: An Integrated History*. London: Laurence King.

Pflugfelder, Gregory M. 1999. *Cartographies of Desire: Male-Male Sexuality in Japanese Discourse, 1600–1950*. Berkeley: University of California Press.

Smith, Thomas C. 1959. *The Agrarian Origins of Modern Japan*. Stanford, CA: Stanford University Press.

4

Gender and Modernity, 1860–1912

GLOBAL CONTEXT

East Asians' quests to transform their societies, including developing new ideas about gender, between the mid-nineteenth century and the eve of World War I took place against a backdrop of unprecedented European and North American expansion in power and wealth. During that time, Great Britain secured its hold over India by defeating the Indian (Sepoy) Rebellion in 1857, the Berlin Conference (1884–1888) carved the African continent into European colonies, and France consolidated its control of Indochina (Vietnam, Cambodia, and Laos) in the 1880s. The United States justified nineteenth-century expansion from the Atlantic to the Pacific by the religiously inspired ideology of Manifest Destiny and followed that up at the turn of the twentieth century with territorial acquisitions in the mid-Pacific (Hawai'i) and western Pacific (Guam and the Philippines). Russia conquered territories on its eastern side (close to China's Qing empire) and on its western side (where it incorporated territories of the declining Ottoman Empire). This led to a powerful rivalry, called the "Great Game," between the British Empire and the Russian Empire. The Great Game later drew in Japan. The modernizing Japanese nation joined the Western imperialists in the last two decades before World War I, colonizing Taiwan and Korea and aligning itself with England.

The changing global configuration of power, accompanied by the challenge from Europe and the United States presented in the form of treaties that denied China, Korea, and Japan diplomatic, economic, and legal equality with the West, inspired many East Asians to attempt to modernize their societies to withstand imperialist threats. Modernity came in many forms in this half century, and these changes were often as stunning in their countries of origin as they were in East Asia. Armaments became far more deadly, inspiring both pride in one's country's success at using those armaments and resistance to war by transnational peace movements, many of whose members were women. Movements of people and ideas were radically accelerated by railroads, automobiles, airplanes, transoceanic steamships, telegraph lines, telephones, and mass-circulation newspapers. Higher levels of education helped to transmit ideas and create citizens, men and women alike, who demanded greater rights. Public health became a national project in industrialized and industrializing countries, and new understandings of the role of germs in transmitting diseases led to urban sewage systems and to antisepsis in hospitals, among other improvements. Electricity was harnessed for power in the late nineteenth century, and electric lighting turned night into day, a change of extraordinary importance. Electricity also ran factories, which had implications for national wealth as well as gender relations, as many women and girls were employed in those factories. It powered trolleys that transported working-class women and men to those jobs and young people to potential marriage partners beyond walking distance from their neighborhoods. East Asian observers of these physical emblems of modernity in the West understood them to be part of the power of the imperialist states.

Gender and sexuality were among the cultural and social aspects of civilizations that may be compared among societies in the half century before World War I. In Western Europe and the United States, mandatory education in the late nineteenth and early twentieth centuries created a supply of women workers for new occupations necessary for the support of industrializing states, such as in teaching, nursing, office work, and sales. Just as with the industrial jobs and domestic service jobs that employed working-class women, these middle-class jobs also represented a gendered division of labor. To be sure, the content of girls' and boys' education continued to be different in most of the West throughout the nineteenth century, with, for example, girls more likely to attend religious schools (in France) or study homemaking (in the United States and elsewhere). Western missionaries founded schools for girls around the world, where they stressed Western practices and ideas about motherhood, the family, and sexual purity alongside literacy, geography, and arithmetic. In both Western countries and their colonial offshoots, boys and girls were supposed to be educated, whether in states' mass education systems or in private and religious schools, to become loyal and obedient state subjects and company employees.

But education increasingly led women, working-class people, and minorities to question legal inferiority in law and social customs. In some cases, that inferiority actually worsened during the nineteenth century, as in the case of married women's loss of the right to make contracts in Mexico in 1870, several decades after that country gained independence from Spain. With few exceptions (notably New Jersey from 1790 to 1807), European and American legal systems did not grant the rights of citizenship to women until the early twentieth century. Only in a few limited areas, where middle-class white women demanded the vote as part of their role in nation and empire building, did women gain the vote (Wyoming, Utah, Idaho, and Colorado in the United States between 1869 and 1893; New Zealand in 1893; and Australia in 1902). Elsewhere biology defined women's rights in the nineteenth century. The Napoleonic Code of 1804 placed French wives under the control of their husbands. Although notions of marital companionship and spiritual equality had come to be the norm in Western societies by the end of the eighteenth century, the law of coverture required that wives be legally subordinate to their husbands in England and the United States.

Exposure through education to the rhetoric of a better and more just society (often one in which women "tamed" men through their sexual and ethical purity) led women to respond to their subordination in several different ways beginning in the middle of the nineteenth century. In some areas these responses took the form of periodicals that advocated for women's rights, such as Egypt's *Al Fatah* (*The Young Woman,* 1892) or the numerous women's periodicals published in Bengali, Hindi, English, Urdu, and Gujarati in colonial India beginning in the 1880s. Islamic women in Cairo, Istanbul, and Tehran published journals from the 1890s on that stressed women's "awakening." Women's journals in the West, both stand-alone periodicals and newsletters of feminist organizations, are too numerous to list here.

The other type of reaction was political activism through movements—women demanding the end of legal restrictions such as coverture and the promotion of civil rights and social/marital equality. These movements were not exclusively undertaken by middle-class and elite women, but as in the case of women whose literacy allowed them to publish periodicals, educated women were more likely to be involved. When a desire for improved status of women evolved into a movement, it became what we call "feminism." That term has changed its meaning over time and now is also used in circumstances that are not necessarily centered on social and political rights. The best definition is perhaps that of historian Estelle Freedman: "Feminism is a belief that women and men are inherently of equal worth. Because most societies privilege men as a group, social movements are necessary to achieve equality between women and men, with the understanding that gender always intersects with other hierarchies" (Freedman 2002, 7). The word itself originated in France in the 1830s and was first used in English in 1895. By 1910, Japanese women's rights advocates discussed the English usage of the term.

In the seventeenth century, some advocates for improving the status of women in England linked that improvement to women's education; with education, they contended, women would have the tools to be full-fledged members of their society. These ideas were expanded in the Americas (by Anne Hutchison in the seventeenth century and Abigail Adams in the eighteenth), in France (by Olympe de Gouges's famous *Declaration of the Rights of Woman and the Female Citizen* in 1791), and in England (by Mary Wollstonecraft's *A Vindication of the Rights of Women*, 1792), among many others. But it was the nineteenth century that gave birth to feminist movements for full civil rights. Women organized for rights in various places in the world, and the American movement begun in 1848 at Seneca Falls, New York, is arguably the most representative of these nineteenth-century movements. The feminist movement developed alongside other social reform movements, such as the antislavery movement and family reform movement, many of which were inspired by reformist Christianity. For the next seventy years, until women gained the vote in the United States (1920), the movement that began at Seneca Falls divided into contesting factions over issues of maternalism versus individualism and feminists' classism and racism (the failure of educated white women to see that they were ignoring the rights of working-class women and women of color by basing their arguments for their own rights on their often better education). By the turn of the twentieth century, women's support for full civil rights was not yet universal, but all sorts of organizations, using divergent tactics, had adopted feminist goals, most significantly Christian reformist organizations such as the Woman's Christian Temperance Union (WCTU) and the Young Women's Christian Association (YWCA). These groups also had evangelistic strategies and would influence women around the world, especially in East Asia.

JAPAN

The Tokugawa government in Japan became increasingly concerned about the world outside their borders by the middle of the nineteenth century. The new manufacturing-based wealth of Europe and the United States following the Industrial Revolution and the increasing speed of sea travel intensified Western pressure on East Asia to expand trade and formal diplomatic relations. Throughout the Tokugawa period, Japan had maintained trade relations with China, Korea, Holland, and the Ryūkyū Islands. Beginning in the late eighteenth century, the Russians, Americans, French, and British tried unsuccessfully to add themselves to that list by opening relations with Japan. In 1853, Commodore Matthew Perry of the U.S. Navy sailed four gunboats into a bay near the shogun's capital at Edo. He returned in 1854 to sign a treaty that opened several ports to the Americans. A decade earlier, the great Qing empire had unexpectedly been defeated by the British in the Opium War. This frightened the shogun's government into negotiating with the Americans.

Four years later, the Americans forced Japan to sign a more significant trade treaty that granted the United States wide-ranging trade concessions. This agreement, similar to those imposed on the Qing after the Opium War, treated Japan and its cosigner unequally. Soon other Western powers signed similar treaties, gaining comparable concessions from Japan that remained in place until they were renegotiated in the 1890s and 1900s. These treaties gave the Western nations the right to set Japan's tariffs and exempted foreigners from Japanese laws, a policy called extraterritoriality.

In the decades before these humiliating treaties, domestic problems had emerged in Japan. Crop failures produced famines, and the social changes described in Chapter 3 were eroding cooperation among villagers. Urban uprisings and village riots erupted in many areas. The unequal treaties of the late 1850s had led to a disastrous currency outflow. Japan temporarily benefited from silkworm blight in Europe in 1868. Japanese silk, produced by farm girls and women, filled the European demand for silk, but even this boom in trade was insufficient to offset the economic consequences of the unequal treaties. Anti-Tokugawa forces arose in the late 1860s as a result of foreign pressures and domestic troubles. After a brief military struggle, these forces overthrew the Tokugawa and proclaimed the restoration of the emperor, who had been powerless for more than six hundred years.

The period from the establishment of the new government in 1868 to the death in 1912 of Japan's first emperor of the modern era—the emperor Meiji—is called the Meiji period. Japan's new leaders embarked on modernizing the country to defend themselves against Western imperialism. They developed a modern monarchy like those in many European countries at the time (in practice, the Japanese emperor was relatively powerless despite his "restoration"). By 1912, Japan became one of the world's leading economics and a Pacific power.

Creating a New Society

Government and private-sector leaders as well as average people throughout Japan created new economic systems, developed new discourses of citizenship, ended the old Tokugawa status groups, redefined relations with the outside world, and studied and selectively borrowed ideas from abroad. The government was keenly interested in the construction of new types of citizen-subjects to serve the new nation. These citizens embodied new definitions of masculinities and femininities. The construction of gender and sexuality was deeply connected to the development of the modern state and economy in a global context.

The leadership group in 1868 was small and composed overwhelmingly of young men (mostly under age thirty-five) of samurai background. But many other Japanese also worked to change their society. Advocates and opponents of modernization, supporters of changes in Japan's foreign and cultural relations with the world, and enthusiasts of foreign cultures, arts, and technologies all joined public discussions in the late nineteenth century. For the first time, many felt liberated to voice their opinions. This worried the new government, which created laws to limit free speech. Many people struggled for the right to contribute to public discussions, and some of those who demanded a voice were women.

The young leaders moved quickly to mold a nation-state out of the Tokugawa-era society, which had been divided vertically into separate domains and horizontally into status groups. Although imperialism like that inflicted by Western powers on China no longer worried Japan's leaders by the early 1870s, the continuing humiliation of the unequal treaties inspired them to strengthen Japan in the competitive international context by adopting changes to persuade the West to renegotiate the treaties.

But would adopting Western ways to achieve respect destroy Japan's identity? Some Japanese held that view, while others called for adopting foreign culture and ideas they called "civilization and enlightenment" (*bunmei kaika*). Supporters of "civilization and enlightenment" borrowed foreign texts, ideologies, and technologies to help mold a Japanese nation-state, for which a new word, *kokka* (literally, "nation-family"), was coined. The character *ka* (family) paralleled the concept of shared ethnicity that was the foundation of the modern European nation-state. But the term "family" suggested more than shared ethnicity; it also implied gender and community. Thus gender was baked into the construction of the nation from its very beginning.

Japan experienced a torrent of change from 1868 to the mid-1870s. In 1868, the leaders stressed the centrality of the new emperor-centered government by moving the emperor from Kyoto to Edo, which they renamed Tokyo (meaning "eastern capital"). By 1871, the new government converted all domains to prefectures under direct central rule. The emperor, initially represented as a "perfumed Mikado" in ancient court dress—a style Westerners viewed as "effeminate"—was portrayed in an 1873 official photograph wearing the military uniform of a European king, "arrayed in the symbols used to endow Western monarchs with emblematic competency and dynastic virility"(Cook 2005, 261). His clothing represented modern masculinity.

Although the emperor and the men who emulated him clothed themselves in Western masculine garb, Westerners continued to view Japan itself in gendered terms—that is, as "feminine" in contrast to the West's manliness—until Japan won two foreign wars, the Sino-Japanese War (1894–1895) and the Russo-Japanese War (1904–1905). Numerous studies of colonialism show that this gendered attitude was not limited to Japan; it was common for nineteenth-century Westerners to imagine Asian societies, including their men, as feminine. Japan was portrayed as feminine (and therefore weak) in a variety of ways, including art and culture. Giacomo Puccini's opera *Madam Butterfly* (1904), which depicted a Japanese woman victimized by her American lover, exemplifies this attitude. To be sure, the Japanese adopted a similar gender binary themselves. Artistic images of China's surrender to Japan in the Sino-Japanese War showed Japanese officers wearing their Western-style uniforms in a posture of manliness, connoting strength; Chinese officers' long robes presented a more feminine aspect, intended to suggest weakness.

Gendering New State Institutions

In March 1868, the leadership group developed a set of broad objectives that would later be developed into more specific policies. These objectives called for establishing deliberative assemblies, eliminating class- and status-based restrictions on people's occupations, rejecting what they called "evil customs of the past," and searching for knowledge throughout the world to strengthen imperial rule.

The government acted on the first objective within a few months, creating the short-lived National Deliberative Assembly. Elected prefectural assemblies were established in 1878 and a national parliament (called the Diet, *kokkai* in Japanese) in 1890. The elimination of status-based restrictions made the other changes possible. The leaders decided that rule through Tokugawa-style status groups had prevented the formation of a modern state. Thus they eliminated the status system to allow men (though not women) to pursue their own callings and, more immediately important, to save the government vast sums of money by ending the payments to samurai that had continued since the early seventeenth century. In 1873, the government began to terminate those payments and simultaneously prohibited the wearing of samurai swords. This double blow to the samurai's sense of manhood was more than some could bear. Although most quietly entered new types of work, a number rebelled violently against the new government.

That same year, yet another government decision angered many samurai. Concerned about Japan's strategic vulnerability vis-à-vis the West, the government created a European-style military staffed by male conscripts. But thousands of commoners, previously exempt from service, protested by attacking military registration centers in 1873 and 1874, and samurai complained about the loss of prestige they suffered by sharing their right to bear arms with those they called "dirt farmers." Despite this resistance, a surprisingly small percentage of young Japanese men—fewer than 5 percent of those eligible before the Sino-Japanese War and about 10 percent after that war—were actually drafted. Although few were conscripted, Japanese political observers at that time remarked on the growth of soldiers' commitment to the nation and of their desire for citizenship rights, while foreign commentators praised Japan for abandoning "effeminacy" and adopting masculine military discipline. These observations reflected contemporary commentators' linkage of the construction of Japanese masculinity through military conscription to the construction of the modern nation and the strengthening of Japan's international standing.

The institution of public education also generated debate. In 1872, the government required four years of elementary schooling for all children. Although elementary schools were coeducational, middle schools and secondary schools were sex-segregated. Public universities were open only to male students. Schools were required to teach practical subjects to all children. For boys, this meant science, math, Japanese language, history, and ethics. Girls also had to take sewing classes, leaving them fewer hours for academic subjects.

Not all educators agreed that sewing classes were practical. Tsuda Umeko (1864–1929), for one, stressed science and English as important tools for women to be able to serve society. One of five girls selected in 1871 to study in the United States, Tsuda, six years old when placed in an American family, returned to Japan a dedicated educator. But by the time she returned, the government's approach to women's education had shifted to creating "good wives, wise mothers" (*ryōsai kenbo*), the Japanese counterpart of America's nineteenth-century "republican mothers," tasked with training their sons to become productive citizens of the new nation. Tsuda's interest in science, religion (Christianity), and language no longer fit the government's model of education for girls, so she created a private school that offered women rigorous training in English. Other educators followed in her footsteps, creating schools of medicine and other practical subjects for girls.

While many children and their parents enthusiastically viewed education as the route to personal opportunity, others resisted sending their economically valuable children to school and paying taxes to fund local education. Rioters burned thousands of elementary schools during the 1870s. By the end of the 1890s, however, 98 percent of boys and 93 percent of girls attended school, and the state reached its goal of an educated, disciplined populace.

The effect of educating the entire population was significant. A literate workforce increased productivity. The state could directly convey the responsibilities of imperial subjects to all men and women. Literacy, together with the launching of hundreds of newspapers and magazines, allowed Japanese to overcome regionalism and to seek knowledge throughout the world. But educated men and women could—and did—demand rights of citizenship, something feared by conservatives in the government. Indeed, advocates of women's rights in the 1880s drew a direct line between women's education and women's development as full, competent persons.

Gender and Rights

In a modern democracy, the state defines individuals as citizens, which implies the possession of rights, including the right to protection as a member of the national community and the right to exercise the same political rights granted other citizens. Today we assume all individuals should have equal rights. In the eighteenth and nineteenth centuries, however, many Western countries granted rights of citizenship based on one's ability to carry out military service. In those countries, this differentiated men from women. In Japan, military service did not guarantee all men citizenship rights, as men who did not pay sufficient taxes were not allowed to vote until 1925. Japanese women in feminist movements in the late nineteenth and early twentieth centuries used arguments developed in Europe and the United States to advocate for rights, but they, too, failed to obtain full citizenship rights until the mid-twentieth century.

The earliest demands for rights accompanied economic changes. In the Tokugawa period, commerce had been officially disdained, although both officials and commoners had welcomed its benefits. It took faith in modernity for Meiji-era Japanese to support economic development. But few had personal wealth, so the government invested in telegraph lines (1869), a postal service (1871), harbors and lighthouses, and Japan's first railroad, from Tokyo to Yokohama (1872). The government set up production in textiles, ships, mining, munitions, and consumer goods, building factories that served as demonstration plants before being sold off. All this development, in addition to public education and the new military, cost a lot of money.

Dependable revenue sources were needed. Consumer goods were taxed, but agricultural taxes were the greatest sources of government income. Many farmers protested this tax, and its implementation was one of the reasons for antigovernment political activism in the 1870s. The tax was paid by the head of household, usually the senior male, although a small number of families were headed by women. In 1878, when the government extended the right to vote in local elections to taxpaying heads of households, some women tried to claim that right. One of them was Kusunose Kita (1836–1920), a forty-two-year-old widowed household head, who petitioned for the right to vote in local elections. The government denied her request, and she appealed that decision. Women's rights advocates, who called her the "people's rights grandma," contended that she should not be taxed without representation and protested the use of gender in establishing an individual's relationship to the state (Sievers 1983, 30). While Kusunose failed to gain the vote in 1878, women continued to advocate for rights into the mid-twentieth century.

The earliest advocates for women's rights were part of a larger People's Rights Movement, most but not all of whose members were men. The People's Rights Movement began as a reaction to what some supporters of "civilization and enlightenment" considered government authoritarianism in the early 1870s. In 1871, some of the most powerful men in the government took off for an eighteen-month tour of Europe and America, with the goals of renegotiating the unequal treaties and learning about modern Western institutions. When they heard in 1873 that the officials who had remained in Tokyo to run the government were planning to send a military expedition to Korea to force it to expand foreign contacts (as Perry had done in Japan twenty years earlier), they rushed home to stop the proposed invasion, believing that Japan should not pursue an aggressive foreign policy before completing reforms at home.

Calling the returning officials dictators who silenced the voice of the Japanese people, two of the men who had stayed in Tokyo, Saigō Takamori and Itagaki Taisuke, resigned from the government. Saigō responded to the "dictatorial" officials with armed insurrection. He returned to his far western prefecture (formerly Satsuma) and opened a military academy to train soldiers in the old ways of samurai manhood. In 1877 he raised an army, eventually numbering forty thousand, and attacked a government garrison. In three weeks of combat, Saigō's forces suffered twenty thousand casualties. Saigō committed suicide rather than allow himself to be captured by the conscript army he pejoratively called "dirt farmers."

Unlike Saigō, Itagaki Taisuke went home and founded Japan's first political party. This was part of the nascent People's Rights Movement. The ideas of Jean-Jacques Rousseau and John Stuart Mill, among others, inspired advocates for human and civil rights. By reforming Japan's political and social systems, People's Rights Movement advocates contended, Japan could create a modern society and claim equality with the foreigners. In 1873, men who advocated modernization created the Meiji Six Society and began publishing a journal with articles on civil rights, women's role in the new Japan, family life, and other issues of modernity, ideology, and daily life. For the rest of the decade, political groups emerged throughout the country.

Many of these groups included the neologism "rights" in their name and agenda. The concept of rights was an import from the West, and no term initially existed for it in East Asian languages. Japanese rights advocates found useful the Chinese term *quanli* (pronounced "kenri" in Japanese), coined by the American missionary and translator W. A. P. Martin to mean "rights" in his Chinese translations of Western legal texts, and they adopted it. Japanese progressives then used the character *ken* (*quan*) to devise additional neologisms such as *danjo dōken* (male-female equal rights) and *joken* (women's rights). In a kind of reverse transmission of ideas common in the late nineteenth century, Chinese and Korean progressives soon adopted their own languages' pronunciations of the characters used for concepts of women's rights, people's rights (*minken*), and other forms of rights coined in Japan (Molony 2010, 94).

The Japanese government supported modernization but feared the People's Rights Movement. In 1875 it imposed press censorship laws, and in 1883 Kishida Toshiko (c. 1861–1901), a feminist orator and People's Rights Movement member, was arrested for publicly calling for women's rights. Kishida inspired women all over Japan. Thousands of men and women heard her proclaim that women's equality in society and the family was an indicator of civilization, and that equality would elevate Japan in international eyes. After her arrest, Kishida returned briefly to public speaking, but she soon abandoned it for essay writing—mainly in the influential feminist journal *Jogaku zasshi* (*Women's Education Magazine*)—and teaching. One of those inspired by Kishida was Fukuda Hideko (1865–1927). Fukuda created a women's organization to bring in women's rights speakers, for which the authorities punished her by shutting down the school she and her mother established for boys ages six to ten and girls and women ages six to sixty. This did not stop her. In the first decade of the twentieth century, she worked with antiwar and socialist men and women and was the founding editor (in 1907) of the feminist newspaper *Sekai fujin* (*Women of the World*).

Repression of women's and men's speech occurred throughout the 1870s and 1880s, leading to demands for a constitution and greater rights of political representation. By 1881, more than 250,000 signatures were submitted to the government calling for a constitution. Government leaders themselves also desired a constitution, since the Western powers all had them. The Meiji constitution, the first constitution outside Europe and America, was presented to the people as a gift of the emperor in 1889. It was not a progressive document, however. Modeled on the conservative constitution of Prussia (after 1871 a part of Germany), Japan's constitution made the emperor sovereign, and, erasing a history of women sovereigns, codified for the first time in Japan's history that the emperor must be male. The constitution established a Diet with an elected House of Representatives and a mostly appointed House of Peers (aristocratic men). It set up a powerful bureaucracy and exempted the military from parliamentary oversight.

The constitution included some civil rights but stipulated that they could be limited by law. The government began creating those limits immediately. First they restricted women who wished to observe parliamentary sessions

BOX 4.1

Kishida Toshiko and Women's Rights

One of the articles Kishida published after she abandoned public speaking was a powerful demand for equality entitled "To My Brothers and Sisters," which appeared in a Tokyo newspaper in 1884. She wrote:

> *In ancient times there were various evil teachings and customs in our country, things that would make the people of any free, civilized nation terribly ashamed. Of these, the most reprehensible was the practice of "respecting men and despising women." . . . We are trying, through a cooperative effort, to build a new society. That is why I speak of equality and equal rights. (Sievers 1983, 38)*

to an upper balcony of the Diet. The following year (1890) another law prohibited women from joining political parties or attending political rallies, thereby denying them the rights of speech and assembly. This prohibition was continued in 1900 as part of the Public Peace Police Law. That law's infamous Article 5, which restricted women's rights, would become the target of women's activism for the next two decades. By the end of the decade of the 1890s, women's rights were further limited by the Civil Code. Under this code, all members of a household (*ie*), including the wife, were subordinated to the head of household. Japanese were registered with the state as members of a household rather than as individuals.

Inequality between men and women in the family was the most important stimulus for feminist actions in the late nineteenth century. Although women could no longer agitate for political rights with the spoken word, they had more flexibility with the written word. During the next several decades, women published numerous articles calling for equality in the family and women's rights in the public sphere.

Supporters of women's rights expressed profound disappointment with the gendered legal restrictions on rights. Novelist Shimizu Toyoko (1868–1933) articulated these disappointments in her article "To My Beloved Sisters in Tears," published in *Jogaku zasshi* in 1890 (Sievers 1983, 101). Members of the Japan Woman's Christian Temperance Union (JWCTU), founded in 1886 as a branch of the transnational WCTU, were also distressed by the codification of inequality, but recognized that women's organizing to overturn the limits on political expression was itself prohibited. Interestingly, their focus on social reforms, including campaigns against licensed prostitution, polygamy (Japanese men were legally allowed just one wife but many had legally recognized concubines at that time), and alcohol consumption, appeared less overtly political to the authorities. These morality-based movements were therefore within the bounds of the law. Moreover, the Christian organizations that supported these reforms framed them in the patriotic terms of elevating the status of the nation by improving the status of women (Lublin 2010).

Other women's organizations emerged in the first decade of the twentieth century. On the conservative, nationalistic side, the Aikoku Fujinkai (Patriotic Women's Association), established in 1901, offered comfort to wounded soldiers and solace to the families of Japan's war dead. Some of the members of this organization were also members of more rights-focused groups such as the JWCTU. On the other end of the political spectrum, some advocates for women's rights joined antiwar and socialist movements. A group of women within a larger antiwar socialist and Christian group that emerged in 1903 (the year before the Russo-Japanese War started) persuaded the Diet to take up the question of amending Article 5 to allow women to speak and assemble publicly in 1907. Their activities were chronicled in the pages of *Sekai Fujin* (Fukuda Hideko was one of their members) until that newspaper died in 1909 due to government repression. But the conservative House of Peers repeatedly rejected the proposed amendment of Article 5 until the early 1920s.

Another important antiwar feminist was the poet Yosano Akiko (1878–1942), one of Japan's leading literary figures. During the Russo-Japanese War, she wrote a famous poem begging her brother not to fight: "Brother, do not give your life," she wrote. "His Majesty the Emperor goes not himself into the battle" (Rabson 1991, 46). In the years after that war, women trod the stage in feminist plays such as Henrik Ibsen's *A Doll's House*, which shocked viewers. Numerous women entered classrooms as teachers and hospitals as nurses, the latter profession encouraged by the need for battlefield nurses in the Russo-Japanese War. Middle-class and working-class women gained mobility with bicycles, trolleys, and trains. Japan's New Woman was beginning to come into her own. In 1911, Hiratsuka Raichō (1886–1972) began publishing *Seitō* (Bluestocking), which highlighted the work of members of the Bluestocking Society and other educated feminists. The journal included Hiratsuka's famous "Feminist Manifesto" of 1911: "In the beginning, woman was the sun," suggesting the powerful image of the Sun Goddess, the mythical founder of Japan's imperial family (Hiratsuka 2006, vii).

Japan's victory in the Sino-Japanese War impressed the West and accelerated the process of treaty revision. Most important, defeating China fundamentally altered Japan's position in East Asia, making it one of the imperialist powers when it acquired Taiwan as a colony in 1895. A decade later, Japan defeated Russia in a war over geopolitical dominance in Northeast Asia; after that war, Japan controlled the Korean government and in 1910 forced Korea to become its colony. While the Japanese empire expanded and stifled the independence of its neighbors, the new Japanese men and women created by modernization—graduates of the new schools, workers in modern factories, and soldiers returning from overseas wars—demanded a public voice. Ironically, their struggle for inclusion paralleled Japan's quest for international respect through building an empire. The linking of democracy and imperialism, which seems so contradictory to us today, was unquestioned by most late Meiji-era Japanese—as well as by Americans, British, French, and other Europeans whose democracies were also accompanied by their expanding empires at that time.

Gender and Economic Modernity

Japan's leaders planted the seeds of modern economic development in the 1870s and 1880s. The first part of the economy to grow was farming. Farm families were linked to the modernizing state in different ways than urban dwellers were. Poor farmers' small, dark homes did not have the luxuries of modern life enjoyed by the urban and rural rich. Their teenage daughters trudged through snow-covered mountain passes to work in textile mills. The labor of these poor young women—in 1900, women were more than 80 percent of textile workers and 15 percent of mine workers—linked Japan to European, American, Chinese, and Korean markets.

Both the silk and cotton industries employed young rural women, but the conditions of work and the technologies of these two sectors differed. Many silk mills were located in the countryside, where silkworms were raised. Young girls, most in their mid-teens and with little education, worked shifts as long as eighteen hours a day. The mills closed down for two months in winter, and the girls returned home for those months. Their fathers or elder brothers stamped (the Japanese equivalent of signing) the girls' ten-month contracts because under Japanese law at that time, male family heads had to sign contracts for their family members.

Company recruiters scoured the countryside for families willing to send daughters to the mills. The girls' families received an advance from the recruiters, often the families' largest cash income, for the workers' indentured labor. Workers lived in dormitories, wore work uniforms, and earned between 10 and 30 sen per day (US$ 0.05–0.15), from which they had to pay for their own meals. Disease spread easily in the dormitories, most terrifyingly tuberculosis, incurable at that time. Transmission of disease to the girls' villages linked farm and factory when the factories' sick workers returned home.

Silk reeling was the first mechanized industry in Japan. But the mechanization process remained highly dependent on skilled manual labor. Before mechanization, the worker dropped living cocoons into boiling water, reached bare-handed into the water to lift them out, and then carefully peeled off a thread from each cocoon, placing the thread on a spool she rotated by hand. Mechanization replaced hand rotation with steam power and, later, electricity. The even rotation of the power-driven mechanized spool made for a finer product, but the difficulty of work increased, as the worker no longer controlled its pace. And mechanization did not eliminate the worst part of silk reeling, which was removing cocoons from boiling water by hand.

Cotton spinning was more mechanized than silk reeling and required less skill. At first workers came from the same villages that supplied silk workers,

Silk workers in a factory owned by Mitsui reach into boiling water to retrieve silk cocoons in the late Meiji period. LIBRARY OF CONGRESS, LC-USZ62-125030

but as the industry grew, recruiters sought girls from impoverished areas in Japan's far northeast and Okinawa in the far south. Cotton workers' contracts were of one to two years' duration, and male heads of household also stamped girls' contracts and received their advance payment. Most workers were interested in helping their families with their earnings. Recruiters promised girls further schooling after work, comfortable dormitories, good meals, clean baths, and the opportunity to enjoy city life.

But these promises were deceptive. Workers were too tired to attend classes after twelve-hour shifts; meals were usually just thin soup and rice, with a bit of fish once a week; baths were lukewarm water covered by a film of body oil; and workers were not permitted to leave the factory until their advance payment had been worked off. Cotton mills ran twenty-four hours a day before 1929, when women and children were prohibited from working between 11:00 p.m. and 5:00 a.m. Companies assigned two girls on alternating twelve-hour shifts a single set of bedding, which led to disease transmission. Tuberculosis infected 20 to 30 percent of workers. Cotton lint, which caused respiratory illnesses, filled the air. Excessive summer heat and winter cold debilitated young workers. If one of their threads broke, they could be punished with a fine or beating.

Many girls sought out factory work despite their parents' fears for their health and safety, especially for their sexual morality. Many felt that work in the factories, especially the cotton mills, would be better than the other jobs available to poor girls and women—farm labor, prostitution, domestic service, and mining. Once at the factory, many workers were not passive; when necessary, they organized resistance. Because they ate and bathed together, they could discuss actions without raising suspicion. Although men dominated the labor movement after the turn of the century and ignored women's pioneering contributions, women organized Japan's first industrial strike, at the Amamiya Silk Mill in 1885. The following year, a much larger group at that mill struck for better pay and work hours that would not require them to walk to work in darkness, which exposed them to possible sexual harassment. Other workers resisted by escaping the factory. A large number of these escapees remained in the cities to seek better jobs, eventually marrying there and contributing to Japan's demographic shift from farm to city.

Workers did not protest their conditions alone. Journalists wrote about workers' terrible conditions beginning in the 1890s, and Christian reformers soon joined them. Government welfare officials reported on the appalling health, welfare, and safety conditions in the mills in 1903. The Diet eventually passed the Factory Law of 1911 to protect women and children from the worst workplace abuses, although businesses persuaded the government to postpone the law's implementation until 1929, claiming that workplace reforms would make Japanese textiles uncompetitive in the global market.

Men, women, and children also worked in coal mines under appalling conditions. Until the Factory Law went into effect, coal miners often worked as couples (in addition to limiting work hours, the law outlawed female and child labor underground). Husbands hewed the coal from the mine face, and wives hauled 100-kilogram tubs of coal through narrow shafts and loaded them into coal cars. Managers preferred married couples, believing this strengthened men's commitment to their jobs. Pregnant women hauled heavy containers until right before childbirth, and some babies were born in the mines. Small children sometimes accompanied their parents, crawling into the tiniest shafts to find extra pieces of coal. Young women who sought cleaner labor could work aboveground sorting coal, but their pay was low—about one-third that of male laborers. Women who worked underground were less educated, more prone to sickness, and more likely to be married than those who worked aboveground, but they earned up to 75 percent of their husbands' wages, excellent pay at that time. Conditions underground in the mines were dangerous, but many women chose higher wages over safety.

Gender and Diaspora in the Modernizing Japanese State

Diaspora accompanied modernity. Between 1868 and 1870 a small number of Japanese sailed to Hawai'i (141 men, 6 women, and 1 child) and to California (a few dozen). Emigration was technically illegal until 1886, but the Japanese government did issue some passports. At first, most emigrants were sojourners—temporary migrants—to Korea, Manchuria, and China. Some went to Hawai'i, where Japanese men worked as indentured laborers on sugar plantations and some women were in the sex trades.

Much larger numbers of women emigrated, many without documents, to East Asia. During the Meiji period, poverty pushed many women from western Japan, especially the Amakusa region, to seek work as prostitutes throughout East Asia (Mihalopoulos 2011). Initially, many went to British colonies in Southeast Asia; later, many went to Korea and Manchuria. Miners and other workers in the British colonies tended to be single men from South China and India, creating a clientele for Japanese sex workers. Young Japanese women either bought tickets or stowed away on ships to Northeast and Southeast Asia, Hawai'i, and the North American Pacific coast. Some had been tricked into sex work by recruiters' promises of factory work. Others went on their own, knowing that sex work awaited them overseas. Without proper papers, many found their way into the brothel districts of port cities. This horrified Japanese consular officials in those areas, who feared that the presence of Japanese sex workers would besmirch the reputation of Japan just as it was trying to persuade the Europeans and Americans that it was modern and civilized. Thus, the Japanese government tried to limit women's emigration to avoid the possibility that many would be sex workers at the same time as Japan was protesting restrictions on Japanese men's immigration to the United States and Canada. But the Japanese government found it hard to control women's emigration. For example, as late as 1917, more than 60 percent of Japanese residents in Singapore were women sex workers.

The U.S. government was also part of the gendered diaspora of Japanese citizens through its attempts to placate white Americans' anti-Asian sentiments. In 1907, without totally outlawing Japanese immigration (that came later; Chinese had been excluded since 1882), the United States severely limited Japanese immigration by class and gender. Under the so-called Gentlemen's Agreement, Japanese working-class men were no longer permitted to immigrate into the United States (a similar Canadian agreement was signed in 1908). As a humanitarian gesture, family members were allowed to join husbands and fathers already in the United States. Unlike prostitutes, wives from Japan, many of them married by proxy—which was legal in Japan at that time—were allowed into the United States. (They were called "picture brides," but this is something of a misnomer, as the wedding ceremony was conducted in Japan using a picture of the groom rather than the bride, although the groom usually saw a picture of his future wife before the wedding as well.) Their American-born children were U.S. citizens, and this exacerbated racist sentiment in California. After 1924, no East Asians were permitted to immigrate to the United States.

KOREA

From Isolation to Engagement with the World

The Chosŏn dynasty was remarkably resilient, although the five-century-long Neo-Confucian social order that defined the dynasty was beginning to erode at the dawn of the nineteenth century, as discussed in Chapter 3. However, the final blow to Chosŏn came in the last third of the nineteenth century when full-fledged, powerful challenges stemming from both internal and external forces fundamentally destabilized the already weakened dynasty and forced it to make the transition into the modern era.

As noted in Chapter 3, the premises of the Chosŏn social order were being subverted by a variety of forces. Political corruption at all administrative levels and economic distress resulted in frequent peasant rebellions, the best-known of these being the Chinju Uprising of 1862 in the southern provinces (Kim 2007). The growing popularity of new religions, such as Catholicism and Tonghak (Eastern Learning), presented more attractive philosophical alternatives to the Neo-Confucian moral order.

In addition to these pressures from within, Western countries started to demand that Korea open its doors for trade and diplomacy. The intervention that China suffered after the First Opium War (1839–1842) and the Second Opium War (1856–1860) served as a cautionary tale of the dangers of contact with those Western countries. To avoid a similar fate, the Chosŏn government under the Taewŏn'gun—the father of the young king Kojong (r. 1864–1907)—insisted on an isolation policy, refusing to enter into trade relationships with foreign countries.

Another response to what many in Korea saw as undue external influence was the harsh policies that Chosŏn instituted to slow the spread of Catholicism. In one notorious case, nine French priests and about eight thousand Korean converts were martyred. In what is known in Korea as the Foreign Disturbance of 1866 (*pyŏngin yangyo*), the French launched a military response, which Korean forces turned back. In that same year an American merchant ship, the *General Sherman*, appeared on the Taedong River in P'yŏngyang. Feeling threatened, villagers and soldiers banded together to attack the ship, setting it afire and killing all aboard. Five years later, the U.S. government used this incident as a pretext for dispatching five warships to the Kanghwa Strait to demand that Korea open its doors. In this incident, called the Foreign Disturbance of 1871 (*sinmi yangyo*), Korean troops were again able to repel the foreign military force. To be sure, the Koreans were resolute in defending themselves against foreign incursions; however, it should be borne in mind that both the French and American governments decided to withdraw from the peninsula rather than engage further, as they were more concerned about their interests in other parts of the world and chose to retreat from Korea rather than invest time and resources there. At the time France was preoccupied by concerns about controlling Annam (Vietnam), while the United States had its priorities oriented toward the settlement and economic development of its western regions after the Civil War. Nonetheless, their victories in these "foreign disturbances" gave Korea confidence in its ability to resist foreign powers.

In the meantime, Japan quickly learned the lessons of gunboat diplomacy from its own experience with the 1853 Perry expedition (see the Japan section in this chapter) and embarked on the Meiji Restoration in 1868. In 1875, Japan sent the navy ship *Unyō* to the Kanghwa area in an effort to force Korea to recognize the authority of the Japanese emperor and the new government. Korean soldiers fired upon the ship. The incident provided Japan with cover to demand that Korea enter into treaty negotiations. In 1876, despite strong opposition from the majority of its own high officials, Korea entered into the Treaty of Kanghwa with Japan, its first modern treaty. The terms of the treaty were not equal in that, among other things, it allowed Japan to exercise extraterritoriality in the open ports in Korea (Pusan, Inch'ŏn, and Wŏnsan), meaning that Japanese settlers were exempt from Korean law and subject only to Japanese law.

Korea's transition from the isolation to an "open-door policy" did not go smoothly. Many Confucian scholars encouraged the king to resist "barbarian nations" (Japan and Western countries) in order to preserve orthodox Neo-Confucian precepts. On the other hand, a cadre of scholars and officials put forward proposals that advocated "enlightenment" and encouraged proactive learning from the examples of Japan and the Western countries in the areas of law, science, technology, commerce, and material goods. It is important to note that even those who advocated Western learning did not necessarily accept the superiority of everything Western or modern.

Yu Kilchun (1856–1914), a leading "enlightenment" intellectual who had been educated in Japan and the United States, argued for a balanced approach to the imminent challenges Korea was facing in the late nineteenth century. He wrote: "Enlightenment entails not only learning the advanced skills of others but also preserving what is good and admirable in one's own society. The purpose in learning others' skills is to improve what is already good and admirable in one's own society" (Lee 1996, 344–345).

Korea's engagement with the outside world began at a time when Western imperial expansion was about to reach its height and Japan had begun its rise as a powerful modern nation. The urgency of the need to catch up with other modern nations led to a series of political and social reforms. At the same time, the influx of new and modern ideas from Europe and North America, often via Japan and China, put Korea on a path to reexamine its old customs and moral precepts. Discourse on new, modern forms of masculinity and femininity emerged in the Korean quest to build a stronger nation. The new masculinity idealized physical prowess and a patriotic mind (Tikhonov 2007), a stark contrast to the image of men of the upper class (*yangban*) as weak and effete. The traditional icon of the woman confined to the inner quarters began to be seen as a reflection of national stagnation. In this vein, the "woman question" arose as a key issue in the public discourse on the modern nation-state.

The Woman Question for a Modern Nation

The discourse on "civilization" led by Europeans and Americans generally placed Western nations at the top of a hierarchical order of "civilization." In that discourse, the status of women was used as one criterion in evaluating the level of civilization that a society had achieved. Societies in which women had low status were considered to be inferior. Customs such as child marriage, footbinding, or confinement of women to the inner chambers, which were practiced in some Asian countries, were often cited in Western texts as evidence of inferior, backward societies.

Korea's enlightenment-oriented intellectuals and policy makers, like their contemporaries in Japan, began to reflect on the Neo-Confucian precepts that had placed women in a position subordinate to men. One of those early enlightenment politicians was Pak Yŏnghyo (1861–1939). Pak had helped to organize a coup d'état in 1884, known as *kapsin chŏngbyŏn*, to try to bring about rapid social reforms in Korea; however, within three days the insurrection was put down by the Chinese military under the direction of powerful Korean conservative groups. For his role in the attempted coup, Pak was forced to go into exile in Japan. It was from there that he submitted his 1888 "Memorandum on Domestic and Political Reforms" to the king. The memorandum was the first statement of a new ideal for gender relations that attempted to integrate Confucian ethics and Western ideas and institutions. Pak drew some elements of his reform ideas from classical Confucian teachings; however, his belief in social Darwinist ideas about the evolution of modern society led him to advocate for the equal status of women as a way of bringing greater prosperity to the nation. In addition to explicitly proclaiming the principle of gender equality, he proposed specific policies to enact the principle, including providing equal education for girls and boys after age six, abolishing the concubine system and early marriage, permitting remarriage for widows, and condemning violence against wives and drug-induced abortion.

Some of these proposals were implemented within a decade during the Kabo Reform of 1894 and 1895. The significance of the Kabo Reform in modern gender relations is twofold. First, it was the earliest attempt to provide women with more equitable status and rights and to remove the social traditions that were most inimical to them, such as child marriage and the ban on remarriage for widows. Second, it signaled a shift in the geopolitical dynamics of the region, where the influence of China went into decline while the power of Japan, the United States, and the countries of Europe grew. The reform came about at the conclusion of the Sino-Japanese War (1894–1895), in which Japan defeated China. The two countries entered into the Treaty of Shimonoseki, which officially ended the tributary relationship between China and Korea. The waning of China's influence and the rise in prominence of Japan, America, and Europe helped to expedite the critical reexamination of Confucian-prescribed gender relations.

In addition to the government's efforts to implement policies that would rectify unfair gender practices, newly emerging Korean newspapers played a key role in challenging old gender norms and practices and calling for major transformations. A particularly noteworthy example is *Tongnip sinmun* (*The Independent*, 1896–1899), the first Korean-language newspaper. It was the unofficial organ of the Independence Club, which was a pioneering modern organization led by Sŏ Chaep'il (1864–1951) that pressed for enlightenment-oriented social reforms. *Tongnip sinmun* aimed to introduce modern ideas such as literacy training for both women and men of the lower classes, who had in the past been denied opportunities for education. An editorial essay from April 21, 1896, begins by stating that "the most pitiful being in this world is the Korean woman." It describes the treatment of women in Korea as "barbaric," offering a sharp critique of the Confucian patriarchal social prescriptions that had effectively deprived women of basic rights and human dignity. The essay identifies oppressive customs, such as concubinage, the ban on remarriage for women, and the "inside-outside rule" (*naeoepŏp*; see Chapter 2), as measures that were designed to control women's sexuality and ensure men's dominance over women's lives. Bringing the woman question into the discourse of "civilization and enlightenment," the editorial stresses equal rights for men and women under universal law. This type of discourse led to new ways of thinking about the family and its human relationships. Most prominently, child marriage was condemned, and a full critique of the practice of concubinage promoted the idea of monogamy as the only just marital system.

In addition to newspapers, women's magazines served as an important forum for distributing knowledge about the new roles and responsibilities for women in the modern era. From the earliest examples—*Kajŏng chapchi* (*Home Journal*) and *Yŏja chinam* (*Guide for Women*), founded in 1906 and 1908, respectively—these women's magazines offered information on scientific child rearing, healthy diet, and hygiene, as well as basic knowledge of arithmetic, history, and geography. They also introduced idealized examples of the "wise mother, good wife" from foreign countries. Protestant Christian periodicals published in Korea are another example of print media that contributed to the recasting of gender norms and practices. In addition to presenting theological issues, influential Christian journals such as *Kŭrisdo sinmun* (*The Christian News*, founded in 1897) and *Sinhak wŏlbo* (*Monthly Magazine on Christian Theology*, founded in 1900) also took up social and cultural problems, advocating reforms born out of Christian ethics. Based on the premise that men and women were equal in the eyes of God, writers argued for nondiscriminatory treatment of women, abolition of concubinage, and a woman's right to move freely in the public space.

Educating Women for the Family and the Nation

The most important agenda item in the discourse on gender and civilization was women's education. Intellectuals attributed the low status of Korea in the world hierarchy to women's general ignorance and lack of awareness of world affairs, and they called for women's education as a remedy. However, despite this rhetoric and the growing interest in women's education, the government and the general population were slow to implement formal education for girls and women. Ironically, the first modern educational opportunities for girls and women were offered by Protestant missionaries

An American Mission School circa 1890. Moffett Korea Collection at Princeton Theological Seminary Library

from the United States, Canada, and Australia. In the beginning, Koreans, especially those of the upper class, were not inclined to allow their daughters to go to foreign-run mission schools. As a result, the most accessible pool of potential students for the missionaries' schools were orphan girls or the daughters of impoverished families who were willing to send their children to the mission schools to be assured they would be fed and clothed.

Ewha Girls' School, founded in 1886 by Mary F. Scranton, an American Methodist missionary, was the first educational institution for girls in Korea. Following Ewha, a number of mission schools were established by American, Canadian, and Australian women missionaries from various denominations,, and these filled the gap in women's education until Koreans themselves began to establish schools in the 1900s. The mission schools had clear goals centering on the Christian faith, but they led the way in offering women basic literacy in Korean vernacular (*han'gŭl*), Chinese, English, mathematics, geography, science, and other modern subjects. The leadership role that mission schools took in women's education continued throughout the first half of the twentieth century, producing the first cadre of educated women, who in turn constituted a new class of professional women in education, medicine, journalism, art, and literature. As a result, the vast majority of New Women (*sin yŏsŏng*) in colonial-era Korea (1910–1945) had some kind of connection with Christianity, either as former mission school students or as employees of one of the various mission-related organizations, including the YWCA (see Chapter 5 for further discussion).

Korean women themselves also began to voice their opinion about the importance of education and gender equality. Largely coming from the upper or middle classes in the capital, these women were exposed to new modern knowledge through print media such as *Tongnip sinmun* or their male family members. In particular, "A Circular for the Establishment of a Girls' School," published in *Tongnip sinmun* in 1898, is noteworthy, as it was the first public statement by women that argued that the government should establish a girls' school in order to prepare girls and women for the modern era. Signed by two women, it raised a set of critical questions about the status of women in Korea, and it advocated for women's education based on the idea of gender equality.

The significance of "A Circular" lies in the fact that here in a public pronouncement women had openly expressed their concerns about whether women were adequately prepared for the modern era because of the lack of educational opportunities and the narrow scope of life centered on the home. The expression inspired others to take up the cause. Following models that had been observed in "civilized" countries, women publicly challenged the oppressive gender customs that had been borne out of the high value placed on women's obedience to the men in their lives (father, husband, and son) as well as their purity and chastity. What is perhaps more important is that "A Circular" explicitly pledges fealty to the emperor—following the Independence Club's recommendation that the Korean king be recoronated as an emperor in 1897—and presents its agenda as being in the interest of the national prosperity, stating: "We 20 million people should faithfully embrace the will of the Emperor by abandoning indolent old customs and emulating new ways of enlightenment." In this way, the authors of "A Circular for the Establishment of a Girls' School" aligned their movement with the interests of the nation, linking the necessity of women's education with the national project of enlightenment and modernization.

The piece drew a great deal of attention from intellectuals and reform-minded policy makers. After reports on the article appeared in newspapers, a group of interested women and men in Seoul were spurred to meet and discuss the founding of a girls' school. Their efforts eventually produced Sunsŏng Girls School, the first private school for girls established by Koreans. To support this school, they organized a society called Ch'anyanghoe, the first women's organization in Korean history. It is estimated that it had a membership of nearly four hundred, largely from the upper class in Seoul. The organization attracted

BOX 4.2

Demanding for a Girls' School

An excerpt from "A Circular for the Establishment of a Girls' School" (1898)

Why is it that we women hang on to old customs like senseless idiots? Who knows? Don't women have capable bodies and working senses? Shouldn't they work? Why should they sit idly by, waiting to be clothed and fed through the labor of men? Why should women allow themselves to be confined to the inner chambers for their entire lives, constrained from any public activity by others? If we look at countries that were civilized earlier than ours, we see that they provided men and women with equal rights. In those countries, women attend school from a young age, attain various levels of learning, and expand their perspectives. When they reach adulthood and get married, they coexist with their husbands as equals for the rest of their lives. They aren't suppressed; to the contrary, they are highly respected. The reason why women in those countries are esteemed rather than oppressed by their husbands is because they learn as much as men and have equal rights. Isn't this beautiful?

Alas, when we reflect on the past, [Korean] men have tried to oppress women in the name of the so-called classics that teach women not to talk about the outside world, to dedicate themselves only to making food and drink. Why should women allow themselves to be removed from life and kept ignorant of world affairs by men when there is no difference between men and women? It is time for us to eradicate old customs and strive for enlightenment and progress (Tongnip sinmun, *September 9, 1898).*

support not only from Korean women but also from some prominent Korean dignitaries and foreign residents, who offered donations, advice, and free lectures at weekly meetings. It also acted strategically to keep its agenda in the public consciousness. For instance, it organized a demonstration in which about one hundred members of the organization kneeled in front of the Royal Palace to convince the government to start a public girls' school. The government rejected this plea, claiming that no funds were available for the undertaking. In this connection, it is important to note that Ch'anyanghoe had a close working relationship with the progressive Independence Club, which had been forced to shut down in 1899 after being charged with sedition. The government's decision not to support the girls' school may very well have been motivated by its antagonism toward progressive groups rather than its concern over costs. Ch'anyanghoe itself had disbanded by 1901; however, despite its brief history, the group was a key force in an incipient women's movement in modern-era Korea that challenged oppressive social practices, demanded equal opportunities for education and a decent life, and demonstrated the strong desire on the part of women to join in the efforts to build a modern nation.

Women in the Patriotic Enlightenment Movement

The discourse on women's education reached its height when Korea became a protectorate of Japan in 1905 as a result of the Russo-Japanese War (1904–1905). Japan actively intervened in the internal governance of the country, and Korean sovereignty in representing itself in the world was only nominal. In 1907, King Kojong (r. 1864–1907) secretly dispatched Korean envoys to the Second Hague Peace Conference to make an appeal to the assembled countries to do something to address the injustice that Japan had perpetrated on Korea. When that secret mission was discovered, Japan forced Kojong to abdicate the throne and installed his son Sunjong (r. 1907–1910) as a puppet, thereby taking tighter control of all aspects of governing in Korea.

The period between 1905 and 1910, the year Korea officially became a Japanese colony, is often called the era of "patriotic enlightenment" (*aeguk kaemong*). At that time a number of patriotic movements erupted, ranging from military resistance by bands of guerrillas (known as "righteous armies") to groups focused on specific social and economic reforms. There is some evidence indicating that women participated in the military resistance, providing assistance to the guerrillas behind the front lines by preparing food, caring for the wounded, and raising funds. However, women were most prominently visible in social movements for women's education. Education became a national priority. People believed that modern education would save the nation from Japanese aggression and turn the country into a strong modern state. In that regard, there was a growing sense that fostering good mothers and wives would be crucial for building the new nation, and in the interest of preparing young women to fulfill that role, the cause of education for women was more broadly adopted. As a result, the number of schools for girls and women grew rapidly in that period.

The life trajectory of Ha Nansa (1868–1919) dramatically captures the exceptionally close ties between women's education and patriotism. Ha was born in P'yŏngyang in 1875 and later became a second wife to a government official. When she sought to enroll at Ewha Girls' School in Seoul, she was refused admission because she was a married woman. Undeterred, she arranged to meet one evening with Lulu Frey, an American missionary teacher at Ewha. In the middle of that meeting, she blew out the lantern and reportedly told Frey, "Our country is stuck in darkness, just like this. To bring light we mothers need to learn so that we can teach our children. If you do not admit me, how can I help my children?" Impressed by Ha's seriousness and determination, the missionary teachers decided to admit her in 1896. In 1900, eager to continue her education beyond what she had learned at Ewha, she went to Japan for a year to study, and then in 1902, with financial support from her husband, she went to the United States to enroll in college. She received a degree from Ohio Wesleyan University in 1906, becoming the first Korean woman to obtain a bachelor's degree from an American university. After returning to Korea, Ha taught at Ewha and local churches, becoming an inspiration for girls and women of all classes. She also became involved in the independence movement. She was chosen to be a delegate to the Paris Peace Conference in 1919. She embarked on the trip to Paris, making a planned stopover in Beijing, where she died suddenly under circumstances that remain mysterious (Choi 2009a, 93–94).

Like Ha Nansa, a small number of Korean women undertook advanced-level study overseas—mainly in Japan and the United States—pioneering a new path for future generations of women. Women who had acquired modern knowledge were highly esteemed, and their accomplishments were lauded within the context of the strong desire for national strength and independence. This new attitude can be seen in the public celebration in 1909 of three women who had studied overseas: Ha Nansa; Pak Esther, the first Korean woman to receive a medical degree from the United States; and Yun Chŏngwŏn, one of the first Korean women to study in Japan. This celebration was something of a media event of that time, with more than seven hundred luminaries invited to take part.

Beyond the accomplishments of those contemporary Korean women, writers and intellectuals were eager to bring the inspirational stories of patriotic women from around the world to the Korean public, so they told the life stories of such figures as Joan of Arc, a folk heroine in France for her leadership during the Hundred Years' War, and Marie-Jeanne Roland, an influential figure during the French Revolution, among others. These legendary figures were portrayed as active participants in national affairs, serving to construct a new image of women as citizens (*kungmin*) and patriots, and they were presented to the Korean public as models for Korean women to emulate (Hyun 2003).

Korea's future in the face of imminent threats from modern Japan nurtured a strong sense of nationalism among the populace. Women were not simply part of the nationalist discourse; they were actively incorporated into actual political participation in the modern era as the "mothers" of male citizens. Group activities for women in the public sphere, such as debates on the topics of women's education and gender equality, began in earnest through the Independence Club. Women also played an active role in the 1907 National Debt Repayment Movement, a nationwide campaign to collect money to pay back loans from Japan. Koreans considered the national debt that it owed Japan to be a great humiliation, and thus it launched various social projects to try to pay off that debt as quickly as possible. These efforts included an antismoking campaign that was organized to encourage people to refrain from smoking and donate the money they saved to the government so the debt could be paid off. In addition, many women donated their family jewelry or money they had earned by sewing, or they participated in a number of small-scale campaigns, including "reducing the number of side dishes" to discourage unnecessary food consumption. The thing that needs to be noted about these campaigns is how women were organized for the national cause, publicly embracing the feeling that they had the same duties and rights to help the nation as men did. Furthermore, women from traditionally despised classes, such as entertainers (*kisaeng*), joined their fellow women, signaling the sense that women from all social classes were uniting to meet nationalist goals.

However, while women began to be incorporated into the public sphere for the sake of the development of the modern nation, it is also clear that women were still locked into their traditional roles in the family structure. In this, we see a number of parallels with Meiji-era Japan. The nation (*kukka*) was understood as an extension of the family, and women made their contribution to the national family by performing the traditional role of wife and mother. As a result, the prevalent focus in women's education was on training girls under the model of the "wise mother, good wife" (*hyŏnmo yangch'ŏ*). The term was first used in 1906 in the mission statement of Yanggyu Ŭisuk, a private school following the Japanese model. Although there were strategic adjustments to changing realities, the ideal of "wise mother, good wife" continued to have a lasting impact throughout the twentieth century—arguably the most powerful gender ideology in twentieth-century Korea. This all-pervasive gender ideology was a modern construct significantly influenced by Korea's traditional Confucian norms of *pudŏk* (womanly virtue); Japan's Meiji gender ideology of *ryōsai kenbo* (good wife, wise mother), which had been transmitted through Japanese colonial education policies; and the Victorian idea of true womanhood that was advocated by American missionaries in Korea (Choi 2009b; Yoo 2008, 85–94).

CHINA

Rebellion and Challenges to Gender Order

In the middle of the nineteenth century, China was racked by three major rebellions that engulfed most of the country. By far the largest and most devastating was launched by Hong Xiuquan, a village schoolteacher from the Hakka ethnic minority in southeastern Guangdong province who repeatedly failed the civil service examinations. In a series of visionary dreams inspired by a Christian tract given to him by a missionary in Canton, he came to see himself as the younger brother of Jesus Christ, destined to return China to an ancient Christian path that had been abandoned for Confucianism. His God-Worshipers Society rapidly attracted a huge popular following across regions of the south beset by economic crisis, social unrest, and disillusionment with the Qing government in the wake of the Opium War. In 1851 he pronounced himself king of the Heavenly Kingdom of Great Peace (Taiping Tianguo) and launched a war against the Qing that would devastate the richest areas of the empire over the next fifteen years. His forces swept up into central China and down the Yangzi River valley to Jiangnan, where the Taipings established a capital in Nanjing from which they launched attacks that brought the civil war almost to Beijing and Shanghai.

Unable to turn the tide against the Taiping army with its own forces, the Qing state commissioned powerful local elites from the regions at the heart of the war, Zeng Guofan from Hunan and Li Hongzhang from Jiangnan, to assemble armies consisting of local militias to defend their regions. After Hong Xiuquan died in 1864, Zeng's Hunan Army captured Nanjing amid great slaughter, and the Heavenly Kingdom fell apart. The Taiping wars were a critical turning point for the dynasty. As many as thirty million people were killed, making this the deadliest civil war in human history. Many of the cities and much of the countryside of central China and the Lower Yangzi region were utterly destroyed, and refugees flooded into the remaining urban centers, most notably Shanghai, which soon became the largest city in China.

As the Taipings attacked the Confucian political order and enacted policies to collectivize property, they presented an unprecedented challenge to Confucian gender order. In the relative calm of occupied Nanjing, they promoted a new version of chastity linked to gender equality and opposed to female seclusion and family patriarchy. They banned footbinding and prostitution, called women into service as officials, laborers, and soldiers, and organized the population into sex-segregated communal quarters separated from their families (Kazuko 1989). Although there were female-led military units, most of their soldiers were essentially rogue males under the direct control of the militarized state.

Amid the fighting, women committed suicide in huge numbers to avoid rape. The civil war destroyed families and communities on a vast scale, leaving behind wastelands filled with corpses. As local elites endeavored to rebuild their communities in the wake of this devastation, veneration of the martyrdom of chaste women and men loyal to the Qing became a crucial mechanism for remembering and reviving the old order and the orthodox values people died to defend (Meyer-Fong 2013).

The chastity cult, which had been a prominent indicator of the state's power to define moral norms (see Chapter 2), became instead a desperate mechanism for emphasizing the legitimacy and importance of the state in the midst of the nearly fatal challenge by the Taipings. The rolls of martyrs canonized by the state ballooned into the tens of thousands, but amid the chaos all pretense of proper vetting to meet state standards of virtue was gone. Despite rhetoric about a revival of orthodox values, full restoration of the old gender order was no longer possible.

The war caused massive displacement and poverty that led to an increase in trafficking of women and girls. As refugees flooded into Shanghai and the urban population swelled, the city developed a huge commercial sex market catering to a diverse array of clients. At the top of its complex hierarchy of prostitution were old-style courtesans catering to wealthy literati and merchants who took up residence there after the war. Lower down in the hierarchy were less educated and cultured women whose clients had less money to spend, and at the very bottom were common prostitutes and streetwalkers whose clients were poor single men drawn in large numbers to find work in what would soon become China's largest and wealthiest city. As this treaty port city with growing numbers of Western residents modernized into a global metropolis over the next few decades, Shanghai prostitutes were a prominent presence in new public spaces: riding in open Western-style carriages, strolling in parks, dining in Western-style restaurants, and attending theaters in the foreign-governed concession areas. They were cultural trendsetters, introducing Western fashions and challenging norms of gender propriety (Yeh 2006).

Western Imperialism and Critique of Chinese Women

At the height of the Taiping wars, in 1856, the British provoked another war with the Qing to force them to fully legalize the opium trade. They occupied the city of Tianjin, next to Beijing, and in the ensuing treaty extracted not only legalization of opium but the right to station Western ambassadors in Beijing, ten new treaty ports, freedom of travel for missionaries in the interior, and millions more taels of silver in reparations (at that time, one tael was worth approximately one U.S. dollar). When the Qing balked at enforcement of these provisions in 1860, British troops occupied the capital and burned the Imperial Summer Palace to the ground, looting palaces and princely residences along the way.

In response to these multiple military threats to the integrity of the empire, Zeng Guofan and Li Hongzhang, who occupied powerful political positions after their success against the Taipings, fostered the Self-Strengthening Movement to respond to Western imperialists by borrowing their methods for military modernization and industrialization focused initially on defense-related heavy industries—shipyards, arsenals, and translation bureaus (to open access to Western scientific and technical knowledge). The limits of this pursuit of "wealth and power," as Self-Strengtheners called it, were revealed when China was defeated in 1895 in the Sino-Japanese War as it tried to prevent its imperialist prerogatives in Korea from being taken over by Japan (see the Japan and Korea sections in this chapter). China's humiliating defeat by a country it had always considered inferior indicated to many reformers that a more radical approach to modernization, like that adopted by Meiji Japan, was essential for China to survive.

Modern Chinese feminism developed in the context of a growing sense of cultural crisis as reformers began to argue that the root of the country's political, economic, and military weakness was Confucian civilization, which was incompatible with modern nationhood. In the radical journals that proliferated in the last two decades of the Qing, male and later female intellectuals identified the gender system as a key impediment to progress. They were deeply affected by negative views of Chinese society propagated by Western missionaries, who saw the status of women as a key indicator of a society's level of civilization or barbarism. As missionaries' presence in China grew and permeated the interior over the nineteenth century, they became actively involved in projects to civilize Chinese women. Missionaries founded the first school for girls in 1844 in the newly opened treaty port of Ningbo. The Rev. John McGowan from the London Missionary Society founded the first anti-footbinding group, the Heavenly Foot Society, in the treaty port of Xiamen (Amoy) in 1875. Missionary writings on China emphasized the degraded status of Chinese women—uneducated and hobbled by practices of footbinding, seclusion, and widow chastity—as emblematic of China's backwardness (Ko 2007).

As intellectuals began to wrestle with the role of women in a nation under threat, they evaluated Chinese norms within a global comparative framework, starting with the assumption that they were an impediment to progress. The China in which female chastity, gender segregation, and footbinding made sense was being displaced by a China enmeshed in global processes and conversations about progress and modernity (Ko 2007). Among the things perceived to be irrelevant to the emerging gender order was the tradition of women's writing that represented the pinnacle of women's achievements in a Confucian gender system. Reformist commentaries erased the significance of women's influence as writers and their economic role as producers of household income. China's reformist intellectuals evaluated past exemplars of women's learning and participation in national politics in comparison with new models of heroines from the West whose stories were often introduced through translations from Japanese reformers (Judge 2001).

Two of the most influential early male voices on women's status were the Cantonese scholar Kang Youwei (1858–1927) and his student Liang Qichao (1873–1929), who led a political movement to pressure the young Guangxu emperor (r. 1875–1908) to adopt Meiji-style reforms in 1898. These men examined the role of women through the lens of the social Darwinist paradigm of competition between nations and peoples in which the fittest would survive and the weak would be conquered and colonized. For Kang, footbinding not only was inhumane and unhealthy but also weakened the military strength of the Chinese "race" and caused Westerners to see the country as barbaric. He ensured that his own daughters did not have bound feet, founded one of the first Chinese anti-footbinding societies in 1892, and advocated to the throne for a ban on the practice. Anti-footbinding societies whose members pledged not to bind their daughters' feet or marry their sons to women with bound feet began to appear across the country.

Liang Qichao focused on the issue of women's education and employment, which, he argued, "fundamentally determines whether a nation will survive or be destroyed and whether it will prosper or languish in weakness." In his seminal 1897 essay, "On Women's Education," he describes education as "the mother of occupations." Dismissing both the critical role of women's labor in household economics and the broader economy and the significance of elite women's education, he declares all of China's women to be consumers rather than the producers needed for nation building. He opines, "When I seek out the root causes of national weakness, I find that they inevitably lie in women's lack of education. . . . Owing to women's inability to support themselves and their dependence on other people, men raise women as livestock or slaves. . . . Women sit in idleness while men toil. But leading a life of leisure and being despised as inferior is by no means a naturally happy life." Describing Chinese women as "ignorant, apathetic, and sequestered," he is particularly scathing in his criticism of elite poets, the "talented women" who represented the pinnacle of female education: "In ancient times there were so-called talented women [*cainü*] whose best achievements were nothing more than several stanzas of ditties upon the beauty of the wind and moon, verses describing the flowers and the grasses, or poems lamenting the passage of spring or the loss of a friend. Such activities cannot be called learning." Citing America as the country where women's education is most advanced, he calls for women to receive the same education as men to enable them to earn a livelihood and educate their children to be productive citizens (translations from Liu, Karl, and Ko 2013).

Kang and Liang's reform effort ended tragically when conservatives allied with the Dowager Empress Cixi (1835–1908) placed the emperor under house arrest, executed many of the reformers, and forced Kang and Liang into exile. The virulently anti-foreign Cixi threw the weight of the court behind a populist movement known as the Boxers United in Righteousness that was killing foreigners and Chinese Christian converts across much of North China. When the uprising encompassed Beijing, the Western powers and Japan sent in an Allied Expeditionary Force that crushed the Boxers and occupied the capital. The ensuing Boxer Protocol signed by China and the Allied powers, forcing on China an indemnity so large it was scheduled to be paid out over forty years, marked the nadir of Qing sovereignty.

In the wake of the Boxer debacle, reformers took control of the court and launched new policies to reform the state structure at every level, including forming elected provincial assemblies, creating a modern army and police force, fostering industrialization and commerce, and building railroads. For many people, however, these reforms could not restore the legitimacy of the dynasty. The Boxer Rebellion proved that the Manchus were unfit to govern a Chinese nation and that the imperial political system was incapable of adapting to a modern world. In the last decade of the dynasty, radicalized reformers argued for the abolition of the monarchy and took up open opposition, often violent, to the Qing government. In 1905, Sun Yat-sen and other Chinese revolutionaries studying in Tokyo formed the Revolutionary Alliance to launch uprisings against the Qing.

The Boxer disaster also galvanized reform-minded women, many of whom concluded that men could not save the Chinese nation without the full participation of women. Amid the horrific violence of the foreign assault against the Boxers, some 570 women and girls from a city just next to Beijing had killed themselves to escape rape by foreign soldiers. While some commentators extolled the virtuous self-sacrifice of these chastity martyrs, radical women castigated their passivity in the face of foreign aggression. According to He Xiangning (1878–1972), the first woman to join the Revolutionary Alliance, such women lacked the patriotism necessary for citizenship in a modern nation and indeed "did not know what the nation was" (Judge 2002, 167). Late Qing feminists wanted women to be activists, not martyrs. He Xiangning's long career as a revolutionary for the Nationalist Party and later the Communist Party exemplified her conviction that women bore equal responsibility with men for the fate of the nation, though she continually emphasized the differences in men's and women's contributions. As overseas students in Tokyo, she and her husband, Liao Zhongkai (1877–1925), were pillars of the community of Chinese radicals in exile in the last decade of the Qing, hosting meetings of the secret Revolutionary Alliance at their home.

Women's Education and the Emergence of Chinese Feminism

The new policies that had the greatest impact on women were educational reforms. In 1905 the civil examination system was abolished, severing the link between education and political authority for men. It was replaced with a modern school system with a Western-style curriculum. In 1907 the Qing government opened the first public elementary schools for girls and teachers' schools for women, which greatly expanded access beyond the handful of private Chinese-run schools for girls founded since the 1890s. The number of female students increased from 20,557 in 1908 to 141,130 in 1913 and 417,820 in 1923 (Bailey 2004, 221). Many new schools were run by anti-Qing radicals, such as the Patriotic Girls' School, founded in Shanghai in 1902, where the curriculum included bomb making and the history of the French Revolution in addition to the more standard modern subjects of foreign languages, history, geography, psychology, economics, ethics, physical education, and needlework. Despite the radical elements of its curriculum, the school, like most girls' schools at the time, imposed restrictions on student behavior and dress intended to assure those opposed to women's education that it did not undermine propriety or obedience to family authority.

In the last decade of the Qing, many Chinese students pursued overseas study. By far the largest number went to study in Japan, which they saw as a model of successful modern nation building to compete with the West. Between 1898 and 1906 the number of male students in Japan increased from two hundred to thirteen thousand. While the number of female students was much smaller (about one hundred women were in Japan in 1907), they had a disproportionately large influence back home. Most attended the Practical Arts Girls' School run by Shimoda Utako (1854–1936), who saw the education of women across East Asia as integral to Japan's pan-Asian policies. By 1914 Shimoda's school had graduated more than two hundred Chinese women. The curriculum centered on the nationalist patriarchal values of "good wife, wise mother" that emphasized women's education to become mothers of modern citizens (see the Japan and Korea sections in this chapter). Shimoda also sought to instill respect for Japan's leadership in modernization in East Asia among her Chinese students (Judge 2001).

Overseas study was transformative for young people as they explored Western political concepts such as nationalism, democracy, constitutionalism, people's rights, anarchism, and socialism in Japanese translation while experiencing Japan's adaptation of Western modernity. Shimoda's Chinese women students were more impressed with Japanese women's high levels of literacy, independence, late marriage age, and freedom to be out in public than they were with the modern version of domestic virtue, the "good wife, wise motherism" they learned in the classroom. Many students were radicalized by their experiences in Japan and became active in anti-Manchu cells while in Tokyo. Back home in China, radicals returning from overseas study took up the cause of revolution, becoming teachers, journalists, writers, and activists, publishing journals, making bombs, and plotting assassinations of Manchu officials in anti-Qing revolutionary cells.

The first manifesto for women's political rights, *The Women's Bell* (Nüjie zhong), published in 1903, was written by a man, Jin Tianhe (1874–1947), who, like Liang Qichao and other early male advocates of women's rights, was responding to the assaults of Western imperialism justified, in part, by the "uncivilized" treatment of women in China and other Asian societies. Educated women quickly became active in publishing their own periodicals and newspapers. In journals such as *China's New Women's World*, *Women's World*, and *Women's Studies News*, a first generation of Chinese feminists examined the sources of their oppression in Chinese society and the linkages between patriarchy and the nation's political crisis. They explored solutions such as education, family reform, political empowerment, and economic independence. A song published in *Women's World* captured the sense of urgency, optimism, disdain for tradition, and global connectedness that empowered women and men to devote their lives to reform and revolution in the early twentieth century: "Speed, speed, speed! The energy of civilization is moving through East Asia. The spirit of independence is red in the sunrise, and the currents of freedom are flooding forth. The world of women's rights is weighty, and the principle of equality is mighty. Then turning back we see the gold, powder, paints, and rouge of the ordinary pitiful insects" (quoted in Edwards 2008, 60).

Many Chinese radicals were attracted to anarchism, with its combined critiques of social and class hierarchy, traditional morality and family customs, and imperialism. Anarchist feminists saw the oppression of women not just as a legacy of traditional culture but as a component of class hierarchy. The most prominent of them was He-Yin Zhen (c. 1884–c. 1920), who had studied at the Patriotic Girls' School and then moved to Tokyo in 1907 with her husband, the anarchist Liu Shipei, where she founded the Society for the Restoration of Women's Rights, an anarchist women's group, and was active in the circles of radical women associated with the journal *Bluestocking* (see Japan section). She was a prolific writer and editor of an influential anarcho-feminist journal, *Natural Justice* (*Tianyi*), which offered a feminist critique of the systematic patriarchy built into the Chinese family system, Confucian culture, and political order, including analysis of how the Chinese language is structured to reflect the subjugation of women to men.

Noting the ironic "reversal of attitude" of men (like Liang Qichao and Kang Youwei) who were suddenly calling for women's liberation after they had long worked "to confine women within the boudoir and regarded the oppressive treatment of women as their given duty," she argued that male feminism was entirely self-serving in three ways. First, men believed that since limited freedom for women is linked to the success of modern nations in the West and Japan, by liberating their wives and daughters they would "acquire distinction." Second, with growing poverty in China, men needed the labor of women to support the family's livelihood and "alleviate men's burden." Third, "Chinese men view the family as their personal property and treat having progeny as a top priority, but the task of running the household and raising the children is not something they can bear," so they promoted women's education to make them better, more "civilized" household managers. True liberation, she argued, can only come through women's "active" efforts, not passive reliance on men to set them free (Liu, Karl, and Ko 2013, 53–70).

As an anarchist, He-Yin Zhen argued that women's oppression was rooted not just in patriarchal culture, but in economic systems that relied on exploitation of women's labor, especially that of housemaids, prostitutes, and factory workers. Since the roots of women's subjugation are economic, she argued, the West cannot provide a good model for Chinese women, and Western feminists' focus on suffrage would not bring about the "fundamental transformation of society" because "parliamentary politics has been the source of many inequities in the world" (Liu, Karl, and Ko 2013, 65). She envisioned that women's liberation required the liberation of men: "What we mean by equality between the sexes is not just that men will no longer oppress women. We also want men no longer to be oppressed by other men and women no longer to be oppressed by other women" (quoted in Zarrow 1988, 810). The linkage between feminism, nationalism, and class struggle would later become central to the thinking of the women's movement.

The life and career of the revolutionary Qiu Jin (1877–1907) exemplifies the emergence of this new generation of activist women and the depth of their challenges to old ideals of female propriety. Trapped in an unhappy marriage, she unbound her feet and left her husband and two children in 1904 to study at Shimoda's school. She joined the Revolutionary Alliance in Tokyo, and upon returning to China founded a newspaper and a public speaking training society for women. Evoking woman warriors of the ancient past, she often dressed in men's clothing and ran a physical education school to provide military training for women revolutionaries. Explaining the urgency of women's activism, she said, "We all know the nation is about to perish, and men are incapable of saving it. Can we still think of relying on them?" (quoted in Judge 2001, 791). In 1907 she joined a plot to assassinate a Qing official but was caught and executed.

BOX 4.3

Qiu Jin's Call to Action for Women

During her studies in Tokyo, Qiu Jin edited a journal titled *Baihua bao* (*Colloquial Magazine*), which published articles promoting revolution and radical social reform in vernacular language that was more accessible to a broad audience than the classical language used in examination education. In a 1904 issue, she published "A Proclamation to Two Hundred Million Fellow Countrywomen," in which she outlined specific actions for women to take to liberate themselves from the shackles of the patriarchal family system in order

(continued)

to work for the Chinese nation. The piece is notable for echoing Liang Qichao's harsh criticism of women for their passivity in the face of injustice. She wrote:

> *Alas! The greatest injustice in this world must be the injustice suffered by our female population of two hundred million. . . . Why is there no justice for women? . . . Dear sisters, you must know that you'll get nothing if you rely upon others. You must go out and get things for yourselves. In ancient times, when decadent scholars came out with such nonsense as "men are exalted, women are lowly," "a virtuous woman is one without talent," and "the husband guides the wife," ambitious and spirited women should have organized and opposed them. . . . Men feared that if women were educated they would become superior to men, so they did not allow us to be educated. Couldn't the women have challenged the men and refused to submit? It seems clear now that it was we women who abandoned our responsibilities to ourselves and felt content to let men do everything for us. . . . When men said we were useless, we became useless; when they said we were incapable, we stopped questioning them even when our entire female sex had reached slave status. . . . When we heard that men like small feet, we immediately bound them just to please them, just to keep our free meal tickets. . . . Think about it, sisters, can anyone enjoy such comfort and leisure without forfeiting dearly for it? . . . Whom can we blame but ourselves since we have brought this on ourselves? . . . Let us all put aside our former selves and be resurrected as complete human beings. . . . Don't be lazy, don't eat idle rice. . . . You must know that when a country is near destruction, women cannot rely on men anymore because they aren't even able to protect themselves. If we don't take heart now and shape up, it will be too late when China is destroyed (Ebrey 1993, 343–344).*

Invoking the tradition of cross-dressing woman warriors, Qiu Jin often dressed like a man to free herself from conventions of femininity.
ORIGINAL SOURCE UNKNOWN

For many women reformers and revolutionaries such as Qiu Jin, the main purpose of education and rights for women was strengthening the nation by producing women who could serve society and, as mothers, raise children who were productive citizens. But as women began to encounter opposition from male nationalists and revolutionaries to their pursuit of equality, there was a growing tension between women's rights and nationalist goals that would become sharper after the fall of the Qing dynasty.

Women and the End of the Qing

The fall of China's last dynasty in 1911 was brought about by a mutiny in a New Army unit in Hubei province that triggered the provincial assembly to declare secession from the Qing empire. Provinces all over China quickly followed in secession, and the court abdicated on behalf of the three-year-old emperor. Women formed militias to participate in the fighting against the Manchu regime. Sun Yat-sen's Revolutionary Alliance, which led the anti-Qing fight and the new provisional government, officially supported equal political rights for women, so women activists expected to participate fully in the new republican political order after the fall of the dynasty. With the formation of a provisional parliament in Nanjing that excluded them, women inspired by suffrage movements in other countries lobbied for equal political participation as a recognition of their natural rights, though they accepted in principle the new government's restriction of male suffrage rights to those with education and property. When the 1912 constitution of the new republic excluded them from voting or holding office, outraged women, feeling betrayed by the Revolutionary Alliance, of which many were long-standing members, created several new organizations dedicated to the cause of women's suffrage and political rights. Some 380 women, many of them returned students from Japan, formed the Women's Suffrage Alliance in 1912 under the leadership of Tang Qunying (1871–1937), the first woman to join the Revolutionary Alliance in Japan. A journalist and activist, Tang was one of the founding members of the women's militia, the Women's Northern Attack Brigade, that participated in the fighting that accompanied the collapse of the Qing. With her militant style, the Women's Suffrage Alliance became the most radical of the new groups. It requested that the word "sex" be included in the proposed line in the new constitution stating that "all people are equal regardless of race, class, or religion." Tang led women activists into the parliamentary chamber to observe debate on the issue, and when the head of the parliament tabled the matter, the women argued with him virulently. When their entry to the chamber was blocked by troops, the women smashed windowpanes and demonstrated raucously for some five hours, even kicking a policeman who tried to interfere. Rebuffed by troops again the next day and unable to get parliamentary leaders to meet with them, they stormed the chambers and were forcibly removed amid shouts that they were armed. Suffragists had some limited and short-lived success at the provincial level in the southeast province of Guangdong, where they briefly held seats in the local parliament. But women's rights quickly fell off the agenda as Sun Yat-sen's Revolutionary Alliance joined the conservative coalition that created the Nationalist Party (Kuomintang or Guomindang, hereafter referred to as KMT), and the new government, led by General Yuan Shikai (1859–1916), curtailed all democratic activities and banned the Women's Suffrage Alliance.

In their struggles for political rights, Chinese feminists explicitly modeled their tactics on the actions of radical British suffragists and understood themselves to be participating in a global movement. In 1912, American suffragist Carrie Chapman Catt and a delegation from the International Woman Suffrage Alliance visited China and participated in rallies in Nanjing, Shanghai, and Beijing. Observing women sitting in the Guangdong parliament, Chapman Catt reported back to her fellow American feminists that Chinese women had progressed beyond them in their struggle for political rights. Events of the next decades would complicate that comparison.

CONNECTIONS

All three East Asian countries sought to transform their societies in the late nineteenth and early twentieth centuries in response to unprecedented Western imperialism. As the Qing had discovered during the Opium War in the 1840s, military resistance against the wealth and power of the West would be very difficult. A more effective way to deal with the rising power of the West, many East Asian advocates of reform came to believe, was to study the roots of that power and adopt significant measures to strengthen their own states and societies. During the last decades of the nineteenth century, many of them understood that ideological, religious, social, and cultural changes that Western nations had adopted earlier in the nineteenth century were critical to their success. East Asian reformers—in some cases men who were part of their governments and in other cases men and women who challenged their governments—called the adoption of Western thought about rights, citizenship, feminism, and other progressive notions (for which new terms had to be created, as they did not yet exist in East Asia) "enlightenment" (often paired with "civilization").

Some other Western ideologies, such as social Darwinism, were humiliating and, while accepted by many, were significantly modified in East Asia. Social Darwinism refers to the application of Charles Darwin's (1809–1882) biological insights on the origins and evolution of species to human groups, usually called "races." Nineteenth-century Western thought viewed races as having a scientific reality, a notion that modern science rejects. Social Darwinist thought assumed that the races on top owed their position to their inherent genetic superiority in a worldwide struggle for survival. East Asians accepted the notion that some societies were at that time dominant—how could they doubt that in an imperialistic world? But the racial interpretation of the West's dominance was obviously unacceptable to people outside of Europe, North America, and Australia. Superiority, they said, was not in the genes (or race) but rather was connected to society and culture. If East Asia could move toward Western-style "civilization" and modernity, this line went, they could win the battle for survival of the fittest.

The advocacy of "civilization and enlightenment" was closely tied to national strengthening in Japan, Korea, and China in the last decades of the nineteenth century. The process of nation building included, in all three of these countries, new definitions of masculinities and femininities, and even a desire to reframe one's own country as "masculine" rather than as "feminine." Weak women—usually defined by reformers in Japan and Korea as uneducated and less active in society, and in China as both uneducated and restrained by bound feet—were emblematic, these reformers contended, of backward nations. Women (and men, of course) would have to be educated for Japan, Korea, and China to begin to be viewed as advanced societies. This idea was shared by a significant group of foreigners active in East Asia as well: Christian missionary women, who played an early and important role in women's education. The content of women's Christian education reflected the missionaries' Victorian-era ideas about women's morality and behavior.

Government officials had a different view of education, which was that education was intended to produce loyal male and female subjects. In all three countries, however, some recipients of that education subverted their governments' goals. Some men became revolutionaries or reformers. Some educated women were early advocates of the expansion of women's rights within the family, upsetting the gender order. Other women used their education for politically revolutionary purposes. Still others advanced the opportunities available to women in the professions. In all three countries in the late nineteenth and early twentieth centuries, women's rights were linked to nationalism, although this nationalism took different forms in each country: anti-imperialism in Korea, anti-Qing activism in China, and the desire in Japan to be part of a modern empire.

Other aspects of modernity affected gender as well, in particular the rise of the industrial economy and the recruitment of a female labor force, but this was more evident in Japan in the nineteenth century. The development of industrial workforces in China and Korea and other opportunities for working women in all three countries will be discussed in later chapters.

REFERENCES AND SUGGESTIONS FOR FURTHER READING

GLOBAL CONTEXT

Freedman, Estelle B. 2002. *No Turning Back: The History of Feminism and the Future of Women.* New York: Ballantine Books.

Kent, Susan Kingsley. 2004. "Gender Rules: Law and Politics." In *A Companion to Gender History*, edited by Teresa A. Meade and Merry E. Wiesner-Hanks. Oxford: Blackwell.

Lipset-Rivera, Sonya. 2004. "Latin America and the Caribbean." In *A Companion to Gender History*, edited by Teresa A. Meade and Merry E. Wiesner-Hanks. Oxford: Blackwell.

Marks, Robert B. 2007. *The Origins of the Modern World: A Global and Ecological Narrative from the Fifteenth to the Twenty-First Century*. Lanham, MD: Rowman and Littlefield.

Miller, Pavla. 2004. "Gender and Education Before and After Mass Schooling." In *A Companion to Gender History*, edited by Teresa A. Meade and Merry E. Wiesner-Hanks. Oxford: Blackwell.

Nye, Robert. 2004. "Sexuality." In *A Companion to Gender History*, edited by Teresa A. Meade and Merry E. Wiesner-Hanks. Oxford: Blackwell.

Tucker, Judith. 2004. "Rescued from Obscurity: Contributions and Challenges in Writing the History of Gender in the Middle East and North Africa." In *A Companion to Gender History*, edited by Teresa A. Meade and Merry E. Wiesner-Hanks. Oxford: Blackwell.

Winslow, Barbara. 2004. "Feminist Movements: Gender and Sexual Equality." In *A Companion to Gender History*, edited by Teresa A. Meade and Merry E. Wiesner-Hanks. Oxford: Blackwell.

JAPAN

Anderson, Marnie S. 2010. *A Place in Public: Women's Rights in Meiji Japan*. Cambridge, MA: Harvard University Press.

Cook, Theodore F. 2005. "Making Soldiers: The Imperial Army and Japanese Man in Meiji Society and State." In *Gendering Modern Japanese History*, edited by Barbara Molony and Kathleen Uno. Cambridge, MA: Harvard University Press.

Faison, Elyssa. 2007. *Managing Women: Disciplining Labor in Modern Japan*. Berkeley: University of California Press.

Gluck, Carol. 1985. *Japan's Modern Myths: Ideology in the Late Meiji Period*. Princeton, NJ: Princeton University Press.

Hiratsuka, Raichō. 2006. *In the Beginning, Woman Was the Sun*. Translated by Teruko Craig. New York: Columbia University Press.

Lublin, Elizabeth Dorn. 2010. *Reforming Japan: The Woman's Christian Temperance Union in the Meiji Period*. Vancouver: University of British Columbia Press.

Mackie, Vera. 2003. *Feminism in Modern Japan*. Cambridge: Cambridge University Press.

Mihalopoulos, Bill. 2011. *Sex in Japan's Globalization, 1870–1930: Prostitutes, Emigration and Nation-Building*. London: Pickering and Chatto.

Molony, Barbara. 2010. "Crossing Boundaries: Transnational Feminisms in Twentieth-Century Japan." In *Women's Movements in Asia: Feminisms and Transnational Activism*, edited by Mina Roces and Louise Edwards. London: Routledge.

Rabson, Steve. 1991. "Yosano Akiko on War: To Give One's Life or Not—A Question of Which War." *Journal of the Association of Teachers of Japanese* 25, no. 1: 45–74.

Sievers, Sharon L. 1983. *Flowers in Salt: The Beginnings of Feminist Consciousness in Modern Japan*. Stanford, CA: Stanford University Press.

Tsurumi, E. Patricia. 1990. *Factory Girls: Women in the Thread Mills of Meiji Japan*. Princeton, NJ: Princeton University Press.

KOREA

Choi, Hyaeweol. 2009a. *Gender and Mission Encounters in Korea: New Women, Old Ways*. Berkeley: University of California Press.

———. 2009b. "'Wise Mother, Good Wife': A Trans-cultural Discursive Construct in Modern Korea." *Journal of Korean Studies* 14, no. 1: 1–34.

———. 2013. *New Women in Colonial Korea: A Sourcebook*. London: Routledge.

Hyun, Theresa. 2003. *Writing Women in Korea: Translation and Feminism in the Colonial Period*. Honolulu: University of Hawai'i Press.

Jager, Sheila Miyoshi. 2003. *Narratives of Nation Building in Korea: A Genealogy of Patriotism*. Armonk, NY: M. E. Sharpe.

Kim, Sun Joo. 2007. "Taxes, the Local Elite, and the Rural Populace in the Chinju Uprising of 1862." *Journal of Asian Studies* 66, no. 4: 993–1027.

Kim, Yung-Hee. 1995. "Under the Mandate of Nationalism: Development of Feminist Enterprises in Modern Korea, 1860–1910." *Journal of Women's History* 7, no. 4: 120–136.

Lee, Ji-Eun. 2015. *Women Pre-Scripted: Forging Modern Roles Through Korean Print*. Honolulu: University of Hawai'i Press.

Lee, Peter, ed. 1996. *Sourcebook of Korean Civilization, Volume 2: From the Sixteenth to the Twentieth Centuries*. New York: Columbia University Press.

Tikhonov, Vladimir. 2007. "Masculinizing the Nation: Gender Ideologies in Traditional Korea and in the 1890s–1900s Korean Enlightenment Discourse." *Journal of Asian Studies* 66, no. 4: 1029–1065.

Yoo, Theodore Jun. 2008. *The Politics of Gender in Colonial Korea: Education, Labor, and Health, 1910–1945*. Berkeley: University of California Press.

CHINA

Bailey, Paul J. 2004. "'Modernising Conservatism in Early Twentieth-Century China: The Discourse and Practice of Women's Education." *European Journal of East Asian Studies* 3, no. 2: 217–241.

Ebrey, Patricia Buckley. 1993. *Chinese Civilization: A Sourcebook*. New York: The Free Press.

Edwards, Louise. 2008. *Gender, Politics, and Democracy: Women's Suffrage in China*. Stanford, CA: Stanford University Press.

Hu, Ying. 2000. *Tales of Translation: Composing the New Woman in China, 1899–1918*. Stanford, CA: Stanford University Press.

———. 2002. "Naming the First 'New Woman.'" In *Rethinking the 1898 Reform Period: Political and Cultural Change in Late Qing China*, edited by Rebecca Karl and Peter Zarrow. Cambridge, MA: Harvard University Press.

Judge, Joan. 2001. "Talent, Virtue, and the Nation: Chinese Nationalisms and Female Subjectivities in the Early Twentieth Century." *American Historical Review* 106, no. 3: 765–803.

———. 2002. "Reforming the Feminine: Female Literacy and the Legacy of 1898." In *Rethinking the 1898 Reform Period: Political and Cultural Change in Late Qing China*, edited by Rebecca Karl and Peter Zarrow. Cambridge, MA: Harvard University Press.

Karl, Rebecca. 2002. "'Slavery,' Citizenship, and Gender in Late Qing China's Global Context." In *Rethinking the 1898 Reform Period: Political and Cultural Change in Late Qing China*, edited by Rebecca Karl and Peter Zarrow. Cambridge, MA: Harvard University Press.

Kazuko, Ono. 1989. *Chinese Women in a Century of Revolution*. Stanford, CA: Stanford University Press.

Ko, Dorothy. 2007. *Cinderella's Sisters: A Revisionist History of Footbinding*. Berkeley: University of California Press.

Liu, Lydia He, Rebecca E. Karl, and Dorothy Ko. 2013. *The Birth of Chinese Feminism: Essential Texts in Transnational Theory*. New York: Columbia University Press.

Meyer-Fong, Tobie. 2013. *What Remains: Coming to Terms with Civil War in 19th Century China*. Stanford, CA: Stanford University Press.

Yeh, Catherine Vance. 2006. *Shanghai Love: Courtesans, Intellectuals, and Entertainment Culture, 1850–1910*. Seattle: University of Washington Press.

Zarrow, Peter. 1988. "He Zhen and Anarcho-Feminism in China." *Journal of Asian Studies* 47, no. 4: 796–813.

5

Nationalism and Feminism in the Interwar Period

GLOBAL CONTEXT

Modern feminism—the struggle to attain social and political equality and improved social status regardless of one's gender—has long been linked to nationalism. Nationalism did not require the existence of the sovereign state. In cases where a country did not have national sovereignty, nationalism represented a yearning for the nation, which could be—and usually was—seen in a positive light as a quest for liberation. In the interest of achieving national independence, women were actively incorporated into nationalist endeavors. The nationalist program initiated a number of activities oriented toward family and society that were designed to bring women into the effort to build the new nation. In Korea and China in the first half of the twentieth century, feminists' struggles for rights and status were intertwined with the struggle to create a modern nation, though often in an uneasy balance.

The link between nationalism and feminism in early twentieth-century Japan, where the nation-state already existed, was far more problematic because the quest for equality implied a desire to share in the rights and privileges of citizenship. But the Japanese government's construction of gender roles, a capitalist economy, and an empire seemed to contradict many feminists' desires for peace, gender equality, social and labor justice, and transnational cooperation with women worldwide. This led many into an oppositional stance toward the government, even while the primary goal of most was inclusion in the nation-state with full rights of citizenship (Mackie 2003).

The decades following the end of Japan's Meiji period, China's Revolution of 1911, and Korea's loss of independence as it fell under Japanese colonial domination in 1910 coincided with World War I in Europe, during which more than ten million soldiers died and twenty million were left maimed and wounded. That war emerged from rivalries among Britain, France, Germany, and the Austro-Hungarian, Ottoman, and Russian Empires. These rivalries were cemented in alliances that acted as a trip wire for a multinational war in August 1914 following the assassination of the heir to the Austro-Hungarian throne by a Serbian nationalist. Austria's response, supported by its ally Germany, drew in Russia in support of Serbia, which in turn led Russia's allies, England and France, to join the war against the Austrians and Germans. The Ottomans came to the Austrian-German side, and soon the rest of Europe, as well as England's allies—Japan and the Commonwealth countries of Canada, Australia, and New Zealand—entered the war. The United States entered in 1917. World War I was made particularly deadly by the technological breakthroughs in munitions production in the decades before the war, especially the chemical process that fixed atmospheric nitrogen in a form that could be used for both explosives and agricultural fertilizers (Molony 1990, chap. 3).

Russia withdrew from the war when the Communists came to power in that country after the overthrow of the czarist monarchy in 1917. The German, Austro-Hungarian, and Ottoman Empires were defeated in November 1918, signaling the beginning of the end of the nineteenth-century imperialist order. But while European territories formerly under the control of the defeated empires were molded into new nation-states, the old imperialist order managed to hold on for another three decades in Asia and Africa. The thirty nations that convened at Versailles in 1919 to produce the peace treaty that ended World War I claimed to create a new world order to end all wars. This included punishing the losers and constructing the League of Nations. Requests by representatives of colonies outside of Europe for the right to "self-determination," another goal for the postwar era articulated by American president Woodrow Wilson, were ignored. In fact, England, France, and Japan, among others, extended their imperial reach through colonies and mandates in the Middle East, Africa, India, and East Asia, inspiring stronger movements for independence in those regions. As we shall see in this chapter, imperial expansion led to the March First Movement in Korea and the May Fourth Movement in China in 1919 (Manela 2007).

Nationalist movements in colonial territories were often radical, while those in the imperialist countries increasingly focused on a conservative pride in their nations' strength. Ironically, nationalism, including its feminist forms, was also encouraged by the education of colonial subjects in the imperialist countries' languages and ideologies of self-government and citizenship rights (Blom 1995). Transnational women's organizations, such as Christian and secular groups headquartered in the United States and Europe, sought allies in both colonies and independent countries, extending the reach of global feminism and linking it to the quest for national self-determination as well.

In addition to the Russian Revolution, revolutionary and/or independence movements emerged in the 1910s in Mexico, Vietnam, Palestine, Egypt, and India, among other places. Change, even if not politically revolutionary, was the global order of the day in the 1920s. Many people throughout the world rejected pre–World War I culture as reflective of the environment that had produced the horrific war. They turned to modernist artists such as the painter Pablo Picasso, the composer Igor Stravinsky, the psychologist Sigmund Freud, and the writer Virginia Woolf, whose works deconstructed the worldview that had seemed so normal and stable and yet had come apart at the seams with the destruction wreaked by war. Culture traveled rapidly across borders in the 1920s, bringing jazz and movies, short skirts and hairstyles, and hopes of greater rights for workers, students, women, and marginalized peoples throughout the world. The 1920s appeared to be a time of cultural optimism in many parts of the world.

The postwar recovery was supported to a significant extent by loans from American banks and other forms of global financial interconnectedness. Multinational treaty systems, such as the Washington Naval Conference treaty system of the 1920s (discussed in this chapter), also underwrote a globally connected system, this time in the area of military security. When the American banks and stock exchange at the heart of the global financial system crashed in October 1929, much of the world plunged into the Great Depression (Hobsbawm 1996, chap. 3). (The Soviet Union was not linked to the capitalist economies, and while it faced its own economic problems, these were not generated by the global depression.) The worldwide crisis of capitalism led countries to respond in a variety of ways, some of them extreme. One obvious way was the calling into question of the mutual security regime; if the global financial system failed miserably, why should any country expect the military security system to succeed? As we will see in Chapter 8, militarism and fascism were some of the responses to the crisis of globally interconnected capitalism; under those conditions, nationalism took on an extreme jingoistic form, and feminism was one of the victims of this turn to extremism.

This is not to say that feminist movements everywhere disappeared in the 1930s, but in places such as Japan, as we will see in Chapter 8, they were dealt a hard blow before succumbing in the early 1940s. In the interwar period, however, feminisms and women's rights advocacy around the world appeared very successful. Women gained the vote in Scandinavian, Baltic, and Northern European countries as well as the United States (women had gained the right to vote in Australia and New Zealand decades earlier), and even in countries and colonies where women still did not have civil rights, they were becoming more outspoken. Their exercise of freedom of expression was often connected to nationalism. For example, in India, where male independence leaders argued that India's freedom required women's freedom, some, such as Mohandas K. Gandhi, stressed women's unique maternalist and nonviolent virtues, while others, such as Jawaharlal Nehru, called on men and women to be equally educated to serve the new nation. Women leaders in the All India Women's Conference, founded in 1927, advocated equal political, social, and economic rights, while at the same time claiming that women had a special role in the nationalist struggle. In 1925, women's rights advocate Sarojini Naidu became the first woman president of the Indian National Congress (founded 1885), the most important organization of the Indian independence movement (Molony 2005a, 514–517).

In Egypt, under British rule from 1882 to 1922, women and men advocated independence and worked together in the Revolution of 1919 (Freedman 2002, 100–105). Progressive men had argued that Islam allowed women to be educated, and in 1911, one such educated woman, nationalist reformer Malak Hifni Nasif (who wrote under the pen name Bahithat al-Badiyah), petitioned the Egyptian legislative assembly to expand women's education, economic opportunities, and equality in the family. Following independence, Huda Sha'arawi founded and presided over the Egyptian Feminist Union from 1923 to 1947. Similar feminist-nationalist movements emerged in other colonial situations throughout the world. In all of these cases, feminism was seen by its opponents as an ideology of the Western imperialists, and so advocates for gender equality were careful to link it to nation building.

While bringing together feminism and nationalism, women were also increasingly forging transnational links in the interwar era. Before the end of World War I, Christian and secular organizations such as the WCTU, the YWCA, the International Suffrage Alliance, and the Women's International League for Peace and Freedom brought women together transnationally, but their leaders were mostly Americans, Europeans, and Australians. The Christian organizations had extensive outreach and branches in East Asia, beginning in the nineteenth century, but after the war non-Western women began to claim more active participation and leadership positions. In particular, East Asian women soon assumed a leading role in the Pan-Pacific Women's Association, which had initially been led by American feminists. Among socialist women, it was initially Europeans who led transnational movements as well. As we will see in this chapter, transnational ties were significant in East Asian women's rights movements at a time when women did not have rights at the national level in their own societies.

JAPAN

In Japan, the second and third decades of the twentieth century are commonly called the era of "Taishō democracy," named for the Taishō emperor, who reigned from 1912 to 1926. Millions of Japanese in the 1910s and 1920s believed that they should have access to rights, prosperity, and education, and they mounted movements to achieve them. Historians usually terminate the Taishō period not with the death of the Taishō emperor but with the 1931 Manchurian Incident, which began Japan's fifteen years of hostilities in Asia. After 1931, Japan's government moved increasingly toward militarism, both at home and in the colonies, making democratic movements very difficult and forcing those who wished to gain rights of citizenship to make painful choices. What would the quest for full rights of citizenship and membership in the nation mean under those circumstances?

Motherhood Protection Debate

In Chapter 4, we saw that feminist Hiratsuka Raichō founded the Bluestocking Society, and in Chapter 6, we will examine the role she and the Bluestockings played in the cultural phenomenon known as New Women. But she was also a central figure in the politics of women's rights in the Taishō period. Toward the end of World War I, Hiratsuka was one of several leading feminists who engaged in what became known as the Motherhood Protection Debate. She was joined in this debate by poet Yosano Akiko (see Chapter 4), socialist feminist Yamakawa Kikue (1890–1980), rescued Seattle sex worker turned feminist translator Yamada Waka (1879–1957), and other feminists. The debate was fought out through approximately 115 articles in a variety of women's and general audience journals. Yosano, who gave birth to thirteen children and raised eleven to adulthood, fired the opening salvo, claiming that women should not marry and have children until they could support them on their own. Women's liberation, she asserted, was based on their ability to stand on their own two feet; a mother's dependence on her husband or the state was "slave morality" (Molony 1993, 126–130). In the end, she did support state-sponsored insurance for mothers who needed to take pre- and postnatal time off from work. Hiratsuka replied that Yosano, a very successful poet, could not understand or speak for poor women, who, she said, were not paid well enough to support themselves independently. Instead, Hiratsuka asserted, the state should support mothers—that is, "protect them"—because they performed an essential service to the nation-state by producing children. Yamakawa wrote that such protection for mothers was possible only through changes in social and labor conditions brought about by a socialist revolution. Yamada's view was consistent with the state's "good wife, wise mother" philosophy; she claimed that it was the "sacred mission of women" to educate their children for the sake of the state and to be supported by their husbands or the state. In the end, the four women agreed to disagree and acknowledged that they all cared about improving the status of women. But the debate had two important results: it privileged mothers as child rearers (earlier, fathers had often been seen as better child rearers), and it made the claim that motherhood was a service to the state, an idea that was later expanded as a justification for women's full citizenship.

Economic Growth, Democracy, Imperialism, and Civil Rights

Having fought two wars in the late Meiji period—the first Sino-Japanese War and the Russo-Japanese War—Japan entered World War I in August 1914, following Britain's request for assistance against the German navy in the waters off Germany's leasehold in Shandong, China. Although Japan played only a minor military role, World War I was Japan's "good war." While Europeans and Americans focused their attention on the battles in Europe, Japan was able, for the first time, to compete with the West in Asian markets and to play a radically expanded role in China. The economic benefits of World War I lifted Japan's poorest from poverty and led to the expansion of a middle class who aspired to political and social participation. The development of the middle class opened many doors for women and led to challenges to gender relations.

In addition, the war changed Japan's global strategic position. As one of the victorious allies in World War I, Japan earned major power status at the 1919 Versailles Peace Conference that ended the war. When the victorious powers divided up former colonies of the defeated German empire, Japan expanded territorially in Asia and the Pacific. Even before the Versailles Conference, Japan's allies had allowed Japanese expansion in Asia. Under the 1905 Taft-Katsura Agreement, the United States and Japan recognized each other's dominant positions in the Philippines (a U.S. colony) and Korea (soon to be a Japanese colony), respectively. In 1917, soon after pressuring Japan to give up some of the Twenty-One Demands (1915) that would have allowed Japanese economic and political incursions into China, the United States, under the Lansing-Ishii Agreement, recognized that Japan had "special interests" in China.

World War I also became a "good war" for Japan's economy. Industrial output increased fivefold, as Japanese producers filled munitions orders from the Allies and entered former European and American markets in Asia. The war also opened markets for technologically less advanced products. For instance, when European match producers turned to arms production, Japanese children in destitute families took up match production. Before the war, slums ringed every city, and slum dwellers scraped by doing jobs such as rag picking, piecework, hauling, and street vending. Men, women, and children all worked. Whole families of five or six, who often took in a few boarders, lived in single tenement rooms with one outhouse for several dozen families. Having no cooking facilities of their own, slum dwellers consumed leftover food bought from street vendors. Cooking was not one of the tasks of very poor women (Uno 1993).

Wartime labor demand expanded opportunities for both men and women to work in factories, offering them more predictable incomes as part of an increasingly stable industrial workforce and lifting them out of utter destitution. Working-class families moved into small houses with two or three rooms, a tiny kitchen, and a toilet, thereby escaping their one-room tenement dwellings. As incomes rose, demand for services such as medical care also increased. This, in turn, enhanced opportunities for people interested in professional jobs (Nagy 1991). Instead of entering a factory, a young working-class woman might attend nursing school, pulling her whole family into the middle class as she became a professional. More children stayed in school beyond the required years, increasing the need for teachers. New technologies and modern institutions offered occupations to women in newly middle-class families. Modern companies hired female office workers, newly created department stores needed fashionable sales clerks, the increasing popularity of telephones opened employment to women as operators, and newspapers sought out women reporters to cover issues of interest to middle-class women readers. The new middle class began moving into Western-style homes in the fancier sections of Japan's cities. Adult women of the farming and working classes were increasingly expected to cook meals and care for their households as "good wives and wise mothers," just as their middle-class sisters had been.

But rapid growth during World War I also fueled inflation, leading to a postwar crash. Trouble first appeared in July 1918, when housewives in a fishing village protested the doubling of rice prices between January 1917 and July 1918. During the next two months, "rice riots" broke out all over Japan. Almost a million people, many of them women, took part in more than six hundred demonstrations; a thousand people were killed and twenty-five thousand were arrested before the riots were suppressed. Many historians consider the rice riots, which were started by women, an important early example of Taishō democracy. Another pillar of Taishō democracy was what was called "universal suffrage"—this was actually a movement to expand the vote to all men, regardless of their income level. Men got the vote in 1925, making civil rights a part of manhood. Women's suffrage was not included in "universal" suffrage, but as we shall see later, women also struggled for full civil rights in the 1920s and early 1930s.

The rice riots were the first sign of a growing social and economic divide that emerged even in the good years of the 1920s. Thousands of tiny urban workshops that had sprung up during the war, attracting many thousands of unskilled rural young people, failed when European and American products reentered the Asian marketplace. The economic crash of 1920 led to massive unemployment for these unskilled workers. Many returned to the countryside, where they joined the depressed rural workforce. The increase in rice prices that had produced the rice riots in 1918 had not helped the poorest tenant farmers, but it did cause the government to change colonial policy to import more rice from Taiwan and Korea. Japan's urban consumers got cheaper rice, but Koreans and Taiwanese now had much less rice to eat. In addition, Japanese farmers suffered a dramatic decline in the value of their crops. Tenant farmers organized unions and held thousands of protests, another important aspect of Taishō democracy.

Although the killing fields of World War I were in Europe, far from East Asia, events of the postwar settlement, starting with the 1919 Versailles Peace Conference and continuing into the 1920s, had important effects on the linkages of feminism and nationalism in all three Northeast Asian countries. Inspired by U.S. president Woodrow Wilson's rhetoric of "self-determination of nations" and angered by repressive treatment by Japanese colonial authorities, Korean students and Christian leaders proclaimed Korean independence on March 1, 1919 (Manela 2007). A colonywide outbreak of demonstrations led to brutal suppression by Japanese military police. Japan's examination of its suppression of the March First Movement led to a change in its colonial policy. The impact of the resulting "cultural rule" (*bunka seiji*) will be discussed in detail in the Korean section of this chapter.

Two months after the Korean uprising, the victorious powers at Versailles granted the former German leasehold in Shandong to Japan in exchange for denying Japan's request for a racial equality clause in the Covenant of the League of Nations. This triggered intense anger among Chinese nationalists, who erupted in anti-Japanese demonstrations on May 4, 1919. The impact of the May Fourth Movement will also be discussed later in this chapter.

While the powers were meeting in France, several of them—the United States, France, Britain, Canada, and Japan—still had troops elsewhere in the world. Attempting to turn back the Communist revolution in Russia, they launched in 1917 a costly, unsuccessful, and unpopular action called the Siberian Intervention. This intervention as well as the post–World War I recession made cutting the expenses of a growing global arms race appealing to all the powers, including Japan. The leaders of nine European, American, and Asian countries met in Washington, D.C., in 1921–1922 to take steps toward preserving peace in East Asia and to negotiate cost-saving naval reductions. Japan's feminist peace activists, who will be discussed later in this chapter, added their unofficial voices to the Washington Naval Conference and later global conferences run by male political leaders.

After the Washington Naval Conference, Japan decreased military spending and cut the size of its armed forces by a hundred thousand men. The Siberian Intervention was terminated, and Shandong was returned to China. Because the Japanese military lost prestige after World War I and especially after the failed Siberian Intervention—reflected, for example, in Japanese officers wearing civilian clothes when off duty during the 1920s, rather than the uniforms that had been an esteemed symbol of masculinity earlier—the Army Ministry implemented military education for boys in middle and higher schools to rebuild public support.

Taishō democracy dominated the culture and politics of the interwar decades. Parliamentary government as well as movements of marginalized Japanese who struggled for the right to equality, inclusion, and respect characterized the era. Women's rights movements of varying ideologies focused on both women's equality and difference from men in their quest for rights, respect, and inclusion.

Transnational and Domestic Roots of Interwar Japanese Feminism

Working with transnational women's organizations gave Japanese women in the Meiji and Taishō eras a space for influencing state policy in the absence of national civil rights. Indeed, national feminisms in Japan were strongly linked to transnationalism at a time when women who advocated political change at home found their hands tied by Article 5 of the Public Peace Police Law. Transnationalism took many forms and embraced feminisms with varying primary interests beginning in the Meiji period. As we have seen in Chapter 4, progressives, often influenced by transnational Christianity, embraced rights for women as part of Japan's modernizing project. By the interwar years, Japanese women in global Christian organizations such as the YWCA and the JWCTU played important roles in articulating Japanese feminist theories of citizenship (suffrage and other political rights) and community building (labor and social justice, consumer rights, and reproductive rights).

Transnational linkages had some drawbacks, however. Though inspired by the religious rhetoric of the American leaders of the World WCTU, the JWCTU resisted being treated as if the goal of their participation in global organizations was to learn from their more liberated Western sisters. At the 1920 World WCTU meeting in London, for example, Japanese delegates, who wore kimonos, were seen as "picturesque" by their Western counterparts (Ogawa 2007, 34). To be taken seriously in a transnational context, Japanese abroad often felt compelled to wear Western dress.

At the same time that women in transnational Christian organizations were working to improve the lives of women at home and abroad, secular feminists were intensifying their efforts for greater rights within the nation as well. The climate for women's activism was improving in Japan, and as we will see in Chapter 6, New Women and Modern Girls were part of a new cultural environment that nourished this activism. The Motherhood Protection Debate was one example of the lively atmosphere for discussion of women's rights. In addition to the women involved in that debate—all of whom continued to play important roles in competing Japanese feminist movements for decades to follow—several other leading feminists got their start as activists during World War I.

The most significant twentieth-century suffragist was Ichikawa Fusae (1893–1981), known as the "Susan B. Anthony of Japan" (Molony 2005b). Born in a farming village to a family where her father encouraged both his sons *and* his daughters to pursue an education but subjected her mother to violent domestic abuse, Ichikawa started her life of activism by leading her college classmates' protest against the mandatory "good wife, wise mother" curriculum for female students. After graduation, Ichikawa worked as a schoolteacher and as a journalist in Nagoya, where she heard about feminism while attending a lecture on Christianity. Following her move to Tokyo in 1918, she signed up for English lessons with Yamada Kakichi, Yamada Waka's husband. She met not only Waka but also Hiratsuka

Raichō, who was Kakichi's student as well. This fortuitous meeting led Hiratsuka, already a famous feminist, to ask Ichikawa, the general secretary of the women's division of the *Yūaikai* (Friendly Society, founded in 1912 as a labor organization; the women's division was created in 1916), to introduce her to women in textile mills so she could understand their labor conditions. An important bond was formed between the two women, leading them to found the Shin Fujin Kyōkai (New Woman's Association, NWA) in November 1919. A month later, Ichikawa and Hiratsuka recruited recent college graduate Oku Mumeo (1895–1997) as the third leader of the NWA.

In January 1920, the NWA leaders met with activist women in journalism and in the labor movement and decided to petition the Diet for two changes to Japanese law. Because Article 5 of the Public Peace Police Law made it illegal for women to join political parties or attend political rallies, the NWA knew its first task should be to amend that law. The second petition concerned Japanese family law, which turned out to be much harder to change than political law. Hiratsuka was particularly concerned that men with syphilis were passing the deadly infection to their wives, and submitted a petition to the Diet to require men to submit to syphilis testing before marrying. Under the law proposed by the NWA, a woman could call off her engagement if her fiancé had the disease, and after marriage a wife could divorce a husband who had contracted it. Women would not be required to undergo this medical exam, as Hiratsuka and other feminists believed that women—other than prostitutes—did not go astray sexually, though men did. Hiratsuka argued that making this legal change would protect the health of mothers and children. Had this law passed, it would have given women rights that they did not have in the patriarchal family system at that time. However, men in the Diet refused to support this petition to change the marriage law.

The two proposed legal changes appeared in every issue of the NWA's journal, *Josei Dōmei* (*Women's League*). In 1921 the NWA added a demand for women's suffrage to those petitions. In early 1921 the House of Representatives passed a bill to partially repeal Article 5, but that bill failed in the far more conservative House of Peers. That same year, tensions were developing within the NWA. Hiratsuka and Ichikawa had different ideological approaches to women's rights. While Hiratsuka stressed the principle of mothers' rights (*bokenshugi*), Ichikawa stressed the principle of women's rights (*jokenshugi*) as the foundation for women's citizenship. This clash paralleled ideological clashes in feminist movements worldwide between those who focused on gender differences as justification for women's civil rights and those who claimed women and men should have equal rights because

A meeting of the New Woman's Association. Ichikawa is seated on the far left, Oku is seated holding her baby, and Hiratsuka is seated on the far right.
LIBRARY OF CONGRESS, LC-DIG-GGBAIN-50432

of their essential similarities. Hiratsuka and Ichikawa left the NWA in 1921, but Oku stayed on. Carrying her baby on her back as she lobbied the most conservative aristocrats in the House of Peers, Oku persuaded them that a "good wife and wise mother" could take part in politics. In March 1922, Article 5 was amended to allow women to attend political rallies (although they were not permitted to join political parties until after World War II).

The previous year, socialist women, including Yamakawa Kikue, established the Sekirankai (Red Wave Society). Suffrage would soon be on the agendas of most women's rights advocates. After achieving a partial victory for women's rights, Oku Mumeo turned her attention to helping working women and women as consumers. She joined with suffragists on motherhood issues and with socialists on labor issues, developing a kind of communitarian feminism. That is, she focused on "women's emancipation as a group" (Narita 1998, 145) rather than on individual civil rights, calling for women to be "subjects of the nation." Around the same time, women peace activists, involved in transnational Christian movements, were beginning to make the link between peace advocacy and women's rights. Christian women, including Mary Elkinton Nitobe, a Philadelphia Quaker married to Japanese diplomat Nitobe Inazo, founded the Fujin Heiwa Kyōkai (Women's Peace

Association, WPA) in 1921. Members included both secular women intellectuals and members of the JWCTU and/or the YWCA. The group later became the Japanese affiliate of the transnational Women's International League of Peace and Freedom (WILPF). Although Japanese women did not have civil rights at the national level, transnational feminism gave them a venue to have a national voice and to exercise civic engagement through the international arena. For example, the eighty-nine-year-old founder of the JWCTU, Yajima Kajiko, hand-delivered a petition for peace signed by 10,224 Japanese women to American president Warren Harding at the Washington Naval Conference in 1921 (Tyrell 1991, 189; Ogawa 2007, 35).

JWCTU members took additional steps to claim a space in governance through transnational ties. When the United States outlawed Japanese immigration in 1924, JWCTU members contacted American WCTU members to lobby on behalf of their humiliated nation. They also went straight to secretary of state Charles Evans Hughes (Ogawa 2007, 41–43). The JWCTU believed that Japanese prostitutes and footloose single men had damaged Japan's reputation in the United States. Their patronizing attitude toward less fortunate Japanese kept them from understanding the depth of anti-Japanese racial attitudes among Americans.

Women in transnational feminist organizations were also adopting a more explicitly suffragist platform at the same time the NWA was moving in that direction. Shortly after the 1920 World WCTU meeting mentioned earlier, Gauntlett Tsune (1873–1953), one of the JWCTU delegates, traveled to Geneva to attend the meeting of the International Woman Suffrage Alliance (IWSA) at the invitation of IWSA president Carrie Chapman Catt (Shibahara 2014, chap. 3). Gauntlett's primary interest at that time was the peace movement, and Catt persuaded her that women's suffrage was the way to advance peace. Returning to Japan, and now an advocate for suffrage, Gauntlett was eagerly supported by Kubushiro Ochimi (1882–1972), secretary of the JWCTU. In July 1921, Kubushiro argued for votes for women in an article in the JWCTU's journal, and together with Gauntlett she founded the Nihon Fujin Sanseiken Kyōkai (Japan Women's Suffrage Association).

Ichikawa had left the NWA in 1921, bound for the United States, where she deepened her understanding of the diversity of Western feminisms through meetings with numerous leading feminists, including Jane Addams and especially Alice Paul, author of the U.S. Equal Rights Amendment and standard-bearer for the complete political equality position in American feminism. Paul exerted the strongest influence on Ichikawa. Ichikawa enjoyed working with feminists in the United States, but following the devastating earthquake that killed more than 150,000 people in the Tokyo area on September 1, 1923, Ichikawa knew she needed to return home (Molony 2010, 102). She arrived in early 1924, having been hired to work on women's issues by the International Labour Organization, an agency of the League of Nations. At the same time, she joined women from across the political spectrum who had created the Tokyo Rengō Fujinkai (Tokyo Federation of Women's Organizations) at the end of September 1923 to carry out earthquake relief. One of the subdivisions of this federation was its "government section," which also began to work on women's rights. In December 1924, their relief work done, government-section head Kubushiro Ochimi invited Ichikawa to join her in launching what would become Japan's leading suffrage group, the Fusen Kakutoku Dōmei (Women's Suffrage League, WSL). Members of the WSL included teachers, journalists, writers, housewives, and some workers. The WSL proclaimed as its founding manifesto:

> *1. It is our responsibility to destroy customs that have existed in this country for the past twenty-six hundred years and to construct a new Japan that promotes the natural rights of men and women;*
>
> *2. As women have been attending public schools with men for half a century since the beginning of the Meiji period and our opportunities in higher education have continued to expand, it is unjust to exclude women from universal suffrage;*
>
> *3. Political rights are necessary for the protection of nearly four million working women in this country;*
>
> *4. Women who work in the household must be recognized before the law to realize their full human potential;*
>
> *5. Without political rights we cannot achieve public recognition at either the national or local level of government;*
>
> *6. It is both necessary and possible to bring together women of different religions and occupations in a movement for women's suffrage. (Molony 2000, 656–657)*

From Reconstruction to the Manchurian Incident

Japanese politics had become increasingly democratic after World War I. In 1925, the government of prime minister Katō Takaaki granted suffrage to all males over twenty-five not receiving public welfare. Activists had been agitating for "universal" suffrage since the 1890s. WSL members were hopeful that the political parties would try to attract the new male electorate with promises of greater rights for women. In 1928, during the first national election after the passage of universal male suffrage, the WSL campaigned for fourteen candidates who supported women's rights. Seven of them won seats in the House of Representatives. Until 1931, the number of parliamentary supporters of women's rights continued to grow rapidly. Feminists called these years "the period of hope" (Molony 2005b, 74–75).

In March 1928, the WSL invited five other women's groups, four of them affiliated with proletarian movements such as labor unions, to join them in creating the Fusen Kakutoku Kyōdō Iinkai (Women's Suffrage Coordinating Committee) (Fujin Sansei Dōmei 1928, 5–10). Although government repression forced the proletarian women's groups to disband, leading to the demise of the committee in December 1929, the fact that the committee existed highlighted the possibilities for collaboration among women of different ideologies. In May 1928, Oku Mumeo founded the Fujin Shōhi Kumiai Kyōkai (Women's Consumer Union Association) and stated that the consumer movement would be the "foundation stone of the women's civil rights movement" (Oku 1928). Oku pioneered women's involvement in public actions on behalf of consumers, including lowering the prices of natural gas, electricity, transportation, and water; building hospitals and day care centers; and establishing employment agencies for women. To Oku, consumer activism was a form of civic participation.

Later that year, Japanese feminists turned to transnational activism to build up women's rights within the nation. An eighteen-member delegation of Japanese women, including secular and Christian feminists from a variety of organizations, attended the first Pan-Pacific Women's Conference in August 1928 (Molony 2010, 102–103). They continued to work together after the meeting, creating the Japan Women's Committee for International Relations as an affiliate of the Geneva-based Joint Standing Committee of Women's International Organizations (Yasutake 2009, 17). Matsu Tsuji (of Japan's YWCA) served as president, Gauntlett Tsune (of the JWCTU) as vice president, and Ichikawa Fusae (of the WSL) as secretary of the Women's Committee for International Relations. This was one of a number of transnational women's organizations in Japan at the time. All of them took seriously their role as representatives of Japan as a whole (not just of Japanese women) within global organizations; in 1930, when the heads of the major powers met in London for a disarmament conference that was a follow-up to the 1921–1922 Washington Naval Conference, Japanese women, inspired by Gauntlett Tsune, presented to the male delegates petitions for world peace signed by 750,000 Japanese women. As they had almost a decade earlier, women disenfranchised in national politics used the international stage to find their voice.

Women's civil rights seemed to be advancing in the winter of 1928–1929, when the WSL organized thirteen Tokyo-based women's groups to gather petitions for women's suffrage. The following year, prime minister Hamaguchi Osachi asked women's groups to assist in carrying out the government's economic austerity and savings programs during the recession of the late 1920s. In December 1929 Hamaguchi commended their actions and, because of their civic service, supported giving women (some) political rights so they could continue carrying out public service by reforming politics, consumption, and moral education. This list of responsibilities was gender-stereotyped, but it clearly offered a path toward citizenship based on women's assumed special characteristics and interest in morality and the home. The election of 1930 brought into the House of Representatives 338 members who supported some form of women's voting rights.

The time was ripe to push for the vote. The WSL announced a National Women's Suffrage Convention on April 27, 1930, and four hundred members of secular feminist groups, religious feminist groups such as the YWCA and Young Women's Buddhist Association, the Proletarian Women's League, and teachers' organizations came together. Elected officials did not miss an opportunity to appear before this large audience, and many gave speeches and asserted their support of women's rights. But the bills the government proposed in May 1930 and February 1931 fell far short of equal citizenship rights for women. They would have granted women the right to vote on the municipal level but not on the prefectural or national level. They would have required married women to obtain their husband's approval to run for office. Although these bills were vehemently denounced as inadequate by almost all feminists, they were rejected as too radical by the conservative House of Peers. Because bills needed to pass both houses, women failed to obtain even limited civil rights before everything changed in 1931.

Feminism After the Manchurian Incident

In September 1931, right-wing officers of Japan's Kantōgun (called the Kwantung Army by Western commentators at the time) who were stationed in Manchuria along the Japanese-owned South Manchurian Railway bombed a section of track in order to instigate hostilities in the region. This event, known as the Manchurian Incident, set in motion Japan's fifteen years of war on the continent. Right-wing extremism exploded at home in Japan as well, producing a wave of domestic terror, some of it fueled by hatred of modern society, emblematized by New Women and Modern Girls (see Chapter 6). Japan was closely tied to Western countries through multilateral treaties and trade. The global Great Depression that started with the crash of Wall Street in 1929 dragged Japan down, and anything transnational, whether in diplomacy or trade, was seen by radical right-wingers as the enemy of Japan. Government and business leaders were assassinated, and internationalism was distrusted. In that context, feminism, seen by rightists as Western and selfish, became suspect. Suffrage legislation would not be proposed again until 1945. But the suffragists were pragmatic and adjusted their tactics while retaining, at least until the late 1930s, their strategy of civic engagement as the basis for improving the status of women and children. After 1931 even the limited civil rights the government had proposed in 1930 and 1931 were impossible to achieve. The WSL accepted that civic engagement even without the vote was a step toward rights. As we shall see in Chapter 8, most feminists stressed that women across borders shared values of nurturance and advocacy of peace as "mothers of humanity" even while compromising with the nation-state.

BOX 5.1

International Peace and Women's Suffrage

In 1931, Ichikawa protested against the Manchurian Incident on behalf of "mothers of humanity." In the November 1931 issue of the Women's Suffrage League's journal *Fusen*, she linked the transnational women's efforts to attain peace with women's suffrage at the national level:

> *The hatred of war and the love of peace is an instinct in women. . . . [T]he people must hold the right to object to the outbreak of war. Also we must demand of the authorities to cooperate with other nations in advancing international peace. . . . [C]ivil rights . . . [in] local self-governing bodies [that is, at the local level] are hardly of any use. When we acquire suffrage, namely the right to participate in the law-making of the country, we can reflect our will in the settlement of national affairs. . . . Some may criticize us for demanding suffrage at this critical time, but we believe now is the time when we should advocate for it. (Ichikawa 1931, 2–3; translation in Molony 2011)*

But this attitude would change in the late 1930s and early 1940s (the war years).

Support of women's rights at the national level became problematic, however, because of the militarist imperialism of the Japanese state in the late 1930s and 1940s, in particular the oppressive treatment of Asian women by the Japanese military. The feminist quest for belonging to that state came to be questioned in Japan in the 1980s, tarnishing the reputation of feminists and challenging the link of feminism and nationalism in modernizing states.

KOREA

The official annexation of Korea by Japan in 1910 was further evidence of Japan's geopolitical rise, already seen in the Sino-Japanese War (1894–1895) and the Russo-Japanese War (1904–1905). As discussed in Chapter 4, under the popular motto of "civilization and enlightenment" Korea made a concerted effort to catch up with the modern countries of Europe, the United States, and Japan beginning in the late nineteenth century. Those efforts began to transform people's perceptions of the role and status of women in the family and society. However, Korea's path to a modern nation-state, interrupted by Japanese colonial occupation, posed a number of new challenges to the construction and practice of modern gender relations.

Intellectuals and social reformers were keenly aware of the rapid sociopolitical and cultural changes that were taking place in Korean society. It is important to try to understand the impact these changes in gender relations had on the daily life of the average woman in Korea at that time. How did she perceive these geopolitical shifts? Was she politically aware? If so, did that awareness drive her to participate in nationalist movements? Or was she indifferent to the political situation? Was she merely reacting to social changes? Was she seeking opportunities? Did she even think that she had alternatives?

Generally speaking, gender relations in colonial Korea were reshaped by a number of competing forces. Patriarchal conventions kept women as the subordinate gender. Colonial law and education reinforced hierarchical gender norms while trying to produce obedient and loyal subjects. Korean intellectuals and social reformers often prioritized the nationalist agenda over individual rights and freedoms, including rights for women. However, colonial capitalist developments led to industrialization and urbanization, which brought women into the workforce in unprecedented numbers to labor in factories and commercial agricultural enterprises. In addition, colonial Korea was deeply influenced by Euro-American modernist ideas, and new intellectual trends, including socialism, had made their way into colonial

Korea and were having varying degrees of influence on the discussion of reforms, adding even more complexity to people's lives.

Japanese Colonial Policies in Gender Relations

Japanese colonial rule brought a number of major changes to women's lives. One of the most significant changes under Japanese rule was the adoption of the household head system (*hojuje*) in 1921, based on the Japanese *ie* system. With this new legal arrangement, the patriarch held exclusive and disproportionate legal power in all family matters, ranging from marriage and divorce to property. From the law's point of view, women were practically excluded from any position of authority. A wife had to have permission from her husband to perform any transaction involving property, lawsuits, inheritance, or employment contracts. Thus women were relatively impotent in regard to the legal system. With regard to divorce and adultery, the legal system treated women and men differently. For example, a woman charged with adultery could receive a jail term of up to two years, and the charge could be used as grounds for divorce. In contrast, the law recognized a man's adultery only if the adulterous relationship had been with a married woman.

Along with the changes in the law that helped to reshape gender relations, colonial education for girls and women was designed on the premise that "enlightened" women would have a positive impact on men, the family, and society. The central precept stemmed from the Meiji gender ideology of "good wife, wise mother" (*ryōsai kenbo*) as well as Confucian-prescribed ethics, such as "womanly virtue" (*pudŏk*). In addition, the curriculum designed for girls' schools tended to place heavy emphasis on practical skills rather than humanistic subjects or knowledge of social sciences. Under these directives, the school curriculum devoted more than one-third of the academic program to domestic skills such as sewing, embroidery, child rearing, and home management. After the Manchurian Incident in 1931, Japan began to prepare for an aggressive war campaign, and that effort required the total mobilization of imperial subjects. The motto "Japan and Korea as a single body" (*naesŏn ilch'e* in Korean; *naisen ittai* in Japanese) conveys the message succinctly, and the educational policies for girls placed increasing emphasis on training loyal imperial subjects who would be ready to sacrifice themselves for the Japanese emperor. Later, as Japan's position in the war deepened, a new demand emerged for manual laborers to work in the production of military supplies. Discussion in Chapter 7 will reflect on how the war situation brought a large number of women into the arms industries during the Asia Pacific War.

Another area of importance for understanding the changes that colonial rule made in the lives of women was the adoption of public prostitution. As has been described in previous chapters, premodern Korea did have a system of female entertainers (*kisaeng*) who were to provide pleasure and stimulation for men of the literati class. Despite some opposition, the *kisaeng* system persisted under the rationale that it would protect women of the commoner class from male gaze and sexual advances. However, a more systematic intervention of the government into this form of entertainment began when large numbers of Japanese started to visit and settle in Korea after 1876. In port cities such as Pusan and Inch'ŏn prostitution thrived because of Japanese customers. Especially after the Russo-Japanese War in 1905, the influx of Japanese onto the Korean peninsula spurred the growth of sex industries even further, and the Japanese colonial government designated certain districts for such sexual transactions and managed public health issues that were common to prostitutes in an effort to maintain some measure of control and safety. Still, prostitution was not confined to those officially designated sites. Restaurants, bars, and cafés were also common sites where sexual activities were solicited.

The growth of prostitution was in part a result of colonial agricultural policies that promoted large-scale farming. The large farms bankrupted small family farms, forcing the daughters of those impoverished peasants to seek work in urban areas. Many of those young women, without skills or support, ended up working as prostitutes. Statistics indicate that the number of prostitutes nearly doubled between 1925 and 1931, from three thousand to almost six thousand. Those women from poor peasant families were often sold into service at the pleasure quarters by their families or brokers and exploited as sex slaves for extended periods to help relieve the family's debt. Korean prostitutes got paid significantly less than their Japanese counterparts, and because they were unable to pay back their contractors, they often found themselves indentured as sex slaves. After the Great Depression began in 1929, the sex industries were curtailed in Korea, at which point some of these women were sold into service in China, Japan, or elsewhere.

The Intersection Between Feminism and Nationalism

Korean nationalist endeavors worked in parallel with colonial gender policies to shape the lives of women. The relationship between feminism and nationalism is a matter of continuing discussion. Some argue that women's involvement in anticolonial, nationalist movements advanced the feminist agenda in the sense that under the banner of nationalism women were brought into the public sphere as vital partners, and in the end women were able to pave new paths to political, economic, and cultural engagement that had not been possible previously. Others see obstacles within the nationalist movement for the advancement of women's issues. Nationalist discourse argued that "nationalism works on behalf of all and therefore it is in everyone's interest to work on behalf of nationalism" (Wells 1999, 192). Thus there was a decided lack of focused attention on the issues that needed to be remedied in order to advance the cause of women.

In nationalist discourse, women often figured as the foundation of the family and the nation in their capacity as mothers instead of as individuals with desires and aspirations of their own. The phenomenon of the New Woman and Modern Girl in the 1920s and 1930s, which will be discussed in Chapter 6, illustrates the tensions between the nationalist prescription for women and women's growing desire for selfhood. History shows that the way women related to the nationalist project is complex and multilayered. Furthermore, nationalist groups varied in terms of their ideology and action strategies, ranging from conservative bourgeois ideals to uncompromising socialists. It is reasonable to say that, regardless of its positive or negative impact, the women's movement in colonized Korea was deeply interconnected with the nationalist and anticolonial projects.

One of the significant historical events where nationalist and feminist goals came together was the March First Movement. This independence movement was inspired in part by the doctrine of self-determination for fledgling nations advocated by U.S. president Woodrow Wilson as a part of the peace settlement after World War I. On March 1, 1919, thirty-three Korean intellectuals and religious leaders gathered together to read their Declaration of Independence:

> *We herewith proclaim the independence of Korea and the liberty of the Korean people. We tell it to the world in witness of the equality of all nations and we pass it on to our posterity as their inherent right. We make this proclamation, having back of us five thousand years of history and twenty millions of a united loyal people. We take this step to insure to our children, for all time to come, personal liberty in accord with the awakening consciousness of this new era. This is the clear leading of God, the moving principle of the present age, the whole human race's just claim. It is something that cannot be stamped out, or stifled, or gagged, or suppressed by any means. (Lee 1984, 342)*

News of the Declaration of Independence spread, and popular protests quickly filled the streets. Koreans from all walks of life—men and women, young and old, educated and uneducated, urbanites and peasants—went into the streets to take up the cause, waving the Korean flag and chanting "Long live Korean independence." Approximately two million Koreans participated in more than fifteen hundred separate demonstrations. Consider that figure: one person in every ten living in the country took part in some overt form of protest against the sitting government. Throughout the country, as the crowds grew, the Japanese imperial authorities responded with devastating violence, deploying not only police but also military personnel. According to official reports prepared by the colonial authorities, 46,948 were arrested, 15,961 injured, and 7,509 killed (Lee 1984, 344).

Although the movement was crushed by the Japanese imperial authorities, it did not disappear. The Provisional Government of the Republic of Korea was established in Shanghai in April 1919. This was the first political organ to integrate the various nationalist groups and organizations. In addition, the Japanese colonial administration revisited its governing policies and established "cultural rule" (*munhwa chŏngch'i* in Korean; *bunka seiji* in Japanese), under which Koreans were given more freedom to organize associations and engage in print media, although more sophisticated censorship measures kept politically radical ideas at bay.

The impact of the March First protest and its aftermath on women's movements was far-reaching. Female students actively participated in mobilizing their fellow students and the public to participate in protests in the streets. Some were arrested, spending months in jail. Among the thousands of Korean protesters, Yu Kwansun (1902–1920) is a figure of nearly mythic status. Yu, a student at Ewha Girls' School, was arrested for her involvement in street protests and died in prison after being tortured. She was celebrated as a patriot, a martyr in the struggle against Japan, and the personification of the ideal woman who fully devoted her life to the cause of nationalism.

After the March First Movement, a number of women's groups emerged with a variety of orientations and agendas, ranging from liberal to Christian to socialist. The "liberal" groups, based in urban areas with members who had more advanced educational credentials, prioritized individual freedom and equality, critiquing oppressive patriarchal practices and advocating the inalienable rights of women to equal treatment and opportunity in education, work, and family life. The first feminist magazine, *New Woman* (*Sin yŏja*), was founded in 1920, clearly drawing inspiration from the Japanese feminist magazine *Seitō* (Kim 2013; see Chapter 4). A cohort of educated women shaped the content of the magazine as its staff and contributing writers. Often referred to as "New Women" (*sin yŏsŏng*), they held a modern outlook on such matters as love, marriage, education, work, and family, signifying a new trend for gender relations in modern Korea. At the same time, their novel ideas and bodily practices became a target for criticism and ridicule from conservative intellectuals. Chapter 6 offers a more detailed analysis of the phenomenon of the New Women in the 1920s and 1930s.

Christian women formed the most enduring and best organized groups. Benefiting from the history of interactions with Western Protestant missionaries from the late nineteenth century, Christian women learned how to organize groups for particular purposes, often in connection with the missionary societies. Their religious faith was the central motivating force in the proliferation of Bible study groups, Sunday schools, prayer meetings, and even a national tour for evangelism. Through these activities in conjunction with missionaries, these Korean Christian women also participated in the construction of modern forms of domesticity, including hygienic child-rearing practices, proper home management, and planning a nutritionally balanced diet for the family (Choi 2014; Kim 2014). The culmination of the Christian women's groups and their activities was the establishment of the Korean Young Women's Christian Association (Chosŏn kidokkyo yŏja chŏngnyŏnhoe yŏnhaphoe) in 1922. The Korean YWCA was an organization that had affiliations nationwide and internationally, and it actively utilized this global network in various campaigns to promote women's literacy, hygiene, and economic independence, especially in rural communities.

The first socialist women's organization, Chosŏn yŏsŏng tonguhoe, was founded in May 1924. Korean women educated in Japan, China, and Russia had been exposed to socialist ideas and brought new energy to shaping women's movements with ideological priorities that were distinct from those held by the liberal or Christian groups. Better equipped with systematic knowledge of the origin and causes of gender oppression in relation to the inequalities in the capitalist economic system, socialist women considered economic transformation to be a prerequisite for gender liberation. In the beginning, socialist women mainly focused on women factory workers; however, Korean society was predominantly agrarian, and peasants constituted the vast majority of the population. As the movement grew, socialist women eventually expanded the scope of their work by actively including peasant women in the scheme of social change.

The pivotal moment in the women's movement in colonial-era Korea came when Kŭnuhoe (Friends of the Rose of Sharon) was founded in 1927.

It was the first nationwide women's organization to unify all of the different ideological orientations into a single political entity. It was established as a sister organization to Sin'ganhoe (1927–1931), a coalition of uncompromising nationalist and Communist groups with the shared goal of achieving national independence. The founding document of Kŭnuhoe castigated the lot of women in any society where they were subjected to treatment bound up with "all kinds of contradictions and antagonism," and it held that "women have always been placed in the positions of greatest disadvantage throughout human history" (Kŭnuhoe 1929, 3–4). From that broader historical standpoint, Kŭnuhoe aimed to liberate not only Korean women but also Korean society and eventually all oppressed peoples. The organization held the universal ideal of gender equality while cautioning people not to forget local particulars.

Kŭnuhoe identified a set of goals that needed to be achieved in order to ensure real progress for women, including:

- The eradication of social and legal discrimination against women
- The elimination of feudal customs and superstition
- The abolition of early marriage and the free exercise of a woman's rights to marriage and divorce
- The prohibition of human trafficking and public prostitution
- The economic support of peasant women
- The elimination of wage discrimination and the adoption of paid maternity leave
- The maintenance and enforcement of safe working conditions for women and children
- The abrogation of gender discrimination in education and the expansion of elementary education for girls

Leaders of the organization used its journal, *Kŭnu*, to show how inequality had been propagated by gender-specific norms, rituals, and everyday practices in Korea and elsewhere. Some of the leadership had been significantly influenced by socialism, and thus they attributed gender inequality to the emergence of private property and the capitalist economic system. On the basis of these premises, Kŭnuhoe aimed to mobilize women factory workers and peasants to participate in a broader transformation of society. By 1929 the membership of Kŭnuhoe throughout the country had reached nearly three thousand. The organization led a number of educational, political, and economic initiatives in both urban and rural communities. However, by the early 1930s socialist groups were faced with punishing surveillance and political censorship by the colonial authorities and thus could not engage in public activities. Kŭnuhoe was ultimately dissolved in 1931 because of the internal tensions that had developed between the socialist and the other nationalist factions and increasing political oppression enacted by the Japanese colonial authority.

In the 1930s the women's movement responded to changes in political and economic conditions. The Great Depression had an especially deep and devastating impact on farmers, who constituted 80 percent of the country's population. Furthermore, close to 80 percent of farmers were tenants or

BOX 5.2

"Declaration of the Establishment of Kŭnuhoe," *Kŭnu* 1 (1929): 3–4

Since the beginning of history, there have been all kinds of contradiction and antagonism in human societies. In each historical era, the constant fluctuation in human relationships has resulted in benefits to one group and impediments to others. The grass roots in our society are the underprivileged, and they have had to endure great suffering through most times. Women have always been placed in the positions of greatest disadvantage throughout history. Social contradictions have reached their peak in terms of scale and intensity. As a result, one cannot find even a trace of affection or loyalty among people, and the whole of humanity is pandemonium, fighting with each other out of material greed. The tragic outcomes of war are growing more brutal and far-reaching, and abject poverty and crime are rampant. If one sees a little bit of progress in the status of women in this era, it is nothing more than whimsical imagination. In Korea, the status of women is still very low. They suffer through remnants of the old era that still prevail. On top of that continuing degradation, they must now deal with the added agonies of the present.

(continued)

Inauguration of Kŭnuhoe.
The Independence Hall of Korea

It is readily apparent that all the irrational factors that put women at a disadvantage are essentially linked with factors that haunt Korean society and indeed all societies around the world. Therefore, all the solutions to the problems are intricately connected and cannot be separated from each other. The wretched among us must strain to gain a new life, and history guarantees the inevitable victory that will result from this struggle.

The true meaning of the women's movement in Korea can be understood only after one grasps its broader historical and social background. Our role should never be seen in a narrow sense. Our struggle for liberation should be done simultaneously to liberate Korean society and to further all humanity. However, we must not forget about local particulars in privileging the universal and the general. Therefore, in our attempt to develop a women's movement in Korea, we have established a separate women's organization, giving due consideration to all the particular conditions Korean women face. We realize that such an organization will enable us to guide Korean women more effectively.

The Korean women's movement has taken an important step forward because of circumstances in Korean society and the world, as well as the commitment of Korean women. Fragmented and scattered movements are now organized into a united front. We identify goals and strategies based on challenges women in different social sectors commonly face. In this way, we will be able to expand our women's movement effectively. It is our duty at this stage to overcome any divisive tendencies and solidify our collaborative front.

The essence of the many irrationalities that Korean women are entangled in is due to feudal remnants and contemporary social contradictions. In our fight against these irrational notions, there should not be any disagreement among Korean women. Only women of the reactionary class will fail to participate in this struggle.

From this vantage point, Kŭnuhoe declares its intention to carry out various projects. No matter how horrendous our future paths might be, we are determined to fulfill our historical duty, driven by the power of 10 million sisters.

Women are not weak.
When women are liberated, the world will be liberated.
Korean sisters, let's unite.

semi-tenants, who barely had enough income to support themselves and their families after paying fees to their landlords. The decade saw an enormous increase in the number of disputes between landowners and tenants. In 1931 there were only 667 such cases, but by 1937 the number had grown to 31,799. The colonial authorities deployed a two-pronged strategy to tackle the escalating crisis. On one hand, they tried to suppress such collective disputes, saying that those disputes were a socialist plot. On the other hand, they also instituted a nationwide campaign of "self-reliance and restoration" that gradually led to the implementation of educational and reform programs designed to rescue the devastated rural communities.

These reform-oriented rural movements spearheaded by the colonial government went hand in hand with the rural revitalization movement led by moderate to conservative Korean intellectuals and social reformers. These reformers tried to modernize rural life by introducing new agricultural technology, farming cooperatives, programs to build literacy, and lifestyle reforms. In particular, the YWCA, which had a nationwide network by that time, played an important role in mobilizing women to get involved in rural development. Ch'oe Yongsin (1909–1935), well known for her promotion of the welfare of peasant women and children in the 1930s, was one of the first women workers sent into rural communities by the Korean YWCA. Her life inspired Sim Hun's 1935 novel *Sangnoksu* (Evergreen), which further advanced the idea that educated women must commit themselves to larger social causes rather than self-interest for the betterment of the nation.

Women in Exile

Under colonization, the nation and national independence became a primary concern for Korean intellectuals and social reformers. It became increasingly difficult to build the independence movement within Korea due to Japanese surveillance and restrictions. As a result, some nationalists went into exile to develop military, diplomatic, economic, and educational strategies for taking back the nation. There were prominent exile communities in Shanghai, North Kando (Chien-tao) in Manchuria, Hawai'i and the mainland United States, and the Russian Maritime Territory. Women played a significant role as traditional helpmates as well as active mediators in transmitting information and funds for the independence movement, shuttling between Korea and bases overseas. However, their stories have been more or less invisible in historiography, in part because they did not leave written records of their lives and activities, but also because the idea of woman as helpmate was generally taken for granted and tended to be ignored in the recording of history. Only in recent decades has the crucial role that these emissary women played in the efforts toward independence begun to receive scholarly attention.

One of the few documents from that time that offer insights into the role that women played in independence is the autobiography of Chŏng Chŏnghwa (1900–1991). At the tender age of ten she married the eldest son of a prominent government official. When her husband and father-in-law moved to Shanghai in 1920 to work for the Korean Provisional Government (1919–1948), the center of the national independence movement overseas, she accompanied them to offer assistance. She initially focused on performing household tasks for her family and the families of the other independence fighters, but she soon took up the role of messenger and fund-raiser, making a number of dangerous trips between Shanghai and Korea, carrying messages to underground activists in Korea or bringing funding back to Shanghai to support the work in exile. During one such foray back home, her father expressed his concern about the danger she was putting herself in and suggested that she go to the United States for further study. However, she declined to even consider that option. She firmly believed that, as a daughter-in-law, her role was to take care of her father-in-law. In her autobiography, she writes:

> *I had mixed feelings whenever people talked about me publicly. I never considered myself to be in the vanguard of the nation's struggle for independence from Japan. In truth, I didn't have the strength or skill to do that. I was just an ordinary woman who believed that a person should know his or her place and just go with the flow of life. The conditions of the era created a small space for me in the Provisional Government, and I have been doing my best to faithfully carry out those duties. (Chŏng 1998, 173–175)*

Equally as important a site as Shanghai in the life of Korean migrants was Manchuria. Beginning in the late nineteenth century, a significant number of Koreans migrated to Manchuria in search of new life opportunities. In 1910 the Korean population in Manchuria was approximately 200,000; by 1945 it had reached 1.5 million, and Manchuria became another site where Korean women engaged in the nationalist movement. What is fascinating about the gender politics of Korean peasant women in Manchuria is that they "cooperated with both Korean and Chinese Communists throughout the 1930s to achieve the conjoined goals of changing economic conditions and liberating both Korea and China from the Japanese rule" (Park 1998,

229–230). Korean women's cooperation with the Chinese Communist Party (CCP) initially resulted in challenges to the patriarchal bias in gender relations as the CCP advocated freedom in marriage and divorce and critiqued the oppressive nature of arranged marriages and the practices of early marriage and concubinage. However, beginning in 1934, with the growing resentment among male peasants and the elderly in Manchuria, who saw Communism as a destructive force in family relations and womanly virtues, the CCP adopted more conservative gender policies in order to placate and regain the support of the peasants. As a result, older standards of womanly virtue, such as female chastity and obedience to male authorities, came to be readopted. However, that return to conservative standards did not mean that the women became passive or powerless. Because of the harsh economic realities created by the worldwide depression, inflation, high interest rates, and rising rents and taxation, Korean migrant women had to participate in the ongoing riots in Manchuria simply to survive.

Korean women in Manchuria also filled a supporting role for their male relatives who were leading the fight for independence. They acted as intermediaries by conveying messages from underground guerrillas to other activist cells. The capture and imprisonment of family members by the Japanese military further pushed them to participate in revolutionary activities. For instance, Kim Insuk describes her experience as follows:

> *My son, Tong-gi, and his friends were arrested as suspects in the harvest uprisings. Right after being released by the police due to lack of evidence, Tong-gi and his seven friends went to the mountains to join the guerrilla armies. I heard later that they engaged in attacks of the pro-Japanese, pro-landlord Self-Defense Group (Chawidan) in 1932. My second son and 12 other village people, including my daughter-in-law, were convicted. My second son was tortured and killed during the investigation. Since then, I always carried a hand-made bomb and a knife hidden in my clothes. I was determined to avenge the death of my son. That was 29 years ago [in 1932] and I was 45 years old. I received military training, carrying my baby on my back. I worked in the Storm Corps and the Red Defense Corps. In October 1933, I became the leader of the Women's Committee in Namgol, Pon'gaedong. (Park 1998, 241)*

It is important to note that not all Koreans were engaged in the nationalist movement. Oral histories indicate that emigrating to urban centers outside of

Korea offered the promise of the modern and the opportunity to create a new identity as a New Woman or Modern Girl. In urban centers and concessions such as Tianjin they would be exposed to capitalist consumer cultures. Some women received training in modern professions, such as typing or dressmaking, and they enjoyed the lifestyle of a Modern Girl, essentially free of any Korean identity. Indeed, maintaining an identity as "Korean" was disadvantageous in terms of finding employment because Japanese-run industries and shops discriminated against Koreans in their hiring. Thus many tried to hide their Korean identity in public to get better access to job opportunities.

These examples of women in exile reflect an increasing trend in which Korean women traveled beyond the borders of the country, whether it was for the purpose of supporting male relatives' national independence movement or to find new life opportunities that modernity afforded women. Another example can be found in "picture brides," young women who entered into marriages (generally sight unseen) with men who had emigrated to Hawai'i to work on plantations. Most left home for the promise of escape or opportunity. Elements of modernity had flowed into Korea, and that initial exposure inspired more and more women to venture outward to seek other possibilities.

CHINA

China's new republic was troubled from the start. President Yuan Shikai's regime became increasingly dictatorial, and in 1915 he attempted to declare himself emperor. Events surrounding World War I brought nationalist fervor in China to new heights as the central government lost control of the country. In the midst of the war in 1915, Japan issued its Twenty-One Demands, which called for significant expansion of Japan's control of Chinese territory and economy at the expense of Western powers. The demands included Chinese recognition of Japanese concessions in Manchuria, Japanese takeover of German-controlled territories in Shandong province, and acceptance of Japanese advisors on political, financial, and police affairs. Yuan's acceptance of most of these demands outraged people across China, many of whom were already incensed at his dictatorial policies. There were widespread boycotts of Japanese goods to protest this capitulation, and women, as household managers and consumers, participated in large numbers. After Yuan's death in 1916, the country split into regional regimes controlled by warlords who engaged in constant warfare for the next twelve years, causing chaos across the country. Sun Yat-sen's Revolutionary Alliance regrouped as the Nationalist Party (Kuomintang or Guomindang, hereafter KMT) and established a power base in the southeastern province of Guangzhou in alliance with a regional warlord regime sympathetic to the party's platform of national reunification and modernization.

The New Culture and May Fourth Movements

In Beijing, the old imperial university created by late Qing reforms was restructured as the modern Beijing University under the dynamic leadership of a group of male intellectuals who launched the New Culture Movement, committed to a political and cultural renaissance in China. In 1915, the new dean of letters, Chen Duxiu (1879–1942), who had been educated in Japan, founded a journal, *New Youth*, which became one of the most influential vehicles for promotion of progressive ideas about gender and family reform. Its pages were filled with radical critiques of China's Confucian civilization, social inequality, and political dysfunction by intellectuals representing a diverse array of ideological perspectives, many of whom would later be recognized as China's leading scholars, writers, and political activists. Linking the subjugation of women within the Confucian family to China's lack of political freedoms and individual rights and its weak position on the international stage, Chen placed women's emancipation at the forefront of an anti-Confucian nationalist agenda. In a 1916 article in the journal he wrote, "The three principles that subordinate the subject to the monarch, son to father, and wife to husband have made the subject, son, and wife appendages to the monarch, father, and husband, lacking their own independent and autonomous personhood. . . . Loyalty, filial piety, and chastity are . . . a slavery morality that makes oneself subordinate to others" (quoted in Wang 1999, 45).

In the pages of *New Youth* and similar New Culture journals, family reform and the "woman question," as it was called, were central to the discussion of how to build a strong and modern Chinese nation. Although most New Culture intellectuals were men, they understood women's equality to be a hallmark of modern civilization and national strength in the Western countries they looked to for models. Radical-minded male intellectuals and students felt that their fulfillment as individuals was constrained by filial obedience to family patriarchs who arranged their marriages and controlled their career choices. They argued that customs of concubinage, footbinding, widow chastity, and female seclusion that oppressed women were key elements of a family system that crushed individuality and fostered blind obedience to authority. Confucian family patriarchy fostered an antidemocratic political culture that persisted because most Chinese people had a slavish "emperor mentality" that prevented them from opposing unjust or corrupt political authorities (Glosser 2003). Given the immensity of China's economic backwardness and political weakness, the full participation of women in the economy and civic life was also deemed essential for national survival. Despite its emphasis on cultivating individual personhood as the foundation for modern citizenship, the discourse of the New Culture movement, like most late Qing feminism, justified women's emancipation only as an essential part of nation building and modernization, not as an end in itself.

BOX 5.3

New Culture Gender Ideals

At the height of the May Fourth Movement in 1919, Yang Zhihua (1900–1973) was expelled from the Hangzhou No. 1 Female Normal School for editing a progressive student journal. In 1924 she joined the Communist Party, in which she distinguished herself as an effective labor organizer (see Chapter 7) and leader in Party women's organizations. In a 1922 essay published in the newspaper supplement *Women's Critic,* she elaborated on the obstacles to implementation of New Culture ideals for interaction between women and men in social practice.

> *How many people who are supposedly engaged in the New Culture Movement these days truly mean business? Far too many of them are just wearing masks! As it is, there are more destroyers than builders; if this continues, our future is really in grave danger! . . . Open socializing between men and women is a very important issue. . . . Unfortunately, it has not been easy to carry out. Why not? In my opinion, it is due to the obstacles created by the men and women involved. . . . This is where the obstacles lie. . . .*
>
> *First, when a man and a woman start to socialize by speaking and writing to each other, going to the parks together, or studying together, people jump to the conclusion that this young man and this young woman are in love, even though they are actually just friends. Consequently, some young men and women succumb to these outside pressures and speculations, go ahead and push themselves into the "business of love," and then have sex. After that, they break up, agonize, and part ways. . . .*
>
> *The second is a subjective obstacle. . . . Often, one feels excited when one meets a stranger of the opposite sex. When this happens,*

people behave strangely. . . . For the sole purpose of speeding up the game of love, they discard their personal integrity and try all sorts of tricks to seduce the opposite sex. . . . This kind of union has nothing to do with love. It is nothing but animal desire. . . .

Third, there are some who tend to misunderstand the intention of the other party, assuming that even the slightest agreement in language and thought signifies "love." . . . Suffering from "unrequited love," many of them end up becoming ill, insane, or suicidal. . . . It is my hope that there will be more discussion on socializing between men and women. (Translated in Lan and Fong 1999)

There were very few women in universities at the time. In 1919 Beijing Women's Higher Normal School, the first Chinese-run institution of higher education, was founded. In 1920 Beijing University hired its first woman professor and began to admit women students. But the numbers of female university students grew very slowly. By 1923 there were only 847 women in institutions of higher education in the whole country, the vast majority in Beijing. Although girls made up almost a fifth of the school population by 1928, women still accounted for only 8.5 percent of total university enrollments (Bailey 2007, 108–109). Though their numbers were small, girls' schools were important incubators for young women's political consciousness and the formation of activist networks among women.

Women students and the older generation of suffrage activists enthusiastically took up political organizing when nationalist fervor exploded in 1919 in response to the news that the Treaty of Versailles would give Germany's concessions in the coastal province of Shandong to Japan. Late in World War I, China had allied itself with Britain, France, and the United States and sent some 140,000 laborers to support the Allied effort in Europe. Like their counterparts in colonized countries around the globe, Chinese nationalists were heartened by Woodrow Wilson's talk of a right to self-determination and expected that imperialist privileges and territorial hegemony in various parts of China would be rolled back in recognition of its contributions to the Allied war effort. Upon hearing the news that the Chinese delegation representing the Beijing warlord government was prepared to accept Japanese claims in Shandong, some three thousand students from Beijing University and other schools in the capital launched what would be called the May Fourth Movement, massing in Tiananmen Square in the city center and marching to the legation quarter, where foreign embassies were located, demanding that the warlord government refuse to sign the treaty. Blocked by legation police, they proceeded to the house of a cabinet minister who had negotiated huge loans from Japan, sacked it, and set it on fire. In clashes with police, one student was fatally wounded and hundreds were arrested.

Female students were active participants in the demonstrations, strikes, and boycotts of Japanese goods that erupted across the country in response to the arrests of students in Beijing. The May Fourth Movement inspired widespread nationalist opposition to imperialism and the warlord regimes that fragmented the country. It also galvanized students, intellectuals, professionals, and workers into political activism, and in the twenties political groups representing a variety of ideologies proliferated in an atmosphere of optimism about the potential for meaningful political transformation.

Among these groups was the United Women's Association, which formed branches across the country to advocate for women's rights. Through these groups women suffrage activists succeeded in getting guarantees of gender equality into the provincial constitutions of Guangdong, Hunan, and Zhejiang despite concerted and sometimes violent opposition (Edwards 2008). Some of these groups expanded their advocacy to include economic, educational, and legal rights. In industrialized Shanghai, where foreign control precluded democratic political activities, the women's association was led by leftist women who focused their energies on promoting links between women's issues and the interests of the working class through a journal called *Women's Voice* and the Shanghai Commoners' Girls' School.

In Beijing, where a series of warlord regimes attempted to promulgate constitutions, women suffrage activists created two organizations to lobby for their political rights, both of which soon formed branches in Shanghai and other cities. The Women's Suffrage Association, formed by students in 1922, announced three goals: "overthrow the constitution that was written specifically for men and ensure that there are guarantees for women's rights; overthrow the property and inheritance laws that are designed for men and demand economic independence; and overthrow the education system of the power holders and demand equality in access to knowledge" (Edwards 2008, 132–133). The founders of the more radical Women's Rights League, inspired by anarchism and Marxism, pursued a broader agenda that linked women's inequality to class oppression. In addition to the political, educational, and legal rights demanded by their more moderate rivals, their man-

Female students marching in a demonstration to support the May Fourth Movement.
TRADITIONS.CULTURAL-CHINA.COM

ifesto also called for bans on concubinage, prostitution, trafficking of girls, and footbinding and for equal pay for women factory workers.

Women and the Early Communist Party

From the beginning of the twentieth century, Chinese radicals had been drawn to anarchist and socialist approaches to social transformation and political revolution. After 1911, many young Chinese men and women went to France to participate in work-study programs through which they put anarchist ideals of social equality, communal living, and combined mental and manual labor into practice. Back in China, they formed voluntary associations to enact these new values. The success of the Russian Revolution in 1917 convinced many of these radicals that Marxism-Leninism offered an effective means for expanding revolutionary social change beyond their small communities to society at large and many formed Marxist study societies. In 1921, some twenty radical intellectuals, assisted by representatives of the Communist International (Comintern) in Russia, founded the Chinese Communist Party (CCP) in Shanghai and transformed these groups into party cells. One of these intellectuals was Mao Zedong (1893–1976), an activist from Hunan who had joined a Marxist study society while working at the library at Beijing University.

The men who founded the CCP were steeped in New Culture thinking. They were committed to women's emancipation as part of a vision of radical transformation of social relations that was inspired both by Marxist critiques of women's oppression in the family and by earlier Chinese nationalist assumptions that women's oppression was a key cause of China's weakness as a nation. For early Communists, as for New Culture intellectuals in general, the issue of oppressive marriage practices was personal. Many were in arranged marriages to "old-fashioned" uneducated women from their hometowns. As urban social mores began to condone social interactions between men and women as well as choice of marriage partners, a number of these men left their traditional wives for more educated, modern women. Others continued to support their country wives while pursuing a new, modern relationship.

CCP leaders also understood that, given the persistence of norms of gender segregation, women cadres (political organizers) would be essential for mobilization work with women students and workers. They set about recruiting them into the Party. By 1925 there were about a hundred women Party members. Most had attended provincial schools established in the late Qing, where they participated in May Fourth activities and anarchist study groups in which they learned about Marxism. But most women who became leaders in the party gained their status through their husbands, and their leadership roles were limited to work in the Women's Bureau and organizational support behind the scenes. The CCP was a highly patriarchal organization from its beginning. Despite their rhetoric about the importance of women's emancipation and equality, male CCP members had no interest in sharing power with women and some were quite critical of female comrades they considered to be improperly outspoken. They expected their comrade wives to conform to their whims and manage the household and children so they could focus on their public duties. It appears that CCP women tacitly accepted their inferior status, perhaps because they themselves carried traditional assumptions about women's roles or because they accepted the "mothers of citizens" logic that held that what the nation needed most was women's labor, not their leadership (Gilmartin 1995).

The career of Xiang Jingyu (1895–1928) exemplifies the opportunities and limitations of women's activism in the early CCP (Gilmartin 1995, 71–95). Her father was a prominent businessman from Hunan who was active in the nationalist politics that made the province a center of reformist and anti-Qing activities at the end of the dynasty. Her elder brother, who had joined Sun Yat-sen's Revolutionary Alliance as a student in Japan, was a teacher in the local girls' school where Xiang started her formal education. She completed her secondary education at a girls' normal school in the provincial capital, where she led student demonstrations and boycotts to protest the Twenty-One Demands in 1915. After graduation she founded a school in her hometown to provide girls a nationalist and feminist education that would prepare them to be equal citizens. She joined a Hunan work-study group through which she helped lead Hunan's May Fourth protests. There she met her husband, Cai Hesen (1895–1931), whom she married in public defiance of her father's wishes, becoming a model of revolutionary free choice marriage. The couple went to France in 1919 on a work-study program and joined the Communists. Returning to China in 1921, Cai joined the CCP leadership.

Although Xiang became a member of the Party by virtue of her husband's status, she was soon appointed head of the CCP Women's Bureau in 1922, the first woman to have a formal position. She pushed hard for greater recruitment of women, but she failed to get them positions outside of her Women's Bureau. When she left her husband for another party member, she lost her position and was sent to the Soviet Union. Returning to China as a single woman in 1927, she was no longer part of the leadership.

Political Movements in the 1920s

In 1922, the CCP joined with the Nationalist Party in the United Front to reunify the country through a combined political and military campaign. Communists dominated the mass organizations charged with mobilizing worker, student, and peasant support for the campaign. Xiang Jingyu became head of the joint Shanghai Women's Movement Bureau and led the United Front effort to educate women of all social groups about their importance to the nationalist cause and to coordinate participation of educated women and workers. When women silk workers went on strike that year to demand a ten-hour workday and improved labor conditions, Xiang published numerous essays in the Nationalist periodical *Women's Weekly* to explain their situation and garner support from educated middle-class women in Shanghai, whom she often described as bourgeois ladies of leisure.

In 1923 Sun Yat-sen called for creation of a national assembly to be a foundation for political unification and began negotiations with the Beijing warlord regime. Women in the United Front plunged enthusiastically into the ensuing national assembly movement, creating a Women's National Assembly Promotion Association. Its members lobbied for representatives of women's groups to be included among the participants in the proposed conference in Beijing to plan the assembly and promoted awareness through the press of the issue of women's political rights and the importance of the assembly for China's political development. As leader of the Shanghai Women's Bureau, Xiang Jingyu wrote in a manifesto explaining the urgency of the assembly and the link between women's rights and national salvation:

> *Fundamentally speaking, China's movement for women's rights and suffrage is a progressive movement, an innovative movement,*

> *a movement that carries the style of twentieth-century human liberation. Then its ideal objective does not just consist of achieving equal status with ordinary Chinese men. Rather, on the one hand, it demands legal, economic, educational, and social equality between men and women. On the other, it demands enthusiastic participation in the mass revolutionary movement to overthrow the various big power holders and northern warlords, in order to prevent domestic and foreign oppression of the Chinese. (Quoted in Edwards 2008, 152)*

At the height of the movement in 1924, a meeting of more than six hundred women convened in Shanghai, representing the wide diversity of women activists: moderate social reformers, radicals, Communist women, Christian women, workers, educators, students, and professionals. The collapse of the national assembly effort after Sun's death in 1925 brought an end to the suffrage movement, but the infrastructure women had created provided the base for the next phase of women's activism.

On May 30, 1925, mass demonstrations broke out in Shanghai after a striking worker at a Japanese-owned cotton mill was killed; during these demonstrations, British police killed eleven workers and students. In the ensuing May Thirtieth Movement, people all over the country took to the streets to express their fury, and support for the CCP grew tremendously as it was recognized for its combined focus on workers' rights and nationalist resistance to imperialism. Unprecedented numbers of women took part in strikes and rallies, and female membership in the CCP grew to over a thousand. Xiang Jingyu created the Shanghai All-Women's Association to transform the networks established for the suffrage campaign into a mass organization focused on women workers and elimination of imperialist treaty privileges. Shanghai factories employed more than 170,000 women workers, most in cotton and silk production, and the May Thirtieth Movement inspired some of them to join the party (see Chapter 7).

The CCP-KMT Split and the Women's Movement

In 1926 the United Front army, under the command of Chiang Kai-shek (1887–1975), launched the Northern Expedition to unite the country under KMT rule. Chiang had always reviled the Communists and saw the alliance with them in the United Front as a temporary expediency. As Nationalist troops approached Shanghai early in 1927, he began a purge of CCP members from the Nationalist Party, starting with the execution of labor movement activists who had organized a general strike in the city in anticipation of its liberation from warlord control. The bloody purge, which continued for several years, resulted in the deaths of thousands of Communists and other radicals across the country, including more than one thousand women, some of whom were targeted simply for having bobbed hair. Many executed women had their breasts cut off; mutilation in sexualized ways showed that women's activism was perceived both as a political threat and as a violation of sexual morality. Among those executed was Xiang Jingyu.

As the KMT consolidated control over most of the country, it established new women's associations that abandoned left-wing rhetoric of class struggle and focused on political rights within the Nationalist Party, education, reforms of marriage law, and improved living standards for workers and peasants. Eager to solidify its legitimacy domestically as a modernizing and progressive regime and to win over Western countries as allies, the Nationalist government pursued legal and political reforms to promote gender equality. Despite its association with leftists and the Communist Party, International Women's Day continued to be celebrated by feminists working openly under Nationalist rule. Although they did not establish fully democratic political institutions, the Nationalists did grant women full political rights to vote and be elected to office in their 1935 constitution. Although a few won seats in the 1936 election for the National People's Assembly, implementation of the assembly itself was curtailed by the onset of the Japanese invasion in 1937 (Edwards 2008).

Women activists made more concrete progress with legal reforms, enshrined in the new 1931 legal code, that guaranteed free choice of marriage partners, granted husbands and wives equal rights in divorce, gave sons and daughters equal inheritance rights, and acknowledged limited claims by wives on a husband's property. The legal status of concubinage continued to be controversial. Rather than outlawing the practice, the new code made it possible for a wife to apply for divorce if her husband took a concubine. After a concerted campaign by feminists, the 1935 revision of the code made husbands and wives equally liable for adultery, technically allowing men with concubines to be prosecuted for adultery (Tran 2015). Large numbers of elite and ordinary women, mostly in the cities, took advantage of these laws, filing lawsuits against husbands and other family members to pursue their rights. Nevertheless, implementation of the new laws was slow and uneven in many places because of the persistence of older customs and attitudes within communities and even among judges (Kuo 2012).

The purge decimated the CCP, which was forced to retreat underground and into the remote countryside, where it began the process of rebuilding and refining its revolutionary tactics. In their rural base, known as the Jiangxi Soviet, the CCP experimented with marriage reforms, including freedom of choice of marriage partners, minimum ages of consent, a ban on the purchase of brides, and limited divorce. But full implementation of women's rights was stalled when such policies deterred male peasant recruitment.

Chiang Kai-shek's Nationalist forces launched continuous military assaults against the Jiangxi Soviet, the territory in which the CCP set up a government after fleeing from the Shanghai purge, and its Red Army defenders. In 1934 KMT forces finally routed the CCP's Red Army and forced it to flee the Jiangxi region. CCP forces embarked on what came to be called the Long March across the rugged terrain of southern and western China to the remote region of Yenan, in the north, where they would rebuild for the next round of conflict with the KMT.

Out of the approximately one hundred thousand soldiers who began the march, only some eight thousand survived the skirmishes with Nationalist troops, starvation, and disease that plagued the marchers. Some two thousand women, whose ages ranged from the early teens to early thirties, undertook the trek. They included women who joined the Party as students and peasants who became activists in the base areas. Many were wives or relatives of male cadres or soldiers. They trekked an average of eighteen miles a day with heavy packs on their backs through dangerous mountain passes and grasslands, often with nothing to eat. Along the way they nursed the wounded and sick, did administrative work for the Party, and conducted propaganda work in villages through which they passed. Some married and gave birth to babies along the way. For the women who survived, fellow female comrades became almost like family, supporting each other through harrowing experiences. Deng Liujin, a Long March veteran, described the bonds among women this way: "We women cooperated very well, we were united, all of us were one heart. At that time, we women had to be united. We couldn't quarrel or fight. At that time, we shared everything from food to clothes—we suffered together, enjoyed together" (quoted in Young 2001, 246).

For Communist women, the Long March experience was transformative. It solidified their ties with each other and their indispensability to the revolution. It fostered a militarized party culture with an appearance of gender equality in which women and men dressed alike in military attire and abandoned domestic duties for political work. Yet it also confirmed an emerging consensus among women and men in the party that women's work should be in service to broader revolutionary goals. Within the CCP, women's liberation from this time on was indisputably considered an outcome of revolution, not a prerequisite for it.

CONNECTIONS

In all three countries, feminist movements and ideologies in the interwar period were grounded in the quest for belonging to the nation, whether an independent nation (Japan), a longed-for independent nation (Korea), or a longed-for unified nation (China). In these three countries, nationalism and feminism were also linked by their common origins in modernity. In Korea and China, women inspired by nationalism stood up for their nations in the March First and May Fourth Movements, respectively.

Gender issues in the long interwar period, from the years before World War I to the years right before the outbreak of World War II in 1937, had many similarities in the three counties, despite those countries' enormous structural differences. For example, different types of economic changes produced significant changes in women's work. In Japan, World War I generated major growth in the size of the economy. Many of the desperately poor were able to find factory jobs that gave them greater stability, and many working-class women made a transition to more professional work. At the same time, the end of World War I led to massive inflation in food prices, which sparked nationwide rice riots. Initiated by women consumers, these riots led to changes in policies concerning food imports from Japan's colonies, especially Korea, and a drop in rice prices that devastated Japan's rural population. Japan's middle class continued to grow in the 1920s, opening many new types of work for Japanese women. The pattern of growth seen in Japan during the war was not replicated in Korea, but other types of economic change certainly affected Korean women. Colonial capitalist development changed women's roles in significant ways, with factory work and sex work drawing Korean women from the countryside.

Another commonality was feminist activism on behalf of the nation. Women in all three countries developed middle-class women's suffrage movements that were both challenged by and supported by socialist feminist movements. In Japan, socialist feminists initially stressed the importance of revolutionary class change before women could (or should) demand gender rights. The clash between socialist and liberal feminists was fought out as a war of words in Japan. At other times, socialist feminists, suffragists, consumer activists, Christian feminists, and others collaborated when they had shared goals, which was not that infrequent—coming together, for example, in a series of national women's suffrage conventions beginning in 1930. In Korea, feminists had to maneuver carefully to avoid repression by the colonial authorities, but even in Korea, the Kŭnuhoe was able to bring together socialist, Christian, and liberal feminists between 1927 and 1931 to advocate for equal treatment of women in the family, workplace, and society. In China, starting in the New Culture era and continuing into the early 1920s, feminists linked subjugation of women in the Confucian family with China's weak international position. On the heels of the May Fourth Movement, feminists took up where the earlier generation of suffragists discussed in Chapter 4 had left off. And in 1924, six hundred women professionals, workers, students, Christians, educators, liberals, and Communists came together in Shanghai. Three years later, however, the split between the Nationalists and the Communists severed those kinds of collaborative feminisms.

Other connections among the three countries included the role of maternalism. In Japan, the Motherhood Protection Debate engendered the notion that motherhood was a service to the nation that justified women's political rights. In Korea, women were seen as the maternal foundation of the nation. And in CCP discourse in China, women were viewed as "mothers of citizens." Could these be considered ways of empowering or of essentializing women?

Although transnational feminism may seem to be the opposite of feminist nationalism, it was used to enhance women's roles in their own countries at a time when women did not have rights of citizenship. In all three countries, both secular and Christian transnational linkages inspired many feminists.

REFERENCES AND SUGGESTIONS FOR FURTHER READING

GLOBAL CONTEXT

Blom, Ida. 1995. "Feminism and Nationalism in the Early Twentieth Century: A Cross-Cultural Perspective." *Journal of Women's History* 7, no. 4: 82–94.

Freedman, Estelle B. 2002. *No Turning Back: The History of Feminism and the Future of Women.* New York: Ballantine Books.

Hobsbawm, Eric. 1996. *The Age of Extremes: A History of the World, 1914–1991.* New York: Vintage Books.

Mackie, Vera. 2003. *Feminism in Modern Japan.* Cambridge: Cambridge University Press.

Molony, Barbara. 1990. *Technology and Investment: The Prewar Japanese Chemical Industry.* Cambridge, MA: Harvard University Press.

———. 2005a. "Frameworks of Gender: Feminism and Nationalism in Twentieth-Century Asia." In *A Companion to Gender History*, edited by Teresa A. Meade and Merry E. Wiesner-Hanks. Oxford: Blackwell.

JAPAN

Fujin Sansei Dōmei. 1928. "Fusen Kakutoku Kyōdō Iinkai no ki" [Record of the Women's Suffrage Coordinating Committee]. *Fujin Sansei Dōmei kaihō*, no. 4.

Ichikawa, Fusae. 1931. "Kokusai Heiwa to Fusen" [International peace and women's suffrage]. *Fusen* 5, no. 11.

Manela, Erez. 2007. *The Wilsonian Moment: Self-Determination and the International Origins of Anticolonial Nationalism*. New York: Oxford University Press.

Molony, Barbara. 1993. "Equality Versus Difference: The Japanese Debate over 'Motherhood Protection.'" In *Japanese Women Working*, edited by Janet Hunter. London: Routledge.

———. 2000. "Women's Rights, Feminism, and Suffragism in Japan, 1870–1925." *Pacific Historical Review* 69, no. 4: 656–657.

———. 2005b. "Ichikawa Fusae and Japan's Pre-war Women's Suffrage Movement." In *Japanese Women: Emerging from Subservience, 1868–1945*, edited by Hiroko Tomida and Gordon Daniels. Folkestone, Kent, UK: Global Oriental.

———. 2010. "Crossing Boundaries: Transnational Feminisms in Twentieth-Century Japan." In *Women's Movements in Asia*, edited by Mina Roces and Louise Edwards. London: Routledge.

———. 2011. "From 'Mothers of Humanity' to 'Assisting the Emperor': Gendered Belonging in the Wartime Rhetoric of Japanese Feminist Ichikawa Fusae." *Pacific Historical Review* 80, no. 1: 1–27.

Nagy, Margit. 1991. "Middle-Class Working Women During the Interwar Years." In *Recreating Japanese Women, 1600–1945*, edited by Gail Lee Bernstein. Berkeley: University of California Press.

Narita, Ryūichi. 1998. "Women in the Motherland: Oku Mumeo Through Wartime and Postwar." In *Total War and Modernization*, edited by Yasushi Yamanouchi, J. Victor Koschmann, and Ryūichi Narita. Ithaca, NY: Cornell University Press.

Ogawa, Manako. 2007. "The 'White Ribbon League of Nations' Meets Japan: The Trans-Pacific Activism of the Woman's Christian Temperance Union, 1906–1930." *Diplomatic History* 31, no. 1: 21–50.

Oku, Mumeo. 1928. "Katei fujin to shite no hansei" [Reflections on women in the home]. *Fujin Undō*, 4.

Shibahara, Taeko. 2014. *Japanese Women and the Transnational Feminist Movement before World War II*. Philadelphia: Temple University Press.

Tyrell, Ian. 1991. *Women's World, Woman's Empire: The Woman's Christian Temperance Union in International Perspective, 1880–1930*. Chapel Hill: University of North Carolina Press.

Uno, Kathleen. 1993. "One Day at a Time: Work and Domestic Activities of Urban Lower-Class Women in Early Twentieth-Century Japan." In *Japanese Women Working*, edited by Janet Hunter. London: Routledge.

Yasutake, Rumi. 2009. "The First Wave of International Women's Movements from a Japanese Perspective: Western Outreach and Japanese Women Activists During the Interwar Years." *Women's Studies International Forum* 32: 13–20.

KOREA

Choi, Hyaeweol. 2013. *New Women in Colonial Korea: A Sourcebook*. London: Routledge.

———. 2014. "The Missionary Home as a Pulpit: Domestic Paradoxes in Early Twentieth-Century Korea." In *Divine Domesticities: Christian Paradoxes in Asia and the Pacific*, edited by Hyaeweol Choi and Margaret Jolly. Canberra: ANU Press.

Choi, Kyeong-Hee. 1999. "Neither Colonial nor National: The Making of the 'New Woman' in Pak Wansŏ's 'Mother's Stake 1.'" In *Colonial Modernity in Korea*, edited by Gi-Wook Shin and Michael Robinson. Cambridge, MA: Harvard University Press.

Chŏng, Chŏnghwa. 1998. *Chang'gang ilgi*. Seoul: Hangminsa.

Kim, Elaine H., and Chungmoo Choi, eds. 1998. *Dangerous Women: Gender and Korean Nationalism*. New York: Routledge.

Kim, Sonja M. 2014. "Missionaries and 'A Better Baby Movement' in Colonial Korea." In *Divine Domesticities: Christian Paradoxes in Asia and the Pacific*, edited by Hyaeweol Choi and Margaret Jolly. Canberra: ANU Press.

Kim, Yung-Hee. 2013. "In Quest of Modern Womanhood: *Sinyŏja*, a Feminist Journal in Colonial Korea." *Korean Studies* 37: 44–78.

Kŭnuhoe. 1929. "Declaration of the Establishment of Kŭnuhoe." *Kŭnu* 1: 3–4.

Lee, Ki-baik. 1984. *A New History of Korea*. Translated by Edward W. Wagner with Edward J. Shultz. Cambridge, MA: Harvard University Press.

Park, Hyun Ok. 1998. "Ideals of Liberation: Korean Women in Manchuria." In *Dangerous Women: Gender and Korean Nationalism*, edited by Elaine H. Kim and Chungmoo Choi. New York: Routledge.

Robinson, Michael E. 1988. *Cultural Nationalism in Colonial Korea, 1920–1925*. Seattle: University of Washington Press.

Shin, Gi-Wook. 2006. *Ethnic Nationalism in Korea: Genealogy, Politics, and Legacy*. Stanford, CA: Stanford University Press.

Wells, Ken. 1999. "The Price of Legitimacy: Women and the Kŭnuhoe Movement, 1927–1931." In *Colonial Modernity in Korea*, edited by Gi-Wook Shin and Michael Robinson. Cambridge, MA: Harvard University Press.

CHINA

Bailey, Paul J. 2007. *Gender and Education in China: Gender Discourses and Women's Schooling in the Early Twentieth Century*. London: Routledge.

Edwards, Louise. 2008. *Gender, Politics, and Democracy: Women's Suffrage in China*. Stanford, CA: Stanford University Press.

Gilmartin, Christina. 1995. *Engendering the Chinese Revolution: Radical Women, Communist Politics, and Mass Movements in the 1920s*. Berkeley: University of California Press.

Glosser, Susan. 2003. *Chinese Visions of Family and State, 1915–53*. Berkeley: University of California Press.

Kuo, Margaret. 2012. *Intolerable Cruelty: Marriage, Law, and Society in Early Twentieth-Century China*. Lanham, MD: Rowman & Littlefield.

Lan, Hua R., and Vanessa L. Fong, eds. 1999. *Women in Republican China: A Sourcebook*. New York: M.E. Sharpe.

Tran, Lisa. 2015. *Concubines in Court: Marriage and Monogamy in Twentieth-Century China*. Lanham, MD: Rowman & Littlefield.

Wang, Zheng. 1999. *Women in the Chinese Enlightenment: Oral and Textual Histories*. Berkeley: University of California Press.

Young, Helen Praeger. 2001. *Choosing Revolution: Chinese Women Soldiers on the Long March*. Urbana: University of Illinois Press.

6

New Women in the Interwar Period

GLOBAL CONTEXT

Much of the world was swept up in a quest for modernity that emerged from the killing fields of World War I. This new modernity questioned the previous decades' forms of modernization, such as the new technologies of war that had produced the carnage of World War I. The new modernity undermined what had seemed to be solid values and ways of looking at the world. In addition, new artistic, literary, and musical forms of expression that deconstructed classical forms found adherents throughout the world in the interwar era.

While many of the modernizers in the Western countries that suffered so horribly in World War I rejected the values and culture of the prewar era, their leaders did not abandon the old order that divided the world into the colonized and the colonizers. But many of the indigenous residents of the colonies did reject their colonial status, and for them modernity included the struggle for independence. Ironically, it was the importation of ideas from the metropole—and from other countries that were part of the global flows of culture, ideologies, arts, and sciences—that encouraged the construction of new women and men, new social institutions, and new freedoms in the colonies. These, in turn, accelerated nationalist upsurges after World War I, such as Gandhi's *swaraj* (self-government) movement in India, Sukarno's Partai Nasional Indonesia in Indonesia, anticolonial struggles in North Africa and the Middle East, and nationalist movements in East Asia. The arts and ideas of the imperialists simultaneously inspired some nationalists' thinking and were opposed by other nationalists who found many of those ideas, especially as they pertained to women and gender construction, antithetical to their own cultures. People were often ambivalent about change.

Ambivalence about modernity's effects on the performance and understanding of gender emerged not only in countries outside the West in the 1920s and 1930s but also in Europe and the United States several decades earlier, that is, in the late nineteenth century. "New Women" were represented in novels, theatrical performances, essays, and cartoons in the West as rejecting the notion that heterosexual marriage and motherhood were the only options for women. (The term "New Woman" did not exist before the 1890s, but the characters in plays and novels of the previous decade were retroactively defined as New Women.) Some of these works described New Women as overly educated, autonomous maidens or as bitter and prudish old spinsters—sometimes even mannish women—who focused on women's rights and reformist activism rather than on the stereotypically warm Victorian family. These mocking treatments saw New Women as unlikely candidates for marriage. If they did marry, as some cartoons showed, they would sit comfortably reading the newspaper while their overworked husbands did housework, a role reversal whose irony was lost on both the cartoon's creators and its consumers. Another negative approach to New Women in artistic and literary representations was to present them as sexually promiscuous; Lucy in Bram Stoker's *Dracula* (1897), for example, wondered why she could not marry three men, and in the end she was punished for what was seen as extreme and decadent sexuality. While this sexually decadent image was diametrically opposite to the prudish image, it showed an additional class of modern women who were equally unfit for marriage.

The New Woman was not only attacked but also defended in European and American culture at the turn of the twentieth century. As early as 1879, the character Nora in Henrik Ibsen's play *A Doll's House* abandoned her home because she felt repressed by a husband who treated her as a child. This Norwegian play was performed widely throughout Europe. While Ibsen did not call Nora a New Woman, as the term had not yet been coined, his play engendered much discussion about the appropriateness of Nora's action, not all of it negative. Other literary works depicting women who questioned marriage, especially the double standard that permitted husbands to behave in sexually immoral ways while wives were not so permitted, followed in the 1880s and 1890s.

By the end of the century, positive images of New Women began to replace the ambivalent ones of the previous decade. In the 1890s, many authors praised them as free-spirited, intelligent, and career-minded. New Women were depicted as healthy, athletic women riding bicycles. Many commentators applauded the well-educated real (as opposed to stereotypical) New Women's focus on social reform as an appropriate feminine and nurturing role. New Women in the United States and England in the 1890s did indeed participate in moral reform movements and in urban settlement houses. While most had middle-class backgrounds, they collaborated with working-class women for workers' rights and civil rights. Many American and British New Women supported women's suffrage; those who did not often viewed political involvement as corrupt and therefore unfeminine (Valence 2004, 474).

The term "New Woman" seems to have first been used in 1894 to describe the educated, autonomous women who had appeared in literature and the arts since 1879. British novelist Sarah Grand introduced the term in her essay "The New Aspect of the Woman Question" in the *North American Review* in 1894. A decade later, American author Winnifred Harper Cooley (1874–1967) published a glowing analysis of the modern New Woman in her major work *The New Womanhood.*

> *The new woman, in the sense of the best woman, the flower of all the womanhood of past ages, has come to stay—if civilization is to endure. The sufferings of the past have but strengthened her, maternity has deepened her, education is broadening her—and she now knows that she must perfect herself if she would perfect the race, and leave her imprint upon immortality, through her offspring or her works. (Cooley 1904, 32).*

American historians have used the term "New Women" to describe modern women in different generations (Lowy 2007, 119). The first generation were the educated progressive reformers Cooley describes. They were followed, in the 1910s, by the next generation—bohemian women whose political orientation was more socialist. And finally, in the 1920s, women who came to be called "flappers" or "Modern Girls," depicted as more frivolous and consumption oriented, were the last generation of America's New Women.

Modern Girls appeared throughout much of the world, in every continent, in countries independent and colonial, and in capitalist and communist societies, in the years immediately following World War I (Weinbaum et al., 2008). Young women moved into the workplace in much larger numbers, and postwar consumerism globalized styles and commodities. Like her predecessors, the Modern Girl was simultaneously viewed in many parts of the world positively, as a symbol of modernity that strengthened the nation, and negatively, as representing a type of modernity that undermined the nation and its traditions. The Modern Girl, like the earlier New Woman, was the product of transnational cultural flows, but the types of cultural transmission differed; the flow of feminist ideology in the arts and politics characterized the New Woman of the 1910s and 1920s, while global fashions, advertising, and consumer goods characterized the Modern Girl in the 1920s and 1930s.

As we shall see in this chapter, New Women and Modern Girls also entered the scene in Japan, Korea, and China. New Women appeared a bit earlier in Japan than in the other two countries, but by the 1920s, Modern Girls were highly visible as symbols of modernity in all three countries. The rise of militarism and war at the end of the 1930s, however, led to the demise of the Modern Girl, who had come to be seen as a frivolous, antitraditional emblem of Western decadence.

JAPAN

Japan's liberalizing urban culture of the interwar decades spawned new conceptions of the self, sexuality, and love, which were expressed in art and literature (prose, poetry, and widely read essays), through dress and clothing, and on the theatrical stage. As we saw in Chapter 5, women struggled for rights and citizenship as well as for new roles in civil society during the interwar period, and these were linked to the era's new culture and conceptions of the self and sexualities, to be discussed in this chapter.

From the end of the first decade of the twentieth century through the 1930s, many Japanese women were experimenting with new ways of self-representation. In the 1910s, they were called—and called themselves—New Women (*atarashii onna* or, as in the name of the New Woman's Association discussed in Chapter 5, *shin fujin*). In the mid-1920s, a new type of modern woman emerged—the Modern Girl (*modan gāru*, also abbreviated as *moga*). Japan's New Woman and Modern Girl were part of global phenomena that used the same descriptive names. Both were avatars of modernity, but although the images of each type of modern woman were different, there was considerable overlap in their lived experiences.

The New Women of the 1910s were often educated literary and political figures such as Hiratsuka Raichō and Yosano Akiko (see Chapter 4). Initially the targets of scorn for what social critics considered sexually scandalous or self-centered frivolous behavior, the well-known New Women of the Bluestocking Society took the initiative to redefine the meaning of "New Woman" in a positive manner in 1913. Hiratsuka's statement quoted in

BOX 6.1

Celebrating the New Woman

As this excerpt from Hiratsuka Raichō's January 1913 essay in the widely circulated journal *Chūō Kōron* (*Central Review*) suggests, New Women challenged both "Old Women" and patriarchal institutions by shining like the sun, the potent foundational symbol of the Japanese nation. (The sun goddess, Amaterasu, was an important deity in the Shintō pantheon and the mythical progenitor of Japan's imperial family. The sun had symbolic if not religious meaning to modern readers of Hiratsuka's essay.) The New Woman, Hiratsuka claimed, was not passive but rather an activist with a "mission" to "destroy" patriarchal laws and to "battle" ghosts.

> ***I Am a New Woman . . .***
> *The New Woman is not satisfied with the life of the Old Woman, who was made ignorant, made a slave, made a piece of flesh by the selfishness of men.*
> *The New Woman desires to destroy the old morality and laws that were constructed for the convenience of men. . . .*
> *New Women battle daily all kinds of ghosts.*
> *A moment of neglect and the New Woman is an Old Woman.*
> *I am a New Woman. I am the Sun. I am simply a person. . . .*
> *The New Woman desires every day . . . to create a new realm where new religion, new morality, and new laws will be put into practice.*
> *In fact, herein lies the mission of the New Woman.*
> *(Hiratsuka Raichō, 1913, quoted in Lowy 2007, 82)*

Box 6.1 was part of the Bluestockings' bold reclamation of the New Woman's reputation. New Women increasingly came to be seen as active feminists; some were married, and many were intellectuals.

The Modern Girls of the 1920s were viewed by contemporaries as a product of modern consumer society. The mass media reveled, as they initially had done with New Women during the previous decade, in describing the *moga*'s behavior as transgressive. Stylish, up-to-date, wearing daringly short hair and short skirts, *moga* were young, bright, and representative of sexual liberation. Urban *moga* worked in modern occupations to earn the money they spent in trendy stores and in cinemas, coffeehouses, and jazz bars. Strolling down the Ginza, Tokyo's most fashionable street, they thrilled some people and frightened others. At times, they appeared together with Modern Boys (*modan boi*, or *mobo*), who also wore fashionable Western clothing styles. Some Modern Boys were part of the leftist student movement of the 1920s, but they did not threaten conservative traditionalists the way Modern Girls did. Unlike their male counterparts, who had always had greater sexual freedom, Modern Girls appeared to subvert the patriarchal family by "experimenting with sexuality outside the marital home" (Mackie 2003, 75). On the opposite end of the political spectrum, even some Marxists, who saw Modern Girls as hedonists, found them threatening.

While New Women were concentrated in urban areas and many were educated middle-class women, the new culture they represented spread throughout Japan, among rural and poor women as well, most of whom were literate by the interwar era. Millions of copies of mass-market newspapers and glossy magazines were sold to every segment of society. Radio reached several million households by the late 1920s. Short stories and novels that focused on New Women and Modern Girls were best sellers.

Images of modernity flooded Japan in the 1920s. Hollywood stars were as familiar in Japan as they were in the United States. Middle-class homes, some with Western-style furnishings, were filled with material goods. Japan's mass urban culture was cosmopolitan and modern. Was modernity to be praised for strengthening Japan's reputation in the world's eyes, or was it to be condemned for undercutting "tradition" and thereby weakening Japan? By the 1930s, and especially during the Depression, when many rural people were suffering economically, rightists were criticizing Japan's liberal urban culture as decadent and destructive to Japanese traditions. No part of interwar culture was simultaneously more emblematic of the excitement of this period and yet more criticized than New Women and Modern Girls.

The Emergence of the New Woman in Japan

New Women entered the scene literally from the stage. In the first decade of the twentieth century, theatrical pioneers in Japan were creating a New Theater movement. This movement encouraged women actors to replace the male actors who had played female roles for the previous three hundred years, and called for plays that were much less stylized than the kabuki and puppet productions that defined Japanese theater at the time (Kano 2001). In 1910 scholar and critic Tsubouchi Shōyō, as part of his efforts to promote modern theater, introduced the term "New Women" to the Japanese public in his lectures on the female characters in plays by European writers such as Norway's Henrik Ibsen and Germany's Hermann Sudermann. In September 1911 Tsubouchi's Literary Society mounted Japan's first production of Ibsen's *A Doll's House*. As in the West, the play led to an outpouring of media commentary about the play's protagonist, Nora, as an archetypal New Woman. (Reactions to this play in Korea and China will be discussed later in this chapter.) The same month, the Bluestockings launched their new organization and their magazine of the same name, *Seitō* (Bluestocking). Critics of the Bluestockings called Hiratsuka and her colleagues "Japanese Noras"—New Women who were frivolous and self-absorbed in their quest for self-awareness. Ironically, in January 1912 *Seitō* published a compilation of their members' attitudes toward the play, and some, including Hiratsuka, criticized the Nora character for being shallow herself (Lowy 2007, 21–31).

The Bluestockings' nuanced treatment of Nora did not spare them from media derision, however. Their feminist foremothers, such as the usually married, Christian, and middle-class women of the Woman's Christian Temperance Union and other groups in the late nineteenth century who sought to define personhood through monogamous marriage and social reform (see Chapter 4), had not been attacked in the media as sexually transgressive. But the Bluestockings, who emphasized the development of women's self-awareness as a way to construct a modern identity—an approach they shared with a number of contemporary male literary figures—saw love as a means of attaining self-understanding and articulating identity (Suzuki 2010, 708). Unlike their male counterparts, the Bluestockings were seen as threatening.

In a public letter to her parents, published in *Seitō* in 1914, Hiratsuka explained why she was starting a new life with her male partner, Okumura Hiroshi, writing that she was "determined to . . . see how this love will develop, where it will take me, what unknown world will unfold in front of my eyes, how my thought and life will change" (quoted in Suzuki 2010, 8). Hiratsuka was not alone among New Women in stressing romantic love as modern and progressive; women novelists and short-story writers did as well. The New Women's critics also saw romantic love as modern, but to them, modernity was threatening. Even some otherwise progressive men worried that the New Women's focus on romantic love and self-awareness overshadowed what should be the primary focus for educated women—dedication to nation and family. Love itself was not a problem; indeed, maternal love was respected, as was platonic though romantic love among teenage girls. But adult romantic love, through which a woman would find fulfillment by choosing her own life partner, challenged the traditional family system.

Love relationships among adolescent girls were called *dōseiai*, the same term used for other forms of same-sex love. While sexologists of the early twentieth century were often worried about these kinds of relationships (Pflugfelder 2005), many girls themselves found them exhilarating. These kinds of relationships were portrayed in the numerous magazines targeted to high-school-age girls—many with the word *shōjo* (girl) in their titles—that were first published in 1902. The magazines contained fiction and nonfiction by professional writers as well as letters to the editor, essays, and poems sent in by their teenage readers. A lively and interactive girls' culture grew out of these magazines (Suzuki 2010, 32). *Seitō* contributor Yoshiya Nobuko (1896–1973) began writing short stories for this audience; her most popular work was a collection of fifty-two previously serialized short stories called *Flower Tales* (*Hanamonogatari*). The tales were set in a same-sex girls' world. Although Yoshiya herself lived almost half a century in a romantic relationship with her female partner, her stories suggested that girls' same-sex love would serve as an opening to adult heterosexual love. Other New Women famous for transgressive heterosexual relationships, including Yosano Akiko and Hiratsuka Raichō, also wrote about the passion they had felt in close female relationships that preceded their heterosexual relationships (Suzuki 2010, 30, 35).

In fact, Hiratsuka's adult (and therefore less acceptable in the eyes of the media) relationship with a young woman in the summer of 1912 was one of several scandals that tarnished the Bluestockings' reputation that year. It was these incidents that led to the organization's efforts to reframe the category of New Women in a positive manner. The first of these incidents came to be known as the "five-colored liquor incident," for one of the exotic mixed drinks Bluestocking women were observed drinking. Drinking with gusto in public at fashionable artists' hangouts such as the Swan's Nest Café, as men were entitled to do, was itself quite risqué for women who were not in the sex trades (Lowy 2007, 60–61). What made the drinking of the five-colored liquor even more transgressive were the lively comments in the June and July issues of *Seitō* about Hiratsuka's imbibing these fancy foreign drinks. Written by Bluestocking member Otake Kōkichi (1893–1966), a young woman artist with whom Hiratsuka shared a close emotional bond, the articles suggested that Hiratsuka was having an affair with a beautiful young boy. That Hiratsuka appeared to be a sexy adult woman preying on innocent young boys was scandalous enough; actually, the object of Hiratsuka's affection was the teenage Otake herself, who was deeply enamored of Hiratsuka. Hiratsuka also wrote glowingly about her relationship with the young artist in 1912, but broke with Otake when she began her lifelong cohabitation with Okumura, whom she married decades after giving birth to two children with him. In her autobiography, published in the early 1970s, Hiratsuka dismissed her same-sex attraction to Otake, perhaps unwilling to be thought lesbian or bisexual after those categories became stigmatized in the mid-twentieth century (Pflugfelder 2005, 167).

The next scandalous incident in 1912 was the visit by Hiratsuka, Otake, and a third Bluestocking woman to the Yoshiwara red-light district in Tokyo. This visit was arranged by Otake's uncle. The three women, who visited a geisha and stayed overnight in her house, apparently went to observe the plight of women in the sex trades. To the press, which wrote articles and printed salacious cartoons about the visit, these New Women crossed both class and sexual lines, entering a world that was supposed to be the province of men—other than the female sex and entertainment workers in the district, of course.

A third scandal involved a short story by Araki Ikuko (1890–1943). Araki was a young innkeeper, popular with male Waseda University students and involved in literary and artistic pursuits. She had an affair with a student several years her junior while being courted by a slightly older man who wished to marry her. At first running away from her wealthy suitor to be with her young lover, then returning and running away once more, Araki was attacked in the press as a flighty, scandalous New Woman. Unlike many of the other members of the Bluestockings, Araki did not grow up in middle-class comfort and was not highly educated. When *Seitō* published her short story "The Letter," which praised the protagonist's adulterous affair and criticized her loveless marriage, the police banned that issue of the magazine as contrary to public morals (the civil code prohibited female adultery, though not male). By the middle of 1912 quite a few readers had dropped their subscriptions for fear of losing their jobs if they were found to be readers of the magazine. One of the Bluestockings' founding members even complained to Hiratsuka that *Seitō* was appearing to become "like a tomboy who prides herself on defying convention and doing things women never dare do" (Bardsley 2007, 85).

In response to the theatrical representations of New Women and the scandals of the Bluestockings, male critics—including newspaper reporters, literary critics, and the group of economists, bureaucrats, and businessmen who called themselves the Social Policy Association—made the New Woman an important topic of discussion in 1912. Policy conferences and media articles described her as "vulgar" or "indecent," "an undesirable phenomenon," and a threat, both because of her invasion of the artistic world of men and because of her challenge to the state's patriarchal marriage system. Others took a more positive view and looked forward to New Women having an "intellectual awakening" (Lowy 2007, 72–77). Against this backdrop of lively discussion, Hiratsuka called on Bluestocking members in the December 1912 issue of *Seitō* to contribute to reframing the discourse on the New Woman. The subsequent reframing was quite successful, and while negative images continued to appear, the New Woman gained greater respectability after 1913.

In addition to Hiratsuka's stirring redefinition of the New Woman in *Chūō Kōron* (excerpted in Box 6.1), special supplements to each of the early 1913 issues of *Seitō* carried powerful writings by Bluestockings and other women on a variety of feminist issues. The Bluestockings were clearly articulating a need for social and economic change that went beyond their earlier quest for self-awareness.

Iwano Kiyoko (1882–1920), one of the small group of women who had worked in the first movement to revise Article 5 of the Public Peace Police Law in the first decade of the twentieth century (see Chapter 4), wrote in January 1913:

> ***Men and Women are Equal as Members of the Human Race***
> *When I paid a visit recently to the home of a certain acquaintance and spoke with her husband, he put the comparison [of men and women] this way: "The physical strength of two women equals that of one man. Man is thus naturally the superior of woman." . . . If . . . we were to say that the one with the greater strength is the superior being, then in our nation, a sumo wrestler would necessarily be superior to everyone else. Indeed, even a sumo wrestler would not be the most superior, for bears and great snakes would place ahead of any human. . . . [T]igers, elephants, and crocodiles would be by far the most superior. . . .*
> *Coming to the problem of intelligence . . . I believe it is a mistake to conclude that women have no intellectual ability. [M]en persist in their unfounded denigration of women, taking no account of the fact that we are their subordinates because we have not had the same advantages. In the days of the Meiji Restoration, our people were regarded as an inferior race by the countries of England, the United States, Germany, Russia and France. But we, too, had the ability to understand a level of knowledge equal to theirs. Haven't the last forty-five years proved that? The same is true for today's women. (Iwano 1913, cited in Bardsley 2007, 160–162)*

Itō Noe (1895–1923), the youngest Bluestocking, also contributed to the January 1913 issue. Itō played a significant role in articulating feminist ideology both before and after she assumed the editorship of *Seitō* when Hiratsuka stepped down in 1915. A lively individualist, Itō divorced her first husband—the result of an arranged marriage—to live with her high school teacher. She had two children with him, and she eventually married him. When she discovered he had been involved with another of his students, their love marriage fell apart, and Itō took up with Ōsugi Sakae, who at the time was involved in a common-law marriage with one woman (Hori Yasuko) and romantically involved with another (Kamichika Ichiko, who became a member of the Diet after World War II). All three women were *Seitō* contributors. Ōsugi was a famous socialist anarchist and proponent of "free love." When Kamichika stabbed him in a jealous rage, the love arrangement became yet another scandal for New Women. Ōsugi separated from Hori, Kamichika went to jail, and Itō went to live with him, bearing five additional children, until the couple were murdered by right-wing terrorists after the earthquake of 1923.

Itō's reply to Hiratsuka's call to define the New Woman was a powerful attack on the notion of the New Woman as frivolous. Her use of the trope of the "path" suggests a Buddhist religious journey.

> ***The Path of the New Woman***
>
> *The New Woman does not trudge in endless search of the dusty footprints left by the women who have walked before her. . . . The New Woman will advance beyond the point where so many other women have stopped and, as a pioneer, will dare to tread an entirely new road.*
>
> *All the while the pioneer struggles to open the new way, she denies herself even the smallest of worldly comforts. From beginning to end, she is alone, and every second is one of hardship. . . . Yet the only words she utters are ardent, passionate prayers for the strength to believe in herself. . . . One who would be a pioneer must be a powerful person, a person who gives life to a sense of self that will not crumble. (Itō Noe, cited in Bardsley 2007, 131–133)*

Hori Yasuko also replied to Hiratsuka's call for commentary on the New Woman, but her comment, entitled "I Am the Old Woman," took the Bluestockings to task. That is, the journal wanted to include the opinion of a socialist woman and assumed Hori would necessarily share Ōsugi's ideology. She wrote: "Of course, I am living with a socialist man. However, I do not think of myself as a socialist and I do not recall calling myself one" (quoted in Lowy 2007, 87). In the end, though, she praised the New Woman as one who followed her own way.

Marriage was another issue discussed in the New Woman supplements to *Seitō* in the early months of 1913. One woman wrote that women should ideally remain single to remain true to themselves, but under the current conditions, women still needed men to support them. Hiratsuka wrote a long critique of marriage in the April 1913 issue; because of her piece, that issue of *Seitō* was banned by the government.

> ***To the Women of the World***
> *Why doesn't a most basic doubt occur to most women today about such homilies as . . . "Marriage and motherhood are a woman's whole life"? That this does not happen strikes me as strange. . . . Must a woman's entire life be sacrificed for the necessity of preserving the race? Is there no other vocation for women outside of procreation? . . . Is being a wife and mother the whole of a woman's mission in life? . . . Shouldn't freedom of choice be readily available to each individual? Even if we do not . . . go so far as to oppose marriage itself, we cannot submit at all to . . . the marriage system as it presently operates. In today's social system, doesn't marriage enforce a relationship of authority and subjection? . . . Isn't it true that [wives] have neither property rights nor legal rights to their children? Isn't it true that adultery is not a crime for the husband but is a crime for the wife? . . . Once our eyes have been opened, we cannot fall asleep again. (Hiratsuka, cited in Bardsley 2007, 103–107)*

Seitō continued to be published until 1916. From 1914 to 1916, *Seitō* presented articles on chastity, abortion, and prostitution in which the writers debated one another in strongly worded essays that used strikingly contemporary-sounding language. Should women remain chaste, even if doing so might mean impoverishment of oneself and one's family? Was a fetus a separate human being or was it a part of a woman's body over which she should have control? Was prostitution a social necessity to serve "men's inherent needs" or was it a kind of slavery?

At the same time the Bluestockings were reframing the New Woman in their own journal, mass circulation periodicals that were aimed at a general audience were printing numerous articles, many of them much more nuanced and positive about New Women and women's issues than they had been the previous year. While some continued to assert that New Women were denying their true nature, many articles discussed, in positive terms, women in modern occupations such as medicine, teaching, and office work; the importance of modern women's education; and even the existence of New Women throughout Japanese history, thereby indigenizing what had been seen as a foreign import (Lowy 2007, 94–95).

Another response to the negative view of New Women that had predominated in 1912 was the founding of the True New Woman's Association (Shinshinfujinkai) in early 1913 (Lowy 2007, chap. 6). Although the press made much of the "rivalry" between the Bluestockings and the True New Women, the ideological differences between the two were fairly limited. Both groups acknowledged that the movement should have multiple voices and multiple groups. They both stressed that women should have public voices, equality in marriage and divorce, access to education and to employment opportunity, and the ability to seek self-awareness. Although the True New Women's founders, like the Bluestockings, had had unconventional (even risqué) experiences in their youth, by 1913 they were slightly older married ladies who found the transgressive behavior of the Bluestockings counterproductive. The True New Women's acceptance of the "good wife, wise mother" model as a means of women's empowerment was at odds with the Bluestockings' rejection of that model.

But although the media painted the True New Women as "the New Woman's new foe," this notion of a rivalry among women went much too far. For example, Yosano Akiko, an extraordinarily productive mother and poet and an original Bluestocking, not only published in *Shinshinfujin* (True New Woman) as well but was praised by the latter as an excellent True New Woman. One of the True New Women's founders, Nishikawa Fumiko (1882–1960)—who, like Bluestocking Iwano Kiyoko, had been one of the women who worked unsuccessfully to overturn Article 5 a decade earlier—noted, "Having various women's groups is very necessary for a future large women's movement" (Lowy 2007, 115). The True New Woman's Association, which was the first Japanese organization to openly discuss birth control, was hardly a stodgy organization. Both the Bluestockings and the True New Women claimed the title of New Women, and members of these and other groups went on to build the interwar domestic and transnational women's movements described in Chapter 5. Most immediately, the term "New Woman" was embedded in the political organization, the New Woman's Association, founded by Hiratsuka, Ichikawa, and Oku (see Chapter 5).

The Modern Girl Takes Over

Who was Japan's Modern Girl? The term "Modern Girl" was used for the first time in 1923 (Sato 2008, 264). She was both a real person and a media sensation. As a real person, she was one of the many thousands of young women workers in factories, employees in the newly emerging professional offices, retail workers in both glistening new department stores and tiny mom-and-pop shops, bus conductors and telephone operators, café waitresses, highly trained employees in teaching, medicine, and other sectors, and privileged young women who could easily afford international products and fashions. In other words, the *moga* could be found in every economic class, even among those who were unable to purchase many of those commodities and had to be satisfied with admiring them in magazines. Like their predecessors, many Modern Girls were focused on developing a sense of self-awareness and contributing to social change. Like their predecessors, they were criticized in the press.

As a media sensation, the Modern Girl was transgressive and problematic. One common criticism had to do with her "foreignness." Both Marxist and conservative critics called *moga* "hedonistic" and "decadent." Socialist feminist Yamakawa Kikue was deeply disappointed when she observed young factory workers, who she expected would read works on politics while on their work breaks, reading cosmetics ads in "bourgeois" women's magazines. These women expressed delight in their salaries, which they would presumably use to buy fashions and cosmetics (Sato 2008, 264, 275). Other commentators criticized the Modern Girl as overly sexual. Enamored of dancing and visiting milk bars and other Western-style cafés with Modern Boys, *moga* were described by some male writers as promiscuous. One critic wrote in 1925 that he was surprised when a Modern Girl whom he had met just once sent him a note: "I am lonely sleeping all alone today. Please come visit." He was not sure what the young woman meant—and he did not know if the Modern Girl represented revolutionary possibilities or social decadence—but he did not hesitate to titillate his readers with this suggestive message (Silverberg 1991, 241). Other writers presented the Modern Girl as a consumption-oriented, flirtatious, and foreign fashion plate.

In reality, Modern Girls did exist—they were not simply a media creation. As employed women with some disposable income, even if only enough to buy the magazines that created a dream world of modernity and perhaps a few new pieces of clothing or makeup, Modern Girls in Western styles or Japanese kimonos worn in a sassy modern manner did populate the streets of Japan's cities in the interwar period. Most were not scandalously

This image of a Modern Girl in 1930 shows her with bobbed hair and Western-style clothing and make-up, drinking a liqueur and smoking a cigarette.
TIPSY, KOBAYAKAWA KIYOSHI, JAPANESE, 1889-1948. HONOLULU MUSEUM OF ART

promiscuous, however; the majority were in fact hardworking employees with working-class or middle-class jobs.

Japan's New Women and Modern Girls drew much of their inspiration from Western sources. At the periphery of the empire in Okinawa, however, Tokyo was viewed as the source of feminine modernity. Okinawa, which became part of Japan in 1879, was still being integrated into the nation. Notions of modernity were dependent on flows of ideas and power in multiple directions (Ito 2008, 243).

New Women and Modern Girls as Authors of Fiction

Not only was the written record of women's essays, newspaper articles, letters to the editor, and other forms of social and political commentary voluminous during this period, but the quantity and quality of women's fiction writing was also impressively large. Novels and short stories of the time depicted women taking control of their own lives and sexuality. Many of their authors came from impoverished backgrounds but rose above them to gain professional renown. A large number of them were friends and colleagues with New Women and with the activists discussed in Chapter 5. Many, of course, wrote for *Seitō*, and the younger among them published stories in the mass-circulation media or in the left-leaning feminist literary journal *Nyonin Geijutsu* (*Women's*

Arts), published from 1928 to 1932. Anthologies of translated works by women writers (Lippit and Selden 1991; Selden and Mizuta, 2014; Tanaka 1987) abound. Two of the many writers, Miyamoto Yuriko (1899–1951) and Hayashi Fumiko (1903–1951), will be briefly discussed here.

Miyamoto (the name she took when she married her second husband and by which she is best known) had a well-to-do background, unlike most of her peers in the literary world (Tanaka 1987, 41–45). After achieving success at age seventeen for her first novella, *A Flock of Poor People*, which treated the destitute farmers of a village where her grandfather lived, Miyamoto moved to New York to study at Columbia University. There she met her first husband, a Japanese graduate student fifteen years her senior. Defying her parents, she made her own marriage choice as a passionate Modern Girl. She soon regretted this choice and divorced him. Her novel *Nobuko* was based on that marriage and divorce. Miyamoto's next partner was Yuasa Yoshiko, a scholar of Russian literature; Miyamoto lived with her in the Soviet Union for three years, and came back a dedicated Marxist. In 1930 she met Miyamoto Kenji, who was nine years her junior, as they were both members of the Japan Leftist Writers Alliance. She left Yuasa and married Miyamoto. Following one's emotions was important to New Women and Modern Girls, even if it led to serial relationships with men and women. As a Marxist, Miyamoto Yuriko was arrested several times and spent about two years in jail before and during World War II. She returned to an active life as a writer after the war but died of illness at the height of her career.

In this excerpt from Miyamoto's semi-autobiographical novel *Nobuko*, the young newlywed Nobuko fights with her mother, Takeyo, who objects to Nobuko's marriage to Tsukuda.

> *[Nobuko] "You'd like to see me as your girl, pure and lofty, transcending such things as love affairs."*
>
> *[Takeyo] "I'm not saying you should remain single. I've always thought I'd be happy to see you married to a fine man, who could enlighten you." . . .*
>
> *[Nobuko] "What most girls want is to get married, settle down, and do things in exactly the same manner as their husbands . . . . I'm different. I'm not a bit interested in having a man who grew up just as I did. . . . Tsukuda's good and bad points aside, I don't think you'd be satisfied with any choice I make. I am a bit like a savage, you see, and so I won't be happy unless I can grab what I*

> *want with my own hands." (Miyamoto Yuriko, Nobuko, quoted in Tanaka 1987, 50–51)*

Hayashi Fumiko's life course was quite different from Miyamoto Yuriko's. One of several children her mother had with different lovers, Hayashi moved around frequently as a child and could finish high school only by working in factories and as a maid. She followed a boyfriend from her high school years to Tokyo, but he dumped her when his family objected to the relationship. Hayashi stayed on in Tokyo, taking a variety of menial jobs to support herself that gave her useful material for her later career as a writer. Her break came when *Nyonin Geijutsu* published her long work *Hōrōki* (Vagabond's song) in serial form after it had been rejected by mainstream publishers. This semi-autobiographical work about a woman drifting about on the margins of society was a hit, selling more than six hundred thousand copies in novel form and being made into three films. Her later novels were also made into films. Hayashi went from rags to riches. During World War II, Hayashi continued as a drifter of sorts, albeit a rich one, this time at the fringes of the Japanese empire, working as a reporter with the Japanese military. She was the first Japanese woman to enter Nanjing after the Nanjing Massacre in 1937 (Tanaka 1987, 99–104). Japanese women in the empire will be discussed further in Chapter 8.

In this excerpt from *Hōrōki*, the narrator is working at a café when she receives a postcard from Nomura, a man she calls her "former lover." The narrator states:

> *He says to come by for a visit and thanks me for my recent letter; he received the money. . . . I reach a small apartment building. . . . I'm told Nomura lives . . . on the second floor. I go up and knock. . . . Nomura says he is on his way to eat at a café, and he asks to borrow fifty sen. We leave together. . . . Eating rice with fish and soup, we are like a married couple. . . . I feel cheerful and make a show of answering him agreeably. I forget how miserable I used to be when I lived with him. . . . When I say goodbye in front of his apartment building, Nomura doesn't even look at me before going up the stairs. . . . Remembering our life of poverty together at Tamagawa, I pick up my clogs and go up to the second floor. . . . I find Nomura reading. . . . After sitting for a while, I decide to go back to the café [where I work]. . . . Nomura picks up a knife and flings it at me. . . . Someone knocks at the door. I get up and open*

> *it. . . . To me, he seems like the god of mercy, and . . . I hurry out the door. . . . Nomura comes into the café [where I work]. . . . I leave from the back door. . . . I take my time returning to the café and find that Nomura is still there. . . . I think I would sacrifice anything for him. . . . Feeling that I am about to sink into the ground, I realize that there is no such thing as love. (Quoted in Tanaka 1987, 123–125)*

In the years after the Manchurian Incident in 1931, Modern Girls, who were viewed as acting autonomously in relationships and in life, were increasingly viewed as damaging to Japan's character and national strength. As we will see in Chapter 8, by the end of the decade Japanese women were told that "luxury is the enemy" in time of war. The era of the Modern Girl in Japan was over.

KOREA

Opening a New Gender Discourse

The March First Movement of 1919 resulted in a shift in the colonial governing strategy. After putting down the March First protests, Japanese authorities instituted what they called "cultural rule," a system that brought about greater openness toward publications and interest groups than had been allowed in the previous decade. This led to a boom in publishing in the form of magazines, newspapers, and literary works, offering an important set of platforms for the introduction and discussion of modern ideas on a wide range of issues including gender, family, economy, national identity, and hygiene. Numerous organizations flourished in pursuit of diverse political, cultural, and religious goals. Between 1920 and 1929 about 450 women's societies were founded across the country, with goals ranging from education and enlightenment to religion and socialism. Material culture underwent significant changes as well, spurred by increasing industrialization and urbanization. Theaters, cafés, and department stores sprang up all over Seoul, and the streets of the capital bustled with people venturing out to experience the new and the modern. The discourse and experience of the New Woman and Modern Girl in colonial Korea evolved at this intersection of modernity, colonialism, nationalism, and a variety of ideologies.

The publication in 1920 of the inaugural edition of *Sin yŏja* (*New Woman*), the first feminist magazine, helped to popularize the term "New Woman" and opened the door to a new gender discourse for the modern era. Founded by a small group of women, the magazine aimed to create a platform by women for women. Most magazines had been and would continue to be dominated by male intellectuals, but the key players at *Sin yŏja* were all women, and they held complete control over the direction, content, and administration of the magazine. Although the magazine was in business for only one year, it signaled a new chapter in the discourse on modern gender in Korea.

Emphasizing concepts such as reform (*kaejo*) and liberation (*haebang*), *Sin yŏja* presented the issues of the New Woman as part of a global trend and

BOX 6.2

The Inaugural Editorial of *Sin yŏja* (New Woman), the First Feminist Magazine in Korea

*"Reform [*kaejo*]!" This is the outcry of humankind after painfully grieving over the terrifying gunshots of the past five years [referring to World War I]. "Liberation [*haebang*]!" This is the call of women who have been confined to the deep, dark, inner chambers for thousands of years. Excessively greedy ambition and egoism caused the war, breaking the peace of springtime and bringing mountains of death and oceans of blood. This war went against the will of heaven and the correct path of humankind. Similarly, it is an affront to humanity to treat women as slaves, locking them up in the inner quarters because they are presumed to be weak. If this practice is clearly in opposition to the way of humanity, how much longer can it survive? How much longer can it hold its power and influence? That era has come to an end. It is time to rectify the wrongdoings of the past. The cannon smoke of the prolonged war is lifting, and a bright day will break on earth. The auspicious light of peace has shone through, and a new stage is set, filled with hope. . . .*

We must thoroughly reform our entire society. In order to reform society, we must first reform the family, society's most basic and fundamental unit. In order to reform the family, we have to liberate women, who are the masters of the house. And we must first liberate women if we are to catch up with the rest of the world, to be competitive, to lead lives that can be respected by other states, and to transform our entire social structure. We are not interested in seeking an acknowledgment through empty slogans such as "equality" or "respect for women." We publish our magazine, Sin yŏja, *with the sole purpose of working in society, gaining emancipation, and finding ways in which we can help build a social order that is the envy of the world. (Quoted in Choi 2013, 29–30)* urged readers to awaken to and be prepared for the new modern era. Kim Wŏnju, the editor in chief, and other major contributors to the magazine were educated in Japan in the 1910s and had been influenced by Japanese feminists such as Yosano Akiko and Hiratsuka Raichō. We can infer that *Sin yŏja* was modeled after *Seitō* because one of the stated goals of both magazines was to support "women geniuses" by offering an outlet for their literary talent and modern ideas. Equipped with new knowledge and keenly aware of the global trend, these women emerged as the new leaders of the movement, putting forward their own vision for New Women and giving birth to an intellectual and cultural force for a modern Korea.

So who was the New Woman exactly? There are a variety of definitions in contemporary Korean scholarship, as well as representations from the print media of that time. Education was a central aspect in the image of the New Woman. The conceptions ranged from any woman who had acquired basic literacy skills to someone who had traveled overseas to receive higher education. However, the most popular image of the New Woman in the print media of the 1920s and 1930s was either the "girl student" (*yŏhaksaeng*), a girl of middle or high school age, or the "elite woman," a woman who had achieved some level of prominence as a public figure in literature, education, art, journalism, or politics. In particular, the image of the girl student quickly became emblematic of the new times, new cultures, and the modern. Given Korea's past, in which women were not granted access to formal education, the schooling of girls was a transformative experience, not just for the girls themselves but also for the general public. Intellectuals and the public were deeply concerned about what girl students learned at school and how they would ultimately contribute to the family and society as educated mothers and wives. Magazines in the 1920s and 1930s specifically targeted girl students not only because they were a group of readers in a society where the rate of illiteracy was very high but also because they considered girl students to be the main targets for lessons and instructions on the "proper" application of modern ideas and attitudes.

The high expectations for girl students coexisted with growing anxiety about the content of education for girls. Intellectuals and educators debated whether the curriculum was impractical or too liberal, and in that discussion they offered many opinions about what proper education for girls should include and how it should be conducted. There was considerable resistance to academic offerings, such as physics, chemistry, or English, because many, especially male intellectuals, felt that those subjects would be "irrelevant" once girls were married. Instead, they argued, girls' education should

A Girl Student on the Street. A girl student is roaming around the street with short bangs, dressed in a short skirt, and high heels. A man looks at her disapprovingly, while two other girl students check her out as if to look for fashion tips. SIN YŎSŎNG 3, NO. 6 (1925)

concentrate on practical knowledge such as cooking, sewing, and child rearing to prepare them for their future roles as mothers and wives.

However, the discourse on girls' education reserved its greatest concern for the ethical and moral training of the female students. There was growing apprehension that morality, especially sexual morality, was in decline and that there was excessive interest in luxury and the consumption of frivolous diversions such as romance novels and movies. Some prominent educators with extensive experience with female students published essays dismissing this negative image of girl students. However, the fact that such images prevailed indicates that there was a growing anxiety about the social and cultural implications of having a class of educated women whose interests lay in sensual pleasures.

As the number of educated women increased, so too did anxiety about "unwieldy women" who disrupted the balance of the family unit. The initial image of the New Woman was that of a pioneer in the modern nation who was an educated and informed participant in a rapidly changing world. However, over time the New Woman came to signify something degenerate and unwholesome, a bad example for future generations of women, because she challenged Confucian gender norms, demanded gender equality, enjoyed modern material culture, and experimented with modern love and sexuality. The public perceived the New Woman as one who rejected the sacred nature of motherhood, engaged in scandalous love affairs, and indulged in the "worldly" (read "selfish") pleasures of shopping, drinking coffee at cafés, or going on picnics. This image was often coupled with her reading romance stories, watching "motion pictures of crude Americanism," and wearing Western-style clothing, high heels, and bobbed hair (Choi 2009, 147).

Given the often sensationalized, discursively constructed image of the New Woman in print and visual media (especially in cartoons and illustrations), it is important to make a distinction between the New Woman as a stereotype constructed through the public discourse and the actual exemplars of New Women. The stereotypical image presented had been generated primarily by men, and it was challenged by a number of New Women. In her insightful essay "Urging Men to Critically Reflect on Themselves," published in 1920 in *Sin yŏja*, the prominent educator Kim Hwallan (1899–1970) offered one of the most detailed analyses of the stereotype, detailing how male intellectuals had exaggerated certain aspects of the New Woman in their portrayal. Kim pointed out how male intellectuals often positioned themselves as superior, conferring on themselves the right to decide what constituted "bad behavior" on the part of women and offering advice on how women could keep the proper path, and then reminded men of their own hypocrisy and disreputable behavior in frequenting pleasure quarters, indulging in the company of *kisaeng*, and spending their money on Western clothing and accessories.

While "Modern Girl" (*modŏn kŏl*) was often taken to be an alternate label for "New Woman," in Korea the term connoted distinctive cultural, symbolic, and economic nuances, as it did in Japan. In the popular media of the time it was associated with the image of a frivolous, vainglorious, promiscuous woman, outfitted in Western-style clothing, adorned with jewelry and other accessories, her face made up, her hair cut short. It should be noted that that image seems to have come largely from use of the term in Japan, China, and the West, where these fashions had come to be associated with a rise in sexual promiscuity and materiality, but the image may not have reflected the reality in Korea. The Modern Girl in colonial Korea in the 1920s and 1930s lived in a vastly different situation. First, few Korean women could afford Western-style clothing. The Korean counterpart of the Modern Girl generally wore a reformed version of traditional Korean dress. In Korea there was no significant new middle class, as there was in Japan, and as a consequence, there was not the same economic base of women to consume these luxury items. If commercial advertisements are any indication of what the readership was interested in buying, it is noteworthy that most of the advertisements in *Sin yŏsŏng* (New Women), the most prominent women's magazine of that time, were for books. It was only in the 1930s that a variety of products for women, such as cosmetics and household items, came to be more readily available, but even then the number of women who could afford to purchase such products remained small. Finally, with regard to sexual behavior, there seemed to be a more open attitude in Japan. The topic of sexual freedom was almost taboo in Korea, with the behavior viewed by all ideological persuasions as decadent and empty-headed. The image of the Modern Girl was highly sexualized, and to say that a girl had become "Westernized" was equivalent to saying she was a "bad girl." In the end, it is important to note that in Korea the Modern Girl was a hyperbolic discursive construct that did not have many real-life referents. The term was a dog whistle for those who had grown anxious about the implications of an encroaching modernity, and it came to be used to deride and ridicule the New Woman.

Discourse on Love, Marriage, and Divorce

Sarang (love) and *yŏnae* (romance) were two terms that became highly popular in the 1920s, reflecting a new discourse in the cultural, artistic, and literary realms. Issues ranged from "free love" and "companionate love" to "proletarian love," and the discourse served as a strategic platform for challenging feudal customs of marriage that devalued individuality in favor of collective and familial interests. Both male and female intellectuals revisited the institutional and cultural devices that had perpetuated loveless marriages, and they introduced ideals of modern love and marriage, mostly of Euro-American origin. The Swedish feminist Ellen Key's *Love and Marriage* and the Russian Communist Alexandra Kollontai's *Red Love* are examples of foreign literary works on this topic that were popular among Korean readers.

Those who desired to have the idealized form of love and marriage often faced a less-than-ideal reality because traditional practices such as early marriage and arranged marriage still had a powerful hold in the public consciousness. Parents frequently married off their sons and daughters at an early age. The retention of that traditional practice presented a quandary for educated men and women who wanted to choose their own marriage partners on the basis of love and shared ideals. It was particularly problematic for the new class of educated women, who delayed marriage in order to achieve their educational goals and then faced challenges in finding partners with the appropriate educational background and perspectives on life and work. Some prominent women intellectuals entered into love affairs with married men, and their status as "second wives" drew significant, mostly scornful attention. In some extreme cases, the broad social disapproval led these couples to commit "love suicide." At the same time, such scandals provoked public complaint about the increasingly unstable institutions of marriage and the family.

Another sign of changing attitudes about marriage can be taken from changes in divorce practices. Divorce was still highly stigmatized, and the growing number of divorces generated a great deal of concern. During Japanese rule the proclamation of modern civil law (*Chosŏn minsaryŏng*) in 1912 established a legal basis for divorce, but Article 11 of the civil law stipulated that matters of "family and inheritance" would continue to follow "Korean customs" (*kwansŭp*). The customs inherited from the Chosŏn dynasty (1392–1910) stipulated that a wife could not initiate divorce, nor was consensus divorce available as an option, and any legal action for divorce required prior consent from the parents or the head of the household. However, despite the legal commitment to follow "custom," the 1910s saw a sudden surge in the number of divorce cases; more important, most of these divorce cases were filed by women. The discrepancy between customary practice and actual practice led to a revision of the civil law in 1922 that both eliminated any reference to "Korean customs" in matters having to do with family or inheritance and allowed for divorce suits. Interestingly, while the 1922 civil law reform made it easier for women to file for divorce in the sense that they were not bound by "custom," there was an overall decline in the divorce rate from the late 1910s until the late 1930s. Despite this decline, the print media tended to exaggerate the level and frequency of divorce, suggesting that divorce was an option that was being embraced not only by New Women but also by uneducated peasant women.

It is noteworthy that discussions of these divorced women often invoked the figure of Nora, the heroine of Henrik Ibsen's *A Doll's House*, which had been a global sensation since it was first staged in the late nineteenth century. Korea was no exception. Ibsen was one of many Western writers whose works were translated into Korean, and *A Doll's House* was one of the best-known works of foreign literature among Koreans. A full translation first appeared in 1921 in serialized form in the daily newspaper *Maeil sinbo*. The all-female editorial board of the feminist magazine *Sin yŏja* was instrumental in having the play translated and published for wider distribution.

The character of Nora came to be a cultural icon, an archetype of the New Woman commonly invoked in the heated debates of the 1920s and 1930s. Some viewed the character as an iconic embodiment of the modern self, while others considered her to be a classic example of how perfidious ideas from the West, such as feminism, had destabilized the family. Many people were particularly disturbed by Nora's leaving her children, seeing in that action the abdication of motherhood, the role that most considered to be the essential function for women (Choi 2012a).

Pak Indŏk, a Korean woman intellectual, was famously called "Korea's Nora." She garnered enormous attention from the press when she offered two thousand *won* in alimony, a large sum of money in those days, to the unfaithful husband from whom she was seeking a divorce and custody of her two daughters. It was the first case of a wife paying alimony to her husband in Korean history. It may be inferred that Pak was so desperate to get away from her husband that she broke all precedent and essentially bought her freedom. She filed for divorce in 1931, right after returning to Korea from her studies in the United States and an extended global tour sponsored by American and European Christian groups. In 1934 another prominent New Woman, Na Hyesŏk, published a sensational essay called "A Confession About My Divorce." She had had an extramarital affair while staying in Paris, and she was forced to leave her family in 1930. The act of divorce was already scandalous, but Na took the unprecedented step of presenting her side of the story in full detail and candor.

Chastity and the Body Politics

One of the most visible and sensational aspects of the New Woman was her appearance and sexuality. In traditional Korea women were instructed to cover up their bodies as much as possible and to follow "proper" womanly behavior by remaining quiet, demure, obedient, and modest in their comportment. In contrast, the raised hemline of a skirt, the revealed ankle, the bobbed hair, the high-heeled shoes and silk stockings—these were symbols of the New Woman. There was also a new emphasis on women maintaining a healthy body by engaging in physical activities such as hiking, swimming, skating, volleyball, baseball, and gymnastics.

Intellectuals debated the pros and cons of the "modern look" using scientific, economic, and aesthetic arguments. However, from the perspective of social reformers, the inordinate attention New Women paid to their appearance and the high costs that came with wearing modern clothing and maintaining a Western hairstyle were deeply concerning, given the economic struggles that were common during colonial rule. While only a tiny proportion of the population could afford luxury items, the print media often exaggerated the New Women's desire for those modern products.

However, more worrisome than women's modern fashions were the changing attitudes toward sexual purity and chastity. Some leading feminists pointed to the fact that chastity was generally only expected of women as an anachronism that should be eliminated. In their discussion of true modern love, the traditional notion of woman's chastity was scrutinized. Na Hyesŏk famously said, "Chastity involves neither morals nor laws. It is merely taste. Just as we eat rice [*pab*] when we want to eat rice, and we eat rice cake [*ttŏk*] when we want to eat rice cake, chastity depends on our will and practice. We shouldn't be constrained" (Choi 2013, 147). Her challenge to the old notion of chastity was intended not to promote careless, casual sex but rather to draw attention to the tyrannical nature of man-made norms that had been used to control and restrict a woman's body. This example and others like it represented a fundamental change from the old view that a woman's body was a fragile thing that belonged to the man to whom she was married; the new view saw a woman's body as a resilient and creative vehicle through which she expressed her selfhood.

The desire of women to control their own bodies was also expressed through their interest in contraception. In a society where a woman was under pressure to continue having children until she produced a male heir, the idea of birth control was met with high suspicion. Yun Sŏngsang, a woman intellectual, wrote in 1930, "Upon hearing the phrase 'birth control,' people immediately perceive it as a subversive or sinful subject." Yun offered a number of reasons for people's opposition to birth control: concern about religious prohibitions against birth control; anxiety that access to birth control sanctioned illicit sexual relations by removing the potential for pregnancy; fear that birth control would reduce the number of gifted individuals; and belief that birth control might make it easier for couples to divorce. In addition, some argued that birth control would cause more cases of infertility and female diseases, or *puinpyŏng* (Choi 2013, 152). Yun refuted these claims one by one, arguing that they were largely ideological and hypocritical rather than scientific. Yun argued that, rather than being a complete ban on children, birth control was a means by which a woman could govern her pregnancies so that she could raise a small number of healthy children rather than a large number of weak ones. Although there was some suspicion, it is clear that many women were interested in birth control, and popular magazines invited medical doctors to share advice on proper contraceptive practices. Still, information on birth control was not readily available to the vast majority of women. Abortion was illegal, so it was done in secret and often unsafely. Women from wealthy families could afford to go somewhere for a safe (albeit clandestine) medical abortion, but poor women had to rely on unscientific, dangerous methods such as drinking sodium hydroxide or doing physical harm to themselves to try to cause a miscarriage.

New Women and Transnational Encounters

For centuries, traveling overseas to pursue new knowledge, political missions, or commerce was the exclusive domain of men. However, beginning in the late nineteenth century, a small group of Korean women began to travel overseas for a variety of reasons, most commonly for purposes of advanced study. Given Korea's status as a colony of Japan and the geographical proximity of the two countries, Japan was the most frequent destination for Korean students wanting to study overseas during the colonial era. In 1910 there were only 34 Korean female students in Japan, but by 1942 that number had grown to 2,947. There was an identifiable missionary influence in the pathway that developed between Korea and Japan. That is, graduates from mission schools in Korea often continued their education at mission schools in Japan, including Doshisha Women's College, Kobe Women's College, Kwassui Women's College, and Hiroshima Women's College.

The Japanese colonial government made it difficult for Korean students to go to countries other than Japan, but some students managed to travel to the United States, China, and a few European countries, such as Britain, Germany, and Sweden. Between 1895 and 1940 approximately 148 Korean female students went to the United States for advanced study (Choi 2012b). Korea-based American missionaries played a significant role in sending their students to faith-based U.S. colleges or their alma maters, such as Ohio Wesleyan University.

A small number of women who had traveled overseas for advanced study or professional meetings wrote memoirs that offered some insights into how these transnational encounters helped young women develop a sense of modern personhood. To be sure, they often had to cope with difficulties deriving from limited finances and poor language skills, but they felt those minor inconveniences were the price to pay for the privilege of experiencing a new culture in the liberal environment of a university campus. Some of these memoirs present detailed statistics to demonstrate the higher status of women in Euro-American societies, with the strong implication that Korea should emulate those countries. Still, they were not always in favor of what they observed or experienced overseas. Hŏ Chŏngsuk, a socialist feminist, visited the United States and critiqued the relentless encroachment of material capitalism on people's lives, seeing the United States as the ultimate manifestation of those practices. Even those who admired the civilization of the United States and its technological advancement cautioned against excessive materialism and the "decadent" culture represented by jazz and Hollywood movies. Racism was another negative aspect U.S.-educated Korean students often pointed to. In the words of Chang Iuk, "While the US is known as a pioneer of humanity, freedom, and equality, it is a fact that racism exists in the US. Indeed, no other country seems to be as racist as the US is" (Chang 1925, 29).

Interestingly, some intellectuals found more adequate models to the largely agrarian Korean society in European societies. For instance, the Christian women leaders Kim Hwallan and Pak Indŏk shared the lessons they learned from their time spent in Denmark and Germany, where they visited rural areas to learn more about plans and strategies for the revitalization of rural communities. They highlighted the work ethic, practicality, and frugality of the peasant women in these countries, promoting their lifestyle as a better model for Korean peasant women.

There was a clear fascination with European and American cultures, where these women experienced freedom and opportunities they could have only dreamed about in Korea. Although both financial hardship and linguistic barriers significantly limited the scope of their intellectual and cultural experiences, their exposure to foreign societies and cultures enabled them to reevaluate their own society more clearly and critically with a better sense of the world and keen interest in local conditions in Korea.

CHINA

New Gender Roles and Ideals

New Culture–era feminist discourse presented a politicized view of women's emancipation and gender equality as essential aspects of a strong modern Chinese nation. The development of a modern urban culture in China's largest cities between the world wars brought new ways of being feminine and masculine in public, and new modes and spaces for interaction between men and women. In the 1920s and 1930s, the emergence of modern consumer society and mass media, including magazines, newspapers, radio, and film, created new challenges to traditional gender norms and complicated ideas about the modern woman and her role in modernization of the nation. Although women as consumers, writers, professionals, and activists participated actively in constructing new possibilities for themselves, they were also forced to contend with the images and stereotypes of the modern woman—produced by men—that pervaded mass media. Increasingly visible on the streets of China's rapidly developing cities, in popular pictorials, in print and radio advertisements, and in movies, women became both icons of modern possibilities and touchstones for anxieties about the destabilization of traditional values and social boundaries.

In China, as in Japan and Korea, the global terms "New Woman" (*xin funü, xin nüxing*) and "Modern Girl" (*modeng gou'er*, but often referred to with the English term) described both actual women adopting new styles and behaviors and ideal types that became the focus of praise or criticism. Generally speaking, the New Woman, who emerged in the New Culture Movement of the late 1910s (see Chapter 5), was the educated, patriotic embodiment of a new gender order working to overcome the oppressions of the Confucian family system and traditional society. The Modern Girl appeared a bit later, in the 1930s, and tended to represent a commodified, glamorous, and individualist vision of modern femininity. However, there was considerable overlap between the terms. Female students, for example, displayed aspects of both. Living on their own, with their eyeglasses, short hair, and calf-length skirts revealing unbound feet sometimes iin high-heeled shoes, they were the most visible of the numerous models of modern femininity in the early twentieth century. While reformers across the political spectrum saw women's education as essential for modern progress, these students' independence from family, display of fashion, and open, casual relationships with men drew accusations of frivolity and immorality.

By the 1920s and 1930s, women in new roles—professionals, factory workers, secretaries, department store clerks, shopgirls, entertainers, and prostitutes—were prominent all over China's cities. These changes happened first and most rapidly in Shanghai, the sixth-largest city in the world, the cultural, financial, and industrial center of Republican-period China, and its most globalized city. Cultural trends in Shanghai filtered out to provincial cities through a rapidly expanding commercial press and popular culture industry.

The Woes of the Modern Woman

The concept of the New Woman appeared first in the writings of men in New Culture journals such as *New Youth*. For young urban men coming of age amid the nationalist fervor of the New Culture Movement, the small (nuclear) family centered around a companionate marriage independent of the large extended family was key to fostering the productivity and civic consciousness necessary for building a strong modern nation. The New Woman was both a model of the personal liberation they hoped to attain and an essential partner for the modern family life they hoped to live (Glosser 2003).

Discussion and debate about the education, values, behavior, work, lifestyle, and fashion that were appropriate for the New Woman featured prominently in the many periodicals published for and about women in various cities, including *Ladies' Journal* (*Funü zazhi*, published 1915–1932 in Shanghai) and *New Woman* (*Xin funü*, started in 1920 in Shanghai). Writers often drew on examples of women's emancipation in Western countries and Japan to argue that it was essential for the modern progress of nations. Although the majority of editors and writers were men, such publications reached a growing audience of literate, urban women, and increasing numbers of women writers contributed essays and fiction to them. As we saw in Chapter 5, the early 1920s were an optimistic time for the women's movement, as women's organizations proliferated and an explicitly feminist agenda of educational, economic, legal, and political rights for women was discussed and promoted widely in the press. Female educators, social reformers, writers, journalists, lawyers, doctors, and government workers defined what it meant to be a New Woman for themselves and were prominent at the forefront of these political developments.

Amid the realities of modern city life, optimistic enthusiasm about the possibilities for personal liberation from the constraints of the Confucian family soon gave way to more pessimistic commentaries on the real-life difficulties of economic survival and gender relationships. As in Japan and Korea, Nora, the heroine of Henrik Ibsen's play *A Doll's House,* who leaves her patriarchal marriage to strike out on her own, became a popular icon of modern womanhood in China. In a famous lecture at Beijing Women's Normal College in 1923, "What Happens After Nora Leaves Home," the male writer Lu Xun (1881–1936), one of the leaders of the New Culture Movement, pointed out that without economic rights and the ability to earn a living on their own, New Women faced the inevitability either of returning home or of prostitution.

> *What has [Nora] taken away with her apart from her awakened heart? If she has nothing but a crimson woolen scarf of the kind you young ladies are wearing, even if two or three feet wide it will prove completely useless. She needs more than that, needs something in*

> *her purse. To put it bluntly, what she needs is money. Dreams are fine; otherwise money is essential. . . . Of course money cannot buy freedom, but freedom can be sold for money. Human beings have one drawback, which is that they often get hungry. To remedy this drawback and to avoid being puppets, the most important thing in society today seems to be economic rights. (Lu, quoted in Lan and Fong 2015, 178–179)*

As the numbers of educated women with professional aspirations grew, women confronted the difficulties of balancing an independent career with family duties in a new-style nuclear family. In fiction and essays in the 1920s, women writers, who embodied in many ways the ideals of education and independence of the new woman, began to explore the practical limitations of women's liberation. In "The Woes of the Modern Woman," an essay published in the magazine *New Woman* in 1927, the leftist writer Chen Xuezhao (1907–1991) explained the new phenomenon of women choosing to remain single "to dedicate themselves to society." She wrote:

> *When both partners in the so-called "one husband–one wife new family" have careers, the problem of dependency doesn't arise; however, as soon as the woman has a baby, she is no longer able to keep her job and the family's economic burden falls entirely on the man's shoulders. Since there is no public day care and the average family can't afford a nanny, . . . the woman has no choice but to look after it herself. . . . I can't help recalling all those grand theories that the new men were espousing four or five years ago. Back then, the new men believed that in order to reform the backward family and to construct a superior one, all that was needed was free love: that is, the freedom to marry an educated, talented woman with whom they could relate on an intellectual, emotional, and personal level. . . . The "new family" ought to be blissful, but in fact this is not the case at all! When two people have just fallen in love, the man naturally respects the woman. . . . [H]owever, as soon as they . . . have children, gradually . . . the man becomes the master of the relationship; everything falls under his control and he is no longer able to respect his wife in the way he used to. Since the woman has to take care of the children and the household, she no longer has time to work in society or make a living. (Chen, translated in Dooling and Torgeson 1998, 171)*

For some feminists, such as Chen Xuezhao, the purpose of liberating the New Woman from patriarchal family constraints was to free her to contribute more fully to society. Pursuit of her own personal fulfillment and livelihood was compatible with, and indeed necessary for, active participation in civic life.

Other women writers, such as Ding Ling (1904–1986), used fiction to explore the subjectivity and sexuality of women with cosmopolitan values and the complications they faced making a life for themselves in a modernizing society. Ding's first short story, "Miss Sophia's Diary," published in 1928 at the height of the Communist purge, was a pessimistic exploration of the obstacles to women's self-realization. The main character, inspired by Ibsen's *A Doll's House* and Flaubert's *Madame Bovary*, was a highly educated and self-absorbed young woman living alone in Beijing. Her Western name evoked female revolutionary and literary figures well known to Chinese

BOX 6.3

Ding Ling

Raised in an impoverished literati family from Hunan province in the last years of the Qing dynasty, Ding Ling was part of the first generation of women educated entirely in the new girls' schools, where her classmates included many future women Communist revolutionaries, such as Mao Zedong's future wife. Her first role model was her widowed mother, who was classically educated in the tradition of literati women, but Ding enrolled herself in one of the new women's academies, where she became close friends with classmate Xiang Jingyu (see Chapters 4 and 5) and took up a career as a teacher and activist in the movements for women's suffrage and national sovereignty.

Ding Ling took up political activism in the May Fourth Movement and left Hunan for Shanghai in 1920 to escape a marriage arranged by her uncles. Living and working as a journal editor in an anarchist collective, she was drawn to the radical feminism of women such as Russian Communist Alexandra Kollontai and birth control activist Margaret Sanger (who did a monthlong speaking tour in China in 1922). Like these women, Ding believed that women's emancipation required not only economic independence, but control of their bodies and freedom of sexual expression. Yet she struggled to find paid employment to support her independent—and quite unconventional—lifestyle. As political divisions between the Communist and Nationalist parties hardened during the 1920s, she retreated from politics and embedded

(continued)

herself in the Shanghai social circles of male writers, a number of whom would become her lovers. She loved Hollywood movies (briefly pursuing a career as a film actress) and read widely in translated novels by authors like Flaubert, Alexander Dumas, Tolstoy, and Dostoevsky, drawn especially to the tragic struggles of their romantic heroines. Her early stories, beginning with "Miss Sophia's Diary," also drew on her own experience of fraught relationships with men. Her protagonists are new women whose feminist quest to live life on their own terms is consistently undermined by what she saw as quintessentially feminine qualities like self-delusion, irrationality, and uncontrolled and misdirected sexual desire. Her description of the adulterous main character in "A Woman and a Man" associates modern femininity with confusion about identity and contradictory desires:

> *The woman's name was—well, what was her name? She had deliberately selected more than fifty interesting names and had used them at every conceivable occasion. She mostly allowed her friends to call her Wendy. She was a woman of excessive passion, yet one who would never be able to experience real love. She lives in a constant state of perverse deviancy, in that she loathed expressions of sentiment that reminded her of the desires of the flesh, and that were therefore, to her way of thinking, lacking in sincere love (Barlow 1989, 89).*

urban intellectuals: Sophia Perovskaya, who was executed for her role in the assassination of Tsar Alexander II, and the character of Sophie in Jean-Jacques Rousseau's treatise on the education of citizens, *Emile*. The story describes her rather narcissistic self-examination of her turbulent emotional states as she wrestles with the sexual and emotional frustrations of romantic love as a "liberated" woman in a patriarchal society. She openly expresses her desire for the man for whom she has fallen deeply in love, but depicts him as a sexual object, lamenting, "How could I admit to anyone that I gazed at those provocative lips like a small hungry child eyeing sweets? I know very well that in this society I'm forbidden to take what I need to gratify my desires and frustrations, even when it clearly wouldn't hurt anybody" (Ding 1989, 55). She also expresses homoerotic feelings for her closest friend as she ponders her untimely death. Filled with self-loathing at the thought of allowing herself to fulfill her desire only to become the object of her lover's lust, in the end she chooses her independence over her lover. Critics and readers at the time identified Miss Sophia as a quintessentially modern woman, confused and disillusioned with the incompatibility of romance and independence for women. Her focus on self-fulfillment and self-knowledge presented an alternative mode of modern femininity to the socially minded feminist activism espoused by women like Chen Xuezhao, and, later, Ding Ling herself. (See Chapter 8.)

Gender Modernity and the Mass Media

Highly educated professional female elites represented only a small portion of the women engaged in radically new patterns of work and family life. By choice or necessity, growing numbers of young women worked outside the home in shops, offices, and factories. In Shanghai, and to a lesser extent in other cities, women and men interacted freely with each other in the workplace and socialized together in new public places such as cafés, bars, movie theaters, dance halls, theaters, and the Great World, the famed multistory entertainment center in Shanghai that offered a dizzying array of traditional and modern music, theater, acrobatics, games, movies, teahouses, restaurants, and markets. Many young urbanites dated, chose their marital partners, and set up nuclear family households. As they made their lives in the city, these so-called petty urbanites were avid consumers of popular periodicals full of images of modern women and men, articles about work, family, love, and other aspects of daily existence, and advice about how to deal with the problems of modern life. These mass publications propagated as ideal the vision of modern family life that Chen Xuezhao criticized: husband and wife chose each other freely and lived independently of parents, but while he worked to support the household, she applied her modern education to the scientific rearing of children and domestic management. Letters to the editor revealed just how difficult it was to maintain this small family ideal. Many people described conflicts with parents, marital tensions, and economic woes that frustrated the ambitions for happiness and success created by their modern education.

Scandals, a common feature in the press, often highlighted the contradictions and confusions of new gender norms. The 1922 suicide of Xi Shangzhen, a female secretary working at the offices of a commercial journal, was one example. Her death was particularly troubling to the urban public because, as an educated, unmarried woman supporting herself with an independent career, Xi embodied the New Woman. Yet suicide was behavior associated with the oppressions of the chastity cult of the old society. In the press and in the courts her death was blamed on her employer, Tang Jiezhi, who himself exemplified new modes of masculinity; he was a prominent nationalist reformer, known for his involvement in the May Fourth Movement and for his advocacy of democracy and the stock market. Among the tangle of accusations that emerged in the case was that the two were having an affair and that this modern married man had humiliated her by asking her to become his concubine. Some commentators understood this insinuation of sex into a professional relationship as an offense against Xi's sensibilities as an independent New Woman. For others, it was an affront to her chastity with its traditional connotations. Complicating the sexual intrigue was the fact that Xi had entrusted him with investing a large amount of her family's money in the new Shanghai stock market, but he had lost it in a crash. Accused of defrauding her of money, Tang appeared as both a sexual and financial predator. Modern gender relations were tinged with the threat of sexual promiscuity, while the existence of the stock market symbolized the economic profligacy of modern capitalism (Goodman 2005).

Public Women

Hints of impropriety colored perceptions of the New Woman in part because prostitutes, the only public women of the premodern era, were a persistent foil for women forging new paths in urban spaces. Courtesan culture gradually declined in the first half of the twentieth century, with the disappearance of their old clientele of gentry and merchant elites and the rise of new urban middle and upper classes. Once considered the cultured arbiters of taste, fashion, and even virtue, they were increasingly defined in the media and reformist discourse by their sexuality alone, as sellers of sex at the top of a vast and complex hierarchy of Shanghai prostitutes (Hershatter 1997). Taking their place on the Shanghai social scene in the 1920s were singing hostesses, who accompanied men at parties or worked in teahouses, restaurants, and amusement centers, performing for clients with whom they sometimes developed patronage relationships.

In the 1930s, singing hostesses gave way to dancing hostesses, who sold their services as expert dance partners for men in ballroom dance halls and clubs. Patrons bought tickets for dances and at some establishments could purchase the women's sexual services as well. Popular guidebooks for Shanghai explained the protocol and etiquette of dance halls for men unfamiliar with modern city life. They highlighted the significant role of dance hostesses—who numbered in the thousands in their heyday—in instructing men newly arrived from the countryside or small towns not only on the latest dance steps but also on the fashion and comportment appropriate for such modern encounters between the sexes. In guidebooks, media commentary, and fiction, men were also warned of the dangers of being scammed or deceived by the allure of artificial intimacy such women created (Field 1999). In fiction and film there were also many sympathetic portrayals of the difficult lives and tragic downfalls of such women entertainers, depicting them as innocent victims of a corrupting urban society.

Films, both Chinese and foreign, became a compelling and widely popular source of ideas about modernity. Though the first Chinese films were made around the turn of the twentieth century, it was not until 1921 that a feature film of a murder mystery galvanized the industry, setting Shanghai on a path to becoming the "Hollywood of the East." "Talkie" films were introduced in China shortly after their debut in Hollywood in 1927, and the first Chinese talkie appeared in 1931. Movie theaters showing both Hollywood and Chinese films mushroomed across the cities in the 1920s, with more than thirty in Shanghai alone by the early 1930s.

Two of China's earliest female movie stars, Wang Hanlun (1903–1978) and Yang Naimei (1904–1960), were educated women from elite families who, like many new women at the time, pursued their acting careers in defiance of their families' wishes. They rose to stardom through promotional tours for their films that connected them to their fan base in person. By the late 1920s, both women were wealthy enough to own their own production companies. They were a prominent presence in Shanghai's elite social circles, as well as fashion trendsetters and influential agents of cultural production.

Their success belied the negative social commentary on actresses in the 1920s, which associated them with prostitutes and lower-class dancing girls who lacked genuine talent and were hoping to improve their social status through film careers. An essay in the *Ladies' Journal* in 1927 caustically criticized film actresses: "Almost all of the women who step onto the stage are the wives of actors, lowly women, and prostitutes, who generally lead the disgusting lives of streetwalkers. We can guess what their values, their principles, and their hopes are." The author labeled four types of actresses: those who had no other livelihood, those pursuing high salaries, prostitutes seeking fame and fortune, and prostitutes tired of selling sexual services. He concludes, "They simply cannot imagine what morality or art are. The male side of the film world and those playboys look down upon them and thus hunt them as so many pieces of meat" (quoted in Chang 1999, 139–140). The implication of this kind of criticism was that when such women portrayed virtuous and admirable characters, they were deceiving a naive public.

In the 1930s, with the emergence of the Chinese studio system, female stars were created by the film industry and popularized through the industry's own glossy movie magazines, promoting fan mail in exchange for autographed photos. In contrast with the derogatory discourse of the past, the new mass media image of film stars emphasized their talent, their virtue, and their authenticity as "good girls" who modeled a respectable form of modern femininity for the urban masses. They were the quintessential Modern Girls.

The Modern Girl

For China's urban public, movie stars and dance hostesses were the most iconic examples of the Modern Girl ethos that exploded as a mass media phenomenon in the late twenties and thirties. Highly popular pictorial magazines such as *The Young Companion* (*Liangyou*, started in 1926) and *Women's Pictorial* (*Furen huabao*, 1933–1935) promoted a Westernized standard of beauty and a cosmopolitan lifestyle as hallmarks of the Modern Girl. On their covers, they featured photos or drawings of glamorous young women sporting the new look: bobbed or permed hair, formfitting *qipao* or *cheongsam* (often with a long slit up the side), high heels, face powder, rouge, and lipstick. Inside, such magazines provided practical how-to advice on clothing, hairstyles, skin care, and makeup, complemented by advertisements for the modern and foreign products required to achieve the right look. There were articles about Chinese and Western film stars and celebrities, illustrated with photographs and essays on the proper hobbies and knowledge of sports, jazz and classical music, and literature that a woman should develop for social success. *The Young Companion* also published photos of fashionable college students and the wives and daughters of prominent families, highlighting the respectability of the new style.

While the perfect package of modern fashion and lifestyle was perhaps attainable only by a minority of women, elements of the Modern Girl style were widely adopted and adapted across social classes. Variations on the *qipao* and short hairstyles were common among urban women, including professional women, middle- and upper-class wives, factory workers, shopgirls, secretaries, students, actresses, dance hall girls, and prostitutes.

The pervasiveness of the Modern Girl look highlighted its chief danger: it obscured class and status lines and signaled that modern femininity was a commodity that could be purchased by anyone. Stories of low-class women who seduced respectable men with their Modern Girl looks and of respectable Modern Girls who fell into prostitution abounded in the media; they highlighted the superficiality and deceptiveness of the Modern Girl while

The revealing Western-style swimwear and alluring film-star pose in this cover of Liangyou highlight the global and risqué aspects of the Modern Girl image. LIANGYOU (THE YOUNG COMPANION), NO. 93, SEPT. 1, 1934

celebrating the Modern Girl style. She was a figure full of ironies that spoke to the anxieties caused by modernization. The Modern Girl was praised for her confidence and independence in her relations with men, her ability to choose her romantic partners, her choice to marry for love, and even her choice to divorce to preserve her integrity or her interests. Yet she was often depicted as preying upon innocent men and taking advantage of their naiveté, selfishly failing to fulfill her domestic duties as wife and mother. She represented the allure of modern commodities, yet was criticized for being decadent and materialistic (Dong 2008).

The Demise of the Modern Girl

After Japan's 1931 invasion of Manchuria, leftist and conservative criticisms of modernization, focusing on individual fulfillment, style, and consumption, intensified as national salvation became the dominant priority. The Modern Girl was an easy target for denunciation. For leftist feminists, she represented a bourgeois femininity: selfish, materialistic, shallow, and unaware of the capitalist forces of commodification and consumerism that shaped her life and image. For conservative reformers she embodied the corrosive effect of modernization on traditional values. In 1934, the governing Nationalist

Party launched the New Life Movement, which aimed to purge society of decadent Western influences and to promote a Confucian modernity centered on family, frugality, and obedience to an increasingly fascist state authority. The Nationalist Party began a heavy-handed campaign to regulate fashion and cultural life, issuing bans on Westernized fashion, permed hair, and nail polish; regulating the length of women's clothes; raiding dance halls to arrest and fine patrons engaged in licentious activity; and patrolling city streets with "Brigades of Destroyers of the Modern" that cut women's clothes if they appeared too modern and arrested women wearing "strange clothes" (Dong 2008, 215–216). The conservative entrepreneur You Huaigao articulated a new, decidedly conservative definition of the new woman in the magazine he published:

> *Some people think that modern dress is the sign of a new woman. Others think that if they have studied and can understand applications of the past to the present, or even speak a Western language, that is a sign of distinguishing the New Age Woman. Some of these views are outright mistaken, others are deficient. The New Age Woman should be a figure in society, a companion in the home and a mother of children. . . . Her role is one of bitter work and heavy responsibility. So fastidiousness of dress, extent of knowledge or life achievements are not distinguishing signs of a New Age Woman. (Quoted in Glosser 2003, 163–164)*

Though You was referring to middle-class women, ironically, as we will see in Chapter 7, "bitter work and heavy responsibility" were the lot of the vast majority of those poor and working-class women whose lives were transformed in very different ways by the forces of economic modernization. Although progressive women would continue to reject such reassertions of family patriarchy, they also became increasingly disillusioned with the partial victories offered by the ideology of the New Woman and its failures to address the deep inequalities and military crisis that beset China in the 1930s.

CONNECTIONS

New Women and Modern Girls were simultaneously global phenomena and specific to their national contexts. They were both real people and creatures of media and discourse. They appeared in all three East Asian countries—as well as throughout the West—at about the same time. They were praised, and saw themselves, as emblems of modernity in societies struggling with rapid change and the rejection of a recent past that had led to the battlefields of World War I. The world was turned around as a result of that war, and much that had been seen as normal was deconstructed, to be built anew. Gender norms, behaviors, and discourses, which had already come under review in the modernization movements before the turn of the century, were also taken apart. But the evolution of New Women and later Modern Girls, who were real people as well as the creation of media imaginations, induced anxiety among some segments of the population and excitement among others.

New Women had much in common in the three East Asian countries, but they differed in significant ways as well. In Japan, where East Asia's New Women first appeared in the form of the Bluestocking Society, these women were mostly educated adults, often though not exclusively in the arts. Many Bluestockings wrote brilliant essays, fiction, and poetry that have enjoyed a long shelf life. The Bluestockings, who challenged traditional marriage by stressing romantic love, were sometimes sneered at as Japanese "Noras," following the Ibsen play. But they succeeded in combating the completely scandalous image of the New Woman that initially characterized them. The term "New Women" came to be largely noncontroversial by the mid-1910s, as seen by its adoption by the True New Women's Association, a group of women who claimed that they were even better New Women than the Bluestockings because of their professed greater respectability. Like the Bluestockings, the True New Women stressed that women should have a public voice, marriage equality, and employment opportunities. Picking up the theme of social, economic, and political rights, the pioneering women's rights organization New Woman's Association also adopted the term for its own progressive title in 1919.

By the 1920s, Modern Girls, the figurative "daughters" of the New Women, emerged in Japan. Criticized as frivolous and materialistic, Modern Girls came from all walks of urban life and included white-, pink-, and blue-collar workers. They were characterized by their fashionable clothes, both Western and Japanese styles, even if they only wore them one day a week to stroll down the Ginza. Even more than their New Women forebears, Modern Girls were the subject of press commentary. Traditionalists saw them as hedonistic, overly sexual, threateningly foreign, and leading to the downfall of Japan, while on the opposite side of the political spectrum, leftists bemoaned Modern Girls' materialism and apparent self-absorption.

New Women in Korea were also part of a transnational trend of reform and liberation with parallels in the West and in Japan. But under Korea's colonial conditions, the question of pursuing one's personal independence ran up against the equally important goal of struggling for national independence. In Korea, New Women in the 1920s were often depicted as either girl students or elite adult women, although the former was a more common image. The character of Nora in *A Doll's House* was, as in Japan, sometimes used to describe Korea's New Women. Educators defended their students against the charge that they were frivolous and materialistic. But although Korea's New Women were initially considered pioneers of the modern nation, they increasingly came to be seen in the same negative light as Japan's Modern Girls. Indeed, "Modern Girl" came to be used as a term of derision against New Women in Korea. Seeking equality by challenging Confucian gender and sexuality norms, including favoring love-based relationships and marriages, some New Women were caricatured as degenerate. A number studied abroad, often in Christian colleges, after completing their education in Korean missionary schools.

China's New Women first appeared in articles, often written by men, in progressive magazines and journals such as *New Youth* in the 1910s. By the time of the May Fourth Movement, women were markers both of modernity and for the anxieties about the destabilization of traditional values, as they were in Japan and Korea at that time as well. Some men in the May Fourth era saw China's women as pitiable and deserving of reformists' help, but some New Women of that era stressed women's strength. They asserted that to serve society women needed personal freedom, thereby minimizing the clash that emerged in Korea between serving the country and developing one's own personal independence. There was a growing number of modern married couples in the 1920s in cities such as Shanghai; women in the entertainment trades were another type of New Women who helped to guide male customers in modern relations between the sexes.

Modern Girls appeared in films in the 1920s, and some actresses, who were considered Modern Girls, became respected leading members of the Chinese cinema community. In theory, anyone could purchase the kinds of clothing that made up the Modern Girl "look," but that, in turn, made the Modern Girl seem superficial. In any case, Modern Girls were criticized in China after the Manchurian Incident in 1931; as in Japan and Korea, leftists saw them as materialistic and selfish at a time of national crisis, and conservatives scorned them as Western and therefore corrosive to traditional society.

In all three societies, New Women opened up discussions about social and political equality. But in the end, New Women and Modern Girls were forced to take a backseat as the threat of war and repression began to rise in the 1930s.

REFERENCES AND SUGGESTIONS FOR FURTHER READING

GLOBAL CONTEXT

Cooley, Winnifred Harper. 1904. *The New Womanhood*. New York: Broadway.

Lowy, Dina. 2007. *The Japanese "New Woman": Images of Gender and Modernity*. New Brunswick, NJ: Rutgers University Press.

Valence, Deborah. 2004. "Gender in the Formation of European Power, 1750–1914." In *A Companion to Gender History*, edited by Teresa A. Meade and Merry E. Wiesner-Hanks. Oxford: Blackwell.

Weinbaum, Alys Eve, Lynn M. Thomas, Priti Ramamurthy, Uta G. Poiger, Madeleine Yue Dong, and Tani E. Barlow, eds. 2008. *The Modern Girl Around the World: Consumption, Modernity, and Globalization*. Durham, NC: Duke University Press.

JAPAN

Bardsley, Jan. 2007. *The Bluestockings of Japan: New Woman Essays and Fiction from* Seitō, *1911–16*. Ann Arbor: Center for Japanese Studies, University of Michigan.

Frederick, Sarah. 2006. *Turning Pages: Reading and Writing Women's Magazines in Interwar Japan*. Honolulu, HI: University of Hawai'i Press.

Hiratsuka Raichō. 2006. *In the Beginning, Woman Was the Sun: The Autobiography of a Japanese Feminist*. Translated by Teruko Craig. New York: Columbia University Press.

Ito, Ruri. 2008. "The 'Modern Girl' Question in the Periphery of Empire: Colonial Modernity and Mobility Among Okinawan Women in the 1920s and 1930s." In *The Modern Girl Around the World: Consumption, Modernity, and Globalization*, edited by Alys Eve Weinbaum et al. Durham, NC: Duke University Press.

Kano, Ayako. 2001. *Acting Like a Woman in Modern Japan: Theatre, Gender, and Nationalism*. New York: Palgrave.

Lippit, Noriko Mizuta, and Kyoko Irie Selden. 1991. *Japanese Women Writers: Twentieth Century Short Fiction*. Abington, UK: Routledge.

Lowy, Dina. 2007. *The Japanese "New Woman": Images of Gender and Modernity*. New Brunswick, NJ: Rutgers University Press.

Mackie, Vera. 2003. *Feminism in Modern Japan: Citizenship, Embodiment and Sexuality*. Cambridge: Cambridge University Press.

Pflugfelder, Gregory M. "'S' is for the Sister: Schoolgirl Intimacy and 'Same-Sex Love' in Early Twentieth-Century Japan." In *Gendering Modern Japanese History*, edited by Barbara Molony and Kathleen Uno. Cambridge, MA: Harvard University Press.

Sato, Barbara, 2008. "Contesting Consumerisms in Mass Women's Magazines." In *The Modern Girl Around the World: Consumption, Modernity, and Globalization*, edited by Alys Eve Weinbaum et al. Durham, NC: Duke University Press.

Selden, Kyoko, and Noriko Mizuta. 2014. *More Stories by Japanese Women Writers: An Anthology*. Abington, UK: Routledge.

Silverberg, Miriam. 1991. "The Modern Girl as Militant." In *Recreating Japanese Women, 1600–1945*, edited by Gail Lee Bernstein. Berkeley: University of California Press.

Suzuki, Michiko. 2010. *Becoming Modern Women: Love and Female Identity in Prewar Japanese Literature and Culture*. Stanford, CA: Stanford University Press.

Tanaka, Yukiko, ed. 1987. *To Live and to Write: Selections by Japanese Women Writers, 1913–1938*. Seattle, WA: Seal Press.

Tomida, Hiroko. 2004. *Hiratsuka Raichō and Early Japanese Feminism*. Leiden: E. J. Brill.

Weinbaum, Alys Eve, Lynn M. Thomas, Priti Ramamurthy, Uta G. Poiger, Madeleine Yue Dong, and Tani E. Barlow, eds. 2008. *The Modern Girl Around the World: Consumption, Modernity, and Globalization*. Durham, NC: Duke University Press.

KOREA

Barraclough, Ruth. 2014. "Red Love and Betrayal in the Making of North Korea: Comrade Hŏ Jŏng-suk." *History Workshop Journal* 77 (Spring): 86–102.

Chang, Iuk. *Uraki* 1, 1925: 29.

Choi, Hyaeweol. 2009. *Gender and Mission Encounters in Korea: New Women, Old Ways*. Berkeley: University of California Press.

Choi, Hyaeweol. 2012a. "Debating the Korean New Woman: Imagining Henrik Ibsen's 'Nora' in Colonial Era Korea." *Asian Studies Review* 36, no. 1: 59–77.

———. 2012b. "In Search of Knowledge and Selfhood: Korean Women Studying Overseas in Colonial Korea." *Intersections: Gender and Sexuality in Asia and the Pacific* 29. Online at http://intersections.anu.edu.au/issue29/choi.htm.

———. 2013. *New Women in Colonial Korea: A Sourcebook*. London: Routledge.

Choi, Kyeong-Hee. 1999. "Neither Colonial nor National: The Making of the 'New Woman' in Pak Wansŏ's 'Mother's Stake 1.'" In *Colonial Modernity in Korea*, edited by Gi-Wook Shin and Michael Robinson. Cambridge, MA: Harvard University Press.

Hyun, Theresa. 2004. *Writing Women in Korea*. Honolulu: University of Hawai'i Press.

Jeong, Kelly Y. 2011. *Crisis of Gender and the Nation in Korean Literature and Cinema: Modernity Arrives Again*. Lanham, MD: Lexington Books.

Kim, Iryop. 2014. *Reflections of a Zen Buddhist Nun*. Translated by Jin Y. Park. Honolulu: University of Hawai'i Press.

Kim, Sonja. 2008. "'Limiting Birth': Birth Control in Colonial Korea." *East Asian Science, Technology, and Society: An International Journal* 2, no. 3: 335–359.

Kim, Yung-Hee. 1997. "From Subservience to Autonomy: Kim Wŏnju's 'Awakening.'" *Korean Studies* 21: 1–21.

———. 2002. "Creating New Paradigms of Womanhood in Modern Korean Literature: Na Hye-sŏk's 'Kyŏnghŭi.'" *Korean Studies* 26: 1–60.

———, trans. 2010. *Questioning Minds: Short Stories by Modern Korean Women Writers*. Honolulu: University of Hawai'i Press.

———. 2013. "In Quest of Modern Womanhood: *Sinyŏja*, a Feminist Journal in Colonial Korea." *Korean Studies* 37: 44–78.

Kwon, Insook. 1998. "'The New Women's Movement' in 1920s Korea: Rethinking the Relationship Between Imperialism and Women." *Gender and History* 10, no. 3: 381–405.

Park, Sang Mi. 2006. "The Making of a Cultural Icon for the Japanese Empire: Choe Seung-hui's US Dance Tours and 'New Asian Culture' in the 1930s and 1940s." *Positions: East Asia Cultures Critique* 14, no. 3: 597–632.

Suh, Jiyoung. 2013. "The 'New Woman' and the Topography of Modernity in Colonial Korea." *Korean Studies* 37: 11–43.

Wells, Kenneth. 1999. "The Price of Legitimacy: Women and the Kŭnuhoe Movement, 1927 – 1931." In *Colonial Modernity in Korea,* edited by Gi-Wook Shin and Michael Robinson. Cambridge, MA: Harvard University Press.

Yoo, Theodore Jun. 2008. *The Politics of Gender in Colonial Korea: Education, Labor, and Health, 1910–1945*. Berkeley: University of California Press.

CHINA

Barlow, Tani. 2008. "Buying In: Advertising and the Sexy Modern Girl Icon in Shanghai in the 1920s and 1930s." In *The Modern Girl Around the World: Consumption, Modernity, and Globalization*, edited by Alys Eve Weinbaum et al. Durham, NC: Duke University Press.

Carroll, Peter. 2003. "Refashioning Suzhou: Dress, Commodification, and Modernity." *Positions: East Asia Cultures Critique* 11, no. 2: 443–478.

Chang, Michael. 1999. "The Good, the Bad, and the Beautiful: Movie Actresses and Public Discourse in Shanghai, 1920s–1930s." In *Cinema and Urban Culture in Shanghai, 1922–1943*, edited by Yingjin Zhang. Stanford, CA: Stanford University Press.

Ding Ling. 1989. *I Myself Am A Woman: Selected Writings of Ding Ling*. Edited by Tani E. Barlow with Gary J. Bjorge. Boston: Beacon Press.

Dong, Madeleine Y. 2008. "Who is Afraid of the Chinese Modern Girl?" In *The Modern Girl Around the World: Consumption, Modernity, and Globalization*, edited by Alys Eve Weinbaum, et al. Durham, NC: Duke University Press.

Dooling, Amy D. and Kristina M. Torgeson, eds. 1998. *Writing Women in Modern China: An Anthology of Women's Literature from the Early Twentieth Century*. New York: Columbia University Press.

Field, Andrew D. 1999. "Selling Souls in Sin City: Shanghai Singing and Dancing Hostesses in Print, Film, and Politics, 1920–1949." In *Cinema and Urban Culture in Shanghai, 1922–1943*, edited by Yingjin Zhang. Stanford: Stanford University Press.

Finnane, Antonia. 1996. "What Should Chinese Women Wear? A National Problem." *Modern China* 22, no. 2: 99–131.

———. 2008. *Changing Clothes in China: Fashion, History, Nation.* New York: Columbia University Press.

Glosser, Susan. 2003. *Chinese Visions of Family and State, 1915–1953.* Berkeley: University of California Press.

Goodman, Bryna. 2005. "The New Woman Commits Suicide: The Press, Cultural Memory and the New Republic." *Journal of Asian Studies* 64, no. 1: 67–101.

Hershatter, Gail. 1997. *Dangerous Pleasures: Prostitution and Modernity in Twentieth-Century Shanghai.* Berkeley: University of California Press.

Lan, Hua R., and Vanessa L. Fong. 2015. *Women in Republican China: A Sourcebook.* London: Routledge.

7

Gender, Labor Markets, and the Economy in the Interwar Era

GLOBAL CONTEXT

World War I benefited the American economy, as it had the Japanese, because both nations were allied with the victors but were far from the battles that had ravaged much of Europe. While many American soldiers gave their lives in that war, U.S. soil was not touched, and the engines of American industry had been accelerated to supply the Allied forces. After the war, new consumer products entered the market, and many American workers, both men and women, who had enjoyed high levels of employment during the war, were able to buy those products. Not all families benefited equally, however, as new forms of racism separated African American and white workers. The first stage of the Great Migration of African Americans from the rural South to the industrial North, in response to the demand for workers during World War I, offered new opportunities to African Americans, but it also lit the fires of racist resistance against them in northern cities. As we will see in this chapter, not all working-class and middle-class employees were treated equally in any part of the world; gender, class, and ethnicity must be taken into consideration in analyzing labor and the economy in all countries.

In a number of industrial countries, the end of World War I also meant the return of soldiers and sailors. During the war, women had taken many of the jobs men left behind when they went to war, and in some cases, particularly in England, women were rewarded for their exceptional wartime contributions with expanded civil rights. But many working-class women in England were pushed out of work to make way for the returning servicemen. Upon losing their better-paid factory jobs, women were next hit with inequality in unemployment benefits. These benefits were denied to women if they did not agree to accept menial jobs such as domestic service, thereby reinforcing the gendered division of labor. If no such "women's" jobs were available, women did receive unemployment benefits, but the British government paid women who managed to qualify for benefits much less than they paid men.

Middle-class women in England encountered problems different from those faced by their working-class sisters. On one hand, the Sex Disqualification Act of 1919 had opened the doors for British women to attend universities and develop careers as teachers, nurses, and other professionals. Civil service jobs were also opened to women, although most were in the lowest clerical grades. In the early 1930s, about one-third of women over fifteen worked outside the home, and about one-third of these were in domestic service. But 90 percent of married women did not work outside the home. This was not due entirely to choice: positions in teaching, the civil service, and various new professions usually had a "marriage bar" that required women to resign upon marriage. Thus, while working-class women were most adversely affected by sexism in the British workplace, middle-class women were also treated unequally. Similar kinds of gender and racial discriminations in the workplace continued in other countries as well, even before the Great Depression, which began in 1929, exacerbated discriminatory practices.

Overall, World War I affected the industrialized countries in vastly different ways. In addition to the devastation of Europe's industrial economies, the financial world underwent an enormous shift. The global center of finance moved from London to New York. European countries had large wartime debts to repay, and to do so, they needed the reparations from Germany stipulated in the Versailles Treaty of 1919. But the German economy was in even worse shape than the victorious Allies' economies. The German economy was undermined by hyperinflation in 1922–1923, when the currency went from an exchange rate of about 320 German marks to the U.S. dollar to more than 4.2 trillion marks to the dollar. Germany defaulted on its debts in 1923 and was unable to pay Britain and France, which in turn could not repay their own debts. In 1924, the United States stepped in with a plan to buy German bonds to stabilize the economy, which allowed Germany to make its payments to England and France. The whole system was dependent on the U.S. economy, and when Wall Street, the financial heart of the American economy, crashed in 1929, the world was plunged into the Great Depression.

A number of factors led to the collapse of Wall Street. American consumers' purchasing power, which had been strong right after World War I, declined throughout the 1920s as workers' wages failed to keep pace with the growth of wealth among the super-rich. Products continued to be produced, but consumers could not afford them. Weak consumer demand and a vastly overinflated stock market were two of several factors that led to the crash. By 1932, the stock market had fallen to 10 percent of its pre-crash value. Banks collapsed around the world.

In the United States and Canada, extraordinarily serious drought coincided with the financial crash, devastating the agricultural sector of the economies of North America and forcing hundreds of thousands of farmers onto the road as migrant workers. World trade collapsed, too, and the response in many countries was to impose high taxes on imports, which made it even harder for world trade to recover. Under these protectionist policies, international trade fell to one-third of its pre-1929 level by 1934. East Asian economies, which had been heavily dependent on exports of textiles—especially silk, which was largely produced by women workers—lost their global markets.

Extremist governments came to power. In Germany, Adolf Hitler (1889–1945) and his Nazi Party came to power in 1933. In Italy, Benito Mussolini (1883–1945), who had been in power since the 1920s, claimed state control of most of the Italian economy in 1935. In the Soviet Union, Joseph Stalin (1878–1953) collectivized agriculture, leading to the death by starvation or execution of perhaps thirteen million people. And in Japan, the government moved radically to the right after the Manchurian Incident (1931) and a series of assassinations, oppressing people both at home and in the colonies.

Just as countries turned to unilateralist protectionism in a misguided attempt to restore their economies, they also turned to unilateralist foreign policies. The League of Nations, a product of the post–World War I optimism about ending war through multilateral international cooperation, was shown to be no match for the forces of unilateral foreign policy and militarism. When Japan annexed Manchuria in 1932, Italy invaded Ethiopia in 1935, and Germany and Italy supported fascist rebels against the Spanish government in 1936, the League was powerless to respond. As we will see in Chapter 8, these actions led to World War II.

Below the government level, societies saw other economic changes in the interwar period. While women were often fired or pressured to leave the workforce when men returned from World War I, it is also noteworthy that many women had experienced new opportunities during that war. In industrialized Europe, North America, and Australia, as well as in Japan, Korea, and China in the 1920s, women workers claimed a voice they had not so fully expressed earlier. Women did not accept inferior conditions without a protest. Many took part in militant strikes. Sometimes discriminatory treatment came from fellow workers. For example, labor unions in England, led by men, had called for greater wage equality during the war to entice women into unions so that they would not undermine male wages by accepting the lower wages management routinely offered women. But after the war, male union leaders, still worried about women being cheap labor, dropped the demand for equal pay and instead tried to keep women out of "men's" jobs.

In the United States, the Depression's massive unemployment led the government to pass the Economy Act of 1932, section 213 of which prohibited married couples from both working in the federal civil service—and that usually meant the wife was the one to lose her job. So ingrained was the notion that women were stealing jobs from unemployed men that noted journalist and progressive social commentator Norman Cousins (1915–1990) attacked the widespread idea, which he paraphrased sarcastically, that firing women would end the Depression.

> *There are approximately 10,000,000 people out of work in the United States today. . . . There are also 10,000,000 or more women, married and single, who are jobholders. Simply fire the women, who shouldn't be working anyway, and hire the men. Presto! No unemployment. No relief rolls. No depression. (Cousins 1939, 14)*

Cousins marshaled strong evidence showing the fallacy of this argument, but that does not mean that the idea was not widely held in the United States and in other countries. Gender continued to play an important role in deciding who should work and in what types of jobs, especially against the backdrop of global unemployment, political extremism, the agricultural disasters that led to poverty in North America and starvation in East Asia, and the reemergence of war.

JAPAN

The overwhelming majority of industrial workers in Japan in the early years of industrialization were women (see Chapter 4 for descriptions of labor conditions in Japan's early textile and mining industries). Textile production employed 80 percent of industrial workers until World War I, but wartime economic development drew hundreds of thousands of male factory laborers into new technology-intensive and heavy industries, as well as numerous well-educated men into middle-class professions. In the mid-1930s, mobilization for Japan's next war, which will be discussed in Chapter 8, intensified the trend toward the masculinization of the industrial workforce. By 1940, men made up 60 percent of Japan's factory workers. Middle-class occupations also expanded for women after World War I, for a number of reasons. For example, men left teaching positions for better-paying jobs, and families' consumption patterns led to new employment opportunities for women in modern fields such as teaching, nursing, and retail sales.

The labor force changed in additional ways during the interwar period. Protective legislation that limited women's and children's work hours and types of employment was passed in 1911 and fully implemented in 1929, although it was rescinded in the late 1930s for the duration of World War II. Advocates for workers, both domestic and international, gained a voice during the era of Taishō democracy. Policies on birth control and reproduction were debated in terms of both women's health and their ability to maintain employment. Finally, demographic changes modified the employment market as workers from Japan's empire joined Japan's workforce. Each of these issues will be discussed in this chapter.

Protection of Women Workers' Bodies

As early as the late nineteenth century, social reformers in Japan first proposed that women's unhealthy working conditions in factories and mines be improved and that women and children be barred from working in those sites during overnight shifts. As we saw in Chapter 4, pressure from reformers led to the passage of the Factory Law in 1911. The process of getting that law implemented after its passage, however, was long and difficult, as employers fought against any measures that might cut into their profits. Male reformers in Japan decried the selfishness of such employers, arguing that women's bodies and morality must be protected for the sake of their future motherhood. One noted male intellectual stated in 1911, "If we subject our fragile womenfolk to the extremes of harsh employment we cannot have healthy mothers" (Molony 1993, 125). A male journalist decried potential moral threats by male supervisors and coworkers to young women working the night shift, overlooking the fact that sexual harassment need not be limited to the night hours (Molony 1993, 125). These types of arguments in favor of the Factory Law focused on women and girls as future mothers; that is, they highlighted the workers' identity as women rather than as workers.

Male and female voices in interwar discourse about protective legislation and women's roles in the workforce tended to diverge more along gender lines than along class or ideological lines. Women workers' natural allies should have been men in the labor movement in Japan, but these men were ambivalent about whether they should support protective legislation. While they agreed with liberal social reformers that women's and girls' bodies needed protection to support their future motherhood, some found it harder to accept the proposed limitations on women's work hours. Since the nineteenth century, women in cotton mills worked twelve-hour shifts, while silk workers often worked up to eighteen hours a day. Prohibiting women and children under sixteen years of age from working the midnight shift might have little effect on silk workers, but it definitely would cut cotton workers' shifts from twelve hours to nine or ten, as existing twelve-hour shifts relied on workers alternating their use of shared dormitory bedding. However, such a reduction in women's hours meant that their workday would still be longer than the eight-hour workday for which organized male laborers were struggling. Thus, some men were reluctant to endorse a law that would help women but which might also challenge the benefits for which those men had struggled (Hunter 1989, 254–255). Had these men viewed women workers as *workers*, they could have drawn them into their movements as full-fledged members, but they did not. They saw them, rather, as auxiliary members. In the eyes of both reformers and male union members, women and girl workers were women first and workers second. Since their role was to carry out future motherhood for the sake of the nation, their bodies should be protected by limiting their access to an unhealthy workplace. These concerns about young working women as potential maternal bodies in service to the nation were increasingly shared by the state as well, although the government's view was ambivalent because it also wished to support Japanese businesses that demanded cheap labor.

The women involved in the Motherhood Protection Debate (see Chapter 5) framed motherhood differently. Each of the participants, even when arguing in opposition to the others, saw motherhood as existing in the here and now. That is, a mother was a woman with one or more children; she was not simply a body that might produce a child in the future. The Motherhood Protection Debate focused on who should support those children. To the debaters, mothers were real people, not symbols of a gender role.

One of the feminists involved in the Motherhood Protection Debate was socialist feminist Yamakawa Kikue. In 1925 she and other socialist women struggled unsuccessfully to persuade the leftist union Hyōgikai to accept their demand for a women's division, at the national level, that would support key reforms to help workers who were mothers, as opposed to future mothers, retain their jobs. These demands included leave with pay before and after childbirth—a benefit that women teachers had earned nationwide in 1922—as well as an eight-hour workday and equal pay for equal work. The eight-hour day and equal pay were intended to help mothers get home in a timely manner to take care of children and to have sufficient financial resources to improve that care. This formulation saw women workers as *workers* who also happened to be mothers and who needed help with the home in order to maintain their identity as workers. Unfortunately, the union's male leadership neither approved those demands nor created a women's division, although they did support women workers' strike demands for improved maternity leave during the late 1920s (Molony 1993, 129–131).

Women workers made other body-centered demands in the interwar period. The one most curious to Western observers was menstruation leave, euphemistically called "physiological leave" (*seiri kyūka*). Decades later, in the 1980s, when the Equal Employment Opportunity Law (see Chapter 11) was debated, this policy was framed as necessary to preserve working women's future maternal health. No one recalled that the demand for this provision, which became part of the post–World War II Labor Standards Law of 1947, had nothing to do with maternal health. Rather, it was based on working women's need to find a way to continue to work under difficult conditions related to their bodies.

The first time the issue of menstruation leave was raised was in 1928, when five hundred women bus conductors staged a strike for better working conditions against the Tokyo Municipal Bus Company (Molony 1993, 135). One of their key demands was menstruation leave. Bus conductors had to spend long hours on their feet in crowded, moving buses that had no toilet facilities. Metropolitan buses could not stop to find a toilet when a conductor might need one, which might be quite frequently because the more effective kinds of sanitary towels or pads available to later generations of women were not available at that time. But quitting their jobs because they could not take care of their monthly period was not an option for many women who needed work. So Tokyo's female bus conductors demanded several days off to accommodate this bodily function; their demand was not inspired by consideration of future childbearing.

Feminists joined the menstruation-leave chorus in the late 1930s. The April and May 1937 issues of the women's magazine *Fujin Kōron* contained articles entitled "Let's Have Menstruation Leave!" Feminists from across the political spectrum, including Yamakawa Kikue, Miyamoto Yuriko (see Chapter 6), and Kaneko Shigeri, a prominent women's suffrage advocate, voiced their support for menstruation leave in the May issue. A decade later, after Japan's near-complete destruction in World War II, the demand for menstruation leave was reintroduced by women factory workers. Cotton or rags that could be used for sanitary purposes were in short supply at that time. Most factories had no heat or clean toilets, and where toilets existed, many had broken or missing windows. Again, women who needed to keep their jobs (for war widows and orphans, working was not optional at that time) required provisions that addressed their gendered needs. The interwar and postwar feminists discussed menstruation leave, maternity leave, and other gendered forms of health care not primarily to bar women from working, in order to make them healthier future mothers, but to allow them to continue to work both before and after bearing children.

International pressure also played a role in debates about protecting women workers' bodies. As a signatory of the Versailles Treaty that ended World War I, Japan joined the International Labour Organization (ILO). The first meeting of the ILO took place in Washington, D.C., in 1919, with the goal of developing and implementing international labor standards. The ILO, an organization that continues to this day, was structured to bring together representatives of each member nation's employers, workers, and government officials. The selection processes for representatives of those constituencies as well as for the policies they would support were bound to be contentious. These conflicts were reflected in the debates about protections for women workers. As in Japan, global advocates for women were concerned about women's bodies and workplace exploitation. In the United States, for example, women workers had an eight-hour workday, while men's workday was not limited under federal law before 1937 (organized labor in many industries had won that right decades earlier, but it was not legally mandated until 1937). Most other industrialized countries had limited hours as well.

But Japanese women, despite the passage of the Factory Law in 1911, would not be protected by a required shortened workday until 1929. Employers' representatives at the first ILO meeting argued vigorously that Japan's factories did not need to implement the Factory Law yet because employers practiced benevolence toward their women workers. Moreover, they said, Japanese industry would not be competitive with the rest of the world if forced to abide by international standards. In addition, they asserted that the maternity leave policies being discussed by ILO member states were not appropriate for Japan. These employers viewed Japanese female factory workers, many of them girls rather than adult women, in terms of their gender—as temporary and expendable workers who would return home to their calling as wives and mothers—rather than as workers who needed gender-specific accommodations to retain their jobs.

Japanese feminists and women workers had a different approach. In the run-up to the first ILO meeting, Ichikawa Fusae, who was the general secretary of the Yūaikai labor union's women's division at that time (see Chapter 5), called a meeting to discuss the issues to be brought to Washington and the possible women's representative to that meeting. The Japanese government had no intention of appointing a woman as an official voting delegate, but the ILO required that at least one woman be a nonvoting member of the delegation, in order to address women workers. Tanaka Taka, American-educated and deeply sympathetic to women workers despite her privileged origin (she was the niece of one of Japan's leading entrepreneurs), presented herself to the women's division as a representative who would support the division's demands. The workers in the audience rejected her in spite of her sympathy for their cause because of her class background, but the Japanese government ignored the workers and appointed her (Yamanouchi 1975, 55). Ichikawa tried to get a teenage textile worker, Yamanouchi Mina—who also supported feminist causes—added to the delegation, but she declined under pressure from her union.

Despite the rocky start of Tanaka's role as a representative, she went on to speak eloquently on behalf of Japanese women workers at the ILO meeting on November 8, 1919. Charged with translating and reading the speech of an official government delegate who opposed the protections the ILO was working to advance globally, Tanaka boldly inserted her own unscheduled speech, decrying the terrible labor conditions and gender inequality in Japan and demanding extensive reforms. When that government delegate and a major textile business owner who represented Japanese employers realized what Tanaka was saying, they got into a public altercation with her. The employers' representative claimed she was incompetent because she was pregnant, and she was pulled from the delegation a few days later. Tanaka fought back against the smear that pregnancy made her incompetent, but in the end she was marginalized (Cobble 2015, 14). During the 1920s, the ILO eventually pressured Japan into accepting the protections. As we saw in Chapter 5, Ichikawa Fusae served on behalf of women workers as the representative of the ILO in the mid-1920s. By 1929, the Factory Law of 1911 was fully implemented.

Physical protection of women workers' bodies through the implementation of the Factory Law in 1929 had the ironic result of engendering more powerful images of women laborers. At least some women took advantage of the shortened workday to attend classes at the Workers' School for Women (Rōdō Jojuku), established one month after the prohibition of night work went into effect. Students read material on working women, feminism, and women in unions, and studied handicrafts—not to become the "good wives and wise mothers" that their companies attempted to train them to be, but rather to have marketable skills (Faison 2007, 81–87). Many of these women went on to lead one of the most militant strikes of the interwar period, the Tōyō Muslin Strike of 1930.

The Tōyō Muslin Strike was one of several hundred labor actions in which women workers played a major role in the last years of the 1920s. Some strikes were inspired by gendered demands, such as maternity leave or the right to leave their company dormitories during their off hours before they had worked off their prepaid wages. (Restriction in dormitories was ostensibly to protect women from rapacious men in the city, but was more likely the company managers' way of limiting workers' flight from undesirable working conditions.) The onset of the Great Depression in 1929 led to pay cuts and the closing of some factories, both of which were devastating to women who wished to continue working and to make decent wages to help support their families. Tōyō Muslin workers staged a successful strike in 1927 for more freedom to leave their dormitories. In February 1930 their strike in protest of layoffs was unsuccessful. Both of these were small compared to the famous two-month-long strike that began on September 20, 1930, over the issue of layoffs. Many of the male workers involved in this strike agreed to a negotiated settlement, but thousands of female workers did not (Faison 2007, 93–97).

As they had in the February strike, the company managers called in rightist thugs to put down the workers on September 27. But the two hundred strikebreakers were no match for the twenty-five hundred headband-wearing women. Two days later, the police came in to assist the strikebreakers, and a number of police officers were lifted up by the women and carried on their shoulders. These were no weak women in need of protection. Moreover, they were skilled at organizing, setting up committees for security, propaganda, communications, and the like. On October 24, the Tōyō Muslin women were joined by male unionists and sympathetic neighborhood residents in a march to the factory. Police and strikebreaking thugs met them in the street, and what historians have called the "street battle" (*shigaisen*) erupted (Faison 2007, 97–98). Ultimately, the strikers were defeated on November 19, winning none of their demands. Many workers were fired.

The workers were vanquished not only by the superior fighting force of the police and the thugs hired by the company but also by the company's mobilization of tropes of proper gender behavior. The company undertook a massive letter-writing campaign to the families of female workers, asking them to rescue their daughters and sisters from the evils of the city and from mingling with male strikers who could compromise their virtue. A number of families took their daughters home to the countryside, but many young women hid from their families and refused to abandon the strike. Striking male workers' wives received letters saying that their husbands, by striking, were not carrying out their manly duty to support their families. The company attempted to shame female workers into leaving the strike by writing to them that they were letting down their families, who needed their income, and that they were violating the paternalistic care of their supposedly generous companies. An October 9, 1930 letter explained: "The company is waiting for all of you to even one day sooner, go back to the way you were before the strike and return to the bosom of the company. Your original selves! For that, the company will greet you joyously with arms outstretched" (quoted in Faison 2007, 103).

Although both the trope of the dutiful daughter and its opposite, the scare-tactic image of the sexually compromised woman, were employed by management, another image of working women emerged from the Tōyō Muslin strike: the street-fighting woman. Calling themselves *fujin tōshi* (women warriors), they used a term associated with fighters for a just cause. This image stood in contrast to the narrative of failure often associated with women workers' activism and to the "housewife-mother ideal promoted by the company and to its opposite, the fallen-woman image against which the company promised to protect all workers under its charge" (Faison 2007, 100). These conflicting images of women would reemerge throughout the war and postwar years as well.

The Birth Control Movement

In the early part of the twentieth century, Japanese intellectuals had begun to discuss birth control as a means of controlling overpopulation and the resulting strain on national resources. In 1922, with the visit of American birth control advocate Margaret Sanger (1879–1966), reproductive control was taken up by feminists as a way of helping all women, but especially poor and working-class women. Sanger's conviction that poor women's ability to control their fertility would improve the lives of their families and affect society for the better was shared by Katō Ishimoto Shidzue (1897–2001), who met Sanger while living in New York. (See Box 7.1.) The aristocratic Ishimoto Shidzue (her name at that time, while married to Baron Ishimoto) came to be called the "Margaret Sanger of Japan" for her work to protect the bodies of working women. In 1921, when the Ishimotos returned to Japan from New York, the Japanese press claimed that she was preparing to introduce the "dangerous thoughts" of American-style birth control in Japan (Molony 1984, xviii). The press reacted with even more sensational reports when Sanger herself, hosted by Ishimoto, toured Japan in 1922 for ten days at the invitation of a prominent news magazine.

Although the Japanese consulate in San Francisco refused to grant Sanger a visa, she was able to obtain one from a Japanese diplomat, returning from his stint as a delegate at the Washington Naval Conference (see Chapter 5), who was also a passenger on Sanger's ship across the Pacific. The agitation about her visit and the fact that the police were not going to permit her to speak as an advocate for birth control were covered breathlessly in the press, bringing Sanger's message about birth control to a far wider audience than could have been achieved through public speaking alone. Shortly after Sanger's visit, the Ishimotos were joined by medical doctors, university professors, the founder of the Yūaikai labor union, and socialist-feminist Yamakawa Kikue in a combined effort to study birth control, establish a small clinic, and publish informational pamphlets (Ishimoto 1984, 228–236).

Together with other ladies of her elite circle, Ishimoto Shidzue next created a society to study labor and social problems. In 1923, a young leader in the Japanese miners' union invited her to speak to miners and their wives at Japan's largest copper mine. (That leader was Katō Kanjū, whom Ishimoto would marry two decades later.) Ishimoto and an American missionary woman traveled to the copper mine and spoke to two thousand workers, trying to avoid language that would cause the police, who were monitoring their talks for violations of morality, to shut them down. But a foreign missionary and an aristocrat giving speeches about sexual topics made for such an unusual sight that they managed to get through the four-hour session. This began Ishimoto's active work on behalf of birth control for working women. In 1932, just as Japan was entering a militarist period, she formed the Birth Control League of Japan, and in 1936, after a three-month internship at Sanger's New York clinic, she opened a clinic of her own in Tokyo. In December 1937 she was arrested. Her international friends at the *New York Times*, the *Christian Science Monitor*, and the *New York Herald-Tribune* mounted a campaign to have her released from her miserable, unheated cell. Their pleas were unsuccessful, but Ishimoto was eventually released for

BOX 7.1

Men, Women, and Children in the Coal Mines

In *Facing Two Ways*, initially published in 1935 in the United States for an English-reading audience, Ishimoto Shidzue wrote in detail about her observations of men and women working in the mines. Here we see how she first connected her analysis of the plight of workers to the question of birth control.

> *The miners I knew were usually desperate. . . . Men beat women and children. . . . Many men literally drank nearly all their pay before they brought home any pennies to their families. But it would be rash to blame them! Who would dare preach family obligations to men who got only $20 for a month's work? . . . [A]nd $12 was the maximum pay for women for their monthly labor. Now this pay has been raised a little. . . . The women usually went down with their husbands, sometimes taking their babies on their backs. . . . As soon as the children were old enough, both boys and girls went to work, competing for wages with adults. But there was no other way for the population to keep alive unless it could manage to control the overflooded market of cheap labor by exercising birth control. (Ishimoto 1984, 162–163)*

the reason—unfathomable under the circumstances—that, as an aristocrat, she was expected to pay New Year's respects to the emperor (Molony 1984, xix–xx). Her clinic was closed down in January 1938, and the birth control movement was moribund until the end of World War II.

Diversity Among Women in the Labor Force in Japan

Women's roles in the interwar Japanese economy varied according to class and ethnicity. As we have seen, protective legislation was directed primarily at working-class women in factories and mines, although it had no impact on two other large categories of employed women—household maids who labored behind closed doors, often as the single employee of a household, and prostitutes and other entertainment workers, who could not be prevented from working a midnight shift. Protective legislation could be used to limit the work hours of middle-class working women, but their kinds of employment (office work, teaching school, nursing, retail work) were less likely to require protection from night work.

Almost half of all women in the workforce were farmers who worked with other members of their families. Working in the family economy was a 24/7 job, and no one would have considered applying protective laws to women who worked with their families. Their labor was not defined as differentiated from family responsibilities, and therefore it was usually not counted as labor force participation. This undercounting of women who contributed to family income as wives and daughters, especially in the agricultural sector, was common in all countries and was not limited to Japan. But these women did work, making significant economic contributions throughout history (see Chapters 1 through 4), and were as much a part of the nation's labor force as their husbands, fathers, and brothers on the farm.

The horrific impact of the Great Depression on farm families in the early 1930s, especially in the less fertile northeastern section of Japan, led many to make desperate attempts to survive by selling their underage daughters into sex work. Economically weakened small landlords and newly unemployed factory workers returned to their farms to try to feed their own families, thereby displacing tenant farming families living on the land. At the same time, the bottom fell out of sericulture—which had long kept many marginal farmers afloat—when Western markets for luxury silk items such as stockings collapsed in the face of Depression-era unemployment and poverty. The selling of daughters into sex work was covered extensively by the press as an unavoidable tragedy. The *Tokyo Asahi News* published a series of articles in June 1932 that highlighted several rural problems, including the sale of daughters, high rates of tenancy, and suicide. The *Tokyo Nichi Nichi News* held a forum attended by academics, activists, and politicians on June 11, 1932, to come up with solutions to these problems, followed by the publication of a study called "What Should Be Done to Rescue the Villages?" (Smith 2001, 112–113).

The influx of women into teaching and nursing as the economy expanded during World War I, the development of new opportunities in both government and private-sector offices in the increasingly global economy of the 1920s, and the creation of new jobs for middle-class women as retail sales clerks, telephone operators, and newspaper reporters as technology advanced and the consumer market expanded raised concerns among social conservatives about non-working-class women in the workforce. By the mid-1920s there were approximately sixty thousand nurses and thirty thousand women government workers. Surveys indicated that middle-class women went to work because of "economic necessity, awakened women's consciousness, and job availability" (Nagy 1991, 204).

Some desperately poor farmers in Japan's northeast were forced to sell their daughters into prostitution during the Great Depression.
KAGEYAMA KŌYŌ, ONE POOR FAMILY, THE SEVERE BAD HARVEST IN TŌHOKU, 1934, MEAD ART MUSEUM/BRIDGEMAN IMAGES

While no one had previously worried about the children of employed women in working-class families, commentators now began to express concern about the possibility of juvenile delinquency and other social problems arising from mothers in the workforce. Shouldn't middle-class women, especially those with higher levels of education, be good wives and wise mothers? Those higher levels of education may have inspired some women to cultivate themselves as employees who could make a contribution to society and the nation, but many were most concerned about helping their families maintain middle-class status, something that often required the incomes of both parents in the family. The government, responding to surveys that indicated the economic importance to the family of the wife's employment, decided to redouble their efforts to improve married men's incomes and opportunities. Special efforts were made by Tokyo public job exchanges to find better opportunities for white-collar men. And the government worked to encourage wives to stay at home by improving the status and importance of housewives. These actions took the form of minor modifications of the civil code that had placed women under the legal jurisdiction of the male family head (see Chapter 4), as well as the encouragement of efforts to optimize the efficiency of the home to save the housewife time, money, and labor though the Seikatsu Kaizen Undō (Daily Life Reform Movement), a movement in both urban and rural areas. (For more on this movement, see Nagy 1991, 214; Sato 2003, 102; Tipton 2000; and Sand 2005.)

Gendered employment patterns were greatly affected by ethnicity as well. Japan's workforce included migrants from the far reaches of the empire. Okinawa became part of Japan in 1879, so technically it was not a colony, but many of the young workers who migrated to the main islands of Japan in the interwar period still spoke Okinawan in addition to the Japanese they learned in school. (However, they could be punished by management if they were caught speaking Okinawan.) The Okinawan mill workers also differed from the main-island Japanese in that they preferred different foods and they were perceived as more docile and cooperative. Because they had been recruited from great distances, unlike most of the main-island Japanese workers, they could not easily run home, so they had few alternatives to staying on the job. For these reasons, employers loved them—in some factories they made up more than a quarter of the workforce (Molony 1991, 227–230; Faison 2007, 111–115). But their cultural differences often made them the object of ridicule by other factory workers.

Korean immigration to work in the metropole and elsewhere in the Japanese empire took different forms (Kim 2014). Almost three hundred thousand Koreans had come to Japan by 1930, with about one-third of that population residing in Osaka. Most came in search of work and expected to return to Korea one day, although, like immigrants elsewhere in the world, many remained in the empire outside of Korea for decades. A large number of interwar Korean migrant women worked in the textile mills, where they were supervised in a very different manner than Okinawan and main-island Japanese workers. Korean female employees, most of whom did not speak much Japanese (unlike the Okinawans, they were not punished for speaking their own language in the textile mills), reported to Korean male employees—most of whom did have some knowledge of Japanese—or to representatives of the Sōaikai (Mutual Care Society), a Korean-led pro-Japan organization founded in 1921 that mediated between Koreans and the Japanese authorities. In both cases, women workers were under the control of men, rather than under female supervisors (who were usually workers with seniority, as was the case among Japanese textile workers).

The Sōaikai saw their main purpose as maintaining the discipline of the Korean community in Japan. They illegally recruited Koreans to work in Japan and used strong-arm tactics to suppress demonstrations by Korean workers, but because they also taught classes on how to assimilate to Japanese society and helped newcomers find housing, most Korean workers in Japan had an ambivalent attitude toward the Sōaikai. The organization skimmed off a percentage of the workers' pay (already lower than the pay Japanese workers received) and forced mediation of labor disputes, in addition to serving as supervisors. Despite the Sōaikai's stated goal of assimilating Koreans to the Japanese empire, they actually helped maintain a segregated and unequal workplace where the Korean women workers' ethnicity mattered more than their gender (Faison 2007, 121–135).

Gender played a very different role in the coal mining industry. Japanese married couples worked side by side in the coal mining industry until women were prohibited from working underground when the Factory Law went into effect. Young unmarried Japanese women tended to work aboveground in cleaner tasks but were paid less than the women working the more dangerous jobs underground (see Chapter 4). However, virtually no Korean women worked underground with their husbands. Family responsibilities and the immodest conditions of work attire (miners worked almost naked) made it more difficult for Korean women to work underground. Some worked aboveground, but the overall percentage of Korean women in the coal industry in Japan was far lower than the percentage of Japanese women. In addition, there was little labor solidarity among the Japanese and Korean male workers, and when the latter went on strike, the former did not join them (Smith 2005). Thus, the gender and ethnic conditions of employment differed between industries and according to social customs within the empire, and diversity must be taken into consideration when discussing gender and the economy in interwar Japan.

KOREA

The 1920s and 1930s saw the emergence of a class of women holding salaried employment in factories and service sectors. Considering that Korea had been a largely agrarian society and that women rarely left their communities prior to the 1910s, the scope of women's participation in the labor market during the interwar period was unprecedented. This new phenomenon of women as wage-earning laborers was an integral part of the broader economic transformation from an agrarian economy into an early form of capitalist economy under Japanese colonial rule. Korea's industrialization and urbanization as well as Japan's imperial ambitions in Northeast Asia brought about a major change in labor structures and the gendered division of labor. In these rapidly changing economic conditions a large number of girls and women moved from farms in the rural countryside to urban areas to work in factories or in the service sector.

A key factor in bringing about these structural changes in the colonial economy was the Land Survey, which was conducted by the colonial government between 1910 and 1918. The survey was designed to rationalize and codify the ownership and productivity of various lands in Korea, although its ultimate aim was to create a more effective system for the collection of taxes. The survey required all landowners to register and present the proper documents to prove their rights to the land. The survey allowed the owners of large tracts of land to strengthen the claims on their holdings, but because it did not adopt the rights that had traditionally been conferred on tenant farmers, it had a devastating impact on them. A significant proportion of smaller landowners also lost land claims due to their failure to register. The bankruptcy and impoverishment of subsistence farmers and tenant farmers contributed to the erosion of the rural community. When these small-lot farmers could no longer support their families, the farmers or their family members would drift away from home to search for work, either in large urban areas in Korea or in neighboring regions, such as Manchuria. The daughters of those impoverished farming families, in particular, began to migrate to urban areas looking for jobs so that they could contribute their wages, no matter how meager, to help the family. These young women often sought out jobs as factory workers, housemaids, or sales clerks. If no such positions were available, they often ended up in sectors of the economy that were even more exploitative, like prostitution.

Colonial Korea also underwent major changes in terms of its labor and industrial structures. Even before colonization in 1910 there were a significant number of Japanese entrepreneurs, but once the Japanese colonial government enacted the new Company Law and removed most tariffs in 1920, Japanese investment in the Korean economy swelled, which led to the building of major industrial centers, primarily on the eastern and northwestern coasts. In 1911 the number of factories in Korea was a mere 250, but by 1927 that number had grown to nearly 44,000. The proliferation of industry led to rapid growth in nonagricultural employment. As a result, an exodus of peasants from rural areas to industrial and urban sites transformed the nature of labor and the economy.

It is important to note that colonial Korea was still a largely agrarian society. According to the colonial government census of 1930, about 80 percent of the population worked in agriculture and only 2.1 percent in mining and factory work. The vast majority of women working for wages were employed in the agricultural and fishery sectors (Park 1999, 133; Kim 2004, 347). However, the rise of industrial capitalism within the broader scheme of Japan's imperial expansion into Northeast Asia significantly contributed to the unprecedented level of women's participation both in the manufacturing and service sectors and in consumer culture.

Travails of Factory Workers

In 1910 the total number of factory workers—both men and women—was only 8,203. However, by 1933 the number of women workers alone had grown to more than 30,000, which constituted 33.5 percent of the industrial workforce (Kim 2009, 27). Women workers were primarily employed in the textile and food processing industries. As of 1921, about 28 percent of women factory workers were engaged in textile-related work and 53.7 percent in food processing. The rate of female workers in textiles had jumped to 51.6 percent by 1930 and continued at that high level, while in the same period the number of women working in food processing followed the opposite trajectory, falling to 22.2 percent. Significantly, the number of women in the chemical industry rapidly increased during this period, from 1.2 percent in 1921 to 21.3 percent in 1930. With Japan's increasing militarization after the Manchurian Incident in 1931 and during the Pacific War, "a large number of women worked in traditionally male-dominant industries, such as mining, machinery, shipbuilding and construction" (Kim 2009, 104). By comparison, in Japan most women either worked on farms, as domestic servants, as part of a family team in a small business, or in the sex trade, but among the 1,758,000 women who were in manufacturing and mining in 1919, 86 percent were in spinning, reeling, and weaving, 6.5 percent were in mining, 3 percent were in chemical manufacturing, 1 percent were in food processing, and 2.5 percent were in miscellaneous manufacturing (the total does not reach 100 percent). In 1929, after the application of protections in the mining industry, of 1,348,400 women in mining and manufacturing, 81 percent were in textiles, 4 percent were in mining, 3 percent were in chemical manufacturing, 1.5 percent were in food processing, and 4.5 percent were in miscellaneous manufacturing (Nishinarita 1994, 4–5).

The print media of the time presented gripping images of young factory girls from their early teens to early twenties working in textile, tobacco, or rubber factories for more than twelve hours a day in order to help their impoverished families in the countryside. Their pale complexions and malnourished or injured bodies testified to the inhumane and miserable working conditions these young women were subject to. A diary kept by a female worker in a silk mill in 1930 offers a glimpse of the working environment inside the factory:

> *August 7th, Thursday, sunny: It is so hot today. People are saying that the temperature inside the factory is 105 degrees. . . . I couldn't*

really sleep last night so now I feel tired and sleepy. The manager noticed me drooping and yelled at me several times. He said he will pour hot water on anyone who dozes off. I was so scared. Today Suni was given another demerit. She worked so hard, but still they made her pay a penalty. The manager went crazy. He beat Suni, and she came back to her seat limp and disheveled. Pongnyŏ also earned a penalty point. The manager took her in front of everyone and made her stay on her feet holding a water bucket. She had been sick for a couple of days, and she ultimately fainted. The manager beat her, shouting "Get up!" The only thing we get for our 13 hours of hard labor a day is a severe beating. Who said people who work hard will receive blessings and become rich? . . .

August 9th, Saturday, sunny: Although we put our strength and skill to work for them, they treat us no better than prisoners, cursing at us constantly. I'm saying, they could speak to us civilly, for God's sake. Whenever there is even a short break, they never fail to gather us together and give us "a big lecture." They say, "This year's harvest is bad, so you and your family could have starved. But how lucky you are that we feed you? (Are you kidding? You give us only cheap barley and bowls of rotten miso soup with maggots!) It's a privilege to work, so work harder to repay." They deceive us with this kind of sweet talk. Do they mean for us to give up our lives and work harder than we already do? They don't have the ability to comprehend that human capacity has limits. They don't understand that the work will destroy our health. (U 1930, 72–73)

The harsh reality of labor conditions and substandard sustenance wages led to frequent strikes. The number of labor disputes almost doubled in the 1920s and peaked between 1929 and 1932, as the world tumbled into the Great Depression. With rapid industrialization in the northern part of Korea and the growth of the communist movement, workers' strikes became more militant than they had been in the past.

While Japan itself underwent labor reforms that put in place regulations on working hours, overtime pay, and child labor, no such policies were implemented in Korea. Under Japanese colonial rule, Korean workers were not guaranteed a minimum wage nor any legal provisions that protected their rights. Factory owners were essentially free to exploit cheap labor—particularly female workers—to maximize their profits. Korean female workers were at the

BOX 7.2

A Rooftop Strike for the Fellow Workers

One of the most legendary labor strikes broke out in P'yŏngyang in May 1931. Kang Churyong, a woman who worked at the P'yŏngwŏn Rubber Factory, climbed up to the roof of the famous pavilion named Ŭlmiltae to protest the factory owner's plan to cut wages. Prior to this demonstration Kang had been one of forty-nine workers who occupied the factory to conduct a hunger strike; however, they were removed from the factory by the police shortly after they began their protest. At that moment, Kang decided to sacrifice herself so that the workers' pleas for fairness would be heard by the public. The choice of Ŭlmiltae was strategic. Kang knew that many people would pass the structure in the morning, providing maximal visibility and impact for her protest. From the roof of Ŭlmiltae, she declared:

> *The reduction of wages for our group of forty-nine workers is not that important. What is important is that it will ultimately affect 2,300 other workers in the rubber factory in the P'yŏngyang area. Therefore we will accept death before we accept this wage reduction. I am more than happy to die in order to prevent my fellow workers from further suffering. The most valuable thing I have learned is that it is an honorable thing to die for the masses. I came up here prepared to die. I will not come down until the owner of the factory comes right here and tells me to my face that he will give up his plan to cut wages. If he fails to do so, it will be my great honor to die as a representative of the working populace. (Muho Hyang'in 1931, 40)*

The police forced Kang to descend from the roof, and she was put in jail, where she continued her hunger strike. Her labor activism and imprisonment took an enormous toll on her health, and probably led to her death shortly after in August of 1932.

Kang Churyong rooftop strike.
TONGGWANG 23 (1931)

bottom of the pay scale, earning approximately one-quarter of the wage earned by Japanese male workers (Barraclough 2012, 17–18). Even within the category of Korean working women, factory workers were the lowest-paid, earning only about one-third of what was earned by women professionals in nursing, education, or journalism. Thus with regard to wages it can be seen that "women workers were triply discriminated by their gender, class and nationality" (Kim 2009, 3).

In addition to the meager wages that they provided, factories often lacked adequate facilities to accommodate all their female employees, and they generally had no safety measures in place. These young women had to work inhumanely long hours, sometimes up to fifteen hours a day, on a crowded factory floor without proper ventilation. Working in these conditions commonly resulted in exhaustion, injury, and disease. The lack of workplace safety regulations allowed accidents that left workers disfigured and mutilated. Furthermore, female workers were subjected to physical assault and sexual harassment by male managers and foremen, both Japanese and Korean. The proletarian literature of the mid-1920s vividly captures the degradation and misery that women factory workers suffered from the continuing patriarchy and class violence. Kang Kyŏngae's (1906–1944) novel *In'gan munje* (The human predicament, published in English as *From Wonso Pond*) depicts the heart-wrenching travails that factory workers experienced in colonial Korea (Perry 2013, Park 2013). At the same time, it is also important to recognize the agency that female factory workers demonstrated in real life. They were not passive. They organized and participated in numerous protests to demand their basic rights and better working conditions.

In the 1930s the colonial government shifted its labor policy from noninterference to active intervention, which effectively curtailed the number of labor disputes. By the time the second Sino-Japanese War broke out in 1937, labor movements went underground as Japan deployed wartime emergency rule and the compulsory assimilation policies of *naisen ittai* (Japan and Korea as a single body), practices that will be discussed in more detail in Chapter 8.

Urbanity, Modernity and Consumer Culture

The population of the capital, Seoul (called Kyŏngsŏng in Korean, Keijō in Japanese) more than tripled in less than twenty years, going from 343,000 in 1925 to 1,114,000 in 1942. This remarkable growth is a clear indicator of the rapid urbanization Korea was undergoing (Park 1999, 137). The pace of urbanization was driven by the rapid expansion of the manufacturing and service industries, along with the further development of transportation and communication. The urban and commercial improvements created a wide range of jobs that attracted a large number of young girls and women, who came from rural areas to the cities in search of gainful employment and a modern life. They most often found jobs in retailing, clerical work, domestic service, or entertainment.

An interesting survey of employers presented in the newspaper *Tonga ilbo* on November 10, 1933, reveals a clear preference for hiring young women workers, for a variety of reasons. According to the survey, female clerks at retail shops were valued for having an eye for detail in business transactions and maintaining a docile and cheerful attitude toward customers. As bookkeepers and accountants, women were seen as more honest and less likely to embezzle than men. Young women were preferred to men as bus conductors because they were more amiable and better able to interact with passengers than men. As office workers, female workers were seen as more manageable and not ambitious for promotion.

Despite the advantages women had in getting hired in the service sector, job opportunities for women remained very small and highly competitive. According to statistics in 1930, about 10 percent of working women were engaged in the service sector (retail, transportation, entertainment, or domestic work). Positions as telephone operators, bus conductors, or department store clerks were the most coveted. Given the level of competition for jobs, employers began to set higher requirements on the educational credentials of applicants. For instance, when the first group of female telephone operators was hired in 1920, applicants were required to have completed common school (elementary school) and have basic Japanese-language proficiency, but by 1936 applicants for the same job were required to have a diploma from a higher common school or a commercial (vocational) school (Yun 2009).

The first female bus conductors received a great deal of attention. It was said that people would buy a ticket to ride the bus just for the novelty of seeing a female conductor at work. There was also a great deal of attention paid to them in the media, especially to how they dressed. An article in *Tonga ilbo* on April 25, 1928, includes a photo of a bus conductor, along with a description of her hat, her cobalt uniform cinched at the waist by a belt, her red necktie, and her white socks, which revealed the contours of her calves.

The most coveted and glamorous job among young women was to work as a salesclerk in a department store. To these young women, and the general public as well, the department store symbolized modernity, urban chic, and sophisticated taste. Visiting department stores became a favorite pastime, especially for folks from the countryside. Students would even take field trips to department stores. Furthermore, young men flocked into department stores to look for future spouses among *dep'atŭ gŏl* (department store girls), also called *uriko* (salesgirls) in Japanese. In other words, department stores were not only modern retail outlets but hot "marriage markets" where young men could check out *dep'atŭ gŏl* as potential partners for dating and marriage. By 1934, there were five department stores in Seoul and three in P'yŏngyang. The criteria to be hired as a *dep'atŭ gŏl* were quite high. Most were graduates of higher common schools, including the most prominent girls' schools, such as Ewha and Chŏngsin. In fact, the educational background of department store clerks was high enough that they were even labeled as "intellectuals." However, the most important qualification was appearance—it was assumed that pretty female clerks would attract more customers and that those customers would buy more.

The increase in the number of working women initially appeared highly beneficial to both employers and employees: employers had a bigger applicant pool, and the young women gained a measure of economic independence and a sense of modernity and sophistication. However, once a large number of women were in the labor market in urban areas, there was a growing anxiety about the potential threat these women workers posed for the family and society. The print media used a variety of terms for working women in different sectors of the urban service economy. With the single exception of housekeepers, who were called *kasa sayong'in*, all other terms used the English loanword *gŏl* (girl), as in *bŏsŭ gŏl* (female bus conductor), *elibet'ŏ gŏl* (elevator girl), *dep'atŭ gŏl* (department store girl), *gasŭ gŏl* (girl working at gas station), *cap'e gŏl* (café girl), or even *biladŭ gŏl* (billiard girl). This trend was influenced by metropolitan Japan, where stylish women, many of them employed, were called *modan gāru* (see Chapter 6). The borrowing of "girl" from English is significant in that it attached a modern flavor to these new jobs in urban areas. As wage earners, women became a significant population of consumers. While most female workers did not earn enough to indulge deeply in consumer culture, the print media of the time set up a discursive representation of working "girls" that suggested they frequently indulged their cravings for luxurious clothing and accessories or Western-style food.

Even more sensational discourse was devoted to women workers in the entertainment business. The entertainment business was thriving not only in traditional entertainment houses (*kisaeng chip*) but also in modern cafés, bars, and restaurants. *Yŏsŏng* (*Voice of Women*), a short-lived magazine founded in 1934 with the specific aim of addressing the lives of café girls, offers valuable insight into the inner workings of café culture. Unlike the typical portrayal of café girls and bar girls as passive victims of poverty and male violence, *Yŏsŏng* presented an alternative account of how these young women lived. Here a café girl called White Rose presents her viewpoint with a tone of mockery toward male customers, revealing the complexity of the experiences of women in the entertainment business.

> *We should all be impressed with women who have become typists, company workers, clerks, waitresses, and pilots, all bravely fighting against the men who used to rule over us. Let us go into the job front with strength and courage! Contemporary women are happier than the women of former times because they have freed themselves from men's oppression like birds that have escaped from their cages. With new physical and psychological freedom, they are achieving individual rights equal to those of men.*
>
> *Listen to me, women on the job front! Never be satisfied with your current state. Although we have earned some freedom, it is too early to declare true liberation from men's unreasonable and persistent oppression. Therefore, we need to strive further to bring full freedom for all women in all circumstances.*
>
> *Pay attention! The violence of men continues. They trample upon our freedoms and personal rights, and then they exchange congratulatory shouts as if they've achieved some great victory. They have figured out a way to deprive women of some of their newly acquired freedom to work by denying them of promotions and bonuses. For instance, if the male director of a play requires an actress to perform in a way that would defile her chastity and she refuses, he will cast her in a smaller role. This is a simple illustration of the general experience of many female professionals who, having won the initial battle to gain access to jobs, have to suffer through the capricious control wielded by men. In the end they may have no solution to the uncertainty other than leaving the job market completely. . . .*
>
> *I personally think that my current position meets all the necessary requirements. Perhaps the most gratifying aspect of it is that it is in a liberal, dynamic workplace that allows us women to treat men as playthings, in return for the mockery they subjected us to. Through this profession I am also able to witness the nonsense men*

> *do. Some of them see café girls as sexual objects and mistreat us as worthless people. Some of these bastards even use violence to get us to service them sexually. They must think we are the same as the prostitutes in the red light districts. It's not just out of my duty as a café girl that I feel obliged to inject some common sense and slivers of enlightenment into these fuddled minds.*
>
> *Wake up, women! Do not hesitate to march to the job front. Fight! My comrades on the job front, let us sacrifice ourselves and fight with all our might to overcome all the societal obstacles and advance into the professional territories that men have held for ages. This is the way that will lead us into the bright future. It is also a happy solution for those women tormenting themselves with vanity and fantasy. (Paekjangmi 1934, 8–11)*

By 1933, more than ten thousand women were engaged in a wide variety of entertainment venues to provide "ero-service" to male customers, and half of that group was made up of Korean women. As discussed in chapter 5, after Korea became a Japanese protectorate in 1905, there was a surge in the number of Japanese settlers in and visitors to Korea, and the Japanese authorities created regulations for licensed prostitution (*kongch'ang*) in pleasure districts. By 1916, pleasure districts were under the control of the police, and entertainment workers were subject to regulations designed to contain sexually transmitted diseases. Unlicensed prostitution also continued to thrive in a variety of entertainment sites, including cafés, bars, and restaurants. Young girls from impoverished homes were often lured into work as "café girls" or "bar girls." When the Great Depression hit the entertainment business in the early 1930s, many sex workers sought out or were sold into positions overseas.

Rural Women

Despite the rapid pace of industrialization and urbanization, the vast majority of the Korean populace—nearly 80 percent—still resided in the rural areas. This rural population was most devastated by the Great Depression, as the price of rice fell rapidly from its mid-1920s high. As a result, indebtedness and starvation became widespread. In addition, worsening tenant-landlord conflicts led to an increasingly unstable rural sector throughout the 1920s.

To restore stability in the rural community, the Japanese colonial government initiated the Rural Revitalization Campaign (RRC) in 1931, which was supposed to improve the rural economy and the living standard of peasants. This policy was a major shift from earlier policies that largely focused on agricultural production (to feed metropolitan Japan) with landlord-based local control. The RRC intended to increase state control over rural affairs by creating village-based, semiofficial associations that would report directly to the state. Through the RRC, the colonial state used consent and coercion to gain more effective control over the rural population (Shin and Han 1999).

Besides the colonial government, both Korean nationalists and the educated class were deeply concerned about the rapidly deteriorating conditions in the rural communities. They saw the revitalization of the rural economy and people's livelihoods as necessary to ensure Korea's survival into the future. As a result, moderate, reform-oriented Korean leaders allied themselves with and were eventually co-opted by the Japanese colonial state under the banner of rural rehabilitation and self-sufficiency.

Women's organizations of varying ideological orientations joined this broader movement to help organize rural women so that they could gain self-sufficiency. With the large-scale exodus of men from the rural areas into the cities to find employment, the women who were left behind were forced to assume greater responsibilities. Women not only engaged in their traditional chores, such as weaving, but also worked in the fields, doing tasks that normally would have been done by male family members. However, the rapid mechanization of textile production deprived rural women of the small income they had earned from selling their weaving, leaving them with much less revenue to support their families.

In 1925, Hŏ Chŏngsuk (1902–1991), a woman leader in the Communist movement, made an urgent plea to girl students, encouraging them to recognize the terrible economic conditions in Korea, especially the miserable lot of rural women, who worked in the fields all day long in sweat-soaked rags, their skin burned by the hot sun (Choi 2013, 53–55). The harsh workload and limited opportunities for education left rural women highly vulnerable to poverty and disease. The rates of infant mortality indicate that rural women had little access to proper medical care. According to one study of the conditions of the rural life in Korea in 1941, "32.7 percent of all births were stillbirths, and 35 percent of babies died before age one" (Yoo 2008, 109).

Given these circumstances, women's movements became deeply intertwined with nationwide rural movements during the interwar period. As discussed in Chapter 5, Kŭnuhoe (Friends of the Rose of Sharon) was the first national women's organization to unify women of differing ideological positions into a single political entity, and it attempted to use the power of this coalition to advocate for economic welfare for rural women, including the establishment of medical clinics and child care centers for peasant women. However, when Kŭnuhoe was dissolved in 1931, it had not made any major progress in achieving these goals other than raising awareness of the dire conditions in rural areas.

It was the farmers' associations in villages and religious organizations, in particular the Religion of the Heavenly Way (Ch'ŏndogyo) and the Korean YMCA and YWCA, that actively addressed the welfare of peasant women and men. Significantly inspired by Danish cooperative systems, the programs designed for rural women in those organizations commonly focused on both educational and economic issues. These organizations' literacy campaigns were a major undertaking, as the vast majority of girls and women were illiterate. Leaders also advocated the abolition of early marriage, anachronistic feudal customs, and laws that oppressed women. They worked to establish child care centers and free midwifery service. They also introduced modern agricultural methods and techniques, and taught women how to secure extra money through such activities as sericulture, beekeeping, or raising pigs.

Korea had predominantly been an agricultural society prior to its colonization by Japan. However, the Japanese colonial state's Land Survey and its drive for industrialization began to transform the Korean economy and society. The Land Survey created a systematic program for collecting taxes, but it primarily benefited the landlord class, offering little to tenants. Intense class conflicts between landlords and tenants destabilized the rural community, resulting in an exodus of farmers. Large numbers of girls and women from impoverished peasant families migrated to urban industrial areas in search of jobs and new lives. While a tiny elite class of women thrived in newly created professional positions in medicine, journalism, and education, the vast majority of women had little or no education and had to work in the textile, rubber, or food processing industries or various service industries. They were often at the bottom of the occupational hierarchy. They received the lowest wages, worked the longest hours, and suffered in the harshest working environments; they were also subject to sexual harassment. Perceived as docile, cheap, and compliant, women workers were preferred in certain jobs; however, as shown by numerous strikes and walkouts led by women factory workers, they also organized to protest wage cuts and bad working conditions.

CHINA

In the first half of the twentieth century, the forces of global capitalism wrought major changes in China's economy, most noticeably in the treaty port cities connected to global markets, but also in rural areas in many parts of the country. The Treaty of Shimonoseki, which ended the Sino-Japanese War in 1895, permitted foreigners to open factories in China, and in its wake foreign-owned factories sprouted up rapidly, especially in Shanghai. By the end of the Qing dynasty in 1911, the city had a large cotton industry dominated by British, American, and Japanese companies. During the interwar period, the largest textile conglomerate in Shanghai, with eleven mills, was the Japanese Naigai Wata Company, which also owned cotton mills in Japan. The dramatic decline of foreign imports, most notably textiles, into the country during World War I created an opening for Chinese industrialists, who quickly became major players in the industrial sector. The Rong family came to own six cotton mills in Shanghai and three in other cities. The Guo family pioneered the development of department store chains with their Wing On stores in Hong Kong, Shanghai, San Francisco, and Australia (to which they had immigrated) before establishing four cotton mills in Shanghai. In the 1920s, nearly half of Shanghai's factory workers (about 140,000) labored in cotton mills.

Silk was China's largest export in the late nineteenth and early twentieth centuries and, in response to rising global demand, mechanized silk filatures proliferated in the traditional centers of sericulture in the Yangzi delta and Canton delta regions. Many young women who had been responsible for raising silkworms and spinning silk in the household now took up jobs in the new silk spinning and weaving factories. The silk industry was dominated by the Chinese-owned Meiya Silk Company, one of the largest in China, with more than thirteen hundred employees. Meiya's general manager, the American-educated Cai Shengbai, was an advocate of American technology and factory management practices, and he provided his highly skilled workers in ten factories with generous wages and services such as cafeterias, clinics, night schools, and recreational activities. Believing women workers to be cheaper and more productive than men, Cai hired an unusually high proportion of them. Overall, about half of Shanghai's silk workers were women (Perry 1992).

By 1929, women workers made up more than 60 percent of the industrial workforce in Shanghai, by far China's largest industrial city. The vast majority of these workers engaged in textile production: cotton spinning and weaving and silk reeling and weaving. In addition, significant numbers of women labored in factories processing tobacco, eggs, and paper, making matches, and knitting. If child laborers, the vast majority of whom were girls, are included in the total, nearly 70 percent of the industrial workforce and nearly 80 percent of textile mill hands were female, although the most highly skilled and best-paying jobs were occupied by men. In contrast, in the northern city of Tianjin, with an economy dominated by trade rather than industrial production, only 10 percent of mill workers were women. Most women laborers in Tianjin were employed in household-level or small workshops spinning wool, gluing matchboxes, weaving mats, sewing military uniforms, and performing other handicraft-type production (Hershatter 1986). In Beijing and other cities that had little industry in this period, women engaged primarily in various forms of piecework in the home, producing paper flowers, soles for shoes, and embroidery and other needlework.

Women Factory Workers

Although some factory workers came from families that lived in suburbs of Shanghai, most were migrants from the countryside of the Yangzi delta region. The most skilled workers, those who occupied the highest-paid jobs in silk and cotton spinning and weaving, came from the relatively prosperous Jiangnan counties south of the city, which had been the traditional centers of women's household textile production. As the proliferation of industrially produced textiles in the market undermined the handicraft sector, many families sent their daughters to work in factories in Shanghai. Recruitment of these women was facilitated by the fact that many mill owners and managers were from this region. Geographically, it was close enough that managers and workers could return home for festivals and other visits, which in turn became opportunities for recruiting new workers. Many of these workers from the nearby countryside were literate consumers of Shanghai's mass media and participated in the cosmopolitan culture of the city's dance halls and movie theaters.

The other region that supplied a large portion of the Shanghai labor force was Subei, comprising the poor cotton-growing counties north of the city where women had traditionally done much agricultural labor. This area was beset by flooding and famine in the latter half of the nineteenth and early twentieth centuries, compelling many families to migrate to survive. Many ended up in Shanghai, where the women worked as prostitutes or in unskilled factory jobs such as reeling, and the men as rickshaw pullers, coolie laborers, and beggars. Noticeable because of their dialect, unfashionable dress, and tastes that were considered vulgar, Subei migrants were the underclass of Shanghai society, widely denigrated not just by the middle classes but by more prosperous and educated segments of the working class as well (Honig 1986).

The social, cultural, and economic divide between migrants from Jiangnan and Subei was manifested in prejudicial treatment by factory managers and rivalry between workers. Such native-place identities, maintained in the big city through residence patterns, dialect, food, customs, and popular culture preferences, helped new migrants to form communities and to find jobs and social support. Many workers who shared native-place ties formed sisterhoods of women who pledged loyalty, support, and friendship, helping each other out in hard times and socializing together. One woman remembered her sisterhood this way:

> *Maybe four of us girls got together. Each month, when we got our wages we would each donate a certain amount to the kitty. Then we would determine who needed the money the most that time. For example, it was very hard for us to buy a* qi pao *in those days, a good blue one. So sometimes we would use the money to make a* qi pao *for whichever person needed it. Or maybe someone would use [the money] to make a coat. If one of the members had family problems, like someone needed to see a doctor, or someone had died, they would use the money for that. (Quoted in Honig 1986, 212)*

Silk weavers, about half of whom were women, were at the top of the hierarchy of industrial workers, Shanghai's "labor aristocracy." Many were the children of peasants from the surrounding countryside who had received at least an elementary school education in new-style schools and migrated to the city with ambitions of upward mobility and dreams of a modern lifestyle. These young workers occupied the plum skilled jobs in the bigger modern factories such as Meiya and shared interests in Western fashion and food, movies, and romance with urban students. In contrast, the somewhat older workers in smaller factories that paid less were from rural families that had done home silk weaving for generations but could no longer support themselves because of competition from mechanized weaving factories. They were likely to be illiterate and maintained many aspects of a rural lifestyle, including clothing, religious practices, family rituals, and customs of networking through sworn sisterhoods and secret societies (Perry 1993, 185–188).

Outside of Shanghai, women's entrance into textile factories was sometimes, though not always, associated with greater autonomy from family authority. In Canton, as women silk workers shifted their labor from home to factory, they adapted an older practice called delayed transfer marriage, in which women postponed permanent residence with their new husbands until the birth of a child or even longer while they continued to earn income to support their natal families. In the new variant of this practice women organized sworn sisterhoods, often resided in spinster houses, and pledged not to marry, sometimes developing sexual relationships with each other. Some scholars have interpreted this practice as a form of resistance to patriarchal marriage. Others have seen it as an alternative form of marriage that may have meant greater independence for young women but was sanctioned by families to maintain control over the income produced by their girls (Topley 1975, Stockard 1989).

The Lower Yangzi city of Wuxi shifted from cotton to silk production after the Taiping Rebellion of the 1860s, which devastated traditional silk-producing cities such as Hangzhou and Suzhou just as global demand was growing. By 1930, there were some fifty filatures in Wuxi, and these required labor and supplies of cocoons. Some young women got jobs in those factories, but most continued to work within the household, shifting their household labor from spinning and weaving cotton to cultivating silkworms (Bell 1994). With a dense population and small farms, Wuxi households depended on the supplementary income women brought in, but the work was hard and silkworm disease was a constant threat in the local climate. When silkworm batches failed, families blamed not the weather but the women workers for offending the local spirits and polluting the worms. Here the expanded sericulture economy did not enhance the independence or status of women.

Working Lives

In the industrial metropolis of Shanghai, most women workers moved from one industry to another, beginning factory careers as children doing the least skilled jobs. Many started in silk filatures, which had some of the worst industrial working conditions. Constituting 95 percent of the workforce, women and children performed every step of the production process: cocoon drying, peeling, selection, and boiling; plus silk reeling, stretching, inspection, and packaging. Children undertook the painful process of beating cocoons in boiling water to prepare them for reeling. Managers often beat girls for making mistakes or even threw boiling water at them. One woman recalled,

> *There were two big cauldrons. They would be filled with boiling water, and . . . we would have to keep pushing the cocoons down under the water. The cocoons would have to be boiled until they were very soft before the thread could be pulled off.*
> *When we worked in the silk filature our hands would swell up every night. So we would go to the medicine store and buy an ointment. We would put that on and then wrap up our hands. They would hurt and hurt at night. (Quoted in Honig 1986, 172).*

Under such conditions silk spinners typically left their factories by their early teens. Most would end up in cotton mills, which were noisy, dusty, and poorly ventilated, but which employed workers year-round and were thus considered the best factories in which to work. But many workers also did stints in other kinds of factories. To work their way up into the better-paid jobs, girls learned new skills from friends. A lucky few were selected as apprentices, paid lower wages during a training period, and then promoted to a new position if they demonstrated skill. A tiny handful of those with some education could hope to become "number ones," the most important women on the shop floor, who supervised departments and had enormous power to hire, assign jobs, and dismiss workers (Honig 1986).

Most women workers married by age twenty-four, somewhat later than their peers in the countryside. Like rural women, however, factory workers' husbands, often migrants from their home villages, were typically chosen for them by their parents with the assistance of a matchmaker or mutual acquaintance. Even if workers lived apart from their families in factory dormitories or housing shared with other women, they sent most of their wages home. Still adhering to small-town values and standards of comportment, they did not live the life of freewheeling modern girls. Most continued to work after they married, and some even brought their first children to the factory floor, taking off only a few days after giving birth. A worker's factory career often would last until one of her children was able to step in as a wage earner for the family.

At the very bottom of Shanghai's industrial working classes were contract laborers. The contract labor system was an adaptation of China's long-standing systems of human trafficking. This system was dominated by the powerful underworld Green Gang, which controlled much of Shanghai and was notorious not only for running opium and prostitution rackets but also for operating as thugs for the Nationalist regime as it turned toward fascism in the 1930s. Buying and selling girls as domestic servants,

Women workers sorting silk cocoons for size, color, and quality, the first stage in the silk textile production process, in a Shanghai factory in the 1920s. PHOTO BY PHOTOQUEST/ GETTY IMAGES

concubines, and prostitutes continued to be a pervasive part of China's economy, even as reformed legal systems and new police forces attempted to curtail or at least minimize the Green Gang's most egregious violations of the new laws against slavery. Extending their trafficking know-how to recruiting for Shanghai's factories, labor contractors, many of whom were related to factory managers, bought peasant girls from poverty-stricken families and brought them to the city. Parents signed a contract stipulating the terms of the deal:

> *The undersigned, X, because of present economic difficulties, on this day wishes to hire out his daughter, Y, to recruiting agent of the name Z, who will take her to work in a cotton mill in Shanghai. The hiring payment will be thirty yuan for a period of three years. The money will be paid in three annual installments of ten yuan, to be paid in March of each year.*
>
> *From the time she enters the factory, the girl will owe full obedience to the recruiting agent, and must not violate his instructions. In the event of her abscondence or death, the undersigned takes full responsibility. If she should fall ill, the recruiting agent will be responsible. Throughout the three-year contracted period, the girl will be clothed and fed by the recruiting agent. If any working time is lost, the girl will have to make it up at the end of the contracted period. After the contract expires, the recruiting agent has no further responsibility for the girl. (Quoted in Honig 1983, 426–427)*

During the contracted time the girls were virtually slaves of the contractor, who kept their wages while housing them in overcrowded, airless dormitories and fed them so little that they were undernourished and often ill. If they disobeyed their contractor or supervisor or attempted to escape, they were beaten. Sexual abuse by contractors was common. If the contractor failed to procure a slot for a worker at a factory, it was common for the contractor to sell the worker to a brothel. This most exploitative yet highly secretive system in Shanghai's industrial economy emerged in part because of factory owners' increasing concerns about labor activism after the May Thirtieth Movement, a labor uprising in 1925 (see Chapter 5). In 1936 the leftist writer Xia Yan exposed the contracting system's abuses to public view in a popular piece of reportage titled "Contract Labor," which was based on his own investigations. Yet despite numerous investigations and much public outcry, the system persisted because of the power of the Green Gang.

Women and Labor Activism

Women workers were a target of interest for social reformers and revolutionaries. But with the Communist Party banned and forced underground until 1937, it was the international Young Women's Christian Association that had the greatest impact on reforming working conditions. The YWCA had had a presence in China since the 1890s. In the 1920s it focused its Christian mission on enhancing the social welfare of the poor. In 1928 the YWCA launched a major program to improve the well-being and working conditions of women workers under the leadership of Cora Deng (see Box 7.3). Disturbed by workers' poverty and miserable working conditions, YWCA activists ran night schools in every factory district to teach literacy, arithmetic, history, current events, and electives on industrial problems, unions, and labor legislation. The progressive Western and Chinese YWCA staff explicitly intended these schools to teach women how to become labor organizers. Many women who later became labor leaders got their start in these schools.

Contrary to the assumptions of factory managers, who expanded recruitment of women in the 1920s precisely because they thought women would be more docile than men, women frequently went on strike to demand higher wages or improvements in working conditions. In that decade, unskilled female workers such as spinners and tobacco workers were more active strikers than men, although on the whole women were not interested in the union organizing projects of early CCP cadres, most of whom were men with little understanding of women's concerns. One notable exception was Yang

BOX 7.3

Cora Deng

Like many women reformers and revolutionaries, Cora Deng (Deng Yuzhi, 1900–1996) grew up in the province of Hunan and started her education at Zhounan Girls' School, the same progressive school attended by Xiang Jingyu (Chapter 5) and Ding Ling (Chapter 6), but she charted her own path as a leftist Christian reformer. After her parents' death, her Christian grandmother enrolled her in the missionary Fuxiang School for Girls, where, as president of the Student Self-Government Association, she led demonstrations and boycotts of Japanese goods during the May Fourth Movement in 1919. Recalling her thinking at the time, she described how Christianity and nationalism meshed for her: "Since God does not want people to be exploited or suppressed by others, we thought that fighting for national survival was carrying out God's will."

Influenced by New Culture publications such as *New Youth* and by the example of her Chinese and American missionary teachers, who were single women living independently, Deng developed radical ideas about the role of women in society. After graduation, she fled an arranged marriage and moved to the city of Nanjing to enroll in the missionary Jinling Women's College (see Chapter 8) but had to flee again to Shanghai in 1921 when her husband's family tried to pressure her to return. For the next decade, Deng alternated work for the YWCA and study at Jinling and at the London School of Economics on a YWCA scholarship.

Mentored by the American YWCA secretary Maud Russell, Deng learned about socialism and the plight of women workers. In 1930 she became head of the YWCA's Labor Bureau and, inspired by Communist ideals, researched working conditions for factory girls, interviewed cotton mill workers about their lives, and wrote exposés of the contract labor system. She led the YWCA effort to establish night schools that would teach literacy, arithmetic, geography, history and Christian values to women workers in China's cities, but she also sought to raise their class and nationalist consciousness by teaching them about labor issues, capitalism, and imperialism.

Although she never joined the CCP, Deng saw Communism and Christianity as compatible approaches to social revolution and worked closely with CCP activists in the night schools. She stayed in China after the revolution in 1949 and worked to reconcile the interests of Chinese Christians and religious organizations such as the YWCA with the CCP (Honig 1999).

Zhihua (1900–1973, see Chapter 5 textbox), a Communist leader in the Shanghai General Labor Union who successfully led women tobacco workers in the longest work stoppage in Shanghai history, the four-month strike at the British American Tobacco Company during the strike wave of the May Thirtieth Movement. Yang came from the same rural area as many of the women workers and integrated herself into their social networks, dressing like a worker, swearing sisterhood with many of them, and expressing interest in their personal lives. To evade detection by the authorities, she had the women meet at a Buddhist temple, disguised as pilgrims (Perry 1993).

In 1924, under the leadership of Mu Zhiying—a female gangster whose close working relationships with factory forewomen allowed her to wield great authority over women workers—women of Subei origin organized the Shanghai Silk and Cotton Women Workers Association. When one silk factory fired all of its Subei workers in response, over 14,000 silk workers from fourteen filatures went on strike demanding a wage increase, reduced working hours, and recognition of the new union. Mu was able to negotiate a deal whereby the Cocoon Guild factory owners supported the union with a subsidy, in exchange for the union's assurance that there would be no more strikes. Communist organizers viewed gangster labor leaders like Mu as scabs who did not represent the real interests of the workers. But these gangster leaders were prominent in the Shanghai labor movement, and many workers trusted them.

Male and female silk weavers were the most skilled and educated workers, garnered the highest wages, and had the most say in their working conditions in the 1920s and early 1930s. As their wages and terms of employment declined during the Depression, they became some of the most active labor militants, launching frequent and highly organized strikes to protest the decline of their status. Their walkouts were accompanied by sophisticated public relations campaigns to win support from other workers and the broader public. Some of the earliest Communist Party organizers in the ranks of workers were silk weavers, whose literacy facilitated access to Party tracts and Marxist texts and whose organizing skills made them effective mobilizers of fellow workers.

One of the largest strikes occurred at the Meiya Silk Company. Meiya weathered the Depression better than most companies and by 1934 ran half the looms in Shanghai. But as Japanese competition cut into his profits in the early 1930s, owner Cai Shengbai decided to slash wages. This triggered a massive strike wave. When a group of Meiya workers (several of whom had secretly joined the Communist Youth League) issued calls for workers to strike, women weavers at an all-female factory—whom managers assumed to have passively accepted the wage cut—were the first to join in. As the strike spread to all of the Meiya factories, CCP cadres successfully recruited women by building on shared native-place ties. Women were active in street demonstrations, picket lines, and a hunger strike. One was killed and dozens were wounded by police in Shanghai's French concession, who were called in by the owner to rebuff workers' efforts to meet for negotiations. A few days later, a woman worker was arrested on suspicion of being a Communist. The Meiya strike marked the emergence of politicized labor activism among women in Shanghai (Perry 1993).

The Sex Industry

Brothels were a staple feature of China's urban economy, and sex work was a key source of income for many of the working poor, the unemployed, and the displaced. With its huge population of sojourning men of all social classes, Shanghai had a particularly large and complex sex industry. It was estimated that one in every six residents in the city was a prostitute, but there were vast differences in the economic status, lifestyle, and work experience of the women who were lumped together under this term. At the top were elite courtesans who still provided cultured companionship for wealthy men in upscale brothels. At the bottom were desperately poor streetwalkers, called "wild chickens," many of whom were refugees from famine areas. Like factory workers, streetwalkers often organized themselves into sisterhoods under the patronage of a man, usually with Green Gang affiliations, for mutual support and protection. In between were brothels that catered to men of middle-class economic status, which were staffed by women who sometimes had jobs as factory workers, singing hostesses, or dance hall hostesses but who occasionally supplemented their incomes by selling sexual services. There was a fine and permeable line between entertainment work and sex work. Managers of dance halls often took a cut of the proceeds from sexual services provided by their girls. Most brothels were run by women under the protection of Green Gang patrons. These brothel "mothers" established fictive kin relationships with the women who worked for them, though many also engaged in trafficking themselves (Hershatter 1997, Henriot 2001).

Prostitution was legal and taxed by the Nationalist government. Yet many reformers saw it as a scourge on the nation that ought to be eliminated, or at least subject to heavy regulation. During the 1920s the Shanghai municipal government, which governed the concession areas, issued a series of regulations attempting not only to curtail organized prostitution and prostitution at dance halls, teahouses, and other entertainment venues but also to keep records of the women who worked there. Police kept these places under constant surveillance and often conducted raids to monitor illicit behavior. These policies were an utter failure, however, since they merely forced the businesses underground, and thus they were abandoned in favor of a licensing system for brothels.

Despite regulation, prostitution was widely seen as a social danger. Although they posited different arguments about the causes of and solutions for prostitution, Nationalists, Chinese Christians, and New Culture reformers all condemned it as emblematic of the corruption of traditional culture that made the Chinese nation weak and unhealthy. A variety of state, private, foreign, and Chinese institutions emerged to rescue women from lives of prostitution through education, job training, marriage, and medical treatment. One of the most prominent was the Door of Hope, founded by foreign missionary women in 1900. Funded in part by the Shanghai municipal council, which governed the foreign-controlled International Settlement, the organization took in women who had been sent by the courts and the police, found by Door of Hope workers, or escaped on their own. Most of those who stayed learned literacy and handicraft skills and were married off, many to Christian husbands. Such efforts, however, did not reduce the scale of the industry, which was fueled increasingly by the dislocations of war. Not until after the Communist victory in 1949 would prostitution be effectively eliminated (Hershatter 1997).

Rural Women's Work

Huge gaps exist in our knowledge of how economic changes affected the work patterns and experiences of the vast majority of women in rural villages across China in the first half of the twentieth century. Industrial production of textiles gradually worked to undermine the income potential of home production, but many rural women continued to make clothing for their families and to engage in textile-related work such as silk cocoon production, spinning, weaving, and embroidery. In many regions of China, including Yunnan, Fujian, and Sichuan, women continued to engage in significant work in the fields. In the early twentieth century, commercialization of agriculture in North China and the Yangzi delta appears to have increased women's participation in the fields alongside their male family members or, for a growing number of impoverished families, as wage laborers. Some rural surveys conducted in the 1930s suggest that as villages became more tied to markets, women had more opportunities for income generation, which increased their economic value to their families and thus led to later marriages and higher bride prices.

Changes in the practice of footbinding are a telling indicator of changes in women's labor. Footbinding declined, though not uniformly, in rural as well as urban areas in the early twentieth century. In many rural counties in Sichuan, 40 percent or more of girls were still having their feet bound in the mid-1920s. The percentage actually increased in two counties among cohorts of girls born in the 1910s and 1920s. Rates were even higher—over 65 percent—in parts of Henan, Hebei, and Shaanxi in the north. In Hunan and Jiangxi, rates were below 40 percent by the late 1920s, while in one county in Yunnan they remained above 80 percent until the 1940s. Despite these figures, only about 35 percent of women who had ever had their feet bound still had bound feet at the time of marriage (Brown et al. 2012).

Oral histories indicate that quite often families gave up on the binding when girls resisted, or else bound the girls' feet very loosely, without breaking the arch, so they could be easily unbound. If girls had no access to income-generating work that was compatible with bound feet—such as spinning—families were more amendable to unbinding. Although interviews with women who had had their feet bound indicate that most believed or were told that binding was necessary for marriage (in particular, allowing them to marry above their economic status), recent research suggests that, with few exceptions, there was no correlation between marrying at all or marrying up (hypergamy) and footbinding. The same research indicates that the areas where the practice persisted longest appear to be those where female handicraft labor in the household continued to be important (Brown et al. 2012). Footbinding was, among other things, a form of labor control, and as industrialization undermined the profitability of household-produced thread and cloth, footbinding lost its utility (Bossen 2002, Gates 2015).

Across much of rural China in the first half of the twentieth century, but especially in the north, droughts and floods exacerbated by ecological crises (population pressure, deforestation, and depletion of land and water resources) brought deepening rural crisis, and the country became known as the "Land of Famine." Millions died and millions more were displaced as refugees in massive famines in 1920–1921, 1928–1930, and 1936. Chronic famine was gendered: it brought about increased female infanticide, destabilization of marriage, and sale of women and children into marriage, prostitution, and servitude of various kinds. The pressures of poverty on family life and gender norms would only increase with the onset of the Sino-Japanese War.

CONNECTIONS

The interwar years were a time of great growth and structural changes in women's labor force participation. In Japan, women's industrial participation began to boom in the late nineteenth century, and many of the harsh conditions of employment in textile work that accompanied the emergence of cotton and silk production in Korea and China in the 1920s had already plagued Japan's workers a few decades earlier (see Chapter 4). By the interwar period, some reforms were beginning to take root in Japan, despite employers' resistance to pressure from the International Labour Organization to improve working and residential conditions for women workers. Most of these reforms took the form of gendered protectionism, such as menstruation leave and limits on the hours and places women could work. Women workers were often preferred by employers, as they were thought to be docile and willing to accept wages that were lower than men's. Male union leaders also treated women workers disdainfully, viewing them as women first and workers second. Socialist feminists struggled against male socialists who, contrarily, refused to acknowledge women's real special needs, such as maternity leave.

Despite the image of women as passive, some of the most militant strikes were carried out by women demanding better wages and working conditions. Divisions within the labor force did not stop with gender; in Japan, ethnicity and class also divided workers who had similar interests. Workers from throughout the empire, especially Okinawa and Korea, were drawn into Japanese factories, where their ethnicity conditioned the kinds of treatment they experienced. The interwar era was also a time of great growth of middle-class women's employment in Japan. While no commentators had worried about the social effects of working-class women's work outside the home, many raised concerns about middle-class women. To encourage them back into the home, some government officials called for better salaries for men so that women would not have to work; in the end, however, those higher salaries were not offered.

Administrative changes under Japanese colonialism had a tremendous impact in Korea. The Land Survey's codification of land ownership for the purpose of tax collection led to the loss of many farmers' lands. The passage of the Company Law attracted numerous Japanese firms to Korea in the 1920s. Both of these policies led to an exodus of workers from rural areas, many of them farm daughters. Most workers continued to be farmers in the 1930s, but factory employment, especially in textiles and chemical production, grew exponentially. The reforms that came into effect in Japan in the 1920s were not extended to Korea, where labor conditions were particularly bleak. As in Japan, women workers were thought to be docile, but their strike activity showed that Korean women workers were anything but that.

As in Japan, urban middle-class occupations grew. Seoul's population doubled from 1925 to 1942, and the range of jobs grew commensurately. Women joined the urban workforce as bus conductors, department store clerks, and café waitresses, among others. Sex work in Korea was increasingly performed by Korean women rather than Japanese, as it had been previously. Meanwhile, life on the farm was difficult during the Depression, offering an opportunity for the Japanese colonial authorities to embark on the Rural Revitalization Campaign. In the end, this extended the reach of the authorities into the everyday life of villagers, but many rural residents appeared to welcome the help they were given. At the same time, religious organizations such as the YWCA and the Religion of the Heavenly Way offered similar kinds of rural help and advice.

China's textile workforce also grew during this period. In 1929 women made up 60 percent or more of the industrial workforce in Shanghai, although the numbers were smaller in other cities. Migrants from different neighboring provinces poured into Shanghai, and tensions among people of different native origins were exploited by their employers. Workers were further exploited by labor contractors, especially the members of the Green Gang, who worked with employers to recruit the workforce. As in Japan and Korea, women workers were not as docile as employers thought, and carried out strikes. But unlike the case in Japan and Korea, gangsters played a role in mediating strikes, often getting better wages for the workers while suppressing their strikes on behalf of the factory owners. By 1934 the CCP was also making use of workers' anger to politicize labor activism. As in Japan and Korea, sex work employed large numbers of women in China.

REFERENCES AND SUGGESTIONS FOR FURTHER READING

GLOBAL CONTEXT

Cousins, Norman. 1939. "Will Women Lose Their Jobs?" *Current History* 51, no. 1.

JAPAN

Cobble, Dorothy Sue. 2015. "Who Speaks for Workers? Japan and the 1919 ILO Debates over Rights and Global Labor Standards." *International Labor and Working-Class History* 87: 213–234.

Faison, Elyssa. 2007. *Managing Women: Disciplining Labor in Modern Japan*. Berkeley: University of California Press.

Hunter, Janet. 1989. "Factory Legislation and Employer Resistance: The Abolition of Night Work in the Cotton Spinning Industry." In *Japanese Management in Historical Perspective*, edited by Tsunehiko Yui and Keiichiro Nakagawa. Tokyo: University of Tokyo Press.

Ishimoto, Shidzue. 1984. *Facing Two Ways: The Story of My Life*. Stanford, CA: Stanford University Press.

Kim, Jaeeun. 2014. "The Colonial State, Migration, and Diasporic Nationhood in Korea." *Comparative Studies in Society and History* 56, no. 1: 34–66.

Molony, Barbara. 1984. "Afterword." In *Facing Two Ways: The Story of My Life*, by Ishimoto Shidzue. Stanford, CA: Stanford University Press.

———. 1991. "Activism Among Women in the Taishō Cotton Textile Industry." In *Recreating Japanese Women, 1600-1945*, edited by Gail Lee Bernstein. Berkeley: University of California Press.

———. 1993. "Equality Versus Difference: The Japanese Debate over 'Motherhood Protection.'" In *Japanese Women Working*, edited by Janet Hunter. London: Routledge.

Nagy, Margaret. 1991. "Middle-Class Working Women During the Interwar Years." In *Recreating Japanese Women, 1600–1945*, edited by Gail Lee Bernstein. Berkeley: University of California Press.

Sand, Jordan. 2005. *House and Home in Modern Japan: Architecture, Domestic Space, and Bourgeois Culture, 1880–1930*. Cambridge, MA: Harvard University Press.

Sato, Barbara. 2003. *The New Japanese Woman: Modernity, Media, and Women in Interwar Japan*. Durham, NC: Duke University Press.

Smith, Kerry. 2001. *A Time of Crisis: Japan, the Great Depression, and Rural Revitalization*. Cambridge, MA: Harvard University Press.

Smith, W. Donald. 2005. "Sorting Coal and Pickling Cabbage: Korean Women in the Japanese Mining Industry." In *Gendering Modern Japanese History*, edited by Barbara Molony and Kathleen Uno. Cambridge, MA: Harvard University Press.

Tipton, Elise. 2000. *Being Modern in Japan: Society and Culture from the 1910s to the 1930s*. Honolulu: University of Hawai'i Press.

Yamanouchi, Mina. 1975. *Jiden*. Tokyo: Shinjuku Shobō.

KOREA

Barraclough, Ruth. 2012. *Factory Girl Literature: Sexuality, Violence, and Representation in Industrialized Korea*. Berkeley: University of California Press.

Choi, Hyaeweol. 2013. *New Women in Colonial Korea: A Sourcebook*. London: Routledge.

Eckert, Carter. 1996. *Offspring of Empire: The Koch'ang Kims and the Colonial Origins of Korean Capitalism, 1876–1945*. Seattle: University of Washington Press.

Kang Kyong-ae. 2009. *From Wonso Pond.* Translated by Samuel Perry. New York: Feminist Press.

Kim, Janice. 2009. *To Live to Work: Factory Women in Colonial Korea, 1910–1945.* Stanford, CA: Stanford University Press.

Kim Kyŏngil. 2004. *Yŏsŏng ŭi kŭndae, kŭndae ŭi yŏsŏng.* Seoul: P'urŭn yŏksa.

Muho Hyang'in. 1931. "Ŭlmiltae ŭi ch'egongnyŏ yŏryu t'usa Kang Churyong hoegyŏn'gi" (An Account of my meeting with Kang Churyong, a female militant worker on Ŭlmiltae Pavilion). *Tonggwang* (July): 40–42.

Nishinarita, Yutaka. 1994. "Introduction: Types of Female Labour and Changes in the Workforce, 1890–1945." In *Technology Change and Female Labour in Japan,* edited by Masanori Nakamura. Tokyo: United Nations University Press.

Paekjangmi. 1934. "Chosŏn ŭi yŏsŏng tŭra! Chujŏ malgo chigŏp chŏnsŏn ŭro!" Yŏsŏng 1: 8–11.Park, Soon-Won. 1999. "Colonial Industrial Growth and the Emergence of the Korean Working Class." In *Colonial Modernity in Korea,* edited by Gi-Wook Shin and Michael Robinson. Cambridge, MA: Harvard University Press.

Park, Sunyoung. 2013. "Rethinking Feminism in Colonial Korea: Kang Kyŏngae and 1930s Socialist Women's Literature." *Positions: East Asia Cultures Critique* 21, no. 4: 947–985.

Perry, Samuel. 2013. "The Context and Contributions of Kang Kyŏng-ae's Novel *In'gan munje.*" *Korean Studies* 37: 99–123.

Shin, Gi-Wook, and Do-Hyun Han. 1999. "Colonial Corporatism: The Rural Revitalization Campaign, 1932–1940." In *Colonial Modernity in Korea,* edited by Gi-Wook Shin and Michael Robinson. Cambridge, MA: Harvard University Press.

U, Sunok. 1930. "Ŏnŭ chesa hoesa yŏgong ilgi" (A Diary of a Female Factory Worker in a Silk Mill). *Pyŏlgŏn'gon 27: 72-73.*

Yoo, Theodore Jun. 2008. *The Politics of Gender in Colonial Korea: Education, Labor, and Health, 1910–1945.* Berkeley: University of California Press.

Yun Chihyŏn. 2009. "1920–30 nyŏndae sŏbisŭjik yŏsŏng ŭi nodong silt'ae wa sahoe chŏk wisang." *Yŏsŏng kwa yŏksa* 10: 93–139.

CHINA

Bell, Lynda S. 1994. "For Better, for Worse: Women and the World Market in Rural China." *Modern China* 20, no. 2: 180–210.

Bossen, Laurel. 2002. *Chinese Women and Rural Development: Sixty Years of Change in Lu Village, Yunnan.* Lanham, MD: Rowman and Littlefield.

Brown, Melissa, Laurel Bossen, Hill Gates, and Damian Satterthwaite-Phillips. 2012. "Marriage Mobility and Footbinding in Pre-1949 Rural China: A Reconsideration of Gender, Economics, and Meaning in Social Causation." *Journal of Asian Studies* 71, no. 4: 1035–1067.

Cheng, Weikun. 2011. *City of Working Women: Life, Space, and Social Control in Early Twentieth-Century Beijing.* Berkeley: Institute of East Asian Studies, University of California.

Gates, Hill. 2015. *Footbinding and Women's Labor in Sichuan*. New York: Routledge.

Henriot, Christian. 2001. *Prostitution and Sexuality in Shanghai: A Social History, 1849–1949*. Cambridge: Cambridge University Press.

Hershatter, Gail. 1986. *The Workers of Tianjin, 1900–1949*. Stanford, CA: Stanford University Press.

———. 1997. *Dangerous Pleasures: Prostitution and Modernity in Twentieth-Century Shanghai*. Berkeley: University of California Press.

Honig, Emily. 1986. *Sisters and Strangers: Women in the Shanghai Cotton Mills, 1919–1949*. Stanford, CA: Stanford University Press.

———. 1983. "The Contract Labor System and Women Workers: Pre-Liberation Cotton Mills of Shanghai." *Modern China*. 9, 4: 421–454.

———. 1999. "Christianity, Feminism, and Communism: The Life and Times of Deng Yuzhi." In *Christianity in China: From the Eighteenth Century to the Present*, edited by Daniel H. Bays. Stanford: Stanford University Press.

Mann, Susan. 1992. "Women's Work in the Ningbo Area, 1900–1936." In *Chinese History in Economic Perspective*, edited by Thomas G. Rawski and Lillian M. Li. Berkeley: University of California Press.

Perry, Elizabeth. 1992. "Strikes Among Shanghai Silk Weavers, 1927–1937: The Awakening of a Labor Aristocracy." In *Shanghai Sojourners*, edited by Frederic Wakeman Jr. and Wen-hsin Yeh. Berkeley: Institute of East Asian Studies, University of California.

———. 1993. *Shanghai on Strike: The Politics of Chinese Labor*. Stanford, CA: Stanford University Press.

Stockard, Janice. 1989. *Daughters of the Canton Delta: Marriage Patterns and Economic Strategies in South China, 1860–1930*. Stanford, CA: Stanford University Press.

Topley, Marjorie. 1975. "Marriage Resistance in Rural Kwangtung." In *Women in Chinese Society*, edited by Margery Wolf and Roxane Witke. Stanford, CA: Stanford University Press.

Walker, Kathryn Le Mons. 1993. "Economic Growth, Peasant Marginalization, and the Sexual Division of Labor in Early Twentieth-Century China: Women's Work in Nantong County." *Modern China* 19, no. 3: 354–386.

8

Gender and World War II

GLOBAL CONTEXT

The period from 1931 to 1945 started off with the Great Depression and ended with the deaths of sixty million people worldwide in the Second World War. The Depression was unprecedented in its global reach and in the depth of economic dislocation it produced. Economic disasters helped to fuel extremist policies in a number of industrialized countries. Immediately following the Depression, World War II produced far greater levels of suffering. Both the Depression and the war led to major changes in gender relations as governments and civilians responded aggressively to economic and military crises.

Beginning in 1929, all the industrialized countries in the world (except for the Soviet Union, which had a state-managed economy and was cut off from trade relations with most of the rest of the world at that time) were plunged into massive unemployment, with levels reaching 25 percent. For example, the German economy was still reeling from the hyperinflation of the 1920s, and it suffered a 33 percent unemployment rate in the early 1930s. In addition to massive unemployment and widespread bank failures, the United States and Canada were struck by the loss of hundreds of thousands of farms in the Great Plains, a result of the years of drought known as the "Dust Bowl." Workers had no money to pay for commodities; this led to plummeting prices, which in turn led to a crash in world trade. This had particularly harsh effects on those countries that needed to sell luxury products on the world market to survive, such as Japan and China (silk) or Germany and the United States (automobiles). International trade fell by 66 percent from 1929 to 1934.

Trading nations adopted protectionist policies, but in the end, these hurt everyone except the USSR, as each country was willing to impoverish the others to protect itself. This protectionist tendency began to emerge in foreign policy as well, as governments saw less reason to cooperate with each other through the League of Nations or other multilateral bodies. In 1932 Japan was the first country to abandon the League when it objected to Japan's annexation of Manchuria as a puppet state called Manzhouguo. The League was powerless to oppose the invasion of Ethiopia by Italy's fascist government under Benito Mussolini, or the assistance provided by Nazi Germany and fascist Italy to the fascist rebellion against the government of Spain, which ended with the rebels' victory and the imposition of the dictatorship of Francisco Franco (1892–1975).

Mussolini governed Italy from 1922 on, calling himself "Il Duce" (the leader). He nationalized 75 percent of the Italian economy in the early 1930s. In Germany, Adolf Hitler and his Nazi Party came to power in 1933 and immediately began dismantling democracy and building up military-industrial production, in violation of the 1919 Versailles Treaty. Hitler styled himself as "Führer" (leader), following Mussolini's example. The Soviet Union began its first Five-Year Plan at the same time, collectivizing agriculture throughout the country and deporting or killing millions of *kulaki* (rich farmers). This led to the horrific famine of 1932–1933, in which eleven million people starved to death. To silence his critics, the Soviet leader Joseph Stalin purged two million people, sending them to labor camps or executing them.

Meanwhile, as its war in China escalated, Japan had moved ideologically closer to Nazi Germany and fascist Italy, and the three countries signed the Anti-Comintern Pact against Russia in 1936–1937. At that time, the three came to be known in the West as the Axis powers. Japan battled the USSR in a series of skirmishes at Nomonhan, a small village on the border between Manzhouguo and Mongolia, beginning in May 1939, but this did not stop the Germans from secretly humiliating their Japanese ally by signing the Nazi-Soviet Non-Aggression Pact in August 1939. The Nomonhan Incident ended in September with approximately ten thousand casualties each on the Russian and Japanese sides; at around the same time the Germans invaded Poland from the west and the Russians invaded it from the east. The German occupation of Poland was brutal—their extermination camp at Auschwitz opened in 1940—and the Soviets arrested and executed thousands of Poles as "counterrevolutionaries." The Nazis murdered between two million and four million people, mostly Jews, at Auschwitz.

Bound to Poland by treaty, France, Britain, and the Commonwealth countries declared war on Germany in September 1939. (Britain's colony in India did not actively join the fight against the Axis powers; many Indians joined the Indian National Army, which sided with Japan against Britain, although many more joined Gandhi's call to resist fascism while also carrying out massive civil disobedience against Britain in the "Quit India" movement.) By May 1940, Germany had conquered Norway, Denmark, Belgium, Holland, and France. Germany was bombing Britain in advance of a planned invasion, Italy attacked British colonies in Africa, and Japan moved its armies into French Indochina (Vietnam). The world was at war.

Of the major powers, only the United States and the Soviet Union were not yet involved in World War II by the first months of 1940. (Latin American countries, which were not major powers at that time, joined the war against the Axis between 1942, when Mexico and Brazil declared war, and 1945, when Argentina did.) In 1940, Germany, Italy, and Japan signed one more mutual security pact, the Tripartite Pact, which was directed against the United States. Then Germany violated its Non-Aggression Pact with Russia by invading that country in June 1941. This occurred just as Japan was negotiating a Non-Aggression Pact of its own with the USSR. (The Japanese-Soviet Pact held until August 8, 1945, the last week of World War II, but Germany had again humiliated its ally.) The United States was not yet at war, although it had begun to supply the Russians and British with armaments. As Japanese forces moved toward the southern part of the French colony of Vietnam, the British colony of Malaya (which included Singapore), and the Dutch colony of the Dutch East Indies (Indonesia), the United States placed severe economic sanctions on Japan, especially an oil embargo. Negotiations to end the embargo failed, and Japan bombed Pearl Harbor on December 7, 1941, which pulled the United States into World War II.

Wartime always alters gender relations, and the prewar and wartime years were no exception. Ideological changes came earlier in the Soviet Union, as the notion of gender equality was embedded in Communist thought (Clements 2004). Changes in daily life followed in the 1920s, with women being pushed into factories as the USSR ramped up industrialization. At the same time, however, there was ambivalence about the role of women in the home. The "New Soviet Woman" was told to be both excellent at work and dedicated to the home, which was to be a place of refuge for her husband (who needed to rest from his labors) as well as a place of nurturance for the children. The New Soviet Man would be made over from a rough country fellow to a bold and hardworking man who might rise to become a Party leader.

In Latin America, the modern secular state elevated men and virility (Besse 2004). In Mexico, for example, the post-1917 revolutionaries associated nationalism with virility, and they even silenced women revolutionaries because they believed women were inherently conservative. At the same time, the nationalist populism that the Mexican government espoused focused on social and economic justice and helped to ease some of the patriarchal dominance within the family in order to allow women to better serve the nation as wives and mothers. In Argentina, the Peronist government forged close ties with male labor union leaders and emphasized "manly" responsibility to protect the weak (women, workers, and others).

In North America and Western Europe, with the exception of France and Switzerland, most women earned the vote in the interwar period (Sowerwine and Grimshaw 2004). In the 1930s, the fascist governments of Italy, Spain, and Greece snatched the vote away from women after they had already earned it. German women did not lose the vote with the rise of Hitler, but that did not make any difference, as the vote became meaningless when all Germans lost their political voice. Mussolini announced that a woman's function was to bear children, and to get women back in the household, he cut women's wages to half those of men. Hitler's Germany closed birth control clinics, dissolved feminist groups, labor unions, and socialist parties, and disallowed women from running for public office. Women were to focus on the three K's—*Kinder, Kirche, Küche* (children, church, kitchen).

Women in the democracies fared better, although gender continued to divide them from men. France's conservative climate in the 1930s meant that, even with a socialist prime minister, women still did not get the vote. On the other hand, France enacted provisions to support mothers financially and repealed the part of the Napoleonic Code that required women to obey their husbands. France, Britain, Australia, Denmark, Sweden, the Netherlands, and pre-fascist Italy and Germany all developed policies to support mothers financially after World War I. The United States lagged behind, creating the Aid to Dependent Children program in 1935.

World War II and the subsequent mobilization of millions of men for military service drew women into the workplace in unprecedented numbers. In the United States, for example, female employment rose from 12 million in 1940 to 19 million in 1945; in Canada, the number of women in the workforce rose from 600,000 in 1940 to 1.2 million in 1943. Australian and New Zealand women were mobilized in "land armies" to grow food for Britain. In those European countries invaded by Germany that had enjoyed greater democratic rights before conquest, many women worked in order to survive, but not to support their conqueror.

JAPAN

Feminism and Politics in the War Years

Following the Manchurian Incident in 1931 (see Chapter 5), Japanese feminists struggled with the question of supporting their nation—a key element in the quest for women's rights—or opposing the increasing repression at home and the expanding warfare on the Asian continent. At first most of them opposed Japan's foreign policy and continued to work for women's rights at home while recognizing that the struggle for voting rights was increasingly hopeless. By the end of the 1930s feminists abandoned even these efforts. During the period the Japanese call the Fifteen-Year War, from 1931 to 1945, almost all progressives and advocates of civil rights either went to jail, abandoned their activist movements and lived quietly in the countryside, or tried to find a way to live through the bad times by cooperating with the government.

In the years immediately after the Manchurian Incident, feminists, speaking as "mothers of humanity," outspokenly condemned the war (Ichikawa, quoted in Mackie 2002, 101). "Mothers of humanity" was a maternalist description of women that women's suffrage advocate Ichikawa Fusae had used in a November 1931 newspaper column blasting the Japanese incursion into Manchuria. Feminists' opposition was to military expansionism in China, and not to Japanese colonialism in Korea, which few opposed. By the end of the decade, feminists and others appeared to shift their views on a variety of topics in addition to the war. For example, Ichikawa framed the quest for civil rights as a way for women to "assist the Emperor" (Ichikawa 1935). Today, historians note that the emperor system (*tennōsei*) was one of the roots of Japanese prewar illiberalism and militarism (Ienaga 1978), although in the 1930s few Japanese would have considered the idea of serving the emperor to be any different from the idea of serving the country. Because prewar feminists tried to become part of a now discredited government system, later feminist historians have critiqued them.

When Japan's presence in China and Manchuria became militarized, those Japanese feminists who had been involved in transnational movements felt torn between nationalism and transnationalism. They were disheartened by the differences between what they called the Japanese civilian government's "pacific assurances" about the conflict in Manchuria following the Manchurian Incident of 1931, on one hand, and the aggressive actions of the Japanese military, on the other. Japanese WCTU representatives who traveled to the continent in the early 1930s were naively stunned by their Chinese counterparts' anger at Japan's military actions (Ogawa 2007, 165). The U.S. branch of the Women's International League for Peace and Freedom, previously allies of Japan's WCTU and Women's Peace Association, lobbied the U.S. government to impose sanctions against Japan after the Manchurian Incident. In 1934, Japan's WCTU and YWCA leaders lamented this turn of events in *Japanese Women Speak: A Message from the Christian Women of Japan to the Christian Women of America*, an English-language book published in Boston and targeted to a trans-Pacific American audience:

> *The writer wishes to emphasize the difficult position in which Japanese Christians, and especially Japanese women, who are promoters of international peace and harmony, have been placed.... To some [Japanese] nationalists, the term "internationalism" is synonymous with "Communism," and they regard Christians as dangerous and disloyal; while the peace-workers and pacifists of other countries brand them as cowards, kowtowing humbly before militarism. (Kawai and Kubushiro 1934, 168)*

What these Christian peace advocates in the WCTU and YWCA did not recognize was that their statements of support for transnational friendship through Christianity did not go far enough. In a letter from the Japanese Women's Peace Association to the Chinese Women's Suffrage League in 1932, the Peace Association asked for forgiveness for the Japanese government's actions, thereby placing the onus of unresolved differences on the Chinese victims (Kawai and Kubushiro 1934, 180–181). This failed to address the root causes of transnational tensions—the imperialistic actions of the Japanese government—and, in fact, assumed a kind of "imperialist privilege," which is ironic since Japanese Christian women resented being treated with "white privilege" by Western women, who similarly did not recognize that form of privilege. Gauntlett Tsune, a member of the Japanese WCTU and YWCA, president of Japan's Women's Peace Association, and the international president of the Pan-Pacific Women's Association, also did not anticipate the resistance she would encounter when the Chinese delegates to the 1937 meeting of the Pan-Pacific Women's Association in Vancouver, British Columbia, initially refused to attend because Gauntlett was presiding over that meeting.

Japanese Christian women tried to maintain transnational ties across the Pacific in the late 1930s but were increasingly unable to do so. In 1938, to counter negative images of Japan, the WCTU began publishing an

English-language journal, *Japan Through Women*, to highlight the positive deeds of Japan's women. But this effort failed, and the Japanese WCTU severed its ties to the World WCTU at the outset of the Pacific War in December 1941 (Ogawa 2007, 175). The Japanese WCTU and other Christian groups then refocused their transnationalism toward Asia, rather than toward the Anglo-American countries. To reach out to China, the Japanese WCTU built schools and a medical settlement house called Airinkan (Hall of Neighborly Love) in Beijing and undertook social reform projects, believing these acts of sisterhood would improve Japan's image in China. But these projects were possible only because they were under the umbrella created by Japanese military and colonial protection, and rather than improving Japan's image, they tied the knot of imperialism more tightly (Ogawa 2007, 172).

Like their Christian sisters, with whom they often collaborated in social reform and suffrage organizations, secular feminists also had long-existing links with feminists across the Pacific that were strained by Japan's militarist actions. The secular feminists at first opposed the war, then attempted to persuade their Asian, American, European, and Australian friends that they represented good transnationalism; finally they made accommodations with Japan's wartime government, pivoting away from the West and toward Asia.

Ichikawa Fusae was the secular feminist most often criticized after the war for having replaced her earlier opposition to the state with the kind of wartime collaboration in government-sponsored activities on the home front undertaken by most other secular and Christian feminists. These feminists were almost all immediately reestablished as leaders in government or civil society after the war, but Ichikawa, who later became one of the most highly respected members of the Diet, was purged by the postwar U.S. military occupation (one of only eight women, out of a total of two hundred thousand Japanese, who were purged). She did not deny, as did many of her compatriots, that she had supported the war. Despite or, perhaps, because of this, the occupation recast her in the immediate postwar years as the archetypal feminist nationalist who "sold out" to gain a political voice during the war.

The transnational feminist links of both Christian and secular feminists were severely challenged by Japan's military aggression. The Women's Suffrage League tried to maintain ties to Western friends by publishing *Japanese Women*, an English-language newsletter whose goal was similar to that of the WCTU's *Japan Through Women*, that is, to maintain transnational unity among women. The journal, edited by Ichikawa, printed sixteen issues from 1938 through July 1940. In an introductory essay in the first issue, Ichikawa noted that the goal of the publication was to maintain ties with feminists overseas in time of war: "It is our earnest desire to have our co-workers abroad recognize and be acquainted with the work, insignificant perhaps but nevertheless assiduous effort, of the Japanese women" (Ichikawa 1938).

The November 1938 issue contained an article by the YWCA that recognized that both *Japanese Women* and *Japan Through Women* were explicitly intended to "increase the understanding of foreign women in the problems and interests of Japanese women" (YWCA National Committee 1938). It noted: "In China, although on one hand great destruction is being wrought, on the other hand much sympathy is felt toward the citizens of China, and Japanese women are very eager to participate in medical relief and assistance for civilians and poor people." The writer used the passive voice in the first part of this sentence, not mentioning that the Japanese military was responsible for that destruction. The remaining issues of *Japanese Women*, especially the May 1940 issue, offer much insight into the attempts by the Women's Suffrage League and other transnational feminists to maintain their ties across the Pacific, which were increasingly slipping out of their hands. At the same time, Ichikawa and others wrote enthusiastically about their improving relationships with Chinese women in territory recently pacified and placed under Japanese control. As noted earlier, these ties were possible because of the reach of the Japanese government and military. Japan's feminists appeared unaware of the privileges their nationality conferred.

Ichikawa and two other feminists traveled to Japanese-occupied central China between February 22 and April 11, 1940, and Ichikawa reported on that trip in the May issue of *Japanese Women*. She opened by commenting how deeply she was touched by the devastation of the cities and countryside in that region, and noted that the suffering of war always seemed to hit women and children most heavily. She compared the suffering of the Chinese to that of people in Poland and Norway, countries devastated by the Germans; it is hard to tell if she noticed the irony of the comparison. She wrote that it was a "matter of deep regret that Japan and China found it impossible to solve our mutual problems by peaceful means" (Ichikawa 1940a). Ichikawa went on to write that the new pro-Japan government in Nanjing under Wang Jingwei seemed to be improving conditions for Chinese in that city, and she enthusiastically described meetings with Chinese women leaders who supported Wang's pro-Japanese puppet government. Meetings with other feminists understandably did not go so well, she reported. In addition, she wrote, war between Japan and China might have been avoided if women of the two countries had worked together more closely before the war.

It is clear that she was conflicted between her (vaguely suggested) opposition to Japanese warfare in China, on one hand, and her pride in the improved ties with some Chinese women made possible by that aggression, on the other.

In this article, Ichikawa described her leap from trans-Pacific transnationalism to East Asian transnationalism:

> *We have every reason to regret that educated women of Japan and China have so far only concentrated themselves upon absorbing Occidental civilization and neglected entirely to know each other, paying little attention to our racial affiliation which is extremely close if not identical. . . . I myself have been to America twice, but to China but once, and that very recently.*

But her desire to maintain transnational ties to America was not yet completely eradicated. In fact, she merged Sino-Japanese transnationalism with U.S.-Japan transnationalism. Her belief in the importance and benefit of East Asian transnationalism under the Japanese flag caused her to reach out emotionally for American support:

> *I am really sorry for this war-torn world of ours; there is hardly a spot on earth where some kind of trouble is not threatening. It is indeed a most difficult question how we shall be able to bring about lasting peace out of this chaotic world. . . . I earnestly seek the moral support of the American women deeply concerned with the peace of the world, to help us as best as you can to make our Sino-Japanese women's cooperation a real success.*

In the end, the nationalism of the war years would absorb and unravel the prewar era's transnationalism.

By the middle of the 1930s, women's suffrage was also being challenged, and Japan's militarist government kept suffragists under close surveillance (Molony 2004, 143). In several elections in the early 1930s, the WSL campaigned for candidates they believed to be incorruptible, calling this action an "election purification" movement. They considered this a way to be involved in politics in a uniquely feminine way (they argued that women, who did not have the vote, were inherently purer than men). But increasingly the WSL turned to less overtly political activities as a way of involving disenfranchised women in governance.

The first such issue the WSL turned its attention to was garbage collection and disposal. Since 1932, the residents of Tokyo's Fukagawa ward, where much of Tokyo's trash was dumped and incinerated, had resisted the municipal government's push to increase the number of incinerators (Tamanoi 2009, 835). Rather than moving the incinerators to other areas of Tokyo, the government worked with the WSL to persuade women throughout Tokyo to reduce the overall amount of trash they generated and to separate it into waste that could be incinerated and waste that could not. This was ultimately a political and civic activity, but it masqueraded as a housewives' concern, making it acceptable to Japan's conservative leaders. As two WSL leaders noted in 1934: "It is trash that moves Japan and us women. Although we women have no vote to cast, we can exercise our political rights in local affairs" (Kaneko Shigeri, quoted in Tamanoi 2009). Ichikawa noted that "because [the garbage problem] is related to women's sphere, we were able to receive the support of the authorities and general public without any resistance" (Ichikawa 1934).

The WSL also joined with consumer groups to bring greater competition to the wholesale fish market, which was monopolized by a small group of merchants. The WSL embarked on what they called "the politics of the kitchen" and formed a lobbying group to break up the monopoly. In February 1934 the women's activities achieved success when the Tokyo Municipal Council voted to break up the wholesale monopoly (Ichikawa 1974, 323–325). The last of the feminists' maternalist movements in the 1930s focused on getting the government to pass welfare legislation for poor mothers and children. In 1934 twenty women's organizations lobbied together for the Mother-Child Protection Law. This passed in 1937, giving financial assistance to mothers who were destitute as a result of the loss of their children's fathers in war. The WSL considered this law's passage a victory for women (Tomie 2005, 246). These welfare reforms and women's "politics of the kitchen" activities laid the groundwork for women's greater social and political involvement after the war (see Chapter 9).

The ideological trends in feminism can be seen in the changing resolutions that came out of the annual National Women's Suffrage Conventions that were held throughout the 1930s. The first convention took place in 1930, when feminists were optimistic about getting the vote (see Chapter 5). At the third convention, in May 1932, the participants roundly condemned the recent Manchurian Incident and the rise of "fascism" in Japan (Ichikawa 1932). At the fourth convention, in February 1933, the conveners had hoped to pass a resolution calling for the reduction of military spending, but they were unable to do so since the Social Democratic Women's League, a proletarian suffragist group, had come to view continental expansion as a way of helping the desperately poor in Japan, who were suffering during the Depression. The fifth convention, held in 1934, supported resolutions for peace, for benefits to families of soldiers killed in the war, for cooperation with women around the world, for birth control, and for mother-child protection legislation. By the sixth convention, held in 1935, the suffragists' views had shifted to calling on the government to give women the vote so they might help the government in this time of "emergency" or "crisis" (terms used by the government as euphemisms for war). The conventions were supplanted in 1938 by the Women's National Emergency Congress (also called the Women's Conference on Current Problems) when the rise of militarism at home made suffrage conferences suspect (Nishikawa 1997, 53). That marked the end of conventions focused on women's civil rights until after World War II.

By far the largest women's organizations during the long prewar and war period were those run by the government. In 1931 the Ministry of Education created the Greater Japan Federated Women's Association (Dai Nippon Rengo Fujinkai). In 1932 the army took over an originally independent patriotic women's group called the National Defense Women's Association (Kokubō Fujinkai), and the Home Ministry took over an older nationalist group called the Patriotic Women's Association (Aikoku Fujinkai). The independent women's organizations discussed earlier, both Christian and secular, initially resented these government-affiliated organizations: they were run by men, they took potential members away from the groups dedicated to women's rights, and they dealt with women from the perspective of mobilizing them to serve the state through stereotyped women's roles. When the autonomous groups were forced to disband around 1940, most members of those groups came to accept the government organizations as venues for women's agency outside the home, as well as suitable means for serving the nation. The membership of these organizations, taken together, reached nineteen million by the end of the decade. These women saw soldiers off to war, packed kits for them, and were expected to act as "good wives and wise mothers" to serve the state.

Full-scale warfare between China and Japan broke out in July 1937, and the government increased efforts to mobilize society spiritually, materially, and militarily. In response, the WSL and seven other nongovernmental women's groups, such as the YWCA and the WCTU, joined together in a Federation of Japanese Women's Organizations (Nihon Fujin Dantai Renmei). It was this federation that, together with a dozen other Japanese women's organizations, held the Women's National Emergency Congress that replaced the National Women's Suffrage Convention in 1938. The congress promoted the idea that working with the state was a way for women to empower one another and to serve other women and children on the home front.

In December 1939 the Federation of Japanese Women's Organizations joined with the government-affiliated patriotic women's associations in a huge meeting in Tokyo, during which they called on the government to allow women to serve the state by aiding the economy (Women's Conference 1940). The WSL believed—naively, as it turned out—that this collaboration would persuade the nineteen million members of the government-led organizations to adopt a pro-suffrage position, and that the government could be persuaded to "hand over to women themselves" the leadership of the huge national organizations (Ichikawa 1940b, 4). In addition, Ichikawa wrote, by doing essential work on behalf of the nation, Japanese women would gain rights, just as Western women had after World War I: "We sincerely hope that the day may soon come when we too may be more fully equipped to work not only for the welfare of the nation but for the world and the humanity at large to which one half of the human race belongs" (Ichikawa 1938, 1–2).

In February 1942, the government amalgamated all Japanese women's organizations into one large group, the Greater Japan Women's Association (Dai Nippon Fujinkai), which included the government-directed groups as well as the more progressive feminist, Christian, and social reform groups that had not yet been disbanded. Disappointing many feminists, the leadership of this association continued to be male. Trade unions were terminated and laborers were brought under the Patriotic Industry Association, so union and socialist women's groups ceased to exist as well. Many leaders of formerly autonomous women's groups were placed on national boards. Ichikawa herself was placed on the board of the Patriotic Press Association, which monitored the press; it was her membership on this press board that caused her to be purged by the postwar U.S. occupation (Molony 2005, 60). There were no autonomous women's organizations left in Japan after 1942, and if women wished to have a voice or improve conditions on the home front during the war, they were forced to join the government. As it turned out, women were outnumbered by men and ignored on virtually all the boards on which they served (Ichikawa 1942). Many women's rights activists accepted the wartime government's invitation to join national organizations because they hoped to show that women deserved a role in the state (Garon 1993, 7–8).

In the first decades after World War II, historians and many others considered women's wartime cooperation with the state to have been unavoidable in the context of the times. In addition, they applauded feminists' involvement in national organizations as the first steps toward equality. However, after the widespread exposure of the "comfort women" issue (to be discussed in detail later in this chapter), this attitude gave way to a major reassessment in the 1980s of prewar feminists and their quest for inclusion in a state that had carried out heinous anti-woman atrocities.

Gender, Diaspora, and Empire

Japanese men and women were geographically mobile in the decades after the 1880s, when the Japanese government lifted the restrictions on emigration (see Chapter 4). Although the largest number of migrants intended their stay to be temporary, the overseas stays often became permanent, whether across the Pacific or, more commonly, in Northeast Asia. Potential migrants viewed Taiwan (a colony of Japan since 1895), Korea (a colony since 1910), and Manchuria (a puppet state since 1932) as parts of Japan. But in those territories, gender played a role that was different from that in the Japanese homeland and different from that in Western colonies as well.

Most significant was that Japanese women outnumbered Japanese men in Korea in the first years of colonial possession. This was opposite to the pattern of European and American imperialism, where men vastly outnumbered women in the initial years of those countries' colonies. The largest number of colonial Japanese women were in the sex trades. Japanese-owned newspapers in Korea praised Japanese sex workers for bringing civilization to some of their rough customers, especially Russians in Northeast Asia. Other Japanese women sought work in Korea and Manchuria as professionals, since opportunities to work as journalists, shopkeepers, colonial administrators, and even schoolteachers were more limited in the home country. Middle-class Japanese women also sought occupations in colonial Taiwan (Sokolsky 2014). This pattern was similar to that of European women, who also looked for opportunities in the colonies, often in the professions or in religious proselytizing, that were less available to them at home. In terms of sexuality, Japanese men and women in the colonies behaved differently than each other and differently than European men and women in their colonies. Japanese women were more likely to marry Korean men, but Japanese men greatly preferred wives or mistresses who were Japanese; European colonial men often had affairs with local women, while European women were largely either unmarried or married to European men (Brooks 2005). Korean men who migrated to Japan to work in the interwar period far outnumbered Korean women in Japan. Virtually all the Korean women in Japan were married to Korean men, while a number of Korean men married Japanese women (Smith 2005).

By the 1930s, as Japan was intensifying the development of its possessions in both Northeast Asia and Taiwan, the percentage of diasporic Japanese men jumped rapidly ahead of the percentage of women. Entrepreneurs set up massive production facilities, mining operations, and hydroelectric plants, which for the most part employed both Japanese and local men rather than women. There were more than half a million Japanese of both genders in Korea by 1930 and more than two hundred thousand in Manchuria. Hundreds of thousands more were Japanese military men in Korea and Manchuria. Many Japanese also migrated to the islands the League of Nations had given Japan as protectorates after World War I; in 1935, for example, fifty thousand Japanese lived on tiny Saipan. In addition, large numbers of Japanese migrated to cities throughout non-Japanese-controlled East Asia, including twenty-six thousand in Shanghai, where they played a large role in banking and textiles. Each of those cities had its own Japanese women's groups, newspapers, and medical clinics. These kinds of ethnic communities developed in North and South America as well, where the Japanese, like all other immigrant groups, published their own newspapers and had their own community organizations, Buddhist temples, and Christian churches.

The war years were a terrible time for most Japanese migrants. And yet even during the 1940s some Japanese women and men continued to live adventurous lives in East Asia. For example, Hayashi Fumiko and Yoshiya Nobuko, two highly popular writers (see Chapter 6), were part of the first "Pen Squadron," male and female writers sent by the Ministry of Information to the front lines in China to report on the war and to give encouragement to Japanese soldiers. Hayashi wrote on assignment for major Japanese newspapers; she was the first Japanese woman to enter Nanjing after it fell to Japanese forces, and the first Japanese civilian to enter Hankou. In 1940 and 1941, she lectured throughout the Japanese empire, from Japan to Korea, Manchuria, and occupied China (Horiguchi 2009, 67). As the existence of the Pen Squadron indicates, the extent of the Japanese empire was measured not only by its male soldiers' wartime conquests but also by the reach of some civilian women.

Calling Manzhouguo a "new paradise," the Japanese military tried to entice five million young farmers to settle there to release the pressure of overpopulation at home and to establish a strong ethnically Japanese population base. Village leaders in Japan were recruited to sell this community emigration program, but few people initially took the bait. In 1938 the

BOX 8.1

Japanese Americans in Internment Camps in the United States

In North America, 110,000 native-born American citizens of Japanese ancestry and Japanese immigrants—who were not eligible for citizenship because of racist anti-Asian laws—who resided in the western region of the United States were placed in concentration camps (also called internment camps) under Executive Order 9066 of February 19, 1942. Many remained there until 1946, losing their homes, livelihoods, and property. Young men could get out of the camps by joining segregated units in the U.S. military, but the opportunity to serve in the military did not exist for young women.

Both young women and men, if they were fortunate, could get out by attending universities, most of them east of the Mississippi, and most of them religious schools that did not harbor the anti-Japanese attitudes more common in the western region. Japanese American students began to attend these colleges and universities in 1942 and 1943, and women made up about 40 percent of one group of a thousand students able to leave the camps in this way. Others were approved to leave to take up jobs that needed to be filled during the war. Three hundred women found positions in nursing. Others undertook office work, factory and agricultural work, and domestic service. By 1945, 37 percent of men over the age of sixteen and 63 percent of women over sixteen had left the camps. Most who were able to do so were young; older family members had few such chances to be released. This changed family dynamics radically, as women who left the camps were forced to develop greater self-reliance, living among non-Japanese Americans who might not readily accept them; in addition, their income contributed to their families (Matsumoto 1984, 11–13).

Similar camps were set up by the Canadian government, which incarcerated twenty-two thousand people. And the United States rounded up 2,264 Japanese immigrants in Peru and shipped them to American concentration camps.

colonial authorities began recruiting boys from thirteen to sixteen years of age to be part of Youth Brigades stationed in Manzhouguo. The boys soon became depressed and homesick, so a year later the colonial authorities began recruiting girls they called "continental brides" to join the boys. The Youth Brigades members and their young brides eventually made up one-third of the total of 380,000 Japanese farmers in Manzhouguo. The Japanese military later conscripted the adult male migrants and Youth Brigade boys, leaving the women and children behind to continue farming. In August 1945 the Soviets invaded Manzhouguo. Members of the Japanese military used all available transportation for their own escape, abandoning the women and children to rape, slaughter, and starvation at the hands of the Russians. More than half a million Japanese subjects, including hundreds of thousands of Koreans, were hauled off to Siberia, and at least three hundred thousand were never heard from again. Some thirty thousand Japanese children survived because their Japanese mothers were able to leave them with kindly Chinese neighbors. Raised as Chinese, many of these children tried to find their Japanese families after diplomatic relations between China and Japan resumed in the 1970s (Lipman, Molony, and Robinson 2012, 314–315).

Other overseas Japanese suffered greatly at the end of the war. While soldiers and sailors were the archetypes of Japanese masculinity, women were eventually used as symbols of unflappable resistance to the powerful Anglo-American military. As historian Haruko Cook notes, this symbolism was created by journalists, and it helped to prolong the war (H. Cook, 2005). An American journalist's incorrect report that thousands of women were jumping to their deaths rather than surrender to American forces on Saipan was picked up by the Japanese press and published in Japan as well. (As Cook notes, most civilians actually did surrender.) For American readers, this report was an indication that the Japanese were fanatical and would never surrender. The report had a similar effect on Japanese readers, encouraging the men to keep struggling even as civilian women bravely went to their deaths. But the gendered dichotomy that had long "positioned men exclusively as warriors on the battlefield and women as mere supporters and providers of comfort on the home front" (Frühstück 2014, 163) was itself modified by the end of the war. Nurses worked on the battlefield and high school girls were trained in firing guns, and in June 1945 the Volunteer Military Service Laws were passed: women between seventeen and forty were to be conscripted into the National Volunteer Combat Corps, and the Greater Japan Women's Association was dissolved and its members reorganized into the Combat Corps (Frühstück 2014, 172). Two months later, the war was over.

Women were not, however, inducted into the army as soldiers before the end of the war. The combatant experience belonged entirely to men. For many young men of the war era, "the soldier embodied Japan and what it meant to be a Japanese man" (T. Cook 2005, 259). As we saw in Chapter 4, this was a constructed type of masculinity, as there had been no army tradition for commoners in Japan until the end of the nineteenth century. In many ways, Japanese soldiers resembled those of other industrialized countries; even the brutal atrocities that are still used to define the Japanese military man have parallels in every war and in every country. The most notorious, the Nanjing Massacre, lasted for six weeks after Japanese troops entered the Chinese city of Nanjing on December 13, 1937. During this time, around two hundred thousand people were killed, of whom only about twenty thousand were men of military age (the actual numbers will never be known, but most historians believe these are reasonable estimates). Tens of thousands of women were raped, and an additional sixty thousand refugees outside the city limits were killed or starved to death. The scale of this atrocity is enormous, but the events themselves and the reasons for them are not unique. The historical explanations for these events, as for similar atrocities around the world, include the soldiers' reactions to the loss of their comrades, harsh hierarchical treatment within the Japanese military, a mob mentality, and the dehumanizing of the enemy.

One additional explanation for the soldiers' actions, which was particularly important to Japanese military leaders at that time, was related to their view of masculine sexuality: the atrocities were blamed on a medical notion of uncontrollable male sexuality. This view—that war atrocities are caused by men who cannot control their sexuality—was not common in military thinking elsewhere, nor in Japan today. To control the incidence of rape in areas under Japanese military occupation, they reasoned, the army should set up a system of "comfort stations." Battlefield sex stations had been deployed earlier, but the systematic building of stations to follow the advancing army occurred after the Nanjing Massacre. The workers in these stations were young women who were either enticed with promises of factory work and then turned into sex slaves or simply kidnapped. At the time, the term used for these women was *ianfu* (comfort women), but in reality they were military sexual slaves. Korean, Chinese, Japanese, Vietnamese, Dutch, Filipina, and other women made up this army of sex slaves. Historians dispute the total numbers, but most estimate that there were between 150,000 and 200,000, of whom 80 to 90 percent were Korean women and girls. The experiences of women in this gendered atrocity are discussed later in this chapter.

The Home Front in Japan and the End of the War

In 1940 the prime minister, Konoe Fumimaro, placed all civic organizations, such as labor unions, political parties, and women's groups, under the rule of mass state organizations. One of these was the Imperial Rule Assistance

Association (IRAA), which was intended to coordinate many aspects of daily life. In the end, however, it really had just one important role: the distribution of rationed rice and other commodities. Every population center was organized into neighborhood associations under the IRAA, and because most men were away at war, women came to play a leadership role in these associations, arranging for distribution of rice to all members of the community. These leadership functions helped train women for political roles after the war, when women gained full civil rights.

The National General Mobilization Law, passed in 1938, was intended to control business, labor, and many other parts of the wartime economy. In 1941 a labor draft was set up under this law, requiring all men ages sixteen to forty who were not in the military and all unmarried women ages sixteen to twenty-five to register for the labor draft. Men and women were treated differently because the ideology of "good wife, wise mother" made it difficult to draft women with responsibilities to their husbands and children (Miyake 1991). By the end of the war, one million adult men and one million adult women had been drafted into war production, and three million children had been pulled from school to work in munitions factories. Additionally, two million Koreans and Chinese were taken from their homelands to work in Japan's mines and munitions plants.

"Extravagance," the Japanese state told its subjects from 1938 till 1945, "is the enemy!" (Havens 1978, 10). But what was extravagance? By the end of the war, the average person in Japan was allowed only a starvation-level ration of under 1,000 calories per day (Earhart 2008, 127). Extravagance meant something else—that is, consuming frivolously during difficult times. Here clothing played a role. Because gender was an important part of defining the nation, the control of extravagant clothing was also gendered. But in Japan, unlike other nations at war, just making simpler clothes and using cheaper fabrics would not do. In previous decades, Western-style clothing had been increasingly seen as more "functional"—that is, more practical, cooler in summer, and cheaper. Working women (for example, nurses, teachers, and bus conductors) had worn Western clothing before the war (Ajima 2011, Gordon 2011). But if Japan was fighting a war against Western powers, how could clothing be designed both to save resources and to maintain nationalistic spirits?

The army began to discuss appropriate civilian national clothing as early as 1930. Men's military uniforms, adopted from Western styles more than sixty years earlier, were the original "functional" clothing. Several branches of the government organized committees to design and promote national dress, first for men and later for women. Wearing national dress was encouraged

During World War II, the Japanese government urged women to wear "standard dress"—the simplified dresses on the right—or monpe trousers. This encouraged frugality and allowed women to work more efficiently.
PHOTO BY KEYSTONE-FRANCE\GAMMA-RAPHO VIA GETTY IMAGES

but never required under Japanese law. In 1937 the government announced a plan to develop a *kokuminfuku*—a national uniform or literally "citizen's dress"—for men. When the government eventually got around to convening an advisory board to design clothing for women, in March 1941, there was to be no national uniform for ladies. Instead, the women's designs called for *hyōjun fuku*, or "standard dress." Only men were considered *kokumin*—citizens. Some of the guidelines for the standard dress were the same as for the men's uniform—it had to be economical and easy to move in. But getting women to wear the clothing was difficult. The Greater Japan Women's Association took it as their task to persuade women to wear these simple clothes. The cover of *Nippon Fujin*, the association's magazine, showed a gentle housewife in a standard dress. But *monpe*, the baggy pants worn by women farmers, became the real uniform of Japanese women during the war. *Monpe* were one of the styles approved as standard dress by the government, although it was clear that the government really preferred functional dresses or very simplified kimonos for women. Women made *monpe* out of worn-out dresses and kimonos. No one required women to wear *monpe*, but poverty and shortages drove women into *monpe*, perhaps even more than practicality and a patriotic desire to avoid extravagance.

The war ended with Japan's surrender on August 15, 1945. Almost 3 million Japanese had died, of whom 1.7 million were military men. The rest were civilians who died from starvation (the raw materials used for fertilizer production had been turned over to munitions production, so there was very little food in Japan at the end of the war) or in air raids, most of them firebombings. Two atomic bombs were dropped, on August 6 (Hiroshima) and August 9 (Nagasaki). Nine million people were left homeless. The old Japan came to an end, and as we shall see in Chapter 9, gender relations were one of the areas that changed radically after the war.

KOREA

The outbreak of the second Sino-Japanese War in 1937 and the subsequent Pacific War (1941–1945) had deep ramifications for Korean society, as Korea became the crossroads for Japan's military ambitions throughout Asia and the Pacific. With the passage of the 1938 National General Mobilization Law, the colonial government began to regulate and deploy both material and human resources to support Japan's "sacred war" (*sŏngjŏn*). Heavy industries were actively developed to cater to the war effort. Under the slogan "Japan and Korea as a single body" (*naisen ittai*), the colonial government made full use of educational and community programs to try to turn the Korean populace into completely obedient and loyal subjects who would be willing to sacrifice themselves for the Japanese emperor and Japan's war efforts on the home front as well as on the battlefield. The stated aim of the Greater East Asia Co-Prosperity Sphere propaganda campaign was to free Asian nations from the threat of Western imperialism, but its true motivation was to secure Japan's position as the dominant power in Asia and the Pacific in shaping the new international order.

The total mobilization campaign and the increasingly forceful assimilation policies in late colonial Korea had a significant impact on the lives of women on all fronts—economic, political, cultural, and practical. While the conventional ideal of woman as "wise mother, good wife" continued to be promoted, women were made to feel that they could make a vital contribution to the war effort by saving daily resources, sending their sons to the battlefront, working in military factories and farming lands, serving as nurses on the battlefield, or actively collaborating with the Japanese power in the distribution of wartime propaganda. It was also during this turbulent period that the infamous human trafficking system, euphemistically referred to as the "comfort women" program, was initiated, forcing a vast number of women into service as sex slaves in Japanese encampments throughout Asia and the Pacific.

Mobilization of Women in Heavy Industries

After the Manchurian Incident in 1931, Japan set in place various policies that made the Korean peninsula a strategic location for Japan's ambitions to become the central power in Northeast Asia. As Japan's involvement in military excursions escalated in the late 1930s, there was an increased demand for industrial production of goods for use by the military. Thus a number of legal provisions were enacted to effectively recruit and draft colonized subjects into heavy industries that served the needs of the military. For instance, the 1939 ordinance on the National Labor Draft gave the emperor full power to conscript any of his subjects in Japan or any of its colonies into labor that was vital to the war effort. The 1941 National Registration System required Korean men and women between the ages of twelve and forty "to register with the government for potential enlistment into war-related services." Furthermore, the Patriotic Labor Association Law of 1941 and the establishment of the Wartime Student Organization in 1943 essentially turned secondary and vocational schools into institutes for training laborers (J. Kim 2007, 87–89).

It was within this rapid mobilization of laborers that young girls and women were actively recruited to work in heavy industries that were needed by the military. The Women's Labor Volunteer Corps (*kŭllo chŏngsindae*) was one prominent organization that worked to recruit school-age girls and recent female graduates from elementary and middle schools, as well as unmarried women over fourteen years of age, to work in heavy industries. The promise of higher wages also attracted women who were already in the workforce as factory workers and domestic servants. Schoolteachers, community leaders, local representatives, government officials, and the print media were all instrumental in mobilizing girls and young women to sign up for these new work opportunities. Prior to the war, women laborers were largely concentrated in light industries, and that was also true after the war; however, during wartime an unprecedented range of jobs, particularly in heavy industries, were opened to women. According to an August 26, 1944, article in *Maeil sinbo*, the official newspaper of the colonial government, women worked in "mining, electricity, communications, machinery, aircraft production, shipbuilding, chemicals, ceramics, carpentry, and building and construction" (J. Kim 2007, 91).

Those women laborers were stationed at factories throughout East Asia. They underwent as much as six months of job training before commencing their work. The lives they led in the dormitories and factories were heavily routinized. For example, at the Fujikoshi steel factory in Toyama, Japan, both Japanese and Korean workers had a rigid daily schedule, rising by 5:00 a.m. to greet their dormitory parents and to recite the empire narrative (*hwangminhwa sŏsa* in Korean; *kōminka jiji* in Japanese) before breakfast. They would then report to the factory, where they would work until noon, break for lunch, then go back to work until there was a short afternoon break at 3:00 p.m. They would then return to work until 5:00 p.m., when they would head back to the dormitory to eat dinner and be in bed by 9:00 p.m. (J. Kim 2007, 95). These routines, as well as the radio programs and visual propaganda, such as posters, helped to fashion the identity, mentality and lifestyle of the workers. Very little is known about the actual lives of those women deployed to work in heavy industries in late colonial Korea. However, the Korean labor historian Janice Kim argues that the bits of oral histories available indicate that female workers "became more independent and powerful through the unparalleled experience of wage work." Kim sums up, "Although oppressed and victimized in political memory, many working women of late colonial Korea, in transcending the boundaries of class and gender, saw themselves as pioneers" (J. Kim 2007, 99).

Wartime Domesticity

The escalating demands of the war effort, especially after the outbreak of the Sino-Japanese War in 1937, caused Japan to seek fuller control over human and material resources in its colonies. Various legal provisions, such as the National Spiritual Mobilization program, enacted in 1937, and the National General Mobilization Law, passed in 1938, signaled a dramatic shift in colonial policies. Such mobilization efforts aimed not only to advance economic and military development in support of Japan's war but also to maximize colonial subjects' loyalty to the empire. Under the slogan of *naisen ittai*, the colonial authority implemented policies to compel loyalty to the Japanese emperor through measures that either eliminated old links to Korean identity and culture or established new links to Japan (although Koreans were not invariably passive and managed to complicate the colonial policies in a number of different ways. See Henry 2014; Kim 2013). One strategy was to introduce major educational reforms that emphasized Japanese-language proficiency while eliminating instruction in Korean language, history, and culture—crucial elements in constructing Korean national identity. Other policies mandated attendance at Shintō shrines and required Koreans to adopt Japanese names (*ch'angsi kyemyŏng*). These efforts toward total mobilization were made in virtually every domain of society—families, schools, municipal communities, neighborhood associations, and print media. By 1940, there were some 350,000 Neighborhood Patriotic Associations. Each association comprised ten households, and it served as the basic unit for collecting contributions, drafting soldiers, imposing surveillance on the local community, and mobilizing the populace for everyday rituals (such as "silent prayer time," devoted to prayers for the safety of soldiers fighting on the front lines and the souls of those who had fallen on the battlefield). These associations served to mobilize Koreans in the interest of the Japanese war effort through every conceivable mechanism—formal legal measures, aesthetic images, everyday rituals, and false promises.

During wartime the role of women underwent a major change. The traditional women's role as homemaker and "wise mother, good wife" continued, but in times of military conflict the services of women were needed beyond the private, domestic arena. They were expected to play an important role for the state. The active intervention of the state in the domestic sphere unfolded through a wide range of campaign and reform efforts. In those campaigns, traditional Korean family life was criticized as wasteful, unscientific, and ineffective. Thus the typical Korean home was subject to major reform, and the typical housewife was envisioned as the central figure in enacting those reforms.

At a very mundane level, women were asked to reform their standard daily practices in a way that contributed to management of the emergency situation. For example, instead of the traditional white clothing, they wore simple colored clothing that would require less time and expense to maintain. They were told that the daily diet should be minimalist—a bowl of soup and kimch'i for breakfast, and cold rice for lunch. They had to save energy, recycle waste, eliminate unnecessary rituals and gatherings, and work harder.

Women were also seen as the moral compass for their children, instilling in them a sense of patriotism for the Japanese empire and fealty to the emperor. Mothers were expected to take pride in sending their sons to war to defend the empire. The visual representations of women in late colonial Korea often portrayed them waving Japanese flags for the war effort, reinforcing "their important duties as individuals who could meet both the demands of the family and the state" (M. Kim 2007, 492).

Once Japan's war plans expanded, especially after the Pacific War began in 1941, domestic practices were thought to be crucial to the war effort. On the home front, women were deeply engaged in various forms of "comfort culture." In addition to the horrific history of the "comfort women" (described in the next section), most women were recruited to participate in farewell rituals for the Japanese soldiers heading to the war zone in order to "comfort" them. Japan's spectacular success in military expansion convinced some Koreans that supporting Japan by contributing to its war efforts would be an expedient way for Koreans to gain power and citizenship.

BOX 8.2

A Pledge to Become a "Mother of the Imperial Army": Gender and Wartime Collaboration

In the grand scheme of total mobilization, the role of Korean intellectuals was conspicuous. A group of Korean elites actively participated in giving public lectures and writing essays to urge Koreans to devote themselves to the Japanese emperor and the Japanese Imperial Army. In contemporary Korea, these elites have come to be thought of as "collaborators," and women intellectuals are a subclass who placed special emphasis on the role of woman as mother and housewife. The following essay by Ch'oe Chŏnghŭi (1912–1990), a well-known novelist, captures how deeply the propaganda of naisen ittai penetrated into the everyday life of the Korean populace, including little children. The title of the essay, which was published in *Tae tonga* in June 1942, is "Mother of the Imperial Army."

> *I'm trying not to be weak. I have been trying to be strong. I'm trying hard to build up the courage and strength to block a bullet if I have to. I would swallow fire if it would give me the strength I desire.*
>
> *The thing that inspired this desire for greater courage in me was not the Sino-Japanese War [which broke out in 1937] or Japan's military conflict with the United States and the United Kingdom. Nor was it due to my mother's discipline or my teachers' incitements. It was my 10-year-old child, a student in elementary school, who inspired me.*
>
> *This child, who usually hates being woken up in the morning, embraces the siren signaling Emperor worship. He jumps out of bed and stands firmly facing the East. When pictures of the Emperor or some other person in a position of leadership appear in the newspaper, he straightens his posture and bows before them. He salutes when the Imperial Force appears in the war news at the theatre. When the Emperor appears on screen, he rises to his feet and removes his cap. He*

(continued)

expects everyone to show respect in this way. He always says to me, "Why aren't you standing? Stand with me."

Honestly, it has been some time since I have been able to pay the tribute as unselfconsciously as he does it. I was reluctant to follow along in front of others, but I never tried to stop my son. And gradually I did begin to follow his lead because I realized he was heading in the right direction.

One day, he asked me "Mom, are you going to cry if I die in a war?" This came out of nowhere, and I was dumbfounded. Yes, I know that he is expressing the proper attitude, but he is my one and only child! There is no mother who doesn't adore her child, and I wouldn't trade the world for this dear little one. I couldn't help but be astonished and heartbroken at the thought of his death.

I was struck speechless for a while, and he made a face that implied he thought I was wrong. That made me search my heart once again. And then I embraced my boy and told him, "I won't cry because you're dying for a good cause." And then my child came alive. He said, "Very well, then I shall sing 'My Child, You Were Strong' for you." He rolled up his sleeves as if he were getting ready to run onto the battlefield at that very moment.

I forgot my concerns, and I just hugged my son tightly. "I won't just sing. If you die in war, I'll dance in your honor." I looked at him with a smile as big and bright as the one he was giving me. . . .

Let's fulfill the wishes of our precious sons. Let's become women who follow the will of God. This will make us good mothers. Is it so difficult to entrust our sons to the nation? Women in every other nation on the face of the earth do so. Why don't we do what they do? We have all the same features that they have. Please, I beg of you, reform yourself to become a strong mother who never has to be told by her son, "Mom, you're wrong." I pledge to become such a mother. I make that promise to God. As the old adage says, "A woman is weak but a mother is strong." (Applause)

Sex Slavery: The "Comfort Woman" System

In times of war, unspeakable violence is often visited upon women and children. During the Pacific War, one of history's most appalling examples of this truism was perpetrated against the women of Asia. As many as two hundred thousand Asian women were drafted into service in military brothels for Japanese soldiers throughout Asia and the Pacific. The vast majority of these individuals, between 80 and 90 percent, were Korean women, most of whom came from impoverished peasant families. Although "sexual slavery by the Japanese military" would be a more precise label, the euphemistic term "comfort women" (*wianbu*) has come to be more widely used. The horrific experiences that thousands of women underwent came to be widely known only during the early 1990s, and they remain a critical unresolved "historical problem" in the relations between Japan and neighboring Asian countries. The lack of a formal apology and proper reparations to the victims of the wartime sexual slavery remains a source of tension to this day.

The issue of military sexual slavery must be understood in the context of Japan's total mobilization campaign and its imperial ambitions over Asia and the Pacific. During the Japanese occupation of Nanjing in 1937, members of the Japanese military committed a massive number of civilian rapes. This caused alarm within the military, and in response the general staff devised a plan that involved the operation of military brothels to "comfort" soldiers and build morale. Military brothels had been built by the Japanese military as early as 1905, but it was after the Nanjing Massacre that military brothels were more systematically established in Japanese-occupied territories, including Malaysia, Singapore, Indonesia, the Philippines, Okinawa, Manchuria, China, and the Pacific islands.

The Japanese government has denied playing an active role in the establishment and proliferation of military brothels during the Pacific War. However, in his 1978 memoir, entitled "Nijūsansai de sanzennin no sōshikikan" (Commander of 3,000 men at age 23), Nakasone Yasuhiro, who served as prime minister from 1982 to 1987, offered a depiction of the military sexual slavery system. In 1942 he was a lieutenant paymaster in Japan's Imperial Navy, stationed at Balikpapan on the island of Borneo. His brief was to oversee and complete the construction of an airfield; however, his men were consumed with gambling, fighting, and sexual misconduct, slowing the progress of the project. To better manage these distractions, he decided to build a brothel. His "success in procuring four Indonesian women 'mitigated the mood' of his troops so well that he was commended in a naval report," according to a *New York Times* article published on November 4, 2014. Nakasone's solution was replicated by thousands of Japanese officers in Japanese encampments throughout Asia and the Pacific. Those brothels were under direct orders and received financial support from the Japanese

Ministry of the Army and the Ministry of the Navy. They were largely managed by the Japanese army, although some were run by civilians. Some already established brothels were conscripted for use by the military as well.

Many young girls and women were forcibly drafted or kidnapped to work in these military brothels, while others were lured by local agents with false promises of good jobs in factories. Some have argued that there were also other women who "chose to leave home, not out of economic necessity but in search of independence and freedom from domestic violence" (Soh 2004, 170). Most of the girls pressed into service were between eleven and twenty-four years of age. It is said that Korean girls were particularly targeted because strict adherence to Confucian ideology meant that most young Korean women who had not married were virgins. There were even "virgin clubs" in the southwestern provinces of Korea, from which a large number of girls were drafted to work at the military brothels.

At these brothels, referred to as "comfort stations," each woman was assigned to a very small compartment in a shanty where she was forced to have intercourse with visiting Japanese soldiers. Those who were not obedient were beaten, burned, or sometimes stabbed by the soldiers. Brothels were strictly regulated in terms of allotted time, fees, and other rules. In particular, in order to protect soldiers from contracting venereal diseases, women were periodically checked and treated by visiting doctors. When they contracted a venereal disease, they were given an injection known as "No. 606"—Salvarsan, a notorious antibiotic that contained arsenic and also worked to prevent pregnancy.

According to testimony of both soldiers and victims, after the Japanese were defeated in World War II, many of the women who had worked in the military brothels were either forced to commit suicide or sealed in caves and left to die. Others were simply abandoned, left stranded wherever they were, generally thousands of miles from their homes. Some women managed to get back home despite the obstacles they encountered on the way. Once they had arrived home, however, they were not welcomed by their families. Instead, they were stigmatized as "dirty women" because of the work they had been forced into at the brothels. Abandoned by their own families and scarred by the sexual and medical abuse they had suffered in the military brothels, these women were largely unable to lead normal lives. For decades they lived on the margins of society, ostracized, completely forgotten, erased from history, just barely scratching out a survival existence.

It took more than fifty years to bring out the long-suppressed history of these women. In 1990 South Korean feminist scholars and activists succeeded in breaking the long silence of the comfort women by founding the Korean Council for the Women Drafted into Military Sexual Slavery by Japan. The council made the following demands of the Japanese government:

1. Acknowledgment of the Japanese government's crimes against the former military sex slaves
2. Disclosure of the complete details of those crimes
3. A formal apology for the crimes
4. Erection of a memorial for victims
5. Payment of reparations to the victims and their families
6. Inclusion of the history of military sexual slavery in Japanese school textbooks and educational curricula
7. Appropriate punishment of the criminals (Park 1997, 109)

In 1991 Kim Haksun (1924–1997), a former comfort woman, was the first to come forward to tell her story in public (see Box 8.3). Gradually other comfort women followed suit, and eventually they filed a landmark lawsuit against Japan "for drafting them into service for the sexual satiation of the Japanese soldiers during the Pacific War," although ultimately there was no resolution to the case. In 1993, based on a two-year government investigation, Chief Cabinet Secretary Kono Yohei made an official statement that women were indeed forced to work in the brothels; however, the statement did not explicitly state that the Japanese military was directly involved. Conservative Japanese politicians have continued to assert that comfort women were merely paid prostitutes and the Japanese government was not legally responsible for setting up comfort stations. Those politicians have vehemently rejected any demand for a formal apology. Many Japanese political leaders, including prime ministers, have regularly visited the Yasukuni Shrine, a shrine commemorating the war dead, including a number of high-profile war criminals, which stirs further outrage among people in Asia and beyond.

In addition to the controversy over a formal apology and appropriate reparations, it is worth mentioning that there were major differences between the postwar tribunals in Europe and those held in Asia on the issue of reparations to the former comfort women. In 1948 the Batavia Court charged thirteen Japanese soldiers with conscripting into sexual service Dutch women who were living in Indonesia at that time. Three of those soldiers were ultimately executed. In contrast, no charge has ever been brought to the Tokyo War Crimes Trials for the sexual enslavement of Asian women

(Choi 1997, vi). The issue of comfort women has remained a thorny issue in Asia because of the Japanese government's persistent denial of involvement in the trafficking of Asian women for the purpose of sexual slavery and its refusal to offer proper reparations to the victims.

In a significant way, the military sexual slavery system during World War II was far from a singular tragedy. It can be understood in a larger historical, political, and cultural context. As anthropologist Sarah Soh argues, Korean comfort women embody the issue of "gendered structural violence" because "the wartime exploitation and lifelong suffering of Korean survivors arose not only within the comfort women system and the broader parameters of Japanese colonialism and fifteen years of war, but also within Korean patriarchy and its political economy under colonial rule" (Soh 2008, xii–xiii).

BOX 8.3

Testimony of a Former "Comfort Woman," Kim Haksun

In 1991 Kim Haksun was the first of the Korean comfort women to come forward in public to share her story. The following is a brief description of the life of Kim Haksun. Parts of her testimony were drawn from *True Stories of the Korean Comfort Women* (Howard 1995).

Kim Haksun was born in 1924, in Jilin, Manchuria. Unfortunately, her father died soon after her birth. Unable to find means to support the family in Manchuria, Kim's mother decided to move back to P'yŏngyang, where Kim grew up and attended a missionary school. Kim's mother remarried when Kim was fourteen, and Kim was sent to a foster family that trained *kisaeng* (entertainment girls). Although she graduated from the *kisaeng* academy after two years' training, she was only seventeen years of age, too young to be licensed to work in a *kisaeng* house. In 1941, her foster father took her to Beijing in the hope that she would be able to find work there. While they were in Beijing her foster father was taken away by Japanese soldiers on allegations of "spying," and she was sent to a house used as a comfort station near a Japanese military unit in Tiebizhen, China. On her first night there she was raped twice by the Japanese officer who had arrested her foster father.

Kim recalls that women at the comfort station served seven or eight Japanese soldiers a day, depending on the military activities that the soldiers had been assigned. The women were forced to have intercourse with the soldiers even during their menstruation. Some soldiers were extremely demanding and violent. A military doctor routinely visited the comfort station once a

Celebrating the 1,000th protest on December 14, 2011: This weekly protest began on January 8, 1992, and has continued on every Wednesday in front of the Japanese embassy in Seoul. The protesters call for a formal apology and proper reparations to the victims of wartime sexual slavery. At this 1000th protest, a statue of a "comfort woman" was unveiled. Several surviving "comfort women" were present at this rally.
LEE JIN-MAN/ASSOCIATED PRESS

week to give check-ups. When he detected something wrong, he would inject the women with No. 606. Kim heard from a fellow comfort woman that rank-and-file soldiers paid 1.5 yen a visit and the officers 8 yen to stay the whole night; however, she never received any money.

One day she and some other women were asked to pack quickly, and they were moved to a new, more remote location. There she met a Korean peddler who managed to enter her room when the Japanese soldiers were on an expedition. She begged him to take her with him, and he helped her escape the comfort station. In 1942 they settled in Shanghai, managing a pawn shop. She gave birth to her two children there. They came back to Korea in 1946 after Korea's liberation from Japanese control, but tragedy ensued. Her daughter died during an outbreak of cholera, and in 1953 her husband was killed in an accident. Kim describes how she felt after his death:

> *I had suffered so much, living with this man who had supposedly been my husband. When he was drunk and aggressive, because he knew that I had been a comfort woman, he would insult me with words that had cut me to the quick. After we had returned to Korea I didn't want*

(continued)

> *him to come near me. My life seemed to be wretched. I had refused to do as I was told, and I received more and more abuse from him. When he called me a dirty bitch or a prostitute in front of my son, I cursed him. (Quoted in Howard 1995, 39)*

Kim drifted from one place to another, eking out a meager living to support her son and herself. Tragically, her son drowned while swimming when he was in elementary school. After that, in despair over her daily hardships, she made repeated attempts to end her life. But she had a chance encounter with a woman who had suffered through the aftermath of the atomic bombs being dropped on Japan, someone with whom she shared a great deal of resentment against the Japanese. That encounter inspired her to share her experience as a comfort woman with the larger public. The following is the conclusion of her testimony:

> *I find it very painful to recall my memories. Why haven't I been able to lead a normal life, free from shame, like other people? When I look at old women, I compare myself to them, thinking that I cannot be like them. I want to find the people who took away my innocence and made me as I am and tear them limb from limb. How will I ever appease my bitterness? I would like it if I didn't have to disturb my memories any further. But once I am dead and gone, I wonder whether the Korean or Japanese governments will give any attention to the miserable life of a woman like me. (Quoted in Howard 1995, 40)*

CHINA

The Second World War, followed immediately by civil war between the Nationalists and Communists in China, engulfed the country in the kind of total warfare that it had not experienced since the Taiping wars of the mid-nineteenth century. It is estimated that some twenty million Chinese died during the period of total war between 1937 and 1945, with even greater numbers wounded or left homeless. Women were especially vulnerable to the ravages of war. Millions were killed, raped, kidnapped, or forced into prostitution. The war disrupted or destroyed family and social order, and in the process undermined existing gender norms, making a full return to prewar life impossible. Women were forced into new roles and out of old dependencies and habits.

Although Japan occupied Manchuria in 1931, fighting between China and Japan began in the north with the Marco Polo Bridge Incident, which inaugurated the invasion of North China from Manchuria in 1937. After quickly capturing Beijing and Tianjin, Japanese forces moved swiftly along rail lines to capture northern towns and cities. To slow the Japanese advance, Generalissimo Chiang Kai-shek, leader of Nationalist China, ordered the breaking of Yellow River dikes, which caused massive flooding that drowned at least three hundred thousand people and left more than two million homeless. The Communist Red Army built up guerrilla bases across the north from which they launched attacks on the Japanese, aiming to force them to retreat to the cities, leaving the countryside under the control of the Chinese Communist Party (CCP). This strategy was so effective that the Japanese responded with a campaign of "kill all, loot all, burn all," which for three years unleashed indiscriminate violence on civilians. The Chinese war effort was hampered by ongoing conflict between the Nationalists (KMT) and the Communists. Chiang Kai-shek considered the Communists to pose a greater long-term threat to China than the Japanese, so his forces maintained an economic and military blockade of CCP-held areas and launched military assaults on them.

The worst of the fighting took place in the Yangzi River valley. In 1937 the Japanese defeated Nationalist forces in Shanghai after a bloody three-month battle, with horrific killing of civilians and the loss of nearly two-thirds of the Nationalist forces. In December of that year Japanese troops—frustrated with the unexpected strength of Chinese resistance, and primed to see the Chinese as uncivilized and racially inferior—captured the Nationalist capital, Nanjing, and carried out one of the worst atrocities of the war, the Nanjing Massacre, during which they killed between 200,000 and 300,000 Chinese, most of them civilians. Nationalist troops and the core of the government fled up the Yangzi Valley, first to Wuhan. Under siege and heavily bombed, Wuhan fell to the Japanese by the end of 1938, and the Nationalist capital of Free China moved to Chongqing, up the Yangzi River in Sichuan. Millions of refugees fled Japanese-occupied areas, pouring into the southwest provinces of Sichuan, Yunnan, Guizhou, and Guangxi. Millions more people remained in the occupied areas, where the Japanese set up puppet regimes governed by Chinese collaborators in Beijing and Nanjing (as they had in Manchuria after 1931).

By the end of that year, after the Japanese occupied all of the major cities in northern, central, and coastal China, the fighting reached a stalemate. The Japanese bombed the cities of the Nationalist-controlled regions continuously, launching 268 bombing raids on Chongqing alone. Throughout the war, the Japanese systematically used atrocities—including biological warfare, poison gas, medical experimentation, and brutal occupation policies against civilians—as a military tactic. In 1940 they started epidemics of bubonic plague in three cities in Zhejiang province with airdrops of infected materials. In Manchuria they conducted bacteriological warfare research on Chinese civilians at a facility named Unit 731. Many areas of China's heartland were utterly destroyed and depopulated during the war.

Sexual Assault and Comfort Women

The horrific violence of this total war was acutely gendered, as Timothy Brook explains:

> *Men of fighting age were shot or conscripted for labor because they were, or stood in for, the soldiers of the nation. Women of child-bearing age were raped or forced into prostitution because they were, or stood for, the body of the nation. So rape was widely performed as a gesture of conquest, but not simply as a release for male sexual starvation; it was an act of humiliation. Japanese soldiers performed this act on the bodies of Chinese women, but the target of the humiliation was Chinese men: it was proof of their impotence in all ways. (Brook 2005, 23–24)*

As in Korea, the Japanese instituted a system of military sexual slavery as a tool of conquest. In the midst of its initial assault on Shanghai in 1932, the Japanese military established its first official "comfort station," based on the government's system of licensed brothels that had been in operation since 1907. During the Nanjing Massacre, countless women, including young girls and old women, were raped by Japanese soldiers, who killed many of them and mutilated their bodies. Victims or family members who resisted rape were killed. Westerners who witnessed the massacre and mass rape at Nanjing along with the Chinese expressed outrage at this extreme sexual violence. Concerned about troop control and social order in occupied zones, Japanese commanders accelerated expansion of the comfort station system as the occupation proceeded, shipping in more women, mostly from colonized Korea, but also from Taiwan and Japan.

Between 1932 and 1945 Japanese troops or local Chinese collaborators abducted and detained as sexual slaves many tens of thousands of women, who were kept in more than a thousand comfort stations set up all over occupied China. (An untold number beyond this were raped by soldiers but not detained.) The comfort stations included both officially authorized and regulated stations, run by the military or civilian proprietors, and makeshift stations set up by local military units in their barracks or in a nearby building—or even in the homes of the women themselves. Considered enemies of Japan, Chinese comfort women were subjected to sexual brutality, beaten, bayoneted, or killed outright. Like Korean comfort women, many were injected with toxic Salvarsan to prevent syphilis, but most contracted venereal diseases anyway. Women who became pregnant were routinely killed.

Also like their Korean counterparts, many Chinese young women and girls were deceived with false offers of jobs as domestic servants, nurses, and laundry women, then forced into sexual slavery by the military. But most were abducted when Japanese troops invaded and occupied their communities, often after the women witnessed the killing of their family members. In some areas, Chinese collaborators actively participated in running comfort stations, while in others Chinese civilians working in local administration under Japanese supervision ran them and were required, often under threat of death, to recruit or force young women to work in them. Captured female resistance fighters were also used as comfort women.

After the war, as was the case in Korea, many survivors lived in deep poverty, suffering from chronic physical and psychological problems ranging from post-traumatic stress disorder to injuries to the uterine tract. Many were unable to bear children, exacerbating their poverty and social isolation. Chinese survivors were often vilified as women lacking in virtue who had collaborated with the enemy. Many were targeted for persecution during the numerous political campaigns of the Mao era, 1949 to 1976 (see Chapters 9 and 10), and sentenced to hard labor or imprisonment as counterrevolutionary traitors. Many committed suicide (Qiu 2014, 7–12).

Women and the War of Resistance

During the war, official discourse about women's place in society took a conservative turn in areas under Japanese rule, the collaborationist regimes in Manchukuo (Manchuria) and Central China, and regions under Nationalist government control. While state rhetoric emphasized the importance of traditional virtues of female self-sacrifice for family and society, it also sanctioned a public role for women that extended their domestic nurturing duties into work in nursing, education, and relief efforts. In occupied China, many women became active in religiously inspired redemptive societies such as the Morality Society (Daodehui), which ran schools, clinics, and lecture halls to promote moral reform and syncretic ideas of spiritual salvation. Large numbers of women joined the World Women's Red Swastika Society, modeled on the Western Red Cross Society, founded in 1932 to manage schools, carry out relief work, and even conduct research on women's issues. (The swastika was an ancient Buddhist symbol, and its use was not at all related to German Nazism.) Founded before the war, these popular societies with their apolitical and socially conservative message flourished under wartime conditions of censorship and political repression. Although politically tainted because of their accommodation or outright collaboration with the Japanese, they were important vehicles for encouraging women's activity outside the home (Duara 2004).

Women were also active participants in, and leaders of, resistance efforts in occupied and unoccupied China. In Communist and Nationalist-controlled regions, authorities promoted a militarized lifestyle emphasizing asceticism and self-sacrifice for the nation. Female and male students underwent military training in their schools, and tens of thousands of young women and men volunteered as health and social workers to assist with refugees or joined drama troupes to promote the war effort. Women raised money and in-kind donations for the war effort, nursed wounded veterans and provided support for their families, and engaged in relief work, child care, and education. Women even fought as irregular soldiers in many areas (Li 2010).

Nationalist Party propaganda during the war held up as national heroines New Women who worked to save the nation. Chiang Kai-shek's wife, Song Meiling (1897–2003), a graduate of Wellesley College in Massachusetts and a Christian, was the chief model of patriotic womanhood for Free China. She directed the Nationalist Party's New Life Movement, which was launched in 1934 to promote a syncretic blend of Confucian and Christian values of female duty, family hierarchy, and obedience to state authority as the moral foundation of a nation challenged by growing leftist critiques of the regime and by the Japanese threat. As the war intensified, she led projects to establish schools for war orphans, train women for wartime jobs, and provide refugee relief. Charismatic, elegant, and fluent in English, she also played a major role in Nationalist government diplomacy during the war, addressing the U.S. Congress in 1943 to appeal for financial aid in the war effort and authoring numerous articles on the war situation in China for the American public.

In the midst of the assault on Nanjing, a handful of Westerners in the city established a safe zone for refugees that encompassed the American embassy and several missionary schools as well as Nanjing University, and they negotiated with the Japanese to recognize it as a neutral area. Jinling Women's College, founded by missionaries, was designated specifically as a refugee camp for women and children, sheltering and providing medical assistance to more than ten thousand people. The efforts there were led by its acting president, American missionary Minnie Vautrin (1886–1941), and Tsen Shui-fang (1875–1969), the college nurse and director of its dormitories. The diaries kept by these two women, both of whom had refused to evacuate, provide poignant accounts of the atrocities committed by Japanese troops and of heroic efforts to protect civilians. These two women were in charge of the refugee camp and often personally guarded the front gate against incursions, although troops frequently invaded the campus and killed or kidnapped residents. When the safety zone ceased to exist under Japanese pressure in 1938, the school focused on refugee relief efforts (Hu and Zhang 2010, 5–13).

Another national heroine was Shi Liang (1900–1985), an activist lawyer from a literati family and one of the first Chinese women to graduate from law school. In the early years of the war, she led the countrywide effort to establish women's branches of the National Salvation Association (which promoted military resistance to Japanese encroachment), an activity for which she was arrested in 1936, when Chiang Kai-shek was still opposed to resisting Japan. After her release from prison in 1937, she threw herself into the war effort, moving to Wuhan to organize women there through the National Salvation Association. In 1938, during the ten months when Wuhan served as the wartime capital after the fall of Nanjing, major relief efforts were launched from the city. Shi Liang maintained close relationships with the most powerful women in the country, including the Song sisters: Song Meiling (wife of Chiang Kai-shek), Song Qingling (widow of Sun Yat-sen), and Song Ailing (wife of H. H. Kong, a banker who was the wealthiest man in China).

In 1938, as the refugee crisis worsened, Shi Liang lobbied through this network of powerful women to get the issue of refugee relief on the government's agenda, forming a political coalition that included not only KMT women but also Communists such as Long March veteran Deng Yingchao (whose husband, future premier Zhou Enlai, was in charge of the CCP's operations in Nationalist-controlled regions). Her efforts resulted in the creation of the woman-run National Relief Committee and the Wartime Child Welfare Committee, which became a model for later child welfare organizations in the People's Republic of China and Taiwan. As the war dragged on, more than forty child care centers run by women were set up by the Nationalist Party in the southwest, providing care and education for hundreds of thousands of children. Song Meiling visited many of these and gave speeches to support the effort. In 1938 Shi Liang also organized a national women's committee to mobilize women for the war effort through public rallies. She would later serve as the first minister of justice in the People's Republic of China, from 1949 to 1959 (MacKinnon 2008, 55–59).

After the fall of Wuhan, more than six hundred private industries and some fifty schools and colleges moved their entire operations to the southwest. Many teachers and students from universities and schools in occupied areas, including many girls' middle schools and colleges, migrated inland together to Nationalist-controlled areas. The Southwest Associated University in Kunming, Yunnan, was the wartime union of Beijing, Qinghua, and Nankai Universities. It sheltered many of the country's most respected academics and students. Middle schools formed similar associations. Many single women moved west with their schools and workplaces as those relocated away from the front lines. A number of these schools later became hotbeds of political opposition to the Nationalist regime as repression of dissent against the Nationalists deepened during the war.

Transformations of Family Life

In occupied China, the status of women deteriorated. Epidemics of malaria and other diseases were common amid the wartime chaos. Women, children, and the elderly were particularly vulnerable to disease, starvation, and exposure. At least a hundred million people fled to the interior of the country to escape the violence and chaos of the occupied areas. Women made up at least half of the total number of refugees. Many would never return to their homes. For married women who fled with their husbands, this often meant permanent separation from their natal families.

Family life was utterly transformed by the war, though the changes varied by region. In occupied areas, the threat of mass rape and kidnapping caused many families to increase the sequestering of women at home. Yet many women were forced to leave home as refugees or to find work. All over China, war tore families apart, forced women into prostitution, and led to the abandonment of children and the elderly as able-bodied women and men left to fight or find work. As in most war-torn countries, the number of unmarried women and widows rose significantly. In many occupied areas, women outnumbered men, reversing China's long-standing deficit of women. Many women were left to support their families on their own when their husbands, fathers, and sons went off to fight or were killed by the Japanese. Soldiers' contact with and remittances of pay to their families were

Chinese women receive basic training in guerilla warfare about 1939.
© Pictorial Press Ltd / Alamy Stock Photo

rare. Many women had no idea whether their menfolk were still alive, and there was little if any support for war widows.

Wartime economic collapse, marked by hyperinflation and depression, posed a different kind of threat to family patriarchy, as even husbands who were at home were unable to support their families financially. Legal case records from Beijing, for example, document widespread marital conflict over such economic failure, with many women deserting destitute husbands or suing to divorce them. A vastly expanded modern transportation system of roads and railroads facilitated the quest for autonomy of a growing number of runaway wives, while also fueling expansion of the traffic in women and children. Growing numbers of migrants to cities such as Beijing clustered in crowded tenement neighborhoods, where women developed community support networks and pursued nonmarital sexual relationships that in many ways substituted for tenuous or collapsed family structures (Ma 2015).

War Work

In both occupied and unoccupied China, as in Japan and Korea, war increased both the opportunity for paid work and the necessity for women to join the workforce. Industries that relocated to the interior increased the demand for female factory workers while men were occupied as soldiers. Many rural girls in the southwest who had never left their villages moved to cities such as

Chongqing to work. Educated women took up new kinds of jobs in relief and refugee work, journalism, and government. Refugee women and children were hired to do work such as sewing or making straw sandals for soldiers. Nationalist government publications promoted the image of the career woman working to support the war effort. For many young, single women, the chaos, displacement, and weakening of family authority caused by the war created unprecedented freedom to choose careers and marriage partners.

In the wartime capital of Chongqing, by 1945 nearly 75 percent of the city's women were employed outside the home in industry, commerce, or the service sector. More than thirteen thousand women labored in cotton mills that had been relocated, along with other factories, from the coastal regions occupied by the Japanese. These included some of the Chinese-owned mills that had employed most women workers in Shanghai before the war. Though familiar in large coastal cities, the participation of women in factory work was new to many regions and even at the height of the war was the subject of much controversy. In response to calls for women to stay home and focus on their duties as "worthy wives and good mothers," the government banned discrimination against women in public service and affirmed the patriotism of women workers, promoting the slogan "Big Brother goes to the battleground, Big Sister joins the factory; Big Brother kills the enemy at the front, Big Sister works hard producing at the Rear; the Front and Rear are united, driving off the foreign devils to enjoy the peace" (quoted in Howard 2013, 1903).

The Women's Advisory Committee of the General Association for the Advancement of the New Life Movement, an organization in which both Nationalist and Communist women participated under the terms of the Second United Front during the war, ran education campaigns among women factory workers, most of whom were young and recently arrived from the surrounding countryside. Female instructors taught literacy and the values of the New Life Movement: diligence, patriotism, and respect for authority. However, Communist organizers working under the committee's auspices also mentored workers, often through networks of sworn sisterhoods, on how to present their grievances about harsh working conditions and inequalities in treatment of workers and the mostly male technical and administrative staff. Empowered by their newly acquired literacy and class consciousness, women workers in Chongqing engaged in frequent strikes, slowdowns, and other forms of protest (Howard 2013).

In Shanghai, the textile mills that employed most women workers in the city continued to operate in the early years of Japanese occupation. Wartime inflation fed a boom in production of cloth and yarn and led to soaring profits for British, American, Japanese, and Chinese companies. But many workers fled the occupied areas of the city to live in refugee camps in the International Settlement. With America's entry into the war, the Japanese took over the International Settlement and all textile mills within it. Textile production plummeted, and the number of women workers dropped to below 4,000 from the prewar high of over 116,000. Many factories were repurposed to sew military uniforms. Many unemployed women returned to their home villages during the war, but those who stayed in the city survived however they could, through work such as smuggling in rice from the suburbs, collecting garbage, pulling carts, and growing vegetables.

During the war, the YWCA in Shanghai linked up with the National Salvation Movement, using its night schools to educate women about the Japanese invasion and promote resistance. They organized patriotic schools in refugee camps. Many workers joined the Working Women's Battlefront Service Unit, which sent teams of women in military uniforms out to work with army units, helping with propaganda in local villages, nursing of wounded soldiers, and camp chores (Honig 1986, 223–224). Under the Second United Front, the previously outlawed CCP was legalized in Nationalist-controlled regions, so the Communists took up open mobilization of urban workers again. Communist organizers encouraged women workers to subvert production in Japanese factories by stealing cloth, yarn, and food, setting the machines to run slowly or stopping them, deliberately wasting materials, and producing shoddy cloth (Honig 1986, 228–229). Although the effects of such sabotage on Japanese production are unclear, the Party gained a significant foothold among women workers through these efforts.

Outside of industrial centers, women in most of the country, including cities such as Beijing, still had few opportunities for factory work and faced strong social disapproval for leaving home to work in any kind of job in public. Forced by dire circumstances during the war to earn money for their families, most women in such regions engaged in various combinations of petty trading, brokering, domestic service, home handicraft production, black market trading, trafficking, and prostitution. Through these activities women were crucial to the functioning of the informal economy, through which large portions of the population survived (Ma 2015).

Wartime Culture

Women were prominent in the dynamic wartime popular culture. In the (mostly male-authored) literature of resistance written during the war, women often appeared as prostitutes or rape victims, embodying the violation of the Chinese nation, as traditional heroines whose chastity and filial piety exemplified service to the nation, and sometimes as women warriors in the traditional mode of Mulan. Women also contributed to wartime culture as writers. In the context of Japanese censorship in Shanghai, women writers turned their focus to domestic themes of family life, female identity, and survival. Many expressed a sense of urgency, capturing their perceptions and experiences in writing as their world was falling apart around them. Su Qing wrote:

> *The world has gone crazy. Distress, agitation, depression, and a bizarre joy characterize our mental state. Sometimes it is like dancing on top of a mountain and other times it is like building a jade palace on thin ice. I know only too well that everything is going to collapse soon, but I still hope to grasp this moment and seek serenity and fulfillment right away! Otherwise what am I going to do with these few surviving moments? So I have chosen writing and publishing to consume my time. . . . I want to survive my time. I want to live, and I want to live in a way that most satisfies myself. (Quoted in Huang 2005, 25)*

Women such as Su articulated a new mode of femininity, focused on individual expression and the preservation of self in a dangerous time when life itself was tenuous. Eileen Chang, the most prominent of these writers, commented, "An individual can afford to wait, but an era is transient. Things are being torn apart, and an even larger destruction is on its way. . . . Make yourself famous as early as possible! If success comes too late, it will not be as enjoyable. . . . Hurry! Hurry! Otherwise it will be too late! Too late!" (quoted in Huang 2005, 21).

Yet many women who contributed to the lively press culture in occupied Shanghai emphasized that individual opportunity functioned for the good of the society. One woman, He Jiashui, wrote to a Shanghai journal:

> *The editor might want the contributors to describe their miseries, but I have no miseries to come to terms with. I know I am expected to recount the unequal treatment I have experienced, but I have been treated well anywhere I have been, much better than I deserve. This is a turbulent time; the conflicts between evil and good forces are certainly fiercer than in normal times. There are cannibalistic elements in human relations, but there are also friendship,*

> *integrity, and generosity. . . . During a turbulent time, talents are in great demand, and few can complain that they have no opportunities to make use of their talents. . . . Women often take great advantage of this particular time. For some reason, men of our time feel sorry and are obliged to respect women's rights. In any case, conscientious people can always find a way to be constructive for [the good of] society. (Quoted in Huang 2005, 48–49)*

War created misery for many and opportunity for some, but for most, life was utterly transformed.

Women in Yenan

In the fall of 1935, survivors of the CCP's Long March (see Chapter 5) set up a guerilla base in a poor, remote, mountainous region in northern Shaanxi province, centered on the town of Yenan. This was the headquarters for the CCP during the war, from 1936 to 1945. Throughout the war, in Yenan and other base areas under the control of its Red Army, the CCP built new military and state structures to mobilize the population to join the fight against the Japanese. The Party perfected the political mode of the "mass line," a strategy of going down to the villages to listen directly to the concerns of the peasant masses and then incorporating them into policy. The CCP's populist regime gave many the hope of democratic change, but the Party's main goal was to build a new state, based on broad peasant support, that marginalized the old landlord elites as class enemies of the masses of poor peasants.

Gender norms in the region were, ironically, particularly conservative. In this context, Party cadres deemphasized promotion of women's rights, as they had in the Jiangxi Soviet, out of concern for alienating the male population. In 1936 the CCP called for development of mass organizations (including women's associations) in the northwest border regions, but at the same time it warned of potential divisiveness if women's rights and marriage reforms were pushed too far. Women's associations grew very slowly during the war years, and they placed the greatest emphasis on harnessing women's labor to help the war effort by increasing women's role in agricultural production and in the revival of household textile production (which had diminished due to competition from industrially produced textiles).

In 1938 these associations were consolidated into the Rear Area Enemy Resistance Association, which set up training centers for women cadres to teach local women Party policy and to recruit them as activists in their communities. They organized women into cooperatives to make shoes, blankets, socks, and uniforms for the Red Army. Women were also encouraged to work in the fields, both to make up for the absence of men and to promote local economic self-sufficiency. Women leaders noted at the time that these enhanced economic roles increased women's status and autonomy within the family. The Party also encouraged women to participate in political activities as voters and candidates in local elections. In the 1941 election, 8 percent of township council seats were held by women—far less than the 25 percent in the Jiangxi Soviet (see Chapter 5). There were about seven thousand women Party members in Yenan in 1937, about 15 percent of total Party membership, though most were students and cadres who had come from other regions (Johnson 1983).

As the military and economic crisis deepened in 1941–1942, the Party came to focus exclusively on women's roles in the "production war." It warned cadres to focus on family harmony and wifely loyalty until the dire circumstances of poor men were alleviated. It directed that women's political participation and other rights should remain only slogans and, after 1943, that women should not be summoned for political meetings that would detract from their production.

For cadres in Yenan, the Party itself replaced family authority in key ways, arranging marriages and assigning work. With everyone mobilized for the war effort, a new militarized social life took shape in which women and men wore military uniforms, took military training, and participated in military missions and underground Party work behind Japanese lines. Everyone was subjected to strict Party discipline.

In 1942, as the Nationalist blockade was reaching a critical point, Mao launched a campaign to silence his critics in the Party, unify cadres in support of his ideological line, and indoctrinate the tens of thousands of new recruits, mostly young students and intellectuals, who were fleeing KMT-controlled areas to join the CCP in Yenan. This was called the "rectification campaign." Party members who had criticized Mao or his policies in Yenan were singled out for public criticism in "struggle sessions" and banished to remote villages to be reeducated by doing manual labor and living with peasants. Thousands of people deemed to be unrepentant were executed.

A defining moment of this campaign was the criticism of the writer Ding Ling (see Chapter 6), which clarified the Party's stance toward women and intellectuals. After the Nationalists executed her common-law husband (she shunned the notion of civil marriage as legalized prostitution), she joined the Communist Party, sent her infant son to live with her mother in Hunan, and took up work editing a journal for the Party-sponsored League of Left Wing

Writers. In 1933 the Nationalist secret police kidnapped her and held her under house arrest for three years. In 1937 she escaped to Yenan, where she took up cultural propaganda work and helped organize women's war work. On International Women's Day in 1942 she published an essay, "Thoughts on March 8," in which she criticized gender discrimination among Communist cadres and contradictions in their attitudes about women.

BOX 8.4

Ding Ling's "Thoughts on March 8"

Ding Ling's essay described the paradox of gender politics in Yenan: the Party declared women to be equal to men and expected them to participate fully in the work of revolution, yet their happiness and effectiveness as cadres was hampered by the persistence of sexist assumptions about marriage among male cadres and by women's own emotionality and unrealistic romanticism. She wrote, "When will it no longer be necessary to attach special weight to the word 'woman' and to raise it specially? . . . Women in [Yenan] are happier than women elsewhere in China. . . . It doesn't seem to surprise anyone that women make up a big proportion of the staff in the hospitals, sanatoria, and clinics, but they are inevitably the subject of conversation, as a fascinating problem, on every conceivable occasion. Moreover, all kinds of women comrades are often the target of deserved criticism." As in her early fiction, Ding Ling posited an essentialist view of women and her natural ability as a woman to see and criticize their weaknesses: "I myself am a woman, so I understand the failings of women better than others. But I also have a deeper understanding of what they suffer."

The heart of the essay described the contradictions of sexual politics in Yenan that made it impossible for women to avoid accusations of selfishness and political backwardness. As they tried to balance Party work with marriage and motherhood, women comrades faced gossip and ridicule. They were criticized for their marriage choices, but slandered for remaining single. "I am the first to admit it is a shame when a man's wife is not progressive and retards his progress. But let us consider to what degree [these women] are backward. Before marrying, they were inspired by the desire to soar in the heavenly heights and lead a life of bitter struggle. They got married partly because of physiological necessity and partly as a response to sweet talk about 'mutual help.' Thereupon they are forced to toil away and become 'Noras returned home.'" When

(continued)

they had children, they were "publicly derided" for giving up their autonomy and productive work for domestic life, yet if women comrades employed nannies, then "behind their backs there would also be the most incredible gossip and whispering campaigns." She stated that divorce was almost always initiated by the husband and the pretext was "invariably the wife's political backwardness." Yet women who took their children to nurseries or tried to have abortions were asked, "Why did you get married in the first place?" She concluded, "Under these conditions it is impossible for women to escape this destiny of 'backwardness.' When women capable of working sacrifice their careers for the joys of motherhood, people always sing their praises. But after ten years or so, they have no way of escaping the tragedy of 'backwardness' [i.e., divorce]."

She concluded the essay with advice for her fellow women comrades to take care of their health and emotional well-being: "Use your brain and make a habit of doing so. . . . It is the best way of avoiding the pitfalls of sweet words and honeyed phrases, of being sidetracked by petty gains, of wasting our emotions and wasting our lives. . . . Aware, modern women should identify and cast off all their rosy illusions. Happiness is to take up the struggle in the midst of the raging storm and not to pluck the lute in the moonlight or recite poetry among the blossoms. . . . Not to suffer is to become degenerate. The strength to carry on should be nurtured through the quality of 'perseverance.' People without great aims and ambitions rarely have the firmness of purpose that does not covet petty advantages or see a comfortable existence. But only those who have aims and ambitions for the benefit, not of the individual, but of humankind as a whole can persevere to the end" (Ding 1990, 317–319).

During the rectification campaign, Ding Ling was forced to apologize for her statements, though she did not retract them, and was banned from Party work for two years. The head of the Women's Department castigated her and like-minded women cadres for their "outdated" views, which did not recognize that equality of the sexes had been fully established in Yenan and which instead advocated a one-sided feminism that undermined Party unity (Johnson 1983). Ironically, in her attempt to reconcile feminist goals with the imperatives of nationalism and revolution, Ding Ling had already given up bourgeois notions of individualism. The war's devastating impact social and economic order and ordinary family life justified the new Yenan mode of citizenship for women and men, which was centered on sacrifice to the Party and mobilization to work, first for the war effort and ultimately for the Communist revolution. In the new society created by revolution, women were to be liberated by the Party to participate fully in economic and political transformation, but not to realize feminist goals of self-fulfillment or individual autonomy.

CONNECTIONS

The turbulent years of the Great Depression and World War II, from 1931 to 1945, altered the boundaries of nations and empires and the configurations of their alliances. They changed the relationships of individuals to their governments through the expansion or contraction of civic rights and the creation of welfare states. They drew women in large numbers into the workforce of most combatant nations. And, most important for this book, they fundamentally altered gender relations as nations responded in their own ways to these crises.

In Japan, Korea, and China, the effects of these turbulent years were not limited to the time in which they occurred. They also produced long-lasting changes in the post–World War II era. Depression and war forced great suffering on men, women, and children alike. Millions of civilians died of starvation, from bombing raids, and in atrocities perpetrated by combatants. Additional millions of men were taken away by their countries' military forces (or, in the case of Korea, by Japan's military) to fight and often die on distant battlefields—thereby pushing women to take up what had previously been men's civic and economic tasks. The dynamics of societies devoid of working-age men led to changed family relationships and, in some cases, government-paid welfare policies to support fatherless families. In addition, women either were formally drafted into the workforce, as in Japan and Korea, or entered it because of the need to produce for the war. In each of these countries, as well as in China and in combatant countries outside the East Asian region, the entry of women into the paid workforce led to long-term changes in women's attitudes about their social roles. Women often became more independent and capable of exerting leadership in wartime neighborhood associations, allowing some to make a leap into more public roles in the postwar years. In all three countries the chaos of the times offered the opportunity for some women to write and express themselves, opening new possibilities for them to be involved in cultural production even in difficult times.

An important form of female labor that exploded on a large scale was the performance of sex for the Japanese military. Most of this was not voluntary. Tens of thousands of women in China, one of Japan's wartime enemies, were forced into sexual slavery; even greater numbers of women in colonial Korea, which was not Japan's wartime enemy, suffered the same horrible fate. The legacy of what many people today consider an unresolved war crime against Asian victims (Caucasian "comfort women" were treated as victims, and the men who recruited them were convicted of war crimes) continues to affect Japan's relations with Korea and China seventy years after the end of the war. In December 2015, the foreign ministers of Japan and South Korea made a joint statement outlining elements of an agreement to address the issue of former Korean sex slaves. The statement included an apology on behalf of the Japanese prime minister and a proposal for financial aid to the surviving victims. However, many legal and political issues remain unresolved with both South Korean survivors and survivors in China, the Philippines, and other countries, and the matter is likely to continue to be a point of contention.

The deprivations of war made frugality a necessity, but just in case women did not get the message that they were responsible for maintaining efficient families, in both Japan and colonial Korea women were exhorted to practice thrift. Extravagance, women were told, was the enemy. In the CCP areas in Yenan, women were instructed to focus on production. Hard work and frugality continued to be honored after the war in all three societies.

Some of the prewar connections among women in the three societies were severed by the rise of Japanese militarism in the 1930s, and these were never reestablished after the war. While ties between Japanese and Western women were reconnected after the war, the legacy of the war made this virtually impossible in East Asia. Only under the rubric of larger global feminisms have transnational connections reemerged in recent years.

REFERENCES AND SUGGESTIONS FOR FURTHER READING

GLOBAL CONTEXT

Besse, Susan K. 2004. "Engendering Reform and Revolution in Twentieth-Century Latin America and the Caribbean." In *A Companion to Gender History*, edited by Teresa A. Meade and Merry E. Wiesner-Hanks. Oxford: Blackwell.

Clements, Barbara Evens. 2004. "Continuities Amid Change: Gender Ideas and Arrangements in Twentieth-Century Russia and Eastern Europe." In *A Companion to Gender History*, edited by Teresa A. Meade and Merry E. Wiesner-Hanks. Oxford: Blackwell.

Sowerwine, Charles and Patricia Grimshaw. 2004. "Equality and Difference in the Twentieth-Century West: North America, Western Europe, Australia, and New Zealand." In *A Companion to Gender History*, edited by Teresa A. Meade and Merry E. Wiesner-Hanks. Oxford: Blackwell.

JAPAN

Ajima, Naomi. 2011. "Working Women During the Turning Point from Japanese-Style to Western-Style Clothing." In *Fashion and Luxury: Between Heritage and Innovation*. Paris: Institut de la Mode.

Brooks, Barbara. 2005. "Reading the Japanese Colonial Archive: Gender and Bourgeois Civility in Korea and Manchuria Before 1932." In *Gendering Modern Japanese History*, edited by Barbara Molony and Kathleen Uno. Cambridge, MA: Harvard University Press.

Cook, Haruko Taya. 2005. "Women's Deaths as Weapons of War in Japan's 'Final Battle.'" In *Gendering Modern Japanese History*, edited by Barbara Molony and Kathleen Uno. Cambridge, MA: Harvard University Press.

Cook, Theodore F., Jr. 2005. "Making 'Soldiers': The Imperial Army and the Japanese Man in Meiji Society and State." In *Gendering Modern Japanese History*, edited by Barbara Molony and Kathleen Uno. Cambridge, MA: Harvard University Press.

Earhart, David C. 2008. *Certain Victory: Images of World War II in the Japanese Media*. New York: Routledge.

Frühstück, Sabine. 2014. "'The Spirit to Take Up a Gun': Militarising Gender in the Imperial Army." In *Gender, Nation and State in Modern Japan*, edited by Andrea Germer, Vera Mackie, and Ulrike Wöhr. Abingdon, UK: Routledge.

Garon, Sheldon. 1993. "Women's Groups and the Japanese State." *Journal of Japanese Studies* 19, no. 1: 5–41.

Gordon, Andrew. 2011. *Fabricating Consumers: The Sewing Machine in Modern Japan*. Berkeley: University of California Press.

Havens, Thomas R. H. 1978. *Valley of Darkness: The Japanese People and World War Two*. New York: W. W. Norton.

Horiguchi, Noriko J. 2009. "Migrant Women, Memory, and Empire in Naruse Mikio's Film Adaptations of Hayashi Fumiko's Novels." *U.S.-Japan Women's Journal* 36: 42–72.

———. 2012. *Women Adrift: The Literature of Japan's Imperial Body*. Minneapolis: University of Minnesota Press.

Ichikawa, Fusae. 1932. "Dai sankai Fusen Taikai no ketsugi" [Resolutions of the Third Women's Suffrage Convention]. *Fusen* 6, no. 6.

———. 1934. "Seisō undō no zenkokuteki kōdai to sono igi" [The national expansion and significance of the garbage collection movement]. *Fusen* 8, no. 7.

———. 1935. "Shukusei senkyo no kekka" [The results of election purification]. *Fusen* 9, no. 10: 4–5.

———. 1938. "An Introductory Note." *Japanese Women* 1, no. 1: 1–2

———. 1940a. "On My Return from China." *Japanese Women* 3, no. 3: 1, 4.

———. 1940b. "An Explanation by Miss Ichikawa." *Japanese Women* 3, no. 3: 3–4.

———. 1941. "Fujin dantai no ichigenka" [The unification of women's organizations]. *Asahi Shinbun*, April 11–13.

———. 1942. "Dai Nippon Fujinkai ni tsuite" [On the Greater Japan Women's Association]. *Fujin Jikyoku Kenkyūkai Kaihō* 3.

———. 1974. *Jiden: Senzenhen.* Tokyo: Shinjuku Shobō.

Ienaga, Saburō. 1978. *The Pacific War, 1931–1945.* New York: Pantheon.

Kawai, Michi, and Ochimi Kubushiro. 1934. *Japanese Women Speak: A Message from the Christian Women of Japan to the Christian Women of America.* Boston: Central Committee on the United Study of Foreign Missions.

Lipman, Jonathan, Barbara Molony, and Michael Robinson. 2012. *Modern East Asia: An Integrated History.* New York: Pearson.

Mackie, Vera. 2002. *Creating Socialist Women in Japan: Gender, Labour and Activism, 1900–1937.* Cambridge: Cambridge University Press.

Matsumoto, Valerie. 1984. "Japanese American Women During World War II." *Frontiers* 8, no. 1: 6–14.

Miyake, Yoshiko. 1991. "Doubling Expectations: Motherhood and Women's Factory Work Under State Management in Japan in the 1930s and 1940s." In *Recreating Japanese Women, 1600–1945*, edited by Gail Lee Bernstein. Berkeley: University of California Press.

Molony, Barbara. 2004. "Citizenship and Suffrage in Interwar Japan." In *Women's Suffrage in Asia: Gender, Nationalism and Democracy*, edited by Louise Edwards and Mina Roces. London: Routledge Curzon.

———. 2005. "Ichikawa Fusae and the Pre-war Women's Suffrage Movement." In *Japanese Women: Emerging from Subservience, 1868–1945*, edited by Hiroko Tomida and Gordon Daniels. Folkestone, Kent: Global Oriental.

Nishikawa, Yuko. 1997. "Japan's Entry into War and the Support of Women." *U.S.-Japan Women's Journal, English Supplement*, 12: 48–83.

Ogawa, Manako. 2007. "Estranged Sisterhood: The Wartime Trans-Pacific Dialogue of the World's Woman's Christian Temperance Union, 1931–1945." *Japanese Journal of American Studies* 18: 163–185.

Smith, W. Donald. 2005. "Sorting Coal and Pickling Cabbage: Korean Women in the Japanese Mining Industry." In *Gendering Modern Japanese History*, edited by Barbara Molony and Kathleen Uno. Cambridge, MA: Harvard University Press.

Sokolsky, Anne. 2014. "Reading the Bodies and Voices of *Naichi* in Japanese-Ruled Taiwan." *U.S.-Japan Women's Journal* 46: 51–78.

Tamanoi, Mariko. 2009. "Suffragist Women, Corrupt Officials, and Waste Control in Prewar Japan: Two Plays by Kaneko Shigeri." *Journal of Asian Studies* 68, no. 3: 805–834.

Tomic, Naoko. 2005. "The Political Process of Establishing the Mother-Child Protection Law in Prewar Japan." *Social Science Japan Journal* 8, no. 2: 239–251.

"Women's Conference on War-Time Economy." 1940. *Japanese Women* 3.1.
YWCA National Committee. 1938. "Present Status and Main Problems of Japanese Women." *Japanese Women* 1, no. 5: 2

KOREA

Caprio, Mark. 2009. *Japanese Assimilation Policies in Colonial Korea, 1910–1945.* Seattle: University of Washington Press.
Choi, Chungmoo. 1997. "Guest Editor's Introduction." *positions* 5, no. 1 (special issue, "The Comfort Women: Colonialism, War, and Sex The Comfort"): v–xiv.
Chou, Wan-yao. 1996. "The *Kōminka* Movement in Taiwan and Korea: Comparisons and Interpretations." In *The Japanese Wartime Empire, 1931–1945*, edited by Peter Duus, Ramon H. Myers, and Mark R. Peattie. Princeton: Princeton University Press.
Eckert, Carter J. 1996. "Total War, Industrialization, and Social Change in Late Colonial Korea." In *The Japanese Wartime Empire, 1931–1945*, edited by Peter Duus, Ramon H. Myers, and Mark R. Peattie. Princeton: Princeton University Press.
Henry, Todd A. 2014. *Assimilating Seoul: Japanese Rule and the Politics of Public Space in Colonial Korea, 1910–1945.* Berkeley: University of California Press.
Howard, Keith, ed. 1995. *True Stories of the Korean Comfort Women: Testimonies.* New York: Cassell.
Kim, Janice. 2007. "The Pacific War and Working Women in Late Colonial Korea." *Signs* 33, no. 1: 81–103.
Kim, Michael. 2007. "The Aesthetics of Total Mobilisation in the Visual Culture of Late Colonial Korea." *Totalitarian Movements and Political Religions* 8, nos. 3–4: 483–502.
Kim, Su Yun. 2013. "Racialization and Colonial Space: Intermarriage in Yi Hyosŏk's Works." *Journal of Korean Studies* 18, no. 1: 29–59.
Lee, Helen J. S. 2012. "Eating for the Emperor: The Nationalization of Settler Homes and Bodies in the Kōminka Era." In *Reading Colonial Japan: Text, Context, and Critique*, edited by Michele M. Mason and Helen J. S. Lee. Stanford: Stanford University Press.
Min, Byong Gap. 2003. "Korean 'Comfort Women': The Intersection of Colonial Power, Gender and Class." *Gender and Society* 17, no. 6: 938–957.
Nakasone, Yasuhiro. 1978. "Nijūsansai de sanzennin no sōshikikan." In *Owarinaki kaigun*, edited by Matsuura Takanori. Bunka Hōsō Kaihatsu Sentā Shuppanbu. Tokyo: Bunka Hōsō Kaihatsu Sentā Shuppanbu, 90–98.
Park, Won Soon. 1997. "Japanese Reparations Policies and the 'Comfort Women' Question." *positions* 5, no. 1: 107–136.
Soh, Chunghee Sarah. 2004. "Women's Sexual Labor and State in Korean History." *Journal of Women's History* 15, no. 4: 170–177.
Soh, Sarah. 2008. *The Comfort Women: Sexual Violence and Postcolonial Memory in Korea and Japan.* Chicago: University of Chicago Press.

CHINA

Brook, Timothy. 2005. *Collaboration: Japanese Agents and Local Elites in Wartime China*. Cambridge, MA: Harvard University Press.

Ding Ling. 1990. *I Myself Am a Woman: Selected Writings of Ding Ling*. Edited by Tani E. Barlow. Boston: Beacon Press.

Duara, Prasenjit. 2004. *Sovereignty and Authenticity: Manchukuo and the East Asian Modern*. Lanham, MD: Rowman and Littlefield.

Edwards, Louise. 2008. *Gender, Politics, and Democracy: Women's Suffrage in China*. Stanford, CA: Stanford University Press.

Honig, Emily. 1986. *Sisters and Strangers: Women in the Shanghai Cotton Mills, 1919–1949*. Stanford, CA: Stanford University Press, 1986.

Howard, Joshua H. 2013. "The Politicization of Women Workers at War: Labour in Chongqing's Cotton Mills During the Anti-Japanese War." *Modern Asian Studies* 47, no. 6: 1888–1940.

Hu, Hualing Hu, and Lian-hong Zhang. 2010. *The Undaunted Women of Nanking: The Wartime Diaries of Minnie Vautrin and Tsen Shui-fang*. Carbondale: Southern Illinois University Press.

Huang, Nicole. 2005. *Women, War, Domesticity: Shanghai Literature and Popular Culture in the 1940s*. Leiden: E. J. Brill.

Johnson, Kay Anne. 1983. *Women, the Family, and Peasant Revolution in China*. Chicago: University of Chicago Press.

Lary, Diana. 2010. *The Chinese People at War: Human Suffering and Social Transformation, 1937–1945*. New York: Cambridge University Press.

Lary, Diana, and Stephen MacKinnon. 2001. *The Scars of War: The Impact of Warfare on Modern China*. Vancouver: University of British Columbia Press.

Li, Danke. 2010. *Echoes of Chongqing: Women in Wartime China*. Urbana: Illinois University Press.

Ma, Zhao. 2015. *Runaway Wives, Urban Crimes, and Survival Tactics in Wartime Beijing, 1937–1949*. Cambridge, MA: Harvard University Asia Center.

MacKinnon, Stephen. 2008. *Wuhan, 1938: War, Refugees, and the Making of Modern China*. Berkeley: University of California Press.

Qiu, Peipei. 2014. *Chinese Comfort Women: Testimonies from Imperial Japan's Sex Slaves*. New York: Oxford University Press.

Schoppa, Keith. 2011. *In a Sea of Bitterness: Refugees During the Sino-Japanese War*. Cambridge, MA: Harvard University Press.

9

Reconstructing Gender in the Early Cold War Era, 1945–1953

GLOBAL CONTEXT

The end of World War II marked the beginning of the unraveling of colonialism. It also produced a new set of global blocs—the Communist world, led by the Soviet Union, versus what was known as the free world, led by the United States—that replaced the wartime global blocs of the Axis (Japan, Germany, and Italy) versus the Allies (United States, British Commonwealth, China, France, and Soviet Union). These blocs faced off against each other in what came to be called the Cold War. As colonies in Africa and Asia gained their independence from the empires that had controlled them, many new nations found their interests best served by allying with one of the two blocs. Other new nations struggled to retain nonaligned status.

Tensions between the postwar blocs replaced the prewar tensions between the Axis and the Allies. Although the United States was the world's only nuclear power right after the war, the Soviets joined the nuclear club in 1949 with their first successful test of an atomic weapon. Fear of mutual assured destruction kept the Cold War from turning into a hot war between the major superpowers. Instead, confrontational politics and smaller but nevertheless terribly deadly proxy wars—the first of which was the war in Korea, discussed in this chapter—characterized this global tension. Following the extraordinary death and destruction of World War II, many people throughout the world were convinced that an institution focused on maintaining peace must be established. From that grew the United Nations, established in 1945, where much of the confrontational politics initially played out.

U.S. global policy during the Cold War focused on "containment," intended to restrain Soviet influence and expansionism as well as Communist movements throughout the world. Radicalism in starving, war-torn Western Europe was discouraged by American economic aid under the European recovery program, called the Marshall Plan after its originator, General George Marshall (1880–1959), and by the creation of the North Atlantic Treaty Organization (NATO), a collective security arrangement that included the United States and its allies in Western Europe. (West Germany joined NATO in 1951, and Eastern European and Mediterranean countries such as Turkey are now members as well.) The Americans supplied food and medical aid to Japan and military aid to the Nationalist forces in China right after the war, but a Marshall Plan to rebuild East Asia did not exist. In East and Southeast Asia, the United States encouraged a security perimeter around the USSR that included the Republic of China (ROC), and argued that the ROC should have a permanent seat on the Security Council of the UN, together with the United States, United Kingdom, France, and the USSR.

The military occupations of wartime belligerents and their newly independent colonies were molded by Cold War rivalries as well. Germany was divided into hostile neighbors, West Germany and East Germany, which reunited in 1990. As we will see in this chapter, the United States played a dominant role that excluded the Soviets in postwar Japan, and thus Japan was not divided by rival Cold War spheres. But Korea, Vietnam, and China fell into opposing camps of Cold War politics and suffered many years of war as a result.

As important as the creation of the Cold War blocs in the years after World War II was decolonization. Japan and Germany both lost their overseas colonies, but so, too, did the victorious Allies. The Americans, British, Dutch, and French were all pressured to relinquish their colonies, primarily by nationalist movements in the colonies—but also by the embarrassment of still holding colonies after a war in which colonial masters had treated subject peoples with extreme brutality. The Americans had promised independence to the Philippines before the war, and lived up to their promise, granting independence in 1946. Many other colonies were not let go without continuing warfare, and some of that warfare was tangled up in Cold War rivalries. In addition to their wars against anticolonial nationalist movements in Africa, the French lost an eight-year war in Vietnam against Communist and non-Communist nationalist forces. The British were forced to quit India in 1947 after a decades-long nonviolent independence movement led by Mohandas K. Gandhi. India's long-desired victory was severely marred by the horrors of Partition, the separation of India into two (later three) countries, India and Pakistan (and later Bangladesh), and the separation of families, villages, and communities. The death toll associated with Partition is disputed, but most historians consider it to have been between 250,000 and 500,000 people; 15 million people were displaced. Japanese advances in World War II also loosened Britain's control of other colonies, such as Malaya (now Malaysia and Singapore). In addition, Japan had invaded the Dutch East Indies during the war, and the Indonesian nationalist leader Sukarno collaborated with Japan. After Japan's surrender, Sukarno declared independence, but the Dutch returned and fought a bloody war until 1949, when international pressure finally got the Netherlands to grant independence to Indonesia. Over the course of the next decade, African nationalist movements succeeded in driving out European colonial domination as well.

One of the common denominators of anti-imperialist movements was the recruitment of women to the nationalist side. Seen as important contributors to independence movements, women were often shuffled aside soon after independence. In many cases, anticolonialist women had articulated their demands in what they viewed as powerful maternalist terms, that is, as wives and mothers. This allowed postcolonial leaders of the newly formed states to relegate women to the domestic sphere, where they ceased to be seen as contributing members of their nation-states (Redding 2004, 549–550).

In Europe, Australia, Canada, and the United States in the first years of the Cold War, maternalist ideas increasingly pushed women back into their homes. In most of those countries, women had played a large role in the wartime economies, replacing men who had been drawn to the war front. When the soldiers returned and needed jobs, these women were pushed out of the workforce. Because the removal of women from the workforce after World War I had been so disruptive, governments sought ways to mollify displaced women after World War II (Sowerwine and Grimshaw 2004, 594). This was done by enticing women to return home. A cult of motherhood was fostered through movies, books, and other cultural products. Women's fashions accentuated femininity, featuring longer and fuller skirts, styles that had been impractical for women working in factories during the war. The ideal man in cinema was the bulked-up muscular type (Marlon Brando or Rock Hudson), replacing the thin, sophisticated type (Clark Gable or Fred Astaire). Long-pent-up consumer demand led North Americans and, a decade later, Western Europeans to desire the individual-family-oriented homes, cars, and appliances they could increasingly afford. The new appliances did not decrease the amount of housework women were expected to do, however. American women spent the same amount of time on housework in the 1960s as in the 1920s, and British women doubled their expenditure of time on housework from 1937 to 1961 (Sowerwine and Grimshaw 2004, 595).

Women not only retreated to their single-family homes and apartments but were also pushed into them by economic policy, social conditions, and gendered ideology. The postwar baby boom reached its highest point in the late 1950s, with fertility rates in the United States, Australia, and Canada reaching almost four children per woman. This was about 25 percent higher than in the interwar period, and these rates would drop quickly a decade later. But sexuality was no longer seen as primarily intended for reproduction. Couples increasingly used birth control (the pill was not available until somewhat later, but other forms were on the market in the early 1950s), and *Playboy* magazine, which hit the newsstands in 1953, legitimated sex as part of a modern recreational lifestyle.

Motherhood clearly played a role in women's involvement in the workplace. In 1947 two-thirds of unmarried American women worked outside the home, but only 18 percent of married women were in wage work. This pattern differed in Eastern Europe, which was part of the Soviet bloc until around 1990. Soviet ideas of men's and women's roles were imported into Eastern Europe in the immediate postwar period. Women were expected to work full-time, not only because of the Communist commitment to the idea that work was liberating for women but also because of a severe labor shortage following the massive loss of life, especially of male soldiers, during the war. But women's jobs were generally lower-paying and lower-status than men's. In addition, women were also expected to maintain the household, and this they did often without electricity, indoor plumbing, or adequate sources of food for their families (Clements 2004, 562).

Despite the postwar expectations that they should focus on the home, women did gain political rights in some countries where they had not been able to vote before the war or where the vote had been taken away from them by fascist governments. French women gained the vote in 1944, as did Italian women in 1945, and Greek women regained the vote in 1952. Swiss women finally gained the vote in 1971, and Spanish women regained it in 1976 (Sowerwine and Grimshaw 2004, 594).

KOREA

Division of the Nation in Postcolonial Korea

Korea was liberated from Japanese colonial rule in August 1945, when Japan surrendered to the Allied forces after the atomic bombings of Hiroshima and Nagasaki. Amid the exhilaration of liberation in Korea, the Committee for the Preparation of Korean Independence was immediately established and numerous "people's committees" were quickly organized at the local and regional levels. By early September 1945, the Korean People's Republic, a national coalition, had formed, bringing together delegates from around the country. Progressive reform ideas were proposed, including the right for women to vote.

However, the optimism was soon overshadowed by the brewing geopolitical tensions that came with the onset of the Cold War, as well as internal strife among Koreans who held significantly different visions for the future of their newly liberated country. The seeds of these distractions and conflicts had actually been planted much earlier, beginning in the early part of the twentieth century, when Korea's colonial experiences under Japanese rule inspired a wide range of nationalist movements, colonial capitalist development, and modern political ideologies (including socialism, which was actively introduced into Korea in the 1920s).

Despite the political tensions that had existed between them for decades, as a result of military necessity the two global superpowers of the Cold War—the United States and the Soviet Union—were briefly allied during World War II. In the context of the ongoing competition for global hegemony, one of the outcomes of this calculated collaboration was the "temporary" division of the newly independent Korea along the thirty-eighth parallel into two occupied zones. This arrangement came about because the Americans and the Soviets each wanted to make sure the Korean peninsula would not fall to the competing power. It was agreed that the area north of the thirty-eighth parallel would be occupied by the Soviet Union, while the area south of it would be occupied by the United States. This line of division, which was drawn hastily, was supposed to be temporary until a unified Korean government could be established.

In the north, under the leadership of Kim Il Sung (1912–1994), Korean leftists enacted sweeping economic and social reforms with relatively little guidance from the Soviet Union, which never set up a formal occupation government. As a result, within a few months of independence, Japanese colonial structures had been eliminated, progressive land reforms had been carried out with relatively little resistance, major industrial sectors had been nationalized, labor reforms had been adopted to guarantee equal pay for equal work regardless of gender, and those accused of having "collaborated" with the colonial power had been punished.

In sharp contrast, the U.S. forces that were occupying the South had set up the United States Army Military Government in Korea (USAMGIK), which operated from September 9, 1945, to August 15, 1948. The USAMGIK did not recognize the existing, left-leaning Korean People's Republic and eventually outlawed it. The major social reforms that took place under the USAMGIK tended to be conservative, catering to the concerns of the political right. Furthermore, it resurrected administrative structures from the colonial period and actively recruited former employees of the Japanese colonial government as well as anti-Communist, conservative Korean politicians. The heavy-handedness of the USAMGIK brought about tremendous agitation in the South, evident in a series of violent strikes organized by Koreans and the USAMGIK's drive to put down those insurrections.

The socialist North and capitalist South were unable to negotiate terms to unify the Korean peninsula, and each side declared its own political sovereignty: the Republic of Korea (South Korea) was formed in August 1948, led by Rhee Syngman (1875–1965), and the Democratic People's Republic of Korea (North Korea) was formed in September 1948, led by Kim Il Sung (1912–1994). Tensions between South and North Korea escalated rapidly, ultimately leading to the Korean War, the first armed conflict of the Cold War. The war broke out in June 1950, and the peninsula burst into flames, with millions of human casualties. Furthermore, the conclusion of that civil war in 1953 was not a peace treaty but an armistice, a situation that remains in effect to this day. The long-lasting impact of the Korean War and the division of the nation has been immeasurable, affecting people's lives and virtually all aspects of postcolonial Korean society and culture.

In a significant way, the conflicts and tensions found on the Korean peninsula today are deeply rooted in that postcolonial period between 1945 and 1953, when Korea was endeavoring to build a free, independent nation while caught between the hegemonic powers of the Cold War. The Korean War left deep scars, and the resulting political and economic divisions have often drawn attention away from women's issues, just as during the colonial period national independence was prioritized over "the woman question." Although nationalism was the primary focus during this period, women's concerns garnered new attention in postcolonial Korea, with both intended and unintended outcomes.

Women in the Divided Nation

The period between 1945 and 1948 is commonly referred to as the "liberated space" (*haebang kong'gan*), not simply because Korea gained independence from Japanese colonial rule but also because it was an exhilarating period when a wide range of reform ideas from different political and social groups came under consideration. The openness and energy of the time presented women with tremendous possibilities for active participation in shaping the new nation, and also for their liberation from feudal gender practices. However, as described earlier, "national liberation" was incomplete: the peninsula was divided into two entities and awaited a full and permanent resolution of the division. Thus the goal of liberation for women existed in parallel with the goal of true and full liberation for the nation. As part of the celebration of the twenty-sixth anniversary of the 1919 March First Movement, Ko Myŏngja published an essay entitled "Autonomous Independence and the Direction for Women" (Chaju tongnip kwa punyŏ ŭi kil), which captured some of the goals of the women's movement in the liberated space of that time.

> *Since the beginning of human history, women have been oppressed, a class despised in society, suffering all manner and form of persecution that defied any normal sense of morality or humanity. Now women of the world are putting their utmost efforts into the pursuit of liberation, so as Korean women . . . [there are two tasks ahead of us]. The first is to achieve Korea's autonomous independence, and the second is to find a way to completely liberate all people. . . . A nation-state in which men are liberated and women are not is just like a person whose arms are bound but legs are free. This is not true liberation. The liberation we want would bring liberation to all people, and "all people" means both men and women. (Ko 1946, 87–89)*

Immediately after the declaration of Korea's independence, the Women's Alliance for the Establishment of the State (*Kŏn'guk punyŏ tongmaeng*) was formed on August 17, 1945. The organization boasted an extensive membership of women representing a diversity of ideologies. Its main goal was to help establish a new independent democratic nation in which women's liberation was considered a given. In trying to achieve this goal, the Women's Alliance initially represented a united front of political ideologies and interests, from socialism to the conservative bourgeoisie. However, women's voices and organized actions were soon divided along ideological lines, as domestic politics became fragmented and entangled in the battle for supremacy between the Soviet Union and the United States on the peninsula. Women in the North were influenced by socialist reform ideas under the auspices of the Soviet Union, while women in the South lived under the USAMGIK and the subsequent pro-U.S., anti-Communist regime. Given these circumstances, Korean women in the South and North followed drastically different paths.

Women in the North

In the North, "the woman question" was addressed as an important part of the socialist revolution. Women immediately undertook the task of organizing themselves. The North Korean Democratic Women's League, an umbrella organization that brought together local women's groups that had organized spontaneously throughout the country, was established on November 18, 1945. By the end of 1946, its membership exceeded one million, almost one-third of the female population between the ages of eighteen and sixty-one (Kim 2013, 118–119).

The North Korean Provisional People's Committee instituted gender-related laws and policies that represented progressive reform ideas with considerable influence from Soviet precedents (Armstrong 2003, 92). One of the most significant legal provisions with regard to full equity for women was the Gender Equality Law, promulgated by the North Korean Provisional People's Committee and passed in July 1946. This law explicitly declared that "women have equal rights to men economically, culturally, socially, and politically in all areas of life in the nation" (Kim 2010, 752). It specifically stipulated a woman's right to vote and stand for election, as well as to receive equal wages for equal work and to be entitled to equal opportunities for education. This statute also abolished early marriage, concubinage, and prostitution, and established rights for free marriage and divorce. In addition, it declared that "all Japanese imperial laws and regulations pertaining to Korean women's rights are null and void as of the promulgation of this law," which clearly demonstrated a strong desire to discard all remnants of colonialism (Kim 2010, 752). Although some older-generation politicians expressed deep concern that the Gender Equality Law was too progressive, even radical, North Korea took unprecedented steps—at least on paper—to remedy the "triple subordination" that women were subjected to from family, society, and the political system (Armstrong 2003, 93).

In addition to adopting Gender Equality Law, North Korea abolished the family registry (*hojŏk*), the traditional genealogical system that recorded family histories all the way back to the clan's ancestral seat and gave foremost recognition to the rights and privileges of men. In its place, North Korea created what it called a citizen registration system, which was based on the nuclear family rather than the family's ancestral seat. Other important laws were implemented that would have an impact on women's lives.

For example, the Labor Law (1946) stipulated equal pay for equal work, the protection of women and children in the workplace, an eight-hour workday, and paid maternity leave. The 1947 Law to Eradicate Remnants of Feudal Practices outlawed the traditional practice of dowry exchange.

It should not be assumed that these legal provisions automatically translated into progress on all "feminist causes" in the North Korean revolution. To be sure, the old customs of the feudal system, such as the patrilineal nature of the extended family system, were officially condemned and subject to radical reforms; however, the overall approach to gender issues continued to center on the role of woman, particularly the mother, in the domestic sphere. The significant addition in this approach was that woman was now envisioned to have a critical role not only in the home but also in building the socialist state. The historian Suzy Kim makes the pointed argument that "no legislation or political campaign in North Korea ever denounced tradition or Confucianism per se, as occurred during the Chinese Revolution when the family was configured as the source of women's oppression, a position that aligned nationalism, feminism, and Marxism against a common enemy." In North Korea, "rather than the family being faulted for women's oppression, the family and the home came to symbolize the Korean nation in the North Korean Revolution." The figure of the "revolutionary mother" in a new home became a key building block in the framework of North Korean Communism. The revolutionary mother figure "became the primary trope by which to construct not only women's revolutionary subjectivity but all North Koreans, as everyone was extolled to emulate mothers as the most sacrificial model citizen" (Kim 2010, 745).

Women in the South Under the USAMGIK

As women in the North were aligned with the socialist revolution, women in the South were channeled into anti-Communist paths with significant influence from the United States. The USAMGIK was established in September 1945. Prior to the arrival of U.S. forces, for the sake of unifying as a nation, Korean leaders made an effort to bring together various groups regardless of their ideological beliefs or past wrongdoings such as collaboration with the Japanese colonial authorities. However, when the USAMGIK began to govern in South Korea and needed individuals to serve as government officers, it recruited people who had collaborated with the colonial power, which aggravated preexisting tensions.

As mentioned earlier, immediately after independence the Women's Alliance was organized to bring together left-leaning and right-leaning leaders, but with the beginning of the USAMGIK, right-leaning members left the Women's Alliance and formed their own associations to work to support U.S. policies in the South and actively participate in the anti-Communist movement. After this defection, the socialist women remaining in the Women's Alliance had to reorganize, and in December 1945 they renamed the organization the Korean Women's Alliance (Chosŏn punyŏ ch'ong tongmaeng). At that point it comprised 148 women's associations, with regional and local representatives reporting to the central organization. It aimed to accomplish major reforms that would eliminate feudal practices and improve the status and role of women. Specific action items included the right of women to vote and stand for election, wage equality, an eight-hour workday, paid maternity leave, establishment of child care centers, promotion of communal cooking and laundry facilities, and the abolition of all forms of prostitution as well as old marriage customs. However, the USAMGIK ultimately acted to suppress the activities of this left-leaning organization, while it offered increasing support to right-wing women's organizations. Thus in South Korea the women's movement factionalized, and the USAMGIK was not an impartial player in these dynamics.

In September 1946 the first administrative division for women was established within the USAMGIK. As part of its agenda to mobilize women to vote in the South's election on May 10, 1948, the Women's Department (Punyŏguk) worked closely with conservative women's organizations that supported the establishment of a separate government in the South.

One of the most distinctive changes brought about by the presence of U.S. occupying forces in the post-liberation South is related to women's work in the sex trade. In August 1947 the Korean Provisional Legislature passed a law that made public prostitution (*kongch'ang*) illegal. As described in Chapter 7, the public prostitution system in Korea was established in 1904 by the Japanese, initially for Japanese settlers in Korea and Japanese citizens who traveled there for commerce or other reasons. Prostitution thrived throughout the colonial period and continued after Korea's independence in 1945. Most of the women who worked as prostitutes had no economic resources and turned to the sex trade as a matter of survival. Thus, when the new law made no provisions for alternative livelihoods to help former prostitutes after the law was implemented, sex workers protested that the law would push them even further toward the edges of society.

The presence of U.S. military forces in postliberation South Korea added more complexities to the issue. The Korean government in the South made conscious efforts to "console" U.S. soldiers and enhance their morale by making prostitutes available to satisfy their sexual appetites. The prostitution system that catered to U.S. military personnel was unofficial, but it was also highly regulated nonetheless. In May 1947 the USAMGIK established the VD Control Section under the Department of Public Health and Welfare and introduced a program under which "entertaining girls," including prostitutes, *kisaeng*, bar girls, dancers, and waitresses, were periodically examined and, if necessary, treated for venereal disease (Moon 2010, 45). The image of U.S. troops as "benevolent liberators" was an ironic façade. In reality, the U.S. military was, and remains to this day, complicit in the circumstances that led to the proliferation of military camptown prostitution.

Women's Lives During the Korean War

The growing tensions between North and South Korea soon led to the Korean War, which broke out on June 25, 1950. The war reduced most of Korea to ash and rubble. Nearly three million people were killed, wounded, kidnapped, or unaccounted for. Most research on the Korean War has focused on political and military history. Far less attention has been devoted to the actual experiences of women and men on the ground. But recently there have been a number of oral history projects with surviving women that offer glimpses into women's lives during the war (Hahm 2010).

The Korean War brought unspeakable misery and tragedy to women, who were subjected to rape, violence, hunger, and even death. However, it would be inaccurate to understand these women in the war zone solely as victims. They actively sought opportunities to help their families survive the deprivations brought by war. Furthermore, many economic sectors were left vacant when men were drafted into military service. Thus there were unprecedented opportunities for women to fill factory jobs, cultivate land, or engage in retailing. Women working in the public space, especially in the marketplace, sometimes drew negative comments from the public; however, the war had unexpectedly opened up new arenas where women could find economic independence and a general sense of empowerment as they became breadwinners for their families. According to the July 14, 1952, edition of the daily newspaper *Tonga ilbo*, there was remarkable growth in women's participation in the economy during the war, with about six million women workers in the workforce (compared to eight million men). Once the Korean War ended in 1953, men came back from the war zone to become the primary workforce again. Most Korean women returned to the domestic arena and devoted their time and energy to the traditional womanly duties of the home. However, some women, having found

With her brother on her back a war weary Korean girl tiredly trudges by a stalled M-26 tank, at Haengju, Korea.
NATIONAL ARCHIVES IDENTIFIER 520796, LOCAL IDENTIFIER: 80-G-429691

the experience of the workplace to be fulfilling or lucrative, continued to seek work outside the home as well as further education for professional advancement.

Both men and women were mobilized to support the nation during the war. In North Korea this drew on various preexisting mechanisms for mobilizing the populace, including political and economic slogans. In July 1950 Pak Chŏngae, the head of the Alliance of Democratic Women (Minju yŏsŏng ch'ong tongmaeng) in North Korea, wrote an essay for that group's publication, *Chosŏn yŏsŏng* (*Korean Women*), entitled "All Korean Women Rise in Support of the War of Justice to Wipe Out the Enemy of the People." Her message succinctly captures the range and depth of women's participation in the war:

> *Women laborers and peasants! The People's Army is fighting in the War of Justice. We must participate proactively in the movement to enhance the production in order to provide soldiers with food, clothing, medicine and the other necessities they require to succeed. In addition, women must take up a wide range of jobs and carry out the work that used to be done by men. Women must also take*

> *care of our wounded soldiers, send warm letters of comfort to the People's Army and provide relief efforts to the families those soldiers have left behind. . . . Women are honored to carry out this great and sacred task in pursuit of the complete unification of our nation. There will only be bright victory ahead of us. Let's move forward bravely in order to achieve the unification of the nation, the freedom and rights of women and the happiness of our children! (Quoted in Pak 2006, 11)*

As described above, in the absence of men, women were actively called to participate in re-creating the social order that had been destroyed by the war. They supported soldiers on the battlefield not only by making sacrifices at home so that those soldiers would have the food and clothing they needed on the war front, but also sometimes by taking courageous action themselves against enemy armies. On the home front, women collected funds, conserved daily resources, extended their work hours, donated family treasures, and offered assistance for war orphans and the families of the war dead. They helped transport resources to the war zone, participated in rebuilding bridges and roads that had been destroyed in bombing raids, and worked in factories in the absence of men. The situation was similar in rural areas. Because able-bodied men had been sent to the front, married women undertook the major part of agricultural production under the slogan "Increase agricultural product with women's power!"

The situation in South Korea was similar. Before the war, many women had engaged in farming, but when hostilities began, women's participation in the economy increased, rising from 28.4 percent in 1949 to 63.7 percent in 1951. Women became rice merchants, seamstresses, restaurateurs, and peddlers; others found jobs in factories or transportation, while still others moved into professions such as journalism and medicine. But the vast majority of women continued to engage in the traditional "women's work" of cooking and mending clothes, with the main difference being that during the war the work was done for remuneration in the marketplace, rather than in the service of the family.

The war widowed many women. There were approximately three hundred thousand widows in South Korea in 1953, but two years later the number had grown to half a million. Widows were often the sole breadwinners for their families. The vast majority of them worked as peddlers, cooks, launderers, housemaids, or waitresses. For the sake of their families, many took any work available to support their children and elderly family members.

BOX 9.1

The Lot of War Widows

The journalist Chŏng Ch'ungnyang reports on the nearly unimaginable hardships that war widows had to face in the patriarchal Korean society after the Korean War. By recounting the largely tragic episodes of war widows, Chŏng reminds readers of the hypocrisy and cruelty of male-centered society. Below are some excerpts from her essay.

> *Lady L is in her thirties with five children. She became a widow when her husband was abducted by North Koreans. All of her children attend school, but she finds it difficult to make enough to feed them twice a day. She has given up the pride and dignity of her higher education, seeking any job that would provide enough income to care for her children. She has broken down in front of her friends, pleading with them to find any man who would support her family. She used to say that she would never remarry if it would make her children uneasy, but she is so desperate to feed them that she has abandoned those principles. She visits the friends of her late husband, seeking their help in finding employment, but nothing is on the horizon. . . . A few days ago she informed me that her eldest son had graduated from high school and now works as a clerk at a company. That has offered her some relief in that she no longer has to cover the expense of one tuition. Despite that she recently told me that she feels a family suicide might be her only respite. . . .*
>
> *It is very rare for a widow to remarry happily. For them it is not a matter of remaining chaste; rather, it is simply difficult to find an appropriate partner. If she has two or three children, it's probably wiser for her to give up on the idea of remarriage altogether. (If she has one child, she might still be considered an acceptable candidate for remarriage.) If she finds a reasonably good candidate, there are any number of uncertainties and potential pitfalls—will she be treated well? Will her children be embraced or despised? Even in the event that she finds herself in the best possible circumstances, there is such stigma associated with widows remarrying that she will likely be subjected to questions about her morality and to social ostracism.*
>
> *If a widow has a pension or some other financial resources to rely on, she might be able to prepare a separate household for her children and remarry, but sadly, most don't have such financial independence.*

Thus widows tend to resign themselves to the idea that the only hope they have for a decent life is their children. They love their children, of course, but with the severe constraints imposed by poverty, the burdens of raising them can be overwhelming. If we consider the typical widow's lot of excessive poverty without a male partner to share love with, her unwieldy emotions can be understood. Nonetheless, maternal love is the only way for widows to save their own lives. . . .

We have all heard scandalous rumors of widows who have an inheritance or are hiding some accumulated wealth. It is said they lead promiscuous lives that create disorder in their home lives, driving their children into delinquency. Poor widows are so busy trying to earn enough money to feed their children that they don't have the time to supervise their children, and without that supervision the children go astray. Wealthy widows are so busy dating [in order to find a new husband with whom] to properly raise their children that the children rebel. Indeed, life is not fair. I believe that widows shouldn't suppress their instinct [sexual desire], but the circumstances in this country make it difficult for them to remarry. Many temptations surround them. Furthermore, men's anachronistic ways of thinking view widows as virtually worthless, which makes the prospect of a widow remarrying fairly remote. In the end, can we say their children are the sole source of comfort and the rest of their lives is burdened as if they were carrying the cross on their backs? When the state does not provide these victims of the war with any support, shouldn't the public have a sense of compassion toward them? If there are no welfare programs for widows, then the public should at least be considerate. (Chŏng 1955)

The extreme poverty brought about by the war also drove a large number of women into sex work. As discussed in Chapters 7 and 8, women in poverty were frequently forced into the system of sex service out of financial need. Daughters of impoverished families were the most vulnerable to this aspect of colonial capitalist development and military aggression. The system was also abetted implicitly and explicitly by Korean men, who created and maintained these sex services. The fact that there was such continuity from the colonial to the postcolonial era in the provision of sex services shows how women's bodies have been subject to the congruent power dynamics of patriarchy, (neo)colonialism, and the market economy. The only real shift was the change in clientele from Japanese soldiers in colonial Korea to U.S. soldiers in postcolonial Korea. Thus the practice of women selling sex should be understood within the context of "the presence of imperial troops, the legacy of the comfort station that naturalized both military and civilian authorities' use of women's sexual labor to manage (male) soldiers, and the mass impoverishment generated by Japanese colonial exploitation and the Korean War" (Moon 2010, 40–43).

During the Korean War, prostitution was conducted openly with the unofficial sponsorship of the U.S. military and South Korean government. The South Korean government helped set up "comfort stations," or houses of prostitution, essentially using the model established by the Japanese imperial power during the Pacific War. There were two separate types of "comfort stations," distinguished by the military personnel they were set up to serve. The "UN comfort stations" were designated specifically for use by the Allied forces. With three hundred thousand Allied troops deployed in South Korea during the war, the rationale used to justify the establishment of these comfort stations was that they offered a mechanism to protect respectable Korean women from the sexual aggression of foreign soldiers. The Korean women who provided sexual services at UN comfort stations were called "UN madams" or "Western princesses" (*yang kongju*). The other type of comfort stations, called "special comfort stations," was established to cater to Korean soldiers (Moon 2010, 51). The discussion of military camptowns will continue in Chapter 10.

The Korean War resulted in massive displacement of families and communities, drastic fluctuations in traditional values and interpersonal relations, and highly unstable political and economic conditions. During the postwar reconstruction, which took place in the context of the Cold War at both regional and global levels, both North and South Korea launched major economic development plans following their respective political systems—socialist democracy in North Korea and capitalist liberal democracy in South Korea. Because of the differences in socioeconomic and cultural circumstances in the two different political systems, the lives and experiences of women in North and South Korea diverged significantly.

CHINA

In China, the Japanese surrender did not mark the end of war. Efforts by the United States to broker a truce between the two sides failed, and a civil war immediately erupted between the Communists and the Nationalists. The Nationalist Party's military efforts were severely hampered by economic collapse; rampant inflation was exacerbated by shortages of consumer goods, corruption, and inept monetary policies. In 1949 the cost of rice was more than seven hundred million times what it had been in 1937. As poverty and famine spread across the country, the number of refugees grew to nearly a tenth of the population. Urban dwellers and those in rural areas who had not already been drawn to support the Communists gave up on the Nationalists and began to see the Communists as the best hope for stability, let alone progress.

Chiang Kai-shek's regime responded to mounting criticisms and protests with force: assassinating critics, gunning down demonstrators, and rebuffing calls for political liberalization and pursuit of a truce in the civil war. With superior military strategy and politically committed troops, the People's Liberation Army (PLA), led by Communist Party Chairman Mao Zedong, marched steadily to take over Nationalist-controlled territory, pushing Chiang's forces to retreat to Taiwan. Mao declared the establishment of the People's Republic of China (PRC) on October 1, 1949.

Early PRC economic policies brought about stability, ended the inflationary spiral, and laid the foundations for postwar reconstruction, industrialization, and development. The First Five-Year Plan, modeled on the Soviet Union's state-controlled economic development strategy, started in 1953. With the support of thousands of Soviet technical advisors and loans, China dramatically expanded its industrial output and increased agricultural productivity. In addition to establishing a solid foundation for economic growth, the new regime improved daily life for most of the population, with rising life expectancy and income.

The founding of the PRC was not only about the success of a revolutionary movement in coming to power. It marked the culmination of the Communist Party's long efforts to build a modern socialist state structure. The PRC was governed by the three overlapping bureaucracies of Party, state, and military, but at every level of administration, a Party committee dominated decision making, from the Politburo at the top of the system to the local level. The party held political power, setting policy directions for state organs to follow. Mass campaigns inspired by the governing principles of the mass line (consulting with the masses to develop policy for the masses) and class struggle were the main mechanism for mobilizing the populace to participate in social transformation and construction of the new economic and political order. Gender equality, family modernization, and women's full incorporation into production were integral to the Communist Party's vision of the new society. As Communist forces moved into new areas, they organized struggle meetings, often violent, to politically marginalize the so-called bad classes of landlords, exploitative local bullies, former Nationalist officials, and capitalists. Women in every sector of society were active participants in these political campaigns, both as local party leaders and as victims.

Land Reform and Social Transformation of the Countryside

Land reform began in the areas of North China controlled by the Communists during the civil war, but after 1949 it was implemented across the rest of the country. The economic goal was to increase the productivity of agriculture by transforming the old "feudal" agricultural system, based on landlord ownership and tenant labor, into a new system of collective ownership and labor. The first step in the process of collectivization was distributing land equitably to all peasants. The next step was organizing farmers into mutual aid teams and cooperatives to pool land and share labor, animals, and equipment. In the final stage, completed by 1957, ownership of land, animals, and tools was collectivized and peasants were paid for their labor. Politically the goal was to mobilize peasants to support the new order and integrate villages into the Party-state structure. In the process, those opposed to the new regime were marginalized as political enemies and more than a million landlords were killed.

Although land reform in principle granted women land rights equal to men's by counting them in land allocation, in practice land was distributed to households, most of which were dominated by men. In struggle meetings denouncing landlords, peasants learned that their poverty and suffering were a result not of fate but of class oppression by landlords, and propaganda directed at women linked women's low status and mistreatment to the problems of class division:

> *Only after the liberation of working people as a whole can we women be liberated from feudal oppression. For example, buy-and-sell marriage [that is, with the exchange of bride-price for a wife] was based on the feudal economic system. It does not exist in the Soviet Union because the working people became the masters of the country and do not treat women like oxen and horses. Thus, we have to make clear the relationship between the land reform movement and our women's liberation.* (Quoted in Hershatter 2011, 77)

Struggle meetings gave women a new language for understanding their inferior status in society. They were encouraged to participate in "speaking bitterness" about their exploitation by landlords and their oppression as women in the "old society." Party cadres described the Communist revolution as liberation from this "feudal" past in which women were secluded and abused. In fact, many women's lives had already been dramatically transformed through decades of warfare, famine, and deep poverty. In many regions of China women already worked in the fields, moved from one place to another in search of work, or survived alone as widows. Another goal of these meetings was for Party cadres to identify women of "good" class background—that is, poor peasants—who had potential to be trained as leaders in local branches of the new All-China Women's Federation.

The All-China Women's Federation

The Party reached down to local communities through state-sponsored mass organizations, such as the Communist Youth League and trade unions, which were charged with mobilizing the population to participate in mass campaigns to carry out new policies. One of these was the All-China Women's Federation, founded in 1949 as an umbrella organization that would enfold all existing women's groups. Local branches were set up at each level of administration, from the central government to villages and neighborhoods. Local branches of the federation formed women's congresses, whose elected members communicated women's concerns to Party officials and Party policies to women, and mobilized women to participate in mass campaigns. By 1953 the Federation encompassed more than forty thousand women officials across the country.

In the countryside, the key task of the Women's Federation was mobilizing women to work in fields alongside men, a task assumed to be essential for economic growth in the early years of the PRC. To encourage women and men to work effectively to develop the economy, the Party celebrated labor models who embodied diligence, obedience to Party discipline, skill, and enthusiasm. Female labor models promoted work outside the home and men's acceptance of women's work. The labor models' job was to organize women into production teams, teach them about Party policies and the national importance of their labor, and lead them in building new skills. They were also tasked with mediating family disputes and mobilizing women to participate in campaigns such as those to implement the Marriage Law of 1950 (discussed later in the section on family reform).

Some women had to contend with their husband's opposition to these new leadership roles, but for many these new activities were profoundly transformative. Many gained respect precisely because they exhibited quite traditional feminine virtues such as chaste widowhood and wifely loyalty. These women's lives exemplified the process through which the Maoist party-state replaced a failed traditional patriarchal order. The party gave them a new language for understanding themselves. Fu Guifeng, a labor model from Shaanxi Province, recollected:

> *Although my parents gave birth to me, it was the Party that brought me up: Mao and the Women's Federation. . . . In July 1949, the district . . . sent a cadre to my house. They wanted to select someone who had suffered, who was capable. At that time I had no formal name. . . . My name, Fu Guifeng, was given to me on that date. . . . From that time, every level of the Women's Federation came looking for me. . . . Every level of the Party and government consciously trained and educated . . . me. They spent more on me than what it costs to train a university student. (Quoted in Hershatter 2000, 92)*

Although these women were potent examples of how the revolution could empower poor rural women, Party propaganda made no mention of domestic labor and child rearing or the fact that women continued to be responsible for the bulk of it. Rural labor models and Women's Federation cadres, who enthusiastically worked long hours and were proud of their accomplishments, also struggled to balance their dedication to the Party with motherhood and domestic work. Many placed their children in the care of wet nurses or communal day care and missed important family events because of their duties.

In the cities, the All-China Women's Federation branches included groups of women workers, students, teachers, artists, professionals, and housewives, but the work of these groups overlapped with that of other local units. All city dwellers were organized into work units (*danwei*), equivalent to the workplace or school with which they were affiliated, or they were linked to residents' committees in neighborhoods that reached the retired, self-employed, and unemployed, who did not have work units. These local-level organizations functioned as tools for surveillance, enforcing political conformity and controlling all aspects of daily life: housing, distribution of ration coupons, job changes, dispute mediation, marriage, divorce, birth control, and even funerals. In Shanghai alone, participation in Federation congresses grew to some fifty thousand by 1953. Many of these women were also members of the residents' committees that were in charge of every aspect of neighborhood life, from public health to street repairs to social problems. In Shanghai by

1954 half of these committee members were women. City officials recognized that housewives were particularly useful for this kind of neighborhood work precisely because they were not employed elsewhere (Wang 2005).

A key responsibility of the Women's Federation in the cities was to mobilize women to participate in the nationwide campaigns through which the Party solidified its control. For example, during the Five Antis campaign in 1952 to eliminate corruption, tax evasion, fraud, theft of state property, and theft of financial information among business owners, the federation rallied wives of these men to educate their husbands about the new policies. When China entered the Korean War in November 1950, sending some seven hundred thousand troops into the conflict, the Party rallied a population exhausted from its own decades of war to "resist America and aid Korea" in a mass campaign targeting hundreds of thousands of "counterrevolutionaries" accused of sabotage. The Federation organized efforts to raise money for the war effort and to make care packages to send to soldiers in Korea. Housewives participated in political study groups to encourage patriotism through cutting household expenses to donate money for the war, doing handicraft work, and bolstering their husbands' productivity with the "three cleans": clean homes, streets, and yards; clean food, water, and cooking utensils; and clean beds, bedding, and clothes (Goldstein 1998, 159). Women were also encouraged to identify counterrevolutionaries in their communities.

On International Women's Day in 1951, the Shanghai Women's Federation organized a rally of some three hundred thousand women to protest the rearming of Japan. One woman who joined the rally noted, "Participants in the parade all felt that women have power and status now. Even men said, now women are a big deal" (Wang 2005, 526). As women asserted the equivalence of local Women's Federation congresses with residents' committees and pushed for attention to women's concerns about health, child care, literacy, and vocational training, they encountered hostility and opposition from male officials and men on residents' committees. By the mid-1950s, new regulations clarified that women's congresses were subordinate to residents' committees and thus "women-work"—the mobilization of women for revolutionary activities such as political struggle, social reform, literacy and hygiene campaigns, and production—did not take priority over the Party's "central work." As men questioned the need for a special organization for women, the executive head of the All-China Women's Federation, Zhang Yun, vociferously defended the existence of local women's congresses: "Because the ideas and practices of valuing men over women still exist in our society, women still confront special problems in ideas, work, and personal life. Therefore, we must have a separate women's organization specialized in women-work" (Wang 2005, 536).

Family Reform

Reform of the legal foundations of the family was integral to the new state's agenda. The PRC promulgated the revolutionary Marriage Law in 1950 just as it launched the land reform campaign. The new law articulated a modernist vision of the family and its relationship to the state. It abolished "the feudal marriage system based on arbitrary and compulsory arrangements and the supremacy of man over woman, and in disregard of the interests of children." It established a "new democratic marriage system" based on free choice of partners, monogamy, equal rights for both sexes, and protection of "the lawful interests of women and children." The law set the minimum legal age for marriage at twenty for men and eighteen for women, and all marriages had to be registered with a state office. It also allowed divorce in uncontested cases after mediation by a government registrar. In cases in which only one spouse wanted divorce, it was to be granted only after mediation by the district people's government had failed to bring about reconciliation. Since there were no fees for filing a court case, divorce became in effect easier than it had been in the Republican period (Diamant 2000).

Adopting the New Culture rhetoric (see Chapter 6) promoting the "small family" (i.e., nuclear family) as the foundation of the modern nation, the law stated that the function of marriage was to stabilize not just the family but the larger revolutionary society: "Husband and wife are duty bound to love, respect, assist, and care for their children, and to strive jointly for the welfare of the family and for the building up of the new society." But while the law affirmed the same New Culture movement principles that had inspired legal reforms under the Nationalist regime and in Communist base areas, it also definitively placed the state at the center of family life, replacing the arbitrary and diverse marital arrangements imposed by family heads with universal laws mandated by the state (Glosser 2003). State paternalism to protect women and children was an explicit aim of the law.

Between 1950 and 1953, the All-China Women's Federation led efforts to promote the law through campaigns animated with song, dance, and opera performances in local communities all over the country. These campaigns reinforced the message that the Communist Party had liberated women from feudal patriarchy. The law changed some practices, such as concubinage, faster than others, such as bride price, which persisted in many rural areas. Parental involvement in marriage choices continued in the country-

Excerpt from pamphlet, "Li Feng Jin: How the New Marriage Law Helped One Woman Stand Up," used to educate people about the 1950 law.
EDITED AND TRANSLATED BY SUSAN GLOSSER 2005

side, with "half-free, half-arranged" marriages: matchmakers and parents matched couples, who then were able to express their views about the prospective match. The divorce provision of the Marriage Law threatened marital stability and family hierarchy, and was vociferously resisted, sometimes violently, by many husbands, parents, and parents-in-law. It empowered the younger generation of women, often at the expense of poor peasant men.

Confronted with new responsibility for mediating marital and other family disputes, newly appointed local party officials, many of whom were poor, uneducated, and inexperienced, often resisted implementation of the Marriage Law. Rural women in many regions were most likely to take advantage of the new law in its early years, and many appealed to higher-level courts when their divorce requests were rejected by local officials. In the heyday of campaigns to promote the law, many urban officials, newly arrived from the countryside, also took advantage of the law to divorce their "backward" peasant wives in favor of "cultured" urban women. Ironically, urban intellectuals and workers, more constrained by concerns about reputation and work schedules, were least likely to pursue divorce (Diamant 2000).

BOX 9.2

Implementing the Marriage Law

In 1953, as the Party was preparing a monthlong campaign to push implementation of the Marriage Law, Gan Yifei, the head of the Shaanxi Provincial Propaganda Department, gave a speech to a training meeting for women cadres to explain the significance of the new law not just for women but for men and for larger Party goals.

> *The feudal marriage system is an evil system. It shackles women and men. . . . Because they didn't marry out of love, they didn't have sexual intercourse, fought with each other, quarreled, broke bowls and pots or lay on the kang [North Chinese platform bed] without moving. Many women and men had no way out and jumped into wells or hanged themselves. . . . Because people were not satisfied with their marriages, and didn't have sexual relations they committed adultery. Sometimes one man had a couple of women. Sometimes one woman had a couple of men. Adultery causes murders and affects social security. . . . According to Shaanxi statistics for the first half of 1952, 196 women and 90 men killed themselves or were killed because of marriage problems. This means implementing the Marriage Law is not purely an issue of liberating women. It is also an issue of liberating men. . . . Abolishing the feudal marriage system is most beneficial to women. So women, young women in particular, are most eager to abolish it and the most devoted [to the cause]. This is also an issue for men. . . . How well marriage problems are solved determines whether people will live a happy life or a bitter one, whether the family will be harmonious or not. So, this is not only an issue about husband and wife, about family, but also about liberating social productivity, democracy and solidarity, the unity of nationalities, the campaign Resist America Aid Korea, and production and construction. We shouldn't just take it as women's business. . . . [T]his is the responsibility of all men and women, of all revolutionary comrades. (Hershatter 2011, 111)*

Women and Work

Women's participation in agricultural work expanded steadily in the early 1950s, but in the new cooperatives they earned fewer work points, and thus lower pay, than men. When male co-op leaders argued that gendered divisions of labor justified different work point rates, the Women's Federation took up the cause of wage equality, insisting that "equal pay for equal work means, no matter whether it is women, seniors, or half-laborers, as long as they do the same amount and the same quality as men, they should get the same points" (quoted in Hershatter 2011, 140). Unequal pay continued to be a problem even as women took up an ever greater share of agricultural labor. By the middle of the decade, as men increasingly pursued other kinds of jobs in the collectives and contract work outside their villages, agricultural work became increasingly feminized.

In the cities, all women and men had a right to employment under the new system. Although employee benefits, including housing, health care, accident insurance, child care, and maternity leave, varied among different kinds of work units, typically they were equivalent for women and men. Pay rates were generally the same for men and women in the same jobs with the same seniority. Yet gendered assignment of jobs typically relegated women to lower-level positions, with lower pay and less opportunity for raises and promotions. In many factories, for instance, women were considered most suitable for nontechnical, service, or auxiliary jobs in maintenance or cleaning and in child care centers, cafeterias, or clinics, and in 1952 women accounted for only 11.7 percent of workers in state-owned units. Many urban women were unemployed.

Sex work effectively disappeared during the first decades of the Mao era. Between 1947 and 1951 the PRC government effectively banned prostitution in China's major cities, launching a campaign to reeducate prostitutes to make them into productive female citizens of the new modern socialist society. The rhetoric of the campaign taught the women to see themselves as victims of the poverty, trafficking, crime, and exploitative relationships of the old capitalist society. In Shanghai, which had the largest sex industry, gang leaders who ran brothels were arrested and executed as counter-revolutionaries, and all brothels were shut down in 1951. Police rounded up prostitutes, bar hostesses, taxi dancers, masseuses, and other women who sold sex and detained them in the Women's Labor Training Institute, where they were treated for sexually transmitted diseases and opiate addiction and taught literacy and job skills such as sewing. After their release, they were returned to their families in the villages if possible, assigned to factory work in the cities, or, if they wished, sent to state farms in remote frontier provinces. Most were matched with husbands. In 1958, the government declared that prostitution had been eradicated (Hershatter 1997, 304–325).

Women's Health and Fertility

Even as it promoted gender equality and women's full participation in production, the new regime continued to operate with assumptions of natural gender differences that emphasized women's roles as mothers and housewives (Evans 1997). In the early years of the PRC, although Party leaders were concerned about whether China could produce enough food to feed its huge population, the Party enthusiastically encouraged women to have as many babies as possible to reverse the effects of decades of warfare, high infant mortality, and disease. Early health regulations severely limited access to contraception, sterilization, and abortion. Pro-natalist values were also reflected in labor regulations that gave women special dispensations at work for menstruation, pregnancy, childbirth and breastfeeding.

As part of its campaign to improve public health, the Party launched a program to improve the health and life expectancy of women and children under the slogan "One pregnancy, one live birth; one live birth, one healthy child." The Women's Federation collaborated with the Department of Public Health to organize propaganda teams to educate women and create new local units in charge of women and infants. In training sessions, old-style midwives and young new recruits studied anatomical diagrams and local and national infant mortality statistics. They learned about tetanus, blood poisoning, and the dangers of traditional birthing methods. They were educated in the practices of "scientific childbirth," including sterilizing instruments and prenatal and postpartum care. By the end of the decade, the total number of trained midwives had doubled to over 35,000, and there were 774,983 assistant midwives who had completed a short course. Many newly trained health workers also did vaccinations and other basic medical care. Although they encountered much resistance and misunderstanding at first, over the next two decades, with the exception of the famine years (see Chapter 10), infant mortality gradually fell and overall life expectancy increased (Goldstein 1998).

Women in the Republic of China on Taiwan

As the Communists took over the Chinese mainland, Generalissimo Chiang Kai-shek led his Nationalist troops, party leadership, and many civilians to the island of Taiwan, a former prefecture of Fujian province that had been ceded to Japan after it defeated China in the Sino-Japanese War in 1894–1895. The Taiwan that was finally returned to China in 1945 was significantly different from China culturally and economically. Under Japanese colonial rule between 1895 and 1945, despite political repression and systematic discrimination against the Taiwanese population, the colony experienced much faster industrialization, greater expansion of education, and higher living standards than the mainland. By the end of World War II, some 80 percent of men and 60 percent of women were literate in Chinese, and most could read Japanese as well.

In line with its modernizing mission, the colonial regime had also banned footbinding and trafficking in women and girls, and gave women the right to divorce and remarry. Since the island did not have a university, many young women attended universities in Japan and returned home to do professional work in medicine, nursing, education, commerce, civil service, and journalism. In Japan they also learned about Western and Japanese women's movements. Associating Japan with modern civilization, young Taiwanese New Culture activists drew inspiration from the efforts of Japanese feminists to promote full gender equality, women's economic independence, and marriage choice based on love. The Japanese government actively encouraged women to enter the labor force. Large numbers of women worked in the textile, sugar, tea, and processed food industries and as agricultural laborers. They also began to enter traditionally male occupations such as construction, driving, office work, and radio broadcasting.

During the 1920s, a period of relative political openness, Taiwanese students launched their own New Culture Movement. Their journal, *Taiwan Youth*, like *New Youth* on the mainland, explored progressive ideas about gender and cultural modernity, but it also promoted the development of a distinctively Taiwanese culture and helped to initiate a movement to work toward self-governance and Taiwanese independence from both Japan and China. Taiwanese women students in Japan and at home took up the cause of women's suffrage along with demands for self-rule, though, as in China, feminist concerns were a secondary priority. Women were prominent participants in leftist organizations such as the Taiwan Communist Party and the Taiwan Farmers' Union as well as in key organizations promoting cultural and political autonomy.

Hsieh Hsueh-hung (1901–1970) exemplifies the transnational influences that shaped the women's movement in Taiwan. Sold to be a concubine at the age of twelve, she fled at sixteen and worked in a sugar mill before traveling to Japan to study for three years. As an early activist in the Taiwan Cultural Association, she was forced to escape to Shanghai in 1925 to evade the colonial police; she entered Chinese Communist circles, went to Moscow to study for two years, and became one of the founding members of the Taiwan Communist Party, formed as a branch of the Japanese Communist Party. Like her contemporary Xiang Jingyu (see Chapter 5) on the mainland, Hsieh built the Party's Women's Department while emphasizing that women's liberation could not be separated from the goals of emancipation from colonial rule and proletarian revolution. Yet, having allied with Japanese, Korean, and Chinese women radicals in her travels, she envisioned an East Asian united front in the struggle against patriarchy and capitalism (Chang 2009).

As in Korea, the onset of World War II brought increased political repression, censorship, and rather unsuccessful attempts to replace Chinese culture with Japanese culture by banning Chinese surnames, Chinese opera, and Chinese marriage and funeral ceremonies and imposing Shintoism on the population. During this period, only government-sponsored women's organizations were allowed to operate (see Chapter 8). Taiwanese women were mobilized to volunteer support for the war effort through local chapters of the Patriotic Women's Association, the Japanese Red Cross, the Greater Japan Federated Women's Association, the Greater Japan National Defense Women's Association, and, for school-age girls, the Girls' Youth Corps. Women worked as nurses on the home front and the battlefield; did support work for wounded soldiers and their families; organized literacy classes to teach women Japanese; ran vocational schools to teach handicrafts, home economics, and other income-generating skills for female family members of wounded police and military personnel; coordinated air raid evacuation drills and emergency rescue training; and rallied women to save money, conserve energy, and recycle to support the war effort. The colonial government also ran the Taiwan Women's Philanthropic Association, which organized wives of Taiwanese officials, industrial managers, military officers, and other elites to raise funds through cultural events for social welfare projects in health care, disaster relief, poor relief, and veteran support. As men left for the war front, women replaced them in factory jobs, and by the end of the war more than 40 percent of industrial workers were women. They were employed in power plants, mining, and factories producing metals, fertilizers, coal, cement, alcohol, cigarettes, salt canned foods, matches, paper, and medicine (Chang 2009).

After 1945, the Nationalist Party governed Taiwan much as the Japanese had. Viewing the locals as tainted by their "Japanification" and mentality as colonial slaves, they filled government posts with mainlanders, discriminated against Taiwanese in business dealings and property ownership, and imposed Mandarin as the official dialect of Chinese. When an anti-mainlander rebellion broke out in 1947, the Nationalist rulers imposed martial law (which would not be lifted for nearly forty years) and unleashed a reign of terror, killing some ten thousand people and wounding some thirty thousand more in the infamous February Twenty-Eighth Incident. When Chiang and his troops arrived in 1949 along with tens of thousands of refugees from the mainland, he unleashed a second campaign of terror to root out suspected Communists, killing tens of thousands more.

Committed both to Taiwanese independence and to Communist revolution, Hsieh Hsueh-hung was a central figure in the movement for democratic self-rule and a leader of the armed resistance against the Nationalists in the central city of Taichung where she was known for her radical tactics. As the resistance collapsed, she fled to Hong Kong, founded the Taiwan Democratic Self-Government League, and then moved to Communist China, hoping to find support for the cause of an autonomous Communist Taiwan. However, she was purged along with other Taiwanese Communists in the Anti-Rightist campaign and died in Beijing at the height of the Cultural Revolution (see Chapter 10). There was no tolerance for autonomous political movements under martial law, and so women's activism entered a dormant phase that would last until the 1970s.

JAPAN

Poverty, Gender, and Sexuality in the First Months After the War

Millions of Japanese huddled around radios to hear the voice of the emperor for the first time on August 15, 1945, as he broadcast the news of Japan's surrender. He called on the Japanese people to "endure the unendurable and bear the unbearable." But starvation and homelessness neither started nor ended with the emperor's declaration of defeat. At the end of the war, nine million Japanese were homeless. An additional seven million were scattered throughout the empire and needed to find a way to return to Japan and to find a home when they did return. For millions, the knowledge that their families' loved ones and breadwinners would never come home caused a deep sense of despair, which Japanese psychologists, even before the end of the war, had identified and labeled *kyōdatsu* ("emotional collapse"; see Dower 1999, 89). For others, however, the end of the war represented liberation—from the Japanese government's wartime repression, from the threat of death from the sky via Allied air raids, or from the anticipation of an Allied military invasion (which did not occur because Japan surrendered).

Both men and women suffered, but in many cases it was women, many of them widows, who had to find new ways to help their families survive in the chaotic times right after defeat. Because agricultural production was at a fraction of its prewar level, food was still rationed as it had been during

BOX 9.3

The Hiroshima Maidens

In the late 1940s and early 1950s, Methodist pastor Tanimoto Kiyoshi of Hiroshima, who had been educated at Emory University in Atlanta, ministered to many severely injured survivors of the atomic bomb dropped on Hiroshima. While touring the United States to raise funds to help the injured, he met Norman Cousins, editor of the *Saturday Review of Literature*. By the mid-1950s, Tanimoto had recruited Cousins to develop a plan to raise money to support Hiroshima orphans and to bring twenty-five young women with disfiguring scars to the United States for plastic surgery. The survivors of the atomic bombs dropped in Hiroshima included men, women, and children, but it was believed that men's hard work would allow them to make a life for themselves in postwar Japan, even if they had been disfigured by the blast, while a woman would have no future without being able to get married. As one of these "Hiroshima maidens" explained, "Having a maimed face can . . . deprive you of all incentive to do anything. Whatever people say, the face is what counts if you're a woman" (Shibusawa 2006, 237–238). Cousins and the Americans he recruited to care for the young women while they were in the United States for their surgery shared the 1950s view that women's normal destiny was to be married. The survivors were, of course, in need of medical help, but they also were young women, ostensibly unable to marry (hence "maidens"), and because of their gender not considered responsible for the war. Thus they came to be seen as symbols of peace, a frequently gendered category in postwar Japan and the United States. As the young women treated in the United States had counterparts in other countries as well, with groups of young women in need of medical care being sent to Russia, England, and elsewhere, they unknowingly played a role in Cold War–era scientific competition (which of the Cold War blocs could provide the best care?) while representing universal hopes for world peace.

the war. Families could not survive on the meager rations allotted by the government, and most people depended on food they bought illegally on the black market. Many urban residents trudged long distances to the countryside to exchange whatever clothing or household items they had for small amounts of food. Most businesses had been destroyed during the war, so there were few jobs for urban residents. The firebombing of cities led to the destruction of housing and a resulting mass migration to the countryside before the war ended, but half the population still lived in the cities, often in huts made of wood scavenged from destroyed houses.

Into this situation came the Allied military occupation. Arriving in Japan on August 30, 1945, the American general Douglas MacArthur took over as Supreme Commander for the Allied Powers (SCAP), beginning an almost seven-year period of occupation. (Although SCAP technically refers to MacArthur himself, the acronym was often used to refer to the whole occupation administration; this chapter will do so as well.)

For the first time in seventy-five years, Japan did not focus on relations with Asia. Japan's territory reverted to its 1870s boundaries. The colonies gained their independence, and to the extent that Japanese people interacted with others, it was with Allied military forces. The Americans insisted that the Japanese refer to the war with the term "Pacific War" instead of the previously used "Great East Asia War," thereby erasing the role of Asia in the war from 1931 to 1945. The prewar transnational interactions of Asian feminists and Christians, detailed in Chapters 4, 5, 6, and 8, were not resurrected immediately after the war. Japanese women did return to international feminist collaboration in the postwar period, but their focus would initially shift to links with America and Europe rather than other East Asian nations.

Anticipating the arrival of foreign forces, the Japanese government spent the first two weeks after the war ended destroying government records and setting up sex stations for the army of occupation (Dower 1999, 125). When Japanese government officials learned that MacArthur would oppose official military sex stations, they called on private entrepreneurs to set up brothels, guaranteeing them police protection and government loans. Just as the wartime Japanese government had assumed that Japanese soldiers' uncontrolled sexual urges would lead to greater violence against civilians and, therefore, set up "comfort stations" throughout the Asian war zone (see Chapter 8), they continued to believe that the Allied soldiers would attack Japanese women if their sexual needs were not met. In essence, the government tried to protect the masses of Japanese women by sacrificing between fifty-five thousand and seventy-thousand women and girls in military brothels (Mackie 2003, 136).

Recruiting announcements posted in the weeks after the war called on "new Japanese women" to "participate in the great task of comforting the occupation force" (Dower 1999, 126). The announcements claimed that the government needed female office clerks between eighteen and twenty-five years of age. They would receive clothes and food as part of their compensation. In little more than a week, thirteen hundred young women, many of them widows and orphans who possessed only very shabby clothes, had signed up to work in the newly created Recreation and Amusement Association (RAA). Many who had thought they would find jobs as clerks and typists were aghast to find out what their real work would entail, but others knowingly accepted jobs as sex workers, believing that would be the only way to keep their families and themselves from starvation. At the official inauguration of the RAA on August 28, the women took an oath to "defend and nurture the purity of our race"—that is, the sexual safety of their more fortunate sisters—but most took this work only in order to survive, not for nationalistic reasons. Other women were urged to leave the cities for the countryside and to continue to wear *monpe* pantaloons to ward off sexual attacks.

Sex workers serviced between fifteen and sixty soldiers a day, earning 15 yen (about $1 at that time) for each sexual encounter. This was far more than women in other occupations earned, but the work was degrading and sickening. Some women ran away, and others committed suicide. The brothels represented an intersection of racism and sexism. SCAP asked the head of the Tokyo Hygiene Department (who, ironically, was the son of feminist poet Yosano Akiko; see Chapters 4 and 5) to divide RAA workers into three separate groups to service three types of American soldiers: officers, white enlisted men, and black enlisted men. The RAA was short-lived but historically important. When it was discovered in January 1946 that 90 percent of RAA workers and 70 percent of their American customers in one unit of the U.S. Eighth Army had syphilis, U.S. officials decided to sever ties with the RAA, both because of this high rate of sexually transmitted disease and because the Americans had come to view the official brothels as a violation of women's human rights. The British Commonwealth Occupation Forces in southern Japan continued to operate a military brothel themselves, until the Australian parliament and media discovered this fact and put an end to it (Mackie 2003, 136).

The sex trade did not end with the closing of the RAA brothels, however. Thousands of women became *pan-pan* (the occupation-era term for sex workers who were not affiliated with brothels). Licensed brothels, where women signed contracts to work, continued to exist as well, but unlike the stigmatized *pan-pan*, workers in licensed brothels were seen as dutiful daughters helping their families. Most *pan-pan* streetwalkers worked primarily out of economic desperation, but some others took those jobs because they offered high pay, a degree of freedom to spend their wages that women working in licensed brothels did not have, and working hours that might make it easier to take care of their children.

Japanese Christian feminist organizations, such as the YWCA and WCTU, reestablished themselves after the war. They worked to end all licensed and unlicensed prostitution, thereby attempting to protect the Japanese women in those trades as well as setting themselves against them. They also opposed the U.S. occupation's treatment of all Japanese women as though they were prostitutes, with American military police pulling average working-class and middle-class women from sidewalks or public transportation and publicly humiliating them by forcing them to undergo gynecological exams in front of military examiners. Some of the women so detained were jailed, and others were sprayed with toxic disinfectants. Christian and secular women's organizations vigorously protested this treatment.

Sexuality was part of the atmosphere of decadence and nihilism in the impoverished postwar years. Mimicking what they saw on the streets, children played a popular game of *pan-pan* and customer (Dower 1999, 110–112). This period was also characterized by people's resorting to the black market and other semilegal and illegal activities, combined with many people's attempts to escape from the realities of daily life with alcohol and drugs.

Not all of the relationships between Japanese women and American men were based in the sex trades. SCAP initially restricted friendship-based relationships, which they called "fraternization," between Japanese and Americans, but some long-term, love-based relationships did develop. Although the U.S. Congress passed the War Brides Act in 1945 which allowed European and Chinese brides of American soldiers to enter the United States, it was not until the passage of the Soldier Brides Act of 1947 that American soldiers could marry Japanese and Korean women. Between 1947 and 1964 (the year before the 1965 U.S. Immigration and Nationality Act finally ended nationality-based quotas in the United States), forty-six thousand Japanese wives of American servicemen entered the United States.

Gender and Politics Under the Occupation

The occupation was, in theory, to be carried out by a group of eleven nations called the Far Eastern Commission (FEC). By early 1946, the Allied Council for Japan (ACJ), made up of four of those entities (the United States, the British Commonwealth, the Soviet Union, and China), was created as a more streamlined body in charge of advising MacArthur. But in reality, MacArthur ignored both the FEC and the ACJ and reported only to Washington. Thus the occupation can rightly be considered primarily an American occupation. Officers began to arrive in September 1945, and by 1948 their numbers reached a total of thirty-two hundred civilians and military men and women. This small number of occupation officials was consistent with SCAP's intention to have the Japanese administer their own government, albeit with American guidance and under military control. The Japanese continued to have a prime minister and cabinet, a bureaucracy, and elected officials in the Diet, prefectures, and cities. SCAP disbanded the Japanese military and the state institutions they believed had repressed the Japanese people at home. They carried out massive war crimes trials, most notably the Tokyo War Crimes Trials of 1946–1948. They purged more than two hundred thousand men but only eight women from government (82 percent of the incumbents in the Diet, last elected in 1942, were prevented from running again in 1946), as well as business leaders who were implicated in the war effort. Wartime political prisoners, many of them Communists, were freed. But the United States reinstituted the censorship of all journalistic and artistic works, a form of Japanese government repression that had distressed many Japanese during the war. Under the occupation, all materials had to be translated into English and submitted to SCAP's censors for approval before they could be published or performed.

SCAP was anxious that the bureaucracy and Diet be up and running as quickly as possible, and this offered a new opportunity for women. Anticipating that the Americans would move rapidly ahead on women's rights, and wishing to remind the Japanese government of the contributions of women during the war, Ichikawa Fusae and a few other members of the Women's Suffrage League searched throughout war-torn Tokyo and its environs for survivors of the prewar group. On August 25, 1945, several of these women met to establish the Women's Committee on Postwar Policy. On September 11 they held a fairly large meeting—seventy participants—at which they resolved to promote women's actions to survive the difficult times, including continuing to wear *monpe*, fighting inflation by not selling goods for money, increasing food production, welcoming back Japanese soldiers, and fighting off potential threats posed by Allied soldiers. At a meeting on September 24 they resolved to demand full civil rights, especially the vote. The Japanese cabinet, at its first meeting on October 9, decided that women should be granted political rights; the following day, Ichikawa visited the prime minister and other cabinet ministers, notably the home minister, who verbally confirmed that the government would send a bill to the Diet to amend the election law.

Before the government could make that announcement publicly, MacArthur met with the prime minister the next day, October 11, and presented him with a list of progressive reforms the United States demanded.

At the top of the list was women's full civil rights. Other reforms included freedoms of speech, press, and assembly; the right to form labor unions; redistribution of farmland from landlords to tenant farmers; the breakup of the large industrial conglomerates; and amendment of the nineteenth-century Meiji constitution and civil code (see Chapter 4). Many of these reforms would also affect the gender order in Japan. Ichikawa and other feminists, as well as male supporters in government who wished to credit the suffragists for their hard work over several decades, were deeply disappointed that SCAP would be credited with granting women rights (Koikari 2008, 49–50).

In December, the Diet engaged in a lively debate in which conservatives brought up the tired old arguments about women abandoning their "traditional" roles as wives and mothers should they get the vote. But they were outnumbered by the supporters of women's suffrage when the bill came to a vote on December 17. Women went to the polls in the first postwar election on April 10, 1946. Two-thirds of eligible women voters cast their ballots, an extraordinary percentage when compared to other countries right after women gained the vote (it is estimated that 35–45 percent of eligible women voted in the United States in the decade after gaining the right to vote in 1920).

Thirty-nine women were elected members of the Diet in 1946 (Hastings 1996, 273). The first women Diet representatives were highly educated, and many were professionals. The number of women parliamentarians declined in the second postwar election, in 1947, for a number of reasons, including the redrawing of electoral districts in a way that favored candidates from larger parties. Many of the women candidates did not have party backing, a factor that was less important in 1946, when each electoral district had more than one representative and voters felt that a woman should be one of those representatives.

Feminists of varying political persuasions formed organizations to educate new voters in their rights and to formulate demands for social and political reform. In November 1946 Ichikawa Fusae and other liberal prewar feminists created the New Japan Women's League (renamed the League of Women Voters in 1950) as a successor to the Women's Suffrage League. Women on the left, including Miyamoto Yuriko (see Chapter 6), Katō Ishimoto Shizue (see Chapter 7), and notable educators and labor activists from the prewar period formed the Women's Democratic Club in March 1946. The latter association lost the support of SCAP when SCAP turned against leftist groups in the latter part of the occupation period. Joining Japanese women in undertaking the political education of women was Lt. Ethel Weed, Women's Affairs

Japanese women voted for the first time on April 10, 1946.
LIBRARY OF CONGRESS LC-DIG-GGBAIN-34126

information officer of the Civil Education and Education Section of SCAP, who lectured throughout the country and published articles in newspapers and magazines.

The first thirty-nine women members of the Diet came together across party lines to form the Women Diet Representatives Club (Fujin Giin Kurabu). They worked on issues related to women's roles as mothers, including policies for distributing food, stabilizing milk prices and securing adequate milk supplies, and repatriating soldiers (Mackie 2003, 126).

Although some of these thirty-nine women were members of the Diet for just one year, six of them played a notable role in Japanese political history. These six were among the seventy-two members of the Diet who reviewed the draft of the new constitution. The constitution, which guarantees women's political equality, was actually written not by the Japanese Diet but rather by the American occupation. After MacArthur had demanded that the Japanese revise the Meiji constitution, the prime minister and cabinet dragged their feet and appointed a committee that was stacked with conservatives. The draft they produced was vetoed by SCAP and sent back to the committee for revision. While waiting for the Japanese committee's revision in February 1946, MacArthur secretly appointed a committee of twenty-four Americans (sixteen military officers and eight civilians), of whom four were women.

The most important woman was twenty-two-year-old Beate Sirota, who had grown up in Japan and was therefore one of the few members of the committee appointed by MacArthur who were fluent in Japanese (Gordon 1997). Following her appointment she commandeered a jeep and raced around Tokyo to acquire copies of constitutions from university libraries. Within days the SCAP committee had drafted a new document; technically it was to be a model for the Japanese committee, but instead the two committees simply translated the American document. Sirota had tried to include a wide range of feminist rights but was able to get only two clauses included in the constitution; these two, however, would prove to be important. (And even these two go beyond the U.S. Constitution, which does not include an equal rights clause.) The Japanese constitution stipulates that women and men are equal under the law (Article 14) and that husbands and wives have equal rights in marriage (Article 24). Each of these would be challenged in both the public and private sector, and the Supreme Court of Japan has had to rule numerous times over the years to make sure constitutional equality is preserved. On March 6, 1946, the draft of the Constitution was submitted to the Diet for review. Although, as previously noted, it was drafted by the American team, it was introduced as a purely Japanese-written document that expressed "the will of the Japanese people." After extended debate, the constitution went into effect in May 1947.

Two key prewar feminist leaders who had planned to stand for election in 1947 were purged by SCAP right before the election that year and were therefore prevented from playing any public role. These were Takeuchi Shigeyo, who had served as president of the Women Diet Representatives Club, and Ichikawa Fusae. This came as a big surprise, since many others who were not purged during the occupation years had taken government positions during the war, just as Takeuchi and Ichikawa had. Ichikawa's numerous influential friends in the United States petitioned to have her released from the purge, and the de-purging committee agreed. But for reasons that are not clear, she was not de-purged until the end of the occupation.

Ichikawa did not enter electoral politics immediately after the Americans' departure. Instead, she resurrected a movement against corruption in politics that had been part of the Women's Suffrage League's activities in the 1930s, when the Japanese government had made it impossible to advocate for women's voting rights. As a director of the Clean Election League (Kōmei Senkyo Renmei), founded on June 4, 1952, and primarily though not exclusively seen as a women's political movement, she gave speeches and supported ethical politicians. The following spring, while traveling in the United

States as a guest of Columbia University, she received a letter from Japan's League of Women Voters urging her to run for the House of Councilors (the upper house of the Diet). She entered the race as a candidate from the Tokyo district and won. She spent little, using no trucks or microphones and riding public transportation (Kodama 1985, 92–97), and donated funds left over at the end of her campaign to the League of Women Voters and the Women's Suffrage Hall Building Fund. (The Women's Suffrage Hall is now called the Fusae Ichikawa Center for Women and Governance. It contains archives of the women's movement, a museum, and classrooms for educating women in feminist politics. The center also provides opportunities for mentoring women candidates.) With the exception of the years 1971–1974, Ichikawa remained a member of the Diet, continuing to push for women's rights along with other prewar feminists such as Oku Mumeo (see Chapter 5), Katō Ishimoto Shidzue (see Chapter 7), and Kamichika Ichiko (see Chapter 6), until her death in 1981.

Gender, Work, and Livelihoods

The lives of men and women were radically changed in areas that went beyond electoral politics in the years after the war. The new constitution required major changes in the civil code and the Labor Standards Law. The Meiji-era civil code stipulated that the senior male was the head of the family and that other members of the family had fewer rights, especially in inheritance (which under most circumstances was to go to the eldest son), choice of where to live, and divorce (wives had fewer grounds for divorce). The new civil code, established in 1947, made the grounds for divorce the same for husbands and wives. But in other ways the code continued to carry the baggage of the past, and it has been a long struggle for women to amend it. For example, all family members must be registered as part of a family (not as individuals), and one member must be the family head. While it is not required that this be the husband, in most cases the husband assumes that role and the members of his family take his surname. The struggle for women to retain a surname distinct from their husband's has been a long one; in the fall of 2015, the Japanese Supreme Court ruled that spouses must share a surname, although it can be either spouse's name. This struggle may not be over. Another inequality under the 1947 civil code was the provision that only the father could pass his nationality to his children, so a Japanese mother who had children with a foreign man could not pass her nationality to her children (though this was changed in 1984).

Another of the demands MacArthur made in October 1945, for educational equality, affected the family as well. Before the war, only in elementary school (first through sixth grades) did boys and girls attend school together; after sixth grade, there were separate and unequal middle schools and high schools, and most universities were also segregated by sex. After the war, while some single-sex schools continued to exist, boys and girls at all levels had the opportunity to attend the same schools and study the same curricula. (A gendered curriculum—high school girls, but not high school boys, were required to take home economics—was temporarily in effect from the late 1960s until 1989, as we shall see in Chapter 10.)

Labor law was changed, too. The gender equality article of the constitution required a new Labor Standards Law. The new law, put into effect in 1947, called for equal pay for equal work (Article 4), although what was "equal work" could be defined in ways that discriminated against women, as happened in most other countries as well. Other provisions of the Labor Standards Law included maternity leave and nursing leave. These have been strengthened (and in the case of family leave, extended to fathers) in recent years, as will be discussed in Chapter 11. Other provisions of the Labor Standards Law have been removed in the past three decades. Protective legislation, which was a feminist goal since the early twentieth century, was deemed in Japan, as in other countries in the late twentieth century, to be discriminatory. For example, the Labor Standards Law of 1947 included provisions for menstruation leave and gendered limits on the hours and places women could work. Definitions of workplace policies that would benefit women and equalize opportunities for men and women continue to undergo change (Molony 1995).

Another gender change in the area of labor was the creation of the Women's and Minors' Bureau (Fujin Shōnen Kyoku) in the Ministry of Labor. Women Diet representatives, including Katō Ishimoto Shidzue, sponsored the legislation creating this new government agency. Prewar socialist feminist Yamakawa Kikue (see Chapters 5 and 7) was appointed the first director of this bureau, a post she held until 1963. The agency oversaw the protection of women and children in the workplace, enforced laws against child labor, and carried out surveys of working conditions. Independent labor unions, banned during the war, were initially encouraged by SCAP as a component of democracy. In the late 1940s, unions were organized in three major federations: a conservative one, a Communist one, and a moderate socialist one. Each had women's divisions. As the Cold War heated up, however, the Americans reacted to the rise of Communism in China and began another purge, this time of leftists in labor unions. The unions, including their women's divisions, did not fare well under this repression. At the same time, the male leadership of the unions, just like company managers, treated their women members as housewives first and workers second (Gerteis 2009). This will be further discussed in Chapter 10.

The dynamics of the family were changed by the legalization of birth control and abortion in the postwar years. Deeply concerned about the country's inability to feed the growing numbers of children born during the postwar baby boom (Japan's population grew from 72 million in 1945 to over 83 million in 1950), as well as the families and soldiers returning from Asia after the war, medical doctors and bureaucrats joined with prewar feminist advocates of birth control, such as Katō Ishimoto Shidzue, to propose ways to control Japan's population growth (Molony 1984, xxvi). Katō's goal was legalization of contraception in order to improve the lives of impoverished families and the health of mothers. In 1947 Katō submitted a bill to the Diet to legalize certain forms of birth control (IUDs, condoms, and diaphragms), but it languished in committee when SCAP refused to endorse it, preferring to maintain a neutral position in deference to American Catholic opinion at the time. A revised bill was brought to the Diet later that year. This became the basis for the Eugenic Protection Law (Yūsei Hogo Hō), which was implemented in 1948. Rather than focusing on contraception, which remained technically illegal until 1949, the Eugenic Protection Law focused on abortion. The law outlawed abortion except in cases where the mother's medical or economic condition would be imperiled by carrying a pregnancy to term. This, in effect, made abortion legal in almost all cases because mothers could always claim economic necessity. Katō was disappointed that abortion became the primary means of reproductive control during the last years of the occupation, and continued to work to make contraception legal. The Ministry of Health and Welfare did legalize condoms, spermicides, and diaphragms in 1949, and it set up birth control counseling centers throughout Japan in 1952. Condoms became the primary method of birth control in the 1950s.

CONNECTIONS

Radical changes came to all three countries in the first years after World War II. Japan and Korea faced military occupations and China descended into civil war, complicating the course of gender and sexual liberation that many women, having lived through the gender-redefining social changes of World War II, had hoped for. These military occupations and the brutal civil war in China were key parts of the Cold War in East Asia, and they adversely affected women's autonomous quests for rights. The Chinese civil war ended with the PRC in control of most of China, while the Nationalists set up the Republic of China on Taiwan. Korea was divided into two separate countries.

Taiwan had had a lively feminist movement in the 1920s, but Communist feminists such as Hsieh Hsueh-hung were forced by the Japanese colonial government to flee to Shanghai and elsewhere during that decade. After the colonial occupation ended in 1945, Hsieh struggled to build a Communist movement in an independent Taiwan. Fighting against the Chinese Nationalists who moved into Taiwan after the Japanese departure, Hsieh was forced to flee again, first to Hong Kong and then to the PRC, where she spent her remaining years. Feminist movements in the Republic of China on Taiwan went dormant during the next few decades under the ROC's authoritarian government.

In the weeks following the end of the war, Japanese prewar suffragist activists petitioned the Japanese government for civil equality, only to find that their efforts were preempted by the U.S. occupation. The Women's Democratic Club, an organization of moderates as well as socialist feminists, some of them newly released from jail by the American occupation, was, ironically, suppressed by the SCAP. In Korea, feminists and reformers organized the Women's Alliance to help rebuild the Korean state, with the goal of granting rights to women, in the days immediately following independence from Japanese colonial rule. But they, too, found that the U.S. military government in what later became South Korea suppressed women's groups that were deemed insufficiently anti-Communist. The USAMGIK, furthermore, mobilized the women of right-wing Korean organizations to work in the government's Women's Department. In North Korea, no foreign occupation forces limited women's rights, and the government put into place a series of laws that gave equal rights to women. But here, too, the impetus was to build the state, rather than to liberate women. Self-sacrificing motherhood was esteemed, and the family was never challenged as detrimental to women, as it was in other postwar Communist and non-Communist societies. And in the PRC, the All-China Women's Federation was established in 1949, subsuming the autonomous women's organizations under its umbrella and eventually serving as part of the state. Despite its statism, however, it did serve the needs of women.

The politics of the body, including sexuality, reproduction, and marriage, were addressed in all three culture areas (Japanese, Korean, and Chinese).

Both Japan and South Korea, as occupied territories, encountered the growing problem of the commodification of sex. Japanese leaders tried to handle the threat of U.S. military sexuality by setting up "comfort stations" at the beginning of the occupation, but the United States rejected this model in early 1946, and the sale of sex was turned into a private enterprise during the remaining years of the occupation. Social reformers abhorred the growth of prostitution, both government-sponsored and private, but poverty drove its continuation. In South Korea, public prostitution was officially made illegal in 1947, but the Korean government believed that U.S. soldiers still needed to be "consoled." So prostitution was paradoxically unofficial but regulated, especially in terms of examinations for sexually transmitted diseases. As in Japan, poverty drove many women into this type of work. In both countries, however, some sex workers did appreciate the higher wages and greater ability to control their lives that sex work permitted. In the PRC, prostitution was deemed to be a product of exploitative capitalism, and brothels were outlawed in 1951, with their residents offered retraining in womanly crafts such as sewing.

Marriage laws and practices also changed. In Japan, the civil code was rewritten to eliminate the patriarchal family headship system and the justifications for divorce that had been differentiated by gender, and to guarantee equality in marriage, as stipulated in the new constitution. But the family registration system and nationality laws that favored fathers over mothers continued for several more decades. In North Korea, the family registration system was somewhat improved. In the PRC, the Marriage Law of 1950 stipulated equality in marriage, divorce, freedom of selection of marriage partners, and other rights, but it was watered down by old-fashioned local officials and some men's anger over wives' rights to divorce. In Japan, concern about overpopulation led to changes in abortion and birth control laws, although stubborn resistance to women's rights to control their own bodies made abortion more common than birth control at first. In the PRC, where population policy was to fluctuate over the years, rebuilding the population after years of war was deemed critical; while maternal and infant health were improved, birth control and family planning were not allowed.

China, Japan, and Korea all showed some signs of ambivalence about women in the paid workforce in the postwar years. In Japan, returning soldiers were accommodated, while women were told to go home to take care of their families; at the same time, the large number of fatherless and brotherless families made it necessary for widows and other women to seek work. The Labor Standards Law gave women equal rights at work and in terms of pay, but employers found numerous ways to circumvent these protections. During the Korean War, women in Korea stepped into paid employment while their husbands were at war, but they, too, were told to go home after the war. In China, women's work was esteemed as liberating, but mothers were expected to balance child care and housework with employment; in addition, their pay lagged significantly behind that of men.

What connected these countries when the Cold War, military occupation, and civil war caused them to diverge politically in significant ways was the demand by women for improved status and conditions, some acknowledgment of those demands in government policies, and continuing resistance in both the public and private sectors to full equality.

REFERENCES AND SUGGESTIONS FOR FURTHER READING

GLOBAL CONTEXT

Clements, Barbara Evans. 2004. "Continuities amid Change: Gender Ideas and Arrangements in Twentieth-Century Russia and Eastern Europe." In *A Companion to Gender History*, edited by Teresa A. Meade and Merry E. Wiesner-Hanks. Oxford: Blackwell.

Redding, Sean. 2004. "Women and Gender Roles in Africa Since 1918: Gender as a Determinant of Status." In *A Companion to Gender History*, edited by Teresa A. Meade and Merry E. Wiesner-Hanks. Oxford: Blackwell.

Sowerwine, Charles, and Patricia Grimshaw. 2004. "Equality and Difference in the Twentieth-Century West: North America, Western Europe, Australia, and New Zealand." In *A Companion to Gender History*, edited by Teresa A. Meade and Merry E. Wiesner-Hanks. Oxford: Blackwell.

KOREA

Armstrong, Charles K. 2003. *The North Korean Revolution 1945–1950*. Ithaca, NY: Cornell University Press.

Chŏng Ch'ungnyang. 1955. "Chŏnjaeng mimangin kwa saenghwalgo wa sŏng munje" [War widows' daily hardships and sexual issues]. *Yŏsŏnggye*, September: 168–173.

Hahm, Han-hee. 2010. "Women and the Korean War: Standing in the Margins." *Korea Focus*, July.

Kim, Suzy. 2013. *Everyday Life in the North Korean Revolution, 1945–1950*. Ithaca, NY: Cornell University Press.

———. 2010. "Revolutionary Mothers: Women in the North Korean Revolution, 1945–1950." *Comparative Studies in Society and History* 52, no. 4: 742–767.

Ko, Myŏngja. 1946. "*Chaju tongnip kwa punyŏ ŭi kil*" [Autonomous independence and the direction for women]. *Sin ch'ŏnji*, May.

Lee, Na Young. 2007. "The Construction of Military Prostitution in South Korea During the U.S. Military Rule, 1945–1948." *Feminist Studies* 33, no. 3: 453–481.

Moon, Katharine. 1997. *Sex Among Allies: Military Prostitution in U.S.-Korea Relations*. New York: Columbia University Press.

Moon, Seungsook. 2010. "Regulating Desire, Managing the Empire: U.S. Military Prostitution in South Korea, 1945–1970." In *Over There: Living with the U.S. Military Empire from World War Two to the Present*, edited by Maria Höhn and Seungsook Moon. Durham, NC: Duke University Press.

Pak, Yŏngja. 2006. "6.25 chŏnjaeng kwa pukhan yŏsŏng ŭi nodong segye" [The works of North Korean women during the 6.25 war]. *Asia yŏsŏng yŏn'gu* 45, no. 2: 49–84.

Park, Kyung Ae. 1992–1993. "Women and Revolution in North Korea." *Pacific Affairs* 65, no. 4: 527–545.

Yuh, Ji-yeon. 2002. *Beyond the Shadow of Camptown: Korean Military Brides in America*. New York: New York University Press.

CHINA

Chang, Doris T. 2009. *Women's Movements in Twentieth-Century Taiwan*. Urbana: University of Illinois Press.

Diamant, Neil. 2000. *Revolutionizing the Family: Politics, Love, and Divorce in Urban and Rural China, 1949–1968*. Berkeley: University of California Press.

Evans, Harriet. 1997. *Women and Sexuality in China: Female Sexuality and Gender Since 1949*. New York: Continuum.

Glosser, Susan. 2003. *Chinese Visions of Family and State, 1915–1953*. Berkeley: University of California Press.

Glosser, Susan, editor and translator. 2005 . *Li Fengjin: How the New Marriage Law Helped Chinese Women Stand Up*. Portland, OR: Opal Mogus Books.

Goldstein, Joshua. 1998. "Scissors, Surveys, and Psycho-Prophylactics: Prenatal Health Care Campaigns and State Building in China, 1949–1954." *Journal of Historical Sociology* 11, no. 2: 153–184.

Hershatter, Gail. 1997. *Dangerous Pleasures: Prostitution and Modernity in Twentieth-Century Shanghai*. Berkeley: University of California Press.

———. 2000. "Local Meanings of Gender and Work in Rural Shaanxi in the 1950s." In *Re-Drawing Boundaries: Work, Households, and Gender in China*, edited by Barbara Entwisle and Gail E. Henderson. Berkeley: University of California Press.

———. 2011. *The Gender of Memory: Rural Women and China's Collective Past*. Berkeley: University of California Press.

Johnson, Kay Anne. 1983. *Women, the Family, and Peasant Revolution in China*. Chicago: University of Chicago Press.

Wang, Zheng. 2005. "'State Feminism'? Gender and Socialist State Formation in Maoist China." *Feminist Studies* 31, no. 3: 519–551.

White, Tyrene. 2006. *China's Longest Campaign: Birth Planning in the People's Republic, 1949–2005*. Ithaca, NY: Cornell University Press.

JAPAN

Dower, John. 1999. *Embracing Defeat: Japan in the Wake of World War II*. New York: W. W. Norton.

Gerteis, Christopher. 2009. *Gender Struggles: Wage-Earning Women and Male-Dominated Unions in Postwar Japan*. Cambridge, MA: Harvard University Press.

Gordon, Beate Sirota. 1997. *The Only Woman in the Room: A Memoir*. Tokyo: Kodansha International.

Hastings, Sally A. 1996. "Women Legislators in the Postwar Diet." In *Re-imaging Japanese Women*, edited by Anne E. Imamura. Berkeley: University of California Press.

Kodama, Katsuko. 1985. *Sengo no Ichikawa Fusae*. Tokyo: Shinjuku Shobō.

Koikari, Mire. 2008. *Pedagogy of Democracy: Feminism and the Cold War in the United States Occupation of Japan, 1945–1952*. Philadelphia: Temple University Press.

Mackie, Vera. 2003. *Feminism in Modern Japan: Citizenship, Embodiment, and Sexuality*. Cambridge: Cambridge University Press.

Molony, Barbara. 1995. "Japan's 1986 Equal Employment Opportunity Law and the Changing Discourse on Gender." *Signs* 20, no. 2: 268–302.

———. 1984. "Afterword." In *Facing Two Ways: The Story of My Life*, by Shidzue Ishimoto. Stanford, CA: Stanford University Press.

Ōgai, Tokuko. 1996. "The Stars of Democracy: The First Thirty-Nine Female Members of the Japanese Diet." *US-Japan Women's Journal, English Supplement*, 11: 81–117.

Shibusawa, Naoko. 2006. *America's Geisha Ally: Reimaging the Japanese Enemy*. Cambridge, MA: Harvard University Press.

10

Revolutionary Social and Gender Transformations, 1953 to the 1980s

GLOBAL CONTEXT

The decades from the 1950s through the mid-1980s were a time of revolutionary change throughout the world. Science and technology created new opportunities and challenges, which were often entangled with Cold War politics. For example, after the Russians sent the first human-made satellite, Sputnik I, into space in 1957, the United States launched a vigorous program to promote science and technology. One of the important goals of this science initiative was to best the Soviets' space efforts, which the United States was able to do by 1969 with the landing of American astronauts on the moon. Other achievements in science and technology flowing from the Cold War–era support for research and development included the development of microchips, which in turn fueled the computer revolution. IBM introduced the first personal computer in 1981, which took the exclusive use of computers out of the hands of large companies and placed it—and its spin-offs in smartphones, laptops, and tablets—in everyone's hands. From email to the Internet to various forms of text, image, and verbal messaging, people have become linked in an interconnected global web that could not have been imagined before the 1980s. Some scholars consider the information-technology revolution comparable in world-historical importance to the agricultural and industrial revolutions of previous centuries.

In the world's richest countries, and increasingly in the poorer ones as well, medical discoveries extended and improved the quality of people's lives during this period. These discoveries included new antibiotics, antiviral drugs, artificial organs and the surgical techniques to implant them, the sequencing of DNA, and the birth control pill (which will be discussed later in this chapter). Some horrific diseases, such as polio and smallpox, were almost completely eradicated, and AIDS, first diagnosed in the early 1980s, has been slowly brought under control with advanced drugs in many countries of the world. All of these had revolutionary consequences for human life.

Other technological changes were less beneficial but equally revolutionary. These included advances in atomic weaponry (also stimulated by Cold War tensions); pollution of the air, land, and water and increasingly serious global climate change due to widespread use of fossil fuels, especially oil and coal; depletion of the ozone layer by the release of certain chemicals; acid rain produced by emissions of sulfur dioxide and nitrogen oxides; and adverse health effects of lead in auto emissions. Anti-emissions legislation since the 1980s in a number of countries had lessened the effects of lead, sulfur dioxide, and chemical pollution in recent years, although other types of emissions continue to have adverse environmental effects.

International politics, most strongly influenced by the Cold War until the fall of the Communist regimes in Eastern Europe in the late 1980s, also underwent major changes during these years. Western European countries created a series of increasingly close economic alliances, starting with the six countries of the European Economic Community (1958) and eventuating in the creation of the European Union in 1993, which had twenty-eight member states by 2015. After centuries of bloody warfare, the European continent finally settled down during this period. But Cold War proxy wars and postcolonial revolutions brought violence to other places in the world. In Cuba, revolutionaries under Fidel Castro created a pro-USSR government in 1959. When the Soviet Union attempted to place nuclear-armed ballistic missiles in Cuba, a tense showdown between the United States and the USSR ensued in October 1962. The world was brought back from the brink of nuclear destruction by an agreement that kept Soviet missiles out of Cuba in exchange for America's promise not to invade Cuba and to remove American nuclear missiles from bases in Turkey. With unfortunate long-term consequences, a U.S.- and British-backed military coup removed the democratically elected prime minister of Iran in 1953. Almost three decades later, in 1979, an Islamic revolution overturned the government supported by the Americans and British. Supporters of that revolution took fifty-two American diplomats in Tehran hostage, releasing them only in 1981. Also in 1979, the Soviets invaded Afghanistan in support of a secular Marxist state against Islamic soldiers who came to be called the Taliban. The United States came to the aid of the Taliban, and the Russians' war in Afghanistan dragged on until 1989. The civil war following the Soviets' withdrawal ended in a Taliban victory, with monumental consequences for global history, as we shall see in Chapter 11.

Of greater immediate importance during the decades from the 1950s to the 1980s was the war in Vietnam. Vietnamese revolutionaries had defeated their French colonial masters in 1954, but, fearful of the revolutionaries' Communist ideology, the United States intervened to prevent the formation of a Communist state. An agreement meant to be temporary was signed in Geneva, Switzerland, but this Geneva Convention instead created two separate states, a northern Communist state allied with the USSR and a southern non-Communist state allied with the United States. Brutal warfare broke out between the two sides, fighting to reclaim the whole country. From the early 1960s until 1973, the United States sent massive numbers of troops to support the South Vietnamese government. The war ended with the withdrawal of American soldiers in 1973, the victory of the North's forces, and reunification of Vietnam as a Communist state in 1975. The death toll of the two-decade conflict was appalling: four million Southeast Asians, fifty thousand Americans, and thousands of other soldiers who joined one side or the other. Countries around the world saw anti–Vietnam War demonstrations, from which a global youth revolution emerged that was both political and cultural. The politics of the concurrent American civil rights movement blended with the anti–Vietnam War uprisings, and what came to be called the second wave of the feminist movement emerged at the tail end of the antiwar movement (the international feminist movement will be discussed later in this chapter).

Following the American departure from Vietnam, Southeast Asia remained unstable. Rivalry in the late 1970s between the USSR and the PRC, Communist victories in Laos and Cambodia, and military government in Thailand made life miserable for millions. Most horrific was the takeover of Cambodia by the Khmer Rouge, a Communist faction allied with the PRC, whose reign of terror killed between 1.5 and 2 million Cambodians. In 1979 Vietnam invaded to suppress the Khmer Rouge, but in the process unleashed a civil war in Cambodia that lasted another decade.

Culturally, young people around the world—members of the baby boom generation, born after World War II—created a transnational musical and artistic scene that rejected much of the culture of their parents' generation. Most notably, this included rock-and-roll and modern forms of jazz that originated in African American music (and which were condemned by conservatives). The counterculture, as the complex of the behavior, clothing, music, and relaxed sexuality of the sixties was called, was in many ways revolutionary.

The influence of the American civil rights movement was not limited to the United States. The African American struggle for equality and security that had begun decades earlier was reenergized with the return of soldiers from World War II. Having fought bravely for American values overseas, they now advocated reform at home. The movement gained momentum when the Supreme Court ruled school segregation unconstitutional in 1954, and when Rosa Parks refused to move to the back of a bus in Montgomery, Alabama, in 1955, setting off a bus boycott that lasted more than a year. Martin Luther King Jr. and other civil rights leaders led marches throughout the South and in Washington, D.C., leading to the Civil Rights Act of 1964 and the Voting Rights Act of 1965. Other human rights legislation was passed around that time, including the Immigration and Nationality Act of 1965, which dismantled the eighty-year-old barriers to Asian immigration to the United States. Inspired by American civil rights activism, South African antiapartheid activists began the long and difficult struggle to end segregation in that country as well.

Throughout the world, women who had been involved in their countries' anticolonial movements, civil rights movements, and antiwar movements of the 1950s and 1960s reignited the women's rights movements that had lain dormant during the difficult years of the war and reconstruction (Sowerwine and Grimshaw 2004, 596–605). As we saw in Chapter 9, after the war many women felt compelled to return to the home, where they were supposed to focus on child rearing and homemaking. By the end of the 1950s, the postwar baby boom was winding down, and increasingly well-educated women began to wonder why their lives as housewives did not seem fulfilling. In 1961 American president John F. Kennedy appointed the President's Commission on the Status of Women, and while the commission reported that women's domestic role was primary, it also articulated many of the grievances about inequality in the workplace and society that some women were quietly expressing.

Soon the ideas of this commission were taken one step further with the publication of Betty Friedan's *The Feminine Mystique*, a best seller in the United States and, in its many translations, overseas. Middle-class, primarily white women joined Friedan in founding the National Organization for Women (NOW) in the United States in 1966. In the next half decade, additional feminist groups emerged, including more-radical women's organizations, organizations of feminist women of color, and women's consciousness-raising groups. Access to birth control, especially the contraceptive pill, and legalization of abortion were two critical reproductive rights struggles. Both struggles were won in the United States, but the latter has seen rollbacks in the decades since the U.S. Supreme Court ruled in 1973 that state restrictions on abortion in the first two trimesters of pregnancy were unconstitutional. Books about women's health (for example, *Our Bodies, Ourselves*, published by the Boston Women's Health Book Collective in 1973) and books that challenged sexism (for example, Kate Millett's *Sexual Politics*, 1970) were domestic and overseas best sellers, translated into many languages. Feminism was becoming an increasingly accepted point of view. In 1972 America's Equal Rights Amendment to the Constitution, first proposed in the 1920s (see Chapter 5), was finally passed by Congress and sent to the states for ratification. Unfortunately, the proposed amendment failed to be ratified by enough states to become part of the Constitution, but the favorable climate for state support for feminism was evident in the 1970s.

The American movement was paralleled by women's movements throughout the world in the 1970s and 1980s. In many countries, state support for women's rights went far beyond that in America. France and Germany had ministries of women's rights in the 1980s, and Germany, Ireland, England, New Zealand, Australia, South Korea, Israel, India, Sri Lanka, Argentina, Brazil, and many other countries have had female chancellors, presidents, or prime ministers. Many mainstream Protestant and Jewish denominations have opened their top leadership positions to women, and the militaries in many countries have gradually opened their ranks to women.

The decades from the 1950s through the 1980s were also a time of sexual revolution. Sex increasingly had been seen as more than simply procreative since the 1920s, but it was the availability of birth control—and the evidence that women, as well as men, could have orgasms—that enhanced the recreational view of sex. Although some religions continue to oppose artificial contraception, the majority of women in most countries do practice birth control. Family sizes have plummeted, especially in Europe and East Asia. This fact, as much as the growth of feminist attitudes, has contributed significantly to the changing roles of men and women in families and the workplace.

Pressed by women throughout the world, the United Nations declared 1975 to be International Women's Year, and the decade from 1976 to 1985 to be the UN Decade for Women. The first UN conference on women, held in Mexico City in 1975, was fraught with problems—some a result of the political differences between countries, some a result of conservative countries having sent only men as delegates. Subsequent meetings in Copenhagen, Nairobi, and Beijing were more expressly feminist, and at the last one, in Beijing in 1995, American First Lady Hillary Clinton proclaimed that "women's rights are human rights," thereby encouraging countries that had dragged their feet on women's rights to step up the pace of change. In 1979 the United Nations passed the Convention on the Elimination of All Forms of Discrimination Against Women (CEDAW). This treaty has been signed by most nations of the world, although it has not yet been ratified by the United States. CEDAW inspired legislative changes in many countries (see Chapter 11).

JAPAN

A young Japanese person in the mid-1980s would have found the Japan of the early 1950s almost unrecognizable. Barely 1 percent of Japan's roads were paved in the first few years after the war. Most people lived in the countryside, where they had fled from the wartime bombing of Japan's cities. Half of all boys and girls left school after ninth grade. Both mothers and fathers worked, as did children old enough to do so. Urban families fortunate enough to have their own homes often inhabited tiny wooden houses with a radio, a telephone, and a few electric bulbs but no flush toilets. Family life revolved around home activities and neighborhood festivals at shrines and temples. In the early 1950s, almost all babies were born at home rather than in a hospital.

Japanese economic growth began to pick up with the outbreak of the Korean War in 1950, when American purchases of trucks and other military supplies from Japanese manufacturers provided an enormous stimulus to the Japanese economy. Growth slowed down for a few years after the Korean War but took off again after 1960. In the mid-1970s Japan had the world's second-largest economy and, a decade later, one of the world's highest per capita incomes. (This rapid growth would come to an end around 1990, and the Japanese economy would remain in recession on and off for several decades after that.) By the 1970s highways traversed the countryside; even more important, people could travel more quickly by the world's first high-speed rail, the famous bullet trains (*shinkansen*) that were inaugurated in 1964. Families had moved back to the cities; by 1975 three-quarters of all Japanese lived in urban areas, and only 10 percent of the labor force worked on farms or fisheries. The urban neighborhoods of wooden houses gave way to millions of apartments in huge public housing complexes and millions more comfortable, middle-class single-family homes extending for miles along the commuter rail lines surrounding every Japanese city. Most Japanese identified themselves as "middle-class" by 1975 (60 percent had considered themselves "lower-class" in 1955). Television was ubiquitous, and people throughout the country, who until then had been divided by regional accents, cuisine, and customs, increasingly shared ideas about culture, consumer products, and desirable careers for men and women. Family events such as weddings and funerals that used to take place at home or at a neighborhood shrine or temple now took place in commercial venues such as hotels and restaurants. By 1975, only 1.2 percent of all babies were born at home. The daily lives of men and women (as well as boys and girls) changed radically, diverging from life in the prewar and wartime periods as well as from the daily lives of their neighbors in China and Korea.

When the feminist movement gained steam in the 1970s, many observers at that time believed it was a new challenge to the "traditional" family, made up of a stay-at-home housewife (*shufu*), a hardworking white-collar husband more dedicated to his company than to his family (*sarariman,* "salaryman"), and one or two children driven to academic success by an "education mama" (*kyōiku mama*). But this "tradition" really dated from the 1950s. As we have seen in earlier chapters, Japanese women, men, and children had always worked—in shops, in factories, and on farms. And while they were fewer in number and occupied less prestigious positions than men, women had also held jobs in white-collar sectors such as office work, medicine, and public school teaching before the war. Thus the middle-class household in which the husband was the main breadwinner was primarily a postwar phenomenon in Japan. When 1970s feminists attacked a society divided into a female-dominated home and a male-dominated workplace, they were challenging institutions of relatively recent origin. That did not make the feminist challenge any less important, but we must be careful when we attribute to "tradition" gender relations that are the product of particular historical contexts.

It is also important to note that the very vocal feminist movement of the 1970s did not emerge from thin air. Women had struggled to improve their status since the nineteenth century. In the late 1940s feminist groups silenced during the war regained their voices (see Chapter 9). One of their key efforts was the movement to eliminate licensed prostitution. Christian women's organizations as well as suffragist organizations had been trying to inspire male legislators to outlaw licensed brothels since the late nineteenth century. Licensed brothels were sanctioned by the state, while unlicensed independent sex workers were not. Until the early 1950s, societal attitudes toward women in licensed brothels had been much more supportive (see Chapter 9). During the occupation period, licensed prostitutes were seen as dutiful daughters working to support their parents and siblings, whereas independent streetwalkers were seen as selfish and sexually immoral. Feminists did not generally differentiate between the two groups of sex workers; rather, they considered them all to be exploited by sexist society, on one hand, and sexually degraded, on the other.

By the early 1950s, as Japan was recovering from the war, attitudes had changed among the general population, who came to share the feminists' view that all prostitution should be eliminated (Kovner 2012). But the reasoning of the wider society was somewhat different from that of feminist organizations. That is, the public came to view prostitution as violating *children's* rights not to see sexual immorality on the streets, rather than focusing on prostitutes' rights. It was this societal attitude that women legislators, many of them members of prewar feminist organizations, pragmatically used to push the Prostitution Prevention Law through the Diet in 1956.

Women Diet members, believing that sex workers were fallen women who could be rehabilitated, fought for funds to retrain sex workers and help them find new jobs, although the funds eventually allocated were inadequate to the task. Within ten years of setting up "comfort stations" for the Allied occupation forces after the war, the Japanese government and population had made a complete reversal in their attitudes and policies toward sex work. The law remained controversial, however, as impoverished sex workers organized a union and protested the loss of their livelihoods. Prostitution has, of course, not ended in Japan, but it is no longer licensed by the state.

Other organizations emerged from the ashes of war and adopted a variety of approaches to improve women's status, including, in some cases, reinforcing old gender norms. For example, Oku Mumeo, who had worked with Ichikawa Fusae and Hiratsuka Raichō in the New Woman's Association from 1919 to 1922 and who led a left-leaning women's consumer movement in the 1920s (see Chapter 5), founded the Housewives Association (Shufuren) in 1948. This association was fairly militant in its assertion of women's power as consumers within the household. Marching for better products and economic justice, its members carried giant mock-ups of the rice-serving scoop that symbolized women's primary role as housewives. Today the Housewives Association continues to play a large role in movements against pollution and global climate change.

Another category of activists on behalf of women, the women's divisions of labor unions, also emerged after the war. They marched under their own banners at the first postwar May Day celebrations in 1946. But soon thereafter the male leaders of the major labor unions began to put women workers "in their place," and the women's divisions declined. While formally calling for women's equality in the workplace, male union leaders completely undercut gender equality by pressing working-class women to accept gender norms that resembled the "good wife, wise mother" ideology the government had articulated for middle-class women in the early twentieth century (Gerteis 2010). Instead of seeking better wages and conditions for all their members, unions focused on demands that companies pay their male employees a living wage—an income sufficiently high so that their wives would not have to work outside the home. This demand was seen as progressive at the time, but it was very conservative in terms of gender equality. Women were urged to go home to take care of their children and their hardworking, much better-paid husbands. When women did have jobs, their earnings were viewed as simply supplementary, so their wages could be kept at a low level. The notion that married women should stay at home—while not typically practiced among prewar working-class families—came to be seen as normal and traditional in this historical context.

A number of leading Japanese companies, as well as the government, shared the view that women should take care of the home while their husbands worked very long hours. In 1955, concerned that male employees could not dedicate themselves fully to their work if they had to spend time caring for their children and households, these companies joined with the government in founding the New Life Movement (Gordon 2005). (Despite the similarity of name, this was not at all related to the New Life Movement in China in the 1930s, described in Chapter 8.) The principle behind the Japanese movement was that men could work very long hours (in essence being exploited by their companies) if their wives took care of household matters. This assumed that men were more productive than women in the workplace and that it was wasteful to squander men's time in the home. Both the living wage promoted by the unions and the female-centered home and male-centered workplace promoted by the New Life Movement, while coming from opposite ends of the political spectrum, played a role in formalizing the postwar gender division between men in the workplace and women in the home. Because the unions, employers, and government reinforced the idea that it was normal for married women to stay at home, the number of employed women declined steadily as prosperity returned to Japan after the 1950s. It reached a low point in the 1970s, after which women's employment levels began to climb once again. But even when women's employment was at its lowest levels, a majority of women did continue to work, although many were underpaid part-time workers and all were restricted in the kinds of jobs companies offered them.

Another women's organization that originated in the 1950s, the Mothers' Convention (Hahaoya Taikai), mobilized women politically as mothers. The first meeting, attended by two thousand women, was held in June 1955. The Mothers' Convention, a nonpartisan peace organization, proclaimed its wish for "mothers of the world to join hands to prevent nuclear war and create a world where mothers and children can live without anxiety" (Mackie 2003, 135). The organization had transnational links, similar to the prewar women's peace movements. The Mothers' Convention grew rapidly; thirteen thousand women delegates attended the 1960 annual meeting. Not only mothers but women of all ages and backgrounds came together at that time. Many demonstrated against the renewal of the U.S.-Japan Security Treaty, which they believed would drag Japan into the conflict between the superpowers.

Acting as mothers and housewives for international peace and for their families' economic welfare, women were able to use what was defined by the 1950s as the traditional family to advance their causes. This traditional family was not only seen as a means of empowerment for women but also, conversely, attacked by critics in the Housewife Debate of the mid-1950s for holding women back. This debate, like the Motherhood Protection Debate of the late 1910s (see Chapter 5), was waged in the pages of women's and other mass-circulation journals. At least one debater of the 1910s, Hiratsuka Raichō, contributed to the 1950s debate as well.

The Housewife Debate continued from 1955 until 1976. The opening salvos were particularly interesting. Ishigaki Ayako (1903–1996) opened the debate in February 1955 with an article in a special issue on working women of the women's journal *Fujin Kōron*. Ishigaki was a feminist journalist who had migrated to America in the 1920s, where she married noted Japanese American artist Ishigaki Eitarō. Although both had worked for the American government in the war effort against Japan in the 1940s, Eitarō was expelled from the United States in 1951 as a result of Cold War repression. Ayako followed her husband back to Japan, where she continued working as a feminist journalist. Her 1955 article unleashed a torrent of reactions that reflect 1950s attitudes toward housewives. Ishigaki wrote that 1950s Japanese housewives "spend their time in selfish leisure, working whenever they wish . . . and for this they receive no criticism whatsoever. If they were in the workplace, however, these housewives would face strict training and competition from their colleagues" (quoted in Bardsley 2014, 47). Ishigaki acknowledged the severe discrimination in the workplace that discouraged many women from abandoning their role as housewives. But she also placed some of the blame for workplace inequality on women themselves for being unambitious and thereby helping to reinforce the already existing notion that women did not want real careers.

The April 1955 issue of the same journal carried strong rebuttals to Ishigaki's article. One writer stressed Japanese housewives' important civic work, which she called "domestic feminism," in promoting children's welfare, international peace, and consumer protection (Bardsley 2014, 52). Another respondent, antinuclear activist Shimizu Keiko, wrote that "housewives have taken on the activism which men and employed women cannot . . . and are working with all their might to make this a better place to live" (Bardsley 2014, 59). One male writer asserted that it was natural that women and men occupied different spheres, as men were supposed to protect women and their families. A Marxist feminist argued that corporations exploited women in insecure jobs, so efforts to improve the lot of women workers and housewives, such as establishing day care centers, should be made at the societal level. What almost none of these articles addressed was the larger gender question—that is, how should men's *and* women's roles be changed to improve everyone's work and home life? Similar articles appeared in the pages of journals aimed at educated upper- and middle-class women through the next wave of feminist activism in the 1970s.

The "Traditional" Family

The "traditional" family came under even stronger criticism in the 1970s. What specifically, then, was this family?

The "traditional" family came to be seen as the norm through television shows, literature, movies, and newspapers. Although a large percentage of Japanese families did not have the economic resources to maintain the middle-class lifestyle of the "traditional" family, mass media images led many people to aspire to that type of family and to believe that everyone else did, too. Employers, the government, and unions, as we have seen, had focused on encouraging men to work long hours and to dedicate themselves to the workplace by offering them decent wages and workplace respect. If men were at work all day, their wives would have to focus on taking care of the home and family. Women had less incentive to work under those conditions. Employers encouraged women to accept this division of labor by keeping women's wages very low and by firing women when they got married or had their first child.

The government supported this gendered employment structure by implementing tax policy that prevented wives from earning more than the equivalent of a few thousand dollars per year before higher taxation rates kicked in. (Company policies that dictated vastly different retirement ages for men and women were ruled unconstitutional in 1966, but subtle pressure to force married women and mothers to leave the workplace continued for several decades thereafter.) Job opportunities for women were severely limited—and in many cases much less attractive than jobs for men—until the implementation of the Equal Employment Opportunity Law in 1986, to be discussed in Chapter 11 (Molony 1995).

By the late 1950s, a high school diploma was necessary to get a factory job, and for men, a college degree was usually necessary for an entry-level white-collar job. Men in white-collar occupations were recruited into companies directly from school, and most planned to spend their whole careers with the same firm. They lived in company dormitories until they were married. There they developed loyalty to the company while being molded into salarymen.

The stereotypical salaryman of the 1950s through the 1980s left for work at dawn, after his wife had helped him dress for work. He commuted, packed in like a sardine, by bus or subway for up to ninety minutes. He stayed at his desk till 7:00 or 8:00 p.m. Two or three times a week, salarymen went out drinking with their coworkers for several more hours. Management encouraged these drinking sessions so their employees could bond with one another. Many workers dreaded this essentially mandatory "recreation" that kept them from their families. Their wives might be waiting with dinner, but drunken, exhausted men sometimes rolled into bed at midnight, only to wake up very early the next morning to get to work. The few women employees who joined the men's after-work bar-hopping usually left after the first round of drinks. There was little need for women to build deep rapport with their male colleagues—after all, they were not employed in the same kinds of jobs as the men, and they were not expected to stay with their companies for more than a few years. Men were in jobs that required a good deal of training and could lead to promotion and permanent employment. Women were in auxiliary jobs, often called "office lady" positions, where they did general secretarial work and tea pouring. Considered "flowers in the workplace," office ladies were generally young and unmarried.

Once married, a woman was expected to take care of her family's children, manage the family budget, and make sure her husband got to work in clean clothes and with enough money in his pocket for meals during the day. Japanese women, unlike American women at that time, handled their family budgets. Husbands turned over their weekly pay packets to their wives, who made decisions about expenditures and gave their husbands a weekly allowance. Mothers helped their kids with homework or took them to after-school examination preparation academies. These were the mothers the press called "education mamas." Once the children started school, some wives got jobs while their children were at school, but both social pressure and tax laws tended to restrict mothers to part-time work. When the children finally left for college, mothers often reentered the workplace full-time, but few could find really good jobs. Company loyalty was highly esteemed in Japan—as evidenced by the mandatory after-work socializing for male workers—and women who returned to the workplace after a long break were unable to show that kind of loyalty. As a result, women ended up accepting inferior jobs and lower wages. In recent years the number of women dropping out of the workforce during their childbearing years has noticeably declined as attitudes and laws about balancing family and work responsibilities have changed and men's own job security has decreased.

The "traditional" family became increasingly important in the 1960s with the rapid growth of national wealth and the expansion of Japan's middle class. This economic growth followed intense social unrest in the summer of 1960 over the renewal of the U.S.-Japan Security Treaty. This treaty had originally been signed in 1951, together with the San Francisco Peace Treaty that marked the end of World War II. The U.S.-Japan Security Treaty established American bases in Japan and tied Japan closely to the United States militarily. Many Japanese opposed this treaty because they feared it would draw Japan into war if the Cold War ever erupted into full-scale military conflict between the United States and the Soviet Union. Others resented that Japan had second-class status in the treaty relationship. The scheduled vote over the renewal of the treaty in 1960 appeared to be a good opportunity for Japan to redefine itself as a neutral country tied neither to the United States nor to the Soviet Union. But treaty opponents' hopes were quashed when Prime Minister Kishi Nobusuke rammed the revised treaty through the Diet in May. Millions of Japanese from across the political spectrum, including university students, labor unions, political parties, and many thousands of housewives, mothers, and other women from forty women's organizations—especially groups with antinuclear and peace goals—protested the prime minister's action. In the course of the demonstrations, a woman university student was killed, inspiring more public outrage. Prime Minister Kishi resigned. The new prime minister, Ikeda Hayato (1899–1965), tried to calm the waters, and unveiled his plan to increase Japan's income within a decade. His "income doubling plan" succeeded in making Japan the world's third-largest economy (after the United States and Soviet Union) by 1967, and the second-largest a few years after that.

Women's Activism in the 1970s

The very rapid increase in national income did bring prosperity to many Japanese, but the cost of Japan's focused pursuit of industrial growth was too high. Horrific air pollution forced Tokyo children to stay indoors much of the summer of 1970. Other types of pollution poisoned the land, water, and air throughout Japan, leading to respiratory diseases and mercury poisoning, among other serious health problems. College students took to the streets to protest America's war in Vietnam as well as the U.S.-Japan Security Treaty. Many men came to resent the long working hours that accompanied the economic boom of the 1960s and 1970s, which had made them absentee fathers to their children.

Newly prosperous women grew increasingly tired of their second-class social status in Japan, as elsewhere in the world, and added their voices to the global second wave of feminist movements. Many joined movements to make a better, cleaner, and safer Japan, stating they were doing so as mothers protecting their children. Grassroots housewives' groups sprang up in every neighborhood, many of them making organic food available to their members. By the end of the 1970s, some housewives were contemplating more formal political action and running for office as housewife-citizens (LeBlanc 1999). The antipollution, antiwar, and women's movements all arose in the early 1970s.

Other kinds of women's movements that were more expressly feminist in their ideology and actions sprang up in the early 1970s. These "women's liberation" groups differed from the organizations that stressed women's political and social responsibilities as housewives and mothers. The new feminist organizations' members were often younger. Many had participated in the New Left movements of the 1960s, which had focused on opposition to global capitalism and America's war in Vietnam. The leadership of these New Left groups was male, and many women found themselves marginalized in subordinate and service positions even in supposedly progressive groups. Just as in Europe and the United States, unequal treatment in the

New Left movements led many to become feminists. Consciousness-raising activities led thousands to redefine feminism in new terms, which included questioning sexuality and motherhood and seeing the oppression of women *as women*. Thus motherhood and other aspects of womanhood, which earlier housewife feminists had viewed as a source of strength, came to be seen as contributing to inequality.

These kinds of revolutionary approaches paralleled those in feminist movements in the West. Transnational linkages among radical feminist organizations emerged, in a sense recalling the links among Christian organizations that had been one characteristic of feminism in the interwar period. Japanese feminists in the early 1970s viewed their position in more complex ways than many feminists in the West, however. For example, the Ajia Fujin Kaigi (Asian Women's Conference), founded in the summer of 1970, articulated the view that while Japanese women were oppressed by sexism in Japanese society and by Western imperialism toward people of color, Japanese women were also part of the First World oppression of other Asian women. Thus they were both oppressed and oppressors at the same time. Another group founded in 1970, Tatakau Onna (Fighting Women), got its start by opposing proposed limitations of women's reproductive rights, but soon turned its attention to the broader question of the sexual liberation of women. Means of liberating oneself from sexist attitudes, such as the notion that women were either mothers or whores, were explored at summer camps run by Fighting Women in the early 1970s. The Shinjuku Women's Liberation Center was established in 1972 as an organizing hub and as a women's shelter. And a group called Chūpiren used sensationalist tactics to promote their goals, which included the legalization of birth control pills and putting an end to the sexual double standard that permitted men, though not women, to have affairs outside of marriage. Chūpiren's members, who performed political theater by wearing pink helmets, publicly exposed prominent men for sexual infidelity (Mackie 2003).

Hundreds of small mimeographed magazines and newsletters spread the ideas and public actions of the women's liberation movement. Other, more substantial publications, such as the magazines *Onna: Erosu* (Woman: Eros) and *Feminisuto* (Feminist), founded by scholars and artists, were also widely read. *Feminisuto* consciously referenced the past by adding a subtitle: *The New Bluestocking*. These publications carried not only Japanese news and articles but also translations of works by Western writers. The Femintern Press focused on larger works, publishing several books and pamphlets in the early 1970s. Even mainstream newspapers publicized feminists' actions, but their coverage often left much to be desired. One sympathetic feminist journalist was Matsui Yayori (1934–2002), who wrote for *Asahi*, one of the most respected mainstream newspapers in Japan. In addition to her excellent reporting about women, especially women in Asia, she was also the founder of Ajia no Onnatachi no Kai (Asian Women's Association). Despite all of this activity, in the early 1970s radical feminism was generally mocked by most of the mainstream press, which focused a surprising amount of attention on the pink-helmeted members of Chūpiren.

BOX 10.1

A Feminist Journalist Encounters Asian Women's Oppression

Japanese journalist Matsui Yayori describes her evolution into an activist on behalf of Asian women in her best-selling book, *Women's Asia*, originally published in Japanese as *Onnatachi no Asia* in 1987.

> *When I was a university student, I decided to study abroad. The racial discrimination I encountered in Western society was deeply disappointing and I decided to return to Japan. A month-long journey by ship from Marseilles took me to various Asian ports on the way. This was in the late 1950s and my encounter with the reality of Asia during this journey was one of the most shocking events of my young life. . . . In late 1970 and early 1971 I had an opportunity to spend six months visiting the United States, Europe, and the Soviet Union. . . . While I was in the United States I had a chance encounter with the "Women's Lib" movement. . . . It made me question the first decade of my career. . . .*
>
> *When I returned to Japan I had confidence in myself as a woman for the first time, and decided that I would in future see my job as that of a feminist journalist. . . . This was just before the United Nations Women's Decade . . . and it seemed that I could utilize this event to take women's issues away from the women's or family page, into the social and political pages of our newspaper. As I pursued this course it slowly dawned upon me that Japan's economic growth had been largely achieved by discrimination against women domestically, and by the exploitation and oppression of women in Asia and other regions of the Third World. (Matsui 1989, 1–3)*

This changed in 1975, with the United Nations International Women's Year. In late 1974 Ichikawa Fusae and Tanaka Sumiko, prewar feminists who were by then veteran members of the Diet, coordinated a large number of women's groups, ranging from old-line women's organizations to radical feminists, writers, intellectuals, members of the bureaucracy, academics, and many others, to plan for Japan's participation in the 1975 UN meeting in Mexico City. In January 1975 they founded the International Women's Year Action Group and set out a progressive agenda for change. The Action Group continued long after the Mexico City conference, coordinating the activities of several dozen organizations and addressing a wide range of issues, from organizing for the Equal Employment Opportunity Law and other laws to improve the status of women (see Chapter 11) and protesting sexist television commercials to fighting against sex tourism in South Korea and Southeast Asia.

Japanese television and advertising, like the media elsewhere in the world, portrayed women and men in sexist ways. The Action Group and its affiliates initiated studies and protests about these images in late 1975, first turning its attention to a commercial for instant noodles that offended many women. In the commercial, a young and vibrant woman exclaimed joyfully, "I'm the one who cooks [the noodles]!" And an equally young and exuberant man replied, "I'm the one who eats them!" Viewers seemed to be appalled that such young people were expressing such old-fashioned ideas. Making instant noodles involved nothing more than adding boiling water to a prepared cup of noodles, hardly a task that required training in food preparation—which many women actually had, because during this period high school girls (though not boys) were required to take home economics classes. Moreover, most young men were used to making instant noodles, an inexpensive and easy meal for many college students. So viewers saw it as particularly senseless that the actors in the commercial created artificial gender roles around cooking and eating. The cultural critique of this commercial opened the door to other criticisms of gender representations in the media.

The Action Group next joined with other Japanese women's groups, including the Asian Women's Conference, the Asian Women's Association (whose initial goal was to combat sex tourism), and venerable Christian organizations such as the Japanese WCTU, as well as feminist groups in South Korea, Thailand, and the Philippines, to attack sex tourism by Japanese men in those countries (Matsui 1989). Taiwan had actually been the first country to receive Japanese male sex tourists, who felt at ease there because many Taiwanese were still fluent in Japanese, a legacy of prewar Japanese

Japanese mothers protest against a proposed bill to limit women's access to abortion in 1972. That bill failed, but feminists have continued to rally against subsequent proposals to limit reproductive rights
PHOTO BY THE ASAHI SHIMBUN VIA GETTY IMAGES

colonialism. When Japan shifted its formal Chinese diplomatic relations from Taiwan to the People's Republic of China in 1972, direct flights from Japan to Taiwan decreased, and sex tourism shifted to South Korea, the Philippines, and Thailand. In South Korea, *kisaeng* tourism grew after the 1965 formalization of diplomatic relations with Japan (see the Korea section of this chapter for more on *kisaeng* tourism). By 1973 Korean students were staging huge demonstrations to prevent Japanese male sex tourists' arrival at Kimpo airport, and in 1974 Japanese women's groups joined them on the Tokyo side with their own demonstrations against male tourists' departures from Haneda airport. Ninety percent of the more than half a million Japanese tourists to South Korea in 1979 were men, even after Japanese male sex tourism in South Korea had begun to decline in the late 1970s under the barrage of embarrassing feminist pressure (Moon 2009, 152–153).

The bulk of Japanese sex tourism then moved to Thailand and the Philippines. The structure of the sex tourism industry was exploitative, as the payments made by the sex tourists did not benefit the host country or the women sex workers to any great degree. In the Philippines, for example, sex tourists booked travel packages that included flights on Japan Air Lines as well as lodging and meals in Japanese-owned hotels and restaurants. The women workers kept less than 10 percent of the fees the tourists paid for sexual services (Matsui 1989, 70). By the mid-1980s, pressure from women's groups in Japan and the host countries led to the end of packaged sex tours. Some men continued to go to Asian countries for sexual entertainment purposes, where they joined thousands of American and European men seeking the same kind of entertainment. More important, Japanese business owners and pimps brought into Japan thousands of women from Thailand, the Philippines, and South Korea to work at bars and massage parlors, circumventing Japanese laws against prostitution. These sex workers joined thousands of other undocumented and documented immigrant women who worked in factories and menial jobs in Japan in the 1980s. Many immigrants married Japanese men who were unable to find Japanese wives. This led to discussions about the meaning of Japaneseness, as Japanese ethnicity itself began to change.

Many of the foreign workers, both those working in the sex trades and those holding other jobs, were exploited by their employers. Some had been forced to hand over their passports to their employers, so the workers could not return home if they wished to. Japanese women's groups, especially the WCTU and other nongovernmental organizations, set up shelters for exploited women in the mid-1980s. In addition to providing a safe haven for these immigrant women, volunteers at the shelters helped the women with their unique needs, such as navigating difficult interactions with the Department of Immigration (Mackie 2003, 205–209).

SOUTH KOREA

There are three major characteristics that define the political economy in South Korea from the mid-1950s to the late 1970s. First, South Korea became a crucial battleground in the global politics of the Cold War, and the presence of the U.S. military had an ever-growing influence in virtually all aspects of life in South Korea. Second, a series of dictatorial regimes, beginning with Rhee Syngman (president from 1948 to 1960), followed later by Park Chung Hee (in office 1962–1979) and Chun Doo-hwan (in office 1980–1988), fully utilized the division of the nation and the potential threat from the North to legitimize and strengthen their political power and suppress human rights. Throughout this period there were active social movements against the military dictatorship, which culminated in a large-scale popular uprising in June 1987 that helped force a transition from an authoritarian military regime to a more democratic, civilian political system. Third, state-led economic development plans from the early 1960s were phenomenally successful, laying the foundation to turn South Korea from one of the poorest countries in the world in the 1950s into one of the most developed countries today. The ongoing democratic movement coupled with the rapid and compressed economic development in South Korea made room for women to take active economic and political roles in shaping contemporary South Korea.

In a significant way, South Korea's success in rapid industrialization and urbanization starting in the 1960s can be attributed to its people's pursuit of upward social mobility. The devastation the country underwent during the Korean War uprooted and impoverished the entire population, and that led to the broad public perception that the class distinctions of the old era were less relevant. There was a widespread sense that the country was on the threshold of a new beginning. Upward social mobility was seen as a real possibility, not a mirage. "Education fever" was an integral part of the social milieu; people believed they lived in an open society and that hard work would bring them opportunity. Women, particularly in their capacity as mothers, played a crucial role in helping the family become upwardly mobile (Abelmann 2003). The emergence of the urban middle class in the 1980s came about against this background. The idealized notions of an open society and social mobility were constantly contested, but the period from the 1960s to the 1980s was one in which there was an unprecedented level of optimism among the public. That optimism has been dampened dramatically since the late 1990s, a point that will be further discussed in Chapter 11.

U.S. Hegemonic Power and Gender Politics

The United States Army Military Government in Korea, which was in place from September 1945 until August 1948, and the crucial role the U.S. military played in the Korean War (1950–1953) laid a firm foundation for U.S. influence in virtually every domain of society, backed by a political ideology centering on anti-Communism, national security, and capitalist economics. In the domain of popular culture, the influx of Hollywood films and popular music from the United States began to play a crucial role in shaping postwar culture and gender relations. Against this background, a binary image of woman emerged in the mid-1950s. On one hand, there was the "after-girl" (*après-gurre*, a blend of French and English), who generated public anxiety because of her associations with sexual desire, vanity, and selfish interest. On the other hand, there was the competing, opposed image of the steadfast, selfless mother who would sacrifice anything for the good of her family, stepping into the role of head of household in the absence of her husband. These competing images of women were not entirely new. As discussed in Chapter 6, the popular images of the New Woman and Modern Girl in the 1920s and 1930s were often constructed as a negative model of womanhood, while women who sacrificed for the family and the nation were idealized; however, the intensity of the contrast between these competing images was much more visible in postwar South Korea.

One of the most representative pieces of popular culture during the immediate postwar era was the film *Chayu puin* (*Madame Freedom*), directed by Han Hyŏngmo and released in 1956. Based on a novel by Chŏng Pisŏk, the film was a major hit, attracting a large audience with its sensational storyline. The plot involved a professor's wife who works at a boutique where Western products (*yangp'um*) are sold. She becomes interested in Western-style dancing through her middle-class female friends, and they frequent dance halls together. On one of these excursions she encounters a man with whom she becomes romantically involved. In the meantime, her husband begins to develop feelings for another woman but, not wanting to destroy his marriage, takes no action and waits for his wife to return. Ultimately the wife does regret her actions, and she returns to her home. The film is clearly a cautionary tale about the dangers of freedom and sexual desire on the part of women. As a document of the time, the film vividly reflects the influx of U.S. culture in the form of commercial products, entertainment, and lifestyle that had become available and were enjoyed by the emerging middle class. Intellectuals and the general public were captivated by Western culture, feeling fascinated and anxious at the same time. Once again, a woman's body and her sexual desire were regarded as things to be held in check and controlled in order to preserve "purity" and "virtue."

Along with the growing influence of U.S. popular culture, the semipermanent establishment of numerous military camptowns had a deep impact on gender politics in South Korea. On October 1, 1953, the Korea-U.S. Mutual Defense Treaty was signed to preserve "peace and security" in the Pacific area and to allow South Korea and the United States to "defend themselves against external armed attack." The agreement firmly established the continuing presence of the U.S. military in South Korea, which in turn led to the appearance of camptowns throughout the country to "support" and "console" U.S. military personnel. By 1956 there were about four hundred thousand club girls and barmaids, and 65.5 percent of them were "UN madams" serving U.S. soldiers (Moon 2010, 54). Just as during the colonial period and during the Korean War, the young women who took up work as prostitutes in the camptowns most often came from impoverished families. Many were also refugees from North Korea.

From the 1960s, under President Park Chung Hee, camptown prostitution became organized as a strategic channel not only for "comforting" U.S. soldiers but also for economic development. The ironically named Prostitution Prevention Law in 1961 created "special districts" where prostitution was allowed, catering specifically to U.S. soldiers and foreign visitors; the sex trade became an important source of foreign cash. The South Korean government closely monitored these special districts and the prostitutes that worked in them to control venereal disease and other health problems. In 1962 the number of special districts was 104; by 1964 it had grown to 146 (Moon 2010, 58–69).

Women Workers and the Industrial Transformation

Right after the Korean War, during the government of Rhee Syngman (the First Republic, 1948–1960), the South Korean economy relied heavily on U.S. aid, and the postwar economy was largely based on the production of consumer goods rather than on investment in infrastructure. Three of the most representative industries under Rhee were cotton, flour, and sugar, referred to as the "three white industries." The corrupt Rhee regime was driven out of power by the April Nineteenth Revolution in 1960. At that time South Korea underwent a short period of political adjustment (the Second Republic, 1960–1961), which ended with a military coup led by General Park Chung Hee in May 1961. Park held the office of president of South Korea for close to two decades, from 1963 until October 1979, when he was assassinated.

One of the most spectacular changes to take place during the regime of Park Chung Hee was the state-led drive to revitalize the South Korean economy. Beginning in 1962 the government launched a series of five-year economic plans to modernize and industrialize the Korean economy. By the 1970s those economic plans had transformed South Korea from one of the poorest countries in the world to one of the world's fastest-growing economies. The aggressive economic drive mobilized a large number of young girls and women to participate in the labor market, mostly in manufacturing. According to combined statistical data, 26.8 percent of women were "economically active" in 1960, a figure that increased dramatically to 46.7 percent by 1989 (Moon 2005, 71).

In the 1960s the state began to concentrate on export-oriented, labor-intensive light industries, such as textiles, food processing, and other consumer products. Just as in the 1920s and 1930s, when there was a rural exodus in response to the industrialization and urbanization instituted under Japanese colonial rule, there was another big wave of migration from the countryside into the cities in the 1960s and 1970s to meet the needs of this new state-led drive for industrialization and urbanization. The majority of female factory workers came from poor rural families. In the eyes of the industrialists and the state, these young women were a valuable resource for the accumulation of capital: a steady supply of workers willing to work long hours on the factory floor for low wages (Kim 2001, 56). These factory workers were portrayed as "industrial soldiers" in the public discourse, generally represented as obedient and docile. Despite their service to the economy, these young women were commonly referred to as *kongsuni*, a dismissive label given to factory girls (Kim 1997).

In general, the state-led economic transformation succeeded on the backs of these laborers, who worked without the protections of labor laws—the state suppressed labor unions in order to keep the industrial workforce under tight control. Female factory workers were the part of the workforce that was most disadvantaged in terms of wages, employment opportunities, and safe working conditions. In 1972 "the average wages of female workers employed in manufacturing companies with ten or more employees (where women represented 81.4 percent of the labor force) were among the lowest for all Korean workers, who as a group were already paid far below international standards" (Moon 2005, 77). Even a decade later, female factory workers still earned less than half of the wage that male workers in equivalent jobs were earning. Furthermore, women were constantly discriminated against on the basis of age and marital status. Business interests preferred their female employees to be young and unmarried. Once a female employee had married, she was expected to quit her job. Female workers were also pressured to make extra efforts simply to keep their jobs, so a woman might work overtime without asking for additional compensation. But beyond these unfair practices, the workplace could be downright dangerous for women. Sexual harassment and rape by male supervisors was a fact of life.

The Factory New Village Movement (FNVM) provides another illustration of how deeply the state got involved in creating an environment in which female factory workers would become docile, industrious, and productive workers for the industrial economy. The FNVM began in 1975 as an extension of the New Village Movement, which was launched by the government in 1970 to modernize rural communities and counterbalance the development of urban areas. While in their day-to-day existence female workers were wage earners in the workforce, they were generally thought of as future wives and mothers whose wisdom, thrift, dedication, and rational household management would be crucial for raising the next generation of citizens. To that end, the FNVM provided single female factory workers with a wide range of classes that were designed to instill a strong sense of patriotism and teach efficient household management, womanly etiquette, and proper hobbies such as flower arranging. The fact that the primary focus in those programs was on "femininity" demonstrates how female factory workers were thought of as "women" rather than "laborers," and it is remarkably similar to the effort put into domesticating and "managing" women workers in turn-of-the-twentieth-century Japan).

Labor Struggles and Human Rights

The state and industrialists aimed to domesticate and discipline women workers; however, autonomous labor organizations began to spring up here and there in the 1970s. One of the distinctive aspects of the labor union movement at that time was the critical role played by Christian groups, especially Urban Industrial Missions (UIM), and the alliance between workers and intellectuals. The alliance among workers, Christians, and intellectuals grew even stronger after the death of Chŏn T'aeil, a garment worker who set himself on fire in 1970 to protest inhumane working conditions and extremely low wages. Dissident intellectuals and college students began to get involved to help bring greater attention to the issues of inequality and human rights. Christian organizations were considered "a sanctuary for those involved in the labor movement, protecting them [the dissidents] from ideological attacks by the state and society" (Lee 2007, 223). Christian groups in Korea—both Protestant and Catholic—have been mostly conservative, but a small number of them, such as the UIM and the Christian Academy, were socially engaged with issues of justice and equality. Furthermore, "South Korean society regarded Christianity generally as nationalist, modern, and anticommunist—the trinity of South Korea national identity" (Lee 2007, 223). For this reason, Christian groups were more protected than other dissident groups. College students and progressive intellectuals began to meet with factory workers in night classes and small groups to try to bring about an awakening of conscience in the workers. Political oppression by the Park Chung Hee regime became even harsher, especially after the October 1972 institution of the draconian Yusin System (which allowed the president to remain in office for an unlimited number of terms and to appoint one-third of the members of the National Assembly, essentially giving the president dictatorial powers), so the UIM and other labor unions went underground and relied on small group meetings. In those meetings, female workers learned about issues related to workers' rights in the areas of "wages, dismissal, labor unions, forced overtime, retirement pay, industrial accidents, and sick days, as well as larger political, social, and economic issues, and family or personal problems" (Lee 2007, 225).

BOX 10.2

Women Workers' Fight for Basic Human Rights

Female factory workers led some of the crucial labor disputes of the 1970s, which led to larger changes in workers' rights and labor practices. Most representatively, the 1978 Tongil Textile incident and the 1979 YH dispute are worth mentioning because they revealed the complicit alliance among the state authorities, industries, and industry-friendly unions. The Tongil Textile Company was founded in colonial-era Korea and became one of the biggest textile industries in South Korea. When the female workers at the factory tried to elect female union representatives, they faced strong opposition from management and male workers. Nonetheless, in 1972 they succeeded in electing Chu Kilcha—the first woman chairperson of a labor union in South Korean history. Chu's election inspired other unions to elect women to leadership positions. In a significant way, Chu's election was to be expected, given that over 80 percent of union membership was female. When another female union leader, Yi Yŏngsuk, was elected in 1975, the company and male workers worked to remove her from the position, accusing her of instigating strikes. In July 1976, after locking the women workers in their dormitory, the male workers convened an election. When the women workers emerged from the dormitory and learned what had happened, they staged a sit-in. When riot police broke into the protest site, the women took off their work clothes, thinking that if they were encountered wearing only their underwear, they would appear to be more vulnerable, and it might embarrass the police as well. Tragically, they were mistaken: in one of the most horrifying acts of violence in the history of labor in Korea, the half-naked women workers were ruthlessly beaten by the police and dragged from the building. Many of them were arrested or hospitalized. In the end there was little to show for the sacrifices they had made.

It was the YH dispute in 1979 that brought labor issues to the national political stage and stirred college students, dissident intellectuals, politicians, and ultimately the general populace. In the early 1970s the YH Trading Company was the biggest wig company in the country, but it began to experience a rapid decline in its revenues starting in the mid-1970s. In March 1979 the president of the company made a unilateral decision to shut down operations. When workers learned of this plan, they launched a series of protests. The distinctive feature of this incident is that once the company had refused to negotiate with workers and the state had offered no support or assistance, the workers fled to the offices of the opposition party, the New Democratic Party (NDP), for protection and also to continue their protest. Workers won the support of the NDP leader, Kim Young Sam, and members of the party; nevertheless, the riot police soon entered NDP headquarters and dragged out all who were inside the building. There were a large number of causalities, among them a twenty-three-year-old female worker named Kim Kyŏngsuk who fell from the fourth floor during the police attack and eventually died. The opposition party brought this incident to the National Assembly, demanding a full investigation of the death of Kim Kyŏngsuk and the culpability of the riot police. President Park Chung Hee later forcefully removed Kim Young Sam from his position as the leader of the NDP and his seat in the National Assembly because of his support for the YH workers as well as his vocal criticism of the Park regime. This series of events caused major protests in the Pusan and Masan areas, a stronghold of Kim Young Sam, in October 1979, which are seen as among the events that contributed to the ultimate downfall of the Park regime. In the end, it was the protests of the female workers, the least powerful people in the workforce, who were merely seeking basic survival, that contributed to the end of the long dictatorial regime of Park Chung Hee.

Protest at Tongil Textile.
HTTP://BLOG.HANI.CO.KR/NOMUSA/53780

While labor-intensive industries continued to be central, a shift in focus took place starting in the late 1970s, with emphasis on the development of heavy industries (such as shipbuilding) and the manufacture of electronics, machinery, and automobiles. Women did work in these heavy industries in the 1970s, but skilled male laborers dominated those emerging sectors because there was a decided lack of training programs for women in the skilled trades that were most in demand for those better-paying sectors.

As the economic priorities shifted over time, women laborers gradually moved from textiles and other light industries into the service sector. In 1963 the percentage of women in the service sector was a mere 24.4 percent, but that number grew rapidly over the next few decades, reaching 74.8 percent by 2004 (Kang 2006, 49). The economic boom in the 1980s especially accelerated the development of service sector jobs, particularly in the areas of entertainment and leisure, where a large percentage of women workers found employment.

State Control of Women's Bodies and Female Sexuality

The militant economic drive was intimately linked with the control of women's bodies. The most prominent case in point is the government-led program for family planning and birth control in the 1960s and 1970s. Family planning was presented as an integral part of economic development. This was a dramatic shift from the population policies of the 1950s, when a high birth rate and large population were considered to be important for the future prosperity of the nation. Family planning was officially adopted as a major part of the first five-year economic plan of Park Chung Hee (1962–1966), which assumed that low population growth was positively correlated with a higher standard of living. In March 1962 the Supreme Council for National Reconstruction established the National Family Planning Center, and the year 1966 was designated as the "Great Year of Family Planning," in which the government set a goal of inserting four hundred thousand IUDs in women and performing twenty thousand vasectomies on men (Moon 2005, 84). The state engaged in a large-scale campaign to promote a low birth rate not only through sloganeering and propaganda but also through a variety of contraceptive programs that provided birth control pills, condoms, and other medical options. Rather than encouraging safe methods, such as the use of condoms or the rhythm method, the state "preferred one-shot and permanent contraception" (Moon 2005, 84).

In the 1970s the government focused more on permanent birth control via vasectomy. Men didn't relish the idea of undergoing such a procedure, however, and as a result, tubal ligation for women became the most common method, particularly in the late 1970s, when more advanced surgical techniques for the procedure became available. Consequently, the birth rate dropped dramatically, from 6.3 children per family in the early 1960s to 1.6 in 1988. It is important to recognize that the rapid fall in the birth rate cannot be attributed solely to state policies and campaigns; the desire of individual women to control their own bodies and reproduction also played a significant role and may indeed have been the most crucial factor (Pae 2005).

While maintaining a low birth rate was assumed to contribute to greater affluence in Korean society, the exploitation of female sexuality in the form of *kisaeng* tourism was actively utilized in the 1970s as a way to bring foreign currency into the country—an essential part of the export-led industrial policy that was a part of the country's long-term economic plan. There were other, broader historical and structural circumstances as well that contributed to the growth in *kisaeng* tourism, particularly involving Japanese men. The spectacular economic boom that took place in Japan in the 1960s and 1970s meant that many more Japanese were traveling, for both business and pleasure. Normalization of relations between South Korea and Japan in 1965 meant that Korea opened up to Japanese business interests. Furthermore, when diplomatic ties between Japan and Taiwan ended in 1972, more Japanese men shifted their travel to South Korea (Lie 1995). In 1973, 80 percent of foreign tourists to Korea were Japanese, and the majority of Japanese men came without wives or girlfriends. According to a survey conducted in the same year, 80 percent of Japanese tourists answered that "*kisaeng* parties" at government-designated hotels or restaurants was the most memorable experience from their travels in Korea (Lie 1995, 318). In this vein, *kisaeng* tourism can be understood as "cross-country patriarchal collaboration," because the South Korean government instituted policies that facilitated sex tourism and worked actively with Japanese corporate and state actors to induce Japanese businessmen and tourists to travel to Korea (Norma 2014).

NORTH KOREA

Under the leadership of Kim Il Sung (1912–1994), postwar North Korea underwent a major socialist transformation, and that gave rise to a reconfiguration of gender relations, which was considered to be a critical factor in the construction of the nation and the new economy. Women in North Korea were actively mobilized to participate in economic development as revolutionary mothers and proletarian laborers. While a long-standing conception of proper gender roles persisted in North Korea, socialist reforms and laws, such as land reform and the Gender Equality Law, laid the foundation for the elimination of patriarchal gender bias and the promotion of gender equality, as discussed in Chapter 9. These legal provisions were expedient preparatory steps prior to North Korea's drive for economic development in the 1950s and 1960s. North Korea initiated a series of plans for economic development beginning in 1957, including the Movement of the Flying Horse (*ch'ŏllima undong*). This was similar to China's Great Leap

Forward campaign, calling for a massive mobilization of people for the purpose of enhancing labor productivity and socialist political consciousness. All major economic production sectors were nationalized, with heavy industry being the main focus of production, and these efforts yielded positive results. The North Korean economy grew rapidly in the 1960s.

During the economic boom, North Korean women were hailed as equal participants in the socialist revolution. Kim Il Sung stated that "women . . . can achieve complete emancipation only if they strive with no less devotion and awareness than men to solve the problems arising on the productive fronts of the factories and countryside," and he further emphasized "women's participation in socialist construction" (Park 1992–1993, 534–535). In this political campaign, a woman's role as mother in the "revolutionary family" was seamlessly intertwined with her role as proletarian laborer in building the socialist nation.

In the 1970s North Korea actively pursued the socialization of domestic labor as a means to free women from the domestic sphere of housekeeping and to allow them to participate in the public sector. A series of laws and political commitments were crafted to make domestic labor and maternal duties the collective responsibility of the state, in order to liberate women from those tasks. Specifically, the state introduced policies and facilities that would allow women to cope more easily with the demands of the domestic sphere, such as "maternity leave with pay, maternity hospitals, free nurseries and kindergartens, and reduced working hours for mothers of large families," as well as public laundries and take-out food services (Park 1992–1993, 536). Men in North Korea were subject to a mandatory ten-year period of military service, which inevitably resulted in labor shortages, and, it was necessary to make use of women laborers. The government implemented social programs to help working mothers, and as a result, there was a steady growth of women in the labor force, from a mere 20 percent in 1956 to 64 percent in 1990—a much higher rate of labor force participation than the 40 percent that was found in South Korea (Park 1992–1993, 537).

However, despite some progress in women's rate of economic participation in North Korea, the status of women did not improve as much as it may appear. The passage of laws and the creation of social policies did not necessarily mean that the aims behind those laws and policies were achieved. The North Korean data are incomplete, but there is evidence that the wage structure remained gender-biased, with men receiving higher salaries. It is also clear that gender prejudice continued in the workplace and that there was an unequal representation of genders in many occupations. Women were far less well represented in higher-level political positions in central political organs, such as the Politburo of the Workers' Party of Korea (Park 1992–1993). Furthermore, beginning in the early 1990s North Korea had to cope with catastrophic changes caused by famine, negative economic growth, and an increasingly unstable political sphere after the collapse of the Soviet bloc and the death of Kim Il Sung. Under these circumstances, North Korea started to shift its economic emphasis from heavy industry to light industry and to put forward a policy called Speed of the 1990s to motivate workers to meet the economic goals of that decade. Women were actively mobilized to engage in light industrial production of consumer products. As we will discuss in Chapter 11, women in contemporary North Korea are a vital segment of the economic force, especially in informal (black) markets.

CHINA

Gender Politics in the 1950s

Between 1949 and his death in 1976, Mao Zedong led China through revolutionary social and economic transformation accompanied by tumultuous political upheaval. By the mid-1950s, the Chinese Communist Party had established its legitimacy and firmed up its control of both rural and urban economies through land reform and various campaigns targeted at urban elites. In 1956, under the slogan "Let a hundred flowers bloom and a hundred schools of thought contend," Mao Zedong launched a campaign to elicit public criticisms and suggestions about the direction the revolution was taking. The campaign resulted in an outpouring of criticisms of Party policy and of social phenomena that had emerged in the early years of the PRC. As criticisms of the Party broadened, with some expressing outright hostility toward Mao and the Party leadership, Mao abruptly ended that effort in 1957 and announced an Anti-Rightist Campaign to denounce and purge those who had questioned the Party's policies. Between four hundred thousand and seven hundred thousand people were labeled as "rightists," lost their jobs, and were sent to prison or labor camps.

In the midst of the campaign, the All-China Women's Federation was preparing for its Third National Women's Assembly. By the middle of the 1950s, more than seventy million women had joined the Federation. With branches and cadres in villages and neighborhoods, it had greater reach than any of the other mass organizations, although at every level it was subordinate to the corresponding Party committee. Despite opposition, the Federation had achieved critical success in launching the Marriage Law of 1950, expanding women's employment, and incorporating women into local governance (Wang 2006). Yet the Hundred Flowers campaign revealed hints of tensions over "women-work" (see Chapter 9). For example, there were criticisms of the negative effects of the Marriage Law, especially access to divorce, and of pro-natalist family planning policies that prevented women from getting access to contraception. In 1957 many Federation cadres who had criticized Party policy in the struggle to legitimize the Federation's work were labeled as rightists and lost their positions (Wang 2005a, 542). For example, Zhao Xian, chair of the Shanghai Women's Federation, was denounced for having openly challenged the Party's pro-natalist policies in the early 1950s rather than promoting them.

At a private meeting with top Federation officials to prepare a report to be issued at the assembly, the all-male Party leadership criticized Federation leaders for their mistaken "rightist" view that women were not yet fully liberated and that gender inequality persisted under socialism and for prioritizing women's needs and interests over the central tasks of the Party. These, they contended, were the views of so-called bourgeois feminists. Some Party leaders questioned the need for a Women's Federation at all. They wanted the report issued at the assembly to highlight examples of the revolution's successes in its work with women and children. They mandated that the report state, "Since the socialist revolution was completed, women in our country have already achieved equal rights with men in political, economic, cultural and social aspects and family life. They have forever ended thousands of years of sad history of being oppressed and subjugated, and achieved women's liberation." The federation was tasked to integrate women-work more thoroughly into core Party work by mobilizing women to take up the "two diligences": "diligently, thriftily build the country and diligently, thriftily manage the family" (Wang 2006, 924). The new policy on women-work reaffirmed the Party's long-standing Marxist maternalist view that since women were biologically determined to be mothers, they would "naturally" have a greater role in domestic work than men, even after they were fully engaged in labor outside the home and many aspects of family life were collectivized (Manning 2006).

Women in the Great Leap Forward (1958–1960)

This conservative message, that women's primary role in the nation's socialist construction was management of household and family, was dramatically reversed when the Party plunged the country into the final phase of collectivization in the Great Leap Forward campaign, which began in 1958. The population was organized into communes that controlled all aspects of life. While men were mobilized to leave their villages to work in industry, mining, and large-scale construction and irrigation projects, women took on most of the agricultural work. Private family life disappeared as people labored long hours, ate in communal dining halls, shared housework through collective washing and sewing circles, and deposited their children in commune nurseries and schools, many of which provided boarding. Men and women between the ages of fifteen and fifty were required to do military-style training for several hours a day. With nearly 90 percent of women engaged in production, supposedly freed from the domestic work of child care and cooking, the Great Leap Forward appeared to fulfill Mao's vision of gender equality: women and men working equally for the Party and the nation, unconstrained by individual and family interests.

Women's Federation cadres called attention to the particular health problems, including malnutrition, exhaustion, miscarriages, and prolapsed uteruses, faced by women and children as a result of excessive physical labor and lack of adequate nourishment during the Great Leap. Many rural women, however, saw these hardships as liberating and rejected the idea that women's physiology required them to have special protections that differentiated their labor from that of men. The Great Leap was a transformative experience through which they bonded with other women, learned new skills, became economically self-reliant, and were recognized for their extraordinary accomplishments in labor. One woman recalled, "Every year there are two busy seasons [in which] we must help and support one another. After the busy season [we could] carry out irrigation projects or smooth down the fields. The women were very happy because in the past women were bound by fetters in the home. [After the Great Leap Forward began] they could come out and be in charge. They could talk and laugh during the day [and were] very happy" (Manning 2006, 585).

The Communist utopia promised by the Great Leap collapsed in the largest famine in human history, which killed some thirty million people between 1958 and 1962. Local party cadres, full of revolutionary fervor and fearful of criticizing or questioning Party policy in the wake of the political campaigns that targeted dissenters as rightists and counterrevolutionaries, grossly inflated their grain production targets. The state assessed the amount of grain to be requisitioned as taxes based on these impossibly high figures and thus did not leave enough for local consumption. Drought in many regions and commune mismanagement of harvests compounded the disaster.

Gender and the Cultural Revolution (1966–1976)

The horrific famine caused by the policies of the Great Leap Forward created a deep political schism within the CCP's leadership, setting pragmatists, who recognized that failures of Party policy had led to the famine, against Mao and the defenders of the revolutionary idealism that had fueled the Great Leap. In the wake of the famine, the pragmatists held sway, refocusing Party priorities on material incentives for workers and technical experts to guide the process of development.

BOX 10.3

Love in the Service of Revolution

In the early sixties, as the radicalism of the Great Leap abated, the Party resumed its efforts to educate young people about proper modes of courtship and marriage in the new society. A 1964 handbook for rural cadres to reference in their work with youth explains the official party line on love and sexual morality. Reiterating the logic of the 1950 Marriage Law, the handbook promotes a modern ethos of gender equality and the autonomy of women and men to choose partners based on love, but emphasizes that sex must be linked to monogamous marriage. It also affirms the centrality of the Party in regulating private and emotional life and reiterates the notion that love and marriage are about social stability and progress, not individual fulfillment.

1. *We must clear away the remnants of feudal ideology in our minds and treat the relationship between the sexes correctly. When we see a man and a woman talking together, we should not be greatly surprised. We should, moreover, not gossip or interfere with them. When a man and a woman meet, they should be open-minded and not be suspicious of each other. If you love another person, you must give it serious consideration. After due consideration, if you want to propose, then propose. You need not suppress it in your heart and create suffering. If you and the other person build up a proper relationship and fall in love, even if you do encounter ridicule or interference from others, you need not feel troubled by it and may disregard it. You may also explain it to them and, if necessary, make observations on the situation to the party or the [Youth League] in order to request support.*

2. *When they fall in love, young men and women must be particularly careful to balance well the relationship between love and work. They should not forget everything else when they fall in love, but should change love into a kind of motive power to encourage themselves to work, learn, and progress better.*

3. *In falling in love, one should never have improper sexual relationships as a result of temporary emotional impulses. This is immoral. (Ebrey 1993, 471)*

Seeing this retreat from the radicalism of the Great Leap as a betrayal, Mao Zedong launched an attack on the Communist Party itself in May 1966. This unleashed the Cultural Revolution. The attack was led by a Cultural Revolution Group that consisted of his personal allies, including his wife, Jiang Qing, a former movie actress who took charge of culture and performing arts. The group spearheaded the building of a "cult of Mao" that elevated him to near godlike status. The idea of the Cultural Revolution as a movement that would root out counterrevolutionary forces within the Party bureaucracy was particularly appealing to high school and college students, who had grown up steeped in tales of the heroic revolutionary deeds of their parents' generation but faced the very unexciting challenges of employment and upward mobility in a poor, developing country.

When Mao called for the masses to "bombard the headquarters," male and female students responded by forming Red Guard units. These first attacked teachers, administrators, and intellectuals in their schools in violent struggle meetings that often resulted in victims being beaten to death or committing suicide. In August 1966 Red Guards from all over the country came to a series of mass rallies in Tiananmen Square in Beijing, where Mao, their "supreme commander," told them that "it is right to rebel" and charged them with destroying "the Four Olds": old ideas, old habits, old customs, and old culture. Students rampaged around the country destroying temples, museums, and libraries and ransacking the private homes of people identified as "feudal" or "bourgeois" elements. They tortured, beat, or killed millions of people, including PRC president Liu Shaoqi (who died in solitary confinement) and CCP general secretary Deng Xiaoping (who was exiled to a remote village), the two architects of the reforms following the famines caused by the Great Leap Forward. Turmoil spread as factionalized

Red Guard units allied themselves with rival groups of workers and farmers and fought street battles for control. In 1967–1968 rival factions established alliances with military commanders, seized military weapons, and made war against each other across the country.

Realizing that China was in total anarchy, in 1969 Mao called on the People's Liberation Army (PLA, China's national army) to restore order. For the rest of the Cultural Revolution, until Mao's death in 1976, the military dominated social and political life. Cultural Revolution radicalism continued in the ritualized worship of Mao in daily life amid an atmosphere of extreme political repression. The Red Guards were militarily suppressed, many of them were killed, and more than four million high school and university students, many of whom were Red Guards, were sent out to villages to live with peasants and reeducate themselves through manual labor. Many of these "sent-down youth" were not able to return to their urban homes.

Gender, Sexuality, and Violence

The Cultural Revolution era was marked by profound gender paradoxes. Party rhetoric and policy declared the achievement of a radical version of revolutionary equality encapsulated in Mao's slogans "The times have changed, men and women are the same" and "Women can do anything men can do." The Women's Federation was disbanded in 1966 and feminism of any kind was declared to be bourgeois. The images of women that dominated the propaganda posters and the media were masculinized female Red Guards, military revolutionary heroines from the model operas that were approved for performance, and "iron girls," who did the heavy labor of men. The operatic ballet *Red Detachment of Women*, for example, celebrated female militancy through the story of a slave girl who becomes a Communist guerilla inspired to wage war on oppressive landlords by Mao's dictum that "power grows out of the barrel of a gun."

After Mao, dressed in a military uniform, called on the Red Guards to rebel against Party authorities in mass rallies in Beijing, combat uniforms with leather belts, boots, army caps, and red armbands became the official dress of the movement. Jiang Qing, Mao's wife, who rose to the pinnacle of political power as a leader of the most radical faction, also wore military uniforms and short hair, signaling the political correctness of military attire. Critically, though, Red Guard fashion was not androgynous but male. The Red Guards understood their aggressive behavior to be a radical rejection of feudal gender and class norms—anti-feminine and anti-bourgeois. Many observers noted the particular intensity of foul language and violence female

Red Guards displayed. In one infamous incident in August 1966, female students at the prestigious girls' middle school affiliated with Beijing Normal University beat their female vice principal to death in an orgy of violence against teachers and administrators.

Red Guard violence was distinctly sexualized. During the Cultural Revolution, manuals and books about female hygiene, marital relations, and sexual health ceased to be published. All references to romance, love, and sex were forbidden, and a number of authors were imprisoned for works that dealt with these topics or even with marriage. Local-level cadres often criticized or punished unmarried people for romantic relationships they considered inappropriate. Red Guards who came of age amid this silence about sexuality demonstrated highly puritanical attitudes. They identified political purity with sexual purity when they attacked "the Four Olds." Pornography, dirty jokes, slow dancing, perfume, lipstick, jewelry, feminized clothing such as the *qipao*, and hairstyles were all artifacts of "decadent capitalist culture." They often denounced female class enemies as "whores." Sexually corrupt lifestyles and sexual transgressions, including not only promiscuity, adultery, and rape but also divorce, remarriage, and bigamy, were common accusations in factional conflicts and against men and women identified as class enemies. It was not uncommon for male Red Guards to sexually abuse women as a form of punishment (Honig 2003).

Yet the Cultural Revolution was also, ironically, a time when urban young people were free from social controls, as all schools and universities were closed and parents were preoccupied with political meetings. Many of those too young to join the Red Guards roamed their cities in urban gangs, and sexual liaisons, harassment, and assault were common. Many young people had their first sexual encounters while following Mao's call to travel the country and "exchange revolutionary experiences."

For sent-down youth, many of whom later wrote memoirs of their experiences, living in the countryside gave them their first exposure to the much more open social customs and sexual morality among peasants, including bawdy humor, revealing dress, and casual acceptance of sex. Handwritten copies of romantic and erotic stories circulated widely underground and were especially popular with sent-down youth. Communal living with other urban youth also created new opportunities for sexual encounters, both heterosexual and homosexual, and even cohabitation without marriage. Rape by local cadres and demands for sex in exchange for privileges such as permission to return to the city were pervasive threats for female urban youth and sometimes men as well. Pregnancy outside of marriage was common and caused complications for women who had the chance to return to the cities after the Cultural Revolution, since their children lacked urban residence permits. When these young women were permitted to return home after the Cultural Revolution, many adopted their children out to peasant families or abandoned them (Honig 2003, 155–166).

The "Iron Girls": Women and Work

Under the system of central economic planning, the state assigned urban and industrial jobs according to the priorities of the time. During the Great Leap Forward most women were mobilized for production. In the wake of the famine there was widespread unemployment, so the Party encouraged women to return to domestic labor as housewives. In the 1960s and 1970s rapid industrialization again became the top priority, so the state actively recruited women into industrial jobs. In 1960 women made up 20 percent of the urban workforce, but by the end of the 1970s nearly 90 percent of women were employed. Gendered divisions of labor and thus disparities in pay persisted, with women concentrated in lower-skilled jobs and in smaller collective enterprises rather than in large state enterprises. Moreover, women were still expected to do the bulk of domestic work and child rearing.

One of the most prominent demonstrations of the radical notions of gender equality was the "iron girls"—tough, muscular women who did traditionally male, physically taxing work. During the sixties and seventies, many women were recruited to join Iron Girl Brigades that won accolades for their feats in the electricity, coal mining, transportation, oil production, fishing, and lumber industries. Although working conditions were often very harsh in these heavy industries and women suffered work-related injuries and illnesses, many Iron Girls took pride in their accomplishments and the prestige that came to them. Although such women were a small minority of workers, their images pervaded the media and seem to have affected the girls who became Red Guards and were later sent down to the countryside. Some of these sent-down women embraced heavy labor with enthusiasm and crusaded for labor equality against the objections of rural cadres (Honig 2000).

Marriage and Family Life in the Cultural Revolution

After the Anti-Rightist campaign in 1957, Party surveillance over private life increased. Family life became politicized as the Party encouraged people to draw lines of demarcation between themselves and members of their family labeled as "rightists" or "counterrevolutionaries." Children denounced parents, and people considered political factors in marriages and divorces. It

Poster exhorting women to militancy, in the service of economic development, with the slogan "Study the battle spirit of the Red Army during the Long March, conquer nature, build up our nation." LANDSBERGER COLLECTION, INTERNATIONAL INSTITUTE OF SOCIAL HISTORY (AMSTERDAM)

became increasingly difficult to get a divorce, continuing the decline in the overall number of divorces granted that had begun in 1953.

Yet, as in the prerevolutionary past, concerns about economic and social status continued to shape marriage choices. Many urban workers preferred to marry better-paid workers or technicians, even if their prospective partners had "bad class backgrounds"—associations with groups or ideologies the state opposed. Women in one Shanghai cotton mill told Women's Federation investigators that they preferred to marry cadres not because of their political status but because of their high skill level (and thus higher wages). One investigation discovered that it was common practice for men to inflate their salaries when getting to know potential spouses. Women cadres also reported using marriage as a means of upward mobility, preferring husbands with higher status in the political system because this came with a higher salary.

Preference for life in the city drove many peasants to leave their villages and rural spouses behind and to file for divorce. During the many campaigns in which urban workers and students were sent out to the countryside to learn from the peasants, there was a spike in divorce filings by spouses who remained behind in the cities. In some regions, so many rural women migrated out of the countryside that peasant men had difficulty in finding wives. In the early 1960s, state policies to promote economic recovery by allowing limited market development after the famines of the Great Leap Forward also fostered both greater mobility and more criminal activity. This created the context for a spike in incidences of trafficking of urban women to the countryside through matchmakers, who preyed upon women's political fears of not finding a husband because of bad class backgrounds and lies about the economic and political status of their prospective husbands (Diamant 2000).

China's birth control policy had its origins in 1953, when a groundswell of popular opinion expressed in the context of a campaign to open up communication with state bureaucrats spurred the Party to investigate the effects on a family's living conditions of having a large number of children. This opened up access to contraception. New census results showing a rapid population increase motivated the Party to advocate an explicitly anti-natalist policy of actually promoting birth control in 1954. But as Mao and Party leaders began to discuss the concept of national-scale birth planning as a component of economic five-year plans, they linked it not to women's health or autonomy but to national needs. Mao declared, "With respect to births, mankind is in a state of anarchy; the self is unable to control the self. In the future, we want to achieve the complete planning of births, but without societal strength, unless everyone agrees, unless everyone does it together, then it won't work" (quoted in White 2006). Birth control and population planning became taboo subjects during the Great Leap Forward. Throughout the sixties and early seventies, large families with five or more children were common.

Amid the radical politics of the Cultural Revolution in 1970 Premier Zhou Enlai argued for inclusion of birth planning in the Fourth Five-Year Plan, stating that "birth planning isn't a health question, it is a planning question. If you can't plan the rate of population increase, how can you have any national plan?" (quoted in White 2006). Birth planning as a component of state control over society and the economy was politically uncontroversial. As the policy was implemented throughout the 1970s and 1980s, contraceptives were widely distributed and propaganda encouraged couples to have fewer babies. It was not until 1980 that a policy of one child per family was announced. This required local cadres to adhere to birth-rate targets, track women's fertility, and compel abortion and sterilization if women did not comply. Families with more than one child were subject to fines and loss of welfare and medical benefits. With large numbers of peasant families preferring sons, the policy resulted in a huge increase in female infanticide, which had decreased significantly in the early decades of the PRC. Yet enforcement was difficult, and many exceptions were made for ethnic minority families and peasant families whose first child was a girl.

TAIWAN

Between 1950 and the early 1980s, Taiwan's path as an independent country diverged significantly from China's. Having thoroughly suppressed the Taiwanese independence movement and all political opposition by the early fifties, the Nationalist Party (KMT) established an authoritarian regime under martial law that inherited many of the same institutional structures of a party-state through which it had governed China in the thirties and forties. With substantial economic and military support from the United States, which bolstered Taiwan as a Cold War ally against China and North Korea, it focused on rapid economic development and perpetual military preparedness for a battle to retake the Chinese mainland. As in the other East Asian countries, the government actively encouraged increased participation of women in productive labor as part of a drive to industrialize and modernize the economy. Yet the KMT's effort to harness women's labor for national development was hampered by its continued promotion of the modernized version of a Confucian family-state developed in the New Life Movement of the 1930s (see Chapter 9).

Madame Chiang Kai-shek (Song Meiling), as wife of the nation's patriarch, took up again her wartime role as the chief model of virtuous and nationalist womanhood, exhorting women to excel in their homemaking duties and rear patriotic children. As the head of the KMT's government-sponsored women's organizations, such as the Taiwan Provincial Women's Association and the Chinese Women's Anti-Aggression League, she focused women's public activities on propaganda and philanthropic work to support the military: nursing, sewing uniforms, and raising funds for military housing, nurseries, orphanages, and homes for the disabled and elderly that cared for veterans and their families. The league sponsored weekly radio broadcasts to the mainland extolling Taiwan's economic progress and inciting mainlanders to defect. The Women's Association intervened directly in family life in ways that were reminiscent of both earlier KMT social reform policies and the PRC state's efforts in the 1950s to remold society and the private realm in accord with its own vision of modernity: providing matchmaking services, mediating domestic disputes, and educating women about home economics, child care, health, hygiene, and nutrition.

As on the mainland, the ruling party-state acknowledged women as full participants in the new political order in theory, but the practical effects of such equality were severely limited in undemocratic systems that precluded popular political agency. Although feminist activists had lobbied successfully for inclusion of universal suffrage and full political rights for women in the KMT's 1947 constitution, under martial law national-level elections were suspended indefinitely. The KMT did allow local-level elections, although it nominated almost all candidates, since opposition parties were banned. Dominated by mainlander immigrants, the Party's Women's Working Committee recruited female candidates, including Taiwanese women, to whom they taught political skills and the Mandarin dialect, instilling loyalty to the KMT.

As was the case in Korea, Japan, and mainland China, women entered the paid workforce in ever larger numbers but fell short of achieving full economic self-sufficiency and equality with men. Despite laws mandating equal pay for the same tasks, women continued to earn only two-thirds of men's salaries into the 1980s. Lack of child care and pervasive state rhetoric about women's Confucian family duties led many women to quit their jobs after the birth of their first child, which by the 1970s contributed to a growing labor shortage. To deal with this problem, the government encouraged housewives to take up low-wage piecework production of handicrafts, garments, and toys at home; the Women's Association provided training for them in "mothers' classrooms" and incentivized them with small loans. In the 1960s Japanese and American manufacturers moved production to Taiwan to take advantage of its female workforce, which was literate but accustomed to low wages. Women's production of textiles, garments, shoes, toys, and electronics was a crucial component of the country's rapid industrialization. By the middle of the 1970s, 41 percent of women were in the labor force and a third of unskilled and semiskilled factory workers were women. As wages rose, the government shifted its focus to more capital-intensive industries and women took up jobs in factories producing computers, semiconductors, and precision instruments as well as in the burgeoning service sector (Chang 2009).

The development of an autonomous feminist movement in Taiwan was intertwined with the emergence of democratic opposition to KMT authoritarianism and its pursuit of unity with China. In 1971 the People's Republic of China replaced the Republic of China in the United Nations. This international marginalization of the KMT regime together with the emergence of a prosperous middle class of native Taiwanese created the impetus for an opposition movement calling for democratization and an end to KMT and mainlander domination of the political system. In a climate of limited tolerance for dissent and political activism, a new generation of feminists launched a new women's movement under the leadership of Hsiu-lien Annette Lu (b. 1944). Born into a Taiwanese merchant family that encouraged her education and independence, Lu graduated with top honors from the law school of Taiwan National University and pursued graduate studies in the United States in the late sixties, just as the women's liberation movement there was unfolding. Returning to a government job in Taiwan, she began to publish and lecture on women's issues, such as equal access to higher education and the persistence of the values of the old chastity cult in the sexual double standard. In 1972, when the government refused to allow a permit for her and some thirty supporters to establish the Contemporary Women's Association, she opened a coffee shop called Home of the Pioneers, run by volunteers, to serve as a gathering place for people interested in women's rights and political reform. She established hotlines for victims of sexual assault and domestic violence.

In 1973 she published a book titled *New Feminism* in which she laid out a critique of Confucian-based patriarchy in Taiwanese society and argued that despite seemingly progressive clauses in the law code on gender equality, laws on property and economic right perpetuated women's subordination to their husbands and second-class status as citizens (Rubinstein 2004). Drawing on diverse Western feminists, such as Mary Wollstonecraft and Simone de Beauvoir, as well as Confucian ideas about gender and family order, she argued that there were social and biological differences between men and women and that everyone was obliged to fulfill his or her familial and social roles. Yet she vociferously advocated for full gender equality, including complete equality in educational and work opportunities and pay. Arguing that marriage and childbearing were matters of personal choice, she called for an end to the denigration of women who chose to remain unmarried (like herself) and for women's right to abortion. Although she allowed for some distinction between the roles of husband and wife in the household, she called for men to play a greater role in child rearing and household chores, for shared management of finances, and for an equal standard of sexual virtue that did not condone male promiscuity (Chang 2009).

Like so many Chinese feminists before her, Annette Lu understood the agenda of women's rights to be inextricably linked to larger nationalist goals. While pursuing another graduate degree at Harvard in 1977–1978, Lu turned her focus to Taiwanese history and began to argue for peaceful coexistence between Taiwan and the PRC, in direct contravention of the official KMT insistence on one China. She returned home determined to enter politics by running for a seat in the national assembly as a candidate for the

Dangwai (anti-KMT opposition). After the United States announced normalization of relations with the People's Republic of China and suspension of diplomatic ties with Taiwan in 1979, the KMT cancelled the election, fearing that the Dangwai would make electoral gains. Unable to form an opposition party officially, Dangwai activists, including Lu, created a new journal, *Formosa*, as a platform to promote their cause. On December 10, 1979, the group organized a rally to commemorate the anniversary of the Universal Declaration of Human Rights. Violence broke out when police confronted the demonstrators, and eight *Formosa* leaders were arrested, including Annette Lu, who had made a speech advocating independence. Charged with sedition, she was convicted and sentenced to twelve years in prison. She was not released until 1985, just as Taiwan was on the verge of its democratic transformation, in which she would play a critical role (Chang 2009).

CONNECTIONS

The five countries—PRC, ROC, South Korea, North Korea, and Japan—continued to have vastly different political systems, global positions, and transnational relations from the 1950s through the 1980s. Gender issues were, as a result, treated differently in each of them. Nevertheless, we can find some common concerns and even some common approaches by advocates for reform.

Women and men found their roles increasingly defined by state actors and/or economic interests in the 1960s, and many, especially in South Korea and Japan, resisted these forms of gendering through women's movements in the 1970s and 1980s. Resistance was more difficult in Taiwan in the 1970s, but some brave women resisted nevertheless. The PRC followed a different path, but there, too, the state increasingly defined gender and offered little room for resistance. The discrediting of the All-China Women's Federation during the Hundred Flowers campaign and its dissolution during the Cultural Revolution, as well as the disparaging of feminism itself as bourgeois and counterrevolutionary, made advocating for women difficult throughout much of this period. At the height of the Cultural Revolution in China, women were defined—and many were proud to depict themselves—in masculinized ways. To underscore women's equality with men, gender differences in terms of ability to carry out hard work and to act as violent upholders of political purity were erased. Rather than this equality being one that supported equality through diversity or equality through androgyny, it enforced a masculinization of women in terms of representation (especially in clothing and demeanor). In Japan, South Korea, and Taiwan, by contrast, gender differences were highlighted by government and business interests.

In Japan, a notion of the "traditional family" was promoted by big business through the New Life Movement and by the government through social programs in the countryside, through education (including the teaching of home economics to girls), through tax policies, and through the persistence, until the early 1980s, of laws that gendered the definition of nationality. Women resisted these gendered images of women and the family and the policies of inequality that grew from them in active feminist movements. Some feminists championed maternalist notions of women's ability to change society, and others, especially in the 1970s, stressed complete male-female equality in society, performance of sexuality, the workplace, and the economy. Some second-wave feminists were mocked by sexist traditionalists, as feminists were in the PRC as well, although on different grounds. After International Women's Year in 1975, however, Japanese reformers began to make progress toward feminist reforms.

In South Korea, two contrasting images of women emerged in 1950s movies and literature—the fun-loving after-girl, associated with sexual desire and materialism, and the hardworking, self-sacrificing mother. The maternalistic image paralleled the mother role promoted by Japan's New Life Movement at about the same time. In addition, the South Korean government promoted the Factory New Village Movement in the 1970s, whose purpose was to train young girls working in factories to be docile and to think of themselves as future mothers and not as workers. While the government assumed women would therefore not protest their harsh working conditions and low pay, Christian women reformers recognized women's work as labor and engaged in efforts to improve workers' conditions.

In the Republic of China, Song Meiling, wife of President Chiang Kai-shek, headed up government efforts to organize women to support government policies, such as supporting the military and wooing PRC residents to the Nationalist cause. Her Taiwan Provincial Women's Association promoted Confucian family life and intervened directly in the lives of Taiwan's families in ways similar to the Women's Federation activities in the PRC. After the United Nations shifted its recognition of the official government of China from the ROC to the PRC in 1971, democracy and feminist movements began to emerge. Though repressed and even arrested by the ROC government, some of these women, such as Hsiu-lien Annette Lu, persisted in advocating for women.

Deeply felt concerns about sexual abuse were also shared by advocates for women in most of these countries, although the conditions they decried were often different. In Taiwan, feminists such as Lu set up a hotline for victims of sexual and domestic violence. In Japan, the anti-prostitution movement accomplished its long-held goal of eliminating licensed prostitution, but it succeeded not by stressing the difficult lives of sex workers, many of whom opposed the feminists' actions, but by stressing the adverse effects on children of seeing prostitution in action. Later, second-wave feminists took up as a primary goal opposition to international sex trafficking and sex tours by Japanese men. This transnational activism was the first major feminist activity undertaken simultaneously by Japanese and Korean women since before World War II. In South Korea, sex workers' "comforting" of American military personnel had also been permitted in the "special districts" set up by the ROK government under the ironically named Prostitution Prevention Law of 1961 as a way to contain the diseases associated with sex work and to bring in foreign cash. Although the purchase of sex took place within South Korea, it represented an international sexual nexus, with American, Japanese, and other customers.

In the PRC, sex abuse was domestic as opposed to international, as the dearth of women in the countryside led to kidnapping of urban women to serve as rural brides. Other forms of sexual abuse common in the PRC during the Cultural Revolution were the Red Guards' use of sexual violation to punish women and their claims that their female class enemies were "whores." Because the All-China Women's Federation had been disbanded in 1966 (it would be reinstated in the late 1970s), there was no state institution that could formally resist this type of abuse during the Cultural Revolution.

Thus, although their governmental systems were very different, all of these countries' gender systems experienced significant changes in definitions of masculinities and femininities, gender roles in the home and workplace, responses to feminism both domestic and transnational, and sexual abuse and trafficking from the 1950s to the 1980s.

REFERENCES AND SUGGESTIONS FOR FURTHER READING

GLOBAL CONTEXT

Sowerwine, Charles, and Patricia Grimshaw. 2004. "Equality and Difference in the Twentieth-Century West: North America, Western Europe, Australia, and New Zealand." In *A Companion to Gender History*, edited by Teresa A. Meade and Merry E. Wiesner-Hanks. Oxford: Blackwell.

JAPAN

Bardsley, Jan. 2014. *Women and Democracy in Cold War Japan*. London: Bloomsbury.

Brinton, Mary C. 1993. *Women and the Economic Miracle: Gender and Work in Postwar Japan*. Berkeley: University of California Press.

Gerteis, Christopher. 2010. *Gender Struggles: Wage-Earning Women and Male-Dominated Unions in Postwar Japan*. Cambridge, MA: Harvard University Press.

Gordon, Andrew. 2005. "Managing the Japanese Household: The New Life Movement in Postwar Japan." In *Gendering Modern Japanese History*, edited by Barbara Molony and Kathleen Uno. Cambridge, MA: Harvard University Press.

Kovner, Sarah. 2012. *Occupying Power: Sex Workers and Servicemen in Postwar Japan*. Stanford, CA: Stanford University Press.

LeBlanc, Robin M. 1999. *Bicycle Citizens: The Political World of the Japanese Housewife*. Berkeley: University of California Press.

Mackie, Vera. 2003. *Feminism in Modern Japan*. Cambridge: Cambridge University Press.

Matsui, Yayori. 1989. *Women's Asia*. London: Zed Books.

Molony, Barbara. 1995. "Japan's 1985 Equal Employment Opportunity Law and the Changing Discourse on Gender." *Signs* 20, no. 2: 268–302.

Moon, Okpyo. 2009. "Japanese Tourists in Korea: Colonial and Postcolonial Encounters." In *Japanese Tourism and Travel Culture*, edited by Sylvie Guichard-Anguis and Okpyo Moon. London: Routledge.

KOREA

Abelmann, Nancy. 2003. *The Melodrama of Mobility: Women, Talk, and Class in Contemporary South Korea*. Honolulu: University of Hawai'i Press.

Barraclough, Ruth. 2012. *Factory Girl Literature: Sexuality, Violence, and Representation in Industrializing Korea*. Berkeley: University of California Press.

Cho, Hwasun. 1988. *Let the Weak Be Strong: A Woman's Struggle for Justice*. Bloomington, IN: Meyer Stone.

Höhn, Maria, and Seungsook Moon, eds. 2010. *Over There: Living with the U.S. Military Empire from World War Two to the Present*. Durham, NC: Duke University Press.

Hughes, Theodore. 2012. *Literature and Film in Cold War South Korea: Freedom's Frontier*. New York: Columbia University Press.

Kang, Isu. 2006. "Haebang hu han'guk kyŏngje ŭi pyŏnhwa wa yŏsŏng ŭi nodong kyŏnghŏm" [Changes in economy and women's work experience in post-liberation Korea]. *Yŏsŏng kwa yŏksa* 4: 43–76.

Kendall, Laurel, ed. 2002. *Under Construction: The Gendering of Modernity, Class, and Consumption in the Republic of Korea*. Honolulu: University of Hawai'i Press.

Kendall, Laurel. 1985. *Shamans, Housewives, and Other Restless Spirits: Women in Korean Ritual Life*. Honolulu: University of Hawai'i Press.

Kim, Hyun Mee. 2001. "Work, Nation and Hypermasculinity: The 'Woman' Question in the Economic Miracle and Crisis in South Korea." *Inter-Asia Cultural Studies* 2, no. 1 (2001): 53–68.

Kim, Seung-Kyung. 1997. *Class Struggle or Family Struggle: The Lives of Women Factory Workers in South Korea*. New York: Cambridge University Press.

Lee, Namhee. 2007. *The Making of Minjung: Democracy and the Politics of Representation in South Korea*. Ithaca, NY: Cornell University Press.

Lie, John. 1995. "The Transformation of Sexual Work in 20th-Century Korea." *Gender and Society* 9, no. 3: 310–327.

Moon, Kyoung-Hee. 2007. "Women's Experiences of Employment in South Korean Banks After the 1997 Economic Crisis." *Asian Women* 23, no. 1: 1–29.

Moon, Seungsook. 2005. *Militarized Modernity and Gendered Citizenship in South Korea*. Durham, NC: Duke University Press.

———. 2010. "Regulating Desire, Managing the Empire: U.S. Military Prostitution in South Korea, 1945–1970." In *Over There: Living with the U.S. Military Empire from World War Two to the Present*, edited by Maria Höhn and Seungsook Moon. Durham, NC: Duke University Press.

Nam, Hwasook. 2009. "Shipyard Women and the Politics of Gender: A Case Study of the KSEC Yard in South Korea." In *Gender and Labour in Korea and Japan: Sexing Class*, edited by Ruth Barraclough and Elyssa Faison. London: Routledge.

Nelson, Laura. 2000. *Measured Excess: Status, Gender, and Consumer Nationalism in South Korea*. New York: Columbia University Press.

Norma, Caroline. 2014. "Demand from Abroad: Japanese Involvement in the 1970s' Development of South Korea's Sex Industry." *Journal of Korean Studies* 19, no. 2: 399–428.

Pae, Ŭngyŏng. 2005. "Kajok kyehoek saŏp kwa yŏsŏng ŭi mom" [Women's body and the family planning programs]. *Sahoe wa yŏksa* 67: 260–299.

Park, Kyung Ae. 1992–1993. "Women and Revolution in North Korea." *Pacific Affairs* 65, no. 4: 527–545.

CHINA AND TAIWAN

Chang, Doris T. 2009. *Women's Movements in Twentieth-Century Taiwan*. Urbana: University of Illinois Press.

Davin, Delia. 1976. *Woman-Work: Women and the Party in Revolutionary China*. London: Oxford University Press.

Diamant, Neil. 2000. *Revolutionizing the Family: Politics, Love, and Divorce in Urban and Rural China, 1949–1968*. Berkeley: University of California Press.

Ebrey, Patricia Buckley. 1993. *Chinese Civilization: A Sourcebook*. New York: Free Press.

Evans, Harriet. 1997. *Women and Sexuality in China: Female Sexuality and Gender Since 1949*. New York: Continuum.

Honig, Emily. 2000. "Iron Girls Revisited: Gender and the Politics of Work in the Cultural Revolution, 1966–76." In *Re-Drawing Boundaries: Work, Households, and Gender in China*, edited by Barbara Entwisle and Gail E. Henderson. Berkeley: University of California Press.

———. 2003. "Socialist Sex: The Cultural Revolution Revisited." *Modern China* 29, no. 2: 143–175.

Jin, Yihong. 2006. "Rethinking the 'Iron Girls': Gender and Labour During the Chinese Cultural Revolution." *Gender and History* 18, no. 3: 613–634.

Manning, Kimberley Ens. 2006. "Making a Great Leap Forward? The Politics of Women's Liberation in Maoist China." *Gender and History* 18, no. 3: 574–593.

Rubinstein, Murray A. 2004. "Lu Hsiu-lien and the Origins of Taiwanese Feminism, 1944–1977." In *Women in the New Taiwan: Gender Roles and Gender Consciousness in a Changing Society*, edited by Catherine Farris, Anru Lee, and Murray Rubenstein. New York: M. E. Sharpe.

Wang, Zheng. 2003. "Gender, Employment and Women's Resistance." In *Chinese Society: Change, Conflict and Resistance*, 2nd ed., edited by Elizabeth J. Perry and Mark Selden. London: Routledge Curzon.

———. 2005a. "'State Feminism'? Gender and Socialist State Formation in Maoist China." *Feminist Studies* 31, no. 3: 519–551.

———. 2005b. "Gender and Maoist Organization." In *Gender in Motion: Divisions of Labor and Cultural Change in Late Imperial and Modern China*, edited by Wendy Larson and Bryna Goodman. Lanham, MD: Rowman and Littlefield.

———. 2006. "Dilemmas of Inside Agitators: Chinese State Feminists in 1957." *China Quarterly* 188: 913–932.

White, Tyrene. 2006. *China's Longest Campaign: Birth Planning in the People's Republic, 1949–2005*. Ithaca, NY: Cornell University Press.

11

Gender and Domestic and Transnational Feminisms After the Cold War

GLOBAL CONTEXT

The years from 1980 through the first decade of the twenty-first century were tumultuous. The Communist regimes of Eastern Europe fell in rapid succession, and the Soviet Union broke apart in 1991. Most of the Eastern European countries embraced capitalism, but during those first years their economies were in a shambles, powerful and corrupt oligarchs took the reins of formerly state-owned enterprises, and the people suffered. East Germany had a better fate, as it reunited with West Germany. In the Philippines, the phenomenon known as "People Power" brought the authoritarian regime of Ferdinand Marcos to an end and ushered in democratic elections in 1986. Authoritarian regimes in Argentina, Brazil, and Chile were replaced with democracies in the 1980s and early 1990s. To many, it looked like the world was heading toward better days at the end of the millennium. Yet instability continued to claim many lives. Post-Communist Yugoslavia, for example, fragmented into ethno-religious countries—Serbia, Croatia, Bosnia, Montenegro, and Kosovo—some of which undertook "ethnic cleansing" in an effort to build ethnically pure societies, genocidally murdering between one hundred thousand and two hundred thousand civilians during those tragically dark years.

Economic troubles emerged at the end of the 1990s. In 1997 Thailand's currency collapsed, causing severe recessions in a number of regional economies. In Indonesia, President Suharto was driven from power in 1998 by citizens angry over the state of their economy. When South Korea faced a huge foreign debt crisis, the government looked to the International Monetary Fund for a bailout to shore up their economy, but that led to a severe and painful austerity program that remained in effect for several years. To avoid a recurrence of its debt crisis, South Korea, together with Japan and the PRC as well as Brazil, Russia, and India, bought up large quantities of U.S. debt. This helped the American economy in the short term but contributed to the development of bubbles in the U.S. stock market and housing sector, both of which crashed in 2008 with devastating effects on the world economy.

The end of the Cold War led to hopes for peace and global integration, as there was only one superpower left on the stage in the 1990s. But those hopes were soon dashed as new lines of polarization emerged. Tensions between Western and Middle Eastern countries, in existence since the time of colonialism and frequently reignited by tensions between Israel and Palestine, exploded on September 11, 2001, with a terroristic attack on the World Trade Center and other U.S. sites by a transnational network called Al Qaeda. War between the United States (and its allies) and the Islamic Taliban government of Afghanistan, which had harbored Al Qaeda, was declared within a week. U.S. president George W. Bush declared war on Iraq a few months later, although Iraq's government had no connection to Al Qaeda. The past decade and a half has seen a succession of failing states in the Middle East and North Africa. Some were replaced by stable states, but others have been so weak that they have been unable to stem the growth of deadly militant factions wreaking havoc in the region and beyond.

Women's lives were greatly affected by these global changes at the turn of the millennium. In Latin America, many women who had played a significant role in the movements against authoritarian regimes hoped that the end of those regimes would lead to a greater role for them in governance. Although there have been some important women leaders in that part of the world in the last decade, women were initially ignored as potential leaders as new democracies started to get on their feet. But the new democracies did have good plans for women. Many set up offices of women's affairs at the national level. Quite a few came to recognize the importance of women in government, and several required that political parties run a quota of female candidates to ensure that some would be elected. Some had wide-ranging programs of state feminism: some promoted better work conditions for women, some fought against domestic violence, some advocated better child care, and a small number worked to strike down laws and practices that discriminated against LGBT citizens. Women's reproductive rights, however, were generally not addressed, as the influence of the Catholic Church impeded work in that area. Some Latin American feminists worked with the new institutions of state feminism, but others criticized those institutions for being underfunded and less effective than many had hoped. An important debate emerged among Latin American feminists concerning the best approach to feminist change—that is, should they work through state feminist institutions to make those organizations run more effectively, or should they focus on change through independent advocacy organizations (Besse 2004, 581–584)?

Eastern European feminists confronted a number of issues at the end of the Cold War. Just as during the former Communist era, they complained that male leaders did not bring them into elite government circles. In addition, some of the protections that Communist governments had offered, such as wide employment (even if poorly paid and under bad conditions) and access to reproductive health care, were absent or inadequate under the new governments. One unmistakable gendered horror was the use of sexual violation of women as part of ethnic cleansing strategies during the wars of devolution in the former Yugoslavia. But elsewhere in Eastern Europe better conditions eventually emerged, and new paradigms for modern men and women were created. Many women pushed for feminist egalitarianism, while others stressed a maternalist essentialism to celebrate the contributions of women as mothers. The latter was, unfortunately, co-opted by some Eastern European governments to continue different treatment of women and men. Another paradigm was that of the chic, modern, consumerist career woman and her counterpart, the aggressive entrepreneurial man (Clements 2004, 564–566).

Family change occurred rapidly in the countries of the West (including Western Europe, North America, and Australia). In most of them, marriage age and age of first birth increased. Because of the large number of births to teenage mothers in the United States at the beginning of this period, the average age of first birth was initially lower in the United States. But in the others, the mother's age when her first (and increasingly only) child was born rose to around thirty or above. The percentage of women in the workforce kept rising, especially with the entry of married women with children into the workforce. As men's rates of employment inched downward and women's moved upward, the long-standing differential between men's and women's workforce participation rates narrowed. People working only part-time were measured in the totals for workforce participation, and many of those part-time workers were women. Surveys indicated that most of those women wished for full-time jobs. And the wage gap continued to be painfully large in most Western countries, although less so in Scandinavia. Gendered inequality still needed to be addressed. But one thing did change: the notion that men work outside the home and women stay at home was fast becoming an idea of the past. The changes that occurred as a result of the active feminist movements in Western countries in the 1980s, incomplete though they may have been, engendered a negative reaction in a number of those countries, described in the American case by Susan Faludi in her 1991 book entitled *Backlash* (Sowerwine and Grimshaw 2004, 602–608).

SOUTH KOREA

Spring Forward, Fall Back? Progress and Challenges in Korean Gender Politics

Prior to the late 1980s, social movements in South Korea largely focused on political and economic democratization and on reunification with North Korea. Although women's movements had made steady progress from the 1950s, issues related to women and gender were often considered to be of secondary importance. However, since the late 1980s there have been dynamic and remarkable changes in overall gender relations, perceptions, and everyday practices in the country. A number of landmark legal and institutional changes have led to a larger percentage of women participating in politics and the market economy. The first woman prime minister, Han Myŏngsuk, was appointed in 2006, and Park Geun-hye was elected as the first woman president in South Korea in 2012. Women have gained great prominence not only in Korea but globally as artists, entertainers, and athletes. Furthermore, the general conception of ideal womanhood has become much more fluid and diverse. These transformations can be attributed to three major factors.

First, after decades in which the nation was ruled by a succession of oppressive military regimes, South Korea achieved political democratization in the late 1980s, which opened up new space for activism. The more liberal political, intellectual, and cultural milieu allowed various women's movements to coalesce and devote their energies to a gender-focused agenda that would take the initiative in eliminating feudal legal arrangements such as the family head system (*hojuje*). Second, there is a new autonomy in political, economic, and cultural domains at the regional level of government, and this has provided women with more opportunities to have their voices heard. Not only have they acted as advocates for the rights of women, but they have also participated in various social movements on issues such as consumer rights, protection of the environment, antinuclear activism, labor reforms, youth rights, and democratic and liberal education, through which they endeavor to enhance the status of women and social minorities. And third, the unprecedented pace of globalization has helped women forge networks with international women's organizations to address the challenges that women around the world face. Furthermore, since the 1990s the new phenomena of international marriages (mainly Korean men with women from other parts of Asia) and North Koreans defecting to South Korea have brought about new perspectives on the family, gender roles, national identity, and multiculturalism intersecting at the local, national, and global levels.

Gender, Democracy, and Landmark Laws

The year 1987 was a historical watershed in advancing political democracy and regional autonomy. The authoritarian dictatorships of Park Chung Hee (1963–1979) and Chun Do Hwan (1980–1988) had been challenged by students and intellectuals throughout those years, but authoritarianism finally came to an end in the face of a mass mobilization of the public in June 1987. This mass movement, often referred to as the June Democratic Uprising, demanded direct election of the president and the revival of autonomous regional politics. The success of the movement eventually brought about civilian governments beginning in 1993 and enabled wider segments of the population, including women, to participate in a variety of local, regional, and national politics.

Women's movements benefited significantly from the increasingly democratic society. In particular, under the progressive presidencies of Kim Dae Jung (1998–2002) and Roh Moo Hyun (2003–2007), numerous reform ideas that addressed the issue of gender equity were proposed and implemented in laws and institutional development. At the political and administrative levels, the establishment of the Ministry of Gender Equality in 2001 signaled a shift toward more concerted efforts to establish policies on women's issues and gender discrimination. Women's groups began to demand a quota system for women candidates in party politics. Although the percentage of women political representatives in Korea still has not reached the OECD average, there has been gradual progress: in 2004 women accounted for 13 percent of the National Assembly, the highest level in Korean history.

While more women were participating in government and party politics at the national level, political changes at the regional level may have had a greater impact. Beginning in the 1990s local governments started to regain autonomy from the central power in Seoul, and with that new opportunities opened up for women to shape their own lives. In particular, their status as residents, housewives, and mothers has helped them pursue specific agendas that are closely related to family life and healthy community living. For instance, mothers in the city of Puch'ŏn organized a campaign to prohibit

BOX 11.1

Abolition of the Family Head System (*Hojuje*), 2005

Among the major reforms to take place under the two progressive presidencies, the most significant legal change was the abolition of the family head system (*hojuje*) in 2005. *Hojuje* was the most powerful male-centered family law in Korean society, and it had far-reaching material implications. It gave men exclusive power in the matters of marriage and family lineage, and privileges in the ownership and inheritance of property. The abolition of this system came after many years of struggle through a strong alliance of diverse women's and citizens' groups. The nationwide campaign to eliminate *hojuje* gained traction when President Roh Moo Hyun was elected. One of his pledges during his presidential campaign was to abolish *hojuje*. He appointed Chi Ŭnhŭi, an individual who was exceptionally proactive in this campaign, as the minister of gender equality. Chi argued that "patriarchy is the root cause of many social problems, such as the abortion of female fetuses. The family-head system is at the core of patriarchy in that it defines men as family heads and women as dependents . . . and the family-head system goes against the constitutional mandate of gender equality" (quoted in Kim 2014, 83). *Hojuje* most succinctly represented legal stipulations of the patriarchal gender relations that reproduced and reinforced unequal economic and sociocultural practices in prioritizing men over women and preferring boys to girls. Thus the abolition of that law was a watershed event, shifting gender dynamics toward more equal and democratic relationships between women and men in the family and society.

A protest demanding the abolition of the Family Head System, 2003. Yŏsŏng sinmun (Women News)

the installation of cigarette vending machines in public places in order to make it less easy for minors to purchase cigarettes. Women also led a movement to get politicians to pledge support for a program to deliver meals to children in schools, first in all elementary schools and eventually in middle schools and high schools as well. This agenda became one of the central issues in regional election campaigns. Once the provision of school meals was achieved, women's groups started to insist that the lunches include organic food produced within the region or in Korea rather than imported products. This type of woman-led activism is a good example of the increased participation by women in local and regional politics to improve family and community life.

Neoliberal Economy and Women's Labor

There has been steady growth in the rate of women's participation in the workforce, reaching a little over 50 percent by 2013. Some legal protections for women laborers have been implemented since the late 1980s, including the Equal Employment Law in 1987 and the 1999 Ban on Gender Discrimination. However, despite some progress, there is still a long way to go. Within the context of the increasingly neoliberal economic environment, women have continued to be subjected to bias in terms of job opportunities and career development as well as unspoken rules of male-centered, hierarchical gender practices at work. The income gap that exists between men and women remains a serious problem. In 2012 women earned less than 70 percent of the salary that a man earned for equivalent work. Furthermore, women tend to occupy positions in the workplace that are lower-paying, irregular, or temporary. In top-tier positions women are far less well represented, holding only 20 percent of managerial and professional positions.

The 1997 Asian financial crisis had a significant impact on the labor market and further unsettled the status and prospects of women workers. The reactions to that financial crisis were a painful reminder of the persistence of gender bias in the workplace. For example, under the neoliberal programs of structural adjustment put together to address the economic crisis, both employers and labor unions gave absolute priority to male workers based on the traditional assumption that men would be the primary breadwinners. Female employees were the first group to be fired and the last group to be rehired. Women were seen as a "flexible reserve pool of labor to supplement the labor market in upturns, and return to the home in downturns" (Moon 2007, 2). According to a report from the Korea Labor Institute, only 7.8 percent of newly hired women workers were "regular" employees. The vast majority—92.2 percent—were hired as "nonstandard workers" (Chun 2009, 63).

In addition to the increasingly precarious condition of the national economy, the rapid increase in the general cost of living and in particular the exorbitant expenses associated with children's education have led to a new norm in which families need two incomes just to maintain basic living standards, especially in urban communities. Given this set of conditions, the younger generation generally expects women to work after marriage.

The rise of female labor participation should be considered in conjunction with another critical issue facing South Korea—the very low birth rate. In 2009 South Korea had the world's lowest birth rate for the second consecutive year. Policy makers and pundits consider the low birth rate to be the greatest threat to the country's economy and future prosperity. In 2004 President Roh signed the Framework Act for Healthy Families, "the first effort of the state to reverse Korea's declining birth rate" (Kim 2014, 90). The drop in the birth rate can be related to the lack of social infrastructure and public policies that provide some level of support for women with children. For example, there is no paid maternity leave. A system of child care is only now starting to be developed, and the culture of many companies is still antagonistic to the concept of maternity leave. A woman who takes leave in order to have a baby may lose her job. As a consequence, women in the labor force tend to have fewer children.

In the domain of the family, there is a large gap between ideas and practice. More people today accept the idea that married women and mothers will be part of the labor force. Young men nowadays would prefer to marry a woman with a career than have a stay-at-home wife. That being said, women are still expected to handle most of the work around the household and the care of the children with little or no support from their husbands. In other words, women are doubly burdened, expected to meet the demands of their jobs along with their domestic responsibilities. Beyond that, because it is assumed that women bear the obligations of child care and home maintenance, they are seen as less committed to their jobs and less reliable as workers. This attitude toward women makes them the most dispensable employees, as can be seen from the fact that women employees were the first to be laid off during the 1997 Asian financial crisis, as previously noted, as well as during the global financial crisis in 2008.

While there has been a steady rise of women in the labor force, the workplace is still somewhat inhospitable to women. Because female workers are more likely to fill positions as irregular workers, they are highly vulnerable to job loss. This accelerates the marginalization of the female workforce, which already experiences a higher rate of poverty than male workers do. Furthermore, a new phenomenon has developed in recent years in which workers who are college-educated are unable to find employment. Although this group, referred to as the "new poor," includes both women and men, women are far more likely to find themselves in this situation (Jesook Song 2014). This sets up competition between men and women for the small number of positions that are available. That competition is one of the reasons for the rapid rise in conservative rhetoric that criticizes women for competing for jobs that men should have first claim to.

Sexual Violence and Sex Trafficking

One of the key foci of feminist activism has been the issue of sexual violence. Sexual violence was by no means a new phenomenon, but it had been either hidden as a matter of personal shame or dismissed as unimportant. However, in the 1980s there was growing public outrage after several cases of egregious sexual violence were reported in the news. Women's groups worked actively to raise public awareness of those cases and urged the government to take legal action. To mention one of the most prominent cases, in 1987 Kwŏn Insuk, a female activist at Seoul National University, was among the college students who took jobs in factories in order to help make factory laborers aware of their rights as workers and help them organize themselves for collective bargaining. Taken into police custody for questioning, she refused to reveal the names of other student activists in the movement. Her interrogator subjected her to sexual torture to make her talk. Rather than living with the shame and keeping the experience to herself, she told her fellow inmates what had happened to her. Soon her story had been passed on to women's groups and civilian organizations as well as the mass media. Various civil groups formed a large coalition to support and defend Kwŏn. Eventually, after being in jail for more than a year, she was released, and the police detective who had assaulted her was sentenced to a five-year jail term. This case came to symbolize the oppressive political regime that college students had mobilized to defeat and replace with political and economic democracy. As Kwŏn herself pointed out, "This sexual torture case won't be approached as my personal issue or a chastity issue. The most important thing is the fact that sexual assault was perpetrated on a female worker as a means of oppressing the labor movement" (quoted in Jung 2014, 14).

In addition to sexual violence, the issue of sexual harassment on campuses and in the workplace has become a matter of public concern. In 1993

U Hŭijŏng, a female graduate student at Seoul National University, filed a suit against one of her male professors, charging him with sexual harassment. This landmark case was the first-ever lawsuit in Korea to charge sexual harassment, and the first public airing of the routine ways in which female students were sexually harassed both on and off campus. The plaintiff eventually won the case, which set a precedent for future cases. Furthermore, it stimulated various entities to consider the existing legal provisions and devise guidelines to prevent sexual harassment in the workplace. With the proclamation of the Gender Equality in Employment Act in 1999, businesses with more than five employees were required to give an annual seminar for employees to raise awareness of sexual harassment in an effort to curtail it.

Thanks to a series of lawsuits, the public has come to know that cases of rape and harassment are frequent. At the same time, there have been

BOX 11.2

Ten Commandments for the Gender-Friendly Workplace

A representative feminist group, Han'guk yŏsŏng minuhoe (Womenlink), released their "Ten Commandments" for preventing sexual harassment in the workplace:

1. Stop telling obscene jokes.
2. Use honorific speech with all colleagues.
3. If you are sexually harassed, express your discontent clearly and immediately.
4. Do not misinterpret messages; *no* means "no."
5. Do not force colleagues to drink or dance during after-work social sessions.
6. Do not visit pornographic websites at work.
7. Do not comment on a work colleague's appearance.
8. Avoid unnecessary body contact.
9. Do not emphasize the traditional gender roles.
10. Provide active support for the victims of sexual harassment.

(*Chungang ilbo*, January 12, 1999, reprinted in *Han'guk kŭnhyŏndae yŏsŏngsa* 3, edited by Chŏn Kyŏngok et al. (Seoul: Mot'ibŭ Puk, 2011), 274. Translation by Hyaeweol Choi.)

dramatic changes in the perception and practice of sexual engagement. By the mid-1990s, sex was no longer primarily for procreation but for pleasure, and women were no longer passive objects of sexual desire but active participants. The shift in attitudes about sexual morality was evident in TV dramas, where storylines had female characters engaging in premarital sex and dealing with pregnancy and single motherhood. The long-standing ideology of chastity, especially prior to marriage, has seemingly become a thing of the past.

Although attitudes toward sexual engagement are becoming more liberalized in South Korea, issues related to the sex industry are once again at the heart of heated debates and protests. The sex industry is certainly not new in Korea, but it has rapidly expanded since the 1990s and now constitutes a significant sector in the economy. In 2002 approximately 330,000 women were working in the sex industry, which includes not only brothels in the established red-light districts but also other venues that incorporate sexual services into their business, such as barber shops, karaoke clubs, nightclubs, bars, restaurants, and massage parlors. In addition, foreign "entertainers" started to become a significant presence in military camptowns and private brothels. Most of these women entered Korea on "arts and entertainment" (E-6) visas. Others were trafficked into Korea illegally.

In 2002 the total revenue from sex industries was about U.S. $2.4 billion. That represented 4.1 percent of South Korea's gross domestic product (Kim 2014, 37–38). Many feminists viewed this widespread sex trafficking as the sexual exploitation of women (especially poor women) by men. The Ministry of Gender Equality advocated passage of the Anti–Sexual Trafficking Act (Sŏng Maemae Pangjipŏp) to protect women and punish those who profit from sexual trafficking. That advocacy paid off: the National Assembly passed the act, which went into effect on September 23, 2004. However, prostitutes themselves opposed the Anti–Sexual Trafficking Act, staging major sit-ins and hunger strikes; some even shaved their heads in protest. Their main concern was that the act would deprive them of their livelihood. As noted in Chapter 9, when the Korean Provisional Legislature passed a law that made public prostitution illegal in 1947, prostitutes at that time had a very similar reaction. Women in the sex industry were obviously not consulted during the process of lawmaking, as they were considered to be victims of sexual exploitation by men and thus subjects who needed to be protected and rescued. Their highly publicized protests surprised the public as well as policy makers and feminists.

The vast majority of feminist scholars and activists supported the Anti–Sexual Trafficking Act, but a small minority embraced the arguments of the sex workers. In this latter camp Ko-Chŏng Kaphŭi, a leading feminist scholar and activist, has been spearheading a movement that challenges the long-standing stigmatization of and discrimination against prostitutes and calls for considering sex work as legitimate labor just like any other professions. She has criticized the act for criminalizing prostitution, thereby cutting women off from their existing income stream and offering no alternative means of support. She has argued that prostitutes should be recognized as capable, independent economic actors who choose how they will earn income and who need to be protected from abuse by male customers and pimps and allowed to negotiate their working conditions.

To be sure, prostitutes are victimized by a sex industry that is deeply embedded in the patriarchal capitalist system and the uneven power relations that exist between Korea and foreign powers, mainly the United States and Japan. However, the enactment of the Anti–Sexual Trafficking Act and the sex workers' opposition to it revealed a vast gap between sex workers and activists, a division that continues to exist to this day.

Challenges to Heteronormativity and the Nation of "Pure Blood"

In the early 1990s the dominant heteronormative culture began to be challenged by sexual minorities. In 1993 Ch'odonghoe, the first alliance of sexual minorities, was formed, but within a year it had split into two separate groups—one for gays and the other for lesbians. Since then, a number of gay and lesbian organizations have come into existence to advocate for the rights of sexual minorities and engage in outreach activities such as counseling, publications, and public information events. They have been working closely with human rights advocacy groups as well as other social movement activists. In particular, there has been close collaboration between sexual minority groups and the labor movement. They see the problems that each group confronts as stemming from interlocking interests of the patriarchal and capitalist systems, which privilege heterosexual relations for the production and reproduction of laborers and consumers.

Same-sex marriage is not legally recognized in South Korea. To negotiate the prevailing heteronormative system, some gay men and lesbian women have entered into marriages of convenience, allowing them to meet the expectations of their families and at the same time to maintain a lifestyle in which they can be true to their nature. This type of negotiation concedes the centrality of the heterosexual conjugal system in Korea, but the practice also reveals the distinctive character of the response by Korean sexual minorities to heteronormativity. It offers a sharp point of comparison to the Western model of the "out and proud" gay or lesbian (Cho 2009, 401–422).

With its traditions firmly rooted in the patriarchal family system, South Korean society continues to be antagonistic to sexual minorities. Widespread prejudice and discrimination against gays and lesbians still prevail. However, there are signs of change. The popular media, especially films and TV dramas, have contributed to the increasing awareness of issues related to homosexuality by focusing on the pain and challenges that sexual minorities face in everyday life. In addition, annual cultural festivals such as the Korea Queer Culture Festival and Korea Queer Film Festival have raised the profile of the movement and its ongoing struggles to gain equal rights and fair recognition.

At the same time that sexual minorities have presented challenges to the traditional notions of marriage and family, the rapidly growing population of foreign migrants in South Korea and the increasing frequency of international marriages (usually between Korean men and non-Korean women) have begun to pose critical questions about the family and gender relations. Since the early 1990s, South Korea has been undergoing a major shift from a relatively homogeneous society to an increasingly heterogeneous, multiethnic one. South Korea had always been a country with net emigration until recently, when it has become a country of net immigration, with inbound migrants coming mainly from other Asian countries. Because so many women of marriageable age have migrated from the rural areas to the cities, the ratio of men to women has gone seriously out of balance. As a result, local and regional governments have tried to create opportunities for bachelors in rural communities to find brides in China, Mongolia, and Southeast Asia. Implementing special visas for foreign brides, the Korean government actively sanctioned international marriages and multicultural families. By 2009, 10.8 percent of all marriages in South Korea were international, a drastic increase since the 1990s, when the percentage of cross-cultural unions was negligible. The majority of the foreign brides came from China (where ethnic Koreans were particularly sought-after), Vietnam, Thailand, Mongolia, the Philippines, and Cambodia.

The marital unions of Korean men and non-Korean Asian women are often arranged in haste through commercial agencies. Prospective grooms not infrequently misrepresent themselves in their profiles, exaggerating their living conditions or financial resources to make themselves more appealing. Upon arriving in Korea and discovering the truth, the brides despair, as they are trapped in a new familial and cultural setting with little or no knowledge of the language or local culture and few protections. These marriages have given rise to some notorious cases of domestic violence, abuse by in-laws, and even rape. In the face of these problems, new social organizations have emerged to provide legal, occupational, and cultural programs to assist immigrant brides and multicultural families.

A significant challenge stemming from the emergence of ethnic minorities in Korea is how to deal with the long-held concept of "pure-bloodedness" among Koreans and its importance to the Korean sense of identity and tradition. The idea of pure-bloodedness was historically constructed as part of the program of nation building beginning in the late nineteenth century, and one still finds a strong popular perception of pure-bloodedness among Koreans today. In this vein, the growth of multicultural families (*tamunhwa kajok*) poses a new set of questions, especially with regard to the role of migrant women, who are expected to act "Korean" and preserve Korean traditions (Kim 2012). What constitutes the family and the community? In what ways would ethnic minorities reshape Korean society in terms of gender relations, sociocultural values, religions, citizenship, and national identity? In considering these questions, it is important not to treat migrant women as mere victims who need to be rescued, but rather to understand how migrant women navigate the social terrain in Korea and negotiate the material, legal, and cultural challenges they encounter (Choo 2013).

What's Next for South Korean Women?

The turn of the twenty-first century has been marked with both major victories and new challenges in gender politics. The iconic example of patriarchal law, the family head system, was abolished in 2005. A much higher representation of women legislators in the National Assembly and regional government offices promises further participation by women in policy making, with a consequent impact on women and social minorities. More women than ever have joined the workforce, changing the landscape of the labor market and corporate culture.

However, many new challenges lie ahead, as neoliberal economic structures continue to put women in a vulnerable position, and rapidly growing inequality among social classes tends to affect women more negatively. Furthermore, one can see an ever louder outcry against women. Well-known examples include the derogatory labels "alpha girls" and "soybean-paste girls." Alpha girls are, like "alpha males," very successful in their chosen careers, extremely ambitious, and ruthless in their pursuit of those ambitions. The negative connotation associated with the term hints at the lingering Confucian value of womanly modesty and the sense that a woman's proper place is in the domestic sphere. The term "soybean-paste girl" (*toenjangnyŏ*) refers to a young woman of the new middle class who compulsively purchases luxury goods out of vanity and blindly follows a Western lifestyle. The term critiques such conspicuous consumption by contemporary women, contrasting them with her idealized Confucian counterparts, who were expected to be frugal and industrious (Jee Eun Regina Song 2014).

In this rapidly globalizing world, the visible advancement of women in society has created deep anxiety. There is a sense of déjà vu in the current attitude toward women and feminism, which is reminiscent of the reaction to the New Woman/Modern Girl phenomenon of the 1920s and 1930s, when the emerging class of educated women caused deep male anxiety, as discussed in Chapter 6. Despite such public anxiety over the empowerment of women, South Korea ranks near the bottom among OECD countries when it comes to gender equality in virtually all aspects of society except education. Still, there are many reasons to be optimistic that there will be more equitable gender relations in Korea. Building on major victories in the advancement of the rights of women and keeping abreast of rapidly changing social and global circumstances, feminist and sexual minority groups have been developing fluid, innovative, and sometimes subversive strategies to cope with existing and new challenges in society. Those groups are locally grounded, virtually connected, and creatively mobilized, making strategic alliances for specific agendas on issues relating to gender, labor, the environment, organic farming, migrant workers, and multicultural families.

NORTH KOREA

The collapse of the Soviet Union in 1989 and its ripple effects on the socialist economic bloc had a serious impact on the North Korean economy. North Korea had been a long-term recipient of Soviet aid, which suddenly ended. The economy in North Korea was already reeling, and its weakened state was further aggravated by a series of droughts and floods, which caused a devastating and long-lasting famine. In 1994 the death of Kim Il Sung, who had been the "supreme leader" of North Korea since 1945, created even greater instability in the country. By 1995 the Public Distribution System, which delivered food and basic necessities to North Korean citizens, had practically ceased to function. People struggled merely to survive. Under these circumstances a huge number of North Koreans crossed the border illegally into northeast China in search of food and jobs. Others defected to South Korea or other foreign countries. The vast majority of those refugees have been women. In 2004, "more than three-quarters of North Korean refugees living in China were female. Of the 4,952 North Korean refugees living in South Korea in 2004, 59.5% were women" (Jung and Dalton 2006, 746).

Inside North Korea, a system of "black capitalism" began to grow in the early 1990s. According to Andrei Lankov, "In the late 1990s, the North Koreans would say: 'There are only three types of people in [North] Korea: those who starve, those who beg, and those who trade'" (Lankov 2007, 320). In the face of the continuing famine and failing economy, women, especially married women, began to emerge as a new economic force in the informal markets. A woman who defected from North Korea in that period succinctly describes the changing circumstances: "In 1997–98 men became useless. They went to their workplaces, but there was nothing to be done there, so they came home. Meanwhile their wives traveled to distant places to trade and kept the families going." As a result, "the new North Korean capitalism of dirty marketplaces, charcoal trucks and badly dressed vendors with huge sacks of merchandise on their backs displays one surprising feature: it has a distinctly female face. Women are overrepresented among the leaders of the growing post-Stalinist economy at least at the lower level, among the market traders and small-time entrepreneurs" (Lankov 2007, 323).

From the beginning of the socialist revolution in North Korea, law and policy proclaim that North Korean women are equal to men. Nonetheless, the traditional image of woman as mother has been a consistent trope that places women firmly in the domestic sphere. Despite legal provisions that guarantee equal treatment for women in all social aspects, North Korean women have never been treated as full equals in the workplace or the family. However, the political and economic crises that have battered the country since the early 1990s have provided women with opportunities to claim space in the informal market economy. As Lankov notes, women have become the face of the new black capitalism, which in turn has begun to reshape gender dynamics in the family and society.

JAPAN

In Japan, as elsewhere in East Asia, key issues for women and men at the end of the twentieth century and the beginning of the twenty-first concerned the workplace; politics; sexuality, marriage, family, and declining birth rates; and gender in the arts and media. With the exception of North Korea, the East Asian countries were major industrial powers (and, in the case of Japan and South Korea, postindustrial powers) that were redefining their societies, economies, and political orders through both good economic times and devastating recessions. In Japan a persistent economic recession began in 1991. Interestingly, the years before the recession represented a time of optimism for proponents of gender change in the workplace, while the decade and a half after the beginning of the recession saw some surprising advances for women's rights and feminist redefinitions of gender. Indeed, both feminists and advertisers taking advantage of the excitement engendered by women in new social roles called the late 1980s the beginning of an "age of women," or *onna no jidai* (Kano 2011, 47). And while a backlash against feminist gender policies emerged in the first decade of the twenty-first century, not all of the progress achieved in the preceding years was undone.

Gender and the Workplace

Continuing economic inequality, particularly in the workplace, was the leading issue for most feminists in the late 1980s. Following Japan's ratification of the CEDAW (see Chapter 10) in June 1985, it was clear that Japan would not be in compliance with the convention without passing legislation that promoted gender equality in the workplace. The run-up to the passage of the Equal Employment Opportunity Law (EEOL) in 1985 and its implementation in 1986 highlighted significant ideological differences between employers and workers, between the government and civic organizations, and among feminist groups. The only legislation until that time that addressed gender inequality in the workplace had been Article 14 of the Japanese Constitution of 1947, which prohibited discrimination on the basis of sex; the Labor Standards Law of 1947, which mandated equal pay for equal work and maternity leave for women workers; and the Working Women's Welfare Law of 1972, which called for counseling and training of women workers. None of these had any penalties for employers who failed to hire, pay, or treat women and men equally, however.

At the same time, gendered "motherhood protections" for women did exist in Japanese law, and these were enforced (Molony 1995, 279–280). One such protection called for menstruation leave of two days per month. This leave had been included in the Labor Standards Law to help impoverished women in the years immediately after World War to retain their jobs. Many women at that time found it difficult to hold full-time jobs because they did not have access to cloth or cotton when they needed it for sanitary use, and a few days off might allow many of these women to stay employed (Molony 1993, 135–136). In time people came to believe that this policy was intended to protect women's bodies for future motherhood rather than allow them to overcome postwar material shortages. The Labor Standards Law also gave mothers leave of six weeks before and six weeks after childbirth, as well as two 30-minute breaks a day for breastfeeding during the infant's first year of life. For women who were able to continue to work during pregnancy and after childbirth, these protections were very helpful. But most women were not able to continue to work, because most companies pressured women to quit at the time of marriage or childbirth—despite the decision by the Japanese Supreme Court in 1966 that made different retirement ages for men and women technically illegal. This pressure was called the "tap on the shoulder." Thus, motherhood protections applied to few women of childbearing years.

During the prosperous years of the 1970s and 1980s, many women in their late twenties whose husbands made good salaries responded to the tap on the shoulder by leaving their full-time jobs to become full-time mothers and housewives. When they returned to the workforce in their late thirties, as many did, they were unable to get good full-time jobs. Companies did not hire older workers into promotion-track positions. In addition, the Labor Standards Law had put into practice the pre–World War II feminist demand to protect women from having to work long hours on midnight shifts, and now employers were reluctant to hire women whom they could not force to work the long hours they pressured men to work. Women's work opportunities and pay therefore lagged far behind men's.

In 1976, amidst the excitement generated by the UN International Women's Year (see Chapter 10), some advocates of equality unsuccessfully attempted to have sex added to nationality, creed, and social status as categories of discrimination that were prohibited, with penalties, under the Labor Standards Law. Two years later, the Labor Standards Law Research Association reported that some of the motherhood protection provisions under the law, such as limited work hours, harmed women's chances for employment and promotion. In 1982, a committee of specialists on women's employment, including academics, labor representatives, managers, and lawyers, began to meet to discuss an equal employment bill. Their report agreed that some of the protections harmed women's employment opportunities. In the meantime, employers' associations weighed in. They decried the move toward equality of opportunity for women, claiming that women had no work consciousness and were not by their nature interested in long-term employment (Molony 1995, 281–283). Some public intellectuals claimed that equality would be a form of Western encroachment on Japanese customs; this spurious claim failed to recognize the historical nature of the gendered division of labor in the middle-class Japanese household (see Chapter 10 on the New Life Movement of the post–World War II era).

Feminists also advocated different approaches to changes in labor law. Some wished to get rid of the motherhood protection clauses that differentiated male and female employees, while others wanted to retain some of those provisions, such as maternity leave. Some feminists had to be persuaded that menstruation leave was no longer necessary and had no relationship to women's health or potential for motherhood. In the end, the bill proposed by the Diet in 1984 was opposed by forty-eight women's organizations under the umbrella of the International Women's Year Action Group (see Chapter 10) because it presumed that all men and women must adopt the male employment model rather than a more humane one that balanced work and home for both men and women.

While the law guaranteed maternity leave, it offered little else. Women were told, under the law, to "harmonize" the workplace with their homes, while companies were not required to supply the mechanisms by which this could be done. Two different tracks were created at many firms to circumvent the law's requirement that men and women be treated equally: a "general employee" track that allowed workers to avoid overtime and transfers and a more rigorous managerial promotion track. Women on the managerial track had to accept the conditions of work imposed on men—very long hours of daily work as well as the possibility of being transferred to a branch office far from one's spouse and children—or risk losing their position on that track. In addition, the law only called on employers to "endeavor" to hire without regard to gender. These provisions led the International Women's Year Action Group to call the law *honenuki*, or toothless (literally "boneless"). Because the late 1980s was a time of extraordinary economic boom in Japan, companies actually did hire some young women into promotion-track positions. Terms like *shokuba no hana* (flower in the workplace) and "office lady" (a generalist whose work was supportive of others in the workplace) came to be seen as somewhat pejorative, although they had been accepted terms for young women office workers until that time. The move toward equality of employment opportunity came to an end when recession hit in the 1990s, and the promotion-track women who were the last hired were the first fired. Two steps forward, one step back.

The EEOL increased the number of paid weeks of maternity leave to six before childbirth and eight after birth for women working full-time. The Child Care Leave Law of 1992 allowed either parent to take a partially paid leave of up to a year after the birth of a child. But few parents, especially fathers, initially took this leave, because they were concerned that their absence from the workplace would impede their ability to advance at work (Molony 1995,

289–291). In 1997 the Nursing Care Insurance Law shifted responsibility for caring for the elderly from the family to society, thereby lifting some of the burden of that care from daughters and daughters-in-law, who had traditionally been responsible for it at a time when they might still be trying to juggle work and household responsibilities as well (Kano 2011, 43).

Some of the weaknesses of the EEOL's protections for equality in the workplace were addressed in 1997. Although the original law claimed to support women who were already employees, it had done nothing about equality in the hiring process. Sanctions against discrimination in hiring were included in a revision of the law in 1997. The more comprehensive Gender Equality Law of 2007 stipulated penalties for discrimination in both hiring and workplace conditions, but women's pay equity and access to management positions continued to lag behind those of most industrialized countries. At the end of the first decade of the twenty-first century, women's incomes in Japan averaged about 68 percent of men's incomes, compared to about 78 percent in the United States and about 90 percent in European countries. As for the gender pay gap, in 2013 Japan ranked eighty-seventh in the world and the United States ranked sixty-seventh (Chanlett-Avery and Nelson 2014).

According to the 2015 *World Economic Forum Gender Gap Report*, Japan ranked 104th for women's economic participation out of 142 countries surveyed; the United States was ranked 20th (World Economic Forum 2015). Women's current labor force participation rate is just 65 percent in Japan, compared to men's rate of 82 percent. These kinds of results were an embarrassment to the government, and in 2013 Japanese prime minister Abe Shinzō announced, to great fanfare, his "womenomics" initiative. Intended not only to raise Japan's image in the world, "womenomics" was the government's response to the serious decline in Japan's population and therefore its workforce. The centerpiece of this initiative included plans for improved access to child care, better compensation during child care leave, more flexible work hours, revision of the tax code to remove the tax disincentives for two-income families, recruiting more women to work in government jobs, and pressing the private sector to hire and promote more women (Chanlett-Avery and Nelson 2014). Abe contended that these kinds of conditions would relieve women of needing to choose between having babies and continuing to work. Two years later, in the fall of 2015, the government reported that this initiative failed to meet its employment goals, and it revised those goals downward significantly. Child care facilities have not been built quickly enough, and companies are still dragging their feet on hiring women in managerial-track positions.

Legislation passed in the fall of 2015 required companies with more than three hundred employees to set employment targets, but this would leave out the bulk of women employees, who work in smaller companies. Employment equality is a continuing problem in Japan.

Politics and Feminism

Thirty-nine women were elected to the House of Representatives of Japan's Diet in the first election after World War II. Since then, the number of women in elected offices has persistently lagged behind that in many other countries. In the fall of 2015, Japan ranked 116th out of 190 countries in the percentage of women representatives in the lower house of the national parliament, with about 10 percent of seats held by women; the United States ranked 72nd (Inter-Parliamentary Union 2015). In Japan's upper house, the House of Councillors, the numbers were better—about 16 percent of seats were held by women—but still low by international comparison. The numbers have been higher in the past. For example, in 1989 and 1990, following more than a decade of political and sexual scandals involving male politicians (including prime ministers) of the then ruling Liberal Democratic Party, voters swept into office a large number of women they called "Madonna" candidates (for women's seeming immunity to corruption) (Iwai 1993). The leader of the largest opposition party at the time, the Socialist Party, was a feminist named Doi Takako, and the large electoral gains for her party allowed her to become Japan's first female Speaker of the House of Representatives, from 1993 to 1996. Many of those women could not hold their seats in subsequent elections, however. Similar patterns followed in 2005 and again in 2009, with women first winning and then losing seats in off-year elections. Women's current total of about 10 percent in the House of Representatives and 15 to 19 percent in the House of Councillors seems to be fairly persistent.

Women have not advanced as far in politics and the workplace as feminists—and even nonfeminists in government such as Prime Minister Abe, who wishes to see Japan's economy boom—may have anticipated. In other areas of society and economy, however, there has been greater progress. For example, women are lively contributors to the arts. While several male writers, such as Murakami Haruki (b. 1949) and Nobel Prize winner Ōe Kenzaburō (b. 1935) dominate in world literary markets, many female writers, most prominently Yoshimoto Banana (b. 1954), have large numbers of readers both in Japan and overseas. Numerous other women writers also have large followings in Japan and await translation to bring their work to a global audience. Japanese male and female artists have transnational audiences, and the most famous

BOX 11.3

Doi Takako (1928–2014), Parliamentary Leader

Doi was a role model for women politicians and a champion of world peace and gender equality in Japan. As a teenager during World War II, she and her classmates were sent to work in a munitions factory, narrowly escaping death in the firebombing of Kobe in 1945. This event made her a committed pacifist. She entered academia following graduation from Doshisha Law School, where she was one of just two women in the school. In 1969 she ran for and won a Diet seat as a member of the Socialist Party. During the next two decades Doi spearheaded critical issues in gender equality and peace. She was a leader on the issues of aid to African famine victims; revision of the Nationality Law to permit women married to non-Japanese nationals to pass their Japanese citizenship on to their children, a right only men had had till 1984; elimination of girls-only home economics requirements in schools; and passage of the CEDAW in Japan.

When her party did poorly in the 1985 elections, it turned to Doi to be the new party chair. Doi turned the fortunes of the party around, winning two big electoral victories in 1989 and 1990. While remaining committed to the renunciation of war embedded in Article 9 of the constitution, she gradually moved her party more toward the political center. In 1996 she renamed the party the Social Democratic Party to broaden its appeal. Despite her many successes, her backing in 2003 for North Korea lost her the support she had enjoyed earlier. She stepped down as party chair that year and lost her Diet seat in 2005. Doi was an unusual political woman, but she showed that even in a political environment that is difficult for women, some women can lead (Lipman, Molony, and Robinson 2012, 422–423).

Doi celebrating her election as party chair.
(PHOTO BY SANKEI ARCHIVE/GETTY IMAGES)

living Japanese artist overseas is Yoko Ono (b. 1933). The first woman to win the Pritzker Prize, the highest accolade in world architecture, was Sejima Kazuyo (b. 1956), who received it in 2010. Hanae Mori (b. 1926) was the first Japanese woman designer to display her work in New York and Paris, and in 1977 she was the first Japanese to be elected a member of the Chambre Syndicale de la Haute Couture, the governing body of French fashion.

Women have played a central role in the production of manga since right after World War II, although they have had a smaller role in the production of films and anime. Many, though not all, of the manga produced by women have been written and drawn for a female or mixed audience. Many have found ready audiences overseas, such as the *Sailor Moon* series created by Takeuchi Naoko (b. 1967) in the 1990s and later adapted as an anime series. Manga and anime written by women have been joined by those written by men, notably Miyazaki Hayao (b. 1941), in which the central themes and characters revolve around powerful girls and women. In Miyazaki's *Princess Mononoke*, both the righteous activist for nature and her antagonist, who runs an environmentally destructive firearm-making factory (in fourteenth-century Japan!), are women. Even the "villain" is a fighter for social justice, if not for environmental justice.

The rebirth of the feminist movement in the early 1970s and the excitement of International Women's Year in 1975 (see Chapter 10) encouraged feminist scholarship in a variety of academic fields and gave rise to women's studies courses and programs at many universities. Two major scholarly groups, each with an important journal disseminating feminist research, were established: the Women's Studies Society of Japan (Nihon Joseigaku Kenkyūkai), founded in Kyoto in 1978, and the Women's Studies Association of Japan (Nihon Josei Gakkai), founded in 1979 in Tokyo. Feminist scholars became prominent on talk shows and in government councils, although most were still teaching at smaller colleges before they began to break into the top tier of elite universities in the 1990s. The appointment that made the biggest headlines in the news was that of sociologist Ueno Chizuko in 1993 at the University of Tokyo, Japan's most prestigious university. But she was not alone at the top in those years. In addition to the still small but growing number of women in academia, feminists influenced government policy making in the 1990s. Ōsawa Mari (b. 1953) played a particularly important role in the drafting of feminist legislation.

That legislation became the center of what can be called Japan's state feminism (see Chapter 10 for other forms of state feminism in Japan and elsewhere in East Asia in previous decades). As we will see in this section, the implementation of one key law central to the 1990s version of state feminism led to a backlash in Japan in the first decade of the twenty-first century. At the same time, some feminist legislation passed during this time was not as controversial. For example, some of the laws drafted in the 1990s by the government, with the advice of feminist scholars and of women representatives in the Diet, specifically addressed societal failings that impeded women's progress in the labor force, such as the lack of sufficient child care and elder care (noted previously). Other laws addressed serious social problems that caused gendered bodily harm. These included the 1999 Law for Punishing Acts Related to Child Prostitution and Child Pornography and for Protecting Children, the 2000 Anti-Stalking Law, and the particularly important 2001 Law for the Prevention of Spousal Violence and the Protection of Victims, which criminalized behavior previously overlooked as personal (Kano 2011, 43).

These laws all helped women (and children), but they did not engender the resistance encountered by the 1999 Basic Law for a Gender Equal Society (Danjo kyōdō sankaku kihon hō, literally "male-female joint participation law"). Scholar Ayako Kano points out that the English translation of the law's Japanese title suggests it is more supportive of equality than the official Japanese title, which came about because the law's framers anticipated problems and through the choice of title tried to avoid the possibility of parliamentary resistance (Kano 2011, 43). The passage of the law led to the creation of the Gender Equality Bureau, which was placed within the prime minister's cabinet. Each ministry and agency was also directed to create a division tasked with carrying out gender initiatives. Prefectures, cities, and towns were required to create plans to carry out the law.

The law was passed a few years after the United Nations Fourth World Conference on Women in 1995 at Beijing. Around the same time, though coincidentally, discussions about a concept called *jendā furī* (gender-free) became quite frequent. That term was used in several ways: to mean "free of gender bias" or to mean "free of gender itself." Together, these meanings called for the removal of gendered inequality in society, economy, and government, assuming that men and women were the two genders, as well as the more controversial defining of gender as a constructed concept that could be changed or eliminated. When right-wing nationalists within Japan started to become concerned about the effects of transnational feminism on Japan, they attacked the law as a manifestation of foreign-style "gender-free" ideology. (One of those nationalists in 2005 was Abe Shinzō, prime minister from 2005 to 2006 and then again beginning in 2012.) When the backlash started, feminists in government and academia had already been working, under the 1999 Basic Law, to implement policies based on both meanings of "gender-free."

Compounding conservatives' concerns about Japan's adoption of "foreign" values and conservatives' squeamishness about the possibility of the concept of "gender-free" morphing into greater acceptance of lesbians, gay men, and transgender people (Kano 2011, 50–55) was the government's panic, expressed as early as the 1980s, about Japan's rapidly dropping fertility rate. That stood at about 1.3 children per woman in 2005, and Japan's population was beginning to decline. At 1.4 children per woman in 2015, Japan had a lower fertility rate than all but thirteen countries in the world (five of them in East Asia—South Korea, Taiwan, and Singapore, as well as the Chinese territories of Macau and Hong Kong—and the rest in Europe). The United States had a birthrate of 1.9 children per woman in 2015, closer to the replacement level of 2.1 children per woman.

At the same time, Japan ranked highest among large countries (it is currently beaten out by Monaco) in longevity. The panic had two parts: concern about the "graying of society" and the resulting insufficiency of working-age people to support the growing number of elderly pensioners, and the decline of Japan's global status as it began to drop from being one of the larger countries in the world in terms of population to a middle-sized country. Opining that women should focus on making babies, conservatives struggled to undermine the Basic Law for a Gender Equal Society. (Later, as we have seen, those same conservatives, especially Prime Minister Abe, advocated "womenomics" as a way to simultaneously increase Japan's birth rate and expand the economy.)

The concept of "gender-free" was the first issue to feel the backlash, and familiar bogeymen such as unisex bathrooms in schools were suddenly unearthed. Many feminists felt that they needed to retreat strategically from the more inclusive meanings of "gender-free" if they were to be able to defend the policies that called for equal treatment of men and women. In the meantime, some progress had been made in redefining gender. Sexual reassignment surgery was made legal in 2003, and the Japan Association for Queer Studies was founded in 2007. Feminist scholar and activist Ueno Chizuko resigned from her position at the University of Tokyo in 2011 to take the helm of an Internet site, the Women's Action Network (WAN), which she built into a powerful feminist communications network that publishes in Japanese and English. The WAN site includes archival materials, global feminist news, information about actions in Japan and elsewhere, and many other topics. Some of the more socially transformative aspects of the Basic

Law may have been whittled away, but contemporary feminists continue to work toward building a more equal Japan.

One job in Japan remains resolutely gendered as masculine, although it is more a symbolic status than a real job: the role of emperor of Japan. Although the post was constitutionally important before World War II, when the emperor was deemed sovereign, the emperor was stripped of that definition under the 1947 constitution. Under the revised postwar legal system, all imperial daughters assumed their husband's status and became commoners upon marriage (unless they married a first cousin, they would have to marry a commoner, because the aristocracy had been dissolved), but sons remained members of the imperial family. When Crown Prince Naruhito (b. 1960) persuaded his Harvard- and Oxford-educated sweetheart, foreign service officer Owada Masako (b. 1963), to marry him, feminists expressed disappointment that she had to give up a potentially brilliant diplomatic career. The royal couple's only child was a girl, Aiko (b. 2001), so Japanese politicians set out in 2006 to change the imperial succession law, passed in 1890 and not revised after the war, to allow female succession (Molony 2005). When the crown prince's brother and sister-in-law, who already had two girls and were apparently past their childbearing years, suddenly announced they were expecting, this discussion was paused. The birth of a boy ended it.

Masculinities

The dominant view of Japanese masculinity, even if it was not the type of lifestyle practiced by many, was that of the salaryman (see Chapter 10). This view of masculinity has been challenged in the last quarter century, however. The popping of the Japanese economic bubble in the early 1990s destroyed the economic stability of many salarymen's lives—and even that of many unionized blue-collar workers—by undermining the lifetime employment guarantees they enjoyed in exchange for their hard work and company loyalty. When the persistent recession of the 1990s led to these men being laid off, their loyalty was worthless. This was one reason young men began to have different dreams about adult masculinity. Another reason was the identification in the late 1980s of "death by overwork" (*karōshi*) as a condition for which family members of men (and very occasionally women, though the public discussion was all about men) could receive monetary compensation. Young men questioned whether even striving to obtain one of the declining number of salaryman-style jobs was worth it. An increasing number of young men chose to take short-term jobs in new technology sectors. Their elders found them somewhat hard to understand and labeled them a "new species" (*shinjinrui*). Average marriage ages increased for both sexes, to about thirty for women and thirty-two for men, although those were still somewhat younger than the ages of first marriages in a few European counties and in South Korea (average ages of first marriages in the United States and in the PRC are younger than Japan's). So being employed, married, and a father was no longer the only definition of masculinity.

Being part of the military had been a critical part of the definition of manhood in prewar Japan, but unless Article 9 of the postwar constitution is revised—which some in the Liberal Democratic Party are advocating—the Japanese Self-Defense Forces (SDF, founded in 1954) are prohibited from engaging in combat missions. In addition, the military has long struggled with the negative image it earned as a result of World War II. So where does the military fit into contemporary masculinity? Japan's SDF have about 230,000 men and 12,000 women. Women are predominantly in medical, accounting, administrative, and communications positions. Many of the male recruits have been men who sought a second chance after becoming discouraged at work, failing a college entrance exam, or coming from a poor rural family who could not afford the fees to attend technical training schools (Frühstück 2007, 12). Many have seen the SDF as a good way to gain work skills—a promise recruiters have always made. Overseas assignments, which were illegal until the 1990s, have been to serve as election observers, medics, and support staff for combatant nations such as the United States during the Iraq War. Domestically, the SDF have served as recue forces, most notably at the time of the 2011 earthquake and tsunami. These service actions have been built into a new type of military masculinity that challenges the old warrior type. In fact, when Prime Minister Abe proposed in 2015 that the Diet vote to increase the SDF's role by allowing combat functions in support of the United States in the Pacific, many recruits abandoned their training, saying they had been deceived into believing they would not have to engage in combat. For the past decade, the SDF has used ultra-cute cartoon characters, especially the big-eyed girls popular in manga and anime, to recruit both men and women.

Other types of new Japanese men include the *otaku* type (Napier 2011). *Otaku* can be roughly translated as "geek," but this does not cover the range of meaning in the term, as scholar Susan Napier notes: "As Japanese commentators point out, *otaku* are in some ways the inevitable expressions of a postindustrial society where technology has replaced community, and media products and electronic gadgets have become the main objects of desire" (Napier 2011, 156). This type of male is seen as threatening to modern

Japanese society, as he is as different from the settled-down salaryman as can be. But a recent book, television series, and movie based on an *otaku* and his cohort, called *Train Man* (*Densha Otoko*), shows the humanity in this type of man, even while depicting a wide variety of Internet-obsessed, socially awkward, virtually shut-in young men who fantasized and played with weird dolls and objects. The young woman the *otaku* Train Man attracted by his chivalrous deed on a train was a perfectly proper young lady, and her interest in him suggests that the salaryman is no longer the only ideal of masculinity.

Transnational masculinity, especially the masculinity of South Korean men, also strongly appeals to Japanese women. The most popular male film and television star in Japan around 2005 was Bae Yong-Joon, star of the South Korean series *Winter Sonata*. Middle-aged Japanese women made tours of places in the series and in Bae's life, and young Japanese women traveled to Korea in the hope of meeting a man like Bae (Jung 2011, 35–39). The character Bae played was gentle, empathetic, and very concerned about the woman he loved, traits that early twenty-first-century Japanese women claimed were lacking in the career-driven Japanese salaryman. Thus we see in contemporary Japan many alternatives to the stereotypical salarymen of the postwar era: the young men of the "new species" generation, men in the military, *otaku* types of men, and appealing transnational models of masculinity.

CHINA

Gender in the Era of Post-Mao Reforms

In the 1980s, with the ascent of Deng Xiaoping as leader of the PRC, China embarked on radical reforms, described as the Four Modernizations: reforms in agriculture, industry, national defense, and science and technology. Since then, under a new rubric of "socialist modernization," China has been focused on the development of market capitalism, including rapid economic growth, opening up of the economy to global trade and investment, and creation of a consumer economy. A victim of the political purges of the Cultural Revolution, Deng captured the spirit of this new path with the slogan "It doesn't matter if the cat is black or white, as long as it catches the mouse," signaling a new pragmatism that rejected the dominance of politics in every aspect of life and the overriding fixation on ideological correctness during the Mao era. With the retreat of the Party-state from regulation of intimate private family life and personal decisions, private life has reemerged and there has been a resurgence of individual and family choice about every aspect of life: work, family, and leisure. A society exhausted with the relentless political campaigns of the Cultural Revolution welcomed the new focus on improving standards of living and creating space for ordinary family life.

Economic liberalization, however, was not linked to political liberalization. In the mid-1980s there was growing frustration with inflation, unemployment, rising inequality, and widening corruption within the Party. In the spring of 1989, students inspired by the political ascendance within the Politburo of leaders open to political reform launched a national movement to call for greater political transparency and democracy, an end to nepotism and corruption within the Party, and rehabilitation of dissidents persecuted in campaigns earlier in the decade. At the height of the movement, more than 1.5 million students in cities all over China demonstrated to commemorate the seminal student movement on May 4, 1919. By the end of May, nearly three million were out in the streets. Tiananmen Square, the site of the original May Fourth demonstrations, was the epicenter of the movement, occupied for weeks by students who staged a hunger strike that successfully garnered public sympathy for their cause. Citizens from all sectors of society joined in the demonstrations across the country, and workers formed the new Beijing Workers Autonomous Federation to support the movement. Fearing the collapse of the country into turmoil, Party leaders declared martial law on May 20, and when this failed to quiet the demonstrations, they sent the army into Beijing to crack down on the demonstrators beginning on June 4. Estimates of the death toll in the capital and several other cities vary from the hundreds to the thousands.

The violent quelling of the so-called Beijing Spring resulted in mass disillusionment with the Party and with politics. The Party has crafted a model of political authoritarianism designed to maintain its monopoly on political power while allowing just enough space for public discourse and private life to maintain economic growth and diminish the potential for political opposition. With the notable exception of the one-child policy, the state has retreated from its intense surveillance of and intervention in private life. Calculated censorship of the media, including sophisticated controls of the Internet referred to as "the Great Firewall of China," contains or prevents open discussion of sensitive topics such as Taiwanese independence, human rights, and controversial events that create potential for broader criticism of the Party. Yet there can be open discussion and debate of most subjects, and a vibrant cultural sector produces globally cutting-edge music, arts, film, and literature.

From the nineties through the early years of the new millennium, China's GDP grew at an annual rate of about 11 percent and the economy quadrupled in size. This unprecedented growth brought an explosion of wealth and a consumer revolution, but also increasing wealth disparities and rampant corruption. In a reversal of Mao-era values, Deng Xiaoping explicitly noted that some would get richer faster than others, and new kinds of inequality have emerged as the most enterprising, skilled, and well-connected (especially Party cadres) surged ahead while others remained in poverty.

Although most of the population saw improvements in their standards of living in the early years of reform, there has been a growing prosperity gap between rural and urban areas, between coastal regions most connected to the global economic networks and the more isolated inland, and between the Han Chinese majority and ethnic minorities living mostly in remote regions of the interior. Rapid growth has also created environmental crisis, with air and water pollution undermining health and quality of life across the country. The floating migrant population has reached nearly three hundred million, many of them unemployed or underemployed and lacking access to the amenities of urban life and privileges of official urban registration. These problems have led to growing social unrest.

Women have been integral to all of these trends. They have benefited in many ways, gaining education, higher quality of life, and more choices about work and family. However, they have also faced the persistence of old forms of gender inequality and the emergence of new ones. Women's voices are prominent in public discourse, yet the persistence of authoritarianism has hampered the development of an autonomous women's movement. Women's issues were not on the agenda of the reform movements of the eighties, including the Beijing Spring. While millions of women all over the country participated in demonstrations in 1989, very few were in positions of leadership. The most notable exception was Chai Ling, who served as commander in chief for the students in Tiananmen Square and was known for her radical resistance to any compromise with the regime.

The One-Child Policy

The most obvious realm of ongoing state intervention in family life was the one-child policy, enacted in the early 1980s. Birth rates dropped steadily in the 1980s and 1990s, falling below replacement levels in 1993. In addition to promotion of birth control, the policy was enforced through forced sterilizations and forced abortions. In cities, where the costs of rearing children are high, most people adapted to the one-child ideal. In the countryside, the one-child policy encountered widespread resistance among peasant families as the household once again became the key unit of production. Local state authorities under pressure to adhere to birth planning quotas often resorted to coercive measures, including fines, late-term abortions, sterilization, and insertion of IUDs, with local female cadres playing a key role in enforcement (Greenhalgh 2005).

Among rural families, where marriage continues to be patrilocal, there is still a strong preference for sons, to provide labor and to offer support in old age. Although some wealthy peasants could afford to pay the fines for having more than one child, many more families adopted out, abandoned, neglected, or aborted girls and there was a resurgence of female infanticide. As a result, China has one of the worst sex ratio imbalances in the world. Close to the conventional norm of 106:100 in the sixties, by 2000 the male-to-female ratio at birth was 117:100 nationwide, and even higher in some regions. Such skewed sex ratios mean that, as in the Qing (see Chapter 3), millions of men, mostly poor, cannot find wives, which has led to the re-emergence of trafficking in women.

Amid mounting worries about the social problems caused by men unable to marry and the economic consequences of the population aging too quickly, the state began granting exceptions, first allowing some couples whose first child was a girl to try for a second, then allowing a second child to couples if both were only children and then in 2014 if only one was an only child. Non-Han ethnic minorities were also allowed to have more than one child. In 2015 the government announced that it would end the policy, officially allowing all couples to have two children. Surveys suggest that while many rural couples see two children as ideal, a son to support them financially in old age and a daughter for emotional support, most urban people do not wish to have a second child because of the expense of child rearing.

Women and Economic Reform

The first step in the economic reforms was decollectivization of agriculture through creation of a responsibility system in which households contracted land from the collective for a fifty-year period, were wholly responsible for decisions about production (including development of sideline economic activities), and kept the profits. The result was a doubling of rural per capita income by 1984 and a dramatic improvement in living standards, evident in a housing boom, a better diet, and a surge in acquisition of consumer goods. Urban commerce and industry were also to be controlled through market forces and run with profit making as the key goal. Factory managers, not Party cadres, were responsible for decisions about hiring and firing workers, bringing an end to the "iron rice bowl" that guaranteed job security under

Mao. As in the countryside, urban incomes and standards of living doubled by the late eighties.

To foster development of export-oriented manufacturing, the state created Special Economic Zones (SEZs) offering low tax rates, subsidized infrastructure, and low wages, initially in the coastal southeast provinces bordering Hong Kong, where foreign companies could set up joint venture factories to produce products for export with foreign investment. The state also loosened restrictions on internal migration to allow villagers to migrate to cities and SEZs, although under the rules of the *hukou* household registration system they cannot transfer their official residence status to the cities and thus cannot access the educational, health, and other benefits of urban status.

The effects of all of these changes were gendered. The return of the household as the primary unit of production, consumption, and welfare led to a reemphasis on gendered divisions of labor and opportunity as families developed strategies to advance their interests. Women's labor ran the so-called courtyard economy, focused on small household enterprises, marketing, and running small shops or restaurants. Many work in township and village enterprises. As growing numbers of men pursued job opportunities in construction and industry in cities in the 1980s and 1990s, agriculture became women's work in many regions, and women served as effective heads of household, responsible for managing land, livestock and providing subsistence for the family. At least half of the labor force in SEZs is female and in light industries (producing electronics, toys, garments, and shoes); young, single, migrant women comprise the vast majority of these workers, valued for their low wage cost, dexterity, and docility. Considered long-term migrants, most of these workers live in crowded dormitories, often lacking adequate lighting and ventilation, where supervisors monitor their comings and goings (Lee 1998).

China has enacted a series of protective labor laws that in theory regulate working hours and factory safety, mandate vacation and overtime, guarantee women equal pay for equal work, and offer special dispensations including leaves, rest time, and reassignment of tasks during menstruation, pregnancy, and nursing. However, enforcement of labor regulations is uneven, and many women (and men) work extremely long hours, up to twelve hours a day seven days a week, under terrible conditions and subject to sexual harassment. Protective legislation for women has also had the effect of encouraging factories to discriminate against them in hiring and layoffs, and to segregate them in occupations that tend to be lower-paid (Woo 1994).

Despite all of these difficulties, young women continue to seek factory jobs as opportunities to escape boredom and parental control in the countryside. Most send remittances home (sometimes to support the education of their brothers) but are able to save money on their own. Work in the city allows many to postpone marriage, to take charge of marriage choice, and sometimes to exercise more independence when they return to take up life as married women (Lee 1998). Many female migrants to the cities also find employment as domestics, hostesses, waitresses, secretaries, department store clerks, and sex workers. These jobs offer little, if any, job security or workplace protections. Yet, like factory work, they still hold out the possibility of higher incomes than women can make in the countryside, and women pursue them to save money before marriage, pay for the education of children, and support family members left home in villages.

Women have become a significant force in the educated urban middle and upper classes. During the reform era, girls continued to make progress in equal access to education, though they still lagged behind boys, especially in rural areas, where many parents opt to focus family resources on educating sons, who do not marry out. In cities, the rate of girls pursuing high school and college-level education has steadily increased, and the one-child policy encouraged parents to invest fully in the career success of daughters. Women account for about half of the number of university students and more than a third of students in graduate programs. In the new millennium, the rates of young women applying to universities have surpassed those for men, prompting some elite institutions to adopt discriminatory policies to restrict the number of female students in highly competitive programs by requiring higher test scores of them.

Educated urban women make up a large portion of the ranks of professionals in business, media, government, finance, education, and other sectors. The one-child policy and ready availability of rural migrant women willing to work as nannies facilitated the success of this class of female professionals. A few women have achieved spectacular success and influence (notably the nineteen women on the global list of self-made female billionaires), but many still struggle to rise to the top of their fields and most make far less than their male counterparts. Women account for nearly one-third of business owners and half of all managers in companies, government workers, and professionals in civic organizations. Most businesses have at least one woman in their senior ranks, but overall, less than a quarter of senior-level managers and higher-level government officials are women. Only one-quarter of the Party's total membership of over 85 million are women, and about one-fifth of the delegates to the 2012 National Party

Congress were women. At the top of the political system, the twenty-five-member ruling Politburo has only two women.

The gender wage gap is growing, with women earning 67 percent of men's wages in cities and 56 percent in rural areas. Pay gaps are exacerbated by concentration of women in low-wage industries, obstacles to their promotion to the highest-paying jobs, and higher layoff rates. When state-owned enterprises were restructured in the late nineties, for example, many more women than men were laid off, and women had a higher unemployment rate overall. Women also retire earlier than men because the retirement age for women is five years lower.

Marriage, Property, and the Law

Notions of affection, romantic love, free choice of spouses, conjugal independence, and individual property that were introduced in the Mao era have become increasingly important in shaping family life in the reform era. In both urban and rural China, marital choice, dating, and even premarital sex have become common. Young people's increasing autonomy in matters of marriage and employment has meant a decrease in parental authority and displacement of the parent-son axis by the conjugal unit as the core of family relations. Individual property is also increasingly important, and young people express an increased sense of entitlement in negotiations over property division and inheritance. Young women in many cases have become active agents in family politics, pushing these issues forward (Friedman 2006). However, these changes have not happened without considerable intergenerational family conflict and growing feelings of insecurity among older women and men about their stability in old age as norms of filial piety have been challenged by growing awareness of individual rights (Yan 2003).

Despite the rhetoric and practice of romance and continuous improvements to the laws on marriage and property, marriage continues to be a patriarchal institution that privileges men. The 1980 Marriage Law raised the minimum age of marriage to twenty-two for men and twenty for women. New inheritance laws in 1985 strengthened the rights of daughters. Revised provisions on divorce in 1990 have made it easier to get and allowed a spouse to pursue compensation for bigamy, cohabitation with a third party (that is, concubinage), domestic violence or maltreatment, and desertion. Divorce rates have risen significantly, as high as 33 percent in the big cities, and most divorces are initiated by women.

Revisions in 2001 gave an expanded definition of domestic violence as beating, tying up, maiming, or restricting personal freedom such that physical or mental harm results. However, many women describe a continuing epidemic of domestic violence against women, with about one-fourth of all women reporting that they have experienced it. Yet domestic violence itself is not a crime, nor is marital rape. A significant limitation of the law is that the maltreatment has to be "persistent" and "frequent" to qualify as domestic violence. Even when it meets this standard, in practice it is extremely difficult for women to get help. Family members often counsel victims that such violence is to be expected and that seeking redress disgraces the family. Local authorities routinely press women to seek mediation and refuse to intervene. In 2015, after several sensational cases brought attention to the problem, the National People's Congress issued a draft of a new law that, if enacted, might make it easier for women to seek police intervention.

Women's rights to marital property are also less robust than they would appear in the 2001 revisions to the law. Although the Marriage Law technically recognizes the notion of common marital property that must be divided upon divorce, in 2011 the Supreme Court issued a new ruling stating that residential property acquired during marriage belongs to whoever paid for it. Thus, if a woman's name is not on the deed, she is not entitled to a share of the property in case of divorce. This has become a significant problem for women, especially in the cities. In China's booming economy, property has become the most important family asset as growing numbers of people in the middle class (some three-fifths of the urban population) purchase homes and apartments. Since prices are high, families typically have to pool their assets to afford a home. Most wives, even highly educated and professionally successful women, give their portion of the investment to their husband and allow him to have only his name on the deed, motivated by a romanticized sense of trust and often pressured by family members to recognize the husband's prerogative as homeowner. Parents of daughters are much less likely to contribute to their daughter's purchase of marital property than are parents of sons, who often purchase homes for sons before marriage to help them attract a wife in a marriage market made more competitive by the shortage of women. Only a quarter of couples have both names on the deed. As a result, if there is a divorce, these women lose their investment and may be left without assets. Knowing this, many women who are highly successful in their professional lives persevere in unhappy or abusive marriages (Fincher 2014). Seeking to maintain their autonomy, a small but growing percentage of urban professional women remain single into their thirties or forties, and some are making the unprecedented choice of remaining single for their entire lives.

Images of Women in Cultural Discourse and the Media

The reinterpretation of marital property law is indicative of the lack of women's voices among policy makers and the widespread support for marital patriarchy. Surprisingly, though, many women themselves accept male dominance as inevitable, if not natural. Advertising markets household goods, appliances, food products, and children's merchandise to women as homemakers. Although consumption is packaged as a realm of choice and self-expression, consumer culture also perpetuates the idea that housework and child rearing are women's duties. This has been reiterated by social commentary criticizing the Mao era's attempt to erase gender differences and arguing for the biological basis for women's roles as mothers. Indeed, this was the underlying logic for the 1988 labor regulations creating protections for women in the workplace for menstruation, pregnancy, and breastfeeding.

Criticism of women who remain single or childless is common in the media. There has been mounting pressure on urban middle-class women to ensure that their one child is successful, perfect, and provided with all manner of educational, extracurricular, and material advantages (Milwertz 1997). As growing numbers of professional women are postponing marriage and motherhood or forgoing them altogether, the government and the media have become fixated on the problem of "leftover women" who fail to marry before their mid-twenties and thus risk becoming spinsters. In 2013, a widely reprinted state media editorial (disseminated by the Women's Federation, among others) opined, "In waiting for true love to appear, women squander their precious youth. . . . The problem is that many of these women are too clear-headed, they can't tolerate weaknesses in their partner, especially since more and more women seek the 'three highs'—high education, high professional achievement and high income. Their standards for their careers and their partners are so high, by the time they want to marry they discover that almost all the men who are their equal in education and age are already married. . . . As these unmarried women age, the feeling of loneliness gets worse and worse" (quoted in Fincher 2014). Young professional women offer another view of this problem, complaining that many men are loath to have a wife who is more educated, is older, or makes more money than they do, a phenomenon borne out in social research.

The media offers an alternative to the model of feminine self-sacrifice and familial duty in the proliferation of images of women as sexually attractive and fashionably Western. Fashion and beauty are marketed as aspects of female self-expression and consumer choice, but women are also commodified as objects for the consumption of men. In a modern-day echo of courtesan culture in the past, capitalist development has produced a male business culture featuring women's sexual services and erotic entertainment. As the state has promoted tourism as a strategy for economic development in regions populated by ethnic minorities such as the Miao and the Dai in the southwest, the media has deliberately propagated an eroticized image of minority women, playing off marriage customs and dress that diverge from Han norms (Schein 2000). Such images have inspired a sex tourism industry in many regions, though, ironically, many of the prostitutes are Han migrant women (Hyde 2001).

Alternative Voices

Although dominated by consumerist discourse, the media has spaces for a variety of women's own perspectives on the complex and ever-changing landscape of gender politics. The Women's Federation has played an increasingly complicated role. It operates as an organ of the Communist Party and is thus restricted in how far it can push the issue of women's rights. Yet it has had a significant impact, bringing difficult issues such as female infanticide, domestic violence, the resurgence of female suicide, and various forms of discrimination to public attention and motivating government action to deal with them. It also conducts much important research on women and promotes women's entry into entrepreneurship. It has advocated successfully for maternity leaves, workplace protections, and changes to the laws on marriage, domestic violence, and other issues.

Many feminists have argued for the need for a women's movement that is autonomous of the Party-state, but given the difficulties of registering NGOs in China and censorship around public discussion of political and human rights, progress has been slow. Pioneering the effort to create an autonomous feminist movement was Li Xiaojiang, a scholar at Zhengzhou University in Henan province, who in 1985 founded the first independent women's studies research institute, the Henan Women's Studies Center, which hosted conferences, published books, and established women's studies curricula. Since then women's studies scholarship and feminist discourse have blossomed across the country. Although many of these women's studies scholars are highly critical of Maoist state feminism, many of them grew up in the Mao era and were profoundly influenced by the notion that men and women were the same and women could do anything men could do. Confident in their abilities and their rights, they assume that gender equality is something the state has already accepted and push it to fulfill its own principles (Zheng 2001).

BOX 11.4

Toward a Chinese Feminism

Li Xiaojiang argues that Maoist state feminism asserted the existence of gender equality as an outcome of the revolution that did not require any participation from women or men and calls for the creation of an indigenous Chinese feminism. Thus independent feminist thinking cannot simply borrow Western paradigms because the core concepts of Western feminism make no sense in post-revolutionary China.

Li notes that "under the slogan, 'Men and women are alike,' we relinquished the category of women." Women were "liberated" by the Party without taking responsibility for themselves, so "for Chinese women, the word *liberation* does not necessarily carry the connotation of liberty. . . . Lack of freedom is precisely one of the important characteristics of Chinese women's liberation." The term *equality* is problematic because "for Western women, equality is a goal and a banner. . . .Its frame of reference is men. However, for Chinese women, equality was the very principle that constructed our history and environment. . . .When China was in a miserable state, our equality was to have an equality of misery, so that the sharing of misery was both the price we had to pay for equality as well as an intrinsic part of equality. . . .this period of history has enabled them to thoroughly understand the world of men; in this world still laden with hardships and war, it is indeed difficult to maintain one's attraction to the goal of becoming like men." She also rejects the Western feminist slogan "the personal is political" because, "In the past half-century in China, the personal has, without exception, been political. In everything from relations between men and women to marriage and family relations, the hand of politics was felt everywhere. It penetrated and eventually completely appropriated personal space. Since the family and private life were women's areas of influence, not only were women objects of appropriation but, under the influence and goading of ideology, they easily became the appropriators, too." (Li 1999)

Organizing to press for women's rights has been more difficult. Some organizations that have affiliated with the Women's Federation and focused on social services have been successful. For example, the Women's Research Institute established a Beijing Women's Hotline in 1992, followed by eleven other hotlines around the country that have provided assistance to tens of thousands of women dealing with a wide variety of psychological and social problems, including domestic violence, sexual harassment, and professional difficulties. The United Nations Conference on Women held in Beijing in 1995 was a catalyst for the emergence of a diverse array of independent women's organizations that provide legal services, offer social support and counseling, and conduct research. But on the occasion of the twentieth anniversary of the conference, women activists pointed out that while significant progress has been made, reversals in property rights, a growing wage gap, discrimination in hiring and higher education, and rampant domestic violence and sexual harassment are signs that things are moving backward. Moreover, a restrictive political climate hampers mobilization to address these problems.

A younger generation of grassroots activists who did not experience the Mao era has boldly used creative public protests and performance art to call attention to violence against women and everyday discrimination. In 2015, five women activists, including two openly lesbian women and one bisexual woman, were arrested for planning a public awareness campaign against sexual harassment on public transportation for International Women's Day. While their arrest illustrates the nervousness of the one-party state about the potential linkages between women's rights and broader calls for democracy and human rights, the women were released within weeks and the government moved forward on a landmark domestic violence bill, suggesting that perhaps such activism can be effective.

LGBT rights are prominent on the agenda of this new movement. Homosexuality was decriminalized in 1997, but LGBT women and men still face widespread prejudice and discrimination in employment. In the 1990s, lesbians and gay men became visible on the social landscape with the establishment of new organizations in Beijing. Appropriating the Maoist term for comrade, *tongzhi*, to identify themselves, these activists arrange social and cultural activities for the LGBT community and endeavor to educate the public through lectures, conferences, film showings, and discussion groups. Not mentioned at all in the Maoist era, homosexuality has since then often been portrayed in the media as an aberrant reaction to male mistreatment or a form of mental illness, legacies of Republican-period medical and psychological discourses based on Western sexology (Sang 2003). In 2001 homosexuality was removed from the official classification of mental disorders, and while negative views still abound, there has been expanding room for discussion and debate about LGBT issues and sympathetic portrayals of lesbians and gay men in the cultural sphere.

On Valentine's Day in 2012, feminist activists in Beijing protested against domestic violence dressed in bridal gowns covered in red paint, carrying signs with slogans like: "Beating is not intimacy, scolding is not love, we want good love not violence!"
PHOTO BY SIMON SONG/
©SOUTH CHINA MORNING POST

TAIWAN

As the movement for democracy gained momentum in the 1980s, Taiwan saw a surge of popular protest and activism around all sorts of issues: the environment, consumer rights, and the rights of women and workers. The KMT regime responded by embarking on a path of political transition to democracy. In 1986 the opposition announced the establishment of the Democratic Progressive Party (DPP). Within weeks the government abolished martial law, the ban on creating political parties, and the restrictions on travel to mainland China. With the lifting of martial law in 1987, Taiwan's feminist movement flourished in conjunction with the movement for democracy. Censorship and bans on organization were lifted as well, and women's NGOs and media outlets proliferated, representing a wide array of agendas and political perspectives.

The DPP opposed not just one-party rule but the domination of politics by mainlanders, who made up only 15 percent of the population. Through the nineties, democracy activists pressed the government to work with the DPP on a plan to reform the constitution and restructure the National Assembly and Legislative Yuan (the legislature), which were dominated by mainlanders representing provinces back in China. President Lee Teng-hui was a willing partner in these negotiations, but many KMT leaders were not. After a decade of lobbying and gradual reforms, punctuated by large demonstrations to keep the pressure on in the face of mainlander opposition, the constitution was amended to allow direct election of the president, full representation for Taiwan in the legislature, and term limits for legislators. In elections in 2000, DPP candidate Chen Shui-bian became president with a platform that explicitly stated that full independence for Taiwan was the ultimate goal. The

PRC government was furious, and the question of whether to declare full independence from the mainland continues to be a contentious one in Taiwan's domestic political debate. But in the years since Chen's election, the country has, for all intents and purposes, pursued a political path of its own. With China as its largest trading partner, Taiwan has had enormous economic success, becoming the fifth-largest economy in Asia.

The symbiotic relationship of the movements for democracy and women's rights is clear in the career of feminist activist Hsiu-lien Annette Lu (see Chapter 10), who was at the forefront of the democratic revolution and in 2000 was elected vice president. As she became more focused on DPP politics, the center of gravity in leadership of the women's movement shifted to Lee Yuan-chen and a group of women who coalesced around the magazine *Awakening*, founded in 1982 to encourage women to step out of their emotional and economic dependence on patriarchal family structures and work for their own equality, self-reliance, and human rights. Born to mainland parents, Lee developed a strong Taiwanese identity and became active in the democratic movement. Having personally experienced the injustice of Taiwan's child custody law after her divorce in 1973, she took up study of Western feminist thought and the history of the women's movement. Lee called for democratization of the family and society, a key element of which was that men and women should not be restricted by fixed notions of gender roles but be free to choose their own individual paths. Women should have the freedom to choose to marry or remain single, to have children or not, and even to have children without marrying. *Awakening* played a leading role in petitioning for passage of the Eugenic Bill for the Protection of Health in 1984, which legalized abortion. Feminists associated with *Awakening* were also at the forefront of the emergence of an environmental movement with the establishment of the Homemakers' Union for Environmental Protection in 1987. Their premise was that as primary consumers and mothers, women were in a position to play a catalytic role in raising consciousness of environmental issues in their families and communities and changing habits of consumption.

In the nineties, the *Awakening* group reconfigured itself to develop a mass membership and began to mobilize local activists to lobby the government on various issues, resulting in passage of legislation to mandate equality in all aspects of employment and a series of changes to family law that ended preference for fathers in custody cases, recognized women's property rights in marriage, and established protections and compensation for victims of domestic violence. In 2004 they won passage of the Gender Equity Education Act, which mandated development of a gender-balanced school curriculum and gender studies at the university level and prohibited discrimination based on sexual orientation and against pregnant women and girls in the school system. In the nineties, *Awakening* feminists played a critical role in the development of gender and women's studies at universities and launched an anti-sexual-harassment movement (Chang 2009).

In 1990, lesbian activists from *Awakening* established Between Us, Taiwan's first organization focused specifically on providing support for the lesbian community and increasing their visibility. Since then, Taiwan's dynamic civil society has fostered the emergence of one of the most vibrant movements for LGBT rights in Asia. Discrimination in employment and education based on sexual orientation is illegal, gays and lesbians can serve openly in the military, and the Ministry of Education requires that textbooks promote tolerance for gays and lesbians. In 2015 Taiwan is poised to become the first country in Asia to legalize same-sex marriage. The island has a thriving gay cultural sphere, with clubs, bookstores, and film festivals. Taiwan Pride, first held in 2003, is the largest gay pride event in Asia.

CONNECTIONS

The past quarter century has been an era of enormous economic change throughout East Asia, and this change has had a fundamental impact on gender in each country. The People's Republic of China has lifted itself out of Third World status to become the world's second-largest (soon to be largest) economy. The building of a market economy after decades of state direction has brought improved economic standards to families while at the same time increasing inequalities in wealth. Growth in the PRC has also opened new opportunities for women to leave home for work, thereby expanding their social horizons. Many of those new jobs serve the export economy, especially those in Special Economic Zones, and are difficult and poorly paid. Nevertheless, women seek out these new types of jobs. On the other hand, however, growth in the PRC has led to a regendering of the household division of labor that had been attacked in previous decades. In Japan, South Korea, and Taiwan, rapid economic growth pulled large numbers of women into the workforce in the 1980s as well, but the notion that men were still the primary breadwinners allowed for inequalities in the workplace to remain in place. Even the 1985 Equal Employment Opportunity Law in Japan was unable to offer true equality to working women. In all market economies in East Asia, women continue to lag significantly behind men both in pay and in the opportunity to move into management positions, even when their percentage in the workforce is close to that of men. In North Korea, the collapse of the official (nonmarket) economy has forced many women to take part in informal trading, called "black capitalism," to help their families survive.

Families have changed in many ways in the past quarter century as well. The PRC, South Korea, and Japan have all passed laws against domestic violence, thereby undermining the notion that what went on in the family was private and that men were, in any case, entitled to behave as they wished toward their wives. The PRC legislation is fairly weak by comparison to that of the other countries—acts of violence must be persistent and frequent to count as domestic violence in the PRC—but it is a step in the right direction. South Korean legislators made a major step toward gender justice by responding to feminists' demands to eliminate the patriarchal family head system. Japanese legislation in the 1990s improved parents' abilities to work by making new provisions for child care leave, and shifted part of the burden of elder care from daughters and daughters-in-law to the state. Reforms in divorce laws in the PRC lightened some of the burden faced by women undergoing divorce, but policies concerning ownership of family property still appear to favor the husband.

Same-sex marriage was not yet legal in East Asia in 2015, but Taiwan and Japan allowed same-sex couples to register legally in same-sex partnerships. Polling data in both of those countries indicate that public opinion is moving toward acceptance of marriage equality. Heteronormative marriage continues to be the dominant trend in South Korea. Lesbian, gay, and transgender movements have been increasingly successful throughout the region; in the PRC, lesbians and gays have even appropriated familiar Maoist language, calling one another "comrades."

In yet another way, families are undergoing similar change throughout the region—couples are no longer interested in having a large number of children. South Korea, Japan, and Taiwan have extraordinarily low fertility rates, significantly under the replacement rate. Their governments are dismayed that women do not respond to government incentives to have more babies. The PRC, which had instituted a one-child policy in the late 1970s, discovered by the 1990s that too few babies might mean there would be too few working-age people to support a graying population. When they abandoned their formal policy and encouraged families to have two children, they found that urban Chinese women were no longer interested in having large families. And women were not the only ones to change in East Asian families. Especially in Japan, new masculinities have begun to emerge, replacing Japan's stereotypical salaryman.

Gender continues to be an important issue in government and politics. While a small number of women have made it to the top ranks of government in South Korea, Japan, the PRC, and the ROC, the number of women in formal government positions in all these countries is very small. Autonomous feminist movements in South Korea, Japan, and Taiwan have addressed this issue. Women have made social changes without having to be in elected office in all of these countries. In South Korea and Japan, feminists pushed their governments to establish cabinet-level women's advocacy offices, such as the Ministry of Gender Equality in South Korea and the Gender Equality Bureau in Japan. In Japan, state feminism seemed to be moving forward in the 1990s, only to face a backlash in the 2000s. The Women's Federation continued to advocate for women in the PRC, although it was not an autonomous feminist organization. In all of these countries, nuanced, sophisticated, and intellectually diverse women's studies courses, programs, and journals have blossomed in the past quarter century.

REFERENCES AND SUGGESTIONS FOR FURTHER READING

GLOBAL CONTEXT

Besse, Susan K. 2004. "Engendering Reform and Revolution in Twentieth-Century Latin America and the Caribbean." In *A Companion to Gender History*, edited by Teresa A. Meade and Merry E. Wiesner-Hanks. Oxford: Blackwell.

Clements, Barbara Evans. 2004. "Continuities amid Change: Gender Ideas and Arrangements in Twentieth-Century Russia and East Europe." In *A Companion to Gender History*, edited by Teresa A. Meade and Merry E. Wiesner-Hanks. Oxford: Blackwell.

Sowerwine, Charles, and Patricia Grimshaw. 2004. "Equality and Difference in the Twentieth-Century West: North America, Western Europe, Australia, and New Zealand." In *A Companion to Gender History*, edited by Teresa A. Meade and Merry E. Wiesner-Hanks. Oxford: Blackwell.

KOREA

Cho, John. 2009. "The Wedding Banquet Revisited: 'Contract Marriages' Between Korean Gays and Lesbians." *Anthropological Quarterly* 82, no. 2: 401–422.

Choi, Hyaeweol. 2014. "South Korean 'Alpha Girls' and Workplace Bias." *East Asia Forum,* August 7. (http://www.eastasiaforum.org/2014/08/07/south-korean-alpha-girls-and-workplace-bias/).

———. 2015. "Constructions of Marriage and Sexuality in Modern Korea." In *Routledge Handbook of Sexuality Studies in East Asia*, edited by Mark McLelland and Vera Mackie. London: Routledge.

Choo, Hae Yeon. 2013. "The Cost of Rights: Migrant Women, Feminist Advocacy, and Gendered Morality in South Korea." *Gender and Society* 27, no. 4: 445–468.

Chun, Jennifer Jihye. 2009. *Organizing at the Margins: The Symbolic Politics of Labor in South Korea and the United States*. Ithaca, NY: Cornell University Press.

Han, Ju Hui Judy, and Jennifer Chun. 2014. "Introduction: Gender and Politics in Contemporary Korea." *Journal of Korean Studies* 19, no. 2: 245–255.

Jung, Kyungja. 2014. *Practicing Feminism in South Korea: The Women's Movement Against Sexual Violence*. London: Routledge.

Jung, Kyungja, and Bronwen Dalton. 2006. "Rhetoric Versus Reality for the Women of North Korea: Mothers of the Revolution." *Asian Survey* 46, no. 5: 741–760.

Kendall, Laurel. 1996. *Getting Married in Korea: Of Gender, Morality, and Modernity*. Berkeley, CA: University of California Press.

Kendall, Laurel. 2009. *Shamans, Nostalgias, and the IMF: South Korean Popular Religion in Motion*. Honolulu: University of Hawai'i Press.

Kim, Hyun Mee. 2012. "The Multicultural Family in South Korea." In *Contested Citizenship in East Asia*, edited by Kyung-sup Chang and Brian Turner. London: Routledge.

Kim, Seung-kyung. 2014. *The Korean Women's Movement and the State: Bargaining for Change*. With Kyounghee Kim. London: Routledge.

Lankov, Andrei. 2007. *North of the DMZ: Essays on the Daily Life in North Korea*. Jefferson, NC: McFarland.

Moon, Kyoung-Hee. 2007. "Women's Experiences of Employment in South Korean Banks after the 1997 Economic Crisis." *Asian Women* 23, no. 1: 1–29.

Shim, Y.-H. 2001. "Feminism and the Discourse of Sexuality in Korea: Continuities and Changes." *Human Studies* 24, nos. 1–2: 133–148.

Soh, C.-H. S. 1993. "Sexual Equality, Male Superiority, and Korean Women in Politics: Changing Gender Relations in a 'Patriarchal Democracy.'" *Sex Roles* 28, no. 1: 73–90.

Song, Jee Eun Regina. 2014. "The Soybean Paste Girl: The Cultural and Gender Politics of Coffee Consumption in Contemporary South Korea." *Journal of Korean Studies* 19, no. 2: 429–448.

Song, Jesook. 2014. *Living on Your Own: Single Women, Rental Housing, and Post-Revolutionary Affect in Contemporary South Korea*. Albany, NY: SUNY Press.

JAPAN

Chanlett-Avery, Emma, and Rebecca M. Nelson. 2014. "'Womenomics' in Japan: In Brief." Congressional Research Service, Washington, D.C.

Frühstück, Sabine. 2007. *Uneasy Warriors: Gender, Memory, and Popular Culture in the Japanese Army*. Berkeley: University of California Press.

Inter-Parliamentary Union. 2015. "Women in National Parliaments." http://www.ipu.org/wmn-e/classif.htm.

Iwai, Tomoaki. 1993. "'The Madonna Boom': Women in the Japanese Diet." *Journal of Japanese Studies* 19, no. 1: 103–120.

Jung, Sun. 2011. *Korean Masculinities and Transcultural Consumption: Yonsama, Rain, Oldboy, K-Pop Idols.* Hong Kong: Hong Kong University Press.

Kano, Ayako. 2011. "Backlash, Fight Back, and Back-Pedaling: Responses to State Feminism in Contemporary Japan." *International Journal of Asian Studies* 8, no. 1: 41–62.

Lipman, Jonathan, Barbara Molony, and Michael Robinson. 2012. *Modern East Asia: An Integrated History*. New York: Pearson.

Molony, Barbara. 1993. "Equality Versus Difference: The Japanese Debate over 'Motherhood Protection,' 1915–50." In *Japanese Women Working*, edited by Janet Hunter. London: Routledge.

———. 1995. "Japan's 1986 Equal Employment Opportunity Law and the Changing Discourse on Gender." *Signs: Journal of Women in Culture and Society* 20, no. 2: 268–302.

———. 2005. "Why Should a Feminist Care About What Goes on Behind Japan's Chrysanthemum Curtain? The Imperial Succession Issue as a Metaphor for Women's Rights." In *Japanese Women: Lineage and Legacies*, edited by Amy McCreedy Thernstrom. Washington, D.C.: Woodrow Wilson International Center for Scholars.

Napier, Susan. 2011. "Where Have All the Salarymen Gone? Masculinity, Masochism, and Technomobility in *Densha Otoko*." In *Recreating Japanese Men*, edited by Sabine Frühstück and Anne Walthall. Berkeley: University of California Press.

World Economic Forum. 2015. "World Economic Forum Gender Gap Report." http://reports.weforum.org/global-gender-gap-report-2014/rankings.

CHINA AND TAIWAN

Chang, Doris T. 2009. *Women's Movements in Twentieth-Century Taiwan*. Urbana: University of Illinois Press.

Entwisle, Barbara, and Gail E. Henderson, eds. 2000. *Re-Drawing Boundaries: Work, Households, and Gender in China*. Berkeley: University of California Press.

Fincher, Leta Hong. 2014. *Leftover Women: The Resurgence of Gender Inequality in China*. London: Zed Books.

Friedman, Sara L. 2006. *Intimate Politics: Marriage, the Market, and State Power in Southeastern China*. Harvard East Asian Monographs 265. Cambridge, MA: Harvard University Asia Center.

Gilmartin, Christina K., Gail Hershatter, Lisa Rofel, and Tyrene White, eds. 1994. *Engendering China: Women, Culture, and the State.* Cambridge, MA: Harvard University Press.

Greenhalgh, Susan. 2005. *Governing China's Population: From Leninist to Neoliberal Biopolitics*. Stanford, CA: Stanford University Press.

Hershatter, Gail. 2007. *Women in China's Long Twentieth Century*. Berkeley: University of California Press.

Honig, Emily, and Gail Hershatter. 1988. *Personal Voices: Chinese Women in the 1980s.* Stanford, CA: Stanford University Press.

Hyde, Sandra Teresa. 2001. "Sex Tourism Practices on the Periphery: Eroticizing Ethnicity and Pathologizing Sex on the Lancang." In *China Urban: Ethnographies of Contemporary Culture,* edited by Nancy N. Chen, Constance C. Clark, Suzanne Z. Gottschang, and Lyn Jeffrey. Durham, NC: Duke University Press.

Judd, Ellen R. 2005. *The Chinese Women's Movement Between State and Market.* Stanford, CA: Stanford University Press.

Lee, Ching Kwan. 1998. *Gender and the South China Miracle: Two Worlds of Factory Women.* Berkeley: University of California Press.

Lee, Yuan-chen. 1999. "How the Feminist Movement Won Media Space in Taiwan: Observations by a Feminist Activist." In *Spaces of Their Own: Women's Public Sphere in Transnational China,* edited by Mayfair Mei-Hui Yang. Minneapolis: University of Minnesota Press.

Li, Xiaozhang. 1999. "With What Discourse Do We Reflect on Chinese Women? Thoughts on Transnational Feminism in China." In *Spaces of Their Own: Women's Public Sphere in Transnational China,* edited by Mayfair Mei-Hui Yang. Minneapolis: University of Minnesota Press.

Milwertz, Cecilia N. 1997. *Accepting Population Control: Urban Chinese Women and the One-Child Family Policy.* Richmond, Surrey: Curzon Press.

Rofel, Lisa. 1999. *Other Modernities: Gendered Yearnings in China After Socialism.* Berkeley: University of California Press.

Rubinstein, Murray A. 2004. "Lu Hsiu-lien and the Origins of Taiwanese Feminism, 1944–1977." In *Women in the New Taiwan: Gender Roles and Gender Consciousness in a Changing Society,* edited by Catherine Farris, Anru Lee, and Murray Rubenstein. Armonk, NY: M. E. Sharpe.

Sang, Tze-lan D. 2003. *The Emerging Lesbian: Female Same-Sex Desire in Modern China.* Chicago: University of Chicago Press.

Schein, Louisa. 2000. *Minority Rules: The Miao and the Feminine in China' Cultural Politics.* Durham: Duke University Press.

Yan, Yunxiang. 2003. *Private Life Under Socialism: Love, Intimacy, and Family Change in a Chinese Village, 1949–1999.* Stanford, CA: Stanford University Press.

Wang, Zheng. 1997. "Maoism, Feminism, and the UN Conference on Women: Women's Studies Research in Contemporary China." *Journal of Women's History* 8, no. 4: 126–153.

Woo, Margaret. 1994. "Chinese Women Workers: The Delicate Balance Between Protection and Equality." In *Engendering China: Women, Culture, and the State, edited by* Christina K. Gilmartin, Gail Hershatter, Lisa Rofel, and Tyrene White. Cambridge, MA: Harvard University Press.

Zheng, Wang. 2001. "Call me 'Qingnian' But Not 'Funü': A Maoist Youth in Retrospect." In *Some of Us: Chinese Women Growing Up in the Mao Era,* edited by Xueping Zhong and Wang Zheng. New Brunswick, NJ: Rutgers University Press.

Index

CPSIA information can be obtained at www.ICGtesting.com
Printed in the USA
LVOW10s0950230216

476342LV00001B/1/P